FOCUS ON LITERATURE

ACTION

PEOPLE

VIEWPOINTS

FORMS

AMERICA

IDEAS

HOUGHTON MIFFLIN COMPANY   BOSTON

Atlanta   Dallas   Geneva, Illinois   Hopewell, New Jersey   Palo Alto   Toronto

FOCUS ON LITERATURE

VIEWPOINTS

PHILIP McFARLAND

FRANCES FEAGIN

SAMUEL HAY

STELLA S.F. LIU

FRANK McLAUGHLIN

NORMA WILLSON

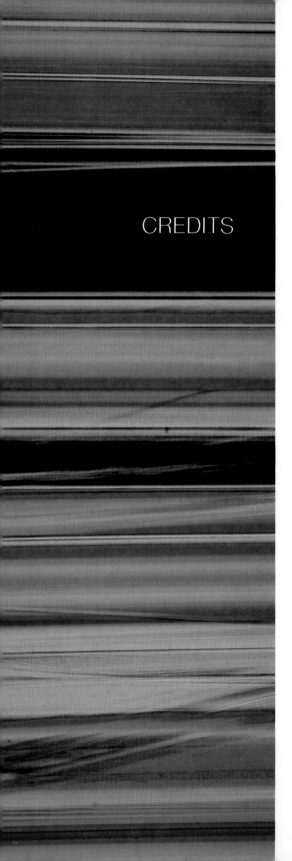

CREDITS

Credits continued on page 592.

ABOUT THE  editors

Philip McFarland teaches at Concord Academy in Massachusetts, where he has served for a number of years as Chairman of the English Department. He earned his B.A. at Oberlin College in Ohio, and he received a Master's Degree and First Class Honors in English Literature at Cambridge University in England. Mr. McFarland has published a novel and a biography of Washington Irving. He is also the co-author of several high school texts in literature and composition.

Frances Feagin is a former teacher of English at Albany High School in Albany, Georgia. She received her B.A. and M.Ed. from Mercer University in Macon, Georgia. She has had extensive teaching experience at the secondary level, including five years as Supervisor of English, and has been involved in the continuing study and revision of local curricula.

Samuel Hay is Chairman of the Department of Communications and Theater Arts at Morgan State University. A graduate of Bethune-Cookman College, he received an M.A. from Johns Hopkins University and a Ph.D. from Cornell University. He has taught high school English, speech, and drama. Dr. Hay is a playwright and the author of numerous articles on black literature.

Stella S.F. Liu is an Associate Professor of Education at Wayne State University in Detroit, Michigan. Dr. Liu received her B.A. from Yenching University in China and her Ph.D. from the University of California at Berkeley; she is a recipient of an outstanding dissertation award from the International Reading Association. Dr. Liu has had extensive experience as a teacher, reading specialist, and reading coordinator at both the elementary and secondary levels.

Frank McLaughlin, co-founder and editor of *Media and Methods* magazine, is an Associate Professor at Fairleigh Dickinson University in New Jersey. A graduate of St. Joseph's College in Philadelphia, Mr. McLaughlin received his M.A. from Villanova University. Formerly an English teacher and department chairman, he continues to work in high schools as coordinator of teaching interns. He has written numerous articles for *Media and Methods* and other publications.

Norma Willson is Chairwoman of the English Department at West High School in Torrance, California. A graduate of Kansas State College, she received an M.A. from the University of Southern California. She is a frequent speaker at national and state conferences on topics relating to the image of women in society and education, particularly in textbooks.

Marcella Johnson is Instructional Supervisor and Specialist in Communication Skills for the Instructional Planning Division of the Los Angeles Unified School District. As consultant for the Focus on Literature Series, she reviewed the selections written by and about members of minority groups.

ConTenTs

SURVIVAL

VIEWPOINTS

IDENTITY

MYSTERY

CHOICES

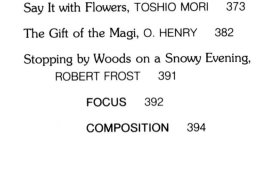

CHALLENGES

THE FLOW OF TIME

SURVIVAL

MY FIRST DEATH

JACQUELINE AURIOL

The flight had begun well enough. Nothing is prettier than the sky of the Ile-de-France on a sunny late afternoon in autumn. I had taken off from Brétigny after the end of a day's work, for this was a practice flight and had no connection with normal test flights, and that kind of flight takes place late in the afternoon so as not to disturb the traffic.

So I took off then into a blue and almost empty sky, with instructions to place one or two sonic booms over Brétigny and to wind up the last sonic boom with a display of aerobatics. On the ground, in the monitoring room, was Guillaume,[1] who guided and controlled my flights.

I was diving along an axis that would cause the sonic boom too far from the aerodrome for Guillaume to hear it, he began to get into a cold sweat as soon as his stop-watch told him that I must have crossed the sound barrier, and he had not heard my 'top'. A few more seconds and the needle would show two minutes or two and a half minutes: for Guillaume this was mathematical proof that I was dead. Mathematically, after two or two and a half minutes in a nose-dive, I would have hit the ground.

The plane was in a tail-spin. The spin was tightening dreadfully and I was in darkness, not yet unconscious, but completely in darkness. I knew it was all over, that this was the catastrophe, the end of which all test pilots think from time to time, and I was filled with a feeling of immense curiosity. Yes, curiosity.

I was saying to myself:

"This is it! This is the moment of your death and the most fascinating moment of your life. No doubt about it. You're going somewhere you've never been before, from where no one has ever returned. Soon, now, you'll know at last. What luck: to spend your last waiting moments in the best circumstances in the world. I am probably going to crash now, but in fact I cannot tell. Maybe right now. Maybe in a few seconds. It's even more fascinating than going to India."

Yes, I thought about India. It was utterly preposterous, for I

Jacqueline Auriol: pronounced zhȧk-lēn' ôr-y-ôl'.
[1] *Guillaume:* pronounced gē-yōm'.

didn't think of İndia as a paradise. Only I had never been to India at that time and for years I had been wanting to go. India was the unknown that fascinated me, and at this instant that I believed to be my last, the name of this country sprang into my mind as the symbol of the unknown. I didn't know whether this unknown was going to be happy or unhappy, but I knew there was going to be something there, something different. And I was filled with an immense curiosity.

In a more diffuse way, but quite separate as if on another level, another thought was also crossing the darkness of my brain: presently someone will telephone my children to tell them I have crashed. They are going to grieve. The thought of their unhappiness saddened me, obviously, but not in any acute way. Deep down I was already terribly withdrawn from life. I also thought of the friends who were waiting for me on the ground, who could hear me and must be in an agony of distress. Their distress mattered to me, but, once again, not too much. I grieved for them all, my children, my friends, but somehow it was only second-degree grief.

Nor was I overmuch saddened by my own fate. I was too curious, too excited by what was going to happen to me. I was living the most exciting moment of my life, because I thought that at last I was going to know.

This is how, on that fine October day in 1956, at the controls of my Mystère IV, I learned so many things. I learned more about myself in two or three minutes than in the course of my whole life.

I realized that I believed in a beyond, whereas I had thought I was no longer a believer. At that moment when I was sure I was going, sure I was about to die, I truly believed that something was going to happen. I was sure there was something on the other side of that barrier, more rarely met and harder to cross than the sound barrier I had just crossed a few seconds before. And I was terribly curious to know what it was. But the really big, the marvelous lesson I learned in that moment in my life that was as decisive as the moment of my birth, was that I was not afraid. Like many people, like many pilots especially, I had always wondered whether I would be afraid at such a moment. And I had always been afraid of being afraid at such a moment. Since that day, I have known that, when things are inexorable, it is not possible to be afraid. In those few moments I realized that in the face of death some kind of gear change takes place in one's brain, one somehow alters speed, and that truly one is not afraid, not afraid at all. At least this is true of myself and I am certain it is equally true for many people at such a moment.

I lost consciousness, and that in itself was a little like death. Then I came to—I shall never know after how long, probably a few seconds. Unconsciously I must have thought of Guillaume and the mechanics who, down on the ground, were dying with me. I first became aware of my cockpit, then of the ground, the position of the plane—I was in a tail-spin.

I was still sure I was going to die, but I began to fight for my life. My mask was disconnected and, just as after an operation, when you have been put to sleep counting nineteen—twenty, and you come out of the anesthetic continuing with twenty-one—twenty-two—twenty-three (or at least that's what happens with me), my hand of its own accord completed my half-finished movement towards the connection point. And I put it back in place. Thanks to my mask, with its built-in mike, I could talk with ground control. Now I had recovered consciousness, one thing mattered greatly to me: to let ground control know what was happening and explain it to them.

'They won't know why I've been killed. And I really don't want it to be the same with me as it has been nearly every time one of my colleagues has been killed. When they find all the bits of the plane with the poor fellow more or less in it, they never know, or almost never, why it happened, and afterwards there are always those big question marks. So, since I do know why I'm being killed, I'm going to tell them. They absolutely must know why this is happening.'

So then I told them:

"I have a stabilizer breakdown. I'm crashing because my stabilizer has jammed in a nose-up position."

This in fact was the second communication I had sent to the ground since the plane had started its tricks. Just before I fainted, I had told them:

"I can't hold the plane any more."

And now, as consciousness returned more and more, I continued to speak to them:

"I'm in a tail-spin."

I am sure that at one moment I even waxed a little theatrical: I was wondering whether or not one ought to say something when one was about to die. I decided it would be

appropriate if I said *au revoir*[2] to them. And so, still spinning like mad, I said:

"*Au revoir* to you all."

At least, I think I said it . . .

But those moments were so charged with emotion that the truth as I saw it is not necessarily the truth as Guillaume saw it, or even the truth at all. Guillaume told me later that he clearly heard my first communications: 'I can't hold the plane any more,' and that he had equally heard my voice announcing that I was in a tail-spin, and, luckily, my very last shout of pure relief 'I've pulled out!' On the other hand, he didn't hear me say anything about the stabilizer, which is a great pity, nor my *au revoir* either.

For his part, Guillaume assured me that he was sending me a series of communications. That he was telling me to do this or do that, yet I heard none of his advice. I suppose my mind was so full of what I was doing, of what I was thinking, that I was incapable of hearing anything coming from ground control.

So we have two completely different versions of the truth, Guillaume and I, for he lived through these moments seeing

[2] *au revoir* (ō rə-vwàr'): French for "good-bye."

nothing, isolated in the monitoring room, and I lived them wholly and with such intensity in the plane. Perhaps I didn't say all I thought I'd said. Perhaps I said it but forgot to press the little button on the stick that switches on the mike. I've no idea. The fact is that I heard Guillaume's voice clearly, and could understand every word he said, only after the danger of death was past.

While I was unconscious, the plane did anything it wanted. First it must have gone into a tighter and tighter spin, and then it must have started spiraling and looping and turning upside down. But with all these turns and loops, it was losing speed. And as it slowed, the centrifugal acceleration diminished accordingly. You get—comparatively speaking—the same thing in a car: when you take a sharp bend at high speed, and you feel the centrifugal pull very strongly, but if the bend is less sharp or your speed is lower, you feel it less.

From the moment I recovered consciousness and started to talk, my friends on the ground felt greatly relieved. My silence had led them to believe I had already crashed. They couldn't have known what had happened, since they couldn't see the plane and I had been silent, unconscious, for an undetermined length of time.

So I was conscious, I could vaguely hear the voices from ground control, and I was beginning to see. My vision was still very limited: at first I could make out only the instrument panel, which wasn't very helpful in view of the circumstances. But then I began to see fields and a little village, between Brétigny and La Ferté-Allais, which was not particularly reassuring either: as a matter of fact I was thinking, that is where I am going to crash.

The tail-spin that was killing me was in a class of its own: I was twisting in every direction, I kept turning upside down, I was dropping and whirling around at all angles. And I couldn't pull out of it. In a healthy spin, the plane dives nose down and turns on its own axis. You can stop it quite easily in a plane with straight wings by returning the controls to a central position. But the Mystère IV was one of the first planes to have swept-back wings, which considerably alter a spin.

As I plunged towards the ground I remembered a lunch I had had a week before with a colleague of mine, Elie Buges, who was working at Bordeaux, where I had gone to make some flights in the Mystère IV. As it happened, he was testing this very plane, and he told me about some trouble he had had a little while previously:

"I had a little bother trying a tail-spin in a Mystère IV," he told me. "Remember, Jacqueline, if ever you get into a tail-spin in this plane, do what I did: shove everything hard down, not central, hard down, Jacqueline."

"When you get into a tail-spin in this plane," he went on, "what you have to do is so contrary to approved procedure that you really have to kick yourself in the backside to make yourself do it. Instead of trying to stop the spin by putting everything in the central position, you must on the contrary accelerate the spin to the maximum by putting the rudder pedals, the control column, absolutely everything into the spin. She's got to have maximum acceleration, because it's only then that the plane dives nose first and the spin becomes healthy. And it's only then that you can return the controls to the central position to stop it."

I went through the maneuver Buges had described and as I did I was thinking very precisely: "I have to do this and that" and then I did it exactly. The tail-spin had become healthy again. And at the right moment, from pure reflex, I returned the controls to central position. I had straightened out. I was still in a nose-dive heading straight for the ground, of course, but I was no longer in a spin.

My eyes functioned properly now—and I could see the ground rushing up to me with dizzy speed. To myself I said: "You *are* a champion and no mistake, but nobody will ever know because you're going to make your little hole just the same. You're too close to the ground. You'll never pull out of it at this rate. There isn't enough room for you to get by."

At that moment I was about twelve and a half miles from Brétigny, near to La Ferté-Allais, and there were some mechanics on the ground who saw me and, as I heard later, said:

"I say . . . that chap's going to kill himself."

Exactly what I was thinking.

But I was thinking it quite calmly. And it is perhaps owing to this feeling of detachment, that, while being certain I was going to kill myself, I still felt a kind of obligation towards the plane and perhaps towards myself too, and went through the necessary actions.

I pulled back on the stick for all I was worth, I throttled back completely, and brought out everything I knew that would affect my turning radius (the slower you're going, the closer you can hug the curve, just as in a car) and . . . I got by.

I made it, over the fields, a few yards from the ground, but I had those few yards and I got by.

I was happy, very happy. "Made it!" I told ground control; "I've pulled out!"

And at that moment—now it was no longer a matter of death but life, now it was a matter of coming back and being infinitely happy to be alive—communications between Guillaume and myself became perfect again. He heard my voice perfectly clearly announcing that I had pulled out, managed to get by, and I could perfectly clearly hear him telling me:

"You needn't be in a hurry to land. Do a lap. Relax."

But I wasn't at all tense. And so I told him: "No. I'm coming in now."

And I landed with a plane that was all out of true. You couldn't tell it was just by looking at it, the wings were still intact and seemed to be in their usual place, but in fact the plane was in an appalling condition, almost beyond salvaging. The terrible pressures to which it had been subjected had turned it into a kind of solidified spin. To land, I had to put the controls in positions in which one simply does not put them. Like turning the steering wheel of a car to the left in order to go to the right.

But I landed first shot and I was filled with happiness. A wild happiness at being alive.

DISCUSSION

1. On "the brink of death," Jacqueline is surprised by her reactions. What are her surprising reactions? Why are her reactions important to her survival?

2. Jacqueline views her almost certain death as "the most fascinating moment" of her life. Why is it fascinating? Why does she think about India?

3. As Jacqueline's plane seems about to crash, some mechanics on the ground say, "That chap's going to kill himself." They assume that the pilot is a man. Why do you think there have been so few woman pilots in the past?

For further activities, see page 44.

MALFUNCTION

RICHARD E. ALBERT

He fell in a sweeping arc
From airplane to earth.

You could almost express it
In an equation:

Speed of the airplane minus   5
Force of the propblast,

Pull of gravity, speed and
Direction of wind,

The slight factor of his jump,
Thrust of leg muscle.   10

I did not witness his fall,
I was too far off,

Too busy trying to slip
Away from the trees,

Pulling the risers, watching   15
The scallops of silk

Ruffled above by the wind.
I heard distant shouts:

"Pull your reserve! Pull! Reserve!"
I looked below me,   20

Saw the earth, the discs of chutes
Sliding to the ground

Like cookies off a tin sheet.
After I landed

It was much too far to walk.   25
I saw men running,

15. *risers:* straps by which a parachutist's harness is
attached to the parachute.   19. *reserve:* extra
parachute, to be used if the regular parachute does
not open.

But the trucks were parked this way.
I know he is dead,

Know we will talk about it
Riding in the trucks   30

Feeling wind in our faces.
By tonight I would

Describe what all will have seen
By then: he fell fast

Without a sound, like a rock   35
In a handkerchief;

I was close by when he hit,
Saw him bounce six feet.

Forgetting to drink a toast
We will press bottles   40

Against our faces and hands,
Clinging to coldness,

Reliving all but the slight
Factor of his death.

DISCUSSION

1. "Pull your reserve!" is the shout which the speaker hears. To whom are the shouts yelled? What happens to that person?

2. At the end, the speaker says that he and the other men relive every detail of their comrade's accident except for "the slight factor of his death." Why do they talk about the details of the accident and not about its result?

3. **Stanza.** A stanza is a unit of poetry made up of two or more lines. In this poem each stanza contains only two lines. What effect is created by these short stanzas?

For further activities, see page 44.

The Most Dangerous Game

RICHARD CONNELL

"Off there to the right—somewhere—is a large island," said Whitney. "It's rather a mystery——"

"What island is it?" Rainsford asked.

"The old charts call it Ship-Trap Island," Whitney replied. "A suggestive name, isn't it? Sailors have a curious dread of the place. I don't know why. Some superstition——"

"Can't see it," remarked Rainsford, trying to peer through the dank tropical night that was palpable¹ as it pressed its thick, warm blackness in upon the yacht.

"You've good eyes," said Whitney with a laugh, "and I've seen you pick off a moose moving in the brown fall brush at four hundred yards, but even you can't see four miles or so through a moonless Caribbean night."

"Nor four yards," admitted Rainsford. "Ugh! It's like moist velvet."

"It will be light enough in Rio," promised Whitney. "We should make it in a few days. I hope the jaguar guns have come from Purdey's. We should have some good hunting up the Amazon. Great sport, hunting."

"The best sport in the world," agreed Rainsford.

"For the hunter," amended Whitney. "Not for the jaguar."

"Don't talk rot, Whitney," said Rainsford. "You're a big-game hunter, not a philosopher. Who cares how a jaguar feels?"

"Perhaps the jaguar does," observed Whitney.

"Bah! They've no understanding."

"Even so, I rather think they understand one thing at least—fear. The fear of pain and the fear of death."

"Nonsense," laughed Rainsford. "This hot weather is making you soft, Whitney. Be a realist. The world is made up of two classes. The hunters and the hunted. Luckily you and I are hunters. Do you think we've passed that island yet?"

"I can't tell in the dark. I hope so."

"Why?" asked Rainsford.

"The place has a reputation—a bad one."

"Cannibals?" suggested Rainsford.

"Hardly. Even cannibals wouldn't live in such a godforsaken place. But it's got into sailor lore, somehow. Didn't you notice that the crew's nerves seem a bit jumpy today?"

"They were a bit strange, now you mention it. Even Captain Nielsen——"

"Yes, even that tough-minded old Swede, who'd go up to the devil himself and ask him for a light. Those fishy blue eyes held a look I never saw there before. All I could get out of him was 'This place has an evil name among seafaring men, sir.' Then he said to me very gravely, 'Don't you feel anything?'—as if the air about us was actually poisonous. Now, you mustn't

¹ *palpable:* capable of being felt.

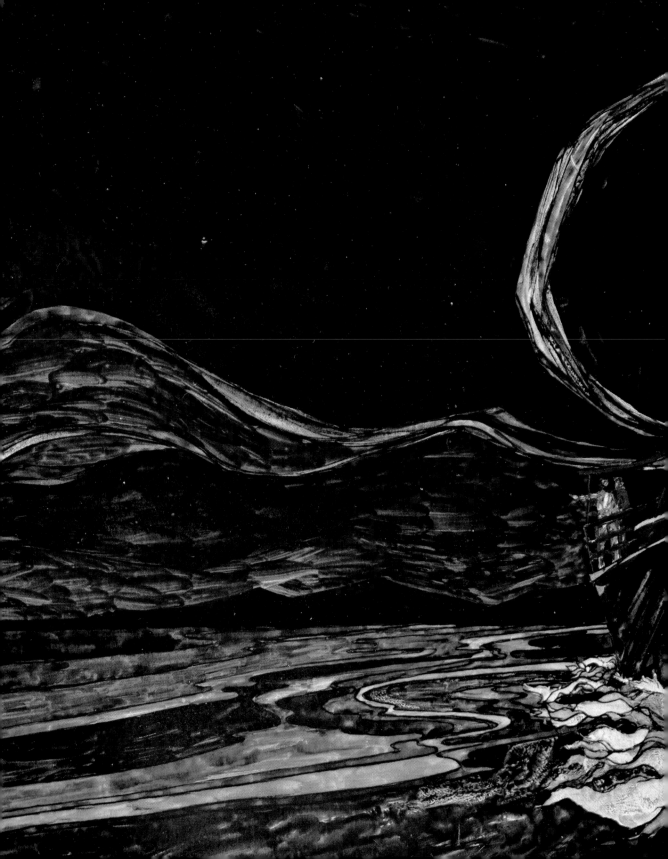

laugh when I tell you this—I did feel something like a sudden chill. There was no breeze. The sea was as flat as a plate-glass window. We were drawing near the island then. What I felt was a—a mental chill—a sort of sudden dread."

"Pure imagination," said Rainsford. "One superstitious sailor can taint the whole ship's company with his fear."

"Maybe. But sometimes I think sailors have an extra sense that tells them when they are in danger. Sometimes I think evil is a tangible thing—with wavelengths, just as sound and light have. An evil place can, so to speak, broadcast vibrations of evil. Anyhow, I'm glad we're getting out of this zone. Well, I think I'll turn in now, Rainsford."

"I'm not sleepy," said Rainsford. "I'm going to smoke another pipe up on the afterdeck."

"Good night, then, Rainsford. See you at breakfast."

"Right. Good night, Whitney."

There was no sound in the night as Rainsford sat there but the muffled throb of the engine that drove the yacht swiftly through the darkness, and the swish and ripple of the wash of the propeller.

Rainsford, reclining in a steamer chair, indolently puffed on his favorite briar. The sensuous drowsiness of the night was on him. "It's so dark," he thought, "that I could sleep without closing my eyes; the night would be my eyelids——"

An abrupt sound startled him. Off

to the right he heard it, and his ears, expert in such matters, could not be mistaken. Again he heard the sound, and again. Somewhere off in the blackness someone had fired a gun three times.

Rainsford sprang up and moved quickly to the rail, mystified. He strained his eyes in the direction from which the reports had come, but it was like trying to see through a blanket. He leaped upon the rail and balanced himself there to get greater elevation; his pipe, striking a rope, was knocked from his mouth. He lunged for it; a short, hoarse cry came from his lips as he realized he had reached too far and had lost his balance. The cry was pinched off short as the blood-warm waters of the Caribbean Sea closed over his head.

He struggled up to the surface and tried to cry out, but the wash from the speeding yacht slapped him in the face, and the salt water in his open mouth made him gag and strangle. Desperately he struck out with strong strokes after the receding lights of the yacht, but he stopped before he had swum fifty feet. A certain cool-headedness had come to him; it was not the first time he had been in a tight place. There was a chance that his cries could be heard by someone aboard the yacht, but that chance was slender and grew more slender as the yacht raced on. He wrestled himself out of his clothes and shouted with all his power. The lights of the yacht became faint and ever-vanishing fireflies; then they were blotted out entirely by the night.

Rainsford remembered the shots. They had come from the right, and doggedly he swam in that direction, swimming with slow, deliberate strokes, conserving his strength. For a seemingly endless time he fought the sea. He began to count his strokes desperately; he could do possibly a hundred more and then——

Rainsford heard a sound. It came out of the darkness—a high, screaming sound, the sound of an animal in an extremity of anguish and terror.

He did not recognize the animal that made the sound; he did not try to; with fresh vitality he swam toward the sound. He heard it again; then it was cut short by another noise, crisp, staccato.

"Pistol shot," muttered Rainsford, swimming on.

Ten minutes of determined effort brought another sound to his ears—the most welcome he had ever heard—the muttering and growling of the sea breaking on a rocky shore. He was almost on the rocks before he saw them; on a night less calm he would have been shattered against them. With his remaining strength he dragged himself from the swirling waters. Jagged crags appeared to jut up into opaqueness; he forced himself upward, hand over hand. Gasping, his hands raw, he reached a flat place at the top. Dense jungle came down to the very edge of the cliffs. What perils that tangle of trees and underbrush might hold for him did not concern Rainsford just then. All he knew was that he was safe from his enemy, the sea, and that utter weariness was on him. He flung himself down at the jungle edge and tumbled headlong into the deepest sleep of his life.

When he opened his eyes, he knew from the position of the sun that it was late in the afternoon. Sleep had given him new vigor; a sharp hunger was picking at him. He looked about him almost cheerfully.

"Where there are pistol shots, there are men. Where there are men, there is food," he thought. But what kind of men, he wondered, in so forbidding a place? An unbroken front of snarled and jagged jungle fringed the shore.

He saw no sign of a trail through the closely knit web of weeds and trees; it was easier to go along the shore, and Rainsford floundered along by the water. Not far from where he had landed, he stopped.

Some wounded thing, by the evidence a large animal, had thrashed about in the underbrush; the jungle weeds were crushed down, and the moss was lacerated; one patch of weeds was stained crimson. A small, glittering object not far away caught Rainsford's eye, and he picked it up. It was an empty cartridge.

"A twenty-two," he remarked. "That's odd. It must have been a fairly large animal, too. The hunter had his nerve to tackle it with a light gun. It's clear that the brute put up a fight. I suppose the first three shots I heard was when the hunter flushed his quarry[2] and wounded it. The last shot

was when he trailed it here and finished it."

He examined the ground closely and found what he had hoped to find—the print of hunting boots. They pointed along the cliff in the direction he had been going. Eagerly he hurried along, now slipping on a rotten log or a loose stone, but making headway; night was beginning to settle down on the island.

Bleak darkness was blacking out the sea and jungle when Rainsford sighted the lights. He came upon them as he turned a crook in the coastline, and his first thought was that he had come upon a village, for there were many lights. But as he forged along, he saw to his great astonishment that all the lights were in one enormous building—a lofty structure with pointed towers plunging upward into the gloom. His eyes made out the shadowy outlines of a palatial chateau; it was set on a high bluff, and on three sides of it cliffs dived down to where the sea licked greedy lips in the shadows.

"Mirage," thought Rainsford. But it was no mirage, he found, when he opened the tall, spiked iron gate. The stone steps were real enough; the massive door with a leering gargoyle for a knocker was real enough; yet about it all hung an air of unreality.

He lifted the knocker, and it creaked up stiffly, as if it had never before been used. He let it fall, and it startled him with its booming loudness. He thought he heard footsteps within; the door remained closed. Again Rainsford lifted the heavy knocker and let it fall. The door opened then, opened as

---

[2] *flushed his quarry:* forced the victim out of hiding.

suddenly as if it were on a spring, and Rainsford stood blinking in the river of glaring gold light that poured out. The first thing Rainsford's eyes discerned was the largest man Rainsford had ever seen—a gigantic creature, solidly made and black-bearded to the waist. In his hand the man held a long-barrel revolver, and he was pointing it straight at Rainsford's heart.

Out of the snarl of beard two small eyes regarded Rainsford.

"Don't be alarmed," said Rainsford, with a smile which he hoped was disarming. "I'm no robber. I fell off a yacht. My name is Sanger Rainsford of New York City."

The menacing look in the eyes did not change. The revolver pointed as rigidly as if the giant were a statue. He gave no sign that he understood Rainsford's words or that he had even heard them. He was dressed in uniform, a black uniform trimmed with gray astrakhan.

"I'm Sanger Rainsford of New York," Rainsford began again. "I fell off a yacht. I am hungry."

The man's only answer was to raise with his thumb the hammer of his revolver. Then Rainsford saw the man's free hand go to his forehead in a military salute, and he saw him click his heels together and stand at attention. Another man was coming down the broad marble steps, an erect, slender man in evening clothes. He advanced to Rainsford and held out his hand.

In a cultivated voice marked by a slight accent that gave it added precision and deliberateness, he said, "It is a very great pleasure and honor to welcome Mr. Sanger Rainsford, the celebrated hunter, to my home."

Automatically Rainsford shook the man's hand.

"I've read your books about hunting snow leopards in Tibet, you see," explained the man. "I am General Zaroff."

Rainsford's first impression was that the man was singularly handsome; his second was that there was an original, almost bizarre quality about the general's face. He was a tall man past middle age, for his hair was a vivid white; but his thick eyebrows and pointed military moustache were as black as the night from which Rainsford had come. His eyes, too, were black and very bright. He had high cheekbones, a sharp-cut nose, a spare, dark face, the face of a man used to giving orders, the face of an aristocrat. Turning to the giant in uniform, the general made a sign. The giant put away his pistol, saluted, withdrew.

"Ivan is an incredibly strong fellow," remarked the general, "but he has the misfortune to be deaf and dumb. A simple fellow but, I'm afraid, like all his race, a bit of a savage."

"Is he Russian?"

"He is a Cossack,"[3] said the general, and his smile showed red lips and pointed teeth. "So am I."

"Come," he said, "we shouldn't be chatting here. We can talk later. Now you want clothes, food, rest. You shall have them. This is a most restful spot."

---

[3] *Cossack:* The Cossacks of Russia were famous as fighters and horsemen.

Ivan had reappeared, and the general spoke to him with lips that moved but gave forth no sound.

"Follow Ivan, if you please, Mr. Rainsford," said the general. "I was about to have my dinner when you came. I'll wait for you. You'll find that my clothes will fit you, I think."

It was to a huge, beam-ceilinged bedroom with a canopied bed big enough for six men that Rainsford followed the silent giant. Ivan laid out an evening suit, and Rainsford, as he put it on, noticed that it came from a London tailor who ordinarily cut and sewed for none below the rank of duke.

The dining room to which Ivan conducted him was in many ways remarkable. There was a medieval magnificence about it; it suggested a baronial hall of feudal times with its oaken panels, its high ceiling, its vast refectory table where two score men could sit down to eat. About the hall were the mounted heads of many animals—lions, tigers, elephants, moose, bears; larger or more perfect specimens Rainsford had never seen. At the great table the general was sitting alone.

"You'll have a cocktail, Mr. Rainsford," he suggested. The cocktail was surpassingly good and, Rainsford noted, the table appointments were of the finest—the linen, the crystal, the silver, the china.

They were eating borsch, the rich, red soup with sour cream so dear to Russian palates. Half apologetically General Zaroff said, "We do our best to preserve the amenities of civilization here. Please forgive any lapses. We are well off the beaten track, you know. Do you think the champagne has suffered from its long ocean trip?"

"Not in the least," declared Rainsford. He was finding the general a most thoughtful and affable host, a true cosmopolite.[4] But there was one small trait of the general's that made Rainsford uncomfortable. Whenever he looked up from his plate, he found the general studying him, appraising him narrowly.

"Perhaps," said General Zaroff, "you were surprised that I recognized your name. You see, I read all books on hunting published in English, French, and Russian. I have but one passion in my life, Mr. Rainsford, and it is the hunt."

"You have some wonderful heads here," said Rainsford as he ate a particularly well-cooked filet mignon. "That Cape buffalo is the largest I ever saw."

"Oh, that fellow. Yes, he was a monster."

"Did he charge you?"

"Hurled me against a tree," said the general. "Fractured my skull. But I got the brute."

"I've always thought," said Rainsford, "that the Cape buffalo is the most dangerous of all big game."

For a moment the general did not reply; he was smiling his curious red-lipped smile. Then he said slowly, "No. You are wrong, sir. The Cape buffalo is not the most dangerous big game." He sipped his wine. "Here in my preserve on this island," he said in the same slow tone, "I hunt more dangerous game."

---

4 *cosmopolite* (kŏz-mŏp'ə-līt): widely traveled and sophisticated person.

Rainsford expressed his surprise. "Is there big game on this island?"

The general nodded. "The biggest."

"Really?"

"Oh, it isn't here naturally, of course. I have to stock the island."

"What have you imported, General?" Rainsford asked. "Tigers?"

The general smiled. "No," he said. "Hunting tigers ceased to interest me some years ago. I exhausted their possibilities, you see. No thrill left in tigers, no real danger. I live for danger, Mr. Rainsford."

The general took from his pocket a gold cigarette case and offered his guest a long black cigarette with a silver tip; it was perfumed and gave off a smell like incense.

"We will have some capital hunting, you and I," said the general. "I shall be most glad to have your society."

"But what game—" began Rainsford.

"I'll tell you," said the general. "You will be amused, I know. I think I may say, in all modesty, that I have done a rare thing. I have invented a new sensation. May I pour you another glass of port, Mr. Rainsford?"

"Thank you, General."

The general filled both glasses and said, "God makes some men poets. Some he makes kings, some beggars. Me he made a hunter. My hand was made for the trigger, my father said. He was a very rich man with a quarter of a million acres in the Crimea, and he was an ardent sportsman. When I was only five years old, he gave me a little gun, specially made in Moscow for me, to shoot sparrows with. When I shot some of his prize turkeys with it, he did not punish me; he complimented me on my marksmanship. I killed my first bear in the Caucasus when I was ten. My whole life has been one prolonged hunt. I went into the army—it was expected of noblemen's sons—and for a time commanded a division of Cossack cavalry, but my real interest was always the hunt. I have hunted every kind of game in every land. It would be impossible for me to tell you how many animals I have killed."

The general puffed at his cigarette.

"After the debacle in Russia [5] I left the country, for it was imprudent for an officer of the Czar to stay there. Many noble Russians lost everything. I, luckily, had invested heavily in American securities, so I shall never have to open a tearoom in Monte Carlo or drive a taxi in Paris. Naturally, I continued to hunt—grizzlies in your Rockies, crocodiles in the Ganges, rhinoceroses in East Africa. It was in Africa that the Cape buffalo hit me and laid me up for six months. As soon as I recovered, I started for the Amazon to hunt jaguars, for I had heard they were unusually cunning. They weren't." The Cossack sighed. "They were no match at all for a hunter with his wits about him, and a high-powered rifle. I was bitterly disappointed. I was lying in my tent with a splitting headache one night when a terrible thought pushed its way into my mind. Hunting was beginning to

---

[5] *debacle in Russia:* 1917 revolution, in which the Czar's government was overthrown.

bore me! And hunting, remember, had been my life. I have heard that in America businessmen often go to pieces when they give up the business that has been their life."

"Yes, that's so," said Rainsford.

The general smiled. "I had no wish to go to pieces," he said. "I must do something. Now, mine is an analytical mind, Mr. Rainsford. Doubtless that is why I enjoy the problems of the chase."

"No doubt, General Zaroff."

"So," continued the general, "I asked myself why the hunt no longer fascinated me. You are much younger than I am, Mr. Rainsford, and have not hunted as much, but you perhaps can guess the answer."

"What was it?"

"Simply this: hunting had ceased to be what you call 'a sporting proposition.' It had become too easy. I always got my quarry. Always. There is no greater bore than perfection."

The general lit a fresh cigarette.

"No animal had a chance with me any more. That is no boast; it is a mathematical certainty. The animal had nothing but his legs and his instinct. Instinct is no match for reason. When I thought of this, it was a tragic moment for me, I can tell you."

Rainsford leaned across the table, absorbed in what his host was saying.

"It came to me as an inspiration what I must do," the general went on.

"And that was?"

The general smiled the quiet smile of one who has faced an obstacle and surmounted it with success. "I had to

invent a new animal to hunt," he said.

"A new animal? You are joking."

"Not at all," said the general. "I never joke about hunting. I needed a new animal. I found one. So I bought this island, built this house, and here I do my hunting. The island is perfect for my purposes—there are jungles with a maze of trails in them, hills, swamps——"

"But the animal, General Zaroff?"

"Oh, said the general, "it supplies me with the most exciting hunting in the world. No other hunting compares with it for an instant. Every day I hunt, and I never grow bored now, for I have a quarry with which I can match my wits."

Rainsford's bewilderment showed in his face.

"I wanted the ideal animal to hunt," explained the general. "So I said, 'What are the attributes of an ideal quarry?' And the answer was, of course, 'It must have courage, cunning, and, above all, it must be able to reason.'"

"But no animal can reason," objected Rainsford.

"My dear fellow," said the general, "there is one that can."

"But you can't mean—" gasped Rainsford.

"And why not?"

"I can't believe you are serious, General Zaroff. This is a grisly joke."

"Why should I not be serious? I am speaking of hunting."

"Hunting? General Zaroff, what you speak of is murder!"

The general laughed with entire good nature. He regarded Rainsford quizzically. "I refuse to believe that so modern and civilized a young man as you seem to be harbors romantic ideas about the values of human life. Surely your experiences in the war——" He stopped.

"Did not make me condone cold-blooded murder," finished Rainsford stiffly.

Laughter shook the general. "How extraordinarily droll you are!" he said. "One does not expect nowadays to find a young man of the educated class, even in America, with such a naive and, if I may say so, mid-Victorian point of view. It's like finding a snuff-box in a limousine. Ah, well, doubtless you had Puritan ancestors. So many Americans appear to have had. I'll wager you'll forget your notions when you go hunting with me. You've a genuine new thrill in store for you, Mr. Rainsford."

"Thank you, I'm a hunter, not a murderer."

"Dear me," said the general, quite unruffled, "again that unpleasant word. But I think I can show you that your scruples are quite ill-founded."

"Yes?"

"Life is for the strong, to be lived by the strong and, if needs be, taken by the strong. The weak of the world were put here to give the strong pleasure. I am strong. Why should I not use my gift? If I wish to hunt, why should I not? I hunt the scum of the earth—sailors from tramp ships—lascars,[6] blacks, Chinese, whites, mongrels—a thoroughbred horse or hound

---

[6] *lascars:* Asian (particularly Indian) sailors.

is worth more than a score of them."

"But they are men," said Rainsford hotly.

"Precisely," said the general. "That is why I use them. It gives me pleasure. They can reason, after a fashion. So they are dangerous."

"But where do you get them?"

The general's left eyelid fluttered down in a wink. "This island is called Ship-Trap," he answered. "Sometimes an angry god of the high seas sends them to me. Sometimes, when Providence is not so kind, I help Providence a bit. Come to the window with me."

Rainsford went to the window and looked out toward the sea.

"Watch! Out there!" exclaimed the general, pointing into the night. Rainsford's eyes saw only blackness, and then, as the general pressed a button, far out to sea Rainsford saw the flash of lights.

The general chuckled. "They indicate a channel," he said, "where there's none; giant rocks with razor edges crouch like a sea monster with wide-open jaws. They can crush a ship as easily as I crush this nut." He dropped a walnut on the hardwood floor and brought his heel grinding down on it. "Oh, yes," he said casually, as if in answer to a question, "I have electricity. We try to be civilized here."

"Civilized? And you shoot down men?"

A trace of anger was in the general's black eyes, but it was there for but a second, and he said, in his most pleasant manner, "Dear me, what a righteous young man you are! I assure you I do not do the thing you suggest.

That would be barbarous. I treat these visitors with every consideration. They get plenty of food and exercise. They get into splendid physical condition. You shall see for yourself tomorrow."

"What do you mean?"

"We'll visit my training school," smiled the general. "It's in the cellar. I have about a dozen pupils down there now. They're from the Spanish bark *San Lucar*, that had the bad luck to go on the rocks out there. A very inferior lot, I regret to say. Poor specimens, and more accustomed to the deck than to the jungle."

He raised his hand, and Ivan, who served as waiter, brought thick Turkish coffee. Rainsford, with an effort, held his tongue in check.

"It's a game, you see," pursued the general blandly. "I suggest to one of them that we go hunting. I give him a supply of food and an excellent hunting knife. I give him three hours' start. I am to follow, armed only with a pistol of the smallest caliber and range. If my quarry eludes me for three whole days, he wins the game. If I find him"—the general smiled—"he loses."

"Suppose he refuses to be hunted?"

"Oh," said the general, "I give him his option, of course. He need not play that game if he doesn't wish to. If he does not wish to hunt, I turn him over to Ivan. Ivan once had the honor of serving as official knouter to the Great White Czar,[7] and he has his own ideas of sport. Invariably, Mr. Rainsford, invariably they choose the hunt."

---

[7] *knouter . . . Czar:* flogger of prisoners of Czar Alexander III, ruler of Russia from 1881 to 1894.

"And if they win?"

The smile on the general's face widened. "To date I have not lost," he said.

The he added hastily, "I don't wish you to think me a braggart, Mr. Rainsford. Many of them afford only the most elementary sort of problem. Occasionally I strike a tartar.[8] One almost did win. I eventually had to use the dogs."

"The dogs?"

"This way, please. I'll show you."

The general steered Rainsford to a window. The lights from the windows sent a flickering illumination that made grotesque patterns on the courtyard below, and Rainsford could see moving about there a dozen or so huge black shapes; as they turned toward him, their eyes glittered greenly.

"A rather good lot, I think," observed the general. "They are let out at seven every night. If anyone should try to get into my house—or out of it— something extremely regrettable would occur to him." He hummed a snatch of song from the Folies Bergères.

"And now," said the general, "I want to show you my new collection of heads. Will you come with me to the library?"

"I hope," said Rainsford, "that you will excuse me tonight, General Zaroff. I'm really not feeling at all well."

"Ah, indeed?" the general inquired solicitously. "Well, I suppose that's only natural, after your long swim. You need a good, restful night's sleep. Tomorrow you'll feel like a new man, I'll

wager. Then we'll hunt, eh? I've one rather promising prospect——"

Rainsford was hurrying from the room.

"Sorry you can't go with me tonight," called the general. "I expect rather fair sport—a big, strong chap. He looks resourceful—well, good night, Mr. Rainsford; I hope that you have a good night's rest."

The bed was good and the pajamas of the softest silk, and he was tired in every fiber of his being, but nevertheless Rainsford could not quiet his brain with the opiate of sleep. He lay, eyes wide open. Once he thought he heard stealthy steps in the corridor outside his room. He sought to throw open the door; it would not open. He went to the window and looked out. His room was high up in one of the towers. The lights of the chateau were out now, and it was dark and silent, but there was a fragment of sallow moon, and by its wan light he could see, dimly, the courtyard; there, weaving in and out in the pattern of shadow, were black, noiseless forms; the hounds heard him at the window and looked up, expectantly, with their green eyes. Rainsford went back to the bed and lay down. By many methods he tried to put himself to sleep. He had achieved a doze when, just as morning began to come, he heard, far off in the jungle, the faint report of a pistol.

General Zaroff did not appear until luncheon. He was dressed faultlessly in the tweeds of a country squire. He was solicitous about the state of Rainsford's health.

[8] *strike a tartar:* discover a dangerous man.

"As for me," sighed the general, "I do not feel so well. I am worried, Mr. Rainsford. Last night I detected traces of my old complaint."

To Rainsford's questioning glance the general said, "Ennui. Boredom."

Then, taking a second helping of crepes suzette, the general explained, "The hunting was not good last night. The fellow lost his head. He made a straight trail that offered no problems at all. That's the trouble with these sailors; they have dull brains to begin with, and they do not know how to get about in the woods. They do excessively stupid and obvious things. It's most annoying. Will you have another glass of Chablis, Mr. Rainsford?"

"General," said Rainsford firmly, "I wish to leave this island at once."

The general raised his thickets of eyebrows; he seemed hurt. "But, my dear fellow," the general protested, "you've only just come. You've had no hunting——"

"I wish to go today," said Rainsford. He saw the dead black eyes of the general on him, studying him. General Zaroff's face suddenly brightened.

He filled Rainsford's glass with venerable Chablis from a dusty bottle.

"Tonight," said the general, "we will hunt—you and I."

Rainsford shook his head. "No, General," he said. "I will not hunt."

The general shrugged his shoulders and delicately ate a hothouse grape. "As you wish, my friend," he said. "The choice rests entirely with you. But may I not venture to suggest that you will find my idea of sport more diverting than Ivan's?"

He nodded toward the corner to where the giant stood scowling, his thick arms crossed on his hogshead of chest.

"You don't mean—" cried Rainsford.

"My dear fellow," said the general, "have I not told you I always mean what I say about hunting? This is really an inspiration. I drink to a foeman worthy of my steel—at last."

The general raised his glass, but Rainsford sat staring at him.

"You'll find this game worth playing," the general said enthusiastically. "Your brain against mine. Your woodcraft against mine. Your strength and stamina against mine. Outdoor chess! And the stake is not without value, eh?"

"And if I win—" began Rainsford huskily.

"I'll cheerfully acknowledge myself defeated if I do not find you by midnight of the third day," said General Zaroff. "My sloop will place you on the mainland near a town."

The general read what Rainsford was thinking.

"Oh, you can trust me," said the Cossack. "I will give you my word as a gentlemen and a sportsman. Of course you, in turn, must agree to say nothing of your visit here."

"I'll agree to nothing of the kind," said Rainsford.

"Oh," said the general, "in that case—but why discuss it now? Three days hence we can discuss it over a bottle of Veuve Cliquot, unless——"

The general sipped his wine.

Then a businesslike air animated him. "Ivan," he said to Rainsford, "will supply you with hunting clothes, food, a knife. I suggest you wear moccasins; they leave a poorer trail. I suggest too that you avoid the big swamp in the southeast corner of the island. We call it Death Swamp. There's quicksand there. One foolish fellow tried it. The deplorable part of it was that Lazarus followed him. You can imagine my feelings, Mr. Rainsford. I loved Lazarus; he was the finest hound in my pack. Well, I must beg you to excuse me now. I always take a siesta after lunch. You'll hardly have time for a nap, I fear. You'll want to start, no doubt. I shall not follow till dusk. Hunting at night is so much more exciting than by day, don't you think? *Au revoir*, Mr. Rainsford, *au revoir*."

General Zaroff, with a deep, courtly bow, strolled from the room.

From another door came Ivan. Under one arm he carried khaki hunting clothes, a haversack of food, a leather sheath containing a long-bladed hunting knife; his right hand rested on a cocked revolver thrust in the crimson sash about his waist.

Rainsford had fought his way through the bush for two hours. "I must keep my nerve. I must keep my nerve," he said through tight teeth.

He had not been entirely clear-headed when the chateau gates snapped shut behind him. His whole idea at first was to put distance between himself and General Zaroff, and to this end he had plunged along, spurred on by the sharp rowels of something very like panic. Now he had got a grip on himself, had stopped, and was taking stock of himself and the situation.

He saw that straight flight was futile; inevitably it would bring him face-to-face with the sea. He was in a picture with a frame of water, and his operations clearly must take place within that frame.

"I'll give him a trail to follow," muttered Rainsford, and he struck off from the rude path he had been following into the trackless wilderness. He excuted a series of intricate loops; he doubled on his trail again and again, recalling all the lore of the fox hunt and all the dodges of the fox. Night found him leg-weary, with hands and face lashed by the branches, on a thickly wooded ridge. He knew it would be insane to blunder on through the dark, even if he had the strength. His need for rest was imperative and he thought, "I have played the fox; now I must play the cat of the fable."[9]

A big tree with a thick trunk and outspread branches was nearby, and taking care to leave not the slightest mark, he climbed up into the crotch, and stretching out on one of the broad limbs, after a fashion, rested. Rest brought him new confidence and almost a feeling of security. Even so zealous a hunter as General Zaroff could not trace him there, he told himself; only the devil himself could follow that

[9] *fox . . . fable:* Rainsford is thinking of the French fable about a fox who used many clever tricks in an unsuccessful attempt to escape some pursuing hounds, and a cat who escaped by using the only strategy it knew—hiding.

complicated trail through the jungle after dark. But perhaps the general was a devil——

An apprehensive night crawled slowly by like a wounded snake, and sleep did not visit Rainsford, although the silence of a dead world was on the jungle. Toward morning, when a dingy gray was varnishing the sky, the cry of some startled bird focused Rainsford's attention in that direction. Something was coming through the brush, coming slowly, carefully, coming by the same winding way Rainsford had come. He flattened himself down on the limb, and through a screen of leaves almost as thick as tapestry he watched. The thing that was approaching him was a man.

It was General Zaroff. He made his way along with his eyes fixed in utmost concentration on the ground before him. He paused almost beneath the tree, dropped to his knees, and studied the ground. Rainsford's impulse was to hurl himself down like a panther, but he saw the general's right hand held something small and metallic—an automatic pistol.

The hunter shook his head several times, as if he were puzzled. Then he straightened up and took from his case one of his black cigarettes; its pungent, incenselike smoke floated up to Rainsford's nostrils. Rainsford held his breath. The general's eyes had left the ground and were traveling inch by inch up the tree. Rainsford froze there, every muscle tensed for a spring. But the sharp eyes of the hunter stopped before they reached the limb where Rainsford lay; a smile spread over his brown face. Very deliberately he blew a smoke ring into the air; then he turned his back on the tree and walked carelessly away, back along the trail he had come. The swish of the underbrush against his hunting boots grew fainter and fainter.

The pent-up air burst hotly from Rainsford's lungs. His first thought made him feel sick and numb. The general could follow a trail through the woods at night; he could follow an extremely difficult trail; he must have uncanny powers; only by the merest chance had the Cossack failed to see his quarry.

Rainsford's second thought was even more terrible. It sent a shudder of cold horror through his whole being. Why had the general smiled? Why had he turned back?

Rainsford did not want to believe what his reason told him was true, but the truth was as evident as the sun that had by now pushed through the morning mists. The general was playing with him! The general was saving him for another day's sport! The Cossack was a cat; he was the mouse. Then it was that Rainsford knew the full meaning of terror.

"I will not lose my nerve. I will not."

He slid down from the tree and struck off again into the woods. His face was set and he forced the machinery of his mind to function. Three hundred yards from his hiding-place he stopped where a huge dead tree leaned precariously on a smaller, living one. Throwing off his sack of food, Rainsford took his knife from its sheath and began to work with all his energy.

The job was finished at last, and he threw himself down behind a fallen log a hundred feet away. He did not have to wait long. The cat was coming again to play with the mouse.

Following the trail with the sureness of a bloodhound, came General Zaroff. Nothing escaped those searching black eyes: no crushed blade of grass, no bent twig, no mark—no matter how faint—in the moss. So intent was the Cossack on his stalking that he was upon the thing Rainsford had made before he saw it. His foot touched the protruding bough that was the trigger. Even as he touched it, the general sensed his danger and leaped back with the agility of an ape. But he was not quite quick enough; the dead tree, delicately adjusted to rest on the cut living one, crashed down and struck the general a glacing blow on the shoulder as it fell; but for his alertness, he must have been smashed beneath it. He staggered, but he did not fall; nor did he drop his revolver. He stood there rubbing his injured shoulder, and Rainsford, with fear again gripping his heart, heard the general's mocking laugh ring through the jungle.

"Rainsford," called the general, "if you are within sound of my voice, as I suppose you are, let me congratulate you. Not many men know how to make a Malay mancatcher. Luckily for me, I too have hunted in Malacca. You are proving interesting, Mr. Rainsford. I am going now to have my wound dressed; it's only a slight one. But I shall be back. I shall be back."

When the general, nursing his bruised shoulder, had gone, Rainsford took up his flight again. It was flight now, a desperate, hopeless flight that carried him on for some hours. Dusk came, then darkness, and still he pressed on. The ground grew softer under his moccasins; the vegetation grew ranker, denser; insects bit him savagely. Then, as he stepped forwards, his foot sank into the ooze. He tried to wrench it back, but the muck sucked viciously at his foot as if it were a giant leech. With a violent effort he tore his foot loose. He knew where he was now. Death Swamp and its quicksand.

His hands were tight closed as if his nerve were something tangible that someone in the darkness was trying to tear from his grip. The softness of the earth had given him an idea. He stepped back from the quicksand a dozen feet or so and, like some huge prehistoric beaver, he began to dig.

Rainsford had dug himself in in France when a second's delay meant death. That had been a placid pastime compared to his digging now. The pit grew deeper; when it was above his shoulders, he climbed out and from some hard sapling cut stakes and sharpened them to a fine point. These stakes he planted in the bottom of the pit, with the points sticking up. With flying fingers he wove a rough carpet of weeds and branches, and with it he covered the mouth of the pit. Then, wet with sweat and aching with tiredness, he crouched behind the stump of a lightning-charred tree.

He knew his pursuer was coming; he heard the padding sound of feet on the soft earth, and the night breeze brought him the perfume of the general's cigarette. It seemed to Rainsford that the general was coming with unusual swiftness; he was not feeling his way along, foot by foot. Rainsford, crouching there, could not see the general, nor could he see the pit. He lived a year in a minute. Then he felt an impulse to cry aloud with joy, for he heard the sharp crackle of the breaking branches as the cover of the pit gave way; he heard the sharp scream of pain as the pointed stakes found their mark. He leaped up from his place of concealment. Then he cowered back. Three feet from the pit a man was standing with an electric torch in his hand.

"You've done well, Rainsford," the voice of the general called. "Your Burmese tiger pit has claimed one of my best dogs. Again you score. I think, Mr. Rainsford, I'll see what you can do against my whole pack. I'm going home for a rest now. Thank you for a most amusing evening."

At daybreak Rainsford, lying near the swamp, was awakened by a sound that made him know that he had new things to learn about fear. It was a distant sound, faint and wavering, but he knew it. It was the baying of a pack of hounds.

Rainsford knew he could do one of two things. He could stay where he was and wait. That was suicide. He could flee. That was postponing the inevitable. For a moment he stood there, thinking. An idea that held a wild chance came to him, and tightening his belt, he headed away from the swamp.

The baying of the hounds drew nearer, then still nearer, nearer, ever nearer. On a ridge Rainsford climbed a tree. Down a watercourse, not a quarter of a mile away, he could see the bush moving. Straining his eyes, he saw the lean figure of General Zaroff; just ahead of him Rainsford made out another figure whose wide shoulders surged through the tall jungle weeds; it was the giant Ivan, and he seemed pulled forward by some unseen force; Rainsford knew that Ivan must be holding the pack in leash.

They would be on him any minute now. His mind worked frantically. He thought of a native trick he had learned in Uganda. He slid down the tree. He caught hold of a springy young sapling and to it he fastened his hunting knife, with the blade pointing down the trail; with a bit of wild grapevine he tied back the sapling. Then he ran for his life. The hounds raised their voices as they hit the fresh scent. Rainsford knew now how an animal at bay feels.

He had to stop to get his breath. The baying of the hounds stopped abruptly, and Rainsford's heart stopped too. They must have reached the knife.

He shinned excitedly up a tree and looked back. His pursuers had stopped. But the hope that was in Rainsford's brain when he climbed died, for he saw in the shallow valley that General Zaroff was still on his feet. But Ivan was not. The knife, driven by the recoil of the springing tree, had not wholly failed.

Rainsford had hardly tumbled to the ground when the pack took up the cry again.

"Nerve, nerve, nerve!" he panted as he dashed along. A blue gap showed between the trees dead ahead. Ever nearer drew the hounds. Rainsford forced himself on toward that gap. He reached it. It was the shore of the sea. Across a cove he could see the gloomy gray stone of the chateau. Twenty feet below him the sea rumbled and hissed. Rainsford hesitated. He heard the hounds. Then he leaped far out into the sea.

When the general and his pack reached the place by the sea, the Cossack stopped. For some minutes he stood regarding the blue-green expanse of water. He shrugged his shoulders. Then he sat down, took a drink of brandy from a silver flask, lit a perfumed cigarette, and hummed a bit from *Madame Butterfly*.

General Zaroff had an exceedingly good dinner in his great paneled dining hall that evening. With it he had a bottle of Pol Roger and half a bottle of Chambertin. Two slight annoyances kept him from perfect enjoyment. One was the thought that it would be difficult to replace Ivan; the other was that his quarry had escaped him; of course, the American hadn't played the game—so thought the general as he tasted his after-dinner liqueur. In his library he read, to soothe himself, from the works of Marcus Aurelius. At ten he went up to his bedroom. He was deliciously tired, he said to himself as he locked himself in. There was a little moonlight, so before turning on his light, he went to the window and looked down at the courtyard. He could see the great hounds, and he called "Better luck another time!" to them. Then he switched on the light.

A man, who had been hiding in the curtains of the bed, was standing there.

"Rainsford!" screamed the general. "How did you get here?"

"Swam," said Rainsford. "I found it quicker than walking through the jungle."

The general sucked in his breath and smiled. "I congratulate you," he said. "You have won the game."

Rainsford did not smile. "I am still a beast at bay," he said in a low, hoarse voice. "Get ready, General Zaroff."

The general made one of his deepest bows. "I see," he said. "Splendid! One of us is to furnish a repast for the hounds. The other will sleep in this very excellent bed. On guard, Rainsford."

He had never slept in a better bed, Rainsford decided.

DISCUSSION

1. Who wins the game? How do you know?

2. "Life is for the strong . . . the weak of the world were put here to give the strong pleasure," said General Zaroff (page 21). Do Zaroff's words recall a similar statement made by Rainsford early in the story? Do you think Rainsford's experience made him change his attitude at all? Explain.

3. **Plot.** Plot refers to the bare outline of the events in the story, in the order in which they occur. The plot is often determined by what the characters in the story are like and where the story takes place. To what extent are the events in this story determined by the characters of Rainsford and Zaroff? For example, how would the story be different if Zaroff had not enjoyed the thrill of the hunt more than the actual kill?

For further activities, see page 44.

STAYING ALIVE

DAVID WAGONER

Staying alive in the woods is a matter of calming down
At first and deciding whether to wait for rescue,
Trusting to others,
Or simply to start walking and walking in one direction
Till you come out—or something happens to stop you.   5
By far the safer choice
Is to settle down where you are, and try to make a living
Off the land, camping near water, away from shadows.
Eat no white berries;
Spit out all bitterness. Shooting at anything   10
Means hiking further and further every day
To hunt survivors;
It may be best to learn what you have to learn without a gun,
Not killing but watching birds and animals go
In and out of shelter   15
At will. Following their example, build for a whole season:
Facing across the wind in your lean-to,
You may feel wilder,
And nothing, not even you, will have to stay in hiding.
If you have no matches, a stick and a fire-bow   20
Will keep you warmer,
Or the crystal of your watch, filled with water, held up to the
        sun
Will do the same, in time. In case of snow,
Drifting toward winter,
Don't try to stay awake through the night, afraid of
        freezing—   25
The bottom of your mind knows all about zero;
It will turn you over

20. stick . . . fire-bow: primitive device for starting a fire.

And shake you till you waken. If you have trouble sleeping
Even in the best of weather, jumping to follow
The unidentifiable noises of the night and feeling   30
Bears and packs of wolves nuzzling your elbow,
Remember the trappers
Who treated them indifferently and were left alone.
If you hurt yourself, no one will comfort you
Or take your temperature,   35
So stumbling, wading, and climbing are as dangerous as flying.
But if you decide, at last, you must break through
In spite of all danger,
Think of yourself by time and not by distance, counting
Wherever you're going by how long it takes you;   40
No other measure
Will bring you safe to nightfall. Follow no streams: they run
Under the ground or fall into wilder country.
Remember the stars
And moss when your mind runs into circles. If it should
      rain,   45
Or the fog should roll the horizon in around you,
Hold still for hours
Or days, if you must, or weeks, for seeing is believing
In the wilderness. And if you find a pathway,
Wheel rut, or fence wire,   50
Retrace it left or right—someone knew where he was going
Once upon a time, and you can follow
Hopefully, somewhere,
Just in case. There may even come, on some uncanny evening,
A time when you're warm and dry, well fed, not thirsty,   55
Uninjured, without fear,
When nothing, either good or bad, is happening.
This is called staying alive. It's temporary.
What occurs after
Is doubtful. You must always be ready for something to come
      bursting   60
Through the far edge of a clearing, running toward you,
Grinning from ear to ear
And hoarse with welcome. Or something crossing and hovering
Overhead, as light as air, like a break in the sky,
Wondering what you are.   65

Here you are face to face with the problem of recognition.
Having no time to make smoke, too much to say,
You should have a mirror
With a tiny hole in the back for better aiming, for reflecting
Whatever disaster you can think of, to show   70
The way you suffer.
These body signals have universal meaning: If you are lying
Flat on your back with arms outstretched behind you,
You say you require
Emergency treatment; if you are standing erect and hold-
    ing   75
Arms horizontal, you mean you are not ready;
If you hold them over
Your head, you want to be picked up. Three of anything
Is a sign of distress. Afterward, if you see
No ropes, no ladders,   80
No maps or messages falling, no searchlights or trails blazing,
Then chances are, you should be prepared to burrow
Deep for a deep winter.

DISCUSSION   1.   "Staying Alive" contains several rules for survival "in the woods." What is the first decision a person must make? What does the poet recommend?

2.   What advice does the poet offer about (a) food, (b) using guns, (c) staying warm, and (d) wild animals?

To School in Keams Canyon

HELEN SEKAQUAPTEWA

In the early 1900s two factions developed among the Hopi Indians: Friendlies, who cooperated with the U.S. Government, and Hostiles, who refused to do so. Helen Sekaquaptewa's traditional family, living on Hopi land in Arizona Territory, were Hostiles, who opposed sending their children to school. This excerpt from her autobiography recounts the result of that opposition.

Very early one morning toward the end of October, 1906, we awoke to find our camp surrounded by troops who had come during the night from Keams Canyon. Superintendent Lemmon called the men together, ordering the women and children to remain in their separate family groups. He told the men that the government had reached the limit of its patience; that the children would have to go to school. Yokeoma angrily defied them and refused to yield. He was taken to a house and put under guard.

All children of school age were lined up to be registered and taken away to school. Eighty-two children, including myself, were listed. It was late in the afternoon when the registration was completed. We were now loaded into wagons hired from and driven by our enemies, the Friendlies. There were not enough wagons, so the bigger boys had to walk. We were taken to the schoolhouse in New Oraibi, with military escort. We slept on the floor of the dining room that night.

The next morning three more wagons were hired, covered wagons drawn by four horses. All were loaded in, boys and girls in separate wagons. We just sat on the floor of the wagon, and still with military escort, started for Keams Canyon. In each wagon the older boys or girls looked after the little ones. I was one of the little ones. One little boy was about five years old. They let him live in the dormitory with the big girls so they

could mother him. Everyone called him "Baby," and he was still called "Baby" when he was a grown man.

It was after dark when we reached the Keams Canyon boarding school and were unloaded and taken into the big dormitory, lighted with electricity. I had never seen so much light at night. I was all mixed up and thought it was daytime because it was so light. Pretty soon they gave us hardtack and syrup to eat. There were not enough beds, so they put mattresses on the floor. When I was lying down I looked up and saw where the light came from just before the matron turned out the lights.

For the next few days we were all curious about our new surroundings. We thought it was wonderful and didn't think much about home, but after a while, when we got used to the school, we got real homesick. Three little girls slept in a double bed. Evenings we would gather in a corner and cry softly so the matron would not hear and scold or spank us. I would try to be a comforter, but in a little while I would be crying too. I can still hear the plaintive little voices saying, "I want to go home. I want my mother." We didn't understand a word of English and didn't know what to say or do.

Our native clothing was taken away from us and kept in boxes until our people came to take them. We were issued the regular school clothes. Each girl had two everyday dresses, three petticoats, two pairs of underwear, two pairs of stockings, one pair of shoes, one Sunday dress, and two white muslin aprons to be worn over the dresses, except on Sunday. The dresses were of striped bed ticking, with gathered skirts and long sleeves.

Some of the Friendly girls and those from other villages used to call us Hostiles and tease us until we would cry. At night when the doors were closed and locked and little girls were supposed to be in bed for the night, our tormentors would take our native clothes from the boxes and put them on and dance around making fun of us.

Boys and girls marched to the dining room from their separate dormitories. Usually the bigger boys got there first. Meals were served on twelve long tables, family style. Older boys and girls set the tables, and one of the older ones sat at the head of the table and served the food. There were Navajos there, even though it was a school for Hopis. It seemed a Navajo was always at the head and the Navajos would have their plates heaping full, while little Hopi girls just got a teaspoonful of everything. I was always hungry and wanted to cry because I didn't get enough food. They didn't give second helpings, and I thought I would just starve. You can't go to sleep when you are hungry.

In the center of the table was a big plate of bread. The big boys would grab it as they went in. By the time little boys and girls got in, there was no bread. Sometimes the big boys would even take bread away from the little ones. There was a matron who was supposed to watch, but she didn't seem to notice these things.

For breakfast we had oatmeal mush, without milk or sugar, and plain bread. The Navajos didn't like the mush, so they took the bread and we had the mush. At noon it was beef, potatoes, and gravy, with prunes or bread pudding for dessert. At night we had the leftovers, sometimes with beans. Another dish often served was salt bacon gravy over bread; bacon was fried in small pieces, flour was added and browned in the grease, water was added, and the mixture was boiled until it was thickened into gravy. Without the bread there wasn't much nourishment. Sometimes we little ones were hunger driven to ask the boys to give us just one slice of bread to go with our gravy, but they would never do it, so we just drank the gravy. Day after day, the food had a sameness. How we longed for some food cooked by our mothers—the kind and quantity we were used to eating.

On the few occasions when the girls did beat the boys to the dining room, we marched right in and did as they did. We took all the bread and piled it on our stools and covered it with our aprons, while we stood waiting until everyone was in place and the blessing on the food was said. Then we would pick up our bread and sit on the stools. Later on they changed the system, and instead of seating the boys on one side of the table and the girls on the other, girls of one age were put at tables by themselves, and the same for the boys. I fared better then.

When you were sick the matron put you to bed in the dormitory. She was sympathetic and tried to comfort you. She brought your meals on a tray, and there was enough food. The trouble was when you were sick you didn't feel like eating.

It seemed like everything was against us at first.

We were a group of homesick, lonesome, little girls, huddled together on the schoolgrounds early one morning, when we wondered what was making the approaching clinking sound. Running to the high, woven wire fence around the playground, we saw a long line of men walking down the road. They were some

of the seventy or so fathers from Hotevilla who had been arrested for resisting the government and had been sentenced to
ninety days of hard labor; the Superintendent was using them
to improve and build a dug-way into the canyon, thereby short-
ening the route by several miles. Supplies for the military post
and the school were hauled along this road, and the traders who
came by team and wagon from Holbrook also used it. What a
thrill as one little girl after another recognized her father and
pressed against the fence, calling out to him.

The construction gang walked four miles out to the job
every morning. They were fastened together in twos with ball
and chain. If one didn't keep step with his partner he might fall
down, but they would only laugh about it. They were not
ashamed of their condition because they knew in their hearts
they had done no wrong; they had only protested having their
lives interfered with. An officer with a stick would see to it that
they did not stop to talk to their little girls. After that, each
morning we ran out to see if our fathers went by. We would cry
if we saw them and cry if we didn't. I recognized my father in
the chain gang only once. He was put on kitchen duty, and I

saw him there once before he was sent to prison at Fort Huachuca.

Being a little girl and away at Keams Canyon, I hardly realized until later the very sad plight of my mother, along with the other exiles back at Hotevilla; there were seven old men and a handful of younger ones who had promised to cooperate, twenty-three children under school age, and sixty-three women—aged ones, middle-aged ones bereft of their children, and young mothers with little babies, all longing and crying for their old homes and fields and for their menfolk and their children who had been taken away. Few had the strength to gather and chop wood and to bring in the water. Their corn baskets were empty. They were so hungry! Sometimes the younger women would organize a rabbit hunt. The best time for this is when snow is on the ground. They wrapped their feet in whatever was available; a piece of sheepskin with the wool inside is good if tied on securely. They had no guns, just rocks and sticks and maybe a dog. If your dog caught it, it was your rabbit. Somehow they managed to survive the winter, while I had three meals each day and a comfortable bed and a warm building to shelter me.

The months passed by, and then it was the last day of school that first year at Keams Canyon. Parents in wagons, on horseback, and burros converged on the campgrounds around the school, from all directions. They had come to take their children home for the summer. There were parents from Hotevilla, but they would not promise to bring us back to school in September, so I was left to spend the summer at the school along with other boys and girls of Hostile parentage.

During the summer we fared better in the dining room because there were only about twenty girls and six boys and no Navajos. The big girls who worked in the kitchen and dining room favored us. In the cellar behind the kitchen there were many sacks of potatoes. Sometimes one of the older girls on kitchen duty would slip a raw potato to us little girls. They tasted good and sweet. I have tasted raw potato many times, but have never found any that tasted as sweet.

Come September, 1907, all the other children were brought back to school by their parents, and we were back in the regular routine again. One October afternoon, our eyes followed a few government wagons as they wended their way down the dugway into the canyon and stopped at the campgrounds, and lo!

the cargo unloaded itself—men, the prisoners being returned from Fort Huachuca. They had come by train to Holbrook, and then by team and wagon on out to Keams Canyon. We watched as the men filed by on their way to the dining room to be fed, and what a thrill, I recognized my own father. He was dressed in an old military uniform and looked fine and young and straight to me, and I was proud of him.

We talked together for a little while that night and again in the morning. My father's Hopi name is Talashongnewa, but he was given the name of Sam at Huachuca, and from then was known as Sam Talashongnewa. He didn't feel mean toward the soldier guards. He said they treated the Hopis well and were loved by them, and that many of them had tears in their eyes when they said "good-bye" to their Indian prisoners. But the prisoners came back still Hostile. My father's attitude had not changed, and it was many years before he could even begin to tolerate any part of the white man's culture. The prisoners were released to walk the forty miles on home to Hotevilla; it probably seemed a short forty miles to them.

As soon as they could, which was a year after we were taken away to Keams Canyon, some of the mothers came to visit their children. They came in a burro caravan of eight to ten. If one did not own a burro she would borrow or hire one on which she packed blankets and food for herself and as much as she could load on of piki,[1] parched corn, dried peaches, and the like to give to her children. Mothers who couldn't make the trip would send bundles to their children. These travelers got everything ready the night before so they could start early in the morning. It was a long day's journey. The women walked most of the way, each driving her burro before her. When a woman got very tired she would stop the burro near a stump or rock and climb on and ride for a while.

Arriving at the school late, they found shelter in the rock rooms built by the big boys and slept in their own blankets and ate their own food during their stay. Meat was not expensive, and the school had lots of meat. If the cook was good natured, he would give a Hopi mother a bone with a little meat on it, which she could boil with her corn.

My mother came two times during the four years I was at Keams. We thought we were sitting on top of the world to have

---

[1] piki: thin cornbread.

our mothers with us for a little while and to have some food
they had cooked over the campfire. After school they were permitted to come over and visit for a little while, bringing with
them some parched corn or some piki. They usually stayed
three days.

We learned by sad experience to have our housemother lock
up our precious bundle of piki or parched corn, otherwise it
would be pilfered. The matrons were usually older women, who
were pretty good to us. On the first visit, the mothers took
home the native clothing that we were wearing at the time we
were—shall we say—kidnaped.

DISCUSSION   1.   Helen Sekaquaptewa uses an unusually strong word to characterize
her being taken from her parents and put into a government school.
What word does she use? Is Helen justified in using this word? Explain.

2.   Helen says that "It seemed like everything was against us at first"
(page 39). What difficulties did the Hopi children encounter at the
school?

3.   The children were not the only ones to suffer when they were sent
away to school. What happened to the children's fathers? What was life
like for the mothers and the others who were left behind at the camp in
Hotevilla?

For further activities, see page 44.

VOCABULARY

My First Death (page 2)

This selection contains several phrases which are common to the vocabulary of pilots. Match each word in list A with the word in list B that correctly completes the phrase

List A
nose   tail   sound   ground   do a   instrument

List B
lap   control   barrier   spin   panel   dive

The Most Dangerous Game (page 11)

Word meaning can often be determined by how the word is used in the sentence. Read the sentences below, and then choose the meaning of the word in bold type from among the choices in parentheses.

1.   The *dank* (damp, smelly, starry) tropical night was *palpable* (frightening, capable of being felt, full of animal sounds) as it pressed its thick, warm blackness in upon the yacht.

2.   There was an original, almost *bizarre* (alarmingly strange, darkly handsome, starkly lonely) quality about the general's face, with its thick eyebrows and pointed moustache.

3.   Rainsford was finding the general a most thoughtful and *affable* (talkative, pleasant, well-dressed) host.

COMPOSITION

My First Death (page 2)

Jacqueline Auriol tells us about a frightening experience, one which she thinks will cause her death. Notice how suspensefully she relates her story. Write an account of one of your most frightening experiences. Try to construct it so that it also contains suspense for the reader.

The Most Dangerous Game (page 11)

How would the story have ended if Rainsford had not felt he had to kill Zaroff? Rewrite the ending, based on the rules of the game and what you know about Rainsford and Zaroff. Include some dialogue in your version.

READING

Malfunction (page 9)

Only one of the following statements accurately summarizes the action of the poem. Select the correct statement.

1. The speaker watches one of his comrades nearly get killed when he waits foolishly too long to open his parachute.

2. The speaker watches a comrade plunge to his death during a practice jump because his chute fails to open.

3. The speaker watches helplessly from the ground as a buddy floating to earth by parachute is shot to death by enemy airplanes.

The Most Dangerous Game (page 11)

Below is a list of characteristics. On separate paper, place *R* next to the number of those which you feel belong to Rainsford and *Z* next to the number of those which you feel belong to Zaroff. Some traits will belong to neither and some to both.

1. skilled woodsman, able to function in the wilds
2. compassionate
3. desperate
4. diabolical
5. sophisticated, knows about and likes fine wines, food, etc.
6. great interest in hunting
7. disturbed by the idea of killing human beings
8. lives for danger

Would you say that the two men are very much alike or very different?

To School in Keams Canyon (page 36)

Below are a series of events in the author's life. On separate paper, place the events in the order in which they occurred in the story.

1. Our native clothing was taken away from us.
2. I saw my father in the construction gang.
3. During the summer we fared better in the dining room.
4. The camps were surrounded by troops.
5. The mothers came to visit the school for the first time.
6. We were loaded into wagons.

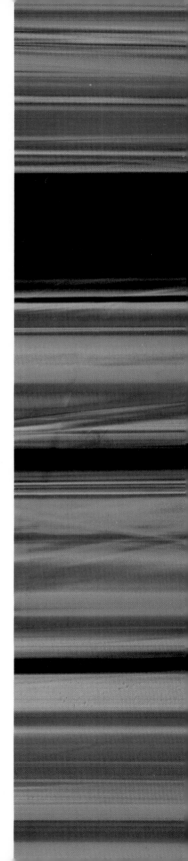

fable for when there's no way out

MAY SWENSON

Grown too big for his skin,
and it grown hard,

without a sea and atmosphere—
he's drunk it all up—

his strength's inside him now,   5
but there's no room to stretch.

He pecks at the top
but his beak's too soft;

though instinct and ambition shoves,
he can't get through.   10

Barely old enough to bleed
and already bruised!

In a case this tough
what's the use

if you break your head   15
instead of the lid?

Despair tempts him
to just go limp:

Maybe the cell's
already a tomb,   20

and beginning end
in this round room.

Still, stupidly he pecks
and pecks, as if from under

his own skull—   25
yet makes no crack . . .

No crack until
he finally cracks,

and kicks and stomps.
What a thrill   30

and shock to feel
his little gaff poke

through the floor!
A way he hadn't known or meant.

Rage works if reason won't.   35
When locked up, bear down.

DISCUSSION   1. After a seemingly hopeless struggle, the chick finally "cracks" his
                    shell. More than anything else, what causes him to break out?

                2. What two factors guide the chick's behavior?

The Sea Devil

ARTHUR GORDON

The man came out of the house and stood quite still, listening. Behind him, the lights glowed in the cheerful room, the books were neat and orderly in their cases, the radio talked importantly to itself. In front of him, the bay stretched dark and silent, one of the countless lagoons that border the coast where Florida thrusts its great green thumb deep into the tropics.

It was late in September. The night was breathless; summer's dead hand still lay heavy on the land. The man moved forward six paces and stood on the seawall. He dropped his cigarette and noted where the tiny spark hissed and went out. The tide was beginning to ebb.

Somewhere out in the blackness a mullet jumped and fell back with a sullen splash. Heavy with roe,[1] they were jumping less often now. They would not take a hook, but a practiced eye could see the swirls they made in the glassy water. In the dark of the moon a skilled man with a cast net might take half a dozen in an hour's work. And a big mullet makes a meal for a family.

The man turned abruptly and went into the garage, where his cast net hung. He was in his late twenties, wide-shouldered and strong. He did not have to fish for a living, or even for food. He was a man who worked with his head, not with his hands. But he liked to go casting alone at night.

He liked the loneliness and the labor of it. He liked the clean taste of salt when he gripped the edge of the net with his teeth, as a cast netter must. He liked the arching flight of sixteen pounds of lead and linen against the starlight, and the weltering crash of the net into the unsuspecting water. He liked the harsh tug of the retrieving rope around his wrist, and the way the net came alive when the cast was true, and the thud of captured fish on the floorboards of the skiff.

He liked all that because he found in it a reality that seemed to be missing from his twentieth-century job and from his daily life. He liked being the hunter, skilled and solitary and elemental. There was no conscious cruelty in the way he felt. It was the way things had been in the beginning.

---

[1] *roe:* their eggs.

The man lifted the net down carefully and lowered it into a bucket. He put a paddle beside the bucket. Then he went into the house. When he came out, he was wearing swimming trunks and a pair of old tennis shoes. Nothing else.

The skiff, flat-bottomed, was moored off the seawall. He would not go far, he told himself. Just to the tumbledown dock half a mile away. Mullet had a way of feeding around old piling after dark. If he moved quietly, he might pick up two or three in one cast close to the dock. And maybe a couple of others on the way down or back.

He shoved off and stood motionless for a moment, letting his eyes grow accustomed to the dark. Somewhere out in the channel a porpoise blew with a sound like steam escaping. The man smiled a little; porpoises were his friends. Once, fishing in the Gulf, he had seen the charter-boat captain reach overside and gaff a baby porpoise through the sinewy part of the tail. He had hoisted it aboard, had dropped it into the bail well, where it thrashed around puzzled and unhappy. And the mother had swum alongside the boat and under the boat and around the boat, nudging the stout planking with her back, slapping it with her tail, until the man felt sorry for her and made the captain let the baby porpoise go.

He took the net from the bucket, slipped the noose in the retrieving rope over his wrist, pulled the slipknot tight. It was an old net, but still serviceable; he had rewoven the rents made by underwater snags. He coiled the thirty-foot rope carefully, making sure there were no kinks. A tangled rope, he knew, would spoil any cast.

The basic design of the net had not changed in three thousand years. It was a mesh circle with a diameter of fourteen feet. It measured close to fifteen yards around the circumference and could, if thrown perfectly, blanket a hundred and fifty square feet of sea water. In the center of this radial trap was a small iron collar where the retrieving rope met the twenty-three separate drawstrings leading to the outer rim of the net. Along this rim, spaced an inch and a half apart, were the heavy lead sinkers.

The man raised the iron collar until it was a foot above his head. The net hung soft and pliant and deadly. He shook it gently, making sure that the drawstrings were not tangled, that the sinkers were hanging true. Then he eased it down and picked up the paddle.

The night was black as a witch's cat; the stars looked fuzzy and dim. Down to the southward, the lights of a causeway made a yellow necklace across the sky. To the man's left were the tangled roots of a mangrove swamp; to his right, the open waters of the bay. Most of it was fairly shallow, but there were channels eight feet deep. The man could not see the old dock, but he knew where it was. He pulled the paddle quietly through the water, and the phosphorescence glowed and died.

For five minutes he paddled. Then, twenty feet ahead of the skiff, a mullet jumped. A big fish, close to three pounds. For a moment it hung in the still air, gleaming dully. Then it vanished. But the ripples marked the spot, and where there was one there were often others.

The man stood up quickly. He picked up the coiled rope, and with the same hand grasped the net at a point four feet below the iron collar. He raised the skirt to his mouth, gripped it strongly with his teeth. He slid his free hand as far as it would go down the circumference of the net so that he had three points of contact with the mass of cordage and metal. He made sure his feet were planted solidly. Then he waited, feeling the tension that is older than the human race, the fierce exhilaration of the hunter at the moment of ambush, the atavistic[2] desire to capture and kill and ultimately consume.

A mullet swirled, ahead and to the left. The man swung the heavy net back, twisting his body and bending his knees so as to get more upward thrust. He shot it forward, letting go simultaneously with rope hand and with teeth, holding a fraction of a second longer with the other hand so as to give the net necessary spin, impart the centrifugal force that would make it flare into a circle. The skiff ducked sideways, but he kept his balance. The net fell with a splash.

The man waited for five seconds. Then he began to retrieve it, pulling in a series of sharp jerks so that the drawstrings would gather the net inward, like a giant fist closing on this segment of the teeming sea. He felt the net quiver, and knew it was not empty. He swung it, dripping, over the gunwale, saw the broad silver side of the mullet quivering, saw too the gleam of a smaller fish. He looked closely to make sure no stingray was hidden in the mesh, then raised the iron collar and shook the net out. The mullet fell with a thud and flapped wildly. The other victim was an angelfish, beautifully marked, but too small to keep. The man picked it up gently and dropped it overboard. He coiled the rope,

---

[2] *atavistic* (ăt-ə-vĭz′tĭk): like that of early ancestors.

took up the paddle. He would cast no more until he came to the dock.

The skiff moved on. At last, ten feet apart, a pair of stakes rose up gauntly out of the night. Barnacle-encrusted, they once had marked the approach from the main channel. The man guided the skiff between them, then put the paddle down softly. He stood up, reached for the net, tightened the noose around his wrist. From here he could drift down upon the dock. He could see it now—a ruined skeleton in the starshine. Beyond it a mullet jumped and fell back with a flat, liquid sound. The man raised the edge of the net, put it between his teeth. He would not cast at a single swirl, he decided; he would wait until he saw two or three close together. The skiff was barely moving. He felt his muscles tense themselves, awaiting the signal from the brain.

Behind him in the channel he heard the porpoise blow again, nearer now. He frowned in the darkness. If the porpoise chose to fish this area, the mullet would scatter and vanish. There was no time to lose.

A school of sardines surfaced suddenly, skittering along like drops of mercury. Something, perhaps the shadow of the skiff, had frightened them. The old dock loomed very close. A mullet broke water just too far away; then another, nearer. The man marked the spreading ripples and decided to wait no longer.

He swung back the net, heavier now that it was wet. He had to turn his head, but out of the corner of his eye he saw two swirls in the black water just off the starboard bow. They were about eight feet apart, and they had the sluggish oily look that marks the presence of something big just below the surface. His conscious mind had no time to function, but instinct told him that the net was wide enough to cover both swirls if he could alter the direction of his cast. He could not halt the swing, but he shifted his feet slightly and made the cast off balance. He saw the net shoot forward, flare into an oval, and drop just where he wanted it.

Then the sea exploded in his face. In a frenzy of spray, a great horned thing shot like a huge bat out of the water. The man saw the mesh of his net etched against the mottled blackness of its body, and he knew, in the split second in which thought was still possible, that those twin swirls had been made not by two mullet, but by the wing tips of the giant ray of the Gulf Coast, *Manta birostris,* also known as clam cracker, devil ray, sea devil.

The man gave a hoarse cry. He tried to claw the slipknot off his wrist, but there was no time. The quarter-inch line snapped taut. He shot over the side of the skiff as if he had roped a runaway locomotive. He hit the water headfirst and seemed to bounce once. He plowed a blinding furrow for perhaps ten yards. Then the line went slack as the sea devil jumped again. It was not the full-grown manta of the deep Gulf, but it was close to nine feet from tip to tip and it weighed over a thousand pounds. Up into the air it went, pearl-colored underbelly gleaming as it twisted in a frantic effort to dislodge the clinging thing that had fallen upon it. Up into the starlight, a monstrous survival from the dawn of time.

The water was less than four feet deep. Sobbing and choking, the man struggled for a foothold on the slimy bottom. Sucking in great gulps of air, he fought to free himself from the rope. But the slipknot was jammed deep into his wrist; he might as well have tried to loosen a circle of steel.

The ray came down with a thunderous splash and drove forward again. The flexible net followed every movement, impeding it hardly at all. The man weighed a hundred and seventy-five pounds, and he was braced for the shock, and he had the desperate strength that comes from looking into the blank eyes of death. It was useless. His arm straightened out with a jerk that seemed to dislocate his shoulder; his feet shot out from under him; his head went under again. Now at last he knew how the fish must feel when the line tightens and drags him toward the alien element that is his doom. Now he knew.

Desperately he dug the fingers of his free hand into the ooze, felt them dredge a futile channel through broken shells and the ribbonlike sea grasses. He tried to raise his head, but could not get it clear. Torrents of spray choked him as the ray plunged toward deep water.

His eyes were of no use to him in the foam-streaked blackness. He closed them tight, and at once an insane sequence of pictures flashed through his mind. He saw his wife sitting in their living room, reading, waiting calmly for his return. He saw the mullet he had just caught, gasping its life away on the floorboards of the skiff. He saw the cigarette he had flung from the seawall touch the water and expire with a tiny hiss. He saw all these things and many others simultaneously in his mind as his body fought silently and tenaciously for its existence. His hand touched something hard and closed on it in a death grip, but it was only the sharp-edged helmet of a horsehoe crab, and after an instant he let it go.

He had been underwater perhaps fifteen seconds now, and something in his brain told him quite calmly that he could last another forty or fifty, and then the red flashes behind his eyes would merge into darkness, and the water would pour into his lungs in one sharp, painful shock, and he would be finished.

This thought spurred him to a desperate effort. He reached up and caught his pinioned wrist with his free hand. He doubled up his knees to create more drag. He thrashed his body madly, like a fighting fish, from side to side. This did not disturb the ray, but now one of the great wings tore through the mesh, and the net slipped lower over the fins projecting like horns from below the nightmare head, and the sea devil jumped again.

And once more the man was able to get his feet on the bottom and his head above water, and he saw ahead of him the pair of ancient stakes that marked the approach to the channel. He knew that if he was dragged much beyond those stakes, he would be in eight feet of water, and the ray would go down to hug the bottom as rays always do, and then no power on earth could save him. So in the moment of respite[3] that was granted him, he flung himself toward them. For a moment he thought his captor yielded a bit. Then the ray moved off again, but more slowly now, and for a few yards the man was able to keep his feet on the bottom. Twice he hurled himself back against the rope with all his strength, hoping that something would break. But nothing broke. The mesh of the net was ripped and torn, but the draw lines were strong, and the stout perimeter cord threaded through the sinkers was even stronger.

The man could feel nothing now in his trapped hand—it was numb—but the ray could feel the powerful lunges of the unknown thing that was trying to restrain it. It drove its great wings against the unyielding water and forged ahead, dragging the man and pushing a sullen wave in front of it.

The man had swung as far as he could toward the stakes. He plunged toward one and missed it by inches. His feet slipped and he went down on his knees. Then the ray swerved sharply and the second stake came right at him. He reached out with his free hand and caught it.

He caught it just above the surface, six or eight inches below high-water mark. He felt the razor-sharp barnacles bite into his hand, collapse under the pressure, drive their tiny slime-covered shell splinters deep into his flesh. He felt the pain, and he welcomed it, and he made his fingers into an iron claw that would hold until the tendons were severed or the skin was shredded from the bone. The ray felt the pressure increase with a jerk that stopped it dead in the water. For a moment all was still as the tremendous forces came into equilibrium.

Then the net slipped again, and the perimeter cord came down over the sea devil's eyes, blinding it momentarily. The great ray settled to the bottom and braced its wings against the mud and hurled itself forward and upward.

The stake was only a four-by-four of creosoted pine, and it was old. Ten thousand tides had swirled around it. Worms had bored; parasites had clung. Under the crust of barnacles it still had some heart left, but not enough. The man's grip was five feet

---

[3] *respite* (rĕs'pĭt): temporary relief.

above the floor of the bay; the leverage was too great. The stake snapped off at its base.

The ray lunged upward, dragging the man and the useless timber. The man had his lungs full of air, but when the stake snapped he thought of expelling the air and inhaling the water so as to have it finished quickly. He thought of this, but he did not do it. And then, just at the channel's edge, the ray met the porpoise coming in.

The porpoise had fed well this night and was in no hurry, but it was a methodical creature and it intended to make a sweep around the old dock before the tide dropped too low. It had no quarrel with any ray, but it feared no fish in the sea, and when the great black shadow came rushing blindly and unavoidably, it rolled fast and struck once with its massive horizontal tail.

The blow descended on the ray's flat body with a sound like a pistol shot. It would have broken a buffalo's back, and even the sea devil was half stunned. It veered wildly and turned back toward shallow water. It passed within ten feet of the man, face down in the water. It slowed and almost stopped, wing tips moving faintly, gathering strength for another rush.

The man had heard the tremendous slap of the great mammal's tail and the snorting gasp as it plunged away. He felt the line go slack again, and he raised his dripping face, and he reached for the bottom with his feet. He found it, but now the water was up to his neck. He plucked at the noose once more with his lacerated hand, but there was no strength in his fingers. He felt the tension come back into the line as the ray began to move again, and for half a second he was tempted to throw himself backward and fight as he had been doing, pitting his strength against the vastly superior strength of the brute.

But the acceptance of imminent death had done something to his brain. It had driven out the fear, and with the fear had gone the panic. He could think now, and he knew with absolute certainty that if he was to make any use of this last chance that had been given him, it would have to be based on the one faculty that had carried man to his pre-eminence above all beasts: the faculty of reason. Only by using his brain could he possibly survive, and he called on his brain for a solution, and his brain responded. It offered him one.

He did not know whether his body still had the strength to carry out the brain's commands, but he began to swim forward, toward the ray that was still moving hesitantly away from the channel. He swam forward, feeling the rope go slack as he gained on the creature.

Ahead of him he saw the one remaining stake, and he made himself swim faster until he was parallel with the ray and the rope trailed behind both of them in a deep U. He swam with a surge of desperate energy that came from nowhere, so that he was slightly in the lead as they came to the stake. He passed on one side of it; the ray was on the other.

Then the man took one last deep breath, and he went down under the black water until he was sitting on the bottom of the bay. He put one foot over the line so that it passed under his bent knee. He drove both his heels into the mud, and he clutched the slimy grass with his bleeding hand, and he waited for the tension to come again.

The ray passed on the other side of the stake, moving faster now. The rope grew taut again, and it began to drag the man back toward the stake. He held his prisoned wrist close to the bottom, under his knee, and he prayed that the stake would not break. He felt the rope vibrate as the barnacles bit into it. He did not know whether the rope would crush the barnacles or whether the barnacles would cut the rope. All he knew was that in five seconds or

less he would be dragged into the stake and cut to ribbons if he tried to hold on, or drowned if he didn't.

He felt himself sliding slowly, and then faster, and suddenly the ray made a great leap forward, and the rope burned around the base of the stake, and the man's foot hit it hard. He kicked himself backward with his remaining strength, and the rope parted and he was free.

He came slowly to the surface.

Thirty feet away the sea devil made one tremendous leap and disappeared into the darkness. The man raised his wrist and looked at the frayed length of rope dangling from it. Twenty inches, perhaps. He lifted his other hand and felt the hot blood start instantly, but he didn't care. He put this hand on the stake above the barnacles and held onto the good, rough, honest wood. He heard a strange noise, and realized that it was himself sobbing.

High above, there was a droning sound, and looking up, he saw the nightly plane from New Orleans inbound for Tampa. Calm and serene, it sailed, symbol of man's proud mastery over nature. Its lights winked red and green for a moment; then it was gone.

Slowly, painfully, the man began to move through the placid water. He came to the skiff at last and climbed into it. The mullet, still alive, slapped convulsively with its tail. The man reached down with his torn hand, picked up the mullet, let it go.

He began to work on the slipknot doggedly with his teeth. His mind was almost a blank, but not quite. He knew one thing. He knew he would do no more casting alone at night. Not in the dark of the moon. No, not he.

DISCUSSION

1. "He was a man who worked with his head, not with his hands" (page 47). Is it his head or his hands that finally save this man's life? Explain how he does free himself in the end. What has he learned from his experience with the sea devil?

2. What did the man like about casting alone at night? How did the solitary fishing contrast with his daily life?

3. **Setting.** The setting of a story is the time and place in which the action takes place. In this story, how does the setting add to the conflict and the tension? Would another setting be just as appropriate?

For further activities, see page 80.

Carmel Point

MARGARET PHYLLIS MacSWEENY

I watched a sea anemone
The color of green jade
Shadowed under water.

I saw a daring crab,
Unafraid and young   5
Touch the velvet petals
Of that princess under water.
Softly she took him in,
Softly she sighed and closed.
The little crab was hushed and still—   10
Never would he swim again
Under crevice, under weed,
Under green and colored water.

Softly she opened—
That princess of rare jade.   15
Softly she gave him back
Sucked of all his pearly flesh
Sucked of all his salty blood.

I ran away to tell my dad,
"Let's go home," I said,   20
"I am sorry to be born,
I am afraid of many things."

1. *sea anemone* (ə-něm′ə-nē): a flowerlike marine animal
which uses its tentacles to capture food.

DISCUSSION   1.   Why is the speaker so horrified and frightened to see the anemone devour the flesh of the crab?

2.   The speaker says, "I am sorry to be born / I am afraid of many things." Why? What has this experience made the speaker realize?

FROM STAYING ALIVE!

MAURICE and MARALYN BAILEY

Fulfilling a longtime dream of living on the water, Maurice and Maralyn Bailey set sail from Panama to the Galápagos Islands on their yacht *Auralyn*. Just before breakfast on March 4, 1973, a whale crashed into the *Auralyn*, leaving an eighteen-inch hole below the water line. Fifty minutes later the Baileys abandoned ship and watched everything they had worked for slowly sink beneath the waves. With a dinghy, a life raft, and few provisions they began an ordeal that was to last one hundred and eighteen days. Here are excerpts from their story, which they began writing aboard their rescue ship.

MARALYN   MARCH 4TH

We settled into the raft as comfortably as possible and before the sun rose too high we had our breakfast which consisted of four biscuits each spread thickly with margarine and a smear of marmalade. At lunch time we had a small handful of peanuts each and our evening meal was one tin of food between us.

At the last moment as I left the yacht I had grabbed our small "Camping Gaz" butane stove. Unfortunately, the gas canister was part used and we had no spare cartridges, but by careful use I reckoned it would last out our supply of tins. I put the contents of a tin in a small saucepan we had managed to salvage and heated the food for three or four minutes. I took one spoonful then handed the pan to Maurice who also took one spoonful. We shared it like this until the food had gone. At meal times all conversation ceased and we concentrated on our food. When the last mouthful had disappeared we were both still very hungry and occasionally for "afters" we would raid the biscuit tin and have one each, or sometimes a date, and drool over its sweetness.

In our emergency kit I had placed two plastic bottles each holding two pints of water and one of these bottles would be our day's ration. When it was empty we would fill it from the main supply kept in the dinghy. For breakfast we would stir approximately three spoons of Coffeemate into a cup of water and the rest of the day we would take turns and have sips from the bottle, finishing the rest after our evening meal. We learned later that our thirst might have been better satisfied if we had drunk our ration at one go.

On leaving the yacht I had rescued two books, one was Eric Hiscock's *Voyaging* which he had kindly autographed for me one day on the Hamble River. The second book was a historical volume, *Richard III* by Paul Murray Kendall. We passed many hours remembering the books we had left behind and usually by starting with the words, "Did you read . . .", we would tell each other the story in minute detail. I remembered one story of the life of Eleanor of Aquitaine; she was imprisoned for sixteen years by her husband and the way in which she kept her mind occupied during that time was fascinating. Another story was of an American soldier captured during the Korean war who was kept in solitary confinement yet retained his sanity by designing and building in his mind his future home. It was this last story that gave us the idea of designing and planning our next boat in detail.

MAURICE

The sun rose higher and the heat became intense and with it a state of languor pervaded the raft. I opened the chart and plotted our Dead Reckoning position. We were, in fact, quite close to the shipping lane. I estimated our position to be 1° 30′ N 85° 47′ W, 250 miles north of Ecuador and 300 miles east of the Galápagos Islands, which was too far north to allow the west-going current to drift us on to the islands.

The wind blew from the southeast and, although light in strength, would drive us even farther north. Could we, perhaps, row the hundred or so miles south to the latitude of the Galápagos? It would take us above twelve days to reach the longitude of the Galápagos drifting at twenty-five miles per day. We would then have to row ten miles per day south to offset the wind and current and to reach their latitude at the same time as attaining the longitude. These calculations depended a lot on the wind and current remaining constant. Were we capable of rowing the dinghy ten miles each day with the raft in tow? Should we abandon the raft to give ourselves a better chance?

I stopped thinking about this problem and contented myself with the knowledge that in the next few days we should be drifting in a shipping lane. Nevertheless, I would have to mention the possibility of rowing to Maralyn. But later; not now.

We noticed a slight loss of pressure in the raft during the afternoon and I pumped air into the tubes with the pump provided in the raft's emergency kit. This made me aware of the appalling vulnerability of our position; only our two small craft to keep us afloat on that vast ocean.

During the late afternoon I explained to Maralyn the desperate half-formed plan to row south to reach the latitude of the Galápagos Islands.

"We'll have to do the rowing at night," she said, "it would be impossible in the heat of the day."

I was depressed by the seriousness of our position and reluctant to make any decision. I found myself renouncing all pretense of leadership, and with her flair for organization Maralyn was taking command. "If it is too dark to see the compass we can steer by the stars," she said simply. Maralyn appeared undaunted. "We'll start rowing immediately after supper. Two-hour spells will be enough." I hated the idea of rowing and asked, "How far do you think you can row in two hours?" She would not be discouraged. "We must try," she said.

The day wore on and the sun slid towards the clear horizon bringing the refreshing coolness we longed for. After our evening meal I argued a case for deferring rowing until the next evening. It was not just laziness that made me argue like this. We were drifting towards the shipping lane which runs to the south of the Galápagos. In another twenty-four hours we should be in the center of this lane and we might just see a ship.

Of course this was wrong, we should have started rowing straight away. The longer we delayed, the more we would have to row on subsequent nights. We settled down for our first night adrift, making ourselves as comfortable as possible. Unable to lie down in the raft together, one of us would curl up on the floor and sleep, whilst the other keeping watch, would sit hunched up in the little remaining space. We would change over every three hours. Maralyn had the worst of the arrangement because, whether sleeping or watch-keeping, I would take up the most room. We found this arrangement satisfactory only when the raft was inflated hard. The watch-keeper therefore had to pump the raft frequently to replace any slight loss of pressure. When several weeks later the raft became damaged and it was impossible to keep fully inflated, we abandoned this system and slept fitfully where we sat.

MARCH 5TH (1)

Dawn arrived and heralded another scorching day. We used some of our precious food, but hardly enough to sustain us, and sipped our daily one-pint ration of water carefully. Even then we found our thirst intolerable but hunger, up to then, was bearable. I examined the water containers in the dinghy and was horrified to discover that four gallons had been contaminated by sea water. It was obvious that we had to have rain soon to replace this foul water.

That night after retrieving the drogue we started rowing. The task of towing the unwieldy bulk of the raft was slow, painful and laborious; we strained our bodies and badly blistered our hands. At each stroke the dinghy would be propelled forward at a good pace, only to be brought up short when the painter between the two craft tautened, thus braking any further progress. The raft, responding to the momentum, would then slowly, Oh! so slowly and sluggishly, move forward for a short distance. Hour followed laborious hour.

When the moon was up we checked our course with the compass;

afterwards we used the stars, using principally the constellations of Orion, Crux and the Plough, with the Pole Star low on the northern horizon.

Eight hours rowing had exhausted us and we found that even though we doubled our water ration we did not find any relief from our thirst. This was indeed a bad thing. I doubted our ability to row enough each night to attain the right latitude before our water ran out. Although she had suffered through this strenuous activity, Maralyn did not complain and I could not disillusion her.

MARCH 6TH–8TH (2, 3 AND 4) My calculations showed that we had only gained a little over four miles to the south, whilst our westerly drift had been nearly thirty miles. I could say nothing to Maralyn; she was very optimistic. In fact, later in the day, when a layer of cumulus cloud appeared on the horizon to the southwest, she was convinced that it lay over the Galápagos Islands.

I kept a check on the accuracy of my wristwatch by frequent comparisons with the compass and ensuring that the sun's maximum altitude coincided with the hands showing twelve o'clock. The accuracy of the watch helped me a lot when waiting to take a noon latitude sextant sight.

Although we placed little reliance on its absolute accuracy, we were indeed surprised to discover that it was only two minutes slow when we were rescued.

During the day we would get an idea of our drift or the wind direction by using the watch as a compass. This was especially helpful after we later lost the boat's compass when the dinghy capsized.

Our efforts at rowing were continued on the third and fourth nights and then, having fixed our position at noon on the fifth day, I explained to Maralyn my misgivings about rowing any more. Surprisingly she agreed, saying that the sooner we drifted into a shipping lane the better.

"You will not find these lanes full of shipping like the English Channel," I said. "Months may pass before a ship will be seen."

"But there will be a chance," Maralyn replied emphatically.

MARALYN
For three nights we had rowed in turn, two hours each throughout the coolness of the evening until the sun rose the next morning. We had taken the ship's compass from the cockpit and Maurice had wedged it between the water carriers and we followed a compass course when there was enough light from the moon. After that we steered by the stars.

At the end of this time we were both exhausted and had blisters on our hands. A feature of this exercise was our alarming consumption of water. I had laid down the ration as one pint of water each per day, as I knew that one of the most dangerous things to do was to let the body dehydrate and this was about the least amount our bodies would need. However, we found that during these three days we were exceeding our ration. It was then that Maurice explained the true position to me. We had only managed by rowing to gain ten miles south and we would have to row for, at least, another ten to twelve days to attain sufficient southing to keep on the same latitude as the Galápagos Islands—but the current was taking us west faster than we rowed south. This, in simple terms, meant that however hard we rowed we would still pass north of the Galápagos Islands.

MAURICE   MARCH 9TH (5)
Maralyn brooded for some time and left the raft and clambered into the dinghy. Picking up the oars she thrust them upright down each side of the thwart and guyed them fore and aft with a thin line. Between these two 'masts' she rigged a sail bag as a sail. In the light southeast wind the sail worked well. "You'll be driving us northwest," I said.

"And toward a shipping lane— and towards the American coast!" Maralyn retorted.

What could I say? It was no use explaining that once we were out of the doldrum belt we would meet the northeast trade winds again and these would drive us southwest away from the American continent. There was only one thing that I could really hope for and that was to meet a possible counter current running east just north of the cold Humboldt current.

Soon after Maralyn had fixed the sail we encountered an electrical storm; more picturesque than violent.

The sky was lit by momentary flashes of light charging from the tall and majestic cumulo-nimbus clouds that now towered above us. Thunder rolled over us like loud and tumultuous gunfire. Yet there was no rain. The display soon finished and left us fractionally cooler.

The four days that followed were even hotter; the sun shining from an almost cloudless sky; there was no wind. We wilted during the hottest part of the day under the raft's canopy, trying to keep cool by means of evaporation, draping our bodies with our spare clothes soaked in sea water. Drop by drop we conserved our depleting water supply.

Our main hope of survival now was to meet a ship. We kept a strict watch, two hours each throughout the day and night and reasoned that, with the colossal amount of shipping going through the Panama Canal, at least one ship would pass our way.

What I had failed to comprehend was the vastness of that ocean and the fact that we were a mere speck of human flotsam.

MARALYN   MARCH 29TH (25)
On March 29th we saw our second ship. We had kept a strict watch throughout the night and as I watched the stars during my watch, I saw one move on the northern horizon. That was odd, I thought, and looked again. I held my breath; it can only be a ship.

It was 3:45 A.M. I didn't want to wake Maurice and raise his hopes if it turned out to be a false alarm but suddenly as the ship rose above a swell I saw a red navigation light as well as the masthead lights. I shook Maurice awake and collected our two remaining flares. The ship, a tanker, its masthead lights nearly in line came steadily on. We saw the deck lights picking out clearly the ship's structure and the warm glow of light from the portholes as the ship came closer. Maurice took the first flare—a red one. The fates were really against us because that flare was also a dud but we had suffered so many misfortunes that this calamity was taken in our stride. Maurice tossed it into the sea without a word and reached for our last flare.

The second flare worked perfectly and illuminated both raft and dinghy and a large area around us. We felt confident that the watch keepers on the boat would see us. As the flare faded Maurice began flashing S O S with the torch. Relentlessly the ship proceeded on its way until its stern light once more became a bright star on the horizon.

Two ships in twenty-five days; I tried to console Maurice by saying "Third time lucky," but it did little to lift our flagging spirits. As if the weather reflected our mood March came to a close with squally, wet, dismal days. The only good thing about this weather was an ample supply of fresh water.

APRIL 8TH (35)

How often I would lean on the edge of the raft dreamily gazing at the multicolored aquarium swimming lazily below me. A sleek white two-masted sailing boat sailed across my

mind's eye, a thing of beauty, yet purposeful. I walked the decks and peeped below into the various cabins noting the furnishings and the varnished woodwork. How could I persuade Maurice that I longed for another yacht just like this dream ship.

For so many years we had planned our life afloat, we couldn't give up now. It was the life we had chosen, the life Maurice was happy with. Yet he was now prepared to give up this life, swallow the anchor, and return to the life he had found so restricting, because he was convinced I would no longer wish to sail. He spoke of the house we would buy, with a large garden for me to potter around in and grow all our vegetables once more, and fill the flowerbeds with a riot of color. Although I talked with enthusiasm I knew that, peaceful as this plan sounded, it was not really what either of us wanted. For a short time it would have been relaxing but deep down within us both was the restless urge to travel "beyond the sunset," a desire to see strange places, different people, and animals in their natural surroundings. We had to go on.

As Maurice stirred I gathered my thoughts together and decided to tell him of the dream ship and the voyages we would make in her. Once I had persuaded him I still loved the sea and ships, we both found an enormous amount of pleasure designing our next yacht and home. We planned to live aboard again as we had done with *Auralyn*.

Hour after hour passed as we discussed our plans down to each minute detail. Maurice drew the outline of the yacht and gradually we filled it out as we decided on the layout. Each section was itemized and I wrote down all the details in our log book. Once we had designed the boat I spent days planning a provision list and stocking the boat for an extended voyage, and when we had decided on the quantity of food we spent a long time discussing its stowage, and the positioning of locker space. These preparations ran into weeks; in fact we had two favorite subjects—our yacht and food.

APRIL 24TH (51)

The day began fine, but dull; the seas were much calmer but lumpy. It was my birthday. As a special treat Maurice started fishing early and kept trying for a large silver milk-fish whose flesh we particularly liked, but he found it a difficult task to catch one with our barbless hooks. We both got excited as time and time again the fish took the bait—but not the hook. It was getting overconfident however and we recognized the signs—soon it would make a mistake.

"I've got it!" yelled Maurice as he struggled with the line. I kept my fingers crossed as I had seen this happen so many times before. The hook was not strong enough to take the weight of such a large fish, and they usually escaped when almost within reach. This time was no exception— within inches of the dinghy it gave a vicious tug and pulled free of the hook; like a catapult the hook flicked back, and to our horror embedded itself in the dinghy.

Automatically Maurice pulled it out and a slow hiss started. Bubbles popped on the surface of the sea as air escaped from the punctured tube. As the puncture was just under water, we knew we would have to lift the dinghy clear to patch it. I took some of the water carriers from Maurice and placed them in the raft, and the rest were floated and tied to the outside. Maurice then returned to the raft and we both knelt in the doorway and lifted the side of the dinghy, resting it on the top tube of the raft. We only had the repair kit which was supplied with the raft and as we read through the instructions, we realized that if we had only had one craft it would have been impossible to repair any leak near the water, and this was the most vulnerable place.

Following the instructions carefully, we dried and cleaned the appropriate area and applied the first coat of glue. We had to wait until this was dry and already my arms began to ache with holding the dinghy in place, but I could not let go as it would get wet. Maurice took over for a while to give me some relief. When the glue was dry, I took hold of the dinghy again while Maurice applied the second coat of glue and then, carefully, a small round patch. We both held on to the dinghy until it was perfectly dry and then surveyed our handiwork. Although it had been an effort in our weakened state, we were pleased with it, and resolved to

be more careful with fish hooks in the future.

We returned the dinghy to the sea and reloaded it. I noticed Maurice looking puzzled and inquired what the matter was.

"I'm sure we had more water containers," he said.

"Are you sure you've counted properly?"

"Well you count and see if I'm right."

I counted, then counted again. He was right, one container had disappeared! We scanned the sea around us, but could see no trace of our water carrier. Our feeling of achievement rapidly dissolved as we realized the cost of one small patch was four days' water supply. To try and raise our spirits I reminded Maurice that today *was* my birthday, and tonight we would celebrate.

That night we opened and shared out our one and only rice pudding topped with the remains of the treacle. It was thick, creamy and wonderful, and we ate it in blissful silence. Afterwards we came back to reality and agreed that it had tasted a bit tinny; the tin was very rusty, but it seemed we had caught it in time, although had we kept it for much longer I think it would have "blown."

MAURICE　　　　APRIL 28TH (54)
As the days progressed, we became shocked at the physical decline in each other. Maralyn's brown, smooth-skinned and supple body had now developed into a thin bony frame motivated by stiff and sore limbs. Her

sunken eyes accentuated the gaunt-
ness of her face.

My beard, to a large extent, must
have disguised the drawn and angular
features of my face but I could feel
the bones as they protruded through
my skin. Our muscles were slack and
wasted.

Our emaciated state horrified us.
There was all this natural food
around us and yet we were not, apparently, getting sufficient nourishment.

Day followed day without making any impact on our minds. We
could make no true distinction between different days of the week.
Only the change from day to night
and the fluctuation of the sun's decli-
nation, proclaiming the changing seasons, were obvious to us. The passage
of the days was noted by Maralyn in
her diary. She also faithfully marked
each day on the inside of the raft's
canopy, putting a circle round family
birthdays, whilst turtle days had a
cross and ship days had a plus sign.
We could thus work out the average
time between events: four-and-a-half
days between turtles, eleven days between ships.

JUNE 16TH (104)

The thunderstorms came and went
with increasing frequency. Then the
wind increased and low, dark clouds
scudded quickly across the sky fore-
telling the coming of another storm.
Apprehensively we watched the
waves heighten between periods of
torrential driving rain. More and

more our discomfort grew with the
violently increasing motion; rain was
now an ever present facet of our daily
routine. It was difficult for us to
imagine what it had been like to be
warm and dry. My salt water sores
were becoming daily more unbearable. The pain from these sapped my
spirit and I found little contentment
in living. I was in a state of abject
misery. Rest had been a luxury that
we had both forgotten. Now all our
efforts went towards survival. There
was no prospect of fishing in those
conditions and we expended our energy ridding the raft of water. Even
when it was not raining waves would
send water crashing over us and we
would start all over again.

Each hour went by slowly and
with tedious monotony. I wondered
just how we could survive the next
hour. Yet Maralyn appeared undaunted, she encouraged me to keep
baling with promises of good things
when the storm subsided. She spoke
of the luxury of sitting there eating
meat and the greenish fat from the
green turtles. We talked while we
worked, describing to each other the
relative merits of the male and female
turtle. We could no longer talk of the
food we would eat had we been rescued, the prospects were too slender
at that time and it would have depressed us further. These discussions
we referred to as 'morale boosters'
and our discomfort was tolerable
while we dreamed of eating our turtle
steaks in warm sunshine.

Reality frequently came upon us

as another load of water had to be cleared, or the raft would need inflating again, or the cloths that we had placed in the gaps that had opened up between the tubes would need wringing or replacing. There was no respite.

The storm continued for four more days and we tried to keep warm beneath our oilskin jackets. This was impossible, however, and the jackets chafed our bodies. White blisters appeared on our paunches and arms. We longed to rid ourselves of those jackets, but we feared the cold. Sitting very cramped in the small space of the raft exercise was difficult and, in any case, I became reluctant to move for fear of shifting on to an ulcerated spot.

Nothing was new and our whole existence was as though we belonged to the sea. We could see and feel and hear only the things directly about us. Our association with the sea was no longer detached. It appeared as though we knew no other life. I had stopped dreaming of our life before or after this misadventure.

MARALYN   JUNE 30TH (118)
The dawn of June 30th was bright and clear with the promise of a hot day. We tipped some water into the bottom of the dinghy and watched our two baby turtles splash around. We fished for most of the morning and as we scrambled back to the raft for our afternoon siesta, Maurice emptied some more sea water into the dinghy "to keep them cool."

MAURICE
For the first time for ages we slept blissfully for longer than one hour. The sun rose higher into a cloudless sky. There was no escape from the aggressive heat and sweat dripped from our naked bodies. The raft bobbed gently in the long ocean swell; there were few waves. At midday we ate the remaining fish and complained that it was not very fresh.

We slept again, longer this time. Everything was still, with just a slight southerly breeze roughing the surface of the sea and cooling us through the ventilation hole. How wonderful sleep was.

Maralyn stirred, she was on her knees. Her movements awoke me and I wondered through the fog of sleep what was the matter; perhaps another turtle. I feel asleep again oblivious of Maralyn's effort of pushing her head through the vent.

For a long time I could not rid myself of the feeling that there were three people in the raft, an impression I had frequently had before. In my half-sleep I imagined clearly Maralyn and myself and an American yachtsman called Wayne, whom we had met briefly in Cristobal.

Someone was shaking me, a disembodied voice was calling, "Maurice," and again "Maurice . . ." I thought, "For pity's sake leave me alone and wake Wayne."

"Get out to the dinghy. A ship is coming," Maralyn's urgent tone had penetrated my sluggish brain. Cursing, I automatically struggled to a kneeling position and scrambled across to the dinghy. I sat on the thwart in a dazed condition, trying to focus my eyes on to different parts of the sea. Maralyn was standing in the raft waving her jacket. Yet I could see no ship; Maralyn must be imagining things.

"Wave your jacket, it's there, behind you."

"All right," I said turning round slowly. Then I saw it; a small white, rust-streaked ship approaching from the east. It would pass very close and I began to wave my oilskin jacket. The ship steamed on a course nearly due west and within a short time it was opposite us, about half a mile away.

"It's a Korean fishing boat," I called to Maralyn. "Remember seeing them in Tenerife?"

Maralyn answered but did not stop waving. Her vigorous movements rocked the raft with its nearly deflated lower section almost under water. The ship went past and I stopped waving. It was no use, the ship was not going to stop. Why waste any more energy? I felt ill and slumped to my knees.

I called to Maralyn, "Stop waving; save your strength." She ignored me and continued to wave as the ship showed its stern to us. It was the first we had seen for 43 days.

"Please come back," Maralyn shouted. "Please. . . ."

I was oblivious now of the ship's movements as I knelt in the dinghy. Maralyn was still imploring the ship to return. Let it go on, I thought, this is our world now on the sea, amongst the birds and the turtles and the fish.

Maralyn had suddenly stopped her entreaties but continued to wave her jacket quietly. I looked up and stared for some time at the ship. I looked long and hard at it in disbelief. Was it returning or was it a trick of my eyes? Maralyn looked across at me, her eyes moist and gleaming. "It's coming back," she said.

MAURICE
"You've found us a ship," I said excitedly, then realizing our nakedness I went on. "Sort some clothes out, quickly."

She passed over a sodden pair of tennis shorts and a rotting shirt and while we struggled into our clothes, the fishing boat maneuvered into the wind to come alongside. I reached down and lifted our two young turtles and lowered them over the side.

A heaving line with a heavy "monkey's fist" on the end descended but it fell short into the sea. Voices shouted from the ship attracting my attention to a second heaving line now draped across the life raft and the stern of the dinghy. I wedged the monkey's fist hard into the rowlock and strong hands on the ship began to haul our rubber craft towards a boarding ladder up forward.

A voice came down to us, "Can you speak English?"

"We are English," I replied.

Alongside the ladder I secured the dinghy with another line and,

holding on to the ladder, I began to haul the raft close so that Maralyn could go on board first. A seaman jumped down and stood beside me and indicated that I should board first. "Go on, I'll follow," Maralyn said. I climbed the ladder and over the bulwarks to be greeted by a number of willing arms to support me. I was led across to a blanket laid on deck, but because of my sores, I could not sit. I half knelt taking most of my weight on my arms and thighs.

MARALYN
Within minutes I too was pulled alongside and another sailor held the raft close to the ladder as I climbed towards the deck.

I was helped over the bulwarks and when they let go of me I sank to my knees. I thought it was the heaving and rolling of the deck but when I tried to stand again I realized it was my legs and not the ship. After four months of sitting my legs refused to take the weight of my body. I looked round for Maurice and saw him sitting on a blanket several feet away. I indicated I wanted to join him and soon I was installed on the blanket next to him.

I remembered the many Korean fishing boats we had seen in the small fishing harbor at Tenerife. Several of the seamen had helped us then to lower the groceries into the dinghy as we loaded up *Auralyn* for her trans-Atlantic crossing. We never expected to meet up with any of them again, but how glad I was that we had.

A beaming cook approached us with two glasses of hot, steaming milk. All around us were happy smiling faces and I found it hard to hold back the tears of joy as, between sips of milk, I tried to express my thanks.

We looked at each other and for the moment we were unaware of the men crowding around us. Maurice said, "We've made it," and I replied: "Now for *Auralyn II*."

DISCUSSION

1. What did Maralyn mean when she said "Now for *Auralyn II*"? Does the remark surprise you? Why, or why not?

2. How many days were Maurice and Maralyn lost at sea? What did they do to keep their physical condition as healthy as possible under those circumstances?

3. As important as their physical condition was their mental condition. What did Maralyn and Maurice do to keep fit mentally, to keep their spirits up?

For further activities, see page 80.

The Sniper

LIAM O'FLAHERTY

The long June twilight faded into night. Dublin lay enveloped in darkness but for the dim light of the moon that shone through fleecy clouds, casting a pale light as of approaching dawn over the streets and the dark waters of the Liffey. Around the beleaguered Four Courts the heavy guns roared. Here and there through the city machine guns and rifles broke the silence of the night spasmodically, like dogs barking on lone farms. Republicans and Free Staters were waging civil war.

On a rooftop near O'Connell Bridge a Republican sniper lay watching. Beside him lay his rifle, and over his shoulders were slung a pair of field glasses. His face was the face of a student— thin and ascetic—but his eyes had the cold gleam of the fanatic. They were deep and thoughtful, the eyes of a man who is used to look at death.

He was eating a sandwich hungrily. He had eaten nothing since morning. He had been too excited to eat. He finished the sandwich, and taking a flask of whiskey from his pocket, he took a short draught. Then he returned the flask to his pocket. He paused for a moment, considering whether he should risk a smoke. It was dangerous. The flash might be seen in the darkness, and there were enemies watching. He decided to take the risk. Placing a cigarette between his lips, he struck a match, inhaled the smoke hurriedly, and put out the light. Almost immediately, a bullet flattened itself against the parapet of the roof. The sniper took another whiff and put out the cigarette. Then he swore softly and crawled away to the left.

Cautiously he raised himself and peered over the parapet. There was a flash, and a bullet whizzed over his head. He dropped immediately. He had seen the flash. It came from the opposite side of the street.

He rolled over the roof to a chimney stack in the rear and slowly drew himself up behind it until his eyes were level with the top of the parapet. There was nothing to be seen—just the dim outline of the opposite housetop against the blue sky. His enemy was under cover.

Just then an armored car came across the bridge and advanced slowly up the street. It stopped on the opposite side of the street

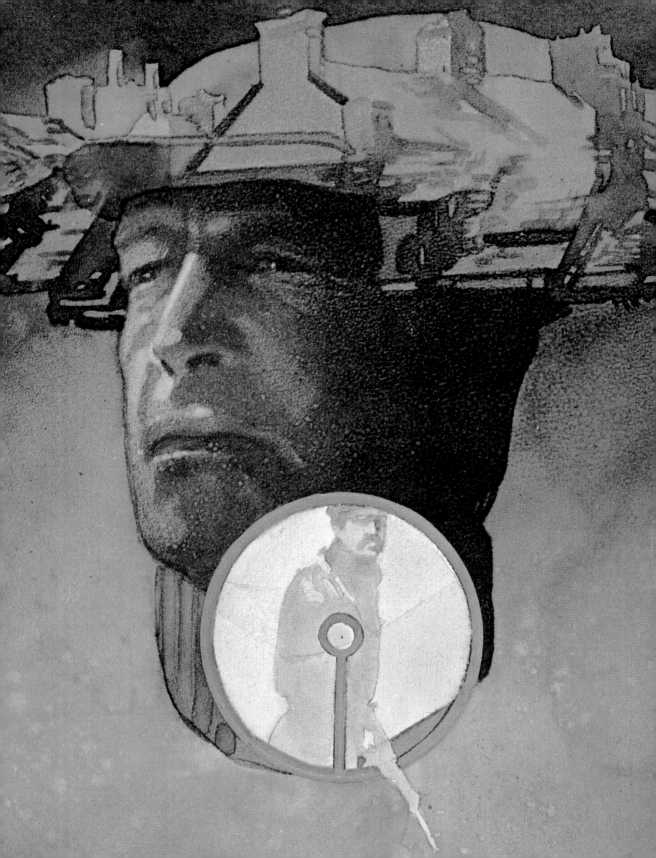

fifty yards ahead. The sniper could hear the dull panting of the motor. His heart beat faster. It was an enemy car. He wanted to fire, but he knew it was useless. His bullets would never pierce the steel that covered the gray monster.

Then round the corner of a side street came an old woman, her head covered by a tattered shawl. She began to talk to the man in the turret of the car. She was pointing to the roof where the sniper lay. An informer.

The turret opened. A man's head and shoulders appeared, looking toward the sniper. The sniper raised his rifle and fired. The head fell heavily on the turret wall. The woman darted toward the side street. The sniper fired again. The woman whirled round and fell with a shriek into the gutter.

Suddenly from the opposite roof a shot rang out, and the sniper dropped his rifle with a curse. The rifle clattered to the roof. The sniper thought the noise would wake the dead. He stopped to pick the rifle up. He couldn't lift it. His forearm was dead. He muttered, "I'm hit."

Dropping flat onto the roof, he crawled back to the parapet. With his left hand he felt the injured right forearm. The blood was oozing through the sleeve of his coat. There was no pain—just a deadened sensation, as if the arm had been cut off.

Quickly he drew his knife from his pocket, opened it on the breastwork of the parapet, and ripped open the sleeve. There was a small hole where the bullet had entered. On the other side there was no hole. The bullet had lodged in the bone. It must have fractured it. He bent the arm below the wound. The arm bent back easily. He ground his teeth to overcome the pain.

Then, taking out his field dressing, he ripped open the packet with his knife. He broke the neck of the iodine bottle and let the bitter fluid drip into the wound. A paroxysm of pain swept through him. He placed the cotton wadding over the wound and wrapped the dressing over it. He tied the end with his teeth. Then he lay still against the parapet, and closing his eyes, he made an effort of will to overcome the pain.

In the street beneath all was still. The armored car had retired speedily over the bridge, with the machine gunner's head hanging lifeless over the turret. The woman's corpse lay still in the gutter.

The sniper lay for a long time nursing his wounded arm and planning escape. Morning must not find him wounded on the roof. The enemy on the opposite roof covered his escape. He must kill that enemy, and he could not use his rifle. He had only a revolver to do it. Then he thought of a plan.

Taking off his cap, he placed it over the muzzle of his rifle. Then he pushed the rifle slowly upwards over the parapet until the cap was visible from the opposite side of the street. Almost immediately there was a report, and a bullet pierced the center of the cap. The sniper slanted the rifle forward. The cap slipped down into the street. Then, catching the rifle in the middle, the sniper dropped his left hand over the roof and let it hang, lifelessly. After a few moments he let the rifle drop to the street. Then he sank to the roof, dragging his hand with him.

Crawling quickly to the left, he peered up at the corner of the roof. His ruse had succeeded. The other sniper, seeing the cap and rifle fall, thought that he had killed his man. He was now standing before a row of chimney pots, looking across, with his head clearly silhouetted against the western sky.

The Republican sniper smiled and lifted his revolver above the edge of the parapet. The distance was about fifty yards—a hard shot in the dim light—and his right arm was paining him like a thousand devils. He took a steady aim. His hand trembled with eagerness. Pressing his lips together, he took a deep breath through his nostrils and fired. He was almost deafened with the report, and his arm shook with the recoil.

Then, when the smoke cleared, he peered across and uttered a cry of joy. His enemy had been hit. He was reeling over the parapet in his death agony. He struggled to keep his feet, but he was slowly falling forward as if in a dream. The rifle fell from his grasp, hit the parapet, fell over, bounded off the pole of a barber's shop beneath, and then cluttered onto the pavement.

Then the dying man on the roof crumpled up and fell forward. The body turned over and over in space and hit the ground with a dull thud. Then it lay still.

The sniper looked at his enemy falling, and he shuddered. The lust of battle died in him. He became bitten by remorse. The sweat stood out in beads on his forehead. Weakened by his wound and the long summer day of fasting and watching on the roof, he revolted from the sight of the shattered mass of his dead enemy. His teeth chattered. He began to gibber to himself, cursing the war, cursing himself, cursing everybody.

He looked at the smoking revolver in his hand, and with an oath he hurled it to the roof at his feet. The revolver went off with the concussion, and the bullet whizzed past the sniper's head. He was frightened back to his senses by the shock. His nerves steadied. The cloud of fear scattered from his mind, and he laughed.

Taking the whiskey flask from his pocket, he emptied it at a draught. He felt reckless under the influence of the spirits. He decided to leave the roof and look for his company commander to report. Everywhere around was quiet. There was not much danger in going through the streets. He picked up his revolver and put it in his pocket. Then he crawled down through the skylight to the house underneath.

When the sniper reached the laneway on the street level, he felt a sudden curiosity as to the identity of the enemy sniper whom he had killed. He decided that he was a good shot whoever he was. He wondered if he knew him. Perhaps he had been in his own company before the split in the army. He decided to risk going over to have a look at him. He peered around the corner into O'Connell Street. In the upper part of the street there was heavy firing, but around here all was quiet.

The sniper darted across the street. A machine gun tore up the ground around him with a hail of bullets, but he escaped. He threw himself face downwards beside the corpse. The machine gun stopped.

Then the sniper turned over the dead body and looked into his brother's face.

DISCUSSION

1. What might be the sniper's thoughts and reactions when he realizes what he has done? What details about the **setting** (see page 57) make possible what he has done?

2. **Point of view.** The position from which a story is told determines its point of view. In the *personal* point of view, the story is told through the eyes of a character *inside* the story. The action is revealed only as it is seen and felt by that character. In the *omniscient* (all-knowing) point of view, the story is told by a narrator *outside* the story who knows what each character is doing and thinking at any moment.

This story is told from the point of view of the sniper. The reader knows only what he knows. Why is that point of view the appropriate one to use in telling this particular story?

For further activities, see page 80.

The Man He Killed

THOMAS HARDY

"Had he and I but met
　By some old ancient inn,
We should have sat us down to wet
　Right many a nipperkin!

"But ranged as infantry,　　　　　　　　5
　And staring face to face,
I shot at him as he at me,
　And killed him in his place.

"I shot him dead because—
　Because he was my foe,　　　　　　　　10
Just so—my foe of course he was;
　That's clear enough; although

"He thought he'd 'list, perhaps,
　Off-hand like—just as I—
Was out of work—had sold his traps—　　15
　No other reason why.

"Yes; quaint and curious war is!
　You shoot a fellow down
You'd treat if met where any bar is,
　Or help to half-a-crown."　　　　　　　20

4. *nipperkin:* a half pint of ale.

DISCUSSION

1. Why did the young man speaking in this poem decide to enlist? What feelings of his about war and killing are revealed in lines 9–16?

2. **Rhyme.** Rhyme is the repetition of the same stressed sound or sounds at the ends of words. There are many examples of rhyme in "The Man He Killed." In the first **stanza** (see page 10) lines 1 and 3 rhyme ("met," "set"), as do lines 2 and 4. What other examples do you see? In the last stanza, lines 17 and 19 are examples of what is sometimes called "eye-rhyme." That is, the endings of the words are spelled alike but they are not pronounced alike. Watch for other examples as you read more poetry.

VOCABULARY

The Sea Devil (page 47)

This story has many words and expressions pertaining in some way to the sea. On separate paper, match these sea terms with their correct definitions. Use your dictionary if necessary.

1. skiff
2. pilings
3. mullet
4. starboard
5. ebb

a. fall back or recede
b. flat-bottomed boat
c. wooden beams used for support
d. righthand side
e. a type of fish

The Sniper (page 74)

On separate paper, write the word following each sentence that is closest in meaning to the word in bold type.

1. A *paroxysm* of pain swept through him.
   dread   infection   emotion   outburst

2. His *ruse* had succeeded.
   gamble   sharpshooting   strategy   insincerity

3. He became bitten by *remorse.*
   pessimism   poison   pleasure   regret

4. Machine guns and rifles broke the silence of the night *spasmodically.*
   rhythmically   irregularly   seasonally   habitually

COMPOSITION

Staying Alive! (page 59)

Write a short survivors' manual for sailors. Base your information and instructions on what you learned from Maralyn and Maurice Bailey but use any other knowledge you may have.

The Sniper (page 74)

Write a letter to a newspaper in which you express your feelings about what happened in "The Sniper." Assume that you read the story in a newspaper.

READING

The Sea Devil (page 47)

On separate paper, write the answer that best completes each statement.

1. In this story the conflict is between

    a. two men
    b. a man and a primitive creature
    c. a man and the weather

2. The author tells us about the man by means of

    a. the man's conversations
    b. description of the man's thoughts and actions
    c. other people's conversations about the man

3. The man realized that he could not overpower the ray by physical strength but only by

    a. reason
    b. mechanical devices
    c. calling his brother for help

4. At the end, the man lets go of the mullet he'd caught because

    a. he was too weak to carry it home
    b. the mullet was dead anyway
    c. he now knew what a wonderful feeling it was to be free

The Sniper (page 74)

Some of the following statements about the story are true; some are false. On separate paper write the numbers of the ones that are false.

1. The sniper wants to defeat the Free Staters.
2. He strikes a blow against the Free Staters by killing three people.
3. The story shows us why Great Britain entered the Irish Civil War.
4. The sniper ignores a serious wound and possible hostile fire to look at the man he has killed.
5. He shows a lot of courage in firing at the armored car.
6. The sniper sits down and sobs when he realizes he's shot his own brother.
7. He cleverly figures out how to kill the man firing at him from across the street.
8. Just before he dies, the victim realizes he's been shot by his own brother.

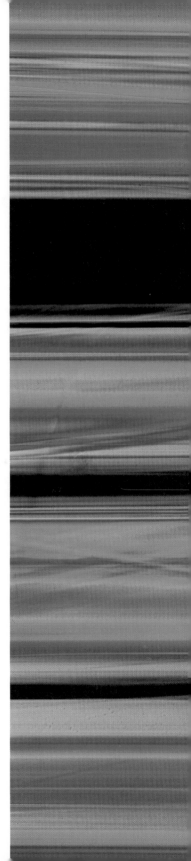

COMPOSITION

Writing is a way of letting others share what is on our minds. We as writers know, more or less, what we want to say, but if others are to understand us, we must search for words that will express our meaning *exactly*.

"They came to visit us," a writer remembers of an incident in her girlhood that she wants to share. But the words are too general. "*The mothers of the children* came to visit. . . ." Even that, however, is not exactly how it was. So the writer states the thought still more precisely: "*Some* of the mothers came to visit their children."

And how did they get there? How did they travel? By burro, the writer remembers. Yet in order to let us see the experience as clearly as possible, she thinks harder about it, remembers more, and writes:

> They came in a burro caravan of eight to ten. If one did not own a burro she would borrow or hire one. . . .

What did the mothers bring along?

Food. Things for the children. But those words, too, are vague. The writer must always strive to remember *exactly:* they brought food for themselves, of course, to eat on the journey, and blankets, but for the children (who would remember precisely) they brought corn, and peaches, and that thin cornbread called piki.

So the general thought, which may originally have been remembered fuzzily as "After a while the mothers came to see their children and brought them things," emerges at last in sharp focus. It is made clear by choices of the precise word, the concrete word, the specific word:

> As soon as they could, which was a year after we were taken away to Keams Canyon, some of the mothers came to visit their children. They came in a burro caravan of eight to ten. If one did not own a burro she would borrow or hire one on which she packed blankets and food for herself and as much as she could load on of piki, parched corn, dried peaches, and the like to give her children (page 42).

By thinking precisely, then choosing words that express your thoughts *exactly*, work toward making your own writing that sharp, that clear.

CHOOSING THE RIGHT WORD

ABOUT THE SELECTIONS

1.   What was the most terrifying moment you read about in the selections in this section? As precisely as you can, describe the moment as you remember it. When you finish your description, look back at the author's description of the same moment. Has he or she used any words that would make your own account even more effective?

2.   Suppose you were a reporter assigned to cover any one of the exciting events described in this section. Report on the event in a way that would be suitable as a news item for your school or local newspaper. Stick to facts and write crisply, with the most important information first. What happened exactly? To whom? Where? When?

3.   Choose one of the poems in the unit and expand the situation it presents into a prose account. "The Man He Killed," for instance, might be made into a little story told by a soldier reminiscing to a friend. "Carmel Point" might be expressed as a prose description of nature. Compare what you have written with the poem itself. What advantages does your version have over the poem? What disadvantages?

4.   What specific details in the following paragraph help to make the experience vivid? Would more general details have worked as well?

> In our emergency kit I had placed two plastic bottles each holding two pints of water and one of these bottles would be our day's ration. When it was empty we would fill it from the main supply kept in the dinghy. For breakfast we would stir approximately three spoons of Coffee-mate into a cup of water and the rest of the day we would take turns and have sips from the bottle, finishing the rest after our evening meal. . . . (page 59)

ON YOUR OWN

1.   Imagine that your survival is threatened by someone (as in "The Most Dangerous Game") or something (as in "My First Death"). Try to experience what you would really feel if your very life were in danger. Then, in a page, describe your feelings. Let the reader know the situation you are in, as well as the emotions you experience and the thoughts that go through your mind.

2.   What does it take to survive in this world? Mention the two or three qualities that you think are most vital for a person's survival. To help explain your choice, include examples of people who you think possess those qualities.

3.   Almost all the selections in this section might have ended differently. Write an alternative ending to any one of them, making your own writing sound as much like the writing in the selection as you can.

4.   Replace the vague words in the following paragraph with more specific ones:

> *Awhile back,* trying to fix *something* on our *animal* pen, my father succeeded only after getting inside the cage, where he was *kept* for *quite a while,* with *some* rabbits and *other creatures.* When he tried to *get up,* he *hit* his *hat* against the *covering* over the top of the pen.

VIEWPOINTS

The STORYTELLER

SAKI

It was a hot afternoon, and the railway carriage was correspondingly sultry, and the next stop was at Templecombe, nearly an hour ahead. The occupants of the carriage were a small girl, and a smaller girl, and a small boy. An aunt belonging to the children occupied one corner seat, and the further corner seat on the opposite side was occupied by a bachelor who was a stranger to their party, but the small girls and the small boy emphatically occupied the compartment. Both the aunt and the children were conversational in a limited, persistent way, reminding one of the attentions of a housefly that refused to be discouraged. Most of the aunt's remarks seemed to begin with "Don't," and nearly all of the children's remarks began with "Why?" The bachelor said nothing out loud.

"Don't, Cyril, don't," exclaimed the aunt, as the small boy began smacking the cushions of the seat, producing a cloud of dust at each blow.

"Come and look out of the window," she added.

The child moved reluctantly to the window. "Why are those sheep being driven out of that field?" he asked.

"I expect they are being driven to another field where there is more grass," said the aunt weakly.

"But there is lots of grass in that field," protested the boy; "there's nothing else but grass there. Aunt, there's lots of grass in that field."

"Perhaps the grass in the other field is better," suggested the aunt fatuously.

"Why is it better?" came the swift, inevitable question.

"Oh, look at those cows!" exclaimed the aunt. Nearly every field along the line had contained cows or bullocks, but she spoke as though she were drawing attention to a rarity.

"Why is the grass in the other field better?" persisted Cyril.

The frown on the bachelor's face was deepening to a scowl. He was a hard, unsympathetic man, the aunt decided in her mind. She was utterly unable to come to any satisfactory decision about the grass in the other field.

The smaller girl created a diversion by beginning to recite "On the Road to Mandalay." She only knew the first line, but she put her limited knowledge to the fullest possible use. She repeated the line over and over again in a dreamy but resolute and very audible voice; it seemed to the bachelor as though some one had had a bet with her that she could not repeat the line aloud two thousand times without stopping. Whoever it was who had made the wager was likely to lose his bet.

"Come over here and listen to a story," said the aunt, when the bachelor had looked twice at her and once at the communication cord.

The children moved listessly towards the aunt's end of the carriage. Evidently her reputation as a storyteller did not rank high in their estimation.

In a low, confidential voice, interrupted at frequent intervals by loud, petulant questions from her listeners, she began an unenterprising and deplorably uninteresting story about a little girl who was good, and made friends with every one on account of her goodness, and was finally saved from a mad bull by a number of rescuers who admired her moral character.

"Wouldn't they have saved her if she hadn't been good?" demanded the bigger of the small girls. It was exactly the question that the bachelor had wanted to ask.

"Well, yes," admitted the aunt lamely, "but I don't think they would have run quite so fast to her help if they had not liked her so much."

"It's the stupidest story I've ever heard," said the bigger of the small girls, with immense conviction.

"I didn't listen after the first bit, it was so stupid," said Cyril.

The smaller girl made no actual comment on the story, but she had long ago recommenced a murmured repetition of her favorite line.

"You don't seem to be a success as a storyteller," said the bachelor suddenly from his corner.

The aunt bristled in instant defense at this unexpected attack.

"It's a very difficult thing to tell stories that children can both understand and appreciate," she said stiffly.

"I don't agree with you," said the bachelor.

"Perhaps *you* would like to tell them a story," was the aunt's retort.

"Tell us a story," demanded the bigger of the small girls.

"Once upon a time," began the bachelor, "there was a little girl called Bertha, who was extraordinarily good."

The children's momentarily aroused interest began at once to flicker; all stories seemed dreadfully alike, no matter who told them.

"She did all that she was told, she was always truthful, she kept her clothes clean, ate milk puddings as though they were jam tarts, learned her lessons perfectly, and was polite in her manners."

"Was she pretty?" asked the bigger of the small girls.

"Not as pretty as any of you," said the bachelor, "but she was horribly good."

There was a wave of reaction in favor of the story; the word horrible in connection with goodness was a novelty that commended itself. It seemed to introduce a ring of truth that was absent from the aunt's tales of infant life.

"She was so good," continued the bachelor, "that she won several medals for goodness, which she always wore, pinned on to her dress. There was a medal for obedience, another medal for punctuality, and a third for good behavior. They were large metal medals and they clicked against one another as she walked. No other child in the town where she lived had as many as three medals, so everybody knew that she must be an extra good child."

"Horribly good," quoted Cyril.

"Everybody talked about her goodness, and the Prince of the country got to hear about it, and he said that as she was so very good she might be allowed once a week to walk in his park, which was just outside the town. It was a beautiful park, and no children were ever allowed in it, so it was a great honor for Bertha to be allowed to go there."

"Were there any sheep in the park?" demanded Cyril.

"No," said the bachelor, "there were no sheep."

"Why weren't there any sheep?" came the inevitable question arising out of that answer.

The aunt permitted herself a smile, which might almost have been described as a grin.

"There were no sheep in the park," said the bachelor, "because the Prince's mother had once had a dream that her son would either be killed by a sheep or else by a clock falling on him. For that reason the Prince never kept a sheep in his park or a clock in his palace."

The aunt suppressed a gasp of admiration.

"Was the Prince killed by a sheep or by a clock?" asked Cyril.

"He is still alive, so we can't tell whether the dream will come true," said the bachelor unconcernedly; "anyway, there were no sheep in the park, but there were lots of little pigs running all over the place."

"What color were they?"

"Black with white faces, white with black spots, black all over, gray with white patches, and some were white all over."

The storyteller paused to let a full idea of the park's treasures sink into the children's imaginations; then he resumed:

"Bertha was rather sorry to find that there were no flowers in the park. She had promised her aunts, with tears in her eyes, that she would not pick any of the kind Prince's flowers, and she had meant to keep her promise, so of course it made her feel silly to find that there were no flowers to pick."

"Why weren't there any flowers?"

"Because the pigs had eaten them all," said the bachelor promptly. "The gardeners had told the Prince that you couldn't have pigs and flowers, so he decided to have pigs and no flowers."

There was a murmur of approval at the excellence of the
Prince's decision; so many people would have decided the other
way.

"There were lots of other delightful things in the park.
There were ponds with gold and blue and green fish in them,
and trees with beautiful parrots that said clever things at a moment's notice, and humming birds that hummed all the popular
tunes of the day. Bertha walked up and down and enjoyed herself immensely, and thought to herself: 'If I were not so extraordinarily good I should not have been allowed to come into this
beautiful park and enjoy all that there is to be seen in it,' and
her three medals clinked against one another as she walked and
helped to remind her how very good she really was. Just then
an enormous wolf came prowling into the park to see if it could
catch a fat little pig for its supper."

"What color was it?" asked the children, amid an immediate quickening of interest.

"Mud color all over, with a black tongue and pale gray eyes
that gleamed with unspeakable ferocity. The first thing that it
saw in the park was Bertha; her pinafore was so spotlessly
white and clean that it could be seen from a great distance. Bertha saw the wolf and saw that it was stealing towards her, and
she began to wish that she had never been allowed to come into
the park. She ran as hard as she could, and the wolf came after
her with huge leaps and bounds. She managed to reach a shrub-
bery of myrtle bushes and she hid herself in one of the thickest
of the bushes. The wolf came sniffing among the branches, its
black tongue lolling out of its mouth and its pale gray eyes glaring with rage. Bertha was terribly frightened, and thought to
herself: 'If I had not been so extraordinarily good I should have
been safe in the town at this moment.' However, the scent of
the myrtle was so strong that the wolf could not sniff out where
Bertha was hiding, and the bushes were so thick that he might
have hunted about in them for a long time without catching

sight of her, so he thought he might as well go off and catch a little pig instead. Bertha was trembling very much at having the wolf prowling and sniffing so near her, and as she trembled the medal for obedience clinked against the medals for good conduct and punctuality. The wolf was just moving away when he heard the sound of the medals clinking and stopped to listen; they clinked again in a bush quite near him. He dashed into the bush, his pale gray eyes gleaming with ferocity and triumph, and dragged Bertha out and devoured her to the last morsel. All that was left of her were her shoes, bits of clothing, and the three medals for goodness."

"Were any of the little pigs killed?"

"No, they all escaped."

"The story began badly," said the smaller of the small girls, "but it had a beautiful ending."

"It is the most beautiful story that I ever heard," said the bigger of the small girls, with immense decision.

"It is the *only* beautiful story I have ever heard," said Cyril.

A dissentient opinion came from the aunt.

"A most improper story to tell to young children! You have undermined the effect of years of careful teaching."

"At any rate," said the bachelor, collecting his belongings preparatory to leaving the carriage, "I kept them quiet for ten minutes, which was more than you were able to do."

"Unhappy woman!" he observed to himself as he walked down the platform of Templecombe station; "for the next six months or so those children will assail her in public with demands for an improper story!"

DISCUSSION

1. Near the end of the selection the bigger of the small girls says, "It's the most beautiful story that I ever heard." What elements in the bachelor's story pleased the children?

2. On page 89 is the first reaction of the aunt to the bachelor's story: "The aunt permitted herself a smile, which might almost have been described as a grin." Explain her feelings. How does she feel at the end of his story?

3. Contrast the aunt's idea of a good story for children with that of the bachelor. With which do you think the author agrees? Give reasons based on the story to support your answer.

For further activities, see page 120.

YOUTH TO AGE

PAULI MURRAY

Aged one and wise,
Were you twenty-two again
Would you risk all for fame?
Conform?
Or go your way alone?

But how can you reply, being seventy-two?
Your path is fogged with memories
As mine with fears.

DISCUSSION   According to the poem, why would a person of seventy-two find it difficult to answer the questions in stanza 1? What exactly is the speaker
asking? The young person must have a reason for asking the question.
What might that reason be?

THE NECKLACE

GUY DE MAUPASSANT

She was one of those attractive pretty girls, born by a freak of fortune in a lower-middle-class family. She had no dowry, no expectations, no way of getting known, appreciated, loved and married by some wealthy gentleman of good family. And she allowed herself to be married to a junior clerk in the Ministry of Public Instruction.

She dressed plainly, having no money to spend on herself. But she was as unhappy as if she had known better days. Women have no sense of caste or breeding, their beauty, their grace, and their charm taking the place of birth and family. Their natural refinement, their instinctive delicacy and adaptability are their only passport to society, and these qualities enable daughters of the people to compete with ladies of gentle birth.

She always had a sense of frustration, feeling herself born for all the refinements and luxuries of life. She hated the bareness of her apartment, the shabbiness of the walls, the worn upholstery of the chairs, and the ugliness of the curtains. All these things, which another woman of her class would not even have noticed, were pain and grief to her. The sight of the little Breton maid doing her simple housework aroused in her passionate regrets and hopeless dreams. She imagined hushed anterooms hung with oriental fabrics and lit by tall bronze candelabra, with two impressive footmen in knee breeches dozing in great armchairs, made drowsy by the heat of radiators. She imagined vast drawing rooms, upholstered in antique silk, splendid pieces of furniture littered with priceless curios, and dainty scented boudoirs, designed for teatime conversation with intimate friends and much sought-after society gentlemen, whose attentions every woman envies and desires.

When she sat down to dinner at the round table covered with a three-days-old cloth opposite her husband, who took the lid off the casserole with the delighted exclamation: "Ah! your good stew again! How lovely! It's the best dish in the world!" she was dreaming of luxurious dinners with gleaming silver and tapestries peopling the walls with classical figures and exotic birds in a fairy

Guy de Maupassant: pronounced gē dŭ mō-på-sàn'

forest; she dreamed of exquisite dishes served on valuable china and whispered compliments listened to with a sphinxlike smile, while toying with the pink flesh of a trout or the wing of a hazel-hen.

She had no evening clothes, no jewels, nothing. But she wanted only those things; she felt that that was the kind of life for her. She so much longed to please, be envied, be fascinating and sought after.

She had a rich friend who had been with her at a convent school, but she did not like going to see her now, the contrast was so painful when she went home. She spent whole days in tears; misery, regrets, hopeless longings caused her such bitter distress.

One evening her husband came home with a broad smile on his face and a large envelope in his hand: "Look!" he cried. "Here's something for you, dear!"

She tore open the envelope eagerly and pulled out a printed card with the words: "The Minister of Public Instruction and Mme. Georges Ramponneau request the honor of the company of

M. and Mme. Loisel[1] at the Ministry on the evening of Monday, January 18th."

Instead of being delighted as her husband had hoped, she threw the invitation pettishly down on the table, murmuring: "What's the good of this to me?"

"But I thought you'd be pleased, dear! You never go out and this is an occasion, a great occasion. I had the greatest difficulty to get the invitation. Everybody wants one; it's very select and junior clerks don't often get asked. The whole official world will be there."

She looked at him crossly and declared impatiently: "What do you think I'm to wear?"

He hadn't thought of that and stuttered: "Why! the frock you wear for the theater. I think it's charming!"

He stopped in astonished bewilderment when he saw his wife was crying. Two great tears were running slowly down from the corners of her eyes to the corners of her mouth; he stammered: "What's the matter? What's the matter?"

But with a great effort she had controlled her disappointment and replied quietly, drying her wet cheeks: "Oh! Nothing! Only not having anything to wear I can't go to the party. Pass on the invitation to some colleague whose wife is better dressed than I."

"Look here, Mathilde! How much would a suitable frock cost, something quite simple that would be useful on other occasions later on?"

She thought for a few seconds, doing a sum and also wondering how much she could ask for without inviting an immediate refusal and an outraged exclamation from the close-fisted clerk. At last with some hesitation she replied: "I don't know exactly but I think I could manage on four hundred francs."

He went slightly pale, for this was just the amount he had put by to get a gun so that he could enjoy some shooting the following summer on the Nanterre plain with some friends who went out lark-shooting on Sundays. But he said: "Right! I'll give you four hundred francs, but try and get a really nice frock."

The date of the party was approaching and Mme. Loisel seemed depressed and worried, though her dress was ready. One evening her husband said to her: "What's the matter? The last three days you've not been yourself."

---

[1] *Loisel:* pronounced lwä-zĕl'.

She replied: "It's rotten not to have a piece of jewelry, not a stone of any kind, to wear. I shall look poverty-stricken. I'd rather not go to the party."

He answered: "But you can wear some real flowers. That's very smart this year. For ten francs you could get two or three magnificent roses."

She was not impressed. "No, there's nothing more humiliating than to look poor in a crowd of wealthy women."

But her husband suddenly cried: "What a fool you are! Go to your friend, Mme. Forestier,[2] and ask her to lend you some of her jewelry. You know her well enough to do that."

She uttered a joyful cry: "That's a good idea! I'd never thought of it!"

Next day she went to her friend's house and explained her dilemma.

Mme. Forestier went to a glass-fronted wardrobe, took out a large casket, brought it over, opened it, and said to Mme. Loisel:

"Take what you like, my dear!"

First she looked at bracelets, then a pearl collar, then a Venetian cross in gold and stones, a lovely piece of work. She tried the various ornaments in front of the mirror, unable to make up her mind to take them off and put them back; she kept asking: "Haven't you got anything else?"

"Yes, go on looking; I don't know what you would like."

Suddenly she found a black satin case containing a magnificent diamond necklace, and she wanted it so desperately that her heart began to thump. Her hands were shaking as she picked it up. She put it round her throat over her high blouse and stood in ecstasy before her reflection in the glass. Then she asked hesitantly, her anxiety showing in her voice: "Could you lend me that, just that, nothing else?"

"But of course!"

She threw her arms round her friend's neck and kissed her wildly, and hurried home with her treasure.

The day of the party arrived. Mme. Loisel had a triumph. She was the prettiest woman in the room, elegant, graceful, smiling, in the seventh heaven of happiness. All the men looked at her, asked who she was, and wanted to be introduced. All the private secretaries wanted to dance with her. The Minister himself noticed her.

---

[2] *Forestier:* pronounced fô-rĕs-tēā'.

She danced with inspired abandon, intoxicated with delight, thinking of nothing in the triumph of her beauty and the glory of her success; she was wrapped in a cloud of happiness, the result of all the compliments, all the admiration, all these awakened desires, that wonderful success so dear to every woman's heart.

She left about four in the morning. Her husband had been dozing since midnight in a small, empty drawing room with three other gentlemen, whose wives were also enjoying themselves.

He threw over her shoulders the wraps he had brought for going home, her simple everyday coat, whose plainness clashed with the smartness of her ball dress. She was conscious of this and wanted to hurry away, so as not to be noticed by the ladies who were putting on expensive fur wraps.

Loisel tried to stop her: "Wait a minute! You'll catch cold outside. I'll call a cab."

But she would not listen and ran down the stairs. When they got into the street they could not find a cab and began to hunt for one, shouting to the drivers they saw passing in the distance. In despair they went down towards the Seine, shivering. At last, on the Embankment they found one of those old carriages that ply by night and are only seen in Paris after dark, as if ashamed of their shabbiness in the daytime. It took them back to their house in the Rue des Martyrs and they went sadly up to their apartment. For her this was the end; and he was remembering that he had got to be at the office at ten o'clock.

She took off the wraps she had put round her shoulders, standing in front of the glass to see herself once more in all her glory. But suddenly she uttered a cry; the diamond necklace was no longer round her neck. Her husband, already half undressed, asked: "What's the matter?"

She turned to him in a panic: "Mme. Forestier's necklace has gone!"

He stood up, dumfounded: "What? What do you mean? It's impossible!"

They searched in the folds of her dress, in the folds of her cloak, in the pockets, everywhere; they could not find it. He asked: "Are you sure you had it on when you left the ball?"

"Yes, I fingered it in the hall at the Ministry."

"But, if you had lost it in the street, we should have heard it drop. It must be in the cab."

"Yes, it probably is. Did you take the number?"

"No! And you didn't notice it, I suppose?"

"No!"

They looked at each other, utterly crushed. Finally Loisel dressed again: "I'll go back along the way we walked and see if I can find it."

He went out and she remained in her evening dress, without the strength even to go to bed, collapsed on a chair, without a fire, her mind a blank.

Her husband returned about seven, having found nothing. He went to the police station, to the papers to offer a reward, to the cab companies, in fact anywhere that gave a flicker of hope.

She waited all day in the same state of dismay at this appalling catastrophe. Loisel came back in the evening, his face pale and lined; he had discovered nothing.

"You must write to your friend," he said, "and say you have broken the clasp of the necklace and are getting it mended. That will give us time to turn around."

So she wrote at his dictation. After a week they had lost all hope and Loisel, who had aged five years, declared: "We must do something about replacing it."

Next day they took the case which had contained the necklace to the jeweler whose name was in it. He looked up his books: "I did not sell the jewel, Madame; I must only have supplied the case."

They went from jeweler to jeweler, looking for a necklace like the other, trying to remember exactly what it was like, both of them sick with worry and anxiety.

At last in the Palais Royal they found a diamond necklace just like the one lost. Its price was forty thousand francs, but they could have it for thirty-six thousand.

So they asked the jeweler to keep it for three days. They made it a condition that he should take it back for thirty-four thousand if the first was found before the end of February.

Loisel had got eighteen thousand francs which his father had left him; he would borrow the rest.

He borrowed one thousand francs from one, five hundred from another, one hundred here, sixty there. He gave I.O.U.'s and notes of hand on ruinous terms, going to the loan sharks and moneylenders of every kind. He mortgaged the whole of the rest of his life, risked his signature on bills without knowing if he would ever be able to honor it; he was tormented with anxiety about the future, with the thought of the crushing poverty about to descend upon him and the prospect of physical privations and mental agony. Then he went and collected the necklace, putting down the thirty-six thousand francs on the jeweler's counter.

When Mme. Loisel took the necklace back to Mme. Forestier, the latter said rather coldly: "You ought to have brought it back sooner; I might have wanted it."

She did not open the case, as her friend had feared she might.

If she had detected the replacement what would she have thought? What would she have said? Would she have considered her a thief?

Now Mme. Loisel learned to know the grim life of the very poor. However, she faced the position with heroic courage. This ghastly debt must be paid and she would pay it. They got rid of the maid; they gave up the apartment and took an attic under the tiles. She did all the heavy work of the house as well as the hateful kitchen jobs. She washed up, ruining her pink nails on the coarse crockery and the bottoms of the saucepans. She washed the dirty linen and shirts and the kitchen cloths and dried them on a line. She carried the rubbish down to the street every morning and brought up the water, stopping on every floor to get her breath. And dressed as a woman of the people, she went to the fruiterer, the grocer and the butcher with her basket on her arm, bargaining in spite of their rudeness and fighting for every penny of her miserable pittance.

Every month some notes of hand had to be paid off and others renewed to gain time. Her husband worked in the evening keeping a tradesman's books and often at night he did copying at twenty-five centimes a page. This life went on for ten years.

After ten years they had paid everything back, including the interest and the accumulated compound interest.

Mme. Loisel now looked an old woman. She had become the strong, tough, coarse woman we find in the homes of the poor. Her hair was neglected, her skirt was askew, her hands were red, and her voice loud; she even scrubbed the floors. But sometimes, when her husband was at the office, she would sit down near the window and dream of that evening long ago, the ball at which she had been such a success.

What would have happened to her if she had not lost the necklace? Who can say? Life is such a strange thing with its changes and chances. Such a little thing can make or mar it!

One Sunday, when she had gone for a stroll in the Champs-Élysées as a change from the week's grind, she suddenly saw a lady taking a child for a walk. It was Mme. Forestier, still young, still beautiful, still attractive.

Mme. Loisel felt a wave of emotion. Should she speak to her? Yes, she would. Now that she had paid, she would tell her everything. Why not?

She went up to her: "Good morning, Jeanne!"

The other woman did not recognize her; surprised at being addressed in this familiar fashion by a common woman, she stammered: "But, Madame . . . I don't know you . . . there must be some mistake."

"No! I'm Mathilde Loisel!"

Her friend exclaimed: "Oh! Poor Mathilde, how you've changed!"

"Yes, I've had a pretty grim time since I saw you last, with lots of trouble—and it was all your fault!"

"My fault? What do you mean?"

"You remember that diamond necklace you lent me to go to the party at the Ministry?"

"Yes, what about it?"

"Well! I lost it!"

"What! But you brought it back to me."

"I brought you back another exactly like it; and for ten years we've been paying for it. You'll realize it hasn't been easy, for we had no money of our own. Well, now it's all over and I'm glad of it!"

Mme. Forestier had stopped: "You say you bought a diamond necklace to replace mine?"

"Yes! And you never spotted it, did you? They were as like as two peas."

And she smiled with simple proud pleasure.

Mme. Forestier, deeply moved, took both her hands: "Oh! my poor Mathilde! But mine was only paste, not worth more than five hundred francs at most!"

DISCUSSION

1. What are Mathilde's feelings when she learns that the necklace is "only paste, not worth more than five hundred francs at most"?

2. How many years do she and her husband work to repay the loss of the necklace? What physical changes come over her during these years of poverty?

3. **Characterization.** The means by which an author creates lifelike people in fiction is called characterization. We come to know what kind of person Mathilde is by what she does, what she says and thinks, what others say and think about her, and what de Maupassant says directly about her. Give examples from the story that show how her selfishness and her determination are revealed.

For further activities, see page 120.

Star-Pudding

ROBERT P. TRISTRAM COFFIN

People wondered what Dan Wholebrook found
To live on, up there on his hungry farm.
His cow was always breaking through her fences
And eating up the neighbors' corn by rows,
The soil was spread too thin between the ledges,   5
And mostly powdered rock, like tiny stars;
The hardtack crowded the potatoes out;
Dan raised a first-rate crop of goldenrod.
The crows used Daniel's farm to crack their clams on,
There was so much of it bare granite rock.   10
Wind-pudding was what Daniel had, folks said,
And lucky for the man he had no wife
And children's mouths to find potatoes for.

The neighbors did not know about the stars.
A man can get a lot of life from them   15
If he knows how to go about it. They came
Closer to Daniel's place than down below,
And being on a hill, he had lots more;
They were as thick as daisies in poor hay.
Seemed so, he always was all tangled up   20
In stars, he had to hoe so long
And get up out of bed so bright and early.
'Twas nothing for him to find a morning star
Beside his shoulder, or an evening one.
It might do for a breakfast or a supper,   25
And Daniel showed it in his burning eyes.

DISCUSSION   1. Why was Dan "always tangled up / In stars" (lines 20–21)?

2. **Image.**   An image is a word picture. Images make use of sensory words to appeal to all of the senses—taste, touch, smell, sight, and sound. This poem is rich in visual images. Coffin might have said that Dan's cow "was always causing him trouble," but in line 4 we can *see* her "eating up the neighbors' corn by rows." Point out two or three other effective images.

Seeing

ANNIE DILLARD

When I was six or seven years old, growing up in Pittsburgh, I used to take a precious penny of my own and hide it for some-one else to find. It was a curious compulsion; sadly, I've never been seized by it since. For some reason I always "hid" the penny along the same stretch of sidewalk up the street. I would cradle it at the roots of a sycamore, say, or in a hole left by a chipped-off piece of sidewalk. Then I would take a piece of chalk, and, starting at either end of the block, draw huge arrows leading up to the penny from both directions. After I learned to write I labeled the arrows: SURPRISE AHEAD or MONEY THIS WAY. I was greatly excited, during all this arrow-drawing, at the thought of the first lucky passer-by who would receive in this way, regardless of merit, a free gift from the universe. But I nev-er lurked about. I would go straight home and not give the mat-ter another thought, until, some months later, I would be gripped again by the impulse to hide another penny.

It is still the first week in January, and I've got great plans. I've been thinking about seeing. There are lots of things to see, unwrapped gifts and free surprises. The world is fairly studded and strewn with pennies cast broadside from a generous hand. But—and this is the point—who gets excited by a mere penny? If you follow one arrow, if you crouch motionless on a bank to watch a tremulous ripple thrill on the water and are rewarded by the sight of a muskrat kit paddling from its den, will you count that sight a chip of copper only, and go your rueful way? It is dire poverty indeed when a man is so malnourished and fatigued that he won't stoop to pick up a penny. But if you cul-tivate a healthy poverty and simplicity, so that finding a penny will literally make your day, then, since the world is in fact planted in pennies, you have with your poverty bought a life-time of days. It is that simple. What you see is what you get.

I used to be able to see flying insects in the air. I'd look ahead and see, not the row of hemlocks across the road, but the air in front of it. My eyes would focus along that column of air, picking out flying insects. But I lost interest, I guess, for I

dropped the habit. Now I can see birds. Probably some people can look at the grass at their feet and discover all the crawling creatures. I would like to know grasses and sedges—and care. Then my least journey into the world would be a field trip, a series of happy recognitions. Thoreau, in an expansive mood, exulted, "What a rich book might be made about buds, including, perhaps, sprouts!" It would be nice to think so. I cherish mental images I have of three perfectly happy people. One collects stones. Another—an Englishman, say—watches clouds. The third lives on a coast and collects drops of seawater which he examines microscopically and mounts. But I don't see what the specialist sees, and so I cut myself off, not only from the total picture, but from the various forms of happiness.

Unfortunately, nature is very much a now-you-see-it, now-you-don't affair. A fish flashes, then dissolves in the water before my eyes like so much salt. Deer apparently ascend bodily into heaven; the brightest oriole fades into leaves. These disappearances stun me into stillness and concentration; they say of nature that it conceals with a grand nonchalance; and they say of vision that it is a deliberate gift, the revelation of a dancer who for my eyes only flings away her seven veils. For nature does reveal as well as conceal: now-you-don't-see-it, now-you-do. For a week last September migrating red-winged blackbirds were feeding heavily down by the creek at the back of the house. One day I went out to investigate the racket; I walked up to a tree, an Osage orange, and a hundred birds flew away. They simply materialized out of the tree. I saw a tree, then a whisk of color, then a tree again. I walked closer and another hundred blackbirds took flight. Not a branch, not a twig budged: the birds were apparently weightless as well as invisible. Or, it was as if the leaves of the Osage orange had been freed from a spell in the form of red-winged blackbirds; they flew from the tree, caught my eye in the sky, and vanished. When I looked again at the tree the leaves had reassembled as if nothing had happened. Finally I walked directly to the trunk of the tree and a final hundred, the real diehards, appeared, spread, and vanished. How could so many hide in the tree without my seeing them? The Osage orange, unruffled, looked just as it had looked from the house, when three hundred red-winged blackbirds cried from its crown. I looked downstream where they flew, and they were gone. Searching, I couldn't spot one. I wandered downstream to force them to play their hand, but they'd crossed the creek and scattered. One show to a customer. These appearances catch at my throat; they are the free gifts, the bright coppers at the roots of trees.

It's all a matter of keeping my eyes open. Nature is like one of those line drawings of a tree that are puzzles for children: Can you find hidden in the leaves a duck, a house, a boy, a bucket, a zebra, and a boot? Specialists can find the most incredibly well-hidden things. A book I read when I was young recommended an easy way to find caterpillars to rear: you simply find some fresh caterpillar droppings, look up, and there's your caterpillar. More recently an author advised me to set my mind at ease about those piles of cut stems on the ground in grassy fields. Field mice make them; they cut the grass down by degrees to reach the seeds at the head. It seems that when the grass is tightly packed, as in a field of ripe grain, the blade won't topple at a single cut through the stem; instead, the cut stem simply drops vertically, held in the crush of grain. The mouse severs the bottom again and again, the stem keeps dropping an inch at a time, and finally the head is low enough for the mouse to reach the seeds. Meanwhile, the mouse is positively littering the field with its little piles of cut stems into which, presumably, the author of the book is constantly stumbling.

If I can't see these minutiae, I still try to keep my eyes open. I'm always on the lookout for antlion traps in sandy soil, monarch pupae near milkweed, skipper larvae in locust leaves. These things are utterly common, and I've not seen one. I bang on hollow trees near water, but so far no flying squirrels have appeared. In flat country I watch every sunset in hopes of seeing the green ray. The green ray is a seldom-seen streak of light that rises from the sun like a spurting fountain at the moment of sunset; it throbs into the sky for two seconds and disappears. One more reason to keep my eyes open.

DISCUSSION

1. On page 104 Dillard says, "What you see is what you get." How does this statement apply to her description of the red-winged blackbirds?

2. Explain the relationship between her childhood experience in hiding a penny and her adult experiences in observing nature.

An Emerald Is As Green As Grass

CHRISTINA ROSSETTI

An emerald is as green as grass,
 A ruby red as blood;
A sapphire shines as blue as heaven,
 A flint lies in the mud.

A diamond is a brilliant stone,
 To catch the world's desire;
An opal holds a fiery spark,
 But a flint holds fire.

All but Blind

WALTER DE LA MARE

All but blind
 In his chambered hole
Gropes for worms
 The four-clawed Mole.

All but blind   5
 In the evening sky,
The hooded Bat
 Twirls softly by.

All but blind
 In the burning day   10
The Barn-Owl blunders
 On her way.

And blind as are
 These three to me,
So, blind to Someone   15
 I must be.

DISCUSSION 1. If their vision is compared to ours, the three creatures in "All but Blind" can barely see. Explain how we also may appear to be "all but blind" to "Someone."

2. In "An Emerald Is As Green As Grass" Rossetti contrasts five precious stones with flint. What are the differences? In what ways might these differences also apply to people?

3. Suppose that line 8 began with "And" instead of "But." How would this change affect the meaning?

For Poets

AL YOUNG

Stay beautiful
but dont stay down underground too
    long
Dont turn into a mole
or a worm
or a root   5
or a stone

Come on out into the sunlight
Breathe in trees
Knock out mountains
Commune with snakes   10
& be the very hero of birds

Dont forget to poke your head up
& blink
think
Walk all around   15
Swim upstream

Dont forget to fly

Dream Deferred

LANGSTON HUGHES

What happens to a dream deferred?

Does it dry up
like a raisin in the sun?
Or fester like a sore—
And then run?   5
Does it stink like rotten meat?
Or crust and sugar over—
like a syrupy sweet?

Maybe it just sags
like a heavy load.   10

Or does it explode?

DISCUSSION

1. Briefly describe the poet—or person—who follows Young's advice in "For Poets."

2. Line 1 in "Dream Deferred" asks a question: "What happens to a dream deferred?" How do the succeeding lines answer that question?

3. **Simile.** In a simile, a comparison is made between two dissimilar things, using the words *like* or *as.* The things compared are usually completely different except for a particular shared quality. In line 3 Hughes compares a deferred dream to a raisin in the sun. What is similar about these two things? What other similes do you find in the poem? What is the total effect of these similes in describing "a dream deferred"?

Puerto Rican Paradise

PIRI THOMAS

Poppa lost his night job—I forget why, and probably it was worth forgetting—and went back on home relief. It was 1941, and the Great Hunger called Depression was still down on Harlem.

But there was still the good old WPA. If a man was poor enough, he could dig a ditch for the government. Now Poppa was poor enough again.

The weather turned cold one more time, and so did our apartment. In the summer the cooped-up apartments in Harlem seem to catch all the heat and improve on it. It's the same in the winter. The cold, plastered walls embrace that cold from outside and make it a part of the apartment, till you don't know whether it's better to freeze out in the snow or by the stove, where four jets, wide open, spout futile, blue-yellow flames. It's hard on the rats, too.

Snow was falling . . . . Momma said, "*Qué frío.*[1] Doesn't that landlord have any *corazón?*[2] Why don't he give more heat?" I wondered how Pops was making out working a pick and shovel in that falling snow.

Momma picked up a hammer and began to beat the beat-up radiator that's copped a plea from so many beatings. Poor steam radiator, how could it give out heat when it was freezing itself? The hollow sounds Momma beat out of it brought echoes from other freezing people in the building. Everybody picked up the beat and it seemed a crazy, good idea. If everybody took turns beating on the radiators, everybody could keep warm from the exercise.

We drank hot cocoa and talked about summertime. Momma talked about Puerto Rico and how great it was, and how she'd like to go back one day, and how it was warm all the time there and no matter how poor you were over there, you could always live on green bananas, *bacalao,*[3] and rice and beans. . . . She said, "I don't think I'll ever see my island again."

[1] *Qué frío:* how cold.
[2] *corazón:* heart.
[3] *bacalao:* salt cod.

"Sure you will, Mommie," said Miriam, my kid sister. She was eleven. "Tell us, tell us all about Porto Rico."

"It's not P*o*rto Rico, it's P*ue*rto Rico," said Momma.

"Tell us, Moms," said nine-year-old James, "about P*ue*rto Rico."

"Yeah, Mommie," said six-year-old José.

Even the baby, Paulie, smiled.

Moms copped that wet-eyed look and began to dream-talk about her *isla verde,* Moses' land of milk and honey.

"When I was a little girl," she said, "I remember the getting up in the morning and getting the water from the river and getting the wood for the fire and the quiet of the greenlands and the golden color of the morning sky, the grass wet from the *lluvia*[4] . . . the *coquís*[5] and the *pajaritos*[6] making all the *música* . . . ."

"Mommie, were you poor?" asked Miriam.

"*Sí, muy pobre,*[7] but very happy. I remember the hard work and the very little bit we had, but it was a good little bit. It counted very much. Sometimes when you have too much, the good gets lost within and you have to look very hard. But when you have a little, then the good does not have to be looked for so hard."

"Moms," I asked, "did everybody love each other—I mean, like if everybody was worth something, not like if some weren't important because they were poor—you know what I mean?"

"*Bueno hijo,*[8] you have people everywhere who, because they have more, don't remember those who have very little. But in Puerto Rico those around you share *la pobreza*[9] with you and they love you, because only poor people can understand poor people. I like *los Estados Unidos,* but it's sometimes a cold place to live—not because of the winter and the landlord not giving heat but because of the snow in the hearts of the people."

"Moms, didn't our people have any money or land?" I leaned forward, hoping to hear that my ancestors were noble princes born in Spain.

"Your grandmother and grandfather had a lot of land, but they lost that."

---

[4] *lluvia*: rain.
[5] *coquís*: crickets.
[6] *pajaritos*: little birds.

[7] *Sí, muy pobre*: Yes, very poor.
[8] *Bueno hijo*: Dear son.
[9] *la pobreza*: poverty.

"How come, Moms?"

"Well, in those days there was nothing of what you call *contratos,*[10] and when you bought or sold something, it was on your word and a handshake, and that's the way your *abuelos*[11] bought their land and then lost it."

"Is that why we ain't got nuttin' now?" James asked pointedly.

"Oh, it——"

The door opened and put an end to the kitchen yak. It was Poppa coming home from work. He came into the kitchen and brought all the cold with him. Poor Poppa, he looked so lost in the clothes he had on. A jacket and coat, sweaters on top of sweaters, two pairs of long johns, two pairs of pants, two pairs of socks, and a woolen cap. And under all that he was cold. His eyes were cold; his ears were red with pain. He took off his gloves and his fingers were stiff with cold.

"Cómo está?"[12] said Momma. "I will make you coffee."

Poppa said nothing. His eyes were running hot frozen tears. He worked his fingers and rubbed his ears, and the pain made him make faces. "Get me some snow, Piri," he said finally.

I ran to the window, opened it, and scraped all the snow on the sill into one big snowball and brought it to him. We all watched in frozen wonder as Poppa took that snow and rubbed it on his ears and hands.

"Gee, Pops, don't it hurt?" I asked.

"Sí, but it's good for it. It hurts a little first, but it's good for the frozen parts."

I wondered why.

"How was it today?" Momma asked.

"Cold . . . ice cold."

Gee, I thought, *I'm sorry for you, Pops. You gotta suffer like this.*

"It was not always like this," my father said to the cold walls. . . .

And Miriam, James, José, Paulie, and me just looking and thinking about snowballs and Puerto Rico and summertime in the street and whether we were gonna live like this forever and not know enough to be sorry for ourselves.

---

[10] *contratos:* contracts.
[11] *abuelos:* grandfathers.
[12] *Como esta?:* How are you?

The kitchen all of a sudden felt warmer to me, like being all together made it like we wanted it to be. . . . I looked at the clock and it was time for "Jack Armstrong, the All-American Boy."

José, James, and I got some blankets and, like Indians, huddled around the radio digging the All-American Jack and his adventures, while Poppa ate dinner quietly. Poppa was funny about eating—like when he ate, nobody better bother him. When Poppa finished, he came into the living room and stood there looking at us. We smiled at him, and he stood there looking at us.

All of a sudden he yelled, "How many wanna play 'Major Bowes' Amateur Hour'?"

"Hoo-ray! Yeah, we wanna play," said José.

"Okay, first I'll make some taffy outta molasses, and the one who wins first prize gets first choice at the biggest piece, okay?"

"Yeah, hoo-ray, *chevere.*"[13]

Gee, Pops, you're great, I thought, *you're the swellest, the bestest Pops in the whole world, even though you don't understand us too good.*

When the candy was all ready, everybody went into the living room. Poppa came in with a broom and put an empty can over the stick. It became a microphone, just like on the radio.

"Pops, can I be Major Bowes?" I asked.

"Sure, Piri," and the floor was mine.

"Ladies and gentlemen," I announced, "tonight we present 'Major Bowes' Amateur Hour,' and for our first number——"

"Wait a minute, son, let me get my ukelele," said Poppa. "We need music."

Everybody clapped their hands and Pops came back with his ukelele.

"The first con-tes-tant we got is Miss Miriam Thomas."

"Oh no, not me first, somebody else goes first," said Miriam, and she hid behind Momma.

"Let me! Let me!" said José.

Everybody clapped.

"What are you gonna sing, sir?" I asked.

"Tell the people his name," said Poppa.

"Oh yeah. Presenting Mr. José Thomas. And what are you gonna sing, sir?"

---

[13] *chevere:* great.

I handed José the broom with the can on top and sat back. He sang well and everybody clapped.

Everyone took a turn, and we all agreed that two-year-old Paulie's "gurgle, gurgle" was the best song, and Paulie got first choice at the candy. Everybody got candy and eats and thought how good it was to be together, and Moms thought that it was wonderful to have such a good time even if she wasn't in Puerto Rico where the grass was wet with *lluvia.* Poppa thought about how cold it was gonna be tomorrow, but then he remembered tomorrow was Sunday and he wouldn't have to work, and he said so and Momma said *"Sí,"* and the talk got around to Christmas and how maybe things would get better.

The next day the Japanese bombed Pearl Harbor. . . .

Poppa said, "We're at war. . . ."

I turned to James. "Can you beat that," I said.

"Yeah," he nodded. "What's it mean?"

"What's it mean?" I said. " You gotta ask, dopey? It means a rumble is on, and a big one, too."

I wondered if the war was gonna make things worse than they were for us. But it didn't. A few weeks later Poppa got a job in an airplane factory. "How about that?" he said happily. "Things are looking up for us. . . ."

A lousy rumble had to get called so we could start to live better. . . .

I couldn't figure it out, and after a while I stopped thinking about it. Life in the streets didn't change much. The bitter cold was followed by the sticky heat; I played stickball, marbles, and Johnny-on-the-Pony. . . . War or peace—what difference did it really make?

DISCUSSION

1. Although the family is poor and circumstances are hard, Thomas creates a feeling of warmth and love. What experiences contribute to this feeling?

2. **Setting** (see page 57) is of great significance in this selection. How does the actual setting in Harlem contrast with the mother's stories of Puerto Rico?

For further activities, see page 120.

TO BE OF USE

MARGE PIERCY

The people I love the best
jump into work head first
without dallying in the shallows
and swim off with sure strokes almost out of sight.
They seem to become natives of that element,   5
the black sleek heads of seals
bouncing like half-submerged balls.

I love people who harness themselves, an ox to a heavy cart,
who pull like water buffalo, with massive patience,
who strain in the mud and the muck to move things forward,   10
who do what has to be done, again and again.

I want to be with people who submerge
in the task, who go into the fields to harvest
and work in a row and pass the bags along,
who stand in the line and haul in their places,   15
who are not parlor generals and field deserters
but move in a common rhythm
when the food must come in or the fire be put out.

The work of the world is common as mud.
Botched, it smears the hands, crumbles to dust.   20
But the thing worth doing well done
has a shape that satisfies, clean and evident.
Greek amphoras for wine or oil,
Hopi vases that held corn, are put in museums
but you know they were made to be used.   25
The pitcher cries for water to carry
and a person for work that is real.

DISCUSSION   1. This poem describes the kind of people the speaker "love[s] the best." Pick out phrases that tell what characteristics they have.

2. The speaker draws a parallel between a pitcher and a person (lines 26–27). What does each need? What is "work that is real"?

VOCABULARY

The Storyteller (page 86)

On separate paper, match the number of the word with the letter of its correct definition or synonym at the right.

1. persistent   **a.** fixed belief; firmness
2. audible   **b.** attack verbally
3. wager   **c.** repeated, continuous
4. conviction   **d.** capable of being heard
5. assail   **e.** bet

The Necklace (page 94)

On separate paper, write the word in bold type. Then from the group of three at the right, write the one that is closest in meaning to it.

1. having no *dowry*   record   idea   property
2. a sense of *frustration*   refinement   encouragement   bafflement
3. *exotic* birds   foreign   domesticated   wild
4. *close-fisted* clerk   miserly   repentant   discouraged
5. various *ornaments*   requirements   adornments   consignments

COMPOSITION

The Storyteller (page 86)

Think of a familiar story from your childhood. Consider how it might be retold to a child today in an improbable or unconventional way. Write the story—perhaps as a story or possibly as a script for radio or TV—to share with the class.

The Necklace (page 94)

Put yourself in the place of either the husband or wife during their ten years of poverty. How would you feel about the sacrifices you have to make? Would there be a change in your attitude toward your marriage partner? What would be your reaction when you discover the real worth of the necklace? In the form of a diary or journal, answer these and other questions that may occur to you.

READING

The Storyteller (page 86)

Below is a list of sentence fragments. Some apply to both the aunt and the bachelor; some, to the aunt only; and some, to the bachelor only. On separate paper, mark *A* for each item that applies to the aunt and *B* for each that applies to the bachelor. Some items will have both *A* and *B*. Briefly tell what in the story supports your choice.

1. would like peace and quiet
2. dislikes noisy, prattling children
3. has a nimble mind and is able to give quick answers
4. understands what amuses and entertains children
5. has a practical, realistic goal
6. has a "proper" goal
7. dislikes being bored
8. likes to play practical jokes
9. has a firm, brisk way of dealing with situations
10. is effective in handling people.

Puerto Rican Paradise (page 112)

Below are twelve words, one of which will best fit each blank space in the sentences that follow. On separate paper, write the word that is best for each sentence.

little	run-down	affectionately	limited
possess	lack	depressed	boundless
great	well-kept	gay	distrustfully

1. The immigrants remember their former home——because their lives now lack the pleasures they once had.
2. The spirits of the immigrants are——because they have not been able to reach a higher standard of living in the United States.
3. Because immigrants have usually been given the worst jobs, the father's income is——.
4. The family is forced to live in——housing.
5. The family has——patriotic enthusiasm when the United States becomes involved in the war.

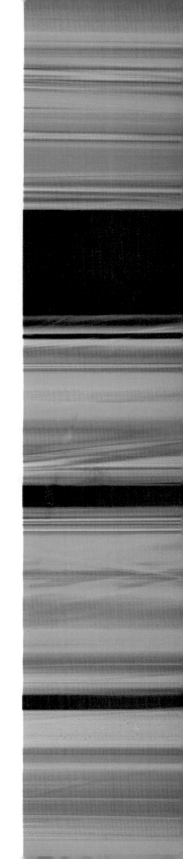

TRINITY PLACE

PHYLLIS McGINLEY

The pigeons that peck at the grass in Trinity Churchyard
  Are pompous as bankers. They walk with an air, they preen
Their prosperous feathers. They smugly regard their beauty.
They are plump, they are sleek. It is only the men who are lean.
The pigeons scan with disfavor the men who sit there,   5
  Listless in sun or shade. The pigeons sidle
Between the gravestones with shrewd, industrious motions.
  The pigeons are busy. It is only the men who are idle.
The pigeons sharpen their beaks on the stones, and they waddle
  In dignified search of their proper, their daily bread.   10
Their eyes are small with contempt for the men on the benches.
  It is only the men who are hungry. The pigeons are fed.

DISCUSSION

1. What is the contrast between the pigeons and the men in Trinity Churchyard? What words or phrases describe each?

2. Explain the significance of the last line of the poem. Are McGinley's sympathies with the men or the pigeons? Cite lines that support your answer.

For further activities, see page 168.

The Fifty-First Dragon

HEYWOOD BROUN

Of all the pupils at the knight school Gawaine le Coeur-Hardy[1]
was among the least promising. He was tall and sturdy, but his
instructors soon discovered that he lacked spirit. He would hide in
the woods when the jousting class was called, although his companions and members of the faculty sought to appeal to his better
nature by shouting to him to come out and break his neck like a
man. Even when they told him that the lances were padded, the
horses no more than ponies, and the field unusually soft for late
autumn, Gawaine refused to grow enthusiastic. The Headmaster
and the Assistant Professor of Pleasance[2] were discussing the case

[1] *Gawaine le Coeur-Hardy:* pronounced gà-'wān lə kər-àr-dē'.
[2] *Pleasance:* recreation.

one spring afternoon, and the Assistant Professor could see no remedy but expulsion.

"No," said the Headmaster, as he looked out at the purple hills which ringed the school, "I think I'll train him to slay dragons."

"He might be killed," objected the Assistant Professor.

"So he might," replied the Headmaster brightly; "but," he added more soberly, "we must consider the greater good. We are responsible for the formation of this lad's character."

"Are the dragons particularly bad this year?" interrupted the Assistant Professor. This was characteristic. He always seemed restive when the head of the school began to talk ethics and the ideals of the institution.

"I've never known them worse," replied the Headmaster. "Up in the hills to the south last week they killed a number of peasants, two cows, and a prize pig. And if this dry spell holds, there's no telling when they may start a forest fire simply by breathing around indiscriminately."

"Would any refund on the tuition fee be necessary in case of an accident to young Coeur-Hardy?"

"No," the principal answered judicially; "that's all covered in the contract. But as a matter of fact he won't be killed. Before I send him up in the hills, I'm going to give him a magic word."

"That's a good idea," said the Professor. "Sometimes they work wonders."

From that day on Gawaine specialized in dragons. His course included both theory and practice. In the morning there were long lectures on the history, anatomy, manners, and customs of dragons. Gawaine did not distinguish himself in these studies. He had a marvelously versatile gift for forgetting things. In the afternoon he showed to better advantage, for then he would go down to the South Meadow and practice with a battle-ax. In this exercise he was truly impressive, for he had enormous strength as well as speed and grace. He even developed a deceptive display of ferocity. Old alumni say that it was a thrilling sight to see Gawaine charging across the field toward the dummy paper dragon which had been set up for his practice. As he ran he would brandish his ax and shout, "A murrain[3] on thee!" or some other vivid bit of campus slang. It never took him more than one stroke to behead the dummy dragon.

[3] *murrain:* (mûr'ĭn): plague.

Gradually his task was made more difficult. Paper gave way to papier-mâché and finally to wood, but even the toughest of these dummy dragons had no terrors for Gawaine. One sweep of the ax always did the business. There were those who said that when the practice was protracted until dusk and the dragons threw long, fantastic shadows across the meadow, Gawaine did not charge so impetuously nor shout so loudly. It is possible there was malice in this charge. At any rate, the Headmaster decided by the end of June that it was time for the test. Only the night before, a dragon had come close to the school grounds and had eaten some of the lettuce from the garden. The faculty decided that Gawaine was ready. They gave him a diploma and a new battle-ax, and the Headmaster summoned him to a private conference.

"Sit down," said the Headmaster. "Have a cigarette."

Gawaine hesitated.

"Oh, I know it's against the rules," said the Headmaster; "but after all, you have received your preliminary degree. You are no longer a boy. You are a man. Tomorrow you will go out into the world, the great world of achievement."

Gawaine took a cigarette. The Headmaster offered him a match, but he produced one of his own and began to puff away with a dexterity which quite amazed the principal.

"Here you have learned the theories of life," continued the Headmaster, resuming the thread of his discourse; "but after all, life is not a matter of theories. Life is a matter of facts. It calls on the young and the old alike to face these facts, even though they are hard and sometimes unpleasant. Your problem, for example, is to slay dragons."

"They say that those dragons down in the south wood are five hundred feet long," ventured Gawaine timorously.

"Stuff and nonsense!" said the Headmaster. "The curate saw one last week from the top of Arthur's Hill. The dragon was sunning himself down in the valley. The curate didn't have an opportunity to look at him very long because he felt it was his duty to hurry back to make a report to me. He said the monster—or shall I say, the big lizard?—wasn't an inch over two hundred feet. But the size has nothing at all to do with it. You'll find the big ones even easier than the little ones. They're far slower on their feet and less aggressive, I'm told. Besides, before you go I'm going to equip you in such fashion that you need have no fear of all the dragons in the world."

"I'd like an enchanted cap," said Gawaine.

"What's that?" asked the Headmaster testily.

"A cap to make me disappear," explained Gawaine.

The Headmaster laughed indulgently. "You mustn't believe all those old wives' stories," he said. "There isn't any such thing. A cap to make you disappear, indeed! What would you do with it? You haven't even appeared yet. Why, my boy, you could walk from here to London, and nobody would so much as look at you. You're nobody. You couldn't be more invisible than that."

Gawaine seemed dangerously close to a relapse into his old habit of whimpering. The Headmaster reassured him: "Don't worry; I'll give you something much better than an enchanted cap. I'm going to give you a magic word. All you have to do is to repeat this magic charm once and no dragon can possibly harm a hair of your head. You can cut off his head at your leisure."

He took a heavy book from the shelf behind his desk and began to run through it. "Sometimes," he said, "the charm is a whole phrase or even a sentence. I might, for instance, give you 'To make the'——No, that might not do. I think a single word would be best for dragons."

"A short word," suggested Gawaine.

"It can't be too short or it wouldn't be potent. There isn't so much hurry as all that. Here's a splendid magic word: 'Rumplesnitz.' Do you think you can learn that?"

Gawaine tried and in an hour or so he seemed to have the word well in hand. Again and again he interrupted the lesson to inquire, "And if I say 'Rumplesnitz' the dragon can't possibly hurt me?" And always the Headmaster replied, "If you only say 'Rumplesnitz,' you are perfectly safe."

Toward morning Gawaine seemed resigned to his career. At daybreak the Headmaster saw him to the edge of the forest and pointed him to the direction in which he should proceed. About a mile away to the southwest a cloud of steam hovered over an open meadow in the woods, and the Headmaster assured Gawaine that under the steam he would find a dragon. Gawaine went forward slowly. He wondered whether it would be best to approach the dragon on the run, as he did in his practice in the South Meadow, or to walk slowly toward him, shouting "Rumplesnitz" all the way.

The problem was decided for him. No sooner had he come to the fringe of the meadow than the dragon spied him and began to charge. It was a large dragon, and yet it seemed decidedly aggressive in spite of the Headmaster's statement to the contrary. As the dragon charged, it released huge clouds of hissing steam through its nostrils. It was almost as if a gigantic teapot had gone mad. The dragon came forward so fast, and Gawaine was so frightened, that he had time to say "Rumplesnitz" only once. As he said it he swung his battle-ax, and off popped the head of the dragon. Gawaine had to admit that it was even easier to kill a real dragon than a wooden one, if only you said "Rumplesnitz."

Gawaine brought the ears home and a small section of the tail. His schoolmates and the faculty made much of him, but the Headmaster wisely kept him from being spoiled by insisting that he go on with his work. Every clear day Gawaine rose at dawn and went out to kill dragons. The Headmaster kept him at home when it rained, because he said the woods were damp and unhealthy at such times and that he didn't want the boy to run needless risks. Few good days passed in which Gawaine failed to get a dragon. On one particularly fortunate day he killed three, a husband and wife and a visiting relative. Gradually he developed a technique. Pupils who sometimes watched him from the hilltops a long way off said that he often allowed the dragon to come within a few feet before he said "Rumplesnitz." He came to say it with a mocking sneer. Occasionally he did stunts. Once when an excursion party from London was watching him he went into action with his right hand tied behind his back. The dragon's head came off just as easily.

As Gawaine's record of killings mounted higher, the Headmaster found it impossible to keep him completely in hand. He fell into the habit of stealing out at night and engaging in long drinking bouts at the village tavern. It was after such a debauch that he rose a little before dawn one fine August morning and started out after his fiftieth dragon. His head was heavy and his mind sluggish. He was heavy in other respects as well, for he had adopted the somewhat vulgar practice of wearing his medals, ribbons and all, when he went out dragon hunting. The decorations began on his chest and ran all the way down to his abdomen. They must have weighed at least eight pounds.

Gawaine found a dragon in the same meadow where he killed the first one. It was a fair-sized dragon, but evidently an old one. Its face was wrinkled and Gawaine thought he had never seen so hideous a countenance. Much to the lad's disgust the monster refused to charge, and Gawaine was obliged to walk toward him. He whistled as he went. The dragon regarded him hopelessly but craftily. Of course it had heard of Gawaine. Even when the lad raised his battle-ax, the dragon made no move. It knew that there was no salvation in the quickest thrust of the head, for it had been informed that this hunter was protected by an enchantment. It merely waited, hoping something would turn up.

Gawaine raised the battle-ax and suddenly lowered it again. He had grown very pale, and he trembled violently.

The dragon suspected a trick. "What's the matter?" it asked, with false solicitude.

"I've forgotten the magic word," stammered Gawaine.

"What a pity!" said the dragon. "So that was the secret. It doesn't seem quite sporting to me, all this magic stuff, you know. Not cricket, as we used to say when I was a little dragon; but after all, that's a matter of opinion."

Gawaine was so helpless with terror that the dragon's confidence rose immeasurably and it could not resist the temptation to show off a bit.

"Could I possibly be of any assistance?" it asked. "What's the first letter of the magic word?"

"It begins with an 'R,' " said Gawaine weakly.

"Let's see," mused the dragon, "that doesn't tell us much, does it? What sort of a word is this? Is it an epithet, do you think?"

Gawaine shook his head.

"Well, then," said the dragon, "we'd better get down to business. Will you surrender?"

With the suggestion of a compromise Gawaine mustered up enough courage to speak.

"What will you do if I surrender?" he asked.

"Why, I'll eat you," said the dragon.

"And if I don't surrender?"

"I'll eat you just the same."

"Then it doesn't mean any difference, does it?" moaned Gawaine.

"It does to me," said the dragon with a smile. "I'd rather you didn't surrender. You'd taste much better if you didn't."

The dragon waited for a long time for Gawaine to ask "Why?" but the boy was too frightened to speak. At last the dragon had to give the explanation without his cue line. "You see," he said, "if you don't surrender you'll taste better because you'll die game."

This was an old and ancient trick of the dragon's. By means of some such quip he was accustomed to paralyze his victims with laughter and then to destroy them. Gawaine was sufficiently paralyzed as it was, but laughter had no part in his helplessness. With the last word of the joke the dragon drew back his head and struck. In that second there flashed into the mind of Gawaine the magic word of "Rumplesnitz," but there was no time to say it. There was time only to strike, and without a word Gawaine met the onrush of the dragon with a full swing. He put all his back and shoulders into it. The impact was terrific, and the head of the dragon flew almost a hundred yards and landed in a thicket.

Gawaine did not remain frightened very long after the death of the dragon. His mood was one of wonder. He was enormously puzzled. He cut off the ears of the monster almost in a trance. Again and again he thought to himself, "I didn't say 'Rumplesnitz'!" He was sure of that, and yet there was no question that he had killed the dragon. In fact, he had never killed one so utterly. Never before had he driven a head for anything like the same distance. Twenty-five yards was perhaps his best previous record. All the way back to the knight school he kept rumbling about in his mind, seeking an explanation for what had occurred. He went to the Headmaster immediately, and after closing the door, told him what had happened. "I didn't say 'Rumplesnitz,' " he explained with great earnestness.

The Headmaster laughed. "I'm glad you've found out," he said. "It makes you ever so much more of a hero. Don't you see that? Now you know that it was you who killed all these dragons, and not that foolish little word 'Rumplesnitz.' "

Gawaine frowned. "Then it wasn't a magic word, after all?" he asked.

"Of course not," said the Headmaster; "you ought to be too old for such foolishness. There isn't any such thing as a magic word."

"But you told me it was magic," protested Gawaine. "You said it was magic, and now you say it isn't."

"It wasn't magic in a literal sense," answered the Headmaster, "but it was much more wonderful than that. The word gave you confidence. It took away your fears. If I hadn't told you that, you might have been killed the very first time. It was your battle-ax did the trick."

Gawaine surprised the Headmaster by his attitude. He was obviously distressed by the explanation. He interrupted a long philosophic and ethical discourse by the Headmaster with, "If I hadn't of hit 'em all mighty hard and fast, any one of 'em might have crushed me like a, like a——" He fumbled for a word.

"Egg shell," suggested the Headmaster.

"Like a egg shell," assented Gawaine and he said it many times. All through the evening meal people who sat near him heard him muttering, "Like a egg shell, like a egg shell."

The next day was clear, but Gawaine did not get up at dawn. Indeed, it was almost noon when the Headmaster found him cowering in bed, with the clothes pulled over his head. The principal called the Assistant Professor of Pleasance, and together they dragged the boy toward the forest.

"He'll be all right as soon as he gets a couple more dragons under his belt," explained the Headmaster.

The Assistant Professor of Pleasance agreed. "It would be a shame to stop such a fine run," he said. "Why, counting that one yesterday, he's killed fifty dragons."

They pushed the boy into a thicket above which hung a meager cloud of steam. It was obviously quite a small dragon. But Gawaine did not come back that night or the next. In fact, he never came back. Some weeks afterwards, brave spirits from the school explored the thicket, but they could find nothing to remind them of Gawaine except the metal parts of his medals. Even the ribbon had been devoured.

The Headmaster and the Assistant Professor of Pleasance agreed that it would be just as well not to tell the school how Gawaine had achieved his record and still less how he came to die. They held that it might have a bad effect on school spirit. Accordingly, Gawaine has lived in the memory of the school as its greatest hero. No visitor succeeds in leaving the building today without seeing a great shield which hangs on the wall of the dining hall. Fifty pairs of dragons' ears are mounted upon the shield, and underneath in gilt letters is "Gawaine le Coeur-Hardy," followed by the simple inscription, "He killed fifty dragons." The record has never been equaled.

DISCUSSION

1. You might expect that Gawaine's self-confidence would be increased by knowing that he, not a magic word, slew the dragons. Why does it have just the opposite effect?

2. Find several examples of humorous statements—for example, the dragon's comment on page 130, "Not cricket, as we used to say when I was a little dragon."

3. This story, lightly told, makes a serious point. What modern dragons might a twentieth-century Gawaine have to overcome? War, for example? What others?

For further activities, see page 168.

FIRST LESSON
Philip Booth

Lie back, daughter, let your head
be tipped back in the cup of my hand.
Gently, and I will hold you. Spread
your arms wide, lie out on the stream
and look high at the gulls. A dead-
man's float is face down. You will dive
and swim soon enough where this tidewater
ebbs to the sea. Daughter, believe
me, when you tire on the long thrash
to your island, lie up, and survive.
As you float now, where I held you
and let go, remember when fear
cramps your heart what I told you:
lie gently and wide to the light-year
stars, lie back, and the sea will hold you.

DISCUSSION

1. This description of a first swimming lesson for a daughter is filled with a parent's concern and gentleness—"let your head / be tipped back in the cup of my hand" (lines 1 and 2), for example. Find two or three similar expressions that show concern.

2. Reread the last five lines slowly and thoughtfully. They sum up the first lesson in swimming. How may they also apply to living?

The Colt

WALLACE STEGNER

It was the swift coming of spring that let things happen. It was spring, and the opening of the roads, that took his father out of town. It was spring that clogged the river with floodwater and ice pans, sent the dogs racing in wild aimless packs, ripped the railroad bridge out and scattered it down the river for exuberant townspeople to fish out piecemeal. It was spring that drove the whole town to the riverbank with pikepoles and coffeepots and boxes of sandwiches for an impromptu picnic, lifting their sober responsibilities out of them and making them whoop blessings on the C.P.R.[1] for a winter's firewood. Nothing might have gone wrong except for the coming of spring. Some of the neighbors might have noticed and let them know; Bruce might not have forgotten; his mother might have remembered and sent him out again after dark.

But the spring came, and the ice went out, and that night Bruce went to bed drunk and exhausted with excitement. In the restless sleep just before waking, he dreamed of wolves and wild hunts, but when he awoke finally, he realized that he had not been dreaming the noise. The window, wide open for the first time in months, let in a shivery draft of fresh, damp air, and he heard the faint yelping far down in the bend of the river.

He dressed and went downstairs, crowding his bottom into the warm oven, not because he was cold but because it had been a ritual for so long that not even the sight of the sun outside could convince him it wasn't necessary. The dogs were still yapping; he heard them through the open door.

"What's the matter with all the pooches?" he said. "Where's Spot?"

"He's out with them," his mother said. "They've probably got a porcupine treed. Dogs go crazy in the spring."

"It's dog days they go crazy."

"They go crazy in the spring, too." She hummed a little as she set the table. "You'd better go feed the horses. Breakfast won't be for ten minutes. And see if Daisy is all right."

[1] *C.P.R.:* Canadian Pacific Railway.

Bruce stood perfectly still in the middle of the kitchen. "Oh my gosh!" he said. "I left Daisy picketed [2] out all night!"

His mother's head jerked around. "Where?"

"Down in the bend."

"Where those dogs are?"

"Yes," he said, sick and afraid. "Maybe she's had her colt."

"She shouldn't for two or three days," his mother said. But just looking at her, he knew that it might be bad, that there was something to be afraid of. In another moment they were both out the door, both running.

But it couldn't be Daisy they were barking at, he thought as he raced around Chance's barn. He'd picketed her higher up, not clear down in the U, where the dogs were. His eyes swept the brown, wet, close-cropped meadow, the edge of the brush where the river ran close under the north bench. The mare wasn't there! He opened his mouth and half turned, running, to shout at his mother coming behind him, and then sprinted for the deep curve of the bend.

As soon as he rounded the little clump of brush that fringed the cutbank behind Chance's, he saw them. The mare stood planted, a bay spot against the gray brush, and in front of her, on the ground, was another smaller spot. Six or eight dogs were leaping around, barking, sitting. Even at that distance he recognized Spot and the Chapman's Airedale.

He shouted and pumped on. At a gravelly patch he stooped and clawed and straightened, still running, with a handful of pebbles. In one pausing, straddling, aiming motion he let fly a rock at the distant pack. It fell far short, but they turned their heads, sat on their haunches, and let out defiant short barks. Their tongues lolled as if they had run far.

Bruce yelled and threw again, one eye on the dogs and the other on the chestnut colt in front of the mare's feet. The mare's ears were back, and as he ran Bruce saw the colt's head bob up and down. It was all right then. The colt was alive. He slowed and came up quietly. Never move fast or speak loud around an animal, Pa said.

The colt struggled again, raised its head with white eyeballs rolling, spraddled its white-stockinged legs and tried to stand. "Easy, boy," Bruce said. "Take it easy, old fella." His mother arrived, getting her breath, her hair half down, and he turned to

---

[2] *picketed:* tied to a stake.

her gleefully. "It's all right, Ma. They didn't hurt anything. Isn't he a beauty, Ma?"

He stroked Daisy's nose. She was heaving, her ears pricking forward and back; her flanks were lathered, and she trembled. Patting her gently, he watched the colt, sitting now like a dog on its haunches, and his happiness that nothing had really been hurt bubbled out of him. "Lookit, Ma," he said. "He's got four white socks. Can I call him Socks, Ma? He sure is a nice colt, isn't he? Aren't you, Socks, old boy?" He reached down to touch the chestnut's forelock, and the colt struggled, pulling away.

Then Bruce saw his mother's face. It was quiet, too quiet. She hadn't answered a word to all his jabber. Instead she knelt down, about ten feet from the squatting colt, and stared at it. The boy's eyes followed hers. There was something funny about——

"Ma!" he said. "What's the matter with its front feet?"

He left Daisy's head and came around, staring. The colt's pasterns [3] looked bent—*were* bent, so that they flattened clear

---

[3] *pasterns:* above a horse's hoof is the pastern, and above the pastern is the *fetlock,* where foot and leg are joined.

to the ground under its weight. Frightened by Bruce's movement, the chestnut flopped and floundered to its feet, pressing
close to its mother. And it walked, Bruce saw, flat on its fetlocks, its hoofs sticking out in front like a movie comedian's too-
large shoes.

Bruce's mother pressed her lips together, shaking her head.
She moved so gently that she got her hand on the colt's poll,[4]
and he bobbed against the pleasant scratching. "You poor
broken-legged thing," she said with tears in her eyes. "You poor
little friendly ruined thing!"

Still quietly, she turned toward the dogs, and for the first
time in his life Bruce heard her curse. Quietly, almost in a whisper, she cursed them as they sat with hanging tongues just out
of reach.

To Bruce, standing with trembling lip, she said, "Go get
Jim Enich. Tell him to bring a wagon. And don't cry. It's not
your fault."

His mouth tightened, a sob jerked in his chest. He bit his
lip and drew his face down tight to keep from crying, but his
eyes filled and ran over.

"It is too my fault!" he said, and turned and ran.

Later, as they came in the wagon up along the cutbank, the
colt tied down in the wagon box with his head sometimes lifting, sometimes bumping on the boards, the mare trotting after
with chuckling vibrations of solicitude in her throat, Bruce
leaned far over and tried to touch the colt's haunch. "Gee
whiz!" he said. "Poor old Socks."

His mother's arm was around him, keeping him from leaning over too far. He didn't watch where they were until he
heard his mother say in surprise and relief, "Why, there's Pa!"

Instantly he was terrified. He had forgotten and left Daisy
staked out all night. It was his fault, the whole thing. He slid
back into the seat and crouched between Enich and his mother,
watching from that narrow space like a gopher from its hole. He
saw the Ford against the barn, and his father's big body leaning
into it pulling out gunnysacks and straw. There was mud all
over the car, mud on his father's pants. He crouched deeper into
his crevice and watched his father's face while his mother was
telling what had happened.

---

[4] *poll:* top of the head between the ears.

Then Pa and Jim Enich lifted and slid the colt down to the ground, and Pa stooped to feel its fetlocks. His face was still, red from windburn, and his big square hands were muddy. After a long examination he straightened up.

"Would've been a nice colt," he said. He brushed his pants and looked at Bruce's mother. "How come Daisy was out?"

"I told Bruce to take her out. The barn seems so cramped for her, and I thought it would do her good to stretch her legs. And then the ice went out and the bridge with it, and there was a lot of excitement." She spoke very fast, and in her voice Bruce heard the echo of his own fear and guilt. She was trying to protect him, but in his mind he knew he was to blame.

"I didn't mean to leave her out, Pa," he said. His voice squeaked, and he swallowed. "I was going to bring her in before supper, only when the bridge——"

His father's somber eye rested on him, and he stopped. But his father didn't fly into a rage. He just seemed tired. He looked at the colt and then at Enich. "Total loss?" he said.

Enich had a leathery, withered face, with two deep creases from beside his nose to the corner of his mouth. A brown mole hid in the left one, and it emerged and disappeared as he chewed a dry grass-stem. "Hide," he said.

Bruce closed his dry mouth, swallowed. "Pa!" he said. "It won't have to be shot, will it?"

"What else can you do with it?" his father said. "A crippled horse is no good. It's just plain mercy to shoot it."

"Give it to me, Pa. I'll keep it lying down and heal it up."

"Yeah," his father said, without sarcasm and without mirth. "You could keep it lying down about one hour."

Bruce's mother came up next to him, as if the two of them were standing against the others. "Jim," she said quickly, "isn't there some kind of brace you could put on it? I remember my dad had a horse once that broke a leg below the knee, and he saved it that way."

"Not much chance," Enich said. "Both legs, like that'" He plucked a weed and stripped the dry branches from the stalk. "You can't make a horse understand he has to keep still."

"But wouldn't it be worth trying?" she said. "Children's bones heal so fast. I should think a colt's would too."

"I don't know. There's an outside chance, maybe."

"Bo," she said to her husband, "why don't we try it? It seems such a shame, a lovely colt like that."

"I know it's a shame!" he said. "I don't like shooting colts any better than you do. But I never saw a broken-legged colt get well. It'd just be a lot of worry and trouble, and then you'd have to shoot it finally, anyway."

"Please," she said. She nodded at him slightly, and then the eyes of both were on Bruce.

He felt the tears coming up again, and turned to grope for the colt's ears. It tried to struggle to its feet, and Enich put his foot on its neck. The mare chuckled anxiously.

"How much this hobble-brace kind of thing cost?" the father said finally.

Bruce turned again, his mouth open with hope.

"Two-three dollars, is all," Enich said.

"You think it's got a chance?"

"One in a thousand, maybe."

"All right. Let's go see MacDonald."

"Oh, good!" Bruce's mother said, and put her arm around him tight.

"I don't know whether it's good or not," the father said. "We might wish we never did it." To Bruce he said, "It's your responsibility. You got to take complete care of it."

"I will!" Bruce said. He took his hand out of his pocket and rubbed below his eye with his knuckles. "I'll take care of it every day."

Big with contrition and shame and gratitude and the sudden sense of immense responsibility, he watched his father and Enich start for the house to get a tape measure. When they were thirty feet away, he said loudly, "Thanks, Pa. Thanks an awful lot."

His father half turned, said something to Enich. Bruce stooped to stroke the colt, looked at his mother, started to laugh, and felt it turn horribly into a sob. When he turned away so that his mother wouldn't notice, he saw his dog, Spot, looking inquiringly around the corner of the barn. Spot took three or four tentative steps and paused, wagging his tail. Very slowly (never speak loud or move fast around an animal) the boy bent and found a good-sized stone. He straightened casually, brought his arm back, and threw with all his might. The rock caught Spot squarely in the ribs. He yipped, tucked his tail, and scuttled around the barn, and Bruce chased him, throwing clods and stones and gravel, yelling, "Get out! Go on, get out of here or I'll kick you apart. Get out! Go on!"

So all that spring, while the world dried in the sun and the willows emerged from the floodwater and the mud left by the freshet hardened and caked among their roots, and the grass of the meadow greened and the river brush grew misty with tiny leaves and the dandelions spread yellow among the flats, Bruce tended his colt. While the other boys roamed the bench hills with .22's, looking for gophers or rabbits or sage hens, he anxiously superintended the colt's nursing and watched it learn to nibble the grass. While his gang built a darkly secret hideout in the deep brush beyond Hazard's, he was currying and brushing and trimming the chestnut mane. When packs of boys ran hare and hounds[5] through the town and around the river's slow bends, he perched on the front porch with his slingshot and a can full of small round stones, waiting for stray dogs to appear. He waged a holy war on the dogs until they learned to detour widely around his house, and he never did completely forgive his own dog, Spot. His whole life was wrapped up in the hobbled, leg-ironed chestnut colt with the slow-motion lunging walk and the affectionate nibbling lips.

Every week or so Enich, who was now working out of town at the Half Diamond Bar, rode in and stopped. Always, with that expressionless quiet that was terrible to the boy, he stood and looked the colt over, bent to feel pastern and fetlock, stood back to watch the plunging walk when the boy held out a handful of grass. His expression said nothing; whatever he thought was hidden back of his leathery face as the dark mole was hidden in the crease beside his mouth. Bruce found himself watching that mole sometimes, as if revelation might lie there. But when he pressed Enich to tell him, when he said, "He's getting better, isn't he? He walks better, doesn't he, Mr. Enich? His ankles don't bend so much, do they?" the wrangler gave him little encouragement.

"Let him be a while. He's growin', sure enough. Maybe give him another month."

May passed. The river was slow and clear again, and some of the boys were already swimming. School was almost over. And still Bruce paid attention to nothing but Socks. He willed so strongly that the colt should get well that he grew furious even at Daisy when she sometimes wouldn't let the colt suck as much as he wanted. He took a butcher knife and cut the long

[5] *hare and hounds:* a game.

tender grass in the fence corners, where Socks could not reach, and fed it to his pet by the handful. He trained him to nuzzle for sugar lumps in his pockets. And back in his mind was a fear: in the middle of June they would be going out to the homestead again, and if Socks weren't well by that time, he might not be able to go.

"Pa," he said, a week before they planned to leave. "How much of a load are we going to have, going out to the homestead?"

"I don't know—wagonful, I suppose. Why?"

"I just wondered." He ran his fingers in a walking motion along the round edge of the dining table, and strayed into the other room. If they had a wagonload, then there was no way Socks could be loaded in and taken along. And he couldn't walk thirty miles. He'd get left behind before they got up on the bench, hobbling along like the little crippled boy in "The Pied

Piper," and they'd look back and see him trying to run, trying to keep up.

That picture was so painful that he cried over it in bed that night. But in the morning he dared to ask his father if they couldn't take Socks along to the farm. His father turned on him eyes as sober as Jim Enich's, and when he spoke it was with a kind of tired impatience. "How can he go? He couldn't walk it."

"But I want him to go, Pa!"

"Brucie," his mother said, "don't get your hopes up. You know we'd do it if we could, if it was possible."

"But Ma. . . ."

His father said, "What you want us to do, haul a broken-legged colt thirty miles?"

"He'd be well by the end of the summer, and he could walk back."

"Look," his father said. "Why can't you make up your mind to it? He isn't getting well. He isn't going to get well."

"He is too getting well!" Bruce shouted. He half stood up at the table, and his father looked at his mother and shrugged.

"Please, Bo," she said.

"Well, he's got to make up his mind to it sometime," he said.

Jim Enich's wagon pulled up on Saturday morning, and Bruce was out the door before his father could rise from his chair. "Hi, Mr. Enich," he said.

"Hello, Bub. How's your pony?"

"He's fine," Bruce said. "I think he's got a lot better since you saw him last."

"Uh-huh." Enich wrapped the lines around the whipstock and climbed down. "Tell me you're leaving next week."

"Yes," Bruce said. "Socks is in the back."

When they got into the backyard, Bruce's father was there with his hands behind his back, studying the colt as it hobbled around. He looked at Enich. "What do you think?" he said. "The kid here thinks his colt can walk out to the homestead."

"Uh-huh," Enich said. "Well, I wouldn't say that." He inspected the chestnut, scratched between his ears. Socks bobbed, and snuffled at his pockets. "Kid's made quite a pet of him."

Bruce's father grunted. "That's just the trouble."

"I didn't think he could walk out," Bruce said. "I thought we could take him in the wagon, and then he'd be well enough to walk back in the fall."

"Uh," Enich said. "Let's take his braces off for a minute."

He unbuckled the triple straps on each leg, pulled the braces off, and stood back. The colt stood almost as flat on his fetlocks as he had the morning he was born. Even Bruce, watching with his whole mind tight and apprehensive, could see that. Enich shook his head.

"You see, Bruce?" his father said. "It's too bad, but he isn't getting better. You'll have to make up your mind——"

"He will get better, though!" Bruce said. "It just takes a long time, is all." He looked at his father's face, at Enich's, and neither one had any hope in it. But when Bruce opened his mouth to say something else, his father's eyebrows drew down in sudden, unaccountable anger, and his hand made an impatient sawing motion in the air.

"We shouldn't have tried this in the first place," he said. "It just tangles everything up." He patted his coat pockets, felt in his vest. "Run in and get me a couple cigars."

Bruce hesitated, his eyes on Enich. "Run!" his father said harshly.

Reluctantly he released the colt's halter rope and started for the house. At the door he looked back, and his father and Enich were talking together, so low that their words didn't carry to where he stood. He saw his father shake his head, and Enich bend to pluck a grass stem. They were both against him; they both were sure Socks would never get well. Well, he would! There was some way.

He found the cigars, came out, watched them both light up. Disappointment was a sickness in him, and mixed with the disappointment was a question. When he could stand their silence no more, he burst out with it. "But what are we going to *do?* He's got to have some place to stay."

"Look, kiddo." His father sat down on a sawhorse and took him by the arm. His face was serious and his voice gentle. "We can't take him out there. He isn't well enough to walk, and we can't haul him. So Jim here has offered to buy him. He'll give you three dollars for him, and when you come back, if you want, you might be able to buy him back. That is, if he's well. It'll be better to leave him with Jim."

"Well. . . ." Bruce studied the mole on Enich's cheek. "Can you get him better by fall, Mr. Enich?"

"I wouldn't expect it," Enich said. "He ain't got much of a show."

"If anybody can get him better, Jim can," his father said. "How's that deal sound to you?"

"Maybe when I come back, he'll be all off his braces and running around like a house afire," Bruce said. "Maybe next time I see him I can ride him."

The mole disappeared as Enich tongued his cigar.

"Well, all right then," Bruce said, bothered by their stony-eyed silence. "But I sure hate to leave you behind, Socks, old boy."

"It's the best way all around," his father said. He talked fast, as if he were in a hurry. "Can you take him along now?"

"Oh, gee!" Bruce said. "Today?"

"Come on," his father said. "Let's get it over with."

Bruce stood by while they trussed the colt and hoisted him into the wagon box, and when Jim climbed in, he cried out, "Hey, we forgot to put his hobbles back on." Jim and his father looked at each other. His father shrugged. "All right," he said, and started putting the braces back on the trussed front legs. "He might hurt himself if they weren't on," Bruce said. He leaned over the endgate, stroking the white blazed face, and as the wagon pulled away he stood with tears in his eyes and the three dollars in his hand, watching the terrified straining of the colt's neck, the bony head raised above the endgate and one white eye rolling.

Five days later, in the sun-slanting, dew-wet spring morning, they stood for the last time that summer on the front porch, the loaded wagon against the front fence. The father tossed the key in his hand and kicked the doorjamb. "Well, good-bye Old Paint," he said. "See you in the fall."

As they went to the wagon, Bruce sang loudly:

"Good-bye, Old Paint, I'm leaving' Cheyenne,
I'm leavin' Cheyenne, I'm goin' to Montana,
Good-bye, Old Paint, I'm leavin' Cheyenne."

"Turn it off," his father said. "You want to wake up the whole town?" He boosted Bruce into the back end, where he squirmed and wiggled his way neckdeep into the luggage. His mother, turning to see how he was settled, laughed at him. "You look like a baby owl in a nest," she said.

His father turned and winked at him. "Open your mouth and I'll drop in a mouse."

It was good to be leaving; the thought of the homestead was exciting. If he could have taken Socks along, it would have been perfect, but he had to admit, looking around at the jammed wagon box, that there sure wasn't any room for him. He continued to sing softly as they rocked out into the road and turned east toward MacKenna's house, where they were leaving the keys.

At the low, sloughlike spot that had become the town's dumpground, the road split, leaving the dump like an island in the middle. The boy sniffed at the old familiar smells of rust and tar paper and ashes and refuse. He had collected a lot of old iron and tea lead and bottles and broken machinery and clocks, and once a perfectly good amber-headed cane, in that old dumpground. His father turned up the right fork, and as they passed the central part of the dump the wind, coming in from the northeast, brought a rotten, unbearable stench across them.

"Pee-you!" his mother said, and held her nose. Bruce echoed her. "Pee-you! Pee-you-willy!" He clamped his nose shut and pretended to fall dead.

"Guess I better get to windward of that coming back," said his father.

They woke MacKenna up and left the key and started back. The things they passed were very sharp and clear to the boy. He was seeing them for the last time all summer. He noticed things he had never noticed so clearly before: how the hills came down into the river from the north like three folds in a blanket, how the stovepipe on the Chinaman's shack east of town had a little conical hat on it. He chanted at the things he saw. "Good-bye, old Chinaman. Good-bye, old Frenchman River. Good-bye, old dumpground, good-bye."

"Hold your noses," his father said. He eased the wagon into the other fork around the dump. "Somebody sure dumped something rotten."

He stared ahead, bending a little, and Bruce heard him swear. He slapped the reins on the team till they trotted. "What?" the mother said. Bruce, half rising to see what caused the speed, saw her lips go flat over her teeth, and a look on her face like the woman he had seen in the traveling dentist's chair, when the dentist dug a living nerve out of her tooth and then got down on his knees to hunt for it, and she sat there half raised in her seat, her face lifted.

"For gosh sakes," he said. And then he saw.

He screamed at them. "Ma, it's Socks! Stop, Pa! It's Socks!"

His father drove grimly ahead, not turning, not speaking, and his mother shook her head without looking around. He screamed again, but neither of them turned. And when he dug down into the load, burrowing in and shaking with long smothered sobs, they still said nothing.

So they left town, and as they wound up the dugway to the south bench there was not a word among them except his father's low "I thought he was going to take it out of town." None of them looked back at the view they had always admired, the flat river bottom, green with spring, its village snuggled in the loops of river. Bruce's eyes, pressed against the coats and blankets under him until his sight was a red haze, could still see through it the bloated, skinned body of the colt, the chestnut hair left a little way above the hoofs, the iron braces still on the broken front legs.

DISCUSSION

1. On page 137 Bruce's mother says to the colt, "You poor broken-legged thing. You poor little friendly ruined thing." She undoubtedly realizes how hopeless the colt's condition is. Why then does she talk her husband into trying to save it?

2. Why does the boy's father lie to him about letting Jim Enich take care of the colt during the summer? What does the father expect will happen to Bruce as the summer passes?

3. Why does Bruce feel responsible for the injury to the colt? How does his feeling of guilt affect his relationship with his friends and his dog?

4. **Foreshadowing.** A writer often gives hints of what will happen later in a story. This is called foreshadowing. There are several examples of this in "The Colt." On page 144 Bruce's father says, "You see, Bruce? It's too bad, but he isn't getting better. You'll have to make up your mind——" Find at least one other example that foreshadows the end of the story.

For further activities, see page 168.

Beach Along L Street

CHIANG YEE

Sea and sky are one color without horizon.
A lonely seagull repeatedly examines me
Asking suddenly who is more leisurely.
"Well, either you or me," echoed I.

A strong wind, and the seagull can no longer stand.
He has to ride the wind and go
Up and up, floating in the air.
How is it better than my freedom?

Seagulls

ROBERT FRANCIS

Between the under and the upper blue
All day the seagulls climb and swerve and soar,
Arc intersecting arc, curve over curve.

And you may watch them weaving a long time
And never see their pattern twice the same   5
And never see their pattern once imperfect.

Take any moment they are in the air—
If you could change them, if you had the power
How would you place them other than they are?

What we have labored all our lives to have   10
And failed, these birds effortlessly achieve:
Freedom that flows in form and still is free.

DISCUSSION   1.   "Beach Along L Street" ends with a question that is not answered directly: "How is it [the seagull's leisure] better than my freedom?" Consider carefully the advantage of the seagull's leisure and that of the speaker's freedom. What do you think is the answer to the question?

2.   In "Seagulls" what do the gulls have that people "have labored all [their] lives to have" (line 10)? How do you explain the last line?

HOME

GWENDOLYN BROOKS

What had been wanted was this always, this always to last—the talking softly on this porch, with the snake plant in the jardiniere in the southwest corner, and the obstinate slip from Aunt Eppie's magnificent Michigan fern at the left side of the friendly door. Mama, Maud Martha, and Helen rocked slowly in their rocking chairs, and looked at the late afternoon light on the lawn, and at the emphatic iron of the fence and at the poplar tree. These things might soon be theirs no longer. Those shafts and pools of light, the tree, the graceful iron, might soon be viewed possessively by different eyes.

Papa was to have gone that noon, during his lunch hour, to the office of the Home Owners' Loan. If he had not succeeded in getting another extension, they would be leaving this house in which they had lived for more than fourteen years. There was little hope. The Home Owners' Loan was hard. They sat, making their plans.

"We'll be moving into a nice flat somewhere," said Mama. "Somewhere on South Park, or Michigan, or in Washington Park Court." Those flats, as the girls and Mama knew well, were burdens on wages twice the size of Papa's. This was not mentioned now.

"They're much prettier than this old house," said Helen. "I have friends I'd just as soon not bring here. And I have other friends that wouldn't come down this far for anything unless they were in a taxi."

Yesterday Maud Martha would have attacked her. Tomorrow she might. Today she said nothing. She merely gazed at a little hopping robin in the tree, her tree, and tried to keep the fronts of her eyes dry.

"Well, I do know," said Mama, turning her hands over and over, "that I've been getting tireder and tireder of doing that firing. From October to April there's firing to be done."

"But lately we've been helping, Harry and I," said Maud Martha. "And sometimes in March and April and in October, and even in November, we could build a little fire in the fireplace. Sometimes the weather was just right for that."

She knew from the way they looked at her that this had been a mistake. They did not want to cry.

But she felt that the little line of white, somewhat ridged with smoked purple, and all that cream-shot saffron, would never drift across any western sky except that in back of this house. The rain would drum with as sweet a dullness nowhere but here. The birds on South Park were mechanical birds, no better than the poor caught canaries in those "rich" women's sun parlors.

"It's just going to kill Papa!" burst out Maud Martha. "He loves this house! He *lives* for this house!"

"He lives for us," said Helen. "It's us he loves. He wouldn't want the house, except for us."

"And he'll have us," added Mama, "wherever."

"You know," Helen sighed, "if you want to know the truth, this is a relief. If this hadn't come up, we would have gone on, just dragged on, hanging out here forever."

"It might," allowed Mama, "be an act of God. God may just have reached down and picked up the reins."

"Yes," Maud Martha cracked in, "that's what you always say—that God knows best."

Her mother looked at her quickly, decided the statement was not suspect, looked away.

Helen saw Papa coming. "There's Papa," said Helen.

They could not tell a thing from the way Papa was walking. It was that same dear little staccato walk, one shoulder down, then the other, then repeat, and repeat. They watched his progress. He passed the Kennedys', he passed the vacant lot, he passed Mrs. Blakemore's. They wanted to hurl themselves over the fence, into the street, and shake the truth out of his collar. He opened his gate—the gate —and still his stride and face told them nothing.

"Hello," he said.

Mama got up and followed him through the front door. The girls knew better than to go in too.

Presently Mama's head emerged. Her eyes were lamps turned on.

"It's all right," she exclaimed. "He got it. It's all over. Everything is all right."

The door slammed shut. Mama's footsteps hurried away.

"I think," said Helen, rocking rapidly, "I think I'll give a party. I haven't given a party since I was eleven. I'd like some of my friends to just casually see that we're homeowners."

DISCUSSION

1. The story ends with Helen's statement, "I'd like some of my friends to just casually see we're homeowners." How does this contrast with her earlier statement, "I have other friends I'd just as soon not bring here" (page 151)? Why do you think she expresses such contradictory opinions?

2. From whose **point of view** (see page 78) are events related? How do we learn of the father's thoughts and feelings?

3. Why is "Home" a better title than "The House"?

TRIFLES

SUSAN GLASPELL

CHARACTERS

COUNTY ATTORNEY		MR. HALE
MRS. PETERS		MRS. HALE
SHERIFF		

SCENE   The kitchen in the now abandoned farmhouse of John Wright, a gloomy kitchen, and left without having been put in order—the walls covered with a faded wall paper. D.R. is a door leading to the parlor. On the R. wall above this door is a built-in kitchen cupboard with shelves in the upper portion and drawers below. In the rear wall at R., up two steps is a door opening onto stairs leading to the second floor. In the rear wall at L. is a door to the shed and from there to the outside. Between these two doors is an old-fashioned black iron stove. Running along the L. wall from the shed door is an old iron sink and sink shelf, in which is set a hand pump. Downstage of the sink is an uncurtained window. Near the window is an old wooden rocker. Center stage is an unpainted wooden kitchen table with straight chairs on either side. There is a small chair D.R. Unwashed pans under the sink, a loaf of bread outside the breadbox, a dish towel on the table—other signs of incompleted work. At the rear the shed door opens and the Sheriff comes in followed by the County Attorney and Hale. The Sheriff and Hale are men in middle life, the County Attorney is a young man; all are much bundled up and go at once to the stove. They are followed by the two women—the Sheriff's wife, Mrs. Peters, first; she is a slight wiry woman, a thin nervous face. Mrs. Hale is larger and would ordinarily be called more comfortable looking, but she is disturbed now and looks fearfully about as she enters. The women have come in slowly, and stand close together near the door.

COUNTY ATTORNEY [at stove rubbing his hands]: This feels good. Come up to the fire, ladies.

MRS. PETERS [after taking a step forward]: I'm not—cold.

SHERIFF [unbuttoning his overcoat and stepping away from the stove to right of table as if to mark the beginning of official business]: Now, Mr. Hale, before we move things about, you explain to Mr. Henderson just what you saw when you came here yesterday morning.

COUNTY ATTORNEY [crossing down to left of the table]: By the way, has anything been moved? Are things just as you left them yesterday?

SHERIFF [looking about]: It's just the same. When it dropped below zero last night I thought I'd better send Frank out this morning to make a fire for us—[sits right of center table]

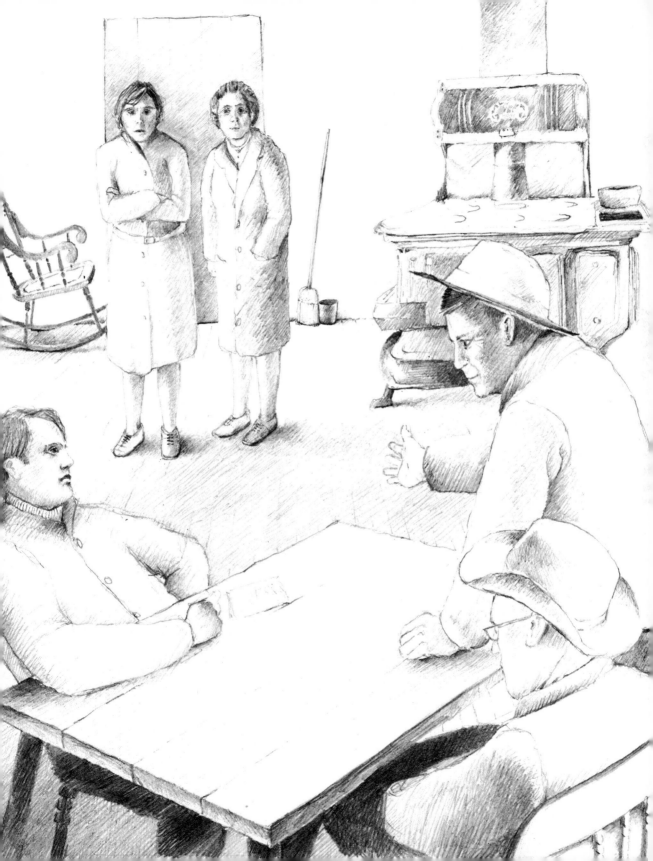

no use getting pneumonia with a big case on, but I told him not to touch anything except the stove—and you know Frank.

COUNTY ATTORNEY: Somebody should have been left here yesterday.

SHERIFF: Oh—yesterday. When I had to send Frank to Morris Center for that man who went crazy—I want you to know I had my hands full yesterday. I knew you could get back from Omaha by today and as long as I went over everything here myself——

COUNTY ATTORNEY: Well, Mr. Hale, tell just what happened when you came here yesterday morning.

HALE [crossing down to above table]: Harry and I had started to town with a load of potatoes. We came along the road from my place and as I got here I said, "I'm going to see if I can't get John Wright to go in with me on a party telephone." I spoke to Wright about it once before and he put me off, saying folks talked too much anyway, and all he asked was peace and quiet— I guess you know about how much he talked himself; but I thought maybe if I went to the house and talked about it before his wife, though I said to Harry that I didn't know as what his wife wanted made much difference to John——

COUNTY ATTORNEY: Let's talk about that later, Mr. Hale. I do want to talk about that, but tell now just what happened when you got to the house.

HALE: I didn't hear or see anything; I knocked at the door, and still it was all quiet inside. I knew they must be up, it was past eight o'clock. So I knocked again, and I thought I heard somebody say, "Come in." I wasn't sure, I'm not sure yet, but I opened the door— this door [indicating the door by which the two women are still standing] and there in that rocker—[pointing to it] sat Mrs. Wright. [They all look at the rocker D. L.]

COUNTY ATTORNEY: What—was she doing?

HALE: She was rockin' back and forth. She had her apron in her hand and was kind of—pleating it.

COUNTY ATTORNEY: And how did she— look?

HALE: Well, she looked queer.

COUNTY ATTORNEY: How do you mean— queer?

HALE: Well, as if she didn't know what she was going to do next. And kind of done up.

COUNTY ATTORNEY [takes out notebook and pencil and sits left of center table]: How did she seem to feel about your coming?

HALE: Why, I don't think she minded— one way or other. She didn't pay much attention. I said, "How do, Mrs. Wright, it's cold, ain't it?" And she said, "Is it?"—and went on kind of pleating at her apron. Well, I was surprised; she didn't ask me to come up to the stove, or to set down, but just sat there, not even looking at me, so I said, "I want to see John." And then she— laughed. I guess you would call it a laugh. I thought of Harry and the team outside, so I said a little sharp: "Can't I see John?" "No," she says, kind o' dull like. "Ain't he home?" says I. "Yes," says she, "he's home." "Then why can't I see him?" I asked her, out of patience. " 'Cause he's dead," says she. *"Dead?"* says I. She just nodded her head, not getting a bit excited, but rockin' back and forth. "Why—where is he?" says I, not knowing what to say. She just pointed upstairs—like that. [*Himself pointing to the room above.*] I started for the stairs, with the idea of going up there. I walked from there to here—then I says, "Why, what did he die of?" "He died of a rope round his neck," says she, and just went on pleatin' at her apron. Well, I went out and called Harry. I thought I might—need help. We went upstairs and there he was lyin'——

COUNTY ATTORNEY: I think I'd rather have you go into that upstairs, where you can point it all out. Just go on now with the rest of the story.

HALE: Well, my first thought was to get that rope off. It looked . . . [*stops, his face twitches*] . . . but Harry, he went up to him, and he said, "No, he's dead all right, and we'd better not touch anything." So we went back downstairs. She was still sitting that same way. "Has anybody been notified?" I asked. "No," says she, unconcerned. "Who did this, Mrs. Wright?" said Harry. He said it businesslike—and she stopped pleatin' of her apron. "I don't know," she says. "You don't *know?*" says Harry. "No," says she. "Weren't you sleepin' in the bed with him?" says Harry. "Yes," says she, "but I was on the inside." "Somebody slipped a rope round his neck and strangled him and you didn't wake up?" says Harry. "I didn't wake up," she said after him. We must 'a' looked as if we didn't see how that could be, for after a minute she said, "I sleep sound." Harry was going to ask her more questions but I said maybe we ought to let her tell her story to the coroner, or the sheriff, so Harry went fast as he could to Rivers' place, where there's a telephone.

COUNTY ATTORNEY: And what did Mrs. Wright do when she knew that you had gone for the coroner?

HALE: She moved from the rocker to that chair over there [*pointing to a small chair in the D. R. corner*] and just sat there with her hands held together and looking down. I got a feeling that I ought to make some conversation, so I said I had come in to see if John wanted to put in a telephone, and at that she started to laugh, and then she stopped and looked at me—scared. [*The County Attorney, who has had his notebook out, makes a note.*] I dunno, maybe it wasn't scared. I wouldn't like to say it was. Soon Harry got back, and then Dr. Lloyd came, and you, Mr. Peters, and so I guess that's all I know that you don't.

COUNTY ATTORNEY [*rising and looking around*]:

I guess we'll go upstairs first—and then out to the barn and around there. [To the sheriff] You're convinced that there was nothing important here—nothing that would point to any motive?

SHERIFF: Nothing here but kitchen things.

The County Attorney, after again looking around the kitchen, opens the door of a cupboard closet in R. wall. He brings a small chair from R.—gets up on it and looks on a shelf. Pulls his hand away, sticky.

COUNTY ATTORNEY: Here's a nice mess.
     [The women draw nearer U. C.]

MRS. PETERS [to the other woman]: Oh, her fruit; it did freeze. [To the Lawyer.] She worried about that when it turned so cold. She said the fire'd go out and her jars would break.

SHERIFF [rises]: Well, can you beat the women! Held for murder and worrying about her preserves.

COUNTY ATTORNEY [getting down from chair]: I guess before we're through she may have something more serious than preserves to worry about.
     [Crosses down R. C.]

HALE: Well, women are used to worrying over trifles. [The two women move a little closer together.]

COUNTY ATTORNEY [with the gallantry of a young politician]: And yet, for all their worries, what would we do without the ladies? [The women do not unbend. He goes below the center table to the sink, takes a dipperful of water from the pail and pouring it into a basin, washes his hands. While he is doing this the Sheriff and Hale cross to cupboard, which they inspect. The County Attorney

starts to wipe his hands on the roller towel, turns it for a cleaner place.] Dirty towels! [Kicks his foot against the pans under the sink] Not much of a house-keeper, would you say, ladies?

MRS. HALE [stiffly]: There's a great deal of work to be done on a farm.

COUNTY ATTORNEY: To be sure. And yet [with a little bow to her] I know there are some Dickson County farm-houses which do not have such roller towels. [He gives it a pull to expose its full length again.]

MRS. HALE: Those towels get dirty awful quick. Men's hands aren't always as clean as they might be.

COUNTY ATTORNEY: Ah, loyal to your sex, I see. But you and Mrs. Wright were neighbors. I suppose you were friends, too.

MRS. HALE [shaking her head]: I've not seen much of her of late years. I've not been in this house—it's more than a year.

COUNTY ATTORNEY [crossing to women U. C.]: And why was that? You didn't like her?

MRS. HALE: I liked her all well enough. Farmer's wives have their hands full, Mr. Henderson. And then——

COUNTY ATTORNEY: Yes——?

MRS. HALE [looking about]: It never seemed a very cheerful place.

COUNTY ATTORNEY: No—it's not cheerful. I shouldn't say she had the home-making instinct.

MRS. HALE: Well, I don't know as Wright had, either.

COUNTY ATTORNEY: You mean that they didn't get on very well?

MRS. HALE: No, I don't mean anything. But I don't think a place'd be any cheerfuller for John Wright's being in it.

COUNTY ATTORNEY: I'd like to talk more of that a little later. I want to get the lay of things upstairs now. [He goes past the women to U. R. where steps lead to a stair door.]

SHERIFF: I suppose anything Mrs. Peters does'll be all right. She was to take in some clothes for her, you know, and a few little things. We left in such a hurry yesterday.

COUNTY ATTORNEY: Yes, but I would like to see what you take, Mrs. Peters, and keep an eye out for anything that might be of use to us.

MRS. PETERS: Yes, Mr. Henderson. [The men leave by U. R. door to stairs. The women listen to the men's steps on the stairs, then look about the kitchen.]

MRS. HALE [crossing L to sink]: I'd hate to have men coming into my kitchen, snooping around and criticizing. [She arranges the pans under sink which the Lawyer had shoved out of place.]

MRS. PETERS: Of course it's no more than their duty. [Crosses to cupboard U. R.]

MRS. HALE: Duty's all right, but I guess that deputy sheriff that came out to make the fire might have got a little of this on. [Gives the roller towel a pull.] Wish I'd thought of that sooner. Seems mean to talk about her for not having things slicked up when she had to come away in such a hurry. [Crosses R. to Mrs. Peters at cupboard.]

MRS. PETERS [who has been looking through cupboard, lifts one end of a towel that covers a pan]: She had bread set. [Stands still.]

MRS. HALE [eyes fixed on a loaf of bread beside

the breadbox, which is on a low shelf of the cupboard]: She was going to put this in there. [Picks up loaf, then abruptly drops it. In a manner of returning to familiar things.] It's a shame about her fruit. I wonder if it's all gone. [Gets up on the chair and looks.] I think there's some here that's all right, Mrs. Peters. Yes—here; [holding it toward the window] this is cherries, too. [Looking again.] I declare I believe that's the only one. [Gets down, jar in her hand. Goes to the sink and wipes it off on the outside.] She'll feel awful bad after all her hard work in the hot weather. I remember the afternoon I put up my cherries last summer.

She puts the jar on the big kitchen table, center of the room. With a sigh, is about to sit down in the rocking chair. Before she is seated realizes what chair it is; with a slow look at it, steps back. The chair which she has touched rocks back and forth. Mrs. Peters moves to center table and they both watch the chair rock for a moment or two.

MRS. PETERS [shaking off the mood which the empty rocking chair has evoked. Now in a businesslike manner she speaks]: Well, I must get those things from the front room closet. [She goes to the door at the R., but, after looking into the other room, steps back.] You coming with me, Mrs. Hale? You could help me carry them. [They go in the other room; reappear, Mrs. Peters carrying a dress, petticoat and skirt, Mrs. Hale following with a pair of shoes.] My, it's cold in there. [She puts the clothes on the big table, and hurries to the stove.]

MRS. HALE [right of center table examining the skirt]: Wright was close. I think maybe that's why she kept so much to herself. She didn't even belong to the Ladies' Aid. I suppose she felt she couldn't do her part, and then you don't enjoy things when you feel shabby. I heard she used to wear pretty clothes and be lively, when she was Minnie Foster, one of the town girls singing in the choir. But that—oh, that was thirty years ago. This all you was to take in?

MRS. PETERS: She said she wanted an apron. Funny thing to want, for there isn't much to get you dirty in jail, goodness knows. But I suppose just to make her feel more natural. [Crosses to cupboard.] She said they was in the top drawer in this cupboard. Yes, here. And then her little shawl that always hung behind the door. [Opens stair door and looks.] Yes, here it is. [Quickly shuts door leading upstairs.]

MRS. HALE [abruptly moving toward her]: Mrs. Peters?

MRS. PETERS: Yes, Mrs. Hale? [At U. R. door.]

MRS. HALE: Do you think she did it?

MRS. PETERS [in a frightened voice]: Oh, I don't know.

MRS. HALE: Well, I don't think she did. Asking for an apron and her little shawl. Worrying about her fruit.

MRS. PETERS [starts to speak, glances up, where footsteps are heard in the room above. In a low voice]: Mr. Peters says it looks bad for her. Mr. Henderson is awful sarcastic in a speech and he'll make fun of her sayin' she didn't wake up.

MRS. HALE: Well, I guess John Wright didn't wake when they was slipping that rope under his neck.

MRS. PETERS [crossing slowly to table and placing shawl and apron on table with other clothing]: No, it's strange. It must have been done awful crafty and still. They say it was such a—funny way to kill a man, rigging it all up like that.

MRS. HALE [crossing to left of Mrs. Peters at table]: That's just what Mr. Hale said. There was a gun in the house. He says that's what he can't understand.

MRS. PETERS: Mr. Henderson said coming out that what was needed for the case was a motive; something to show anger, or—sudden feeling.

MRS. HALE [who is standing by the table]: Well, I don't see any signs of anger around here. [She puts her hand on the dish towel which lies on the table, stands looking down at table, one-half of which is clean, the other half messy.] It's wiped to here. [Makes a move as if to finish work, then turns and looks at loaf of bread outside the breadbox. Drops towel. In that voice of coming back to familiar things.] Wonder how they are finding things upstairs. [Crossing below table to D. R.] I hope she had it a little more red-up up there. You know, it seems kind of *sneaking*. Locking her up in town and then coming out here and trying to get her own house to turn against her!

MRS. PETERS: But, Mrs. Hale, the law is the law.

MRS. HALE: I s'pose 'tis. [Unbuttoning her coat.] Better loosen up your things, Mrs. Peters. You won't feel them when you go out. [Mrs. Peters takes off her fur tippet, goes to hang it on chair back left of table, stands looking at the work basket on floor near D. L. window.]

MRS. PETERS: She was piecing a quilt. [She brings the large sewing basket to the center table and they look at the bright pieces, Mrs. Hale above the table and Mrs. Peters left of it.]

MRS. HALE: It's a log cabin pattern. Pretty, isn't it? I wonder if she was goin' to quilt it or just knot it? [Footsteps have been heard coming down the stairs. The Sheriff enters followed by Hale and the County Attorney.]

SHERIFF: They wonder if she was going to quilt it or just knot it! [The men laugh, the women look abashed.]

COUNTY ATTORNEY [rubbing his hands over the stove]: Frank's fire didn't do much up there, did it? Well, let's go out to the barn and get that cleared up. [The men go outside by U. L. door.]

MRS. HALE [resentfully]: I don't know as there's anything so strange, our takin' up our time with little things while we're waiting for them to get the evidence. [She sits in chair right of table smoothing out a block with decision.] I don't see as it's anything to laugh about.

MRS. PETERS [apologetically]: Of course they've got awful important things on their minds. [Pulls up a chair and joins Mrs. Hale at the left of the table.]

MRS. HALE [examining another block]: Mrs. Peters, look at this one. Here, this is the one she was working on, and look at the sewing! All the rest of it has been so nice and even. And look at this! It's all over the place! Why, it looks as if she

didn't know what she was about!
[After she has said this they look at each
other, then start to glance back at the
door. After an instant Mrs. Hale has pulled
at a knot and ripped the sewing.]

MRS. PETERS: Oh, what are you doing,
Mrs. Hale?

MRS. HALE [mildly]: Just pulling out a stitch
or two that's not sewed very good.
[Threading a needle.] Bad sewing always made me fidgety.

MRS. PETERS [with a glance at door, nervously]:
I don't think we ought to touch
things.

MRS. HALE: I'll just finish up this end.
[Suddenly stopping and leaning forward.]
Mrs. Peters?

MRS. PETERS: Yes, Mrs. Hale?

MRS. HALE: What do you suppose she
was so nervous about?

MRS. PETERS: Oh—I don't know. I don't
know as she was nervous. I sometimes sew awful queer when I'm
just tired. [Mrs. Hale starts to say something, looks at Mrs. Peters, then goes on
sewing.] Well, I must get these
things wrapped up. They may be
through sooner than we think.

[Putting apron and other things together.] I wonder where I can find a piece of paper, and string. [Rises.]

MRS. HALE: In that cupboard, maybe.

MRS. PETERS [crosses R. looking in cupboard]: Why, here's a birdcage. [Holds it up.] Did she have a bird, Mrs. Hale?

MRS. HALE: Why, I don't know whether she did or not—I've not been here for so long. There was a man around last year selling canaries cheap, but I don't know as she took one; maybe she did. She used to sing real pretty herself.

MRS. PETERS [glancing around]: Seems funny to think of a bird here. But she must have had one, or why would she have a cage? I wonder what happened to it?

MRS. HALE: I s'pose maybe the cat got it.

MRS. PETERS: No, she didn't have a cat. She's got that feeling some people have about cats—being afraid of them. My cat got in her room and she was real upset and asked me to take it out.

MRS. HALE: My sister Bessie was like that. Queer, isn't it?

MRS. PETERS [examining the cage]: Why, look at this door. It's broke. One hinge is pulled apart. [Takes a step down to Mrs. Hale's right.]

MRS. HALE [looking too]: Looks as if someone must have been rough with it.

MRS. PETERS: Why, yes. [She brings the cage forward and puts it on the table.]

MRS. HALE [glancing toward U. L. door]: I wish if they're going to find any evidence they'd be about it. I don't like this place.

MRS. PETERS: But I'm awful glad you came with me, Mrs. Hale. It would be lonesome for me sitting here alone.

MRS. HALE: It would, wouldn't it? [Dropping her sewing.] But I tell you what I do wish, Mrs. Peters. I wish I had come over sometimes when *she* was here. I—[looking around the room]—wish I had.

MRS. PETERS: But of course you were awful busy, Mrs. Hale—your house and your children.

MRS. HALE [rises and crosses L.]: I could've come. I stayed away because it weren't cheerful—and that's why I ought to have come. I—[looking out L. window]—I've never liked this place. Maybe because it's down in a hollow and you don't see the road. I dunno what it is, but it's a lonesome place and always was. I wish I had come over to see Minnie Foster sometimes. I can see now——[Shakes her head.]

MRS. PETERS [left of table and above it]: Well, you mustn't reproach yourself, Mrs. Hale. Somehow we just don't see how it is with other folks until—something turns up.

MRS. HALE: Not having children makes less work—but it makes a quiet house, and Wright out to work all day, and no company when he did come in. [Turning from window.] Did you know John Wright, Mrs. Peters?

MRS. PETERS: Not to know him; I've seen him in town. They say he was a good man.

MRS. HALE: Yes—good; he didn't drink, and kept his word as well as most, I guess, and paid his debts. But he was a hard man, Mrs. Peters. Just

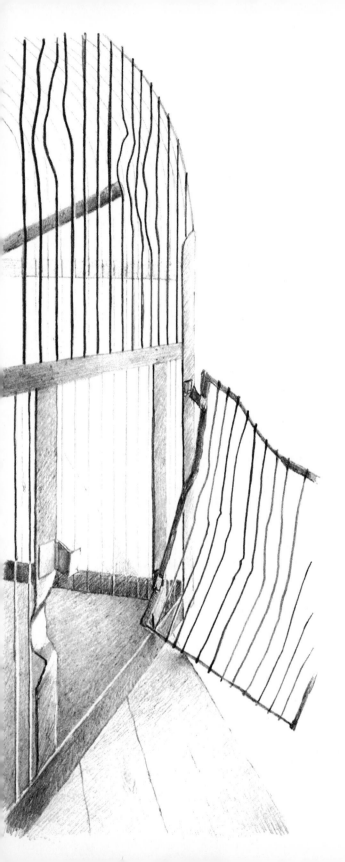

to pass the time of day with him——[Shivers.] Like a raw wind that gets to the bone. [Pauses, her eye falling on the cage.] I should think she would 'a' wanted a bird. But what do you suppose went with it?

MRS. PETERS: I don't know, unless it got sick and died. [She reaches over and swings the broken door, swings it again, both women watch it.]

MRS. HALE: You weren't raised round here, were you? [Mrs. Peters shakes her head.] You didn't know—her?

MRS. PETERS: Not till they brought her yesterday.

MRS. HALE: She—come to think of it, she was kind of like a bird herself— real sweet and pretty, but kind of timid and—fluttery. How—she— did—change. [Silence; then as if struck by a happy thought and relieved to get back to everyday things. Crosses R. above Mrs. Peters to cupboard, replaces small chair used to stand on to its original place D. R.] Tell you what, Mrs. Peters, why don't you take the quilt in with you? It might take up her mind.

MRS. PETERS: Why, I think that's a real nice idea, Mrs. Hale. There couldn't possibly be any objection to it, could there? Now, just what would I take? I wonder if her patches are in here—and her things. [They look in the sewing basket.]

MRS. HALE [crosses to right of table]: Here's some red. I expect this has got sewing things in it. [Brings out a fancy box] What a pretty box. Looks like something somebody would give you. Maybe her scissors are in here. [Opens box. Suddenly puts her hand to her nose.] Why——[Mrs. Peters bends nearer, then turns her face away.] There's something wrapped up in this piece of silk.

MRS. PETERS: Why, this isn't her scissors.

MRS. HALE [lifting the silk]: Oh, Mrs. Peters—it's——[Mrs. Peters bends closer.]

MRS. PETERS: It's the bird.

MRS. HALE: But, Mrs. Peters—look at it! Its neck! Look at its neck! It's all—other side *to*.

MRS. PETERS: Somebody—wrung—its—neck. [Their eyes meet. A look of growing comprehension, of horror. Steps are heard outside. Mrs. Hale slips box under quilt pieces, and sinks into her chair. Enter Sheriff and County Attorney. Mrs. Peters steps D.L. and stands looking out of window.]

COUNTY ATTORNEY [as one turning from serious things to little pleasantries]: Well, ladies, have you decided whether she was going to quilt it or knot it? [Crosses to C. above table.]

MRS. PETERS: We think she was going to—knot it. [Sheriff crosses to right of stove, lifts stove lid and glances at fire, then stands warming hands at stove.]

COUNTY ATTORNEY: Well, that's interesting, I'm sure. [Seeing the birdcage.] Has the bird flown?

MRS. HALE [putting more quilt pieces over the box]: We think the—cat got it.

COUNTY ATTORNEY [preoccupied]: Is there a cat? [Mrs. Hale glances in a quick covert way at Mrs. Peters.]

MRS. PETERS [turning from window takes a step in]: Well, not now. They're superstitious, you know. They leave.

COUNTY ATTORNEY [to Sheriff Peters, continuing an interrupted conversation]: No sign at all of anyone having come from the outside. Their own rope. Now let's go up again and go over it piece by piece. [They start upstairs.] It would have to have been someone who knew just the —— [Mrs. Peters sits down left of table. The two women sit there not looking at one another, but as if peering into something and at the same time holding back. When they talk now it is in the manner of feeling their way over strange ground, as if afraid of what they are saying, but as if they cannot help saying it.]

MRS. HALE [hesitatively and in hushed voice]: She liked the bird. She was going to bury it in that pretty box.

MRS. PETERS [in a whisper]: When I was a girl—my kitten—there was a boy took a hatchet, and before my eyes—and before I could get there——[Covers her face an instant.] If they hadn't held me back I would have——[catches herself, looks upstairs where steps are heard, falters weakly]——hurt him.

MRS. HALE [with a slow look around her]: I wonder how it would seem never to have had any children around. [Pause.] No, Wright wouldn't like the bird—a thing that sang. She used to sing. He killed that, too.

MRS. PETERS [moving uneasily]: We don't know who killed the bird.

MRS. HALE: I knew John Wright.

MRS. PETERS: It was an awful thing was done in this house that night, Mrs. Hale. Killing a man while he slept, slipping a rope around his neck that choked the life out of him.

MRS. HALE: His neck. Choked the life out of him. [Her hand goes out and rests on the birdcage.]

MRS. PETERS [with rising voice]: We don't know who killed him. We don't *know.*

MRS. HALE [her own feeling not interrupted]: If there'd been years and years of nothing, then a bird to sing to you, it would be awful—still, after the bird was still.

MRS. PETERS [something within her speaking]: I know what stillness is. When we homesteaded in Dakota, and my first baby died—after he was two years old, and me with no other then——

MRS. HALE [moving]: How soon do you suppose they'll be through looking for the evidence?

MRS. PETERS: I know what stillness is. [Pulling herself back.] The law has got to punish crime, Mrs. Hale.

MRS. HALE [not as if answering that]: I wish you'd seen Minnie Foster when she wore a white dress with blue ribbons and stood up there in the choir and sang. [A look around the room.] Oh, I *wish* I'd come over here once in a while! That was a crime! That was a crime! Who's going to punish that?

MRS. PETERS [looking upstairs]: We mustn't—take on.

MRS. HALE: I might have known she needed help! I know how things can be—for women. I tell you, it's queer, Mrs. Peters. We live close together and we live far apart. We all go through the same things— it's all just a different kind of the same thing. [Brushes her eyes, noticing the jar of fruit, reaches out for it.] If I was you I wouldn't tell her her fruit was gone. Tell her it *ain't.*

Tell her it's all right. Take this in to prove it to her. She—she may never know whether it was broke or not.

MRS. PETERS [takes the jar, looks about for something to wrap it in; takes petticoat from the clothes brought from the other room, very nervously begins winding this around the jar. In a false voice]: My, it's a good thing the men couldn't hear us. Wouldn't they just laugh! Getting all stirred up over a little thing like a—dead canary. As if that could have anything to do with—with—wouldn't they *laugh!* [The men are heard coming downstairs.]

MRS. HALE [under her breath]: Maybe they would—maybe they wouldn't.

COUNTY ATTORNEY: No, Peters, it's all perfectly clear except a reason for doing it. But you know juries when it comes to women. If there was some definite thing. [Crosses slowly to above table. Sheriff crosses D.R. Mrs. Hale and Mrs. Peters remain seated at either side of table.] Something to show—something to make a story about—a thing that would connect up with this strange way of doing it—— [The women's eyes meet for an instant. Enter Hale from outer door.]

HALE: Well, I've got the team around. Pretty cold out there.

COUNTY ATTORNEY: I'm going to stay awhile by myself. [To the Sheriff.] You can send Frank out for me, can't you? I want to go over everything. I'm not satisfied that we can't do better.

SHERIFF: Do you want to see what Mrs. Peters is going to take in? [The Lawyer picks up the apron, laughs.]

COUNTY ATTORNEY: Oh, I guess they're not very dangerous things the ladies have picked out. [Moves a few things about, disturbing the quilt pieces which cover the box. Steps back.] No, Mrs. Peters doesn't need supervising. For that matter a sheriff's wife is married to the law. Ever think of it that way, Mrs. Peters?

MRS. PETERS: Not—just that way.

SHERIFF [chuckling]: Married to the law. [Moves to D.R. door to the other room.] I just want you to come in here a minute, George. We ought to take a look at these windows.

COUNTY ATTORNEY [scoffingly]: Oh, windows!

SHERIFF: We'll be right out, Mr. Hale.

Hale goes outside. The Sheriff follows the County Attorney into the other room. Then Mrs.

Hale rises, hands tight together, looking intensely at Mrs. Peters, whose eyes make a slow turn, finally meeting Mrs. Hale's. A moment Mrs. Hale holds her, then her own eyes point the way to where the box is concealed. Suddenly Mrs. Peters throws back quilt pieces and tries to put the box in the bag she is carrying. It is too big. She opens box, starts to take bird out, cannot touch it, goes to pieces, stands there helpless. Sound of a knob turning in the other room. Mrs. Hale snatches the box and puts it in the pocket of her big coat. Enter County Attorney and Sheriff, who remains D.R.

COUNTY ATTORNEY [crosses to U.L. door facetiously]: Well, Henry, at least we found out that she was not going to quilt it. She was going to—what is it you call it, ladies?

MRS. HALE [standing C. below table facing front, her hand against her pocket]: We call it—knot it, Mr. Henderson.

DISCUSSION

1. By the end of the play, the two women have discovered what actually happened between the Wrights. What "trifles" gave them the clues they needed to reconstruct the murder? Why do they conceal the evidence from the men?

2. How do the viewpoints of the men investigating the crime differ from the viewpoints of the women?

3. **Setting** (see page 57) is an important element in fiction, and it is particularly important in a play. How does the opening description of the scene add to the mood of this play?

4. **Dialogue.** In literature conversation that is directly quoted is called dialogue. In a play everything given is dialogue except stage descriptions and directions. Through it characters are individualized and the plot moves forward. From the dialogue between Mrs. Peters and Mrs. Hale (pages 161–166), what do we learn about each character? What do we learn about the Wrights?

For further activities, see page 168.

VOCABULARY

Trinity Place (page 122)

On separate paper, head two columns *Pigeons* and *Men.* From the list of adjectives below, place each under the heading it describes.

sleek	lean	hungry	smug	shrewd
pompous	busy	listless	plump	idle

The Fifty-First Dragon (page 124)

Below are phrases from the story with the adjectives in bold type. On separate paper, rewrite each phrase substituting an adjective that will give a completely different meaning from the original. Check in a dictionary if you need to.

1. a *versatile* gift
2. *enormous* strength
3. a *deceptive* display
4. threw *fantastic* shadows
5. your *preliminary* degree
6. seemed decidedly *aggressive*
7. so *hideous* a countenance
8. his best *previous* record
9. a *philosophic* discourse
10. a *meager* cloud of steam

COMPOSITION

The Colt (page 134)

1. Imagine that years later Bruce looks back on the experiences related in this story. What might be his thoughts about the part played by his parents? Suppose that he is talking with a friend about the events. Write down what you think he would say.

2. Perhaps in your own experience with a pet, you have had to face reality and disappointment. If so, describe the experience. It might be easier for you to write as though you were an onlooker rather than a participant, and in a sense you are since the events happened to a younger "you."

Trifles (page 154)

Assume that Mrs. Wright kept a diary. Put yourself in her place—enter into her feelings—and write the entries that she might have included on the day the canary was killed and at the end of her first day in jail.

READING

The Colt (page 134)

Bruce felt that it was his fault that the colt's front legs were broken. His sense of guilt caused him to do a number of things. On separate paper, write the number of each action below that is the result of this feeling.

1. blamed his mother
2. threw a stone at Spot
3. went gopher hunting
4. taught the colt to lie down
5. helped build a secret hideout with his friends
6. waged a war on stray dogs
7. fed the colt by hand
8. learned to accept what was bound to happen

Trifles (page 154)

On separate paper, place these events in the order in which they happened—either *during* the play or *before* the play actually opens.

1. Mrs. Wright is taken into custody.
2. The canary's neck is broken.
3. Mrs. Hale finds the canary's body.
4. Mrs. Wright wears pretty clothes and sings in the choir.
5. Mrs. Hale hides the sewing box in her coat pocket.
6. The sheriff and county attorney search the barn.
7. Mrs. Hale pulls out part of Mrs. Wright's sewing.
8. The sheriff and county attorney search the Wrights' room.
9. Mr. Hale stops by the Wrights'.
10. John Wright is killed.

COMPOSITION

Sentences express ideas. One sentence, in fact, may express two or three ideas, and in several different ways. Here is a sentence that expresses a single thought during an encounter in a back yard. The trees, full of hundreds of blackbirds, are suddenly emptied of them:

I looked again at the tree.

That sentence expresses one idea among the many the writer might have chosen to express.

Here are two sentences that express two different ideas of equal importance:

I looked again at the tree. The leaves had reassembled.

If we combine those two ideas into a single sentence, we can express them in several ways:

a. *I looked again,* and *the leaves had reassembled.*
b. After the leaves had reassembled, *I looked again.*
c. When I looked again, *the leaves had reassembled.*

The first of the three examples *coordinates* the two ideas—keeps them at the same level of importance. There, *I looked again* is neither more nor less important than *the leaves had reassembled.* But in the second and third examples, one of the ideas is *subordinated,* made less important than the other. In the second, what is more important is *I looked again.* The idea of the leaves reassembling is subordinated to that main idea. Similarly, the third example subordinates the looking again—makes it less important—and puts emphasis on the leaves reassembling.

The emphasis stays there in the original sentence in "Seeing" (page 106). That sentence expresses three ideas, one main one and two subordinate ones:

When I looked again at the tree *the leaves had reassembled* as if nothing had happened.

Words within sentences that connect ideas—that join them together—are called *conjunctions.* The principal *coordinate* conjunctions are *and* and *but.* Among *subordinate* conjunctions are such words as *when, if, after, although, since, as,* and *because.* Watch how authors use those words. Become aware of how you, too, can emphasize what seems important, and can play down what is less important, by using the appropriate conjunctions.

EMPHASIZING
IDEAS

ABOUT THE SELECTIONS

1. Which person in this section expresses a viewpoint closest to your own? In a paragraph or two identify the viewpoint and relate it to your own life. Do your views agree with that person's entirely? If not, at what points do they differ?

2. Take a situation from any prose selection in this unit and describe it from another point of view. You might, for example, describe the encounter between Mme. Loisel and Mme. Forestier, at the end of "The Necklace," as Mme. Forestier experienced it. Or a portion of the situation in "The Storyteller" might be described from the aunt's point of view.

3. Choose one of the following.

   a. Write a poem of your own, modeled on "To Be of Use" (page 119) and beginning with the identical opening line, "The people I love the best."

   b. Write a brief poem containing recommendations for a group of people, in the manner of "For Poets" (p. 110).

4. Explain how important ideas in the following sentences are emphasized.

When they got into the street they could not find a cab. In despair they went down towards the Seine, shivering. At last, on the Embankment they found one of those old carriages that ply by night and are only seen in Paris after dark, as if ashamed of their shabbiness in the daytime. It took them back to their house in the Rue des Martyrs, and they went sadly up to their apartment.

ON YOUR OWN

1. Think of some incident that you experienced with several other people, some of whom differed markedly from you—that is, were not your age or at your school or in your family. If the incident was exciting, so much the better. A trip somewhere, a near-accident, an embarrassing quarrel at the supermarket—any such incident will do. Describe it from a point of view other than your own. You will be imagining that you are someone else. Try to observe and respond to the experience as he or she did.

2. Think of some rule or opinion that you disagree with. It may relate to school life, home life, town life, national or international life. Writing as though you were someone who *agrees* with that rule or opinion, make the best case you can for it. Make a case, for example, for why people should not be allowed to drive cars until they are twenty-one.

3. Relate the following ideas in ways that emphasize what seems more important. Subordinate less important thoughts.

Comedians appeared all over the television set. They were laughing. They had a lot of teeth. Peter went into the kitchen. He wanted to get another bunch of grapes. He didn't put on the light in the kitchen. It was odd. A kitchen could look mysterious near midnight. Nobody else was home. There was only the beam of the light from the open refrigerator. It cast shadows from the milk bottles onto the linoleum.

IDENTITY

I'm Nobody! Who Are You?

EMILY DICKINSON

I'm nobody! Who are you?
Are you nobody, too?
Then there's a pair of us—don't tell!
They'd banish us, you know.

How dreary to be somebody!
How public, like a frog
To tell your name the livelong day
To an admiring bog!

Antaeus

BORDEN DEAL

In Greek mythology Antaeus, giant son of the earth goddess
Terra, forced all strangers to his country to wrestle to the
death. No one could defeat him, for he rose with renewed
strength every time he was thrown to his mother earth. Finally
Hercules fought him successfully by holding him in the air and
strangling him. Losing contact with the earth, Antaeus died.

This was during the wartime, when lots of people were coming
North for jobs in factories and war industries, when people
moved around a lot more than they do now and sometimes kids
were thrown into new groups and new lives that were completely different from anything they had ever known before. I
remember this one kid; T. J. his name was, from somewhere
down South, whose family moved into our building during that
time. They'd come North with everything they owned piled into
the back seat of an old-model sedan that you wouldn't expect
could make the trip, with T. J. and his three younger sisters riding shakily atop the load of junk.

Our building was just like all the others there, with families
crowded into a few rooms, and I guess there were twenty-five or
thirty kids about my age in that one building. Of course, there
were a few of us who formed a gang and ran together all the
time after school, and I was the one who brought T. J. in and
started the whole thing.

The building right next door to us was a factory where they
made walking dolls. It was a low building with a flat, tarred roof
that had a parapet all around it about head-high, and we'd
found out a long time before that no one, not even the watchman, paid any attention to the roof because it was higher than
any of the other buildings around. So my gang used the roof as
a headquarters. We could get up there by crossing over to the
fire escape from our own roof on a plank and then going on up.
It was a secret place for us, where nobody else could go without
our permission.

I remember the day I first took T. J. up there to meet the gang. He was a stocky, robust kid with a shock of white hair, nothing sissy about him except his voice—he talked different from any of us, and you noticed it right away. But I liked him anyway, so I told him to come on up.

We climbed up over the parapet and dropped down on the roof. The rest of the gang were already there.

"Hi," I said. I jerked my thumb at T. J. "He just moved into the building yesterday."

He just stood there, not scared or anything, just looking, like the first time you see somebody you're not sure you're going to like.

"Hi," Blackie said. "Where you from?"

"Marion County," T. J. said.

We laughed. "Marion County?" I said. "Where's that?"

He looked at me like I was a stranger, too. "It's in Alabama," he said, like I ought to know where it was.

"What's your name?" Charley said.

"T. J.," he said, looking back at him. He had pale blue eyes that looked washed-out, but he looked directly at Charley, waiting for his reaction. He'll be all right, I thought. No sissy in him . . . except that voice. Who ever talked like that?

"T. J.," Blackie said. "That's just initials. What's your real name? Nobody in the world has just initials."

"I do," he said. "And they're T. J. That's all the name I got."

His voice was resolute with the knowledge of his rightness, and for a moment no one had anything to say. T. J. looked around at the rooftop and down at the black tar under his feet. "Down yonder where I come from," he said, "we played out in the woods. Don't you-all have no woods around here?"

"Naw," Blackie said. "There's the park a few blocks over, but it's full of kids and cops and old women. You can't do a thing."

T. J. kept looking at the tar under his feet. "You mean you ain't got no fields to raise nothing in? No watermelons or nothing?"

"Naw," I said scornfully. "What do you want to grow something for? The folks can buy everything they need at the store."

He looked at me again with that strange, unknowing look. "In Marion County," he said, "I had my own acre of cotton and my own acre of corn. It was mine to plant ever' year."

He sounded like it was something to be proud of, and in some obscure way it made the rest of us angry. "Heck!" Blackie said. "Who'd want to have their own acre of cotton and corn?"

T. J. looked at him. "Well, you get part of the bale offen your acre," he said seriously. "And I fed my acre of corn to my calf."

We didn't really know what he was talking about, so we were more puzzled than angry; otherwise, I guess, we'd have chased him off the roof and wouldn't let him be part of our gang. But he was strange and different, and we were all attracted by his stolid sense of rightness and belonging, maybe by the strange softness of his voice contrasting our own tones of speech into harshness.

He moved his foot against the black tar. "We could make our own field right here," he said softly, thoughtfully. "Come spring we could raise us what we want to . . . watermelons and garden truck[1] and no telling what all."

"You'd have to be a good farmer to make these tar roofs grow any watermelons," I said. We all laughed.

But T. J. looked serious. "We could haul us some dirt up here," he said. "And spread it out even and water it, and before you know it we'd have us a crop in here." He looked at us intently. "Wouldn't that be fun?"

"They wouldn't let us," Blackie said quickly.

"I thought you said this you-all's roof," T. J. said to me. "That you-all could do anything you wanted up here."

"They've never bothered us," I said. I felt the idea beginning to catch fire in me. It was a big idea, and it took a while for it to sink in, but the more I thought about it, the better I liked it. "Say," I said to the gang, "he might have something there. Just make us a regular roof garden, with flowers and grass and trees and everything. And all ours, too," I said. "We wouldn't let anybody up here except the ones we wanted to."

"It'd take a while to grow trees," T. J. said quickly, but we weren't paying any attention to him. They were all talking about it suddenly, all excited with the idea after I'd put it in a way they could catch hold of it. Only rich people had roof gardens, we knew, and the idea of our own private domain excited them.

---

[1] *garden truck:* vegetables grown for market.

"We could bring it up in sacks and boxes," Blackie said. "We'd have to do it while the folks weren't paying any attention to us. We'd have to come up to the roof of our building and then cross over with it."

"Where could we get the dirt?" somebody said worriedly.

"Out of those vacant lots over close to school," Blackie said. "Nobody'd notice if we scraped it up."

I slapped T. J. on the shoulder. "Man, you had a wonderful idea," I said, and everybody grinned at him, remembering he had started it. "Our own private roof garden."

He grinned back. "It'll be ourn," he said. "All ourn." Then he looked thoughtful again. "Maybe I can lay my hands on some cotton seed, too. You think we could raise us some cotton?"

We'd started big projects before at one time or another, like any gang of kids, but they'd always petered out for lack of organization and direction. But this one didn't . . . somehow or other T. J. kept it going all through the winter months. He kept talking about the watermelons and the cotton we'd raise, come spring, and when even that wouldn't work, he'd switch around to my idea of flowers and grass and trees, though he was always honest enough to add that it'd take a while to get any trees started. He always had it on his mind, and he'd mention it in school, getting them lined up to carry dirt that afternoon, saying in a casual way that he reckoned a few more weeks ought to see the job through.

Our little area of private earth grew slowly. T. J. was smart enough to start in one corner of the building, heaping up the carried earth two or three feet thick, so that we had an immediate result to look at, to contemplate with awe. Some of the evenings T. J. alone was carrying earth up to the building, the rest of the gang distracted by other enterprises or interests, but T. J. kept plugging along on his own, and eventually we'd all come back to him again, and then our own little acre would grow more rapidly.

He was careful about the kind of dirt he'd let us carry up there, and more than once he dumped a sandy load over the parapet into the areaway below because it wasn't good enough. He found out the kinds of earth in all the vacant lots for blocks around. He'd pick it up and feel it and smell it, frozen though it was sometimes, and then he'd say it was good growing soil or it wasn't worth anything and we'd have to go on somewhere else.

Thinking about it now, I don't see how he kept us at it. It was hard work, lugging paper sacks and boxes of dirt all the way up the stairs of our own building, keeping out of the way of the grownups so they wouldn't catch on to what we were doing. They probably wouldn't have cared, for they didn't pay much attention to us, but we wanted to keep it secret anyway. Then we had to go through the trap door to our roof, teeter over a plank to the fire escape, then climb two or three stories to the parapet and drop down onto the roof. All that for a small pile of earth that sometimes didn't seem worth the effort. But T. J. kept the vision bright within us, his words shrewd and calculated toward the fulfillment of his dreams; and he worked harder than any of us. He seemed driven toward a goal that we couldn't see, a particular point in time that would be definitely marked by signs and wonders that only he could see.

The laborious earth just lay there during the cold months, inert and lifeless, the clods lumpy and cold under our feet when we walked over it. But one day it rained, and afterward there was a softness in the air and the earth was alive and giving again with moisture and warmth. That evening T. J. smelled the air, his nostrils dilating with the odor of the earth under his feet.

"It's spring," he said, and there was a gladness rising in his voice that filled us all with the same feeling. "It's mighty late for it, but it's spring. I'd just about decided it wasn't never gonna get here at all."

We were all sniffing at the air, too, trying to smell it the way that T. J. did, and I can still remember the sweet odor of the earth under our feet. It was the first time in my life that spring and spring earth had meant anything to me. I looked at T. J. then, knowing in a faint way the hunger within him through the toilsome winter months, knowing the dream that lay behind his plan. He was a new Antaeus, preparing his own bed of strength.

"Planting time," he said. "We'll have to find us some seed."

"What do we do?" Blackie said. "How do we do it?"

"First we'll have to break up the clods," T. J. said. "That won't be hard to do. Then we plant the seed, and after a while they come up. Then you got you a crop." He frowned. "But you ain't got it raised yet. You got to tend it and hoe and take care of it, and all the time it's growing and growing while you're awake and while you're asleep. Then you lay it by when it's growed and let it ripen; and then you got you a crop."

"There's those wholesale seed houses over on Sixth," I said. "We could probably swipe some grass seed over there."

T. J. looked at the earth. "You-all seem mighty set on raising some grass," he said. "I ain't never put no effort into that. I spent all my life trying not to raise grass."

"But it's pretty," Blackie said. "We could play on it and take sunbaths on it. Like having our own lawn. Lots of people got lawns."

"Well," T. J. said. He looked at the rest of us, hesitant for the first time. He kept on looking at us for a moment. "I did have it in mind to raise some corn and vegetables. But we'll plant grass."

He was smart. He knew where to give in. And I don't suppose it made any difference to him really. He just wanted to grow something, even if it was grass.

"Of course," he said, "I do think we ought to plant a row of watermelons. They'd be mighty nice to eat while we was a-laying on that grass."

We all laughed. "All right," I said. "We'll plant us a row of watermelons."

Things went very quickly then. Perhaps half the roof was covered with the earth, the half that wasn't broken by ventilators, and we swiped pocketfuls of grass seed from the open bins in the wholesale seed house, mingling among the buyers on Saturdays and during the school lunch hour. T. J. showed us how to prepare the earth, breaking up the clods and smoothing it and sowing the grass seed. It looked rich and black now with moisture, receiving of the seed, and it seemed that the grass sprang up overnight, pale green in the early spring.

We couldn't keep from looking at it, unable to believe that we had created this delicate growth. We looked at T. J. with understanding now, knowing the fulfillment of the plan he had carried alone within his mind. We had worked without full understanding of the task, but he had known all the time.

We found that we couldn't walk or play on the delicate blades, as we had expected to, but we didn't mind. It was enough just to look at it, to realize that it was the work of our own hands, and each evening the whole gang was there, trying to measure the growth that had been achieved that day.

One time a foot was placed on the plot of ground . . . one time only, Blackie stepping onto it with sudden bravado. Then he looked at the crushed blades, and there was shame in his face. He did not do it again. This was his grass, too, and not to be desecrated. No one said anything, for it was not necessary.

T. J. had reserved a small section for watermelons, and he was still trying to find some seed for it. The wholesale house didn't have any watermelon seed, and we didn't know where we could lay our hands on them. T. J. shaped the earth into mounds, ready to receive them, three mounds lying in a straight line along the edge of the grass plot.

We had just about decided that we'd have to buy the seed if we were to get them. It was a violation of our principles, but we were anxious to get the watermelons started. Somewhere or other, T. J. got his hands on a seed catalogue and brought it one evening to our roof garden.

"We can order them now," he said showing us the catalogue. "Look!"

We all crowded around, looking at the fat, green watermelons pictured in full color on the pages. Some of them were split open, showing the red, tempting meat, making our mouths water.

"Now we got to scrape up some seed money," T. J. said, looking at us. "I got a quarter. How much you-all got?"

We made up a couple of dollars between us, and T. J. nodded his head. "That'll be more than enough. Now we got to decide what kind to get. I think them Kleckley Sweets. What do you-all think?"

He was going into esoteric[2] matters beyond our reach. We hadn't even known there were different kinds of melons. So we just nodded our heads and agreed that yes, we thought the Kleckley Sweets too.

"I'll order them tonight," T. J. said. "We ought to have them in a few days."

Then an adult voice said behind us: "What are you boys doing up here?"

It startled us, for no one had ever come up here before, in all the time we had been using the roof of the factory. We jerked around and saw three men standing near the trap door at the other end of the roof. They weren't policemen, or night watchmen, but three men in plump business suits, looking at us. They walked toward us.

"What you boys doing up here?" the one in the middle said again.

We stood still, guilt heavy among us, levied by the tone of voice, and looked at the three strangers.

The men stared at the grass flourishing behind us. "What's this?" the man said. "How did this get up here?"

"Sure is growing good, ain't it?" T. J. said conversationally. "We planted it."

The men kept looking at the grass as if they didn't believe

---

[2] *esoteric* (ĕs-ə-tĕr′ĭk): intended for or understood by only a small group.

it. It was a thick carpet over the earth now, a patch of deep greenness startling in the sterile industrial surroundings.

"Yes, sir," T. J. said proudly. "We toted that earth up here and planted that grass." He fluttered the seed catalogue. "And we're just fixing to plant us some watermelon."

The man looked at him then, his eyes strange and faraway. "What do you mean, putting this on the roof of my building?" he said. "Do you want to go to jail?"

T. J. looked shaken. The rest of us were silent, frightened by the authority of his voice. We had grown up aware of adult authority, of policemen and night watchmen and teachers, and this man sounded like all the others. But it was a new thing to T. J.

"Well, you wan't using the roof," T. J. said. He paused a moment and added shrewdly, "So we just thought to pretty it up a little bit."

"And sag it so I'd have to rebuild it," the man said sharply. He turned away, saying to a man beside him, "See that all that junk is shoveled off by tomorrow."

"Yes, sir," the man said.

T. J. started forward. "You can't do that," he said. "We toted it up here, and it's our earth. We planted it and raised it and toted it up here."

The man stared at him coldly. "But it's my building," he said. "It's to be shoveled off tomorrow."

"It's our earth," T. J. said desperately. "You ain't got no right!"

The men walked on without listening and descended clumsily through the trap door. T. J. stood looking after them, his body tense with anger, until they had disappeared. They wouldn't even argue with him, wouldn't let him defend his earthrights.

He turned to us. "We won't let 'em do it," he said fiercely. "We'll stay up here all day tomorrow and the day after that, and we won't let 'em do it."

We just looked at him. We knew that there was no stopping it. He saw it in our faces, and his face wavered for a moment before he gripped it into determination.

"They ain't got no right," he said. "It's our earth. It's our land. Can't nobody touch a man's own land."

We kept on looking at him, listening to the words but knowing that it was no use. The adult world had descended on

us even in our richest dream, and we knew there was no calculating the adult world, no fighting it, no winning against it.

We started moving slowly toward the parapet and the fire escape, avoiding a last look at the green beauty of the earth that T. J. had planted for us . . . had planted deeply in our minds as well as in our experience. We filed slowly over the edge and down the steps to the plank, T. J. coming last, and all of us could feel the weight of his grief behind us.

"Wait a minute," he said suddenly, his voice harsh with the effort of calling. We stopped and turned, held by the tone of his voice, and looked up at him standing above us on the fire escape.

"We can't stop them?" he said, looking down at us, his face strange in the dusky light. "There ain't no way to stop 'em?"

"No," Blackie said with finality. "They own the building."

We stood still for a moment, looking up at T. J., caught into inaction by the decision working in his face. He stared back at us, and his face was pale and mean in the poor light, with a bald nakedness in his skin like cripples have sometimes.

"They ain't gonna touch my earth," he said fiercely. "They ain't gonna lay a hand on it! Come on."

He turned around and started up the fire escape again, almost running against the effort of climbing. We followed more slowly, not knowing what he intended. By the time we reached him, he had seized a board and thrust it into the soil, scooping it up and flinging it over the parapet into the areaway below. He straightened and looked us squarely in the face.

"They can't touch it," he said. "I won't let 'em lay a dirty hand on it!"

We saw it then. He stooped to his labor again and we followed, the gust of his anger moving in frenzied labor among us as we scattered along the edge of earth, scooping it and throwing it over the parapet, destroying with anger the growth we had nurtured with such tender care. The soil carried so laboriously upward to the light and the sun cascaded swiftly into the dark areaway, the green blades of grass crumpled and twisted in the falling.

It took less time than you would think . . . the task of destruction is infinitely easier than that of creation. We stopped at the end, leaving only a scattering of loose soil, and when it was finally over, a stillness stood among the group and over the factory building. We looked down at the bare sterility of black tar, felt the harsh texture of it under the soles of our shoes, and the anger had gone out of us, leaving only a sore aching in our minds like overstretched muscles.

T. J. stopped for a moment, his breathing slowing from anger and effort, caught into the same contemplation of destruction as all of us. He stooped slowly, finally, and picked up a lonely blade of grass left trampled under our feet and put it between his teeth, tasting it, sucking the greenness out of it into his mouth. Then he started walking toward the fire escape, moving before any of us were ready to move, and disappeared over the edge while we stared after him.

We followed him, but he was already halfway down to the ground, going on past the board where we crossed over, climbing down into the areaway. We saw the last section swing down with his weight, and then he stood on the concrete below us, looking at the small pile of anonymous earth scattered by our throwing. Then he walked across the place where we could see him and disappeared toward the street without glancing back, without looking up to see us watching him.

They did not find him for two weeks. Then the Nashville police caught him just outside the Nashville freight yards. He was walking along the railroad track; still heading south, still heading home.

As for us, who had no remembered home to call us . . . none of us ever again climbed the escape-way to the roof.

DISCUSSION

1. Why didn't any of the boys ever climb the escape-way to the roof again?

2. After the grass has grown, the boys discover they don't want to walk on it. Why? Then, after they are discovered by the owner of the building, they destroy the grass. Why?

3. In what ways is T. J. different from the other boys? Find examples in the story that show that the boys like and respect T. J. Why do they?

4. **Allusion.** An allusion is a reference to a person or place that the reader is assumed to be familiar with. Sometimes the person or place is real; sometimes not. The allusion in this story is to Antaeus, of Greek mythology. Read the headnote on page 175. Why is "Antaeus" an appropriate title for this story?

For further activities, see page 206.

First Song

GALWAY KINNELL

Then it was dusk in Illinois, the small boy
After an afternoon of carting dung
Hung on the rail fence, a sapped thing
Weary to crying. Dark was growing tall
And he began to hear the pond frogs all   5
Calling on his ear with what seemed their joy.

Soon their sound was pleasant for a boy
Listening in the smoky dusk and the nightfall
Of Illinois, and from the fields two small
Boys came bearing cornstalk violins   10
And they rubbed the cornstalk bows with resins
And the three sat there scraping of their joy.

It was now fine music the frogs and the boys
Did in the towering Illinois twilight make
And into dark in spite of a shoulder's ache   15
A boy's hunched body loved out of a stalk
The first song of his happiness, and the song woke
His heart to the darkness and into the sadness of joy.

DISCUSSION

1. How is the poet's choice of time of day appropriate for the experience the boy has?

2. Why do you think the poet chose the title "First Song"?

3. What might a passer-by think of the music made by the boys with their cornstalk violins?

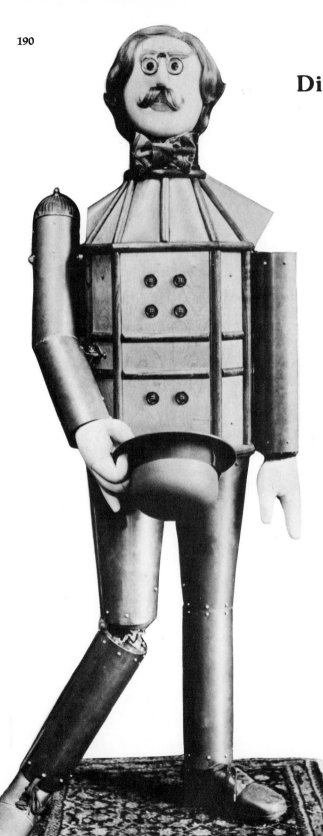

Directions to the Armorer

ELDER OLSON

All right, armorer,
Make me a sword—
Not too sharp,
A bit hard to draw,
And of cardboard, preferably.   5
On second thought, stick
An eraser on the handle.
Somehow I always
Clobber the wrong guy.

Make me a shield with   10
Easy-to-change
Insignia. I'm often
A little vague
As to which side I'm on,
What battle I'm in.   15
And listen, make it
A trifle flimsy,
Not too hard to pierce.
I'm not absolutely sure
I want to win.   20

Make the armor itself
As tough as possible,
But on a reverse
Principle: don't
Worry about its   25
Saving my hide;
Just fix it to give me
Some sort of protection—
Any sort of protection—
From a possible enemy   30
Inside.

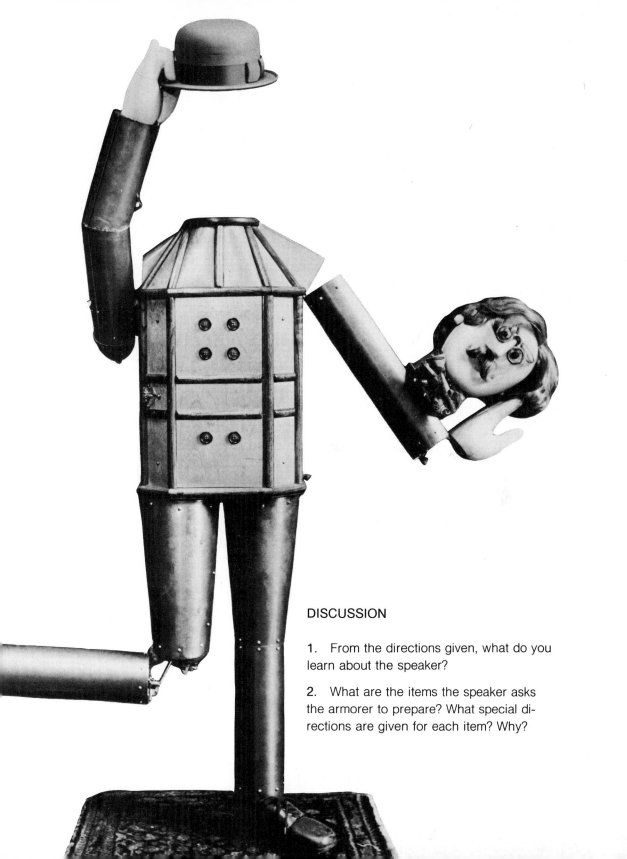

DISCUSSION

1. From the directions given, what do you learn about the speaker?

2. What are the items the speaker asks the armorer to prepare? What special directions are given for each item? Why?

LOST SISTER

DOROTHY M. JOHNSON

Our household was full of women, who overwhelmed my uncle Charlie and sometimes confused me with their bustle and chatter. We were the only men on the place. I was nine years old when still another woman came—Aunt Bessie, who had been living with the Indians.

When my mother told me about her, I couldn't believe it. The Indians had killed my father, a cavalry lieutenant, two years before. I hated Indians and looked forward to wiping them out when I got older. (But when I was grown, they were no menace any more.)

"What did she live with the hostiles[1] for?" I demanded.

"They captured her when she was a little girl," Ma said. "She was three years younger than you are. Now she's coming home."

High time she came home, I thought. I said so, promising, "If they was ever to get me, I wouldn't stay with 'em long."

Ma put her arms around me. "Don't talk like that. They won't get you. They'll never get you."

I was my mother's only real tie with her husband's family. She was not happy with those masterful women, my aunts Margaret, Hannah, and Sabina but she would not go back East where she came from. Uncle Charlie managed the store the aunts owned, but he wasn't really a member of the family—he was just Aunt Margaret's husband. The only man who had belonged was my father, the aunts' younger brother. And I belonged, and someday the store would be mine. My mother stayed to protect my heritage.

None of the three sisters, my aunts, had ever seen Aunt Bessie. She had been taken by the Indians before they were born. Aunt Mary had known her—Aunt Mary was two years older—but she lived a thousand miles away now and was not well.

There was no picture of the little girl who had become a legend. When the family had first settled here, there was enough struggle to feed and clothe the children without having pictures made of them.

Even after army officers had come to our house several times and there had been many letters about Aunt Bessie's delivery from the Indians it was a long time before she came. Major Harris, who made the final arrangements, warned my aunts that they would have problems, that Aunt Bessie might not be able to settle down easily into family life.

This was only a challenge to Aunt Margaret, who welcomed challenges. "She's our own flesh and blood," Aunt Margaret trumpeted. "Of course she must come to us. My poor, dear sister

---

[1] *hostiles:* enemies or unfriendly people.

Bessie, torn from her home forty years ago!"

The major was earnest but not tactful. "She's been with the Indians all those years," he insisted. "And she was only a little girl when she was taken. I haven't seen her myself, but it's reasonable to assume that she'll be like an Indian woman."

My stately aunt Margaret arose to show that the audience[2] was ended. "Major Harris," she intoned, "I cannot permit anyone to criticize my own dear sister. She will live in my home, and if I do not receive official word that she is coming within a month, I shall take steps."

Aunt Bessie came before the month was up.

The aunts in residence made valiant preparations. They bustled and swept and mopped and polished. They moved me from my own room to my mother's—as she had been begging them to do because I was troubled with nightmares. They prepared my old room for Aunt Bessie with many small comforts—fresh doilies everywhere, hairpins, a matching pitcher and bowl, the best towels, and two new nightgowns in case hers might be old. (The fact was that she didn't have any.)

"Perhaps we should have some dresses made," Hannah suggested. "We don't know what she'll have with her."

"We don't know what size she'll take, either," Margaret pointed out. "There'll be time enough for her to go to the store after she settles down and

rests for a day or two. Then she can shop to her heart's content."

Ladies of the town came to call almost every afternoon while the preparations were going on. Margaret promised them that as soon as Bessie had recovered sufficiently from her ordeal, they should all meet her at tea.

Margaret warned her anxious sisters, "Now, girls, we mustn't ask her too many questions at first. She must rest for a while. She's been through a terrible experience," Margaret's voice dropped way down with those last two words, as if only she could be expected to understand.

Indeed Bessie had been through a terrible experience, but it wasn't what the sisters thought. The experience from which she was suffering, when she arrived, was that she had been wrenched from her people, the Indians, and turned over to strangers. She had not been freed. She had been made a captive.

Aunt Bessie came with Major Harris and an interpreter. Aunt Margaret swung the door open wide when she saw them coming. She ran out with her sisters following, while my mother and I watched from a window. Margaret's arms were outstretched, but when she saw the woman closer, her arms dropped and her glad cry died.

She did not cringe, my Aunt Bessie who had been an Indian for forty years, but she stopped walking and stood staring, helpless among her captors.

The sisters had described her often as a little girl. Not that they had ever

seen her, but she was a legend, the captive child. Beautiful blond curls, they said she had, and big blue eyes—she was a fairy child, a pale-haired little angel who ran on dancing feet.

The Bessie who came back was an aging woman who plodded in moccasins, whose dark dress did not belong on her bulging body. Her brown hair hung just below her ears. It was growing out; when she was first taken from the Indians, her hair had been cut short to clean out the vermin.

Aunt Margaret recovered herself, and instead of embracing this silent, stolid woman, satisfied herself by patting an arm and crying, "Poor dear Bessie, I am your sister Margaret. And here are our sisters Hannah and Sabina. We do hope you're not all tired out from your journey!"

Aunt Margaret was all graciousness, because she had been assured beyond doubt that this was truly a member of the family. She must have believed—Aunt Margaret could believe anything—that all Bessie needed was to have a nice nap and wash her face. Then she would be as talkative as any of them.

The other aunts were quick-moving and sharp of tongue. But this one moved as if her sorrows were a burden on her bowed shoulders, and when she spoke briefly in answer to the interpreter, you could not understand a word of it.

Aunt Margaret ignored these peculiarities. She took the party into the front parlor—even the interpreter, when she understood there was no avoiding it. She might have gone on

battling with the major about him, but she was in a hurry to talk to her lost sister.

"You won't be able to converse with her unless the interpreter is present," Major Harris said. "Not," he explained hastily, "because of any regulation, but because she has forgotten English."

Aunt Margaret gave the half-blood interpreter a look of frowning doubt and let him enter. She coaxed Bessie. "Come, dear, sit down."

The interpreter mumbled, and my Indian aunt sat cautiously on a needlepoint chair. For most of her life she had been living with the people who sat comfortably on the ground.

The visit in the parlor was brief. Bessie had had her instructions before she came. But Major Harris had a few warnings for the family. "Technically, your sister is still a prisoner," he explained, ignoring Margaret's start of horror. "She will be in your custody. She may walk in your fenced yard, but she must not leave it without official permission.

"Mrs. Raleigh, this may be a heavy burden for you all. But she has been told all this and has expressed willingness to conform to these restrictions. I don't think you will have any trouble keeping her here." Major Harris hesitated, remembered that he was a soldier and a brave man, and added, "If I did, I wouldn't have brought her."

There was the making of a sharp little battle, but Aunt Margaret chose to overlook the challenge. She could not overlook the fact that Bessie was not what she had expected.

Bessie certainly knew that this was her lost white family, but she didn't seem to care. She was infinitely sad, infinitely removed. She asked one question: "Ma-ry?" and Aunt Margaret almost wept with joy.

"Sister Mary lives a long way from here," she explained, "and she isn't well, but she will come as soon as she's able. Dear sister Mary!"

The interpreter translated this, and Bessie had no more to say. That was the only understandable word she ever did say in our house, the remembered name of her older sister.

When the aunts, all chattering, took Bessie to her room, one of them asked, "But where are her things?"

Bessie had no things, no baggage. She had nothing at all but the clothes she stood in. While the sisters scurried to bring a comb and other oddments, she stood like a stooped monument, silent and watchful. This was her prison. Very well, she would endure it.

"Maybe tomorrow we can take her to the store and see what she would like," Aunt Hannah suggested.

"There's no hurry," Aunt Margaret declared thoughtfully. She was getting the idea that this sister was going to be a problem. But I don't think Aunt Margaret ever really stopped hoping that one day Bessie would cease to be different, that she would end her stubborn silence and begin to relate the events of her life among the Indians in the parlor over a cup of tea.

My Indian aunt accustomed herself, finally, to sitting on the chair in her room. She seldom came out, which was a relief to her sisters. She preferred to stand, hour after hour, looking out the window—which was open only about a foot, in spite of all Uncle Charlie's efforts to budge it higher. And she always wore moccasins. She never was able to wear shoes from the store but seemed to treasure the shoes brought to her.

The aunts did not, of course, take her shopping after all. They made her a couple of dresses; and when they told her, with signs and voluble explanations, to change her dress, she did.

After I found that she was usually at the window, looking across the flat land to the blue mountains, I played in the yard so I could stare at her. She never smiled, as an aunt should, but she looked at me sometimes, thoughtfully, as if measuring my worth. By performing athletic feats, such as walking on my hands, I could get her attention. For some reason, I valued it.

She didn't often change expression, but twice I saw her scowl with disapproval. Once was when one of the aunts slapped me in a casual way. I had earned the slap, but the Indians did not punish children with blows. Aunt Bessie was shocked, I think, to see that white people did. The other time was when I talked back to someone with spoiled, small-boy insolence—and that time the scowl was for me.

The sisters and my mother took turns, as was their Christian duty, in visiting her for half an hour each day. Bessie didn't eat at the table with us—not after the first meal.

The first time my mother took her

turn, it was under protest. "I'm afraid I'd start crying in front of her," she argued, but Aunt Margaret insisted.

I was lurking in the hall when Ma went in. Bessie said something, then said it again, peremptorily, until my mother guessed what she wanted. She called me and put her arm around me as I stood beside her chair. Aunt Bessie nodded, and that was all there was to it.

Afterward, my mother said, "She likes you. And so do I." She kissed me.

"I don't like her," I complained. "She's queer."

"She's a sad old lady," my mother explained. "She had a little boy once, you know."

"What happened to him?"

"He grew up and became a warrior. I suppose she was proud of him. Now the army has him in prison somewhere. He's half Indian. He was a dangerous man."

He was indeed a dangerous man, and a proud man, a chief, a bird of prey whose wings the army had clipped after bitter years of trying.

However, my mother and my Indian aunt had that one thing in common: they both had sons. The other aunts were childless.

There was a great to-do about having Aunt Bessie's photograph taken. The aunts, who were stubbornly and valiantly trying to make her one of the family, wanted a picture of her for the family album. The government wanted one too, for some reason—perhaps because someone realized that a thing of historic importance had been accomplished by recovering the captive child.

Major Harris sent a young lieutenant with the interpreter to discuss the matter in the parlor. Bessie spoke very little during that meeting, and of course we understood only what the half-blood *said* she was saying.

No, she did not want her picture made. No.

But your son had his picture made. Do you want to see it? They teased her with that offer, and she nodded.

If we let you see his picture, then will you have yours made?

She nodded doubtfully. Then she demanded more than had been offered: If you let me keep his picture, then you can make mine.

No, you can only look at it. We have to keep his picture. It belongs to us.

My Indian aunt gambled for high stakes. She shrugged and spoke, and the interpreter said, "She not want to look. She will keep or nothing."

My mother shivered, understanding as the aunts could not understand what Bessie was gambling—all or nothing.

Bessie won. Perhaps they had intended that she should. She was allowed to keep the photograph that had been made of her son. It has been in history books many times—the half-white chief, the valiant leader who was not quite great enough to keep his Indian people free.

His photograph was taken after he was captured, but you would never guess it. His head is high, his eyes stare with boldness but not with scorn, his long hair is arranged with care—dark hair braided on one side and with a tendency to curl where the other side hangs loose—and his hands hold the pipe like a royal scepter.

That photograph of the captive but unconquered warrior had its effect on me. Remembering him, I began to control my temper and my tongue, to cultivate reserve as I grew older, to stare with boldness but not scorn at people who annoyed or offended me. I never met him, but I took silent pride in him—Eagle Head, my Indian cousin.

Bessie kept his picture on her dresser when she was not holding it in her hands. And she went like a docile, silent child to the photograph studio, in a carriage with Aunt Margaret early one morning, when there would be few people on the street to stare.

Bessie's photograph is not proud, but pitiful. She looks out with no expression. There is no emotion there, no challenge, only the face of an aging woman with short hair, only endurance and patience. The aunts put a copy in the family album.

But they were nearing the end of their tether.[3] The Indian aunt was a solid ghost in the house. She did nothing because there was nothing for her to do. Her gnarled hands must have been skilled at Indian women's work, at butchering meat and scraping and tanning hides, at making tepees and beading ceremonial clothes. But her skills were useless and unwanted in a civilized home. She did not even sew when my mother gave her cloth and needles and thread. She kept the sewing things beside her son's picture.

[3] *tether:* here, endurance.

She ate (in her room) and slept (on the floor) and stood looking out the window. That was all, and it could not go on. But it had to go on, at least until my sick Aunt Mary was well enough to travel—Aunt Mary, who was her older sister, the only one who had known her when they were children.

The sisters' duty visits to Aunt Bessie became less and less visits and more and more duty. They settled into a bearable routine. Margaret had taken upon herself the responsibility of trying to make Bessie talk. Make, I said, not teach. She firmly believed that her stubborn and unfortunate sister needed only encouragement from a strong-willed person. So Margaret talked, as to a child, when she bustled in:

"Now there you stand, just looking, dear. What in the world is there to see out there? The birds—are you watching the birds? Why don't you try sewing? Or you could go for a little walk in the yard. Don't you want to go out for a nice little walk?"

Bessie listened and blinked.

Margaret could have understood an Indian woman's not being able to converse in a civilized tongue, but her own sister was not an Indian. Bessie was white; therefore she should talk the language her sisters did—the language she had not heard since early childhood.

Hannah, the put-upon aunt, talked to Bessie too, but she was delighted not to get any answers and not to be interrupted. She bent over her embroidery when it was her turn to sit with Bessie and told her troubles in an unending flow. Bessie stood looking out the window the whole time.

Sabina, who had just as many troubles, most of them emanating[4] from Margaret and Hannah, went in like a martyr, firmly clutching her Bible, and read aloud from it until her time was up. She took a small clock along so that she would not, because of annoyance, be tempted to cheat.

After several weeks Aunt Mary came, white and trembling and exhausted from her illness and the long, hard journey. The sisters tried to get the interpreter in but were not successful. (Aunt Margaret took that failure pretty hard.) They briefed Aunt Mary, after she had rested, so the shock of seeing Bessie would not be too terrible. I saw them meet, those two.

Margaret went to the Indian woman's door and explained volubly who had come, a useless but brave attempt. Then she stood aside, and Aunt Mary was there, her lined white face aglow, her arms outstretched. "Bessie! Sister Bessie!" she cried.

And after one brief moment's hesitation, Bessie went into her arms, and Mary kissed her sun-dark, weathered cheek. Bessie spoke. "Ma-ry," she said. "Ma-ry." She stood with tears running down her face and her mouth working. So much to tell, so much suffering and fear—and joy and triumph, too—and the sister there at last who might legitimately hear it all and understand.

But the only English word that Bessie remembered was Mary, and she

---

[4] *emanating:* coming forth.

had not cared to learn any others. She turned to the dresser, took her son's picture in her work-hardened hands, reverently, and held it so her sister could see. Her eyes pleaded.

Mary looked on the calm, noble face of her half-blood nephew and said the right thing: "My, isn't he handsome!" She put her head on one side and then on the other. "A fine boy, sister," she approved. "You must"—she stopped, but she finished—"be awfully proud of him, dear!"

Bessie understood the tone if not the words. The tone was admiration. Her son was accepted by the sister who mattered. Bessie looked at the picture and nodded, murmuring. Then she put it back on the dresser.

Aunt Mary did not try to make

Bessie talk. She sat with her every day for hours, and Bessie did talk—but not in English. They sat holding hands for mutual comfort while the captive child, grown old and a grandmother, told what had happened in forty years. Aunt Mary said that was what Bessie was talking about. But she didn't understand a word of it and didn't need to.

"There is time enough for her to learn English again," Aunt Mary said. "I think she understands more than she lets on. I asked her if she'd like to come and live with me, and she nodded. We'll have the rest of our lives for her to learn English. But what she has been telling me—she can't wait to tell that. About her life, and her son."

"Are you sure, Mary dear, that you should take the responsibility of having her?" Margaret said dutifully, no doubt shaking in her shoes for fear Mary would change her mind now that deliverance was in sight. "I do believe she'd be happier with you, though we've done all we could."

Margaret and the older sisters would certainly be happier with Bessie somewhere else. And so, it developed, would the United States government.

Major Harris came with the interpreter to discuss details, and they told Bessie she could go, if she wished, to live with Mary a thousand miles away. Bessie was patient and willing, stolidly agreeable. She talked a great deal more to the interpreter than she had ever done before. He answered at length and then explained to the others that she had wanted to know how she and Mary would travel to this far country.

It was hard, he said, for her to understand just how far they were going.

Later we knew that the interpreter and Bessie had talked about much more than that.

Next morning, when Sabina took breakfast to Bessie's room, we heard a cry of dismay. Sabina stood holding the tray, repeating, "She's gone out the window! She's gone out the window!"

And so she had. The window that had always stuck so that it would not raise more than a foot was open wider now. And the photograph of Bessie's son was gone from the dresser. Nothing else was missing except Bessie and the decent dark dress she had worn the day before.

My uncle Charlie got no breakfast that morning. With Margaret shrieking orders, he leaped on a horse and rode to the telegraph station.

Before Major Harris got there with half a dozen cavalrymen, civilian scouts were out searching for the missing woman. They were expert trackers. Their lives had depended, at various times, on their ability to read the meaning of a turned stone, a broken twig, a bruised leaf. They found that Bessie had gone south. They tracked her for ten miles. And then they lost the trail, for Bessie was as skilled as they were. Her life had sometimes depended on leaving no stone or twig or leaf marked by her passage. She traveled fast at first. Then, with time to be careful, she evaded the followers she knew would come.

The aunts were stricken with grief—at least Aunt Mary was—and bowed with humiliation about what Bessie had done. The blinds were drawn, and voices were low in the house. We had been pitied because of Bessie's tragic folly in having let the Indians make an Indian of her. But now we were traitors because we had let her get away.

Aunt Mary kept saying pitifully, "Oh, why did she go? I thought she would be contented with me!"

The others said that it was, perhaps, all for the best. Aunt Margaret proclaimed, "She has gone back to her own." That was what they honestly believed, and so did Major Harris.

My mother told me why she had gone. "You know that picture she had of the Indian chief, her son? He's escaped from the jail he was in. The fort got word of it, and they think Bessie may be going to where he's hiding. That's why they're trying so hard to find her. They think," my mother explained, "that she knew of his escape before they did. They think the interpreter told her when he was here. There was no other way she could have found out."

They scoured the mountains to the south for Eagle Head and Bessie. They never found her, and they did not get him until a year later, far to the north. They could not capture him that time. He died fighting.

After I grew up, I operated the family store, disliking storekeeping a little more every day. When I was free to sell it, I did, and went to raising cattle. And one day, riding in a canyon after strayed steers, I found—I think—Aunt Bessie. A cowboy who worked for me was along, or I would never have let anybody know.

We found weathered bones near a little spring. They had a mystery on them, those nameless human bones suddenly come upon. I could feel old death brushing my back.

"Some prospector," suggested my riding partner.

I thought so too until I found, protected by a log, sodden scraps of fabric that might have been a dark, respectable dress. And wrapped in them was a sodden something that might have once been a picture.

The man with me was young, but he had heard the story of the captive child. He had been telling me about it, in fact. In the passing years it had acquired some details that surprised me. Aunt Bessie had become once more a fair-haired beauty, in this legend that he had heard, but utterly sad and silent. Well, sad and silent she really was.

I tried to push the sodden scrap of fabric back under the log, but he was too quick for me. "That ain't no shirt, that's a dress!" he announced. "This here was no prospector—it was a woman!" He paused and then announced with awe, "I bet you it was your Indian aunt!"

I scowled and said, "Nonsense. It could be anybody."

He got all worked up about it. "If it was *my* aunt," he declared, "I'd bury her in the family plot."

"No," I said, and shook my head.

We left the bones there in the canyon, where they had been for forty-odd years if they were Aunt Bessie's. And I think they were. But I would not make her a captive again. She's in the family album. She doesn't need to be in the family plot.

If my guess about why she left us is wrong, nobody can prove it. She never intended to join her son in hiding. She went in the opposite direction to lure pursuit away.

What happened to her in the canyon doesn't concern me, or anyone. My aunt Bessie accomplished what she set out to do. It was not her life that mattered, but his. She bought him another year.

DISCUSSION

1. Find examples that show the change in the narrator's opinion of Indians. How does he feel about his aunt Bessie?

2. Why will Bessie speak to Mary but not to her other sisters?

3. What special part does the interpreter play in the story?

4. It is partly through **dialogue** (see page 167) that we learn what characters in a story are like. From their dialogue, what do you learn about the sisters and their feelings about Bessie? What do you learn about Bessie from her dialogue?

For further activities, see page 206.

THE SILVER CELL
Mari Evans

I have
never been contained
except I
made
the prison, nor
known a chain
except those forged
by me

O I am slave
and I am master
am at once
both bound
and
free

DISCUSSION

1. Which of the following statements best expresses the meaning of the poem: (a) I cannot help being influenced by the previous experiences in my life; (b) I can at least choose the duties and commitments that I undertake; (c) no one is ever really free.

2. Why do you suppose the poet described the cell as "silver"? What does the word suggest that "iron" would not?

I KILL HER ENEMIES

NORMAN H. RUSSELL

i wear the blanket of my wife
she wears the bracelet i have made
i raised the sheep
she dug the turquoise
i teach the son she gave me   5
she cooks the food i gave her
my wife paints me for war
i kill her enemies

when i go on the hunt
my wife goes in my heart   10
when my wife stays in the hogan
i also stay in her heart

we are two
we are one.

DISCUSSION

1. The speaker says "we are two / we are one."
What does he mean?

2. The speaker does not mention the word *love*.
How do you know he and his wife love each other?
Who are the enemies the husband kills?

VOCABULARY

Antaeus (page 175)

On separate paper, write the word or phrase that is closest in meaning to the word in bold type.

1. His voice was **resolute** with the knowledge of his rightness. . . .

repulsive   firm   shaky   high-pitched

2. But T. J. kept the vision bright within us, his words **shrewd** and calculated toward the fulfillment of his dreams.

biased   clever   loud   impartial

3. This was his grass, too, and not to be **desecrated**.

questioned   abused   concealed   criticized

4. He stooped to his labor again and we followed, the gusts of his anger moving in **frenzied** labor among us. . . .

aggressive   worthless   disordered   systematic

5. . . . the sun **cascaded** swiftly into the dark areaway. . . .

ascended   descended   escaped   mounted

Lost Sister (page 192)

"My stately aunt Margaret arose to show that the audience was over" (page 193). Here, the word *audience* means a formal hearing or conference. What other meaning does the word have? It comes from the Latin *audire,* to hear. So do the words listed below. What do they mean?

audible   audit   auditorium   audio visual   audition

COMPOSITION

Antaeus (page 175)

Tell what happens in this story from T. J.'s point of view. Write a letter to a friend back in Alabama as you think T. J. would write it. Try to use words and expressions you think he might use.

Lost Sister (page 192)

Create a legend about Bessie. Include all the details given in the story, and add other specific adventures. Be sure to include how Bessie was captured by Indians and how she later met and fell in love with her Indian husband. Include what happened after Bessie escaped from the aunt's house. If you wish, write your legend in verse or song form.

READING

Antaeus (page 175)

On separate paper, write the phrase that best completes the statements.

1.   Basically this story describes (a) a Southern boy's inability to adapt to the North's industrial life (b) the author's reaction to the hardships of wartime (c) the efforts of a boys' club to beautify an industrial area (d) living conditions in an overcrowded apartment in the North.

2.   T. J.'s response that he came from Marion County and that he raised his own cotton and corn shows (a) his sense of personal identity (b) nothing concerning his character (c) his sure control of the language (d) his fourth-grade level of education.

3.   In working with T. J., the boys (a) complete their other unfinished projects (b) learn to order seeds from a mail ordering house (c) grow to despise T. J. because of his high-pitched voice (d) learn to work together cooperatively toward a goal.

4.   The story is appropriately named since both Antaeus and T. J. (a) are characters in the same story (b) built roof gardens (c) are mythological characters (d) found their strength in the soil.

Lost Sister (page 192)

In this story, some of the things that take place occur because of things that happened before. For each of the events listed below, look back in the story and find the causes.

1.   The narrator looks forward to wiping out Indians when he grows up.
2.   Aunt Bessie refuses to get her picture taken.
3.   Mary is the only sister Bessie responds to.
4.   Aunt Bessie escapes through the window.

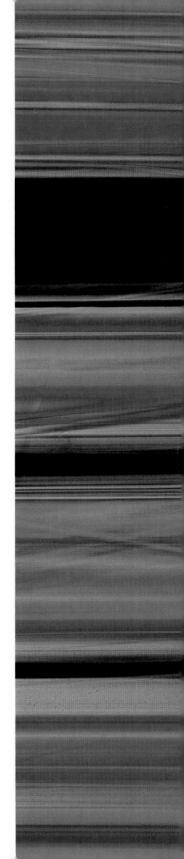

By Any Other Name

SANTHA RAMA RAU

At the Anglo-Indian day school[1] in Zorinabad to which my sister and I were sent when she was eight and I was five and a half, they changed our names. On the first day of school, a hot, windless morning of a north Indian September, we stood in the headmistress's study and she said, "Now you're the *new* girls. What are your names?"

My sister answered for us. "I am Premila, and she"—nodding in my direction—"is Santha."

The headmistress had been in India, I suppose, fifteen years or so, but she still smiled her helpless inability to cope with Indian names. Her rimless half-glasses glittered, and the precarious bun on the top of her head trembled as she shook

[1] *Anglo-Indian day school:* school in India with teachers from England during the days when India was part of the British Empire.

her head. "Oh, my dears, those are much too hard for me. Suppose we give you pretty English names. Wouldn't that be more jolly? Let's see, now—Pamela for you, I think." She shrugged in a baffled way at my sister. "That's as close as I can get. And for *you*," she said to me, "how about Cynthia? Isn't that nice?"

My sister was always less easily intimidated[2] than I was, and while she kept a stubborn silence, I said, "Thank you," in a very tiny voice.

We had been sent to that school because my father, among his responsibilities as an officer of the civil service, had a tour of duty to perform in the villages around that steamy little provincial town, where he had his headquarters at that time. He used to make his shorter inspection tours on horseback, and a week before, in the stale heat of a typically postmonsoon day, we had waved good-bye to him and a little procession—an assistant, a secretary, two bearers, and the man to look after the bedding rolls and luggage. They rode away through our large garden, still bright green from the rains, and we turned back into the twilight of the house and the sound of fans whispering in every room.

Up to then, my mother had refused to send Premila to school in the British-run establishments of that time, because, she used to say, "you can bury a dog's tail for seven years and it still comes out curly, and you can take a Britisher away from his home for a lifetime and he still remains insular." The examinations and degrees from entirely Indian schools were not, in those days, considered valid. In my case, the question had never come up, and probably never would have come up if Mother's extraordinary good health had not broken down. For the first time in my life, she was not able to continue the lessons she had been giving us every morning. So our Hindi books were put away, the stories of the Lord Krishna as a little boy were left in mid-air, and we were sent to the Anglo-Indian school.

That first day at school is still, when I think of it, a remarkable one. At that age, if one's name is changed, one develops a curious form of dual personality. I remember having a certain detached and disbelieving concern in the actions of "Cynthia," but certainly no responsibility. Accordingly, I followed the thin, erect back of the headmistress down the veranda to my classroom feeling, at most, a passing interest in

---

[2] *intimidated:* frightened.

what was going to happen to me in this strange, new atmosphere of School.

The building was Indian in design, with wide verandas opening onto a central courtyard, but Indian verandas are usually whitewashed, with stone floors. These, in the tradition of British schools, were painted dark brown and had matting on the floors. It gave a feeling of extra intensity to the heat.

I suppose there were about a dozen Indian children in the school—which contained perhaps forty children in all—and four of them were in my class. They were all sitting at the back of the room, and I went to join them. I sat next to a small, solemn girl who didn't smile at me. She had long, glossy-black braids and wore a cotton dress, but she still kept on her Indian jewelry—a gold chain around her neck, thin gold bracelets, and tiny ruby studs in her ears. Like most Indian children, she had a rim of black kohl around her eyes. The cotton dress should have looked strange, but all I could think of was that I should ask my mother if I couldn't wear a dress to school, too, instead of my Indian clothes.

I can't remember too much about the proceedings in class that day, except for the beginning. The teacher pointed to me and asked me to stand up. "Now, dear, tell the class your name."

I said nothing.

"Come along," she said, frowning slightly. "What's your name, dear?"

"I don't know," I said, finally.

The English children in the front of the class—there were about eight or ten of them—giggled and twisted around in their chairs to look at me. I sat down quickly and opened my eyes very wide, hoping in that way to dry them off. The little girl with the braids put out her hand and very lightly touched my arm. She still didn't smile.

Most of that morning I was rather bored. I looked briefly at the children's drawings pinned to the wall, and then concentrated on a lizard clinging to the ledge of the high, barred window behind the teacher's head. Occasionally it would shoot out its long yellow tongue for a fly, and then it would rest, with its eyes closed and its belly palpitating, as though it were swallowing several times quickly. The lessons were mostly concerned with reading and writing and simple numbers—things that my mother had already taught me—and I paid very little attention.

The teacher wrote on the easel blackboard words like "bat" and "cat," which seemed babyish to me; only "apple" was new and incomprehensible.

When it was time for the lunch recess, I followed the girl with braids out onto the veranda. There the children from the other classes were assembled. I saw Premila at once and ran over to her, as she had charge of our lunchbox. The children were all opening packages and sitting down to eat sandwiches. Premila and I were the only ones who had Indian food—thin wheat chapatties, some vegetable curry, and a bottle of butter-milk. Premila thrust half of it into my hand and whispered fiercely that I should go and sit with my class, because that was what the others seemed to be doing.

The enormous black eyes of the little Indian girl from my class looked at my food longingly, so I offered her some. But she only shook her head and plowed her way solemnly through her sandwiches.

I was very sleepy after lunch, because at home we always took a siesta. It was usually a pleasant time of day, with the bedroom darkened against the harsh afternoon sun, the drifting off into sleep with the sound of Mother's voice reading a story in one's mind, and, finally, the shrill, fussy voice of the ayah[3] waking one for tea.

At school, we rested for a short time on low, folding cots on the veranda, and then we were expected to play games. During the hot part of the afternoon we played indoors, and after the shadows had begun to lengthen and the slight breeze of the eve-ning had come up we moved outside to the wide courtyard.

I had never really grasped the system of competitive games. At home, whenever we played tag or guessing games, I was al-ways allowed to "win"—"Because," Mother used to tell Premila, "she is the youngest, and we have to allow for that." I had of-ten heard her say it, and it seemed quite reasonable to me, but the result was that I had no idea of what "winning" meant.

When we played twos-and-threes that afternoon at school, in accordance with my training, I let one of the small English boys catch me, but was naturally rather puzzled when the other children did not return the courtesy. I ran about for what seemed like hours without ever catching anyone, until it was time for school to close. Much later I learned that my attitude

---

[3] *ayah* (ä′yə): maid or nurse.

was called "not being a good sport," and I stopped allowing myself to be caught, but it was not for years that I really learned
the spirit of the thing.

When I saw our car come up to the school gate, I broke
away from my classmates and rushed toward it yelling, "Ayah!
Ayah!" It seemed like an eternity since I had seen her that
morning—a wizened, affectionate figure in her white cotton sari,
giving me dozens of urgent and useless instructions on how to
be a good girl at school. Premila followed more sedately, and she
told me on the way home never to do that again in front of the
other children.

When we got home we went straight to Mother's high,

white room to have tea with her, and I immediately climbed onto the bed and bounced gently up and down on the springs. Mother asked how we had liked our first day in school. I was so pleased to be home and to have left that peculiar Cynthia behind that I had nothing whatever to say about school, except to ask what "apple" meant. But Premila told Mother about the classes, and added that in her class they had weekly tests to see if they had learned their lessons well.

I asked, "What's a test?"

Premila said, "You're too small to have them. You won't have them in your class for donkey's years." She had learned the expression that day and was using it for the first time. We all laughed enormously at her wit. She also told Mother, in an aside, that we should take sandwiches to school the next day. Not, she said, that *she* minded. But they would be simpler for me to handle.

That whole lovely evening I didn't think about school at all. I sprinted barefoot across the lawns with my favorite playmate, the cook's son, to the stream at the end of the garden. We quarreled in our usual way, waded in the tepid water under the lime trees, and waited for the night to bring out the smell of the jasmine. I listened with fascination to his stories of ghosts and demons, until I was too frightened to cross the garden alone in the semidarkness. The ayah found me, shouted at the cook's son, scolded me, hurried me in to supper—it was an entirely usual, wonderful evening.

It was a week later, the day of Premila's first test, that our lives changed rather abruptly. I was sitting at the back of my class in my usual inattentive way, only half listening to the teacher. I had started a rather guarded friendship with the girl with the braids, whose name turned out to be Nalini (Nancy, in school). The three other Indian children were already fast friends. Even at that age it was apparent to all of us that friendship with the English or Anglo-Indian children was out of the question. Occasionally, during the class, my new friend and I would draw pictures and show them to each other secretly.

The door opened sharply and Premila marched in. At first, the teacher smiled at her in a kindly and encouraging way and said, "Now, you're little Cynthia's sister?"

Premila didn't even look at her. She stood with her feet planted firmly apart and her shoulders rigid, and addressed herself directly to me. "Get up," she said. "We're going home."

I didn't know what had happened, but I was aware that it was a crisis of some sort. I rose obediently and started to walk toward my sister.

"Bring your pencils and your notebook," she said.

I went back for them, and together we left the room. The teacher started to say something just as Premila closed the door, but we didn't wait to hear what it was.

In complete silence we left the school grounds and started to walk home. Then I asked Premila what the matter was. All she would say was "We're going home for good."

It was a very tiring walk for a child of five and a half, and I dragged along behind Premila with my pencils growing sticky in my hand. I can still remember looking at the dusty hedges, and the tangles of thorns in the ditches by the side of the road, smelling the faint fragrance from the eucalyptus trees and wondering whether we would ever reach home. Occasionally a horse-drawn tonga passed us, and the women, in their pink or green silks, stared at Premila and me trudging along on the side of the road. A few coolies and a line of women carrying baskets of vegetables on their heads smiled at us. But it was nearing the hottest time of day, and the road was almost deserted. I walked more and more slowly, and shouted to Premila, from time to

time, "Wait for me!" with increasing peevishness. She spoke to me only once, and that was to tell me to carry my notebook on my head, because of the sun.

When we got to our house the ayah was just taking a tray of lunch into Mother's room. She immediately started a long, worried questioning about what are you children doing back here at this hour of the day.

Mother looked very startled and very concerned, and asked Premila what had happened.

Premila said, "We had our test today, and She made me and the other Indians sit at the back of the room, with a desk between each one."

Mother said, "Why was that, darling?"

"She said it was because Indians cheat," Premila added. "So I don't think we should go back to that school."

Mother looked very distant, and was silent a long time. At last she said, "Of course not, darling." She sounded displeased.

We all shared the curry she was having for lunch, and afterward I was sent off to the beautifully familiar bedroom for my siesta. I could hear Mother and Premila talking through the open door.

Mother said, "Do you suppose she understood all that?"

Premila said, "I shouldn't think so. She's a baby."

Mother said, "Well, I hope it won't bother her."

Of course, they were both wrong. I understood it perfectly, and I remember it all very clearly. But I put it happily away, because it had all happened to a girl called Cynthia, and I never was really particularly interested in her.

DISCUSSION

1. Why was Santha never particularly interested in "a girl called Cynthia"? Why has she remembered the incident all these years?

2. Although the teacher had been in India for fifteen years, she still called Indian children by English names. What does this tell you about her? Why did Santha say she didn't know her name (page 210)?

3. **Fiction** and **nonfiction.**   Fiction is prose writing about people and events created by an author's imagination. All the other selections in this unit are fiction. This selection is nonfiction. Nonfiction is prose writing about actual events and real people. Does the fact that this selection is nonfiction give it more impact? If so, how?

For further activities, see page 238.

My Grandmother Would Rock Quietly and Hum

LEONARD ADAMÉ

in her house
she would rock quietly and hum
until her swelled hands
calmed

in summer   5
she wore thick stockings
sweaters
and gray braids

(when el cheque came
we went to Payless   10
and I laughed greedily
when given a quarter)

mornings,
sunlight barely lit
the kitchen   15
and where
there were shadows
it was not cold

she quietly rolled
flour tortillas—   20
the papas
cracking in hot lard
would wake me

she had lost her teeth
and when we ate   25
she had bread
soaked in café

always her eyes
were clear
and she could see   30
as I cannot yet see—
through her eyes
she gave me herself

she would sit
and talk   35
of her girlhood—
of things strange to me:
    México
    epidemics
    relatives shot   40
    her father's hopes
    of this country—
how they sank
with cement dust
to his insides   45

now
when I go
to the old house
the worn spots
by the stove   50
echo of her shuffling
and
México
still hangs in her
fading   55
calendar pictures

21. *papas:* potatoes.

DISCUSSION The poet says "she could see / as I cannot yet see" (lines 30–31). What could Grandmother see? Find lines in the poem to support your answer. How much time has passed between the next-to-last and last stanzas? What has happened to Grandmother? What do you think the poet now sees?

Piñones

LEROY QUINTANA

when i was young
we would sit by
an old firewood stove
watching my grandmother make candy,
listening to the stories   5
my grandparents would tell
about "the old days"
                              and eat piñones

now we belong
to a supersonic age   10
and have college degrees.
we sit around color t.v. sets
watching the super bowl
listening to howard cosell,
stories of rioting, war, inflation   15
                              and eat piñones

Piñones: type of pine nut.

DISCUSSION   What has stayed the same for the poet and
what has changed? What is the signif-
icance of the last line in both stanzas? How
do you think the poet might feel about the
way things were and the ways things are?

THE PARSLEY GARDEN

WILLIAM SAROYAN

One day in August Al Condraj was wandering through Woolworth's without a penny to spend when he saw a small hammer
that was not a toy but a real hammer, and he was possessed with
a longing to have it. He believed it was just what he needed by
which to break the monotony and with which to make something.
He had gathered some firstclass nails from Foley's Packing House
where the boxmakers worked and where they had carelessly
dropped at least fifteen cents' worth. He had gladly gone to the
trouble of gathering them together because it had seemed to him
that a nail, as such, was not something to be wasted. He had the
nails, perhaps a half pound of them, at least two hundred of them,
in a paper bag in the apple box in which he kept his junk at
home.

Now, with the ten-cent hammer he believed he could make
something out of box wood and the nails, although he had no idea
what. Some sort of a table perhaps, or a small bench.

At any rate he took the hammer and slipped it into the
pocket of his overalls, but just as he did so a man took him firmly
by the arm without a word and pushed him to the back of the
store into a small office. Another man, an older one, was seated
behind a desk in the office, working with papers. The younger
man, the one who had captured him, was excited and his forehead
was covered with sweat.

"Well," he said, "here's one more of them."

The man behind the desk got to his feet and looked Al
Condraj up and down. "What's *he* swiped?"

"A hammer." The young man looked at Al with hatred.
"Hand it over," he said.

The boy brought the hammer out of his pocket and handed it
to the young man, who said, "I ought to hit you over the head
with it, that's what I ought to do."

He turned to the older man, the boss, the manager of the
store, and he said, "What do you want me to do with him?"

"Leave him with me," the older man said.

The younger man stepped out of the office, and the older man
sat down and went back to work. Al Condraj stood in the office
fifteen minutes before the older man looked at him again.

"Well," he said.

Al didn't know what to say. The man wasn't looking at him, he was looking at the door.

Finally Al said, "I didn't mean to steal it. I just need it and I haven't got any money."

"Just because you haven't got any money doesn't mean you've got a right to steal things," the man said. "Now, does it?"

"No, sir."

"Well, what am I going to do with you? Turn you over to the police?"

Al didn't say anything, but he certainly didn't want to be turned over to the police. He hated the man, but at the same time he realized somebody else could be a lot tougher than he was being.

"If I let you go, will you promise never to steal from this store again?"

"Yes, sir."

"All right," the man said. "Go out this way and don't come

back to this store until you've got some money to spend."

He opened a door to the hall that led to the alley, and Al Condraj hurried down the hall and out into the alley.

The first thing he did when he was free was laugh, but he knew he had been humiliated, and he was deeply ashamed. It was not in his nature to take things that did not belong to him. He hated the young man who had caught him, and he hated the manager of the store who had made him stand in silence in the office so long. He hadn't liked it at all when the young man had said he ought to hit him over the head with the hammer.

He should have had the courage to look him straight in the eye and say, "You and who else?"

Of course he *had* stolen the hammer and he had been caught, but it seemed to him he oughtn't to have been so humiliated.

After he had walked three blocks, he decided he didn't want to go home just yet, so he turned around and started walking back to town. He almost believed he meant to go back and say something to the young man who had caught him. And then he wasn't sure he didn't mean to go back and steal the hammer again, and this time *not* get caught. As long as he had been made to feel like a thief anyway, the least he ought to get out of it was the hammer.

Outside the store he lost his nerve, though. He stood in the street, looking in, for at least ten minutes.

Then, crushed and confused and now bitterly ashamed of himself, first for having stolen something, then for having been caught, then for having been humiliated, then for not having guts enough to go back and do the job right, he began walking home again, his mind so troubled that he didn't greet his pal Pete Wawchek when they came face to face outside Graf's Hardware.

When he got home, he was too ashamed to go inside and examine his junk, so he had a long drink of water from the faucet in the back yard. The faucet was used by his mother to water the stuff she planted every year: okra, bell peppers, tomatoes, cucumbers, onions, garlic, mint, eggplants, and parsley.

His mother called the whole business the parsley garden, and every night in the summer she would bring chairs out of the house and put them around the table she had had Ondro, the neighborhood handyman, make for her for fifteen cents, and she would sit at the table and enjoy the cool of the garden and the smell of the things she had planted and tended.

Sometimes she would even make a salad and moisten the flat old-country bread and slice some white cheese, and she and he would have supper in the parsley garden. After supper she would attach the water hose to the faucet and water her plants and the place would be cooler than ever and it would smell real good, real fresh and cool and green, all the different growing things making a green-garden smell out of themselves and the air and the water.

After the long drink of water he sat down where the parsley itself was growing, and he pulled a handful of it out and slowly ate it. Then he went inside and told his mother what had happened. He even told her what he had *thought* of doing after he had been turned loose: to go back and steal the hammer again.

"I don't want you to steal," his mother said in broken English. "Here is ten cents. You go back to that man and you give him this money and you bring it home, that hammer."

"No," Al Condraj said. "I won't take your money for something I don't really need. I just thought I ought to have a hammer, so I could make something if I felt like it. I've got a lot of nails and some box wood, but I haven't got a hammer."

"Go buy it, that hammer," his mother said.

"No," Al said.

"All right," his mother said. "Shut up."

That's what she always said when she didn't know what else to say.

Al went out and sat on the steps. His humiliation was beginning to really hurt now. He decided to wander off along the railroad tracks to Foley's because he needed to think about it some more. At Foley's he watched Johnny Gale nailing boxes for ten minutes, but Johnny was too busy to notice him or talk to him, although one day at Sunday school, two or three years ago, Johnny had greeted him and said, "How's the boy?" Johnny worked with a boxmaker's hatchet, and everybody in Fresno said he was the fastest boxmaker in town. He was the closest thing to a machine any packing house ever saw. Foley himself was proud of Johnny Gale.

Al Condraj finally set out for home because he didn't want to get in the way. He didn't want somebody working hard to notice that he was being watched and maybe say to him, "Go on, beat it." He didn't want Johnny Gale to do something like that. He didn't want to invite another humiliation.

On the way home he looked for money, but all he found was

the usual pieces of broken glass and rusty nails, the things that were always cutting his bare feet every summer.

When he got home, his mother had made a salad and set the table, so he sat down to eat, but when he put the food in his mouth he just didn't care for it. He got up and went into the three-room house and got his apple box out of the corner of his room and went through his junk. It was all there, the same as yesterday.

He wandered off back to town and stood in front of the closed store, hating the young man who had caught him, and then he went along to the Hippodrome and looked at the display photographs from the two movies that were being shown that day.

Then he went along to the public library to have a look at all the books again, but he didn't like any of them, so he wandered around town some more and then around half-past eight he went home and went to bed.

His mother had already gone to bed because she had to be up at five to go to work at Inderrieden's, packing figs. Some days there would be work all day, some days there would be only half a day of it, but whatever his mother earned during the summer had to keep them the whole year.

He didn't sleep much that night because he couldn't get over what had happened, and he went over six or seven ways by which to adjust the matter. He went so far as to believe it would be necessary to kill the young man who had caught him. He also believed it would be necessary for him to steal systematically and successfully the rest of his life. It was a hot night and he couldn't sleep.

Finally, his mother got up and walked barefooted to the kitchen for a drink of water, and on the way back she said to him softly, "Shut up."

When she got up at five in the morning, he was out of the house, but that had happened many times before. He was a restless boy, and he kept moving all the time every summer. He was making mistakes and paying for them, and he had just tried stealing and had been caught at it, and he was troubled. She fixed her breakfast, packed her lunch, and hurried off to work, hoping it would be a full day.

It was a full day, and then there was overtime, and although she had no more lunch, she decided to work on for the extra money, anyway. Almost all the other packers were staying on, too, and

her neighbor across the alley, Leeza Ahboot, who worked beside
her, said, "Let us work until the work stops, then we'll go home
and fix a supper between us and eat it in your parsley garden
where it's so cool. It's a hot day and there's no sense not making
an extra fifty or sixty cents."

When the two women reached the garden, it was almost nine
o'clock, but still daylight, and she saw her son nailing pieces of
box wood together, making something with a hammer. It looked
like a bench. He had already watered the garden and tidied up the
rest of the yard, and the place seemed very nice, and her son
seemed very serious and busy. She and Leeza went straight to
work for their supper, picking bell peppers and tomatoes and cucumbers and a great deal of parsley for the salad.

Then Leeza went to her house for some bread, which she had
baked the night before, and some white cheese, and in a few minutes they were having supper together and talking pleasantly
about the successful day they had had. After supper they made
Turkish coffee over an open fire in the yard. They drank the coffee and smoked a cigarette apiece, and told one another stories
about their experiences in the old country and here in Fresno, and
then they looked into their cups at the grounds to see if any good
fortune was indicated, and there was: health and work and supper
out of doors in the summer and enough money for the rest of the
year.

Al Condraj worked and overheard some of the things they
said, and then Leeza went home to go to bed, and his mother said,
"Where you get it, that hammer, Al?"

"I got it at the store."

"How you get it? You steal it?"

Al Condraj finished the bench and sat on it. "No," he said. "I
didn't steal it."

"How you get it?"

"I worked at the store for it," Al said.

"The store where you steal it yesterday?"

"Yes."

"Who give you job?"

"The boss."

"What you do?"

"I carried different stuff to the different counters."

"Well, that's good," the woman said.

"How long you work for that little hammer?"

"I worked all day," Al said. "Mr. Clemmer gave me the hammer after I'd worked one hour, but I went right on working. The fellow who caught me yesterday showed me what to do, and we worked together. We didn't talk, but at the end of the day he took me to Mr. Clemmer's office, and he told Mr. Clemmer that I'd worked hard all day and ought to be paid at least a dollar."

"That's good," the woman said.

"So Mr. Clemmer put a silver dollar on his desk for me, and then the fellow who caught me yesterday told him the store needed a boy like me every day, for a dollar a day, and Mr. Clemmer said I could have the job."

"That's good," the woman said. "You can make it a little money for yourself."

"I left the dollar on Mr. Clemmer's desk," Al Condraj said, "and I told them both I didn't want the job."

"Why you say that?" the woman said. "Dollar a day for eleven-year-old boy good money. Why you not take job?"

"Because I hate the both of them," the boy said. "I would never work for people like that. I just looked at them and picked up my hammer and walked out. I came home and I made this bench."

"All right," his mother said. "Shut up."

His mother went inside and went to bed, but Al Condraj sat on the bench he had made and smelled the parsley garden and didn't feel humiliated any more.

But nothing could stop him from hating the two men, even though he knew they hadn't done anything they shouldn't have done.

DISCUSSION

1. Al certainly could have used the job he was offered; his family was poor and his mother worked hard to support them. Why did he refuse the job?

2. Why didn't Al accept his mother's dime and buy the hammer?

3. Al knew that stealing was wrong and that Mr. Clemmer had not been as severe with him as someone else might have been. But still he hated Mr. Clemmer. Why?

For further activities, see page 238.

The Rising of the Moon

LADY GREGORY

CHARACTERS   SERGEANT   POLICEMAN B
                  POLICEMAN X   A RAGGED MAN

SCENE   Side of a quay in a seaport town. Some posts and chains. A large barrel. Enter three Policemen. Moonlight. Sergeant, who is older than the others, crosses the stage to right and looks down steps. The others put down a paste-pot and unroll a bundle of placards.

POLICEMAN B: I think this would be a good place to put up a notice. [He points to barrel.]

POLICEMAN X: Better ask him. [Calls to Sergeant.] Will this be a good place for a placard? [No answer.]

POLICEMAN B: Will we put up a notice here on the barrel? [No answer.]

SERGEANT: There's a flight of steps here that leads to the water. This is a place that should be minded well. If he got down here, his friends might have a boat to meet him; they might send it in here from outside.

POLICEMAN B: Would the barrel be a good place to put a notice up?

SERGEANT: It might; you can put it there. [They paste the notice up. Reading it.] Dark hair, dark eyes, smooth face, height: five feet five—there's not much to take hold of in that. It's a pity I had no chance of seeing him before he broke out of jail. They say he's a wonder, that it's he makes all the plans for the whole organization. There isn't another man in Ireland would have broken jail the way he did. He must have some friends among the jailers.

POLICEMAN B: A hundred pounds is little enough for the government to offer for him. You may be sure any man in the force that takes him will get promotion.

SERGEANT: I'll mind this place myself. I wouldn't wonder at all if he came this way. He might come slipping along there [points to side of quay], and his friends might be waiting for him there [points down steps], and once he got away it's little chance we'd have of finding him; it's maybe under a load of kelp he'd be in a fishing boat, and not one to help a married man that wants it to the reward.

POLICEMAN X: And if we get him itself, nothing but abuse on our heads for it from the people, and maybe from our own relations.

SERGEANT: Well, we have to do our duty in the force. Haven't we the whole country depending on us to keep law and order? It's those that are down would be up and those that are up would be down, if it wasn't for us. Well, hurry on, you have plenty of other places to placard yet, and come back here then to me. You can take the lantern. Don't be too long now. It's very lonesome here with nothing but the moon.

POLICEMAN B: It's a pity we can't stop with you. The government should have brought more police into the town, with him in jail, and at assize[1] time too. Well, good luck to your watch. [They go out.]

SERGEANT [walks up and down once or twice and looks at placard]: A hundred pounds and promotion sure. There must be a great deal of spending in a hundred pounds. It's a pity some honest man not to be the better of that.

A Ragged Man appears at left and tries to slip past. Sergeant suddenly turns.

Where are you going?

MAN: I'm a poor ballad singer, your honor. I thought to sell some of these [holds out bundle of ballads] to the sailors. [He goes on.]

SERGEANT: Stop! Didn't I tell you to stop? You can't go on there.

MAN: Oh, very well. It's a hard thing to be poor. All the world's against the poor.

SERGEANT: Who are you?

MAN: You'd be as wise as myself if I told you, but I don't mind. I'm one Jimmy Walsh, a ballad singer.

SERGEANT: Jimmy Walsh? I don't know that name.

MAN: Ah, sure, they know it well enough in Ennis. Were you ever in Ennis, Sergeant?

SERGEANT: What brought you here?

MAN: Sure, it's to the assizes I came, thinking I might make a few shillings here to there. It's in the one train with the judges I came.

SERGEANT: Well, if you came so far, you may as well go farther, for you'll walk out of this.

MAN: I will, I will; I'll just go on where I was going. [Goes towards steps.]

SERGEANT: Come back from those steps; no one has leave to pass down them tonight.

MAN: I'll just sit on the top of the steps till I see will some sailor buy a ballad off me that would give me my supper. They do be late going back to the ship. It's often I saw them in Cork carried down the quay in a hand-cart.

SERGEANT: Move on, I tell you. I won't have anyone lingering about the quay tonight.

MAN: Well, I'll go. It's the poor have the hard life! Maybe yourself might like one, Sergeant. Here's a good sheet now. [Turns one over.] "Content and a Pipe"—that's not much. "The Peeler[2] and the Goat"—you wouldn't like that. "Johnny Hart"—that's a lovely song.

---

[1] *assize* (ə-sīz'): Assizes are special court sessions held at fixed times in British counties.

[2] *Peeler:* policeman. Robert Peel, British statesman, founded the Irish and British police force.

SERGEANT: Move on.

MAN: Ah, wait till you hear it. [Sings]

> "There was a rich farmer's
> daughter lived near the town of
> Ross;
> She courted a Highland soldier,
> his name was Johnny Hart;
> Says the mother to her daughter,
> 'I'll go distracted mad
> If you marry that Highland sol-
> dier dressed up in Highland
> plaid.' "

SERGEANT: Where are you going?

MAN: Sure you told me to be going,
and I'm going.

SERGEANT: Don't be a fool. I didn't tell
you to go that way; I told you to
go back to the town.

MAN: Back to the town, is it?

SERGEANT [taking him by the shoulder and
shoving him before him]: Here, I'll
show you the way. Be off with
you. What are you stopping for?

MAN [who has been keeping his eye on the notice; points to it]: I think I know
what you're waiting for, Sergeant.

SERGEANT: What's that to you?

MAN: And I know well the man you're
waiting for—I know him well—
I'll be going. [He shuffles on.]

SERGEANT: You know him? Come back
here. What sort is he?

MAN: Come back is it, Sergeant? Do
you want to have me killed?

SERGEANT: Why do you say that?

MAN: Never mind. I'm going. I
wouldn't be in your shoes if the
reward was ten times as much.
[Goes offstage to left.] Not if it was
ten times as much.

SERGEANT [rushing after him]: Come back
here, come back. [Drags him back.]
What sort is he? Where did you
see him?

MAN: I saw him in my own place, in
the County Clare. I tell you, you
wouldn't like to be looking at
him. You'd be afraid to be in the
one place with him. There isn't a
weapon he doesn't know the use
of, and as to strength, his
muscles are as hard as that
board. [Slaps barrel.]

SERGEANT: Is he as bad as that?

MAN: He is then.

SERGEANT: Do you tell me so?

MAN: There was a poor man in our
place, a sergeant from Bal-
lyvaughan—it was with a lump
of stone he did it.

SERGEANT: I never heard of that.

MAN: And you wouldn't, Sergeant. It's
not everything that happens gets
into the papers. And there was a
policeman in plain clothes, too. It
is in Limerick he was. It was after the time of the attack on the
police barrack at Kilmallock.
Moonlight . . . just like this . . .
waterside. Nothing was known
for certain.

SERGEANT: Do you say so? It's a terrible
country to belong to.

MAN: That's so, indeed! You might be
standing there, looking out that
way, thinking you saw him coming up this side of the quay
[points], and he might be coming
up this other side [points], and
he'd be on you before you knew
where you were.

SERGEANT: It's a whole troop of police they ought to put here to stop a man like that.

MAN: But if you'd like me to stop with you, I could be looking down this side. I could be sitting up here on this barrel.

SERGEANT: And you know him well, too?

MAN: I'd know him a mile off, Sergeant.

SERGEANT: But you wouldn't want to share the reward?

MAN: Is it a poor man like me, that has to be going the roads and singing in fairs, to have the name on him that he took a reward? But you don't want me. I'll be safer in the town.

SERGEANT: Well, you can stop.

MAN [getting up on barrel]: All right, Sergeant. I wonder, now, you're not tired out, Sergeant, walking up and down the way you are.

SERGEANT: If I'm tired, I'm used to it.

MAN: You might have hard work before you tonight yet. Take it easy while you can. There's plenty of room up here on the barrel, and you can see farther when you're higher up.

SERGEANT: Maybe so. [Gets up beside him on barrel, facing right. They sit back to back, looking different ways.] You made me feel a bit queer with the way you talked.

MAN: Give me a match, Sergeant. [He gives it, and Man lights pipe.] Take a draw yourself? It'll quiet you. Wait now till I give you a light, but you needn't turn around.

Don't take your eye off the quay for the life of you.

SERGEANT: Never fear, I won't. [Lights pipe. They both smoke.] Indeed, it's a hard thing to be in the force, out at night and no thanks for it, for all the danger we're in. And it's little we get but abuse from the people, and no choice but to obey our orders, and never asked when a man is sent into danger, if you are a married man with a family.

MAN [sings]:

"As through the hills I walked to view the hills and shamrock plain,
I stood awhile where nature smiles to view the rocks and streams.
On a matron fair I fixed my eyes, beneath a fertile vale,
As she sang her song; it was on the wrong of poor old Granuaile."[3]

SERGEANT: Stop that; that's no song to be singing in these times.

MAN: Ah, Sergeant, I was only singing to keep my heart up. It sinks when I think of him. To think of us two sitting here, and he creeping up the quay, maybe, to get to us.

SERGEANT: Are you keeping a good lookout?

MAN: I am; and for no reward too. Amn't I the foolish man? But when I saw a man in trouble, I never could help trying to get

---

[3] *Granuaile* (grăn'vāl): English form of a Gaelic word meaning love and used as a symbol of Ireland.

him out of it. What's that? Did something hit me? [Rubs his heart.]

SERGEANT [patting him on the shoulder]: You will get your reward in heaven.

MAN: I know that, I know that, Sergeant, but life is precious.

SERGEANT: Well, you can sing if it gives you more courage.

MAN [sings]:

"Her head was bare, her hands and feet with iron bands were bound,
Her pensive strain and plaintive wail mingled with the evening gale,
And the song she sang with mournful air, 'I am old Granuaile.'
Her lips so sweet that monarchs kissed—"

SERGEANT: That's not it. "Her gown she wore was stained with gore."
That's it—you missed that.

MAN: You're right, Sergeant, so it is; I missed it. [Repeats line.] But to think of a man like you knowing a song like that.

SERGEANT: There's many a thing a man might know and might not have any wish for.

MAN: Now, I daresay, Sergeant, in your youth you used to be sitting up on a wall, the way you are sitting up on this barrel now, and the other lads beside you, and you singing "Granuaile"?

SERGEANT: I did then.

MAN: And the "Shan Bhean Bhocht"?[4]

SERGEANT: I did then.

MAN: And the "Green on the Cape"?

SERGEANT: That was one of them.

MAN: And maybe the man you are watching for tonight used to be sitting on the wall when he was

[4] *Shan Bhean Bhocht* (shä văn vŏcht): literally, "poor old woman."

young, and singing those same songs. It's a queer world.

SERGEANT: Whisht! I think I see something coming—it's only a dog.

MAN: And isn't it a queer world? Maybe it's one of the boys you used to be singing with that time you will be arresting today or tomorrow, and sending into the dock.[5]

SERGEANT: That's true indeed.

MAN: And maybe one night, after you had been singing, if the other boys had told you some plan they had, some plan to free the country, you might have joined with them—and maybe it is you might be in trouble now.

SERGEANT: Well, who knows but I might? I had a great spirit in those days.

MAN: It's a queer world, Sergeant, and it's little any mother knows when she sees her child creeping on the floor what might happen to it before it has gone through its life, or who will be who in the end.

SERGEANT: That's a queer thought now and a true thought. Wait now till I think it out. If it wasn't for the sense I have, and for my wife and family, and for me joining the force the time I did, it might be myself now would be after breaking jail and hiding in the dark, and it might be him that's hiding in the dark and that got out of jail would be sitting up where I am on this barrel. And it might be myself would be creeping up trying to make my escape from himself, and it might be himself would be keeping the law, and myself would be breaking it, and myself would be trying maybe to put a bullet in his head, or to take up a lump of a stone the way you said he did— no, that myself did. Oh! [Gasps. After a pause.] What's that? [Grasps Man's arm.]

MAN [jumps off barrel and listens, looking out over water]: It's nothing, Sergeant.

SERGEANT: I thought it might be a boat. I had a notion there might be friends of his coming about the quays with a boat.

MAN: Sergeant, I am thinking it was with the people you were, and not with the law you were, when you were a young man.

SERGEANT: Well, if I was foolish then, that time's gone.

MAN: Maybe, Sergeant, it comes into your head sometimes, in spite of your belt and your tunic, that it might have been as well for you to have followed Granuaile.

SERGEANT: It's no business of yours what I think.

MAN: Maybe, Sergeant, you'll be on the side of the country yet.

SERGEANT [gets off barrel]: Don't talk to me like that. I have my duties and I know them. [Looks round.] That was a boat; I hear the oars. [Goes to the steps and looks down.]

MAN [sings]:

"O, then, tell me, Shawn O'Farrel,

---

[5] *dock:* place where a prisoner stands in a courtroom.

Where the gathering is to be.
In the old spot by the river
Right well known to you and
    me!"

SERGEANT: Stop that! Stop that, I tell
    you!

MAN [sings louder]:

"One word more, for signal token,
    Whistle up the marching tune,
    With your pike upon your shoul-
        der,
    At the Rising of the Moon."

SERGEANT: If you don't stop that, I'll
    arrest you. [A whistle from below an-
    swers, repeating the air.] That's a sig-
    nal. [Stands between him and steps.]
    You must not pass this way. Step
    farther back. Who are you? You
    are no ballad singer.

MAN: You needn't ask who I am; that
    placard will tell you. [Points to plac-
    ard.]

SERGEANT: You are the man I am look-
    ing for.

MAN: [takes off hat and wig; Sergeant seizes
    them]: I am. There's a hundred
    pounds on my head. There is a
    friend of mine below in a boat.
    He knows a safe place to bring
    me to.

SERGEANT [looking still at hat and wig]: It's a
    pity! It's a pity. You deceived me
    well.

MAN: I am a friend of Granuaile. There
    is a hundred pounds on my head.

SERGEANT: It's a pity, it's a pity!

MAN: Will you let me pass, or must I
    make you let me?

SERGEANT: I am in the force. I will not
    let you pass.

MAN: I thought to do it with my
    tongue. [Puts hand on breast.] What
    is that?

Voice of POLICEMAN X outside: Here, this is
    where we left him.

SERGEANT: It's my comrades coming.

MAN: You won't betray me—the friend
    of Granuaile. [Slips behind barrel.]

Voice of POLICEMAN B: That was the last of
    the placards.

POLICEMAN X [as they come in]: If he makes
    his escape, it won't be unknown
    he'll make it.

Sergeant puts hat and wig behind his back.

POLICEMAN B: Did anyone come this
    way?

SERGEANT [after a pause]: No one.

POLICEMAN B: No one at all?

SERGEANT: No one at all.

POLICEMAN B: We had no orders to go
    back to the station; we can stop
    along with you.

SERGEANT: I don't want you. There is
    nothing for you to do here.

POLICEMAN B: You bade us to come back
    here and keep watch with you.

SERGEANT: I'd sooner be alone. Would
    any man come this way and you
    making all that talk? It is better
    the place be quiet.

POLICEMAN B: Well, we'll leave you the
    lantern anyhow. [Hands it to him.]

SERGEANT: I don't want it. Bring it with
    you.

POLICEMAN B: You might want it. There
    are clouds coming up and you
    have the darkness of the night
    before you yet. I'll leave it over
    here on the barrel. [Goes to barrel.]

SERGEANT: Bring it with you, I tell you.
    No more talk.

POLICEMAN B: Well, I thought it might be a comfort to you. I often think when I have it in my hand and can be flashing it about into every dark corner [doing so] that it's the same as being beside the fire at home, and the bits of bogwood blazing up now and again.[Flashes it about, now on the barrel, now on Sergeant.]

SERGEANT [furious]: Be off the two of you, yourselves and your lantern! [They go out. Man comes from behind barrel. He and Sergeant stand looking at one another.] What are you waiting for?

MAN: For my hat, of course, and my wig. You wouldn't wish me to get my death of cold? [Sergeant gives them. Going towards steps.] Well, good night, comrade, and thank you. You did me a good turn tonight, and I'm obliged to you. Maybe I'll be able to do as much for you when the small rise up and the big fall down . . . when we all change places at the Rising [waves his hand and disappears] of the Moon.

SERGEANT [turning his back to audience and reading placard]: A hundred pounds reward! A hundred pounds! [Turns towards audience.] I wonder now, am I as great a fool as I think I am?

CURTAIN

DISCUSSION

1. "Did anyone come this way?" Policeman B asks the sergeant. The sergeant pauses before answering. What do you suppose flashes through his mind during that pause?

2. Four times during their meeting, the hunted man interrupts his conversation to sing bits from popular Irish ballads. What is his reason for doing that? What effect do the songs have upon the sergeant?

3. Why did the playwright have the sergeant ask the audience a question at the end of the play? How would you answer the sergeant's question? Why?

4. **Climax.** The high point in the action of a play or story is called the climax. It is the decisive moment in the **plot** (see page 31). Before the climax, the plot may develop in many ways. But when the climax is reached, only one logical ending is possible. Think about the end of the play. Then review what has happened from the beginning. Where is the climax?

For further activities, see page 238.

VOCABULARY

By Any Other Name (page 208)

An antonym is a word whose meaning is the opposite of the meaning of another word. For example, *hot* and *cold* are antonyms. To the left below are six words from "By Any Other Name." Match each word with the correct antonym in the right-hand column.

provincial — involved
valid — gently
detached — cosmopolitan
palpitating — false
fiercely — still
sedately — excitedly

The Rising of the Moon (page 229)

In the Irish expressions of the characters in "The Rising of the Moon" there are certain distinctive ways of putting words together. Rewrite each of the following phrases in the way that would be natural in your speech.

1. it's he makes all the plans
2. it's little chance we'd have of finding him
3. sure, it's to the assizes
4. till I see will some sailor buy a ballad off me
5. no, that myself did

COMPOSITION

By Any Other Name (page 208)

Assume that you are going to conduct an interview for your school paper with an Indian student who has been placed in your class. Write ten questions that you feel would help you learn the most about the Indian student's experiences. Be sure to phrase your questions so that the student won't answer merely *yes* or *no.*

The Rising of the Moon (page 229)

If it became known that the sergeant did not arrest the hunted man when he had the chance, the sergeant might have to explain his actions. Write the explanation you think he might give to his superior officer.

READING

The Parsley Garden (page 220)

On separate paper, write the item that best completes each statement.

1. Al's mother said "Shut up"
   a. every time she talked to Al
   b. whenever she didn't know what else to say
   c. at the end of every conversation
   d. only when she was tired

2. Al hated the two men at Woolworth's because they
   a. were both mean to him
   b. had hit him hard
   c. had spoken unkindly to his mother
   d. had caught him stealing the hammer

3. Al probably would not have been so humiliated if he
   a. hadn't known that he was doing something wrong
   b. hadn't cried at the store
   c. hadn't been taken to the police
   d. hadn't been made to work to pay off his debt

4. Al got the hammer for working at Woolworth's for one hour, but he worked a full day without pay because he wanted
   a. to regain the manager's confidence
   b. to please his mother
   c. to regain his own self-respect
   d. to impress the young man who caught him

The Rising of the Moon (page 229)

Place the following items in the order in which they occurred in the play.

1. The sergeant tries to get the man to move on.
2. The man identifies himself as Jimmy Walsh, a ballad singer.
3. The sergeant realizes who the man really is.
4. The policemen paste up a placard of the wanted man.
5. The man begins to sing Irish ballads.

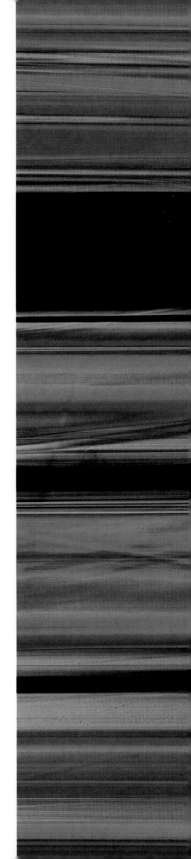

COMPOSITION

**KINDS OF
SENTENCES**

Sentences may be classified as simple, compound, or complex. A *simple* sentence has a subject and a verb: "Ma put her arms around me." "Ma" is the subject, and "put" is the verb. But if the sentence contains a subject and a verb, then a coordinate conjunction (page 170) such as *and* or *but* introducing another subject and verb, the sentence is *compound,* compounding or joining two ideas of equal importance: "The interpreter mumbled, and my Indian aunt sat cautiously on a needlepoint chair."

If one of the two ideas is subordinated, by means of a subordinate conjunction such as *although* or *if* or *because* or *when* the result is a *complex* sentence: "I was lurking in the hall when Ma went in."

Writers may—and should—use all three of those kinds of sentences to give their prose variety and emphasis. But there are other ways to classify sentences. Some sentences (called *declarative* sentences) make, or declare, statements: "I don't like her." Others (called *interrogative* sentences) ask questions: "What happened to him?" Still others (*exclamatory* sentences) exclaim: "She's gone out the window!"

Sentences may be *long* ("And after one brief moment's hesitation, Bessie went into her arms, and Mary kissed her sun-dark, weathered cheek."). Or they may be *short* ("Bessie spoke."). They may be *specific* ("She could butcher meats or tan hides or make tepees.") or *general* ("Her skills were useless and unwanted there."). They may be *abstract,* dealing purely with ideas: "There was so much suffering and fear—and joy and triumph, too." Or they may be *concrete,* mentioning what can be seen and touched: "We found weathered bones near a little spring."

The combinations of all those varieties are almost endless. Don't fall into the habit of writing the same kinds of sentences again and again. For emphasis, do you think to write an idea occasionally as a question? Compound sentences are sometimes effective, and you should use them. Make some sentences short. And if you want to help your reader understand what is important, place less important ideas in subordinate positions. In all these ways, you will be able to put stress where you want it and keep your reader interested in what you are writing.

ABOUT THE SELECTIONS

1.   Which person in this section do you feel you *understand* best? You may not *like* that person best, but you do feel that you can understand why he or she behaves in such-and-such a way. In a paragraph or two, try to account for that understanding. What is there about the person's identity— age, sex, intelligence, place of residence, or other factors—that may explain why you understand him or her as you do?

2.   Choose one of the following:

   a.   Using "Piñones" (page 219) as a model, write a brief poem of two stanzas that evoke two different moments—one past, one present—in your life. Select details to make contrasts between the two moments clear, but join the two moments by some one detail (like the piñones) that they have in common.

   b.   Think of a moment in your own life that was as unexpectedly filled with joy as is the moment in "First Song" (page 189). Then in a brief poem create the moment for your reader.

3.   Bessie, the lost sister (page 192), taken from her family as a child, raised in a different culture entirely, was returned to her home forty years later as a stranger. How much of what we are depends on where we live? In a page or so, consider which is more important in determining who a person is: where he or she lives (environment), or what he or she is born with (heredity). Use examples from this section, and from your own experience, to make your opinion persuasive.

ON YOUR OWN

1.   You are many things to many people—student, friend, brother or sister, daughter or son, customer, future voter, neighbor. But which is the real you? As fairly and specifically as possible, describe your real identity.

2.   Observe yourself after the passage of three years. In a clear composition of two or three paragraphs describe yourself as you were in the sixth grade. Write as though you are describing someone else— accurately, but honestly and without emotion. How did that sixth-grader look and behave?

3.   What you want to become is part of what you are. Specifically, explain what you want to make of your life. Be reasonable, but don't underestimate either your capabilities or your opportunities.

4.   Rewrite the following sentences in ways that make for more variety and that put emphasis on what is important:

   The man worked alone for half an hour. He was fixing the rusted rails. Meanwhile, the woman and the boy ran along the shore. They came back with a dozen dripping shells. They also had some beautiful pink pebbles. Then the boy sat and did homework. His mother helped him. He worked on a pad. He used a pencil. At high noon the man came down. He had taken off his coat. He had thrown his tie aside. The three of them drank orange pop. They watched the bubbles in the bottles. Everything was very quiet.

MYSTERY

THE LANDLADY

ROALD DAHL

Billy Weaver had traveled down from London on the slow afternoon train, with a change at Bristol on the way, and by the time he got to Bath it was about nine o'clock in the evening and the moon was coming up out of a clear starry sky over the houses opposite the station entrance. But the air was deadly cold and the wind was like a flat blade of ice on his cheeks.

"Excuse me," he said, "but is there a fairly cheap hotel not too far away from here?"

"Try The Bell and Dragon," the porter answered, pointing down the road. "They might take you in. It's about a quarter of a mile along on the other side."

Billy thanked him and picked up his suitcase and set out to walk the quarter-mile to The Bell and Dragon. He had never been to Bath before. He didn't know anyone who lived there. But Mr. Greenslade at the Head Office in London had told him it was a splendid town. "Find your own lodgings," he had said, "and then go along and report to the Branch Manager as soon as you've got yourself settled."

Billy was seventeen years old. He was wearing a new navy blue overcoat, a new brown trilby hat, and a new brown suit, and he was feeling fine. He walked briskly down the street. He was trying to do everything briskly these days. Briskness, he had decided, was *the* one common characteristic of all successful businessmen. The big shots up at Head Office were absolutely fantastically brisk all the time. They were amazing.

There were no shops on this wide street that he was walking along, only a line of tall houses on each side, all of them identical. They had porches and pillars and four or five steps going up to their front doors, and it was obvious that once upon a time they had been very swanky residences. But now, even in the darkness, he could see that the paint was peeling from the woodwork on their doors and windows, and that the handsome white façades[1] were cracked and blotchy from neglect.

Suddenly, in a downstairs window that was brilliantly illuminated by a street lamp not six yards away, Billy caught sight of a printed notice propped up against the glass in one of the upper panes. It said BED AND BREAKFAST. There was a vase of pussy willows, tall and beautiful, standing just underneath the notice.

He stopped walking. He moved a bit closer. Green curtains (some sort of velvety material) were hanging down on either side of the window. The pussy willows looked wonderful beside them. He went right up and

[1] *façades* (fə-säds'): the faces or fronts of buildings.

peered through the glass into the room, and the first thing he saw was a bright fire burning in the hearth. On the carpet in front of the fire, a pretty little dachshund was curled up asleep with its nose tucked into its belly. The room itself, so far as he could see in the half-darkness, was filled with pleasant furniture. There was a baby-grand piano and a big sofa and several plump armchairs; and in one corner he spotted a large parrot in a cage. Animals were usually a good sign in a place like this, Billy told himself; and all in all, it looked to him as though it would be a pretty decent house to stay in. Certainly it would be more comfortable than The Bell and Dragon.

On the other hand, a pub would be more congenial than a boarding house. There would be beer and darts in the evenings, and lots of people to talk to, and it would probably be a good bit cheaper, too. He had stayed a couple of nights in a pub once before and he had liked it. He had never stayed in any boarding houses, and, to be perfectly honest, he was a tiny bit frightened of them. The name itself conjured up images of watery cabbage, rapacious landladies, and a powerful smell of kippers in the living room.

After dithering about like this in the cold for two or three minutes, Billy decided that he would walk on and take a look at The Bell and Dragon before making up his mind. He turned to go.

And now a queer thing happened to him. He was in the act of

stepping back and turning away from the window when all at once his eye was caught and held in the most peculiar manner by the small notice that was there. BED AND BREAKFAST, it said. BED AND BREAKFAST, BED AND BREAKFAST, BED AND BREAKFAST. Each word was like a large black eye staring at him through the glass, holding him, compelling him, forcing him to stay where he was and not to walk away from that house, and the next thing he knew, he was actually moving across from the window to the front door of the house, climbing the steps that led up to it, and reaching for the bell.

He pressed the bell. Far away in a back room he heard it ringing, and then *at once*—it must have been at once because he hadn't even had time to take his finger from the bell button—the door swung open and a woman was standing there.

Normally, you ring the bell and you have at least a half-minute's wait before the door opens. But this dame was like a jack-in-the-box. He pressed the bell—and out she popped! It made him jump.

She was about forty-five or fifty years old, and the moment she saw him, she gave him a warm welcoming smile.

"*Please* come in," she said pleasantly. She stepped aside, holding the door wide open, and Billy found himself automatically starting forward into the house. The compulsion or, more accurately, the desire to follow after her into that house was extraordinarily strong.

"I saw the notice in the window," he said, holding himself back.

"Yes, I know."

"I was wondering about a room."

"It's *all* ready for you, my dear," she said. She had a round pink face and very gentle blue eyes.

"I was on my way to The Bell and Dragon," Billy told her. "But the notice in your window just happened to catch my eye."

"My dear boy," she said, "why don't you come in out of the cold?"

"How much do you charge?"

"Five and sixpence a night, including breakfast."

It was fantastically cheap. It was less than half of what he had been willing to pay.

"If that is too much," she added, "then perhaps I can reduce it just a tiny bit. Do you desire an egg for breakfast? Eggs are expensive at the moment. It would be sixpence less without the egg."

"Five and sixpence is fine," he answered. "I should like very much to stay here."

"I knew you would. Do come in."

She seemed terribly nice. She looked exactly like the mother of one's best school friend welcoming one into the house to stay for the Christmas holidays. Billy took off his hat, and stepped over the threshold.

"Just hang it there," she said, "and let me help you with your coat."

There were no other hats or coats in the hall. There were no umbrellas, no walking sticks—nothing.

"We have it *all* to ourselves," she said, smiling at him over her shoulder as she led the way upstairs. "You see, it isn't very often I have the pleasure of taking a visitor into my little nest."

The old girl was slightly dotty, Billy told himself. But at five and six-pence a night, who cares about that? "I should've thought you'd be simply swamped with applicants," he said politely.

"Oh, I am, my dear, I am, of course I am. But the trouble is that I'm inclined to be just a teeny weeny bit choosy and particular—if you see what I mean."

"Ah, yes."

"But I'm always ready. Everything is always ready day and night in this house just on the off chance that an acceptable young gentleman will come along. And it is such a pleasure, my dear, such a very great pleasure when now and again I open the door and I see someone standing there who is just *exactly* right." She was halfway up the stairs, and she paused with one hand on the stair rail, turning her head and smiling down at him with pale lips. "Like you," she added, and her blue eyes traveled slowly all the way down the length of Billy's body, to his feet, and then up again.

On the second-floor landing she said to him, "This floor is mine."

They climbed up a second flight. "And this one is *all* yours," she said. "Here's your room. I do hope you'll like it." She took him into a small but charming front bedroom, switching on the light as she went in.

"The morning sun comes right in the window, Mr. Perkins. It *is* Mr. Perkins, isn't it?"

"No," he said. "It's Weaver."

"Mr. Weaver. How nice. I've put a water bottle between the sheets to air them out, Mr. Weaver. It's such a comfort to have a hot water bottle in a strange bed with clean sheets, don't you agree? And you may light the gas fire at any time if you feel chilly."

"Thank you," Billy said. "Thank you ever so much." He noticed that the bedspread had been taken off the bed, and that the bedclothes had been neatly turned back on one side, all ready for someone to get in.

"I'm so glad you appeared," she said, looking earnestly into his face. "I was beginning to get worried."

"That's all right," Billy answered brightly. "You mustn't worry about me." He put his suitcase on the chair and started to open it.

"And what about supper, my dear? Did you manage to get anything to eat before you came here?"

"I'm not a bit hungry, thank you," he said. "I think I'll just go to bed as soon as possible because tomorrow I've got to get up rather early and report to the office."

"Very well, then. I'll leave you now so that you can unpack. But before you go to bed, would you be kind enough to pop into the sitting room on the ground floor and sign the book? Everyone has to do that because it's the law of the land, and we don't want to go breaking any laws at *this* stage in the proceedings, do we?" She gave him a little wave of the hand and went quickly out of the room and closed the door.

Now, the fact that his landlady appeared to be slightly off her rocker didn't worry Billy in the least. After all, she was not only harmless—there was no question about that—but she was also quite obviously a kind and generous soul. He guessed that she had probably lost a son in the war, or something like that, and had never gotten over it.

So a few minutes later, after unpacking his suitcase and washing his hands, he trotted downstairs to the ground floor and entered the living room. His landlady wasn't there, but the fire was glowing in the hearth, and the little dachshund was still sleeping soundly in front of it. The room was wonderfully warm and cozy. I'm a lucky fellow, he thought, rubbing his hands. This is a bit of all right.

He found the guest book lying open on the piano, so he took out his pen and wrote down his name and address. There were only two other entries above his on the page, and, as one always does with guest books, he started to read them. One was a Christopher Mulholland from Cardiff. The other was Gregory W. Temple from Bristol.

That's funny, he thought suddenly. Christopher Mulholland. It rings a bell.

Now where on earth had he heard that rather unusual name before?

Was he a boy at school? No. Was

it one of his sister's numerous young men, perhaps, or a friend of his father's? No, no, it wasn't any of those. He glanced down again at the book.

> Christopher Mulholland
> 231 Cathedral Road, Cardiff
> Gregory W. Temple
> 27 Sycamore Drive, Bristol

As a matter of fact, now he came to think of it, he wasn't at all sure that the second name didn't have almost as much of a familiar ring about it as the first.

"Gregory Temple?" he said aloud, searching his memory. "Christopher Mulholland? . . ."

"Such charming boys," a voice behind him answered, and he turned and saw his landlady sailing into the room with a large silver tea tray in her hands. She was holding it well out in front of her, and rather high up, as though the tray were a pair of reins on a frisky horse.

"They sound somehow familiar," he said.

"They do? How interesting."

"I'm almost positive I've heard those names before somewhere. Isn't that queer? Maybe it was in the newspapers. They weren't famous in any way, were they? I mean famous cricketers or footballers or something like that?"

"Famous," she said, setting the tea tray down on the low table in front of the sofa. "Oh no, I don't think they were famous. But they were extraordinarily handsome, both of them, I can promise you that. They

were tall and young and handsome, my dear, just exactly like you."

Once more, Billy glanced down at the book. "Look here," he said, noticing the dates. "This last entry is over two years old."

"It is?"

"Yes, indeed. And Christopher Mulholland's is nearly a year before that—more than *three years ago*."

"Dear me," she said, shaking her head and heaving a dainty little sigh. "I would never have thought it. How time does fly away from us all, doesn't it, Mr. Wilkins?"

"It's Weaver," Billy said. "W-e-a-v-e-r."

"Oh, of course it is!" she cried, sitting down on the sofa. "How silly of me. I do apologize. In one ear and out the other, that's me, Mr. Weaver."

"You know something?" Billy said. "Something that's really quite extraordinary about all this?"

"No, dear, I don't."

"Well, you see—both of these names, Mulholland and Temple, I not only seem to remember each one of them separately, so to speak, but somehow or other, in some peculiar way, they both appear to be sort of connected together as well. As though they were both famous for the same sort of thing, if you see what I mean—like . . . well . . . like Dempsey and Tunney, for example, or Churchill and Roosevelt."

"How amusing," she said. "But come over here now, dear, and sit down beside me on the sofa and I'll give you a nice cup of tea and a gin-ger biscuit before you go to bed."

"You really shouldn't bother," Billy said. "I didn't mean you to do anything like that." He stood by the piano, watching her as she fussed about with the cups and saucers. He noticed that she had small, white, quickly moving hands, and red fingernails.

"I'm almost positive it was in the newspapers I saw them," Billy said. "I'll think of it in a second. I'm sure I will."

There is nothing more tantalizing than a thing like this which lingers just outside the borders of one's memory. He hated to give up.

"Now wait a minute," he said. "Wait just a minute. Mulholland . . . Christopher Mulholland . . . wasn't *that* the name of the Eton schoolboy who was on a walking tour through the West Country, and then all of a sudden. . . ."

"Milk?" she said. "And sugar?"

"Yes, please. And then all of a sudden. . . ."

"Eton schoolboy?" she said. "Oh no, my dear, that can't possibly be right because *my* Mr. Mulholland was certainly not an Eton schoolboy when he came to me. He was a Cambridge undergraduate. Come over here now and sit next to me and warm yourself in front of this lovely fire. Come on. Your tea's all ready for you." She patted the empty place beside her on the sofa, and she sat there smiling at Billy and waiting for him to come over.

He crossed the room slowly, and

sat down on the edge of the sofa. She placed his teacup on the table in front of him.

"*There* we are," she said. "How nice and cosy this is, isn't it?"

Billy started sipping his tea. She did the same. For half a minute or so, neither of them spoke. Billy knew that she was looking at him. Her body was half turned toward him, and he could feel her eyes resting on his face, watching him over the rim of her teacup. Now and again, he caught a whiff of a peculiar smell that seemed to emanate directly from her person. It was not in the least unpleasant, and it reminded him—well, he wasn't quite sure what it reminded him of. Pickled walnuts? New leather? Or was it the corridors of a hospital?

"Mr. Mulholland was a great one for his tea," she said at length. "Never in my life have I seen anyone drink as much tea as dear, sweet Mr. Mulholland."

"I suppose he left fairly recently," Billy said. He was still puzzling his head about the two names. He was positive now that he had seen them in the newspapers—in the headlines.

"Left?" she said, arching her brows. "But my dear boy, he never left. He's still here. Mr. Temple is also here. They're on the fourth floor, both of them together."

Billy set down his cup slowly on the table, and stared at his landlady. She smiled back at him, and then she put out one of her white hands and patted him comfortingly on the knee.

"How old are you, my dear?" she asked.

"Seventeen."

"Seventeen!" she cried. "Oh, it's the perfect age! Mr. Mulholland was also seventeen. But I think he was a trifle shorter than you are, in fact I'm sure he was, and his teeth weren't *quite* so white. You have the most beautiful teeth, Mr. Weaver, did you know that?"

"They're not as good as they look," Billy said. "They've got simply masses of fillings in them at the back."

"Mr. Temple, of course, was a little older," she said, ignoring his remark. "He was actually twenty-eight. And yet I never would have guessed it if he hadn't told me, never in my whole life. There wasn't a *blemish* on his body."

"A what?" Billy said.

"His skin was *just* like a baby's."

There was a pause. Billy picked up his teacup and took another sip of his tea, then he set it down again gently in its saucer. He waited for her to say something else, but she seemed to have lapsed into another of her silences. He sat there staring straight ahead of him into the far corner of the room, biting his lower lip.

"That parrot," he said at last. "You know something? It had me completely fooled when I first saw it through the window from the street. I could have sworn it was alive."

"Alas, no longer."

"It's most terribly clever the way it's been done," he said. "It doesn't

look in the least bit dead. Who did it?"

"I did."

"*You* did?"

"Of course," she said. "And have you met my little Basil as well?" She nodded toward the dachshund curled up so comfortably in front of the fire. Billy looked at it. And suddenly, he realized that this animal had all the time been just as silent and motionless as the parrot. He put out a hand and touched it gently on the top of its back. The back was hard and cold, and when he pushed the hair to one side with his fingers, he could see the skin underneath, grayish-black and dry and perfectly preserved.

"Good gracious me," he said. "How absolutely fascinating." He turned away from the dog and stared with deep admiration at the little woman beside him on the sofa. "It must be most awfully difficult to do a thing like that."

"Not in the least," she said. "I stuff all my little pets myself when they pass away. Will you have another cup of tea?"

"No, thank you," Billy said. The tea tasted faintly of bitter almonds, and he didn't care for it.

"You did sign the book, didn't you?"

"Oh, yes."

"That's good. Because later on, if I happen to forget what you were called, then I can always come down here and look it up. I still do that almost every day with Mr. Mulholland and Mr. . . . Mr. . . . ."

"Temple," Billy said. "Gregory Temple. Excuse my asking, but haven't there been *any* other guests here except them in the last two or three years?"

Holding her teacup high in one hand, inclining her head slightly to the left, she looked up at him out of the corners of her eyes and gave him another gentle little smile.

"No, my dear," she said. "Only you."

DISCUSSION   1.   Do you think Billy understands the danger he is in by the end of the story? What is the last point at which you *know* he hasn't caught on? When did you first realize what happened to Gregory Temple and Christopher Mulholland?

2.   What clues can you find early in this story that **foreshadow** (see page 147) the peculiar situation Billy is in?

For further activities, see page 274.

The Skater of Ghost Lake

WILLIAM ROSE BENÉT

Ghost Lake's a dark lake, a deep lake and cold:
Ice black as ebony, frostily scrolled;
Far in its shadows a faint sound whirrs;
Steep stand the sentineled deep, dark firs.

A brisk sound, a swift sound, a ring-tinkle-ring;   5
Flit-flit,—a shadow, with a stoop and a swing,
Flies from a shadow through the crackling cold.
Ghost Lake's a deep lake, a dark lake and old!

Leaning and leaning with a stride and a stride,
Hands locked behind him, scarf blowing wide,   10
Jeremy Randall skates, skates late,
Star for a candle, moon for a mate.

Black is the clear glass now that he glides,
Crisp is the whisper of long lean strides,
Swift is his swaying—but pricked ears hark.   15
None comes to Ghost Lake late after dark!

Cecily only—yes, it is she!
Stealing to Ghost Lake, tree after tree,
Kneeling in snow by the still lake side,
Rising with feet winged, gleaming, to glide.   20

Dust of the ice swirls. Here is his hand.
Brilliant his eyes burn. Now, as was planned,
Arm across arm twined, laced to his side,
Out on the dark lake lightly they glide.

Dance of the dim moon, a rhythmical reel,   25
A swaying, a swift tune—skurr of the steel;
Moon for a candle, maid for a mate,
Jeremy Randall skates, skates late.

Black as if lacquered the wide lake lies;
Breath as a frost-fume, eyes seek eyes;   30

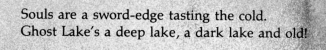

Souls are a sword-edge tasting the cold.
Ghost Lake's a deep lake, a dark lake and old!

Far in the shadows hear faintly begin
Like a string pluck-plucked of a violin,
Muffled in mist on the lake's far bound,   35
Swifter and swifter, a low singing sound!

Far in the shadows and faint on the verge
Of blue cloudy moonlight, see it emerge,
Flit-flit,—a phantom, with a stoop and a swing . . .
Ah, it's a night bird, burdened of wing!   40

Pressed close to Jeremy, laced to his side,
Cecily Culver, dizzy you glide.
Jeremy Randall sweepingly veers
Out on the dark ice far from the piers.

"Jeremy!" "Sweetheart?" "What do you fear?"   45
"Nothing, my darling,—nothing is here!"
"Jeremy?" "Sweetheart?" "What do you flee?"
"Something—I know not; something I see!"

Swayed to a swift stride, brisker of pace,
Leaning and leaning, they race and they race;   50
Ever that whirring, that crisp sound thin
Like a string pluck-plucked of a violin;

Ever that swifter and low singing sound
Sweeping behind them, winding them round;
Gasp of their breath now that chill flakes fret;   55
Ice black as ebony—blacker—like jet!

Ice shooting fangs forth—sudden—like spears;
Crackling of lightning—a roar in their ears!
Shadowy, a phantom swerves off from its prey . . .
No, it's a night bird flit-flits away!   60

Low-winging moth-owl, home to your sleep!
Ghost Lake's a still lake, a cold lake and deep.
Faint in its shadows a far sound whirrs.
Black stand the ranks of its sentinel firs.

DISCUSSION

1. The poem ends the same way it begins—with the dark trees, the cold lake, and the faint sound in the shadows. Where are the skaters? Do you think the ending would be more effective if the poem stopped at line 60? Explain.

2. How does the sound of "muffled in mist" (line 35) fit the word picture? Find other places in the poem where the sound of the words fits what is being described.

3. **Onomatopoeia.** The use of words that sound like what they mean is called onomatopoeia (pronounced ŏn-ə-măt-ə-pē′ə). You have probably already noticed that words like *hiss* and *buzz* are onomatopoetic. Find some examples of onomatopoeia in the poem (the first one is "whirrs," in line 3).

I Followed a Path

PATRICIA PARKER

Do not go gentle into that good night
——Dylan Thomas

I followed a path.
    the path—it led
to somewhere. Curved
around space leading
me from my youth.   5
I met an old man.
"Old man, give back
my youth."
He gave me a
gold pitcher   10
with a hole in it.

I followed a path.
    the path—it led
to marbles & jacks
& dolls, mother,   15
house, school, love.
I met a little girl.
"Little girl, give back
my youth."
She ran away.   20
Her mother had told her not to speak
to strangers.

I followed a path.
   the path—it led
to a mirror.   25
I saw a face—not mine.
A face with lines
leading to pain & joy,
song and dances.
I wanted to dance again.   30
I skipped over guilt;
I laughed at failure.
For one moment,
I chased the lines away.

The lines crept back.   35
"Mirror, give back
my youth."
The face in the mirror
turned away.

I followed a path   40
   the path—it led
to a river.
I bathed myself.
"River, give back
   my youth."   45
The river was muddy.

I followed a path.
   the path—it led
to an unowned grave.
It did not say me,   50
But it was mine.

DISCUSSION

1. What might the "path" in this poem be? In what way were you prepared for the ending?

2. What might the old man of stanza 1 be said to represent, or stand for? The gold pitcher with the hole? The river of the last stanza?

3. Whose face appears in the mirror (line 26)? Give reasons for your answer.

4. The "night" in the Dylan Thomas quotation refers to death. The line is from an intensely emotional poem Thomas wrote about his father's dying. How does the quotation fit this poem?

Thus I Refute Beelzy

JOHN COLLIER

"There goes the tea bell," said Mrs. Carter. "I hope Simon hears it."

They looked out from the window of the drawing room. The long garden, agreeably neglected, ended in a waste plot. Here a little summerhouse was passing close by beauty on its way to complete decay. This was Simon's retreat. It was almost completely screened by the tangled branches of the apple tree and the pear tree, planted too close together, as they always are in the suburbs. They caught a glimpse of him now and then, as he strutted up and down, mouthing and gesticulating, performing all the solemn mumbo-jumbo of small boys who spend long afternoons at the forgotten end of long gardens.

"There he is, bless him!" said Betty.

"Playing his game," said Mrs. Carter. "He won't play with the other children any more. And if I go down there—the temper! And comes in tired out!"

"He doesn't have his sleep in the afternoons?" asked Betty.

"You know what Big Simon's ideas are," said Mrs. Carter. " 'Let him choose for himself,' he says. That's what he chooses, and he comes in as white as a sheet."

"Look! He's heard the bell," said Betty. The expression was justified, though the bell had ceased ringing a full minute ago. Small Simon stopped in his parade exactly as if its tinny dingle had at that moment reached his ear. They watched him perform certain ritual sweeps and scratchings with his little stick, and come lagging over the hot and flaggy grass toward the house.

Mrs. Carter led the way down to the playroom, or garden room, which was also the tea room for hot days. It had been the huge scullery[1] of this tall Georgian house. Now the walls were cream-washed, there was coarse blue net in the windows, canvas-covered armchairs on the stone floor, and a reproduction of Van Gogh's *Sunflowers* over the mantelpiece.

Small Simon came drifting in, and accorded Betty a perfunctory[2] greeting. His face was an almost perfect triangle, pointed at the chin, and he was paler than he should have been. "The little elf-child!" cried Betty.

Simon looked at her. "No," said he.

At that moment the door opened, and Mr. Carter came in, rubbing his hands. He was a dentist, and washed them before and after everything he did. "You!" said his wife. "Home already!"

"Not unwelcome, I hope," said Mr. Carter, nodding to Betty. "Two people canceled their appointments; I decided to come home. I said, I hope I am not unwelcome."

"Silly!" said his wife. "Of course not."

"Small Simon seems doubtful," continued Mr. Carter. "Small Simon, are you sorry to see me at tea with you?"

"No, Daddy."

"No, what?"

"No, Big Simon."

"That's right. Big Simon and Small Simon. That sounds

---

[1] *scullery:* room next to the kitchen where dishes are washed.
[2] *perfunctory:* automatic, showing little interest.

more like friends, doesn't it? At one time little boys had to call
their father 'sir.' If they forgot—a good spanking. On the bottom, Small Simon! On the bottom!" said Mr. Carter, washing
his hands once more with his invisible soap and water.

The little boy turned crimson with shame or rage.

"But now, you see," said Betty, to help, "you can call your
father whatever you like."

"And what," asked Mr. Carter, "has Small Simon been
doing this afternoon? While Big Simon has been at work."

"Nothing," muttered his son.

"Then you have been bored," said Mr. Carter. "Learn from
experience, Small Simon. Tomorrow, do something amusing,
and you will not be bored. I want him to learn from experience,
Betty. That is my way, the new way."

"I have learned," said the boy, speaking like an old, tired
man, as little boys so often do.

"It would hardly seem so," said Mr. Carter, "if you sit on
your behind all the afternoon, doing nothing. Had *my* father
caught me doing nothing, I should not have sat very comfortably."

"He played," said Mrs. Carter.

"A bit," said the boy, shifting on his chair.

"Too much," said Mrs. Carter. "He comes in all nervy and
dazed. He ought to have his rest."

"He is six," said her husband. "He is a reasonable being. He
must choose for himself. But what game is this, Small Simon,
that is worth getting nervy and dazed over? There are very few
games as good as all that."

"It's nothing," said the boy.

"Oh come," said his father. "We are friends, are we not?
You can tell me. I was a Small Simon once, just like you, and
played the same games you play. Of course there were no airplanes in those days. With whom do you play this fine game?
Come on, we must all answer civil questions, or the world would
never go round. With whom do you play?"

"Mr. Beelzy," said the boy, unable to resist.

"Mr. Beelzy?" said his father, raising his eyebrows inquiringly at his wife.

"It's a game he makes up," said she.

"Not makes up!" cried the boy. "Fool!"

"That is telling stories," said his mother. "And rude as well.
We had better talk of something different."

"No wonder he is rude," said Mr. Carter, "if you say he tells lies, and then insist on changing the subject. He tells you his fantasy: you implant a guilt feeling. What can you expect? A defense mechanism. Then you get a real lie."

"Like in *These Three,*" said Betty. "Only different, of course. *She* was an unblushing little liar."[3]

"I would have made her blush," said Mr. Carter, "in the proper part of her anatomy. But Small Simon is in the fantasy stage. Are you not, Small Simon? You just make things up."

"No, I don't," said the boy.

"You do," said his father. "And because you do, it is not too late to reason with you. There is no harm in a fantasy, old chap. There is no harm in a bit of make-believe. Only you have to know the difference between daydreams and real things, or your brain will never grow. It will never be the brain of a Big Simon. So come on. Let us hear about this Mr. Beelzy of yours. Come on. What is he like?"

"He isn't like anything," said the boy.

"Like nothing on earth?" said his father. "That's a terrible fellow."

"I'm not frightened of him," said the child, smiling. "Not a bit."

"I should hope not," said his father. "If you were, you would be frightening yourself. I am always telling people, older people than you are, that they are just frightening themselves. Is he a funny man? Is he a giant?"

"Sometimes he is," said the little boy.

"Sometimes one thing, sometimes another," said his father. "Sounds pretty vague. Why can't you tell us just what he's like?"

"I love him," said the little boy. "He loves me."

"That's a big word," said Mr. Carter. "That might be better kept for real things, like Big Simon and Small Simon."

"He is real," said the boy, passionately. "He's not a fool. He's real."

"Listen," said his father. "When you go down the garden there's nobody there. Is there?"

"No," said the boy.

"Then you think of him, inside your head, and he comes."

---

[3] *Like. . . . liar:* Betty is referring to a movie in which a little girl's lies cause two teachers to be dismissed from a school.

"No," said Small Simon. "I have to make marks. On the ground. With my stick."

"That doesn't matter."

"Yes, it does."

"Small Simon, you are being obstinate,"[4] said Mr. Carter. "I am trying to explain something to you. I have been longer in the world than you have, so naturally I am older and wiser. I am explaining that Mr. Beelzy is a fantasy of yours. Do you hear? Do you understand?"

"Yes, Daddy."

"He is a game. He is a let's-pretend."

The little boy looked down at his plate, smiling resignedly.

"I hope you are listening to me," said his father. "All you have to do is to say, 'I have been playing a game of let's-pretend. With someone I make up, called Mr. Beelzy.' Then no one will say you tell lies, and you will know the difference between dreams and reality. Mr. Beelzy is a daydream."

The little boy still stared at his plate.

"He is sometimes there and sometimes not there," pursued Mr. Carter. "Sometimes he's like one thing, sometimes another. You can't really see him. Not as you see me. I am real. You can't touch him. You can touch me. I can touch you." Mr. Carter stretched out his big, white, dentist's hand, and took his little son by the nape of the neck. He stopped speaking for a moment and tightened his hand. The little boy sank his head still lower.

"Now you know the difference," said Mr. Carter, "between a pretend and a real thing. You and I are one thing; he is another. Which is the pretend? Come on. Answer me. What is the pretend?"

"Big Simon and Small Simon," said the little boy.

"Don't!" cried Betty, and at once put her hand over her mouth, for why should a visitor cry "Don't!" when a father is explaining things in a scientific and modern way? Besides, it annoys the father.

"Well, my boy," said Mr. Carter, "I have said you must be allowed to learn from experience. Go upstairs. Right up to your room. You shall learn whether it is better to reason, or to be perverse and obstinate. Go up. I shall follow you."

"You are not going to beat the child?" cried Mrs. Carter.

---

[4] *obstinate:* extremely stubborn.

"No," said the little boy. "Mr. Beelzy won't let him."

"Go on up with you!" shouted his father.

Small Simon stopped at the door. "He said he wouldn't let anyone hurt me," he whimpered. "He said he'd come like a lion, with wings on, and eat them up."

"You'll learn how real he is!" shouted his father after him. "If you can't learn it at one end, you shall learn it at the other. I'll have your breeches down. I shall finish my cup of tea first, however," said he to the two women.

Neither of them spoke. Mr. Carter finished his tea, and unhurriedly left the room, washing his hands with his invisible soap and water.

Mrs. Carter said nothing. Betty could think of nothing to say. She wanted to be talking for she was afraid of what they might hear.

Suddenly it came. It seemed to tear the air apart. She cried, "What was that? He's hurt him." She sprang out of her chair, her silly eyes flashing behind her glasses. "I'm going up there!" she cried, trembling.

"Yes, let us go up," said Mrs. Carter. "Let us go up. That was not Small Simon."

It was on the second-floor landing that they found the shoe, with the man's foot still in it, like that last morsel of a mouse which sometimes falls unnoticed from the side of the jaws of the cat.

DISCUSSION

1. What has happened to Simon's father?

2. The writer tells us straight out that Simon's father is a dentist, that he makes handwashing motions a lot, and that he finished his tea before he went upstairs to spank Simon. Almost everything else we learn about him, we learn from **dialogue** (see page 167). How would you describe the father from what he says?

3. Simon says, "I love him. He loves me," when his father asked him about Mr. Beelzy. How does this statement help explain the story?

4. There is a big difference between the way Simon sees his father and the way the father sees himself. Find two places in the story where this is obvious.

For further activities, see page 274.

O WHAT IS THAT SOUND

W. H. AUDEN

O what is that sound which so thrills the ear
   Down in the valley drumming, drumming?
Only the scarlet soldiers, dear,
   The soldiers coming.

O what is that light I see flashing so clear   5
   Over the distance brightly, brightly?
Only the sun on their weapons, dear,
   As they step lightly.

O what are they doing with all that gear,
   What are they doing this morning, this morning?   10
Only their usual maneuvers, dear,
   Or perhaps a warning.

O why have they left the road down there,
   Why are they suddenly wheeling, wheeling?
Perhaps a change in their orders, dear.   15
   Why are you kneeling?

O haven't they stopped for the doctor's care,
   Haven't they reined their horses, their horses?
Why, they are none of them wounded, dear,
   None of these forces.   20

O is it the parson they want, with white hair,
   Is it the parson, is it, is it?
No, they are passing his gateway, dear,
   Without a visit.

O it must be the farmer who lives so near.   25
    It must be the farmer so cunning, so cunning?
They have passed the farmyard already, dear,
    And now they are running.

O where are you going? Stay with me here!
    Were the vows you swore deceiving, deceiving?   30
No, I promised to love you, dear,
    But I must be leaving.

O it's broken the lock and splintered the door,
    O it's the gate where they're turning, turning;
Their boots are heavy on the floor   35
    And their eyes are burning.

DISCUSSION

1. How does this poem build suspense? Name all the ways you see.

2. The first speaker seems to become more and more excited. But it is hard to tell very much about the second speaker. What do you think would be the most effective way of reading aloud the second speaker's lines?

3. The poet does not say who the speakers are; why the soldiers are coming; whether one or both of the speakers is in danger. What do you think?

For further activities, see page 274.

OLD CHRISTMAS

ROY HELTON

"Where you coming from, Lomey Carter,
    So early over the snow?
What's them pretties you got in your hand,
    And where you aiming to go?

"Step in, Honey. Old Christmas morning   5
    We hain't got nothing much;
Maybe a bite of sweetness and corn bread,
    A little ham meat and such.

Old Christmas: Because of a calendar change around 1600, the day that once was Christmas became January 6, "old" Christmas.

"But come in, Lomey. Sally Ann Barton's
   Hungering after your face.   10
Wait till I light my candle up.
   Set down. There's your old place.

"Where you been, so early this morning?"
   "Graveyard, Sally Ann:
Up by the trace in the Salt Lick meadow   15
   Where Taulbe kilt my man."

"Taulbe hain't to home this morning.
   Wisht I could scratch me a light:
Dampness gits in the heads of the matches;
   I'll blow up the embers bright."   20

"Needn't trouble. I won't be stopping:
   Going a long ways still."
"You didn't see nothing, Lomey Carter,
   Up on the graveyard hill?"

"What should I see there, Sally Ann Barton?"   25
   "Spirits walk loose last night."
"There was an elder bush a blooming
   While the moon still give some light."

"Yes, elder bushes they bloom, Old Christmas,
   And critters kneel down in their straw.   30
Anything else? Up in the graveyard?"
   "One thing more I saw:

"I saw my man with his head all bleeding
   Where Taulbe's shot went through."
"What did he say?" "He stooped and kissed me."   35
   "What did he say to you?"

"Said Lord Jesus forgive your Taulbe;
   But he told me another word;

---

15. *trace:* path.   26–31. There are traditions that on "Old Christmas" eve the spirits of the dead appear, bushes suddenly blossom,
and animals, especially oxen, kneel down at midnight, as though to
worship.

Said it soft when he stooped and kissed me;
  That was the last I heard."   40

"Taulbe hain't come home this morning."
  "I know that, Sally Ann.
For I kilt him, coming down through the meadow
  Where Taulbe kilt my man.

"I met him up on the meadow trace   45
  When the moon was fainting fast;
I had my dead man's rifle gun,
  And kilt him as he come past."

"I heard two shots." " 'Twas his was second:
  He got me 'fore he died.   50
You'll find us at daybreak, Sally Ann Barton:
  I'm laying there dead at his side."

DISCUSSION   1.   What two characters are talking? (To make sure you know which
person is speaking, watch for the quotation marks at the end of a
speech.)

2.   When can you first tell that Sally Ann Barton is uneasy or worried?
What does she say at the end that lets you know she knew all along that
something had happened?

3.   **Dialect.**   You already know that people from different groups and
from different areas speak English in different ways. These different ways
of speaking are called dialects. Find at least three places in the poem
where the speakers' dialect shows.

For further activities, see page 274.

the stake in
the graveyard

AMÉRICO PAREDES

Well, my grandfather used to tell us this one. He was a physician, and he went to visit a patient one night, and it was raining and there was a high wind. There was a lot of lightning and thunder and I don't know what. And on the way back, he stopped at a little *cantina* before going to bed.

He went inside and sat down at a table somewhat apart, by himself. And then he saw two or three men arguing over at the bar. They were a bit drunk already. And one of them bet another he wouldn't go to the very center of the graveyard that night. It was a little town, and they were agreed more or less as to which grave represented the center of the graveyard. So the other two bet he wouldn't go to the very center and drive a stake into the grave, exactly at midnight.

Grandfather used to say it was about eleven-thirty. So they kept on drinking for a while, until it was twelve. And then this man went off by himself, with a stake and a hatchet. Not a hammer, a hatchet. And he said, "I'll be back in a little while and take all of you to see where I drove the stake. Just to show you I'm not afraid."

Américo Paredes: pronounced ä-mĕ′rē-kō pä-rĕ′dĕs.

So the man left all by himself, and they stayed there in the
cantina drinking. The graveyard was close by, some three, four
blocks. They could see him until he went in the gate, every time
the lightning flashed. It was still raining hard, and the wind was
blowing hard, too.

So the man went off and didn't come back, and Grandfather
decided to stay just to see what would happen. Well, it got to be
12:15, and then 12:20, and finally half-past twelve. And the man
didn't come back.

Well, so they organized a party, with lamps and lanterns and
this and that, and they all went to the graveyard in a group, all
those who had been at the *cantina*. And Grandfather in the bunch.
They went, and they found him there, with the stake driven right
into the center of the grave. But they found him good and dead,
stiff. As if he had tried to run and died like that, all stiff like that.

What happened was that when he squatted down to drive in

the stake, the wind blew his cloak, and he drove the stake over
the cloak. And when he tried to leave, he felt that something
pulled at him, and he died of fright.

   Grandfather used to say that his eyes were opened wide, great
big.

DISCUSSION   1.   How does the narrator use the grandfather to make the story believ-
able?

2.   What role does the weather play in the story? How does it set a
mood?

3.   The man died of fright. How do you know that the people in the *cantina* were scared too? Is there anything wrong with admitting you are
afraid of some things?

FOCUS

VOCABULARY

Thus I Refute Beelzy (page 259)

Write the words on this list on your paper beside the number of the sentence they belong in. Instead of looking up definitions of the words you don't know, find them in the story, and see if the way they are used there can help you place them here.

refute (p. 259)   fantasy (p. 263)
ritual (p. 260)   obstinate (p. 264)
lagging (p. 260)   resignedly (p. 264)
perfunctory (p. 260)   morsel (p. 265)

1. Winding the grandfather clock was his nightly——.
2. The donkey was as——as ever; he simply would not move.
3. The juiciest——is usually eaten first.
4. The runner was——and the crowd was worried.
5. I am going to——your entire argument, point by point.
6. "I see that you won't change your mind," she said——.
7. His favorite——is that he will be adopted by rich relatives.
8. If your hello sounds too——, he'll think you don't want to see him.

COMPOSITION

Thus I Refute Beelzy (page 259)

1. Describe one of your favorite ways of spending a long afternoon when you were a child. Making up games on your own? Playing with everybody you could get together?

2. Simon was much smarter than his father thought he was. That is just one of the things that can lead to misunderstandings between children and adults. Tell about a time you were misunderstood. How did it come out in the end?

O What Is That Sound (page 266)

Make up a story about this poem. Who are the people? How did the events in the poem come about? What had happened just before the events in the poem?

READING

The Landlady (page 244)

When you read this story you probably made some inferences (came to some conclusions) from the details you read. On a separate piece of paper, write two details from the story that back up each of the inferences below. The first one is done for you.

1. Billy was inexperienced and unsophisticated.
    a. He was only seventeen.
    b. He thought briskness was the key to success in business.
2. Billy was drawn to the boarding house almost against his will.
3. The landlady was almost too nice and friendly to be true.
4. The landlady had taken a careful look at Billy before he came in.
5. The landlady had a smell that meant she did something besides just cleaning and cooking.

The Skater of Ghost Lake (page 254)

On separate paper, write T (true) or F (false) for each of these statements and give reasons that support your judgment.

1. Jeremy did not expect Cecily to come.
2. They heard a violin in the distance.
3. They skated close to the shore.
4. Something frightened Jeremy.
5. Something appeared to be chasing the skaters.

Old Christmas (page 268)

Write down what you think each of these statements means, and who said it. Do it first without looking back at the poem. Then check yourself.

1. "Where you aiming to go?"
2. "We hain't got nothing much."
3. "Sally Ann Barton's hungering after your face."
4. "Taulbe kilt my man."
5. "I won't be stopping: going a long ways still."
6. "Taulbe hain't to home this morning."
7. "Dampness gits in the heads of the matches."
8. "Critters kneel down in their straw."

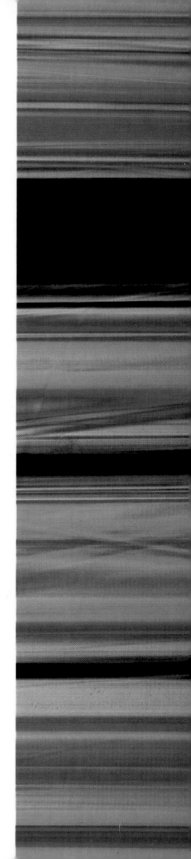

The Tide Rises, the Tide Falls

HENRY WADSWORTH LONGFELLOW

The tide rises, the tide falls,
The twilight darkens, the curlew calls;
Along the sea-sands damp and brown
The traveler hastens toward the town,
   And the tide rises, the tide falls.   5

Darkness settles on roofs and walls,
But the sea, the sea in the darkness calls;
The little waves, with their soft, white hands,
Efface the footprints in the sands,
   And the tide rises, the tide falls.   10

The morning breaks; the steeds in their stalls
Stamp and neigh, as the hostler calls;
The day returns, but nevermore
Returns the traveler to the shore,
   And the tide rises, the tide falls.   15

2. *curlew:* a shore bird.   9. *efface:* wipe out.   12. *hostler:* stable boy.

DISCUSSION   1. Something has happened to the traveler, but the poem does not tell you what it is. How can you tell that something *has* happened?

2. How does the poem give you the feeling of the passing of time? Why is the sea, or tides, appropriate to represent time?

3. Personification. Giving human qualities to nonhuman things is called personification. For example, the United States is often personified as Uncle Sam. What is personified in this poem (see the middle stanza)? How does this personification affect the way you see what happens to the traveler?

The Adventure of the Norwood Builder

SIR ARTHUR CONAN DOYLE

"From the point of view of the criminal expert," said Mr. Sherlock Holmes, "London has become a singularly uninteresting city since the death of the late lamented Professor Moriarty."[1]

"I can hardly think that you would find many decent citizens to agree with you," I answered.

"Well, well, I must not be selfish," said he, with a smile, as he pushed back his chair from the breakfast table. "The community is certainly the gainer, and no one the loser save the poor out-of-work specialist, whose occupation has gone. With that man in the field one's morning paper presented infinite possibilities. Often it was only the smallest trace, Watson, the faintest indication, and yet it was enough to tell me that the great malignant brain was there, as the gentlest tremors of the edges of the web remind one of the foul spider which lurks in the center. Petty thefts, wanton assaults, purposeless outrage—to the man who held the clue all could be worked into one connected whole. To the scientific student of the higher criminal world no capital in Europe offered the advantages which London then possessed.

But now——" He shrugged his shoulders in humorous deprecation of the state of things which he had himself done so much to produce.

At the time of which I speak, Holmes had been back for some months, and I at his request had sold my practice and returned to share the old quarters in Baker Street. A young doctor named Verner had purchased my small Kensington practice and given with astonishingly little demur the highest price that I ventured to ask—an incident which only explained itself some years later, when I found that Verner was a distant relation of Holmes and that it was my friend who had really found the money.

Our months of partnership had not been so uneventful as he had stated, for I find, on looking over my notes, that this period includes the case of the papers of ex-President Murillo, and also the shocking affair of the Dutch steamship *Friesland,* which so nearly cost us both our lives. His cold and proud nature was always averse, however, from anything in the shape of public applause, and he bound me in the most stringent terms to say no further word of himself, his methods, or his successes—a prohibition which, as I have explained, has only now been removed.

[1] *Professor Moriarty:* a master criminal whom Holmes loved to pit himself against.

Mr. Sherlock Holmes was leaning back in his chair after his whimsical protest, and was unfolding his morning paper in a leisurely fashion when our attention was arrested by a tremendous ring at the bell, followed immediately by a hollow drumming sound, as if someone were beating on the outer door with his fist. As it opened, there came a tumultuous rush into the hall; rapid feet clattered up the stair, and an instant later a wild-eyed and frantic young man— pale, disheveled, and palpitating— burst into the room. He looked from one to the other of us, and under our gaze of inquiry he became conscious that some apology was needed for this unceremonious entry.

"I'm sorry, Mr. Holmes," he cried. "You musn't blame me. I am nearly mad. Mr. Holmes, I am the unhappy John Hector McFarlane."

He made the announcement as if the name alone would explain both his visit and its manner, but I could see by my companion's unresponsive face that it meant no more to him than to me.

"Have a cigarette, Mr. McFarlane," said he, pushing his case across. "I am sure that with your symptoms my friend Dr. Watson here would prescribe a sedative. The weather has been so very warm these last few days. Now, if you feel a little more composed, I should be glad if you would sit down in that chair and tell us very slowly and quietly who you are and what it is that you want. You mentioned your name, as if I should recognize it, but I assure you that, be-yond the obvious facts that you are a bachelor, a solicitor,[2] a Freemason,[3] and an asthmatic, I know nothing whatever about you."

Familiar as I was with my friend's methods, it was not difficult for me to follow his deductions and to observe the untidiness of attire, the sheaf of legal papers, the watch-charm, and the breathing which had prompted them. Our client, however, stared in amazement.

"Yes, I am all that, Mr. Holmes, and in addition I am the most unfortunate man at this moment in London. For heaven's sake, don't abandon me, Mr. Holmes! If they come to arrest me before I have finished my story, make them give me time so that I may tell you the whole truth. I could go to jail happy if I knew that you were working for me outside."

"Arrest you!" said Holmes. "This is really most grati— most interesting. On what charge do you expect to be arrested?"

"Upon the charge of murdering Mr. Jonas Oldacre, of Lower Norwood."

My companion's expressive face showed a sympathy which was not, I am afraid, entirely unmixed with satisfaction. "Dear me," said he, "it was only this moment at breakfast that I was saying to my friend Dr. Watson that sensational cases had disappeared out of our papers."

---

[2] *solicitor:* lawyer.
[3] *Freemason:* member of a secret, fraternal organization.

Our visitor stretched forward a quivering hand and picked up the *Daily Telegraph,* which still lay upon Holme's knee. "If you had looked at it, sir, you would have seen at a glance what the errand is on which I have come to you this morning. I feel as if my name and my misfortune must be in every man's mouth." He turned it over to expose the central page. "Here it is, and with your permission I will read it to you. Listen to this, Mr. Holmes. The headlines are 'Mysterious Affair at Lower Norwood. Disappearance of a Well-known Builder. Suspicion of Murder and Arson. A Clue to the Criminal.' That is the clue which they are already following, Mr. Holmes, and I know that it leads infallibly to me. I have been followed from London Bridge Station, and I am sure that they are only waiting for the warrant to arrest me. It will break my mother's heart—it will break her heart!" He wrung his hands in an agony of apprehension and swayed backwards and forwards in his chair.

I looked with interest upon this man, who was accused of being the perpetrator of a crime of violence. He was flaxen-haired and handsome in a washed-out, negative fashion, with frightened blue eyes and a clean-shaven face, with a weak, sensitive mouth. His age may have been about twenty-seven, his dress and bearing that of a gentleman. From the pocket of his light summer overcoat protruded the bundle of endorsed papers which proclaimed his profession.

"We must use what time we have," said Holmes. "Watson, would you have the kindness to take the paper and to read the paragraph in question?"

Underneath the vigorous headlines which our client had quoted, I read the following suggestive narrative:

Late last night, or early this morning, an incident occurred at Lower Norwood which points, it is feared, to a serious crime. Mr. Jonas Oldacre is a well-known resident of that suburb, where he has carried on his business as a builder for many years. Mr. Oldacre is a bachelor fifty-two years of age and lives in Deep Dene House, at the Sydenham end of the road of that name. He has had the reputation of being a man of eccentric habits, secretive, and retiring. For some years he has practically withdrawn from the business in which he is said to have amassed considerable wealth. A small timber yard still exists, however, at the back of the house, and last night about twelve o'clock an alarm was given that one of the stacks was on fire. The engines were soon upon the spot, but the dry wood burned with great fury, and it was impossible to arrest the conflagration until the stack had been entirely consumed. Up to this point the incident bore the appearance of an ordinary accident, but fresh indications seem to point to serious crime. Surprise was expressed at the absence of the master of the establishment from the scene of the fire, and an inquiry followed, which showed that he had disappeared from the house. An examination of his room revealed that the bed had not been slept in, that a safe which stood in it was open, that a number of important papers were scattered about the room, and, finally, that there were signs of a murderous struggle, slight traces of blood being found within the room, and an oaken walking-stick, which also showed stains of blood upon the handle. It is known that Mr. Jonas Oldacre had received a late visitor in his bedroom upon that night, and the stick found has been identified as the property of this person, who is a young London solicitor named John Hector McFarlane, junior partner of Graham and McFarlane, of 426, Gresham Buildings, E. C. The police believe that they have evidence in their possession which supplies a very convincing motive for the crime, and altogether it cannot be doubted that sensational developments will follow.

LATER. It is rumored as we go to press that Mr. John Hector McFarlane has actually been arrested on the charge of the murder of Mr. Jonas Oldacre. It is at least certain that a warrant has been issued. There have been further and sinister developments in the investigation at Norwood. Besides the signs of a struggle in the room of the unfortunate builder it is now known that the French windows of his bedroom (which is on the ground floor) were found to be open, that there were marks as if some bulky object had been dragged across to the woodpile, and, finally, it is asserted that charred remains have been found among the charcoal ashes of the fire. The police theory is that a most sensational crime has been committed, that the victim was clubbed to death in his own bedroom, his papers rifled, and his dead body dragged across to the wood stack, which was then ignited so as to hide all traces of the crime. The conduct of the criminal investigation has been left in the experienced hands of Inspector Lestrade, of Scotland Yard, who is following up the clues with his accustomed energy and sagacity.

Sherlock Holmes listened with closed eyes and fingertips together to this remarkable account.

"The case has certainly some points of interest," said he in his languid fashion. "May I ask, in the first place, Mr. McFarlane, how it is that you are still at liberty, since there appears to be enough evidence to justify your arrest?"

"I live at Torrington Lodge, Blackheath, with my parents, Mr. Holmes, but last night, having to do business very late with Mr. Jonas Oldacre, I stayed at a hotel in Norwood and came to my business from there. I knew nothing of this affair until I was in the train, when I read what you have just heard. I at once saw the horrible danger of my position, and I hurried to put the case into your hands. I have no doubt that I should have been arrested either at my city office or at my home. A man followed me from London Bridge Station, and I have no doubt—great heaven! what is that?"

It was a clang of the bell, followed instantly by heavy steps upon the stair. A moment later our old friend Lestrade appeared in the doorway. Over his shoulder I caught a glimpse of one or two uniformed policemen outside.

"Mr. John Hector McFarlane?" said Lestrade.

Our unfortunate client rose with a ghastly face.

"I arrest you for the willful murder of Mr. Jonas Oldacre, of Lower Norwood."

McFarlane turned to us with a gesture of despair and sank into his chair once more like one who is crushed.

"One moment, Lestrade," said Holmes. "Half an hour more or less can make no difference to you, and the gentleman was about to give us an account of this very interesting affair, which might aid us in clearing it up."

"I think there will be no difficulty in clearing it up," said Lestrade, grimly.

"Nonetheless, with your permission I should be much interested to hear his account."

"Well, Mr. Holmes, it is difficult for me to refuse you anything, for you have been of use to the force once or twice in the past, and we owe you a good turn at Scotland Yard," said Lestrade. "At the same time I must remain with my prisoner, and I am bound to warn him that anything he may say will appear in evidence against him."

"I wish nothing better," said our client. "All I ask is that you should hear and recognize the absolute truth."

Lestrade looked at his watch. "I'll give you half an hour," said he.

"I must explain first," said McFarlane, "that I knew nothing of Mr. Jonas Oldacre. His name was familiar to me, for many years ago my parents were acquainted with him, but they drifted apart. I was very much surprised, therefore, when yesterday, about three o'clock in the afternoon, he walked into my office in the city. But I was still more astonished when he told me the object of his visit. He had in his hand several sheets of a notebook, covered with scribbled writing—here they are—and he laid them on my table.

" 'Here is my will,' said he. 'I want you, Mr. McFarlane, to cast it into proper legal shape. I will sit here while you do so.'

"I set myself to copy it, and you can imagine my astonishment when I found that, with some reservations, he had left all his property to me. He was a strange little ferretlike man with white eyelashes, and when I looked up at him, I found his keen gray eyes fixed upon me with an amused expression. I could hardly believe my own senses as I read the terms of the will, but he explained that he was a bachelor with hardly any living relation, that he had known my parents in his youth, and that he had always heard of me as a very deserving young man and was assured that his money would be in worthy hands. Of course, I could only stammer out my thanks. The will was duly finished, signed, and witnessed

by my clerk. This is it on the blue paper, and these slips, as I have explained, are the rough draft. Mr. Jonas Oldacre then informed me that there were a number of documents— building leases, title deeds, mortgages, scrip,[4] and so forth—which it was necessary that I should see and understand. He said that his mind would not be easy until the whole thing was settled, and he begged me to come out to his house at Norwood that night, bringing the will with me, and to arrange matters.

" 'Remember, my boy, not one word to your parents about the affair until everything is settled. We will keep it as a little surprise for them.'

"He was very insistent upon this point and made me promise it faithfully. You can imagine, Mr. Holmes, that I was not in a humor to refuse him anything that he might ask. He was my benefactor, and all my desire was to carry out his wishes in every particular. I sent a telegram home, therefore, to say that I had important business on hand and that it was impossible for me to say how late I might be. Mr. Oldacre had told me that he would like me to have supper with him at nine, as he might not be

[4] *scrip:* stock certificates.

home before that hour. I had some difficulty in finding his house, however, and it was nearly half past before I reached it. I found him——"

"One moment!" said Holmes. "Who opened the door?"

"A middle-aged woman, who was, I suppose, his housekeeper."

"And it was she, I presume, who mentioned your name?"

"Exactly," said McFarlane.

"Pray proceed."

McFarlane wiped his damp brow and then continued his narrative: "I was shown by this woman into a sitting room, where a frugal supper was laid out. Afterwards Mr. Jonas Oldacre led me into his bedroom, in which there stood a heavy safe. This he opened and took out a mass of documents, which we went over together. It was between eleven and twelve when we finished. He remarked that we must not disturb the housekeeper. He showed me out through his own French window, which had been open all this time."

"Was the blind down?" asked Holmes.

"I will not be sure, but I believe that it was only half down. Yes, I remember how he pulled it up in order to swing open the window. I could not find my stick, and he said, 'Never mind, my boy, I shall see a good deal of you now, I hope, and I will keep your stick until you come back to claim it.' I left him there, the safe open, and the papers made up in packets upon the table. It was so late that I could not get back to Blackheath, so I spent the night at the Anerley Arms, and I knew nothing more until I read of this horrible affair in the morning."

"Anything more that you would like to ask, Mr. Holmes?" said Lestrade, whose eyebrows had gone up once or twice during this remarkable explanation.

"Not until I have been to Blackheath."

"You mean to Norwood," said Lestrade.

"Oh, yes, no doubt that is what I must have meant," said Holmes, with his enigmatical smile.

Lestrade had learned by more experiences than he would care to acknowledge that that razorlike brain could cut through that which was impenetrable to him. I saw him look curiously at my companion. "I think I should like to have a word with you presently, Mr. Sherlock Holmes." said he. Now, Mr. McFarlane, two of my constables are at the door, and there is a four-wheeler waiting."

The wretched young man arose and with a last beseeching glance at us walked from the room. The officers conducted him to the cab, but Lestrade remained.

Holmes had picked up the pages which formed the rough draft of the will and was looking at them with the keenest interest upon his face. "There are some points about that document, Lestrade, are there not?" said he, pushing them over.

The official looked at them with a puzzled expression. "I can read the first few lines, and these in the middle of the second page, and one or two at the end. Those are as clear as print," said he, "but the writing in between is very bad, and there are three places where I cannot read it at all."

"What do you make of that?" said Holmes.

"Well, what do *you* make of it?"

"That it was written in a train. The good writing represents stations, the bad writing movement, and the very bad writing passing over points.[5] A scientific expert would pronounce at once that this was drawn up on a suburban line, since nowhere save in the immediate vicinity of a great city could there be so quick a succession of points. Granting that his whole journey was occupied in drawing up the will, then the train was an express, only stopping once between Norwood and London Bridge."

Lestrade began to laugh. "You are too many for me when you begin to get on your theories, Mr. Holmes," said he. "How does this bear on the case?"

"Well, it corroborates the young man's story to the extent that the will was drawn up by Jonas Oldacre in his journey yesterday. It is curious, is it not, that a man should draw up so important a document in so haphazard a fashion. It suggests that he did not think it was going to be of much practical importance. If a man drew up a will which he did not intend ever to be effective, he might do it so."

"Well, he drew up his own death warrant at the same time," said Lestrade.

"Oh, you think so?"

"Don't you?"

"Well, it is quite possible, but the case is not clear to me yet."

"Not clear? Well, if that isn't clear, what *could* be clear? Here is a young man who learns suddenly that, if a certain older man dies, he will succeed to a fortune. What does he do? He says nothing to anyone, but he arranges that he shall go out on some pretext to see his client that night. He waits until the only other person in the house is in bed, and then in the solitude of the man's room he murders him, burns his body in the woodpile, and departs to a neighboring hotel. The bloodstains in the room and also on the stick are very slight. It is probable that he imagined his crime to be a bloodless one and hoped that if the body were consumed it would hide all traces of the method of his death—traces which, for some reason, must have pointed to him. Is not all this obvious?"

"It strikes me, my good Lestrade, as being just a trifle too obvious," said Holmes. "You do not add imagination to your other great qualities, but if you could for one moment put yourself in the place of this young man, would you choose the very night after the will had been made to commit your crime? Would it not seem dangerous to you to make so very

---

[5] *points:* switches, places where a train can switch from one track to another.

close a relation between the two incidents? Again, would you choose an occasion when you are known to be in the house, when a servant has let you in? And, finally, would you take the great pains to conceal the body, and yet leave your own stick as a sign that you were the criminal? Confess, Lestrade, that all this is very unlikely."

"As to the stick, Mr. Holmes, you know as well as I do that a criminal is often flurried and does such things which a cool man would avoid. He was very likely afraid to go back to the room. Give me another theory that would fit the facts."

"I could very easily give you half a dozen," said Holmes. "Here, for example, is a very possible and even probable one. I make you a free present of it. The older man is showing documents which are of evident value. A passing tramp sees them through the window, the blind of which is only half down. Exit the solicitor. Enter the tramp! He seizes a stick, which he observes there, kills Oldacre, and departs after burning the body."

"Why should the tramp burn the body?"

"For the matter of that, why should McFarlane?"

"To hide some evidence."

"Possibly the tramp wanted to hide that any murder at all had been committed."

"And why did the tramp take nothing?"

"Because they were papers that he could not negotiate."

Lestrade shook his head, though it seemed to me that his manner was less absolutely assured than before. "Well, Mr. Sherlock Holmes, you may look for your tramp, and while you are finding him, we will hold on to our man. The future will show which is right. Just notice this point, Mr. Holmes: that so far as we know, none of the papers were removed, and that the prisoner is the one man in the world who had no reason for removing them, since he was heir-at-law, and would come into them in any case."

My friend seemed struck by this remark. "I don't mean to deny that the evidence is in some ways very strongly in favor of your theory," said he. "I only wish to point out that there are other theories possible. As you say, the future will decide. Good morning! I daresay that in the course of the day I shall drop in at Norwood and see how you are getting on."

When the detective departed, my friend rose and made his preparations for the day's work with the alert air of a man who has a congenial task before him. "My first movement, Watson," said he, as he bustled into his frock-coat, "must, as I said, be in the direction of Blackheath."

"And why not Norwood?"

"Because we have in this case one singular incident coming close to the heels of another singular incident. The police are making the mistake of concentrating their attention upon the second, because it happens to be the one which is actually criminal. But it is evident to me that the logical way to approach the case is to begin by trying to throw some light upon the first incident—the curious will, so suddenly made, and to so unexpected an heir. It may do something to simplify what followed. No, my dear fellow, I don't think you can help me. There is no prospect of danger, or I should not dream of stirring out without you. I trust that when I see you in the evening, I will be able to report that I have been able to do something for this unfortunate youngster who has thrown himself upon my protection."

It was late when my friend returned, and I could see by a glance at his haggard and anxious face that the high hopes with which he had started had not been fulfilled. For an hour he droned away upon his violin, endeavoring to soothe his own ruffled spirits.

At last he flung down the instrument and plunged into a detailed account of his misadventures. "It's all going wrong, Watson—all as wrong as it can go. I kept a bold face before Lestrade, but upon my soul I believe that for once the fellow is on the right track and we are on the wrong. All my instincts are one way, and all the facts are the other, and I much fear that British juries have not yet attained that pitch of intelligence when they will give the preference to my theories over Lestrade's facts."

"Did you go to Blackheath?"

"Yes, Watson, I went there, and I found very quickly that the late la-

mented Oldacre was a pretty considerable blackguard. The father was away in search of his son. The mother was at home—a little, fluffy, blue-eyed person, in a tremor of fear and indignation. Of course, she would not admit even the possibility of his guilt. But she would not express either surprise or regret over the fate of Oldacre. On the contrary, she spoke of him with such bitterness that she was unconsciously considerably strengthening the case of the police, for of course if her son had heard her speak of the man in this fashion, it would predispose him toward hatred and violence.

" 'He was more like a malignant and cunning ape than a human being,' said she, 'and he always was, ever since he was a young man.'

" 'You knew him at that time?' said I.

" 'Yes, I knew him well; in fact, he was an old suitor of mine. Thank heaven that I had the sense to turn away from him and to marry a better, if poorer, man. I was engaged to him, Mr. Holmes, when I heard a shocking story of how he had turned a cat loose in an aviary,[6] and I was so horrified at his brutal cruelty that I would have nothing more to do with him.' She rummaged in a bureau, and presently she produced a photograph of a woman, shamefully defaced and mutilated with a knife. 'That is my own photograph,' she said. 'He sent it

---

[6] *aviary:* large birdhouse.

to me in that state, with his curse, upon my wedding morning.'

"'Well,' said I, 'at least he has forgiven you now, since he has left all his property to your son.'

"'Neither my son nor I want anything from Jonas Oldacre, dead or alive!' she cried, with a proper spirit. 'There is a God in heaven, Mr. Holmes, and that same God who has punished that wicked man will show, in His own good time, that my son's hands are guiltless of his blood.'

"Well, I tried one or two leads, but could get at nothing which would help our hypothesis, and several points which would make against it. I gave it up at last, and off I went to Norwood.

"This place, Deep Dene House, is a big modern villa of staring brick, standing back in its own grounds, with a laurel-clumped lawn in front of it. To the right and some distance back from the road was the timber yard which had been the scene of the fire. Here's a rough plan on a leaf of my notebook. This window on the left is the one which opens into Oldacre's room. You can look into it from the road, you see. That is about the only bit of consolation I have had today. Lestrade was not there, but his head constable did the honors. They had just found a great treasure-trove. They had spent the morning raking among the ashes of the burned wood-pile, and besides the charred organic remains they had secured several discolored metal disks. I examined them with care, and there was no doubt that they were trouser buttons. I even distinguished that one of them was marked with the name of 'Hyams,' who was Oldacre's tailor. I then worked the lawn very carefully for signs and traces, but this drought has made everything as hard as iron. Nothing was to be seen save that some body or bundle had been dragged through a low privet hedge which is in a line with the woodpile. All that, of course, fits in with the official theory. I crawled about the lawn with an August sun on my back, but I got up at the end of an hour no wiser than before.

"Well, after this fiasco I went into the bedroom and examined that also. The bloodstains were very slight, mere smears and discolorations, but undoubtedly fresh. The stick had been removed, but there also the marks were slight. There is no doubt about the stick belonging to our client. He admits it. Footmarks of both men could be made out on the carpet, but none of any third person—which again is a trick for the other side. They were piling up their score all the time, and we were at a standstill.

"Only one little gleam of hope did I get—and yet it amounted to nothing. I examined the contents of the safe, most of which had been taken out and left on the table. The papers had been made up into sealed envelopes, one or two of which had been opened by the police. They were not, so far as I could judge, of any great value, nor did the bankbook show that Mr. Oldacre was in such very affluent circumstances. But it seemed to me that all the papers were not there. There were allusions to some deeds—possibly the more valuable—which I could not find. This, of course, if we could definitely prove it, would turn Lestrade's argument against himself, for who would steal a thing if he knew that he would shortly inherit it?

"Finally, having drawn every other cover and picked up no scent, I tried my luck with the housekeeper. Mrs. Lexington is her name—a little, dark, silent person with suspicious and sidelong eyes. She could tell us something if she would—I am convinced of it. But she was as close as wax. Yes, she had let Mr. McFarlane in at half past nine. She wished her hand had withered before she had done so. She had gone to bed at half past ten. Her room was at the other end of the house, and she could hear nothing of what passed. Mr. McFarlane had left his hat, and to the best of her belief his stick, in the hall. She had been awakened by the alarm of fire. Her poor, dear master had certainly been murdered. Had he any enemies? Well, every man had enemies, but Mr. Oldacre kept himself very much to himself and only met people in the way of business. She had seen the buttons and was sure that they belonged to the clothes which he had worn last night. The woodpile was very dry, for it had not rained for a month. It burned like tinder, and by the time she reached the spot, nothing could be seen but flames. She and all the firemen smelled the burned flesh from inside it. She knew nothing of the papers, nor of Mr. Oldacre's private affairs.

"So, my dear Watson, there's my report of a failure. And yet—and yet"—he clenched his thin hands in a paroxysm of conviction—"I *know* it's all wrong. I feel it in my bones. There is something that has not come out, and that housekeeper knows it. There was a sort of sulky defiance in her eyes which only goes with guilty knowledge. However, there's no good talking any more about it, Watson; but unless some lucky chance comes our way, I fear that the Norwood Disappearance Case will not figure in that chronicle of our successes which I foresee that a patient public will sooner or later have to endure."

"Surely," said I, "the man's appearance would go far with any jury?"

"That is a dangerous argument, my dear Watson. You remember that terrible murderer, Bert Stevens, who wanted us to get him off in '87? Was there ever a more mild-mannered, Sunday-school young man?"

"It is true."

"Unless we succeed in establishing an alternative theory, this man is lost. You can hardly find a flaw in the case which can now be presented against him, and all further investigation has served to strengthen it. By the way, there is one curious little point about those papers which may serve us as the starting point for an inquiry. On looking over the bank-book, I found that the low state of the balance was principally due to large checks which have been made out during the last year to Mr. Cornelius. I confess that I should be interested to know who this Mr. Cornelius may be with whom a retired builder has such very large transactions. Is it possible that he has had a hand in the affair? Cornelius might be a broker, but we have found no scrip to correspond with these large payments. Failing any other indication, my researches must now take the direction of an inquiry at the bank for the gentleman who has cashed these checks. But I fear, my dear fellow, that our case will end ingloriously by Lestrade hanging our client, which will certainly be a triumph for Scotland Yard."

I do not know how far Sherlock Holmes took any sleep that night, but when I came down to breakfast I found him pale and harassed, his bright eyes the brighter for the dark shadows round them. The carpet round his chair was littered with cigarette ends and with the early editions of the morning papers. An open telegram lay upon the table.

"What do you think of this, Watson?" he asked, tossing it across.

It was from Norwood, and ran as follows: "IMPORTANT FRESH EVIDENCE TO HAND. MCFARLANE'S GUILT DEFINITELY ESTABLISHED. ADVISE YOU TO ABANDON CASE. LESTRADE."

"This sounds serious," said I.

"It is Lestrade's little cock-a-doo-dle of victory," Holmes answered, with a bitter smile. "And yet it may be premature to abandon the case. After all, important fresh evidence is a two-edged thing and may possibly cut in a very different direction to that which Lestrade imagines. Take your breakfast, Watson, and we will go out together and see what we can do. I feel as if I shall need your company and your moral support today."

My friend had no breakfast himself, for it was one of his peculiarities that in his more intense moments he would permit himself no food, and I have known him presume upon his iron strength until he has fainted from pure inanition. "At present I cannot spare energy and nerve force for digestion," he would say in answer to my medical remonstrances. I was not surprised, therefore, when this morning he left his untouched meal behind him and started with me for Norwood.

A crowd of morbid sightseers were still gathered round Deep Dene House, which was just such a suburban villa as I had pictured. Within the gates Lestrade met us, his face flushed with victory, his manner grossly triumphant. "Well, Mr. Holmes, have you proved us to be wrong yet? Have you found your tramp?" he cried.

"I have formed no conclusion whatever," my companion answered.

"But we formed ours yesterday, and now it proves to be correct, so you must acknowledge that we have

been a little in front of you this time, Mr. Holmes."

"You certainly have the air of something unusual having occurred," said Holmes.

Lestrade laughed loudly. "You don't like being beaten any more than the rest of us do," said he. "A man can't expect always to have it his own way, can he, Dr. Watson? Step this way, if you please, gentlemen, and I think I can convince you once for all that it was John McFarlane who did this crime."

He led us through the passage and out into a dark hall beyond. "This is where young McFarlane must have come out to get his hat after the crime was done," said he. "Now look at this." With dramatic suddenness he struck a match and by its light exposed a stain of blood upon the whitewashed wall.

As he held the match nearer, I saw that it was more than a stain. It was the well-marked print of a thumb.

"Look at that with your magnifying glass, Mr. Holmes."

"Yes, I am doing so."

"You are aware that no two thumbmarks are alike?"

"I have heard something of the kind."

"Well, then, will you please compare that print with this wax impression of young McFarlane's right thumb, taken by my orders this morning?"

As he held the waxen print close to the bloodstain, it did not take a magnifying glass to see that the two

were undoubtedly from the same thumb. It was evident to me that our unfortunate client was lost.

"That is final," said Lestrade.

"Yes, that is final," I involuntarily echoed.

"It is final," said Holmes.

Something in his tone caught my ear, and I turned to look at him. An extraordinary change had come over his face. It was writhing with inward merriment. His two eyes were shining like stars. It seemed to me that he was making desperate efforts to restrain a convulsive attack of laughter.

"Dear me! Dear me!" he said at last. "Well, now, who would have thought it? And how deceptive appearances may be, to be sure! Such a nice young man to look at! It is a lesson to us not to trust our own judgment, is it not, Lestrade?"

"Yes, some of us are a little too much inclined to be cocksure, Mr. Holmes," said Lestrade. The man's insolence was maddening, but we could not resent it.

"What a providential thing that this young man should press his right thumb against the wall in taking his hat from the peg! Such a very natural action, too, if you come to think of it." Holmes was outwardly calm, but his whole body gave a wriggle of suppressed excitement as he spoke. "By the way, Lestrade, who made this remarkable discovery?"

"It was the housekeeper, Mrs. Lexington, who drew the night constable's attention to it."

"Where was the night constable?"

"He remained on guard in the bedroom where the crime was committed, so as to see that nothing was touched."

"But why didn't the police see this mark yesterday?"

"Well, we had no particular reason to make a careful examination of the hall. Besides, it's not in a very prominent place, as you see."

"No, no—of course not. I suppose there is no doubt that the mark was there yesterday?"

Lestrade looked at Holmes as if he thought he was going out of his mind. I confess that I was myself surprised both at his hilarious manner and at his rather wild observation.

"I don't know whether you think that McFarlane came out of jail in the dead of the night in order to strengthen the evidence against himself," said Lestrade. "I leave it to any expert in the world whether that is not the mark of his thumb."

"It is unquestionably the mark of his thumb."

"There, that's enough," said Lestrade. "I am a practical man, Mr. Holmes, and when I have got my evidence, I come to my conclusions. If you have anything to say, you will find me writing my report in the sitting room."

Holmes had recovered his equanimity, though I still seemed to detect gleams of amusement in his expression. "Dear me, this is a very sad development, Watson, is it not?"

said he. "And yet there are singular points about it which hold some hopes for our client."

"I am delighted to hear it," said I, heartily. "I was afraid it was all up with him."

"I would hardly go so far as to say that, my dear Watson. The fact is that there is one really serious flaw in this evidence to which our friend attaches so much importance."

"Indeed, Holmes! What is it?"

"Only this: that I *know* that that mark was not there when I examined the hall yesterday. And now, Watson, let us have a little stroll round in the sunshine."

With a confused brain, but with a heart into which some warmth of hope was returning, I accompanied my friend in a walk round the garden. Holmes took each face of the house in turn and examined it with great interest. He then led the way inside and went over the whole building from basement to attic. Most of the rooms were unfurnished, but nonetheless Holmes inspected them all minutely. Finally, on the top corridor, which ran outside three untenanted bedrooms, he again was seized with a spasm of merriment.

"There are really some very unique features about this case, Watson," said he. "I think it is time now that we took our friend Lestrade into our confidence. He has had his little smile at our expense, and perhaps we may do as much by him if my reading of this problem proves to be correct. Yes, yes, I think I see how we should approach it."

The Scotland Yard inspector was still writing in the parlor when Holmes interrupted him. "I understand that you are writing a report of this case," said he.

"So I am."

"Don't you think it may be a little premature? I can't help thinking that your evidence is not complete."

Lestrade knew my friend too well to disregard his words. He laid down his pen and looked curiously at him.

"What do you mean, Mr. Holmes?"

"Only that there is an important witness whom you have not seen."

"Can you produce him?"

"I think I can."

"Then do so."

"I will do my best. How many constables have you?"

"There are three within call."

"Excellent!" said Holmes. "May I ask if they are all large, able-bodied men with powerful voices?"

"I have no doubt they are, though I fail to see what their voices have to do with it."

"Perhaps I can help you to see that and one or two other things as well," said Holmes. "Kindly summon your men, and I will try."

Five minutes later, three policemen had assembled in the hall.

"In the outhouse you will find a considerable quantity of straw," said Holmes. "I will ask you to carry in two bundles of it. I think it will be of the greatest assistance in producing the witness whom I require. Thank you very much. I believe you have some matches in your pocket, Watson. Now, Mr. Lestrade, I will ask you all to accompany me to the top landing."

As I have said, there was a broad corridor there, which ran outside three empty bedrooms. At one end of the corridor we were all marshaled by Sherlock Holmes, the constables grinning and Lestrade staring at my friend with amazement, expectation, and derision chasing each other across his features.

Holmes stood before us with the air of a conjuror who is performing a trick. "Would you kindly send one of your constables for two buckets of water? Put the straw on the floor here, free from the wall on either side. Now I think that we are all ready."

Lestrade's face had begun to grow red and angry. "I don't know whether you are playing a game with us, Mr. Sherlock Holmes," said he. "If you know anything, you can surely say it without all this tomfoolery."

"I assure you, my good Lestrade, that I have an excellent reason for everything that I do. You may possibly remember that you chaffed me a little some hours ago when the sun seemed on your side of the hedge, so you must not grudge me a little pomp and ceremony now. Might I ask you,

Watson, to open that window and then to put a match to the edge of the straw?"

I did so, and driven by the draft, a coil of gray smoke swirled down the corridor while the dry straw crackled and flamed.

"Now we must see if we can find this witness for you, Lestrade. Might I ask you all to join in the cry of 'Fire!'? Now then, one, two, three——"

"Fire!" we all yelled.

"Thank you. I will trouble you once again."

"Fire!"

"Just once more, gentlemen, and all together."

"Fire!" The shout must have rung over Norwood.

It had hardly died away when an amazing thing happened. A door suddenly flew open out of what appeared to be solid wall at the end of the corridor, and a little, wizened man darted out of it like a rabbit out of its burrow.

"Capital!" said Holmes, calmly. "Watson, a bucket of water over the straw. That will do! Lestrade, allow me to present you with your principal missing witness, Mr. Jonas Oldacre."

The detective stared at the newcomer with blank amazement. The latter was blinking in the bright light of the corridor and peering at us and at the smoldering fire. It was an odious face—crafty, vicious, malignant, with shifty, light gray eyes and white lashes.

"What's this, then?" said Les-trade, at last. "What have you been doing all this time, eh?"

Oldacre gave an uneasy laugh, shrinking back from the furious red face of the angry detective. "I have done no harm."

"No harm? You have done your best to get an innocent man hanged. If it wasn't for this gentleman here, I am not sure that you would not have succeeded."

The wretched creature began to whimper. "I am sure, sir, it was only my practical joke."

"Oh! a joke, was it? You won't find the laugh on your side, I promise you. Take him down and keep him in the sitting room until I come. Mr. Holmes," he continued when they had gone, "I could not speak before the constables, but I don't mind saying in the presence of Dr. Watson that this is the brightest thing that you have done yet, though it is a mystery to me how you did it. You have saved an innocent man's life, and you have prevented a very grave scandal which would have ruined my reputation in the Force."

Holmes smiled and clapped Les-trade upon his shoulder. "Instead of being ruined, my good sir, you will find that your reputation has been enormously enhanced. Just make a few alterations in that report which you were writing, and they will understand how hard it is to throw dust in the eyes of Inspector Lestrade."

"And you don't want your name to appear?"

"Not at all. The work is its own

reward. Perhaps I shall get the credit also at some distant day when I permit my zealous historian to lay out his foolscap[7] once more—eh, Watson? Well, now, let us see where this rat has been lurking."

A lath-and-plaster partition had been run across the passage six feet from the end, with a door cunningly concealed in it. It was lit within by slits under the eaves. A few articles of furniture and a supply of food and water were within, together with a number of books and papers.

"There's the advantage of being a builder," said Holmes, as we came out. "He was able to fix up his own little hiding place without any confederate—save, of course, that precious housekeeper of his, whom I should lose no time in adding to your bag, Lestrade."

"I'll take your advice. But how did you know of this place, Mr. Holmes?"

"I made up my mind that the fellow was in hiding in the house. When I paced one corridor and found it six feet shorter than the corresponding one below, it was pretty clear where he was. I thought he had not the nerve to lie quiet before an alarm of fire. We could, of course, have gone in and taken him, but it amused me to make him reveal himself. Besides, I owed you a little mystification, Lestrade, for your chaff in the morning."

"Well, sir, you certainly got equal with me on that. But how in the world did you know that he was in the house at all?"

"The thumbmark, Lestrade. You said it was final, and so it was, in a very different sense. I knew it had not been there the day before. I pay a good deal of attention to matters of detail, as you may have observed, and I had examined the hall and was sure that the wall was clear. Therefore, it had been put on during the night."

"But how?"

"Very simply. When those packets were sealed up, Jonas Oldacre got McFarlane to secure one of the seals by putting his thumb upon the soft wax. It would be done so quickly and so naturally that I daresay the young man himself has no recollection of it. Very likely it just so happened, and Oldacre had himself no notion of the use he would put it to. Brooding over the case in that den of his, it suddenly struck him what absolutely damning evidence he could make against McFarlane by using that thumbmark. It was the simplest thing in the world for him to take a wax impression from the seal, to moisten it in as much blood as he could get from a pinprick, and to put the mark upon the wall during the night, either with his own hand or with that of his housekeeper. If you examine among those documents which he took with him into his retreat, I will lay you a wager that you find the seal with the thumbmark upon it."

---

[7] *foolscap:* long sheets of paper.

"Wonderful!" said Lestrade. "Wonderful! It's all as clear as crystal, as you put it. But what is the object of this deep deception, Mr. Holmes?"

It was amusing to me to see how the detective's overbearing manner had changed suddenly to that of a child asking questions of its teacher.

"Well, I don't think that is very hard to explain. A very deep, malicious, vindictive person is the gentleman who is now awaiting us downstairs. You know that he was once refused by McFarlane's mother? You don't! I told you that you should go to Blackheath first and Norwood afterward. Well, this injury, as he would consider it, has rankled in his wicked, scheming brain, and all his life he has longed for vengeance but never seen his chance. During the last year or two, things have gone against him—secret speculation, I think—and he finds himself in a bad way. He determines to swindle his creditors,[8] and for this purpose he pays large checks to a certain Mr. Cornelius, who is, I imagine, himself under another name. I have not traced these checks yet, but I have no doubt that they were banked under that name at some provincial town where Oldacre from time to time led a double existence. He intended to change his name altogether, draw this money, and vanish, starting life again elsewhere."

"Well, that's likely enough."

"It would strike him that in disappearing he might throw all pursuit off his track and at the same time have an ample and crushing revenge upon his old sweetheart if he could give the impression that he had been murdered by her only child. It was a masterpiece of villainy, and he carried it out like a master. The idea of the will, which would give an obvious motive for the crime, the secret visit unknown to his own parents, the retention of the stick, the blood, and the animal remains and buttons in the woodpile—all were admirable. It was a net from which it seemed to me a few hours ago that there was no possible escape. But he had not that supreme gift of the artist, the knowledge of when to stop. He wished to improve that which was already perfect—to draw the rope tighter yet round the neck of his unfortunate victim—and so he ruined all. Let us descend, Lestrade. There are just one or two questions that I would ask him."

The malignant creature was seated in his own parlor, with a policeman upon each side of him.

"It was a joke, my good sir—a practical joke, nothing more," he whined incessantly. "I assure you sir, that I simply concealed myself in order to see the effect of my disappearance, and I am sure that you would not be so unjust as to imagine that I would have allowed any harm to befall poor young Mr. McFarlane."

"That's for a jury to decide," said Lestrade. "Anyhow, we shall have

---

[8] *creditors:* people to whom money is owed.

you on a charge of conspiracy, if not for attempted murder."

"And you'll probably find that your creditors will impound the banking account of Mr. Cornelius," said Holmes.

The little man started, and turned his malignant eyes upon my friend. "I have to thank you for a good deal," said he. "Perhaps I'll pay my debt some day."

Holmes smiled indulgently. "I fancy that for some few years you will find your time very fully occupied," said he. "By the way, what was it you put into the woodpile besides your old trousers? A dead dog or rabbits or what? You won't tell? Dear me, how very unkind of you! Well, well, I daresay that a couple of rabbits would account both for the blood and for the charred ashes. If ever you write an account, Watson, you can make rabbits serve your turn."

DISCUSSION

1. Could you have solved the mystery with the clues the writer gave you? Do you think he intended you to? Explain.

2. How would you describe the relationship between Sherlock Holmes and Inspector Lestrade? What does each think of the other? What things in the story did you base your answer on?

3. From whose **point of view** (see page 78) is the story told? Imagine that you are going to write a mystery story and that you want to keep the reader in suspense. What would be some of the advantages of telling your story through the eyes of an onlooker rather than having the detective tell it?

4. This story comes from *The Adventures of Sherlock Holmes* by Sir Arthur Conan Doyle, a book containing many other stories you may enjoy.

For further activities, see page 318.

MACAVITY: THE MYSTERY CAT

T. S. ELIOT

Macavity's a Mystery Cat: he's called the Hidden Paw—
For he's the master criminal who can defy the Law.
He's the bafflement of Scotland Yard, the Flying Squad's despair:
For when they reach the scene of crime—*Macavity's not there!*

Macavity, Macavity, there's no one like Macavity,   5
He's broken every human law, he breaks the law of gravity.
His powers of levitation would make a fakir stare,
And when you reach the scene of crime—*Macavity's not there!*
You may seek him in the basement, you may look up in the air—
But I tell you once and once again, *Macavity's not there!*   10

Macavity's a ginger cat, he's very tall and thin;
You would know him if you saw him, for his eyes are sunken in.
His brow is deeply lined with thought, his head is highly domed;
His coat is dusty from neglect, his whiskers are uncombed.
He sways his head from side to side, with movements like a snake;   15
And when you think he's half asleep, he's always wide awake.

Macavity, Macavity, there's no one like Macavity,
For he's a fiend in feline shape, a monster of depravity.
You may meet him in a by-street, you may see him in the square—
But when a crime's discovered, then *Macavity's not there!*   20

He's outwardly respectable. (They say he cheats at cards.)
And his footprints are not found in any file of Scotland Yard's.
And when the larder's looted, or the jewel-case is rifled,
Or when the milk is missing, or another Peke's been stifled,
Or the greenhouse glass is broken, and the trellis past repair—   25
Ay, there's the wonder of the thing! *Macavity's not there!*

---

24. *Peke's been stifled:* Pekinese (small long-haired dog) has been smothered.

And when the Foreign Office find a Treaty's gone astray,
Or the Admiralty lose some plans and drawings by the way,
There may be a scrap of paper in the hall or on the stair—
But it's useless to investigate—*Macavity's not there!*   30
And when the loss has been disclosed, the Secret Service say:
"It *must* have been Macavity!"—but he's a mile away.
You'll be sure to find him resting, or a-licking of his thumbs,
Or engaged in doing complicated long division sums.

Macavity, Macavity, there's no one like Macavity,   35
There never was a Cat of such deceitfulness and suavity.
He always has an alibi, and one or two to spare:
At whatever time the deed took place—MACAVITY WASN'T THERE!
And they say that all the Cats whose wicked deeds are widely known
(I might mention Mungojerrie, I might mention Griddlebone)   40
Are nothing more than agents for the Cat who all the time
Just controls their operations: the Napoleon of Crime!

DISCUSSION   1.   Macavity operates out of England, probably London. What minor
changes would you make in the poem to change the scene to the United
States?

2.   Macavity's activities are mainly in the human area, but one or two of
his crimes are things a criminal cat might do. What are these?

3.   **Alliteration.**   Look at line 18: "For he's a fiend in feline shape, a
monster of depravity." The repetition of the *f* sound is called alliteration.
So is the repetition of any initial consonant sound, like "Peter Piper
picked a peck of pickled peppers." What other examples of alliteration
do you find in this poem? What is the effect of the sounds?

For further activities, see page 318.

The Cask of Amontillado

EDGAR ALLAN POE

The thousand injuries of Fortunato I had borne as I best could; but when he ventured upon insult, I vowed revenge. You, who so well know the nature of my soul, will not suppose, however, that I gave utterance to a threat. At length I would be avenged; this was a point definitely settled—but the very definitiveness with which it was resolved precluded the idea of risk. I must not only punish but punish with impunity. A wrong is unredressed when retribution overtakes its redresser. It is equally unredressed when the avenger fails to make himself felt as such to him who has done the wrong.

It must be understood that neither by word nor deed had I given Fortunato cause to doubt my good will. I continued, as was my wont, to smile in his face, and he did not perceive that my smile *now* was at the thought of his immolation.

He had a weak point—this Fortunato—although in other regards he was a man to be respected and even feared. He prided himself on his connoisseurship in wine. Few Italians have the true virtuoso spirit. For the most part their enthusiasm is adopted to suit the time and opportunity, to practice imposture upon the British and Austrian millionaires. In painting and gemmary[1] Fortunato, like his countrymen, was a quack—but in the matter of old wines he was sincere. In this respect I did not differ from him materially: I was skillful in the Italian vintages myself, and bought largely whenever I could.

It was about dusk, one evening during the supreme madness of the carnival season, that I encountered my friend. He accosted me with excessive warmth, for he had been drinking much. The man wore motley. He had on a tight-fitting parti-striped dress, and his head was surmounted by the conical cap and bells. I was so pleased to see him that I thought I should never have done wringing his hand.

I said to him, "My dear Fortunato, you are luckily met. How remarkably well you are looking today. But I have received a pipe[2]

Amontillado (ə-mŏn-tə-lä′dō): a Spanish wine.
[1] *gemmary:* the art of cutting precious stones.
[2] pipe: a large cask for wines.

of what passes for Amontillado and I have my doubts."

"How?" said he. "Amontillado? A pipe? Impossible! And in the middle of the carnival!"

"I have my doubts," I replied; "and I was silly enough to pay the full Amontillado price without consulting you in the matter. You were not to be found, and I was fearful of losing a bargain."

"Amontillado!"

"I have my doubts."

"Amontillado!"

"And I must satisfy them."

"Amontillado!"

"As you are engaged, I am on my way to Luchesi. If anyone has a critical turn, it is he. He will tell me——"

"Luchesi cannot tell Amontillado from sherry."

"And yet some fools will have it that his taste is a match for your own."

"Come, let us go."

"Whither?"

"To your vaults."

"My friend, no; I will not impose upon your good nature. I perceive you have an engagement. Luchesi——"

"I have no engagement—come."

"My friend, no. It is not the engagement, but the severe cold with which I perceive you are afflicted. The vaults are insufferably damp. They are incrusted with niter."[3]

"Let us go, nevertheless. The cold is merely nothing. Amontillado! You have been imposed upon. And as for Luchesi, he cannot distinguish sherry from Amontillado."

Thus speaking, Fortunato possessed himself of my arm. Putting on a mask of black silk and drawing a roquelaure closely about my person, I suffered him to hurry me to my palazzo.

There were no attendants at home; they had absconded to make merry in honor of the time. I had told them that I should not return until the morning, and had given them explicit orders not to stir from the house. These orders were sufficient, I well knew, to insure their immediate disappearance, one and all, as soon as my back was turned.

I took from their sconces two flambeaux,[4] and giving one to

---

[3] *niter:* potassium nitrate, which forms on the damp walls of caves.
[4] *took . . . flambeaux:* took from their holders two torches.

Fortunato, bowed him through several suites of rooms to the archway that led into the vaults. I passed down a long and winding staircase, requesting him to be cautious as he followed. We came at length to the foot of the descent, and stood together upon the damp ground of the catacombs[5] of the Montresors.

The gait of my friend was unsteady, and the bells upon his cap jingled as he strode.

"The pipe," he said.

"It is farther on," said I; "but observe the white webwork which gleams from these cavern walls."

He turned towards me, and looked into my eyes with two filmy orbs that distilled the rheum of intoxication.[6]

"Niter?" he asked at length.

"Niter," I replied. "How long have you had that cough?"

"Ugh! ugh! ugh!—ugh! ugh! ugh!—ugh! ugh! ugh!—ugh! ugh! ugh!—ugh! ugh! ugh!"

My poor friend found it impossible to reply for many minutes.

"It is nothing," he said at last.

"Come," I said with decision, "we will go back; your health is precious. You are rich, respected, admired, beloved; you are happy, as once I was. You are a man to be missed. For me it is no matter. We will go back; you will be ill, and I cannot be responsible. Besides, there is Luchesi——"

"Enough," he said, "the cough is a mere nothing: it will not kill me. I shall not die of a cough."

"True—true," I replied; "and, indeed, I had no intention of alarming you unnecessarily—but you should use all proper caution. A draught of this Medoc will defend us from the damps."

Here I knocked off the neck of a bottle which I drew from a long row of its fellows that lay upon the mold.

"Drink," I said, presenting him the wine.

He raised it to his lips with a leer. He paused and nodded to me familiarly, while his bells jingled.

"I drink," he said, "to the buried that repose around us."

"And I to your long life."

He again took my arm, and we proceeded.

"These vaults," he said, "are extensive."

---

[5] *catacombs:* underground burial passages.
[6] *orbs . . . intoxication:* eyes that were watery with drunkenness.

"The Montresors," I replied, "were a great and numerous family."

"I forget your arms."

"A huge human foot d'or, in a field azure; the foot crushes a serpent rampant whose fangs are imbedded in the heel."[7]

"And the motto?"

"Nemo me impune lacessit."[8]

"Good!" he said.

The wine sparkled in his eyes, and the bells jingled. My own fancy grew warm with the Medoc. We had passed through long walls of piled bones, with casks and puncheons intermingling, into the inmost recesses of the catacombs. I paused again, and this time I made bold to seize Fortunato by an arm above the elbow.

"The niter!" I said; "see, it increases. It hangs like moss upon the vaults. We are below the river's bed. The drops of moisture trickle among the bones. Come, we will go back ere it is too late. Your cough——"

"It is nothing," he said; "let us go on. But first, another draught of the Medoc."

I broke and reached him a flagon of De Grâve. He emptied it at a breath. His eyes flashed with a fierce light. He laughed and threw the bottle upwards with a gesticulation I did not understand.

I looked at him in surprise. He repeated the movement—a grotesque one.

"You do not comprehend?" he said.

"Not I," I replied.

"Then you are not of the brotherhood."

"How?"

"You are not of the masons."

"Yes, yes," I said; "yes, yes."

"You? Impossible! A mason?"

"A mason," I replied.

"A sign," he said, "a sign."

"It is this," I answered, producing from beneath the folds of my roquelaure a trowel.[9]

---

[7] *foot . . . heel:* a golden foot on a blue background; the foot is crushing a snake with its head raised to strike and its fangs already in the heel.

[8] *Nemo . . . lacessit:* "No one strikes me without being punished for it."

[9] The word *Mason* is the name of a secret society, but it also refers to a person who works with stone. Montresor does not understand Fortunato's secret sign, but then he makes a pun on the word by producing a trowel (a mason's tool) and saying that he *is* a mason.

"You jest," he exclaimed, recoiling a few paces. "But let us proceed to the Amontillado."

"Be it so," I said, replacing the tool beneath the cloak, and again offering him my arm. He leaned upon it heavily. We continued our route in search of the Amontillado. We passed through a range of low arches, descended, passed on, and descending again, arrived at a deep crypt, in which the foulness of the air caused our flambeaux rather to glow than flame.

At the most remote end of the crypt there appeared another less spacious. Its walls had been lined with human remains, piled to the vault overhead, in the fashion of the great catacombs of Paris. Three sides of this interior crypt were still ornamented in this manner. From the fourth side the bones had been thrown down and lay promiscuously upon the earth, forming at one point a mound of some size. Within the wall thus exposed by the displacing of the bones, we perceived a still interior crypt or recess, in depth about four feet, in width three, in height six or seven. It seemed to have been constructed for no especial use within itself, but formed merely the interval between two of the colossal supports of the roof of the catacombs, and was backed by one of their circumscribing walls of solid granite.

It was in vain that Fortunato, uplifting his dull torch, endeavored to pry into the depth of the recess. Its termination the feeble light did not enable us to see.

"Proceed," I said; "herein is the Amontillado. As for Luchesi——"

"He is an ignoramus," interrupted my friend as he stepped unsteadily forward, while I followed immediately at his heels. In an instant he had reached the extremity of the niche, and finding his progress arrested by the rock, stood stupidly bewildered. A moment more and I had fettered him to the granite. In its surface were two iron staples, distant from each other about two feet, horizontally. From one of these depended a short chain, from the other a padlock. Throwing the links about his waist, it was but the work of a few seconds to secure it. He was too much astounded to resist. Withdrawing the key, I stepped back from the recess.

"Pass your hand," I said, "over the wall; you cannot help feeling the niter. Indeed, it is very damp. Once more let me implore you to return. No? Then I must positively leave you. But I must first render you all the little attentions in my power."

"The Amontillado!" ejaculated my friend, not yet recovered from his astonishment.

"True," I replied; "the Amontillado."

As I said these words, I busied myself among the pile of bones of which I have before spoken. Throwing them aside, I soon uncovered a quantity of building stone and mortar. With these materials and with the aid of my trowel, I began vigorously to wall up the entrance of the niche.

I had scarcely laid the first tier of the masonry when I discovered that the intoxication of Fortunato had in a great measure worn off. The earliest indication I had of this was a low moaning cry from the depth of the recess. It was not the cry of a drunken man. There was then a long and obstinate silence. I laid the second tier, and the third, and the fourth; and then I heard the furious vibrations of the chain. The noise lasted for several minutes, during which, that I might hearken to it with the more satisfaction, I ceased my labors and sat down upon the bones. When at last the clanking had subsided, I resumed the trowel, and finished without interruption the fifth, the sixth, and the seventh tier. The wall was now nearly upon a level with my breast. I again paused, and holding the flambeaux over the mason work, threw a few feeble rays upon the figure within.

A succession of loud and shrill screams, bursting suddenly from the throat of the chained form, seemed to thrust me violently back. For a brief moment I hesitated—I trembled. Unsheathing my rapier, I began to grope with it about the recess; but the thought of an instant reassured me. I placed my hand upon the solid fabric of the catacombs, and felt satisfied. I reapproached the wall. I replied to the yells of him who clamored. I re-echoed—I aided—I surpassed them in volume and in strength. I did this, and the clamorer grew still.

It was now midnight, and my task was drawing to a close. I had completed the eighth, the ninth, and the tenth tier. I had finished a portion of the last and the eleventh; there remained but a single stone to be fitted and plastered in. I struggled with its weight; I placed it partially in its destined position.

But now there came from out the niche a low laugh that erected the hairs upon my head. It was succeeded by a sad voice, which I had difficulty in recognizing as that of the noble Fortunato. The voice said—

"Ha! ha! ha!—he! he! he!—a very good joke, indeed—an excellent jest. We will have many a rich laugh about it at the palazzo—he! he! he!—over our wine—he! he! he!"

"The Amontillado!" I said.

"He! he! he!—he! he! he!—yes, the Amontillado. But is it not getting late? Will not they be awaiting us at the palazzo—the Lady Fortunato and the rest? Let us be gone."

"Yes," I said, "let us be gone."

"For the love of God, Montresor!"

"Yes," I said, "for the love of God!"

But to these words I hearkened in vain for a reply. I grew impatient. I called aloud—

"Fortunato!"

No answer. I called again—

"Fortunato!"

No answer still. I thrust a torch through the remaining aperture and let it fall within. There came forth in return only a jingling of the bells. My heart grew sick—on account of the dampness of the catacombs. I hastened to make an end of my labor. I forced the last stone into its position; I plastered it up. Against the new masonry I re-erected the old rampart of bones. For the half of a century no mortal has disturbed them. *In pace requiescat!* [10]

---

[10] *In pace requiescat:* "May he rest in peace."

DISCUSSION

1. The first paragraph is important, because it explains why Montresor, the narrator, chooses this dreadful form of revenge. Read it again, and put his reasoning into your own words. What had Fortunato done to deserve his fate? Does Montresor's revenge meet the requirements he states in this paragraph?

2. What strategy does Montresor use to get Fortunato down into the vaults? What weaknesses in Fortunato's character does he appeal to?

3. What preparations has Montresor made ahead of time?

4. Suppose the story had been told from Fortunato's **point of view** (see page 78). Would the story be more or less horrible? In what ways? Why do you think Poe told it from Montresor's point of view?

5. If you liked this story, look in your library for a collection of Poe's stories and poems.

For further activities, see page 318.

The Raven

EDGAR ALLAN POE

Once upon a midnight dreary, while I pondered, weak and weary,
Over many a quaint and curious volume of forgotten lore—
While I nodded, nearly napping, suddenly there came a tapping,
As of someone gently rapping, rapping at my chamber door.
" 'Tis some visitor," I muttered, "tapping at my chamber door—   5
   Only this and nothing more."

Ah, distinctly I remember it was in the bleak December,
And each separate dying ember wrought its ghost upon the floor.
Eagerly I wished the morrow; vainly I had sought to borrow
From my books surcease of sorrow—sorrow for the lost Lenore,   10
For the rare and radiant maiden whom the angels name Lenore—
   Nameless *here* for evermore.

And the silken, sad, uncertain rustling of each purple curtain
Thrilled me, filled me with fantastic terrors never felt before;
So that now, to still the beating of my heart, I stood repeating,   15
" 'Tis some visitor entreating entrance at my chamber door,
Some late visitor entreating entrance at my chamber door—
   This it is and nothing more."

Presently my soul grew stronger; hesitating then no longer,
"Sir," said I, "or Madam, truly your forgiveness I implore,   20
But the fact is I was napping, and so gently you came rapping,
And so faintly you came tapping, tapping at my chamber door,
That I scarce was sure I heard you"—here I opened wide the door—
   Darkness there and nothing more.

Deep into that darkness peering, long I stood there wondering, fearing,   25
Doubting, dreaming dreams no mortal ever dared to dream before;
But the silence was unbroken, and the stillness gave no token,
And the only word there spoken was the whispered word, "Lenore?"
This I whispered, and an echo murmured back the word, "Lenore!"
   Merely this and nothing more.   30

10. *surcease:* an end.

Back into the chamber turning, all my soul within me burning,
Soon again I heard a tapping somewhat louder than before.
"Surely," said I, "surely that is something at my window lattice;
Let me see, then, what thereat is, and this mystery explore;
Let my heart be still a moment and this mystery explore—   35
    'Tis the wind and nothing more!"

Open here I flung the shutter, when, with many a flirt and flutter,
In there stepped a stately Raven of the saintly days of yore;
Not the least obeisance made he; not a minute stopped or stayed he;
But, with mien of lord or lady, perched above my chamber door,   40
Perched upon a bust of Pallas just above my chamber door—
    Perched, and sat, and nothing more.

Then this ebony bird beguiling my sad fancy into smiling,
By the grave and stern decorum of the countenance it wore,
"Though thy crest be shorn and shaven, thou," I said, "art sure no craven;   45
Ghastly grim and ancient Raven wandering from the Nightly shore,
Tell me what thy lordly name is on the Night's Plutonian shore!"
    Quoth the Raven, "Nevermore."

Much I marveled this ungainly fowl to hear discourse so plainly,
Though its answer little meaning, little relevancy bore;   50
For we cannot help agreeing that no living human being
Ever yet was blessed with seeing bird above his chamber door,
Bird or beast upon the sculptured bust above his chamber door,
    With such name as "Nevermore."

But the Raven, sitting lonely on the placid bust, spoke only   55
That one word, as if his soul in that one word he did outpour.
Nothing further then he uttered—not a feather then he fluttered—
Till I scarcely more than muttered, "Other friends have flown before;
On the morrow *he* will leave me, as my hopes have flown before."
    Then the bird said, "Nevermore."   60

Startled at the stillness broken by reply so aptly spoken,
"Doubtless," said I, "what it utters is its only stock and store
Caught from some unhappy master whom unmerciful Disaster
Followed fast and followed faster till his songs one burden bore,

40. *mien:* manner.   41. *bust of Pallas:* a statue of the head and shoulders of the goddess Athena.

Till the dirges of his hope that melancholy burden bore   65
   Of 'Never—nevermore.' "

But the Raven still beguiling all my fancy into smiling,
Straight I wheeled a cushioned seat in front of bird and bust and door;
Then, upon the velvet sinking, I betook myself to linking
Fancy unto fancy, thinking what this ominous bird of yore—   70
What this grim, ungainly, ghastly, gaunt, and ominous bird of yore—
   Meant in croaking, "Nevermore."

This I sat engaged in guessing, but no syllable expressing
To the fowl whose fiery eyes now burned into my bosom's core;
This and more I sat divining, with my head at ease reclining   75
On the cushion's velvet lining that the lamplight gloated o'er,
But whose velvet-violet lining with the lamplight gloating o'er,
   She shall press, ah, nevermore!

Then, methought, the air grew denser, perfumed from an unseen censer
Swung by seraphim whose footfalls tinkled on the tufted floor.   80
"Wretch," I cried, "thy God hath lent thee, by these angels he hath sent thee
Respite, respite and nepenthe from thy memories of Lenore;
Quaff, oh quaff this kind nepenthe and forget this lost Lenore!"
   Quoth the Raven, "Nevermore."

"Prophet!" said I, "thing of evil! Prophet still, if bird or devil,   85
Whether Tempter sent, or whether tempest tossed thee here ashore,
Desolate yet all undaunted, on this desert land enchanted,
On this home by Horror haunted; tell me truly, I implore,
Is there—*is* there balm in Gilead?—tell me—tell me, I implore!"
   Quoth the Raven, "Nevermore."   90

"Prophet!" said I, "thing of evil! Prophet still, if bird or devil!
By that Heaven that bends above us—by that God we both adore—
Tell this soul with sorrow laden if, within the distant Aidenn,
It shall clasp a sainted maiden whom the angels name Lenore,
Clasp a rare and radiant maiden whom the angels name Lenore."   95
   Quoth the Raven, "Nevermore."

79–84. The speaker imagines that God has sent him angels (seraphim) carrying incense
(burning in a censer), and bringing him an ancient medicine to soothe pain (nepenthe). He
tells himself to drink the nepenthe and forget Lenore.   93. *Aidenn*: heaven.

"Be that word our sign of parting, bird or fiend!" I shrieked, upstarting.
"Get thee back into the tempest and the Night's Plutonian shore!
Leave no black plume as a token of that lie thy soul hath spoken!
Leave my loneliness unbroken! Quit the bust above my door!   100
Take thy beak from out my heart, and take thy form from off my door!"
    Quoth the Raven, "Nevermore."

And the Raven, never flitting, still is sitting, still is sitting
On the pallid bust of Pallas just above my chamber door;
And his eyes have all the seeming of a demon's that is dreaming,   105
And the lamp-light o'er him streaming throws his shadow on the floor:
And my soul from out that shadow that lies floating on the floor
    Shall be lifted—nevermore!

DISCUSSION   1. When the speaker first hears a rapping he says to himself, " 'Tis some visitor . . . only this and nothing more." What does this tell you about his frame of mind?

2. Who does the speaker think might have knocked when he opens the door the first time and finds no one there?

3. **Rhythm.** Rhythm is the pattern of accented and unaccented syllables and words. In this poem the rhythm is easy to feel in the regular beat of the lines and the repetition of "nothing more" and "nevermore." Read a few lines of the poem aloud. You will probably be surprised at how much rhythm there is. How does the rhythm add to the mood of the poem?

For further activities, see page 318.

VOCABULARY

The Adventure of the Norwood Builder (page 278)

This exercise involves two steps. First find the bold type words in the story. Then on separate paper write *true* or *false* beside the number of each statement. For example, the first one is false because Holmes had not *hinted* his wishes to Watson but had bound him in *stringent* terms.

stringent (p. 278)

whimsical (p. 279)

disheveled (p. 279)

languid (p. 282)

enigmatical (p. 285)

haphazard (p. 286)

affluent (p. 290)

paroxysm (p. 291)

suppressed (p. 293)

1. Holmes had once hinted that Dr. Watson should not write about him.
2. Holmes seriously wished for more crime in London.
3. McFarlane looked untidy as he rushed up the stairs.
4. Holmes spoke briskly to Mr. McFarlane.
5. Holmes had a mysterious smile.
6. Oldacre drew up his will very carefully.
7. The bank book did not show that Mr. Oldacre was extremely rich.
8. Holmes waved his hands lightly as he spoke.
9. Holmes tried to hold back his excitement.

COMPOSITION

Macavity (page 301)

Think of a pet you own or know. What kind of person would it be if it suddenly became human? Give the pet a human name, some likes and dislikes, and perhaps a job. Then write a character sketch, personifying the pet.

The Raven (page 313)

Create a one-minute commercial for a product. Use for your setting and cast a small room, a dying fire at midnight, a wild-eyed man, a bust of someone famous, and a bird of some kind who knows only one word and who comes in the window at some point. Include other details of the room, the action that takes place, and dialogue for the man to speak to himself and to the bird. Using as many literary devices as you can (or none at all), build up to the one-word response the bird will give at the end of the commercial.

READING

The Adventure of the Norwood Builder (page 278)

On separate paper, write *true* or *false* beside the number of each statement and be ready to support your choice by reference to the story.

1. McFarlane was a solicitor.
2. The walking stick belonged to McFarlane.
3. McFarlane left his thumbprint on a wall in the hall.
4. Oldacre left his estate to McFarlane.
5. Oldacre was burned in the fire.
6. A third person's footprint was not found in Oldacre's room.
7. Oldacre had an odious face with shifty eyes.
8. Oldacre ran out of a door that appeared to be a solid wall.
9. Oldacre wanted revenge upon his old sweetheart.

The Cask of Amontillado (page 304)

Sometimes people say something with a double meaning. Or a writer has a character say something that is truer than he or she thinks. All the phrases below are of this kind. Decide who said each of the statements below, and write his name beside the number of the statement on your paper.

1. "You are luckily met."
2. "Your health is precious."
3. "I shall not die of a cough."
4. "I drink to the buried that repose around us."
5. "And I [drink] to your long life."
6. "Come, we will go back ere it is too late."
7. "He [Luchesi] is an ignoramus."
8. "Yes, let us be gone."

**UNITY IN
PARAGRAPHS**

COMPOSITION

How long should a paragraph be? Quite simply, it should be long enough to be effective. However, the contents of very long paragraphs are hard to follow. A very short paragraph, on the other hand, can be too brief to develop the idea it is presenting.

A paragraph should develop a single idea:

They looked out from the window of the drawing room. The long garden, agreeably neglected, ended in a waste plot. Here a little summerhouse was passing close by beauty on its way to complete decay. This was Simon's retreat. It was almost completely screened by the tangled branches of the apple tree and the pear tree, planted too close together, as they always are in the suburbs. They caught a glimpse of him now and then, as he strutted up and down, mouthing and gesticulating, performing all the solemn mumbo jumbo of small boys who spend long afternoons at the forgotten ends of long gardens.

Notice that all six sentences help us become aware of Simon's retreat. All six sentences are *unified* around a common purpose.

Consider another example:

He pressed the bell. Far away in a back room he heard it ringing, and then *at once*—it must have been at once because he hadn't even had time to take his finger from the bell button—the door swung open and a woman was standing there.

Here the paragraph is composed of two sentences working together to tell what happens during a sequence of actions. First the bell is rung. Then the door is opened.

Some paragraphs explain something. Others define what something means. (In that case, the first sentence might offer a formal definition, another sentence might give an example, and a third might make clear what items are *not* included in the definition.) Other paragraphs are unified around supplying specific examples or facts to support a general statement.

Because it often takes four or five sentences to develop an idea adequately, many paragraphs will be of approximately that length. But more important than length is *unity*. Every paragraph you write should be unified.

ABOUT THE SELECTIONS

1.   Not all the mysteries in this unit are solved. How had Fortunato insulted Montresor (page 304)? How did the traveler die (p. 276)? What did Lomey Carter's husband whisper to her (p. 268)? Why were the soldiers coming to a certain house (p. 266)? Did Weaver escape the fate of Mulholland and Temple (p. 244)? What was the last thing Simon's father saw (p. 259)? Take any one of these mysteries and solve it in some reasonable way.

2.   Choose one of the prose selections, and in a paragraph or two examine how the author prepared the reader for the ending. Look for foreshadowing, for clues that you notice when you go back to the story but that meant nothing to you the first time through.

3.   What single idea does this paragraph from "The Landlady" develop?

Now, the fact that his landlady appeared to be slightly off her rocker didn't worry Billy in the least. After all, she was not only harmless—there was no question about that—but she was also quite obviously a kind and generous soul. He guessed that she had probably lost a son in the war, something like that, and had never gotten over it.

4.   Look again at "The Adventure of the Norwood Builder." Around what ideas are the fourth, fifth, and sixth paragraphs of that story organized? In a paragraph of your own, explain how each of the three is unified.

ON YOUR OWN

1.   Mystery enters every life. Sometimes it comes inconspicuously, to be sure, and involves small matters: "Whatever happened to my ballpoint pen?" Write a brief account of some mystery in your life, the more perplexing the better. Unify your paragraphs, describing the scene, telling what happened, explaining what can be explained, and emphasizing what remains unexplainable.

2.   Do you believe in ghosts? Why, or why not? Write an effective paragraph or two designed to convince the reader to share your opinion. Specific facts and reasons will help to make your case persuasive.

3.   "Macavity's a Mystery Cat"—and, in a different way, there is something mysterious about Poe's talking raven (page 313). Choose some animal you can observe—a pet, a squirrel, a pigeon, or whatever. What is it thinking? Watch it awhile to solve the mystery. In a page or so, put its thoughts down on paper so that we get to understand something about its world, its personality, and its concerns.

4.   What is the scariest moment you have lived through? In a paper of two or three unified paragraphs, re-create that moment for your reader. Choose details that will make clear why the moment was frightening. The more specifically you write, the more successful will be the results.

CHOICES

Learn to Say Good-bye

JESSAMYN WEST

John Thomas had awakened thinking of Curly—or, rather, when he woke up, he did not stop thinking of Curly, for all night he had been with the young steer, encouraging him, patting him on his curling forelock, leading him before the admiring judges. The boy was wide awake now, yet Curly's image was still as strongly with him as in the dream—the heavy shoulders, the great barrel, the short legs, the red coat shining with health and with the many brushings John Thomas had given it. And Curly's face! The boy's own face crinkled happily as he thought of it, and then turned scornful as he thought of the people who said one baby beef was just like another. Curly looked at you with intelligence. His eyes weren't just hairless spots on his head, like the eyes of most baby beeves. They showed that Curly knew when eating time had come and that he understood the difference between being told he was a lazy old cuss and a prize-winning baby beef. You had only to say to him, "You poor old steer," and he put his head down and looked at you as much as to say he knew it was true and not to kid him about it. John Thomas remembered a hundred humors and shrewdnesses of Curly's, and lay in bed smiling about them—the way he had of getting the last bite of mash out of his feed pail, and his cleverness in evading the vet, and how he would lunge at Wolf when the collie barked at him.

"This is the day!" John Thomas said aloud. "This is the day!"

Across the hall came a girl's sleepy voice. "Johnny, you promised to be quiet."

John Thomas didn't answer. No use arguing with Jo when she was sleepy. He sat up and slipped his arms into the sleeves of his bathrobe, and then stepped onto the floor boards, which were so much cooler than the air, and walked slowly, because he wanted so much to walk fast, to the window.

There Curly was, standing with his nose over the corral fence looking up toward John Thomas's window. Curly acts as if he knows, the boy thought. I bet he does know.

"Hey, Curly!" he called softly. "How you feel this morning? Feel like a prize baby beef? Feel like the best steer in Califor-

nia? First prize for Curly?" Curly swished his tail. "Don't you
worry, Curly. You *are* the best."

John Thomas knew he was going to have to go in and talk
to Jo, even though she'd be mad at being waked so early. If he
stood another minute looking at Curly—so beautiful in his clean
corral, with the long blue early-morning shadows of the eucalyptus[1] falling across it—and listening to the meadow larks off in
the alfalfa[2] and remembering that this was the day, he'd give a
whoop, and that would make both Jo and Pop mad. He tiptoed
across the hall, opened his sister's door, and looked at her room
with distaste. Grownup girls like Jo, almost twenty, ought to be
neater. All girls ought to be neater. The clothes Jo had taken off
before she went to sleep made a path from her door to her bed,
starting with her shoes and hat and ending with her underwear.
Curly's corral's neater, he thought, and said, "It's time to get
up, Jo!"

[1] *eucalyptus* (yōō-kə-lĭp′təs): a tall, straight tree found in the Southwest.
[2] *alfalfa:* a plant raised as food for horses and cattle.

Jo rolled over on her face and groaned. John Thomas stepped over Jo's clothes and sat down on the edge of the bed.

Jo groaned again. "*Please* don't wake me up yet, Johnny," she said.

"You're already awake. You're talking."

"I'm talking in my sleep."

"I don't care if you don't wake up, if you'll talk. I've seen Curly already. He looks pretty good. He looks like he knows it's the day."

"He's dead wrong, then. It's still the night."

John Thomas laughed. If he got Jo to arguing, she'd wake up. "It's six o'clock," he said.

Jo, still face down, raised herself on one elbow and looked at her wristwatch. Then she whirled onto her back, stuck one leg out from under the sheet, and gave her brother a kick that set him down on the floor with a thud. "Why, John Thomas Hobhouse!" she said indignantly. "It's only five-fifteen and Nicky didn't get me home until two. You're so kind to that darned old steer of yours, but you don't care whether your own sister gets any sleep or not."

John Thomas bounced back onto the bed. Jo looked at him sharply and he knew what was to come.

"What have you got on under that bathrobe, John Thomas Hobhouse?" she demanded. "Did you sleep in your underwear last night?"

"I slept in my shorts."

"That's a filthy thing to do."

"You say it's filthy if I don't wear them in the daytime and filthy if I do wear them at night. What's daylight or dark got to do with it? Now, if I——"

"Look, Johnny, let's not get started on that. There are some things you're going to have to do that aren't reasonable. Once school starts, you'll be spending some nights with the other boys, and their mothers will be saying I don't look after you, and let you sleep in your underwear."

"I don't do it away from home, Jo, but it was so hot last night. You tell Mrs. Henny to do my ducks³ up special for today? Boy, wait till you see me and Curly go by the grandstand! Wait till you see us in the ring when Curly wins!"

"When Curly wins! Maybe he won't win, Johnny."

---

³ *ducks:* shirt, slacks, made of heavy, white cotton fabric.

"Maybe the judges *won't* see he's best—but they will if they're any good."

John Thomas lay on his stomach, hanging his head over the edge of the bed until his long pompadour[4] spread out on the floor like a dust mop and his face was out of Jo's sight. "I prayed about today," he said.

"Did you, Johnny?"

"Yep, but I didn't think it was fair to pray for Curly to win." He heaved himself up and down, so that his hair flicked back and forth across the floor. "A lot of kids probably did pray they'd win, though."

Jo regarded him with tenderness and amazement. "I never would have thought most of the kids who go to the fair had ever heard of praying," she said.

"Oh, sure, they all heard of it," Johnny said. "And when it comes to something important like this, they all think you ought to try everything. But I didn't ask for Curly to win. I just prayed the judges would be good and know their stuff. If they do, Curly will get the blue ribbon, all right. With everyone else asking to win, I thought maybe that would kind of make an impression on God."

It made an impression on Jo. Lord, she thought, I'm a heathen. "What do you care whether or not Curly wins, if you know he's best?" she asked.

John Thomas heaved his head and shoulders up onto the bed and lay on his stomach with his face near Jo's. "How can you wear those tin things in your hair?" he asked. Then he answered her question. "I know for sure Curly's best, but *he* don't. He knows he's good, but he don't know he's that good. I want him to win so he can have the blue ribbon on his halter and walk up in front of the people while all the other baby beeves watch him."

"You going to walk with him, kid?" Jo asked.

"Yep, I got to."

"Kinda nice to have the other kids watch, too?"

This slyness tickled John Thomas and he laughed. No use trying to fool Jo about anything. "Anyway, it's mostly Curly," he said.

Jo started taking the curlers out of her hair. She tucked

---

4 *pompadour* (pŏm′ pə-dôr): hair style in which long front hair is brushed up over forehead and straight back.

them, one by one, into Johnny's bush of hair as she took them out. "Remember when Curly got bloated?" she asked. "You weren't much help then. You cried and didn't want the vet to stick him."

"Yeah, but, Jo, it looked so awful. To take a knife and stick it inside him. And Curly was so darned scared." He spoke dreamily, with the satisfaction and relief of dangers past. "He looked like he was going to have a calf, didn't he? And I guess it hurt more."

"Yep, Johnny. A cow's made to have a calf, but a steer isn't made to have gas. Hand me my comb. Top lefthand drawer."

John Thomas got up and stood looking at himself in the mirror. His hair was thick enough to keep the curlers from dropping out.

"You look like an African Bushman," Jo said. "Come on, get that comb."

When John Thomas handed it to her, she began loosening her sausagelike curls. He watched her turn the fat little sausages into big frankfurters.

"Time to get dressed, kid," she said. "Jump into your ducks. They're all done up fresh and hanging in your closet."

"Do you think I've been giving him too much mash, Jo?" Johnny asked. "Does he look kind of soft to you? Too fat?"

"He looks just right to me. But it's all over now. No use worrying any more. This time tomorrow, he'll be someone else's problem."

John Thomas sat down on the window sill and looked out at the tank house. The sunlight lay on it in a slab as heavy and yellow as a bar of naphtha[5] soap. There was already a dance of heat out across the alfalfa fields. White clouds were boiling up from behind purple Tahquitz.[6] The morning-glories were beginning to shut themselves against the sun. This was the day all right, but he could not think ahead until tomorrow, when Curly would have been sold.

The boy made the width of the room in three jack-rabbit hops, and banged the door behind him.

Jo swung herself out of her bed and her nightgown in a single looping movement and stood before her mirror. I guess it's awful to be thirteen and not have a mother, and to love a steer

---

[5] *naphtha* (năf′thə): a strong cleaning agent.
[6] *Tahquitz*: pronounced tä-keets′.

that's going to be beefsteak in forty-eight hours, she thought
somberly. I ought to take better care of Johnny, and Dad ought
to wake up from remembering Mother. He's been that way ever
since she died.

The sound of Johnny's leaps down the stairs—four house-
shuddering thuds—and his cracked voice calling out to Mrs.
Henny made her look at her watch. Almost six. Jo grabbed
fresh underwear from the drawer and ran for the bathroom.

When Jo came downstairs, ten minutes later, all dressed except for putting on the scarf and belt that were hanging over
her shoulders, she saw her father, seated at the table on the
screened porch where they ate breakfast in summer and reading
the morning paper. She was fond of her father, but in one respect he was unsatisfactory: She didn't like his appearance. He
didn't look fatherly to her. There wasn't any gray in his black
hair or any stoop to his shoulders, and her girl friends exasper-
ated her by saying, "I could go for your old man."

He called to her now, "Tell Mrs. Henny we're ready to
eat."

Jo went through the porch door into the sunny kitchen,
where Mrs. Henny was slicing peaches for breakfast. She was
already dressed for the fair, in a lavender dotted swiss with a
lavender ribbon through her bobbed gray hair. "Hello, Mrs.
Henny," Jo said. "Dad says let's eat. Gee, you look swell!"

"I thought I'd better wear something light," Mrs. Henny
said. "It's going to be hot as a little red wagon today. Take
these peaches out with you. Time you've finished them, everything else will be ready."

Jo stopped to buckle on her belt and tie her scarf. Then she
took the peaches out to the porch. Her father put the *Los Angeles Times* under his chair and took his dish of peaches out of her
hand. "Well, Josephine," he said, "considering you only had
three hours' sleep last night, you don't look so bad."

"You hear me come in?"

"Nope, but I heard that fellow drive away. He ran into
everything loose and bangable on the place. What's wrong with
him?"

"Blind with love, I guess," Jo said lightly.

Her father held his third spoonful of sugar poised over his
peaches. "I take it that you have no impairment in your eye-
sight," he said.

"Things look a little rosy, but the outline's still plain, I think."

Mrs. Henny came in with the eggs and bacon and muffins. "I don't want to hurry you," she said, pausing, at the kitchen door, on her way out, "but it's not getting any earlier."

"Where did Johnny go?" Jo asked. "He ought to be eating. He'll be sick this afternoon if he doesn't eat." She took two muffins, buttered them, and put them on Johnny's plate.

"He's out talking to Curly. You'd better call him."

"Dad, what's Johnny going to do about not having Curly any more after today?" Jo asked. "You know he acts as if Curly were a dog—or a brother."

"Oh, Johnny's all right. He knows what the score is," her father said, with his mouth full of muffin and scrambled eggs. "But call him, call him. We've less than an hour to eat and load the steer. I ought to have taken him down last night, but John Thomas was afraid Curly would look peaked today if he spent a night away from home."

"Remember John Thomas's kitten?"

"Kitten?" said her father grumpily. "He's had a dozen."

"This was the one he had when he broke his leg. Don't you remember? He said, 'Let's never let her see herself in a mirror, and then she'll think she's just like us, only smaller.' He's that way about Curly now, you know. He never lets Curly know there's any other difference than size between them."

"Doesn't he know where Curly'll be tomorrow?"

"He *must* know it, but he hasn't felt it yet."

"Well, call him, call him," her father said. He got up from the table and stood with his back to her. "He can't learn to say good-bye any earlier."

He's thinking of Mama, Jo thought, and walked slowly out through the screen door and down the steps into the sunshine, eating a muffin-and-bacon sandwich as she went. She stopped at the foot of the steps to pick up the cat, and balanced him, heavy and purring, on her shoulder, and let him lick the last of the muffin crumbs from her fingers. "Oh, Nicky, Nicky," she murmured, pressing her face close against the cat's soft, furry side. Then she saw Johnny, sitting hunched up on the top rail of the corral, looking at Curly. "Well, bud," she called out, "he looks like silk!"

"He's kind of rough on the left flank," Johnny said as she came and stood beside him. "Been rubbing against something. Can you notice it? I been working on it."

"Can't see a thing," Jo said. "Now, look here, John Thomas, you're going to make him nervous, sitting there staring at him—give him the jitters before he ever gets to the fair. You'll spoil his morale. Dad let you keep him here till this morning when he didn't want to, so don't you gum things up now."

John Thomas slid to the ground. "So long, Curly," he said. "I got to eat now." And he ran for the house.

A little before eight, they all drove in to Verdant, the county seat—Mr. Hobhouse and Mrs. Henny and Jo and Johnny in the car, and Curly in the trailer behind them. "Awnings up early this morning," said Mr. Hobhouse as they moved slowly forward in the already long line of cars. "Going to be a scorcher, I guess. Flags look dead when there isn't any wind, don't they?"

Jo, who was riding beside her father in the front seat,

nodded, but nothing looked dead to her. She loved the begin-ning-again look of a town in the morning—the sidewalks sluiced down, the vegetables fresh and shining, the storekeepers in clean shirts, the feeling that nothing that had been spilled or broken or hurt or wronged the day before need be carried over into the new day. The heat made her sleepy, and because she wouldn't be seeing Nicky until evening, the day seemed dream-like, unimportant. She would move through it, be kind to Johnny, and wait for evening and Nicky again. Her father swerved sharply to avoid hitting a car that had swung, without signaling, out of the line of cars heading for the fair.

"Hey, Pop, take it easy!" John Thomas yelled anxiously from the back seat, where he sat with Mrs. Henny. "You almost busted Curly's ribs then."

"John Thomas ought to be riding back there with that steer," declared Mrs. Henny. "Or else I wish I could have rid in the trailer and the steer could have set here with John Thomas. The boy hasn't done a thing since we started but put his feet in my lunch basket and squirm, till I've got a rash watching him."

"Hold out five minutes longer, both of you, and we'll be there," Mr. Hobhouse said.

Jo roused herself, lifted her eyelids, which seemed weighed down with the heat, and turned around. "Hi ya, Johnny," she murmured.

As soon as they were well inside the fairgrounds, her father maneuvered out of the line of cars and stopped. "Jo, you and Mrs. Henny had better get out here," he said. "It'll take me and Johnny some time to get Curly unloaded."

As Jo climbed out, John Thomas touched her arm. "You'll sure be there, won't you, Sis?" he asked.

"Where?"

"In the grandstand for the parade at ten-thirty. All the baby beeves."

"Johnny, where'd you think I'd be then? Looking at the pickle exhibit, maybe? Of course I'll be there. Just you and Curly listen when you go by the stand. You'll hear me roar."

"Hurry up, you two," said her father. "It's getting late."

"When's the judging, Johnny?" Jo asked.

"Two-thirty. Front of the Agriculture Pavilion," he replied.

"I'll see you then. Don't worry. I think the judges are going to know their business." She poked a finger through the trailer's bars and touched Curly. "So long, Curly. You do your stuff!"

Her father edged the car and trailer back into the line of traffic. Mrs. Henny lumbered off, with a campstool on one arm and the lunch basket on the other, and Jo was left alone. The day was already blistering and she was glad. She took no pleasure in a moderately warm day, but a record breaker, one that challenged her ability to survive, elated her. She went into one of the exhibition buildings and walked through acres of handiwork, wondering if she would ever find life so empty that she would need to fill it with the making of such ugly and useless articles. Children whimpered as mothers jerked them doggedly through the heat. Oh, Nicky, I promise you never to be like them, Jo thought.

She was in the grandstand at ten-thirty when a voice from the loudspeaker announced, "Ladies and gentlemen! The Future Farmers of Riverbank County and their baby beeves will now pass in front of the grandstand for your inspection. At two-thirty, the final judging will take place in front of the Agriculture Pavilion, and after that the steers will be auctioned to the highest bidders. I'm proud to announce that there isn't a first-rate hotel in Los Angeles that hasn't a representative here to bid on one or more of these famous Riverbank beeves. There they come now, ladies and gentlemen, through the west gate. Let's give them a big hand—the Future Farmers of Riverbank County!"

Jo craned forward to watch the long line of steers and boys move proudly in review before the grandstand. The steers were mostly Herefords, shining like bright-russet leather in the blazing sun. Jo had not realized how thoroughly John Thomas had convinced her of Curly's superiority. She looked down the long line, expecting Curly, by some virtue of size or spirit, to be distinct from all the others.

A woman leaned heavily against her to nudge a friend in the row below them. "There they are!" she said excitedly.

Jo followed their glances before it occured to her that they were not talking about John Thomas and Curly. Finally, she saw them, well along toward the end of the line, the steer like the other red steers, the boy like the other white-clothed boys. But unlike, too, for surely no other boy walked with the sensitive, loving pride of her brother. Then she saw that Johnny was the only boy who did not lead his animal by a halter or a rope.

He walked beside Curly, with only a hand on his neck. Idiot, thought Jo, he's put something over on somebody; he ought not to be doing that.

She stood up and, to fulfill her promise, shouted, over and over, "Hi, Johnny! Hi, Curly" until a man behind her jerked her skirt and said, "Sit down Sis, you're not made of cellophane."

After the boys and the steers had circled the grandstand and passed through the west gate again and out of sight, Jo closed her eyes and half slept, hearing as in a dream the announcement of the next event. She fully awakened, though, when someone wedged himself into the narrow space that separated her from the stair railing on her right.

"Dad! Where did you come from?" she exclaimed.

"I was up above you," her father said. "Well, the boy's having his day. You're half asleep, Jo."

"More than half. Where's the car? I think I'll go and sleep in it until the judging. I've seen all the Yo-yo pillows[7] and canned apricots I can take in one day."

"I don't know whether you can find the car or not," her father said. "It's over in the first nine or ten rows of cars back of the dining tents. Here's the key, and don't forget to lock it when you leave."

Jo slept for a long time, doubled up on the back seat of the car, and then awakened with a sudden sick start. She seemed to be drowning in heat, and the velours[8] of the seat she was sleeping on was a quicksand that held her down. She looked at her watch and saw with consternation that it was after four o'clock.

She had a long way to go to reach the Agriculture Pavilion, and because she was so angry with herself and still so sleepy, she ran clumsily, bumping into people. I'm so full of fair promises, she accused herself bitterly, and now I've let poor Johnny down. She wanted to hurt herself running—punish herself—and she finally reached the Pavilion with a sick, cutting pain in her side and a taste of sulphur in her throat. A deep circle of onlookers stood around the judging ring, laughing and talking quietly. At last, she saw Johnny and her father in the front line of the circle, a little to her left. Paying no heed to the sour looks

---

[7] *Yo-yo* pillows: round, handmade pillows.
[8] *velours* (və-lōōr'): velvetlike fabric used for upholstery and clothing.

she got, she pushed her way to them. John Thomas saw what she had done and frowned. "You oughtn't to do that, Jo," he said. "People'll think we can get away with anything just because we own the winner."

"Has Curly won already?" Jo asked.

"No, not yet," Johnny said. "Couldn't you see the judging from where you were?"

"Not very well," Jo said. "No, I couldn't see a thing."

She looked now at the animals that were still in the ring, and saw that Curly was there with three other Herefords and an enormous black Ayrshire. He was wearing a halter now, and one of the judge's assistants was leading him. Unless one of the five steers had a cast[9] in his eye or a tick[10] in his ear, Jo did not see how any man living could say that one was an iota better

[9] *cast:* a condition where muscles of both eyes fail to work together.
[10] *tick:* a small insect that burrows under skin.

than another. She knew the points in judging as well as Johnny himself; she had stood by the corral many half hours after breakfast while Johnny recounted them for her, but while she knew them well, her eye could not limn them out[11] in the living beasts.

"Why're you so sure Curly will win?" she asked Johnny.

"Higgins said he would."

"Who's Higgins?"

Johnny shook his head, too absorbed to answer her question. The judge, an old, bowlegged fellow in a pale-blue sweater, had stopped examining the animals and was reading over some notes he had taken on the back of a dirty envelope. He walked over for another look at the Ayrshire. Seemingly satisfied by what he saw, he took off his gray felt hat and, with the back of his hand, wiped away the sweat that had accumulated under the sweatband. He set his hat on the back of his head, stuffed his envelope in a hip pocket, stepped to the edge of the ring, and began to speak.

"Ladies and gentlemen, it gives me great pleasure to be able to announce to you the winner of the Eighteenth Annual Riverbank Baby Beef Contest."

There was a hush as the spectators stopped talking, and Jo tried to find in her father's face some hint of what he thought the decision would be. She saw nothing there but concern. Johnny, though, had a broad and assured smile. His eyes were sparkling; the hour of Curly's recognition had come.

"And I may say," continued the judge, enjoying the suspense he was creating, "that in a lifetime of cattle judging I have never seen an animal that compares with today's winner."

The fool, thought Jo, the darn fool orator! What got into him? They never do this. Why can't he speak out?

But Johnny looked as if he enjoyed it, as if he knew whose name would be announced when people's ears had become so strained to hear it that it would seem to be articulated not by another's lips but by their own heartbeats.

"The winner, ladies and gentlemen, is that very fine animal, John Thomas Hobhouse's Hereford, Curly!" said the judge.

There was a lot of good-natured hand clapping. A few boys yelled "Nerts!" but the choice was popular with the crowd, most of whom knew and liked the Hobhouses. The judge went on to

---

[11] *limn them out:* recognize or pick them out.

name the second- and third-prize winners and the honorable
mentions. Then he called out, "I would like to present to you
Curly's owner, John Thomas Hobhouse himself. Come take a
bow, Johnny!"

Jo was proud of the easy, happy way Johnny ran over to
his side. The judge put out a hand intended for the boy's shoulder, but before it could settle there, Johnny was pressing his
cheek against Curly's big, flat jowl. The steer seemed actually to
lower his head for the caress and to move his cheek against
Johnny's in loving recognition. This delighted the spectators,
who laughed and cheered again.

"Now, ladies and gentlemen, the show's almost over," said
the judge. "Only one thing left—the auctioning of these animals—and, believe you me, the enjoyment you've had here is
nothing to the enjoyment you're going to have when you bite
into one of these big, juicy baby-beef steaks. Now if you'll all
just clear the ring. Ladies and gentlemen, may I present that
silver-tongued Irish auctioneer, Terence O'Flynn. Terence, the
show is all yours."

The non-prize-winners were disposed of first and in short
order. They fetched fancy prices, but nothing like what would
be paid for the prize winners. The big Los Angeles hotels and
the Riverbank Inn liked to be able to advertise "Steaks from
Riverbank's Prize Baby Beeves." Jo felt sick at her stomach
during the auction. This talk of club steaks and top sirloins
seemed indecent to her, in front of animals of whom these cuts
were still integral parts. But Johnny seemed unaffected by the
auction. "Bet Curly will get more than that," he said whenever
a high price was bid.

"He'll fetch top price," his father answered him shortly.
"You'll have a big check tonight, besides your blue ribbon,
Johnny." The prize winners were auctioned last. All of them except Curly went to Los Angeles hotels, but the Riverbank Inn,
determined not to let outside counties get all the prize winners,
bid Curly in for itself.

"I'm not a Riverbank citizen," boomed O'Flynn, "but I
don't mind admitting, folks, that I'm going to come back the
day my good friend Chef Rossi of the Riverbank Inn serves
steak from Curly. I know that baby beef is going to yield juices
that haven't been equaled since Abel[12] broiled the first steak. If

---

[12] *Abel* (ā′bəl): second son of Adam and Eve.

I was young Hobhouse, I'd never sell that animal. I'd barbecue it and pick its bones myself."

Most of the animals had already been led into slaughter-house vans and trucks, and the rest were being quickly loaded. A van belonging to Mack's Market, the Riverbank Inn's butchers, backed up to the ring, which now held only Curly and the Ayrshire. As O'Flynn finished speaking, two young fellows in jumpers marked "Mack's" leaped out and came over to give Curly a congratulatory pat before sending him up the runway.

"Well, kid," one said pleasantly to John Thomas, "you got a fine animal here."

Johnny didn't hear him. He was looking at O'Flynn, hearing those last words of his.

Now it's come, thought Jo. Now he's really taken in what he's been preparing Curly for. Now he knows for the first time. Don't look that way, Johnny, she pleaded silently. Oh, Johnny, you *must* know you can't keep Curly—you can't keep a fat pet steer.

But Johnny didn't smile. He walked over and stood with one arm about Curly's neck, staring incredulously at O'Flynn. "Nobody's going to pick Curly's bones," he said to the auctioneer. Then he turned to the steer. "Don't you worry, Curly. That guy hasn't got anything to do with you."

There was a sympathetic murmur among the bystanders. "The poor kid's made a pet of him," one man said. "Too bad. Well, he can't learn any earlier."

The men from Mack's Market tried to take the matter lightly. "Look here, bud," said one of them. "Get yourself a canary. This steer don't want to be nobody's pet. He wants to be beefsteaks." And he put a hand on Curly's halter.

Johnny struck it down. "Don't touch Curly!" he shouted. "He's going home, where he belongs! He's won the prize! That's all he came here to do!"

The circle of onlookers came closer, augmented by passers-by whose ears had caught in Johnny's voice the sound of passion and hurt. The buzzards, Jo thought. She saw Johnny press himself still more closely against Curly, keeping his eyes all the time on O'Flynn. She gripped her father's arm. "Dad, do something!" she cried. "Let Johnny take Curly home. There's plenty of food and room. Johnny wouldn't feel this way about him except for you and me. It's our fault!" She was half crying.

"Yes, this nonsense can't go on," her father agreed, and went quickly over to Johnny.

Jo couldn't hear what he said or see his face, for he stood with his back to her, but she could see Johnny's face, and its anguish and disbelief. At last, the boy turned and threw both arms around Curly's neck and buried his face against the steer's heavy muscles. Jo saw his thin shoulder blades shaking.

When her father turned and came toward her, eyes to the ground, she found she could not say to him any of the bitter things that had been on her tongue's tip.

"Dad," she said, and put her hand out to him.

"There's no use, Jo."

"But he loves Curly so."

"Oh, love!" her father said, and then added more quietly, "It's better to learn to say good-bye early than late, Jo."

"I'm going to the car," Jo said, and she turned and ran blindly through the crowd. Because Dad's had to learn, why must Johnny, she thought bitterly.

She got into the front seat and leaned across the wheel, without any attempt to stop crying. Then, as the sobs let up, she pounded the wheel. "No, sir!" she said aloud. "I *won't* learn! I refuse to learn! I'll be an exception!"

DISCUSSION

1. "I *won't* learn! . . . I'll be an exception!" What is this lesson that Jo says she will refuse to learn? Has her father successfully learned it?

2. John Thomas wakes with the thought, "This is the day!" Curly will win the blue ribbon. Although he refuses to let himself think about it (page 328), he knows that Curly will then be sold. When does he suddenly understand what that really means?

3. "It's our fault!" Jo tells her father (page 338). What does she mean? What have they done—or not done—for John Thomas?

4. From what **point of view** (see page 78) is this story written?

5. **Theme.** The theme of any piece of writing is that particular truth or meaning which the author is trying to make us see. The theme of this story is the lesson about human life Jo says she will not learn. How would you state it, in words of your own?

For further activities, see page 364.

Growing Up

KEITH WILSON

A big Jack, cutting outward toward blue,
little puffs of my bullets hurrying him.
Sage crushed underfoot, crisp & clean—

My father, a big Irishman, redfaced & watching,
he who could hit anything within range,   5
who brought a 150-lb buck three miles
out of the high mountains when he was 57

—a man who counted misses as weaknesses,
  he whipped up his own rifle, stopped the Jack
  folding him in midair, glanced at me, stood   10
  silent

My father who never knew I shot pips from cards
candleflames out (his own eye) who would've
been shamed by a son who couldn't kill. Riding
beside him.   15

1. *Jack:* a jack rabbit.   12. *pips:* here, symbols on cards.

DISCUSSION   1. Why does the poem's speaker choose to have his father think him a poor shot rather than know he does not want to kill the rabbit?

2. Which line states the father's approach to life?

3. What does "growing up" mean to the poet? What does it mean to you?

For further activities, see page 364.

THE DRIVER AND THE DEMON

YEVGENY YEVTUSHENKO

All of us when we are starting out in life have our special demons who try to kill our faith in human beings, to make us doubt the very possibility of an unselfish motive in anyone, demons with smooth, enticing hands who try to lure us forevèr into dark labyrinths[1] of cynical distrust.

And when I was young, I too had such a demon.

My demon worked as an engineer in one of the mines in Kazakhstan.[2] He was about forty-five, with a big bald head set on a squat body, and with tiny, mocking eyes.

The demon's arguments were abhorrent yet convincing. All the same, the more they seemed to be supported by facts, the stronger grew my resistance to them.

One day the demon took me by truck to fetch the workmen's pay from a small town across the steppe.[3] Our driver was a taciturn young man with a solid row of steel teeth and tattooed hands.

"Keep an eye on him, he's done time," the demon whispered to me before we set out. "We'll have quite a lot of money on us. I've got something here—" He patted the pocket in which he kept his revolver. "Still, you'd better keep an eye on him."

We called at the bank. The demon carefully counted the packets of creased rubles and put them away in a worn leather brief case. Then we all three got back into the cab of the truck—the

---

Yevgeny Yevtushenko: pronounced yĕv′gĕ-nē yĕv-tōō-shĕng′kō.
[1] *labyrinths* (lăb′ə-rĭnths): mazes of connecting passages.
[2] *Kazakhstan* (kə-zäk′stän): a large republic of the Soviet Union.
[3] *steppe* (stĕp): vast plain found in southeastern Europe.

driver, the demon with the brief case on his knees, and I.

Before us lay a journey of close to three hundred miles through almost trackless desert.

All we could see around us were the dead glimmer of salt lakes and the steppe eagles perched on telegraph poles, majestically turning their tiny heads toward us.

When we were halfway home the demon resumed his philosophizing:

"Isn't life fascinating?" he addressed the driver. "I know that you know that there's money in my brief case which you wouldn't mind taking for yourself. But you also know that I have a revolver in my pocket, and that in any case you couldn't get away with it even if you killed me. . . . But otherwise you'd kill me, wouldn't you?"

The demon chuckled, pleased with himself.

The driver said nothing, but his tattooed hands tightened on the wheel.

"All men are by nature thieves and murderers," the demon went on. "But they're afraid of being punished. Take away the penalties and everyone would steal and kill."

Suddenly the driver jammed his foot on the brake.

I hit the windshield with my head. And when a moment later I recovered from the shock, the revolver was in the driver's hand and pointing at the demon's stomach.

"Get out," the driver said tonelessly. "Every time you open your mouth, toads come hopping out. It stinks too much like a swamp with you in here. Get out and leave the money behind!" He snatched the brief case from the demon's shaking hand, pushed him out, and stepped on the accelerator. We drove on.

"You know what he's thinking about me now?" snorted the driver. "He thinks I'm going to make off with the money. These crooks think everybody's like themselves. Give them half a chance and they'll foul up the whole world."

I looked back. In the distance in the middle of the empty steppe a small demon was shouting inaudibly and grotesquely waving his arms as he ran after us, but he was growing smaller and smaller.

"You needn't worry about him," the driver grunted. "He won't get lost. That kind always falls on their feet—unfortunately."

We drove on.

After a while the truck stopped.

"Water's gone—boiled away," said the driver gruffly after taking a look at the radiator. He glanced around him at the desert. "There's no water here."

He thought for a while, then came to a decision.

"I'll tell you what. . . . You stay here and look after the truck, and I'll go and get help. I'll take the money with me because you never know who might turn up. There's all sorts of people roaming around the steppe. So remember. You wait for me."

He took the bundles of notes from the brief case, stuffed them inside his shirt, and walked away with long, purposeful strides.

I was alone, without food or water in the middle of the huge steppe.

Twice the sun rose and went down.

I wandered around near the truck, chewing the harsh leaves of the desert plants for their slightly acid moisture. I became delirious. Thousands of giggling demons rose before me. And all the demons cackled in triumph: "You see, he's left you, he won't come back. Now do you believe me?"

But throwing myself down in despair, I pounded the ground with my fists and shouted hysterically: "I don't believe you! I don't believe you!"

And on the third night, when I was lying in the cab with no more strength left in me, two white, dazzling beams struck my face. Small dark figures surrounded the truck.

The door flew open, two familiar, tattooed hands were around me, and I recognized the driver's face with its solid row of steel teeth. He was weeping with joy and shouting: "He's alive! He's alive!"

A tattooed hand put a bottle to my lips and poured milk into my mouth.

Since then, many demons have come my way and, no doubt, many others will, but not one of them will ever shake my faith in my fellow men.

DISCUSSION

1. It is easy to find the **theme** (see page 339) of this story from the author's life; it is presented in both the first and last sentences. Try stating it in your own words.

2. Why is the engineer called "the demon" (page 341)?

3. "You needn't worry about him," the driver grunted (page 344). "He won't get lost." The driver returns to rescue the author. Do you think he also returned to aid the engineer?

For further activities, see page 364.

THE LESSON OF THE MOTH

DON MARQUIS

i was talking to a moth
the other evening
he was trying to break into
an electric light bulb
and fry himself on the wires   5

why do you fellows
pull this stunt i asked him
because it is the conventional
thing for moths or why
if that had been an uncovered   10
candle instead of an electric
light bulb you would
now be a small unsightly cinder
have you no sense
plenty of it he answered   15
but at times we get tired
of using it
we get bored with the routine
and crave beauty
and excitement   20
fire is beautiful
and we know that if we get
too close it will kill us
but what does that matter
it is better to be happy   25
for a moment
and be burned up with beauty
than to live a long time
and be bored all the while
so we wad all our life up   30
into one little roll

and then we shoot the roll
that is what life is for
it is better to be a part of beauty
for one instant and then cease to   35
exist than to exist forever
and never be a part of beauty
our attitude toward life
is come easy go easy
we are like human beings   40
used to be before they became
too civilized to enjoy themselves

and before i could argue him
out of his philosophy
he went and immolated himself   45
on a patent cigar lighter
i do not agree with him
myself i would rather have
half the happiness and twice
the longevity   50

but at the same time i wish
there was something i wanted
as badly as he wanted to fry himself
                                   archy

45. *immolated:* sacrificed.   50. *longevity* (lŏn-jĕ'və-
tē): a long duration of life.

DISCUSSION

1. What is it that Archy sometimes wishes
he had?

2. Just what is "the lesson of the moth"?
In which lines is it stated?

THE PEN OF MY AUNT

JOSEPHINE TEY

CHARACTERS   MADAME   STRANGER
                           SIMONE   CORPORAL

SCENE   A French country house during the Occupation by German forces in World War II. The lady of the house is seated in her drawing-room.

SIMONE [approaching]: Madame! Oh, madame! Madame, have you——

MADAME: Simone.

SIMONE: Madame, have you seen what——

MADAME: Simone!

SIMONE: But madame——

MADAME: Simone, this may be an age of barbarism, but I will have none of it inside the walls of this house.

SIMONE: But madame, there is a—there is a——

MADAME [silencing her]: Simone. France may be an occupied country, a ruined nation, and a conquered race, but we will keep, if you please, the usages of civilization.

SIMONE: Yes, madame.

MADAME: One thing we still possess, thank God; and that is good manners. The enemy never had it; and it is not something they can take from *us*.

SIMONE: No, madame.

MADAME: Go out of the room again. Open the door——

SIMONE: Oh, *madame*! I wanted to tell you——

MADAME: —Open the door, shut it behind you—quietly—take two paces into the room, and say what you came to say. [Simone goes hastily out, shutting the door. She reappears, shuts the door behind her, takes two paces into the room, and waits.] Yes, Simone?

SIMONE: I expect it is too late now; they will be here.

MADAME: Who will?

SIMONE: The soldiers who were coming up the avenue.

Simone: pronounced sē-mōn'.

MADAME: After the last few months I should not have thought that soldiers coming up the avenue was a remarkable fact. It is no doubt a party with a billeting order. [1]

SIMONE [crossing to the window]: No, madame, it is two soldiers in one of their little cars, with a civilian between them.

MADAME: Which civilian?

SIMONE: A stranger, madame.

MADAME: A stranger? Are the soldiers from the Combatant branch?

SIMONE: No, they are those beasts of Administration. Look, they have stopped. They are getting out.

MADAME [at the window]: Yes, it is a stranger. Do you know him, Simone?

SIMONE: I have never set eyes on him before, madame.

MADAME: You would know if he belonged to the district?

SIMONE: Oh, madame, I know every man between here and St. Estèphe. [2]

MADAME [dryly]: No doubt.

SIMONE: Oh, merciful God, they are coming up the steps.

MADAME: My good Simone, that is what the steps were put there for.

SIMONE: But they will ring the bell and I shall have to——

MADAME: And you will answer it and behave as if you had been trained by a butler and ten upper servants instead of being the charcoal-burner's daughter from over at Les Chênes. [3] [This is said encouragingly, not in unkindness.] You will be very calm and correct——

SIMONE: Calm! Madame! With my inside turning over and over like a wheel at a fair!

MADAME: A good servant does not have an inside, merely an exterior. [Comforting] Be assured, my child. You have your place here; that is more than those creatures on our doorstep have. Let that hearten you——

SIMONE: Madame! They are not going to ring. They are coming straight in.

MADAME [bitterly]: Yes. They have forgotten long ago what bells are for.

Door opens.

---

[1] *billeting order:* a written order demanding housing for troops.
[2] *St. Estèphe:* pronounced săn-tā-tāf'.
[3] *Les Chênes:* pronounced lā shên'.

STRANGER [in a bright, confident, casual tone]: Ah, there you are, my dear aunt. I am so glad. Come in, my friend, come in. My dear aunt, this gentleman wants you to identify me.

MADAME: Identify you?

CORPORAL: We found this man wandering in the woods——

STRANGER: The corporal found it inexplicable that anyone should wander in a wood.

CORPORAL: And he had no papers on him——

STRANGER: And I rightly pointed out that if I carry all the papers one is supposed to these days, I am no good to God or man. If I put them in a hip pocket, I can't bend forward; if I put them in a front pocket, I can't bend at all.

CORPORAL: He said that he was your nephew, madame, but that did not seem to us very likely, so we brought him here.

There is the slightest pause; just one moment of silence.

MADAME: But of course this is my nephew.

CORPORAL: He is?

MADAME: Certainly.

CORPORAL: He lives here?

MADAME [assenting]: My nephew lives here.

CORPORAL: So! [Recovering] My apologies, madame. But you will admit that appearances were against the young gentleman.

MADAME: Alas, Corporal, my nephew belongs to a generation who delight in flouting appearances. It is what they call "expressing their personality," I understand.

CORPORAL [with contempt]: No doubt, madame.

MADAME: Convention is anathema[4] to them, and there is no sin like conformity. Even a collar is an offence against their liberty, and a discipline not to be borne by free necks.

CORPORAL: Ah yes, madame. A little more discipline among your nephew's generation, and we might not be occupying your country today.

STRANGER: You think it was that collar of yours that conquered my country? You flatter yourself, Corporal. The only result of wearing a collar like that is varicose veins[5] in the head.

MADAME [repressive]: Please! My dear boy. Let us not descend to personalities.

STRANGER: The matter is not personal, my good aunt, but scientific.

[4] *anathema* (ə-năth'ə-mə): something to be shunned.
[5] *varicose veins:* swollen, knotted blood vessels.

Wearing a collar like that retards the flow of fresh blood to the head, with the most disastrous consequences to the gray matter of the brain. The hypothetical[6] gray matter. In fact, I have a theory——

CORPORAL: Monsieur,[7] your theories do not interest me.

STRANGER: No? You do not find speculation interesting?

CORPORAL: In this world one judges by results.

STRANGER [after a slight pause of reflection]: I see. The collared conqueror sits in the high places, while the collarless conquered lies about in the woods. And who comes best out of that, would you say? Tell me, Corporal, as man to man, do you never have a mad, secret desire to lie unbuttoned in a wood?

CORPORAL: I have only one desire, monsieur, and that is to see your papers.

STRANGER [taken off guard and filling in time]: My papers?

MADAME: But is that necessary, Corporal? I have already told you that——

CORPORAL: I know that madame is a very good collaborator[8] and in good standing——

MADAME: In that case——

CORPORAL: But when we begin an affair we like to finish it. I have asked to see monsieur's papers, and the matter will not be finished until I have seen them.

MADAME: You acknowledge that I am in "good standing," Corporal?

CORPORAL: So I have heard, madame.

MADAME: Then I must consider it a discourtesy on your part to demand my nephew's credentials.

CORPORAL: It is no reflection on madame. It is a matter of routine, nothing more.

STRANGER [murmuring]: The great god Routine.

MADAME: To ask for his papers was routine; to insist on their production is discourtesy. I shall say so to your Commanding Officer.

CORPORAL: Very good, madame. In the meantime, I shall inspect your nephew's papers.

MADAME: And what if I——

STRANGER [quietly]: You may as well give it up, my dear. You could as easily turn a steamroller. They have only one idea at a

---

[6] *hypothetical* (hī-pə-thĕt'ĭ-kəl): something stated to be true, but not proven.

[7] *Monsieur* (mə-syœ'): mister, sir.

[8] *collaborator* (kə-lăb'ə-rā-tər): one who assists the enemy.

time. If the Corporal's heart is set on seeing my papers, he shall see them. [Moving towards the door] I left them in the pocket of my coat.

SIMONE [unexpectedly, from the background]: Not in your *linen* coat?

STRANGER [pausing]: Yes. Why?

SIMONE [with apparently growing anxiety]: Your *cream* linen coat? The one you were wearing yesterday?

STRANGER: Certainly.

SIMONE: Merciful Heaven! I sent it to the laundry!

STRANGER: To the laundry!

SIMONE: Yes, monsieur; this morning; in the basket.

STRANGER [in incredulous anger]: You sent my coat, *with my papers in the pocket,* to the laundry!

SIMONE [defensive and combatant]: I didn't know monsieur's papers were in the pocket.

STRANGER: You didn't know! You didn't know that a packet of documents weighing half a ton were in the pocket. An identity card, a *laisser passer,*[9] a food card, a drink card, an army discharge, a permission to wear civilian clothes, a permission to go farther than ten miles to the east, a permission to go more than ten miles to the west, a permission to——

SIMONE [breaking in with spirit]: How was I to know the coat was heavy! I picked it up with the rest of the bundle that was lying on the floor.

STRANGER [snapping her head off]: My coat was on the back of the chair.

SIMONE: It was on the floor.

STRANGER: On the back of the chair!

SIMONE: It was on the floor with your dirty shirt and your pajamas, and a towel and what not. I put my arms round the whole thing and then—woof! into the basket with them.

STRANGER: I tell you that coat was on the back of the chair. It was quite clean and was not going to the laundry for two weeks yet—if then. I hung it there myself, and——

MADAME: My dear boy, what does it matter? The damage is done now. In any case, they will find the papers when they unpack the basket, and return them tomorrow.

STRANGER: If someone doesn't steal them. There are a lot of people who would like to lay hold of a complete set of papers, believe me.

---

9 *laisser passer* (lĕs'ă-pä-sā'): a pass, or travel papers.

MADAME [reassuring]: Oh, no. Old Fleureau[10] is the soul of honesty. You have no need to worry about them. They will be back first thing tomorrow, you shall see; and then we shall have much pleasure in sending them to the Administration Office for the Corporal's inspection. Unless, of course, the Corporal insists on your personal appearance at the office.

CORPORAL [cold and indignant]: I have seen monsieur. All that I want now is to see his papers.

STRANGER: You shall see them, Corporal, you shall see them. The whole half-ton of them. You may inspect them at your leisure. Provided, that is, that they come back from the laundry to which this idiot has consigned them.

MADAME [again reassuring]: They will come back, never fear. And you must not blame Simone. She is a good child, and does her best.

SIMONE [with an air of belated virtue]: I am not one to pry into pockets.

MADAME: Simone, show the Corporal out, if you please.

SIMONE [natural feeling overcoming her for a moment]: He knows the way out. [Recovering] Yes, madame.

MADAME: And Corporal, try to take your duties a little less literally in future. My countrymen appreciate the spirit rather than the letter.

CORPORAL: I have my instructions, madame, and I obey them. Good day, madame. Monsieur.

He goes, followed by Simone—door closes. There is a moment of silence.

STRANGER: For a good collaborator, that was a remarkably quick adoption.

MADAME: Sit down, young man. I will give you something to drink. I expect your knees are none too well.

STRANGER: My knees, madame, are pure gelatine. As for my stomach, it seems to have disappeared.

MADAME [offering him the drink she has poured out]: This will recall it, I hope.

STRANGER: You are not drinking, madame.

MADAME: Thank you, no.

STRANGER: Not with strangers. It is certainly no time to drink with strangers. Nevertheless, I drink the health of a collaborator. [He drinks.] Tell me, madame, what will happen tomorrow when they find that you have no nephew?

---

[10] *Fleureau:* pronounced flœ-rō′.

MADAME [surprised]: But of course I have a nephew. I tell lies, my
    friend; but not *silly* lies. My charming nephew has gone to
    Bonneval[11] for the day. He finds country life dull.

STRANGER: Dull? This—this heaven?

MADAME [dryly]: He likes to talk and here there is no audience. At
    Headquarters in Bonneval he finds the audience sympathetic.

STRANGER [understanding the implication]: Ah.

MADAME: He believes in the Brotherhood of Man—if you can credit
    it.

STRANGER: After the last six months?

MADAME: His mother was American, so he has half the Balkans[12] in
    his blood. To say nothing of Italy, Russia and the Levant.[13]

STRANGER [half-amused]: I see.

MADAME: A silly and worthless creature, but useful.

STRANGER: Useful?

MADAME: I—borrow his cloak.

STRANGER: I see.

MADAME: Tonight I shall borrow his identity papers, and tomorrow
    they will go to the office in St. Estèphe.

STRANGER: But—he will have to know.

MADAME [placidly]: Oh, yes, he will know, of course.

STRANGER: And how will you persuade such an enthusiastic collabo-
    rator to deceive his friends?

MADAME: Oh, that is easy. He is my heir.

STRANGER [amused]: Ah.

MADAME: He is, also, by the mercy of God, not too unlike you, so
    that his photograph will not startle the Corporal too much to-
    morrow. Now tell me what you are doing in my wood.

STRANGER: Resting my feet—I am practically walking on my bones.
    And waiting for tonight.

MADAME: Where are you making for? [As he does not answer immedi-
    ately.] The coast? [He nods.] That is four days away—five if your
    feet are bad.

STRANGER: I know it.

MADAME: Have you friends on the way?

STRANGER: I have friends at the coast, who will get me a boat. But
    no one between here and the sea.

MADAME [rising]: I must consult my list of addresses. [Pausing] What
    was your service?

---

[11] *Bonneval:* pronounced bŏn-ə-văl'.
[12] *Balkans:* countries occupying Balkan Peninsula in southeastern Europe.
[13] *Levant:* countries bordering the eastern Mediterranean.

STRANGER: Army.

MADAME: Which Regiment?

STRANGER: The 79th.

MADAME [after the faintest pause]: And your Colonel's name?

STRANGER: Delavault was killed in the first week, and Martin took over.

MADAME [going to her desk]: A "good collaborator" cannot be too careful. Now I can consult my notebook. A charming color, is it not? A lovely shade of red.

STRANGER: Yes—but what has a red quill pen to do with your notebook?—Ah, you write with it of course—stupid of me.

MADAME: Certainly I write with it—but it is also my notebook—look—I only need a hairpin—and then—so—out of my quill pen comes my notebook—a tiny piece of paper—but enough for a list of names.

STRANGER: You mean that you keep that list on your desk? [He sounds disapproving.]

MADAME: Where did you expect me to keep it, young man? In my corset? Did you ever try to get something out of your corset in a hurry? What would you advise as the ideal quality in a hiding place for a list of names?

STRANGER: That the thing should be difficult to find, of course.

MADAME: Not at all. That it should be easily destroyed in emergency. It is too big for me to swallow—I suspect they do that only in books—and we have no fires to consume it, so I had to think of some other way. I did try to memorize the list, but what I could not be sure of remembering were those that— that had to be scored off. It would be fatal to send someone to an address that—that was no longer available. So I had to keep a written record.

STRANGER: And if you neither eat it nor burn it when the moment comes, how do you get rid of it?

MADAME: I could, of course, put a match to it, but scraps of freshly burned paper on a desk take a great deal of explaining. If I ceased to be looked on with approval my usefulness would end. It is important therefore that there should be no sign of anxiety on my part: no burned paper, no excuses to leave the room, no nods and becks and winks. I just sit here at my desk and go on with my letters. I tilt my nice big inkwell sideways for a moment and dip the pen into the deep ink at the side. The ink flows into the hollow of the quill, and all is blotted out. [Consulting the list.] Let me see. It would be good if you could rest your feet for a day or so.

STRANGER [ruefully]: It would.

MADAME: There is a farm just beyond the Marnay crossroads on the way to St. Estèphe——[She pauses to consider.]

STRANGER: St. Estèphe is the home of the singleminded Corporal. I don't want to run into him again.

MADAME: No, that might be awkward; but that farm of the Cherfils[14] would be ideal. A good hiding-place, and food to spare, and fine people——

STRANGER: If your nephew is so friendly with the invader, how is it that the Corporal doesn't know him by sight?

MADAME [absently]: The unit at St. Estèphe is a noncommissioned one.

STRANGER: Does the Brotherhood of Man exclude sergeants, then?

MADAME: Oh, definitely. Brotherhood does not really begin under field rank, I understand.

STRANGER: But the Corporal may still meet your nephew somewhere.

[14] *Cherfils:* pronounced shĕr-fē'.

MADAME: That is a risk one must take. It is not a very grave one. They change the personnel every few weeks, to prevent them becoming too acclimatized. And even if he met my nephew, he is unlikely to ask for the papers of so obviously well-to-do a citizen. If you could bear to go *back* a little——

STRANGER: Not a step! It would be like—like denying God. I have got so far, against all the odds, and I am not going a yard back. Not even to rest my feet!

MADAME: I understand; but it is a pity. It is a long way to the Cherfils farm—two miles east of the Marnay crossroads it is, on a little hill.

STRANGER: I'll get there; don't worry. If not tonight then tomorrow night. I am used to sleeping in the open by now.

MADAME: I wish we could have you here, but it is too dangerous. We are liable to be billeted on at any moment, without notice. However, we can give you a good meal, and a bath. We have no coal, so it will be one of those flat-tin-saucer baths. And if you want to be very kind to Simone you might have it somewhere in the kitchen regions and so save her carrying water upstairs.

STRANGER: But of course.

MADAME: Before the war I had a staff of twelve. Now I have Simone. I dust and Simone sweeps, and between us we keep the dirt at bay. She has no manners but a great heart, the child.

STRANGER: The heart of a lion.

MADAME: Before I put this back you might memorize these: Forty Avenue Foch, in Crest, the back entrance.

STRANGER: Forty Avenue Foch, the back entrance.

MADAME: You may find it difficult to get into Crest, by the way. It is a closed area. The pot boy at the Red Lion in Mans.

STRANGER: The pot boy.

MADAME: Denis the blacksmith at Laloupe. And the next night should take you to the sea and your friends. Are they safely in your mind?

STRANGER: Forty Avenue Foch in Crest; the pot boy at the Red Lion in Mans: and Denis the blacksmith at Laloupe. And to be careful getting into Crest.

MADAME: Good. Then I can close my notebook—or roll it up, I should say—then—it fits neatly, does it not? Now let us see about some food for you. Perhaps I could find you other clothes. Are these all you——

The Corporal's voice is heard mingled in fury with the still more furious tones of Simone. She is yelling: 'Nothing of the sort, I tell you, nothing of the sort', but no words are clearly distinguishable in the angry row. The door is flung open, and the Corporal bursts in dragging a struggling Simone by the arm.

SIMONE [screaming with rage and terror]: Let me go, you foul fiend, you murdering foreigner, let me go. [She tries to kick him.]

CORPORAL [at the same time]: Stop struggling, you lying deceitful little bit of no-good.

MADAME: Will someone explain this extraordinary——

CORPORAL: This creature——

MADAME: Take your hand from my servant's arm, Corporal. She is not going to run away.

CORPORAL [reacting to the voice of authority and automatically complying]: Your precious servant was overheard telling the gardener that she had never set eyes on this man.

SIMONE: I did not! Why should I say anything like that?

CORPORAL: With my own ears I heard her, my own two ears. Will you kindly explain that to me if you can.

MADAME: You speak our language very well, Corporal, but perhaps you are not so quick to understand.

CORPORAL: I understand perfectly.

MADAME: What Simone was saying to the gardener, was no doubt what she was announcing to all and sundry at the pitch of her voice this morning.

CORPORAL [unbelieving]: And what was that?

MADAME: That she *wished* she had never set eyes on my nephew.

CORPORAL: And why should she say that?

MADAME: My nephew, Corporal, has many charms, but tidiness is not one of them. As you may have deduced from the episode of the coat. He is apt to leave his room——

SIMONE [on her cue; in a burst of scornful rage]: Cigarette ends, pajamas, towels, bedclothes, books, papers—all over the floor like a *flood.* Every morning I tidy up, and in two hours it is as if a bomb had burst in the room.

STRANGER [testily]: I told you already that I was sor——

SIMONE [interrupting]: As if I had nothing else to do in this enormous house but wait on you.

STRANGER: Haven't I said that I——

SIMONE: And when I have climbed all the way up from the kitchen with your shaving water, you let it get cold; but will you shave in cold? Oh, no! I have to bring up another——

STRANGER: I didn't ask you to climb the stairs, did I?

SIMONE: And do I get a word of thanks for bringing it? Do I indeed? You say: "*Must* you bring it in that hideous jug; it offends my eyes."

STRANGER: So it does offend my eyes!

MADAME: Enough, enough! We had enough of that this morning. You see, Corporal?

CORPORAL: I could have sworn——

MADAME: A natural mistake, perhaps. But I think you might have used a little more common sense in the matter. [Coldly] And a great deal more dignity. I don't like having my servants man-handled.

CORPORAL: She refused to come.

SIMONE: Accusing me of things I never said!

MADAME: However, now that you are here again you can make yourself useful. My nephew wants to go into Crest the day after tomorrow, and that requires a special pass. Perhaps you would make one out for him.

CORPORAL: But I——

MADAME: You have a little book of permits in your pocket, haven't you?

CORPORAL: Yes. I——

MADAME: Very well. Better make it valid for two days. He is always changing his mind.

CORPORAL: But it is not for me to grant a pass.

MADAME: You sign them, don't you?

CORPORAL: Yes, but only when someone tells me to.

MADAME: Very well, if it will help you, I tell you to.

CORPORAL: I mean, permission must be granted before a pass is issued.

MADAME: And have you any doubt that a permission will be granted to my nephew?

CORPORAL: No, of course not, madame.

MADAME: Then don't be absurd, Corporal. To be absurd twice in five minutes is too often. You may use my desk—and my own special pen. Isn't it a beautiful quill, Corporal?

CORPORAL: Thank you, madame, no. *We* Germans have come a long way from the geese.

MADAME: Yes?

CORPORAL: I prefer my fountain pen. It is a more efficient implement. [He writes.] "For the 15th and the 16th. Holder of identity card number"—What is the number of your identity, monsieur?

STRANGER: I have not the faintest idea.

CORPORAL: You do not know?

STRANGER: No. The only numbers I take an interest in are lottery numbers.

SIMONE: I know the number of monsieur's card.

MADAME [afraid that she is going to invent one]: I don't think that likely, Simone.

SIMONE [aware of what is in her mistress's mind, and reassuring her]: But I really *do*, know, madame. It is the year I was born, with two "ones" after it. Many a time I have seen it on the outside of the card.

CORPORAL: It is good that someone knows.

SIMONE: It is—192411.

CORPORAL: 192411. [He fills in the dates.]

MADAME [as he nears the end]: Are you going back to St. Estèphe now, Corporal?

CORPORAL: Yes, madame.

MADAME: Then perhaps you will give my nephew a lift as far as the Marnay crossroads.

CORPORAL: It is not permitted to take civilians as passengers.

STRANGER: But you took me here as a passenger.

CORPORAL: That was different.

MADAME: You mean that when you thought he was a miscreant you took him in your car, but now that you know he is my nephew you refuse?

CORPORAL: When I brought him here it was on service business.

MADAME [gently reasonable]: Corporal, I think you owe me something for your general lack of tact this afternoon. Would it be too much to ask you to consider my nephew a miscreant for the next hour while you drive him as far as the Marnay crossroads?

CORPORAL: But——

MADAME: Take him to the crossroads with you and I shall agree to forget your—your lack of efficiency. I am sure you are actually a very efficient person, and likely to be a sergeant any day now. We won't let a blunder or two stand in your way.

CORPORAL: If I am caught giving a lift to a civilian, I shall *never* be a sergeant.

MADAME [still gentle]: If I report on your conduct this afternoon, to-morrow you will be a private.

CORPORAL [after a long pause]: Is monsieur ready to come now?

STRANGER: Quite ready.

CORPORAL: You will need a coat.

MADAME: Simone, get monsieur's coat from the cupboard in the hall. And when you have seen him off, come back here.

SIMONE: Yes, madame.

Exit Simone.

CORPORAL: Madame.

MADAME: Good day to you, Corporal.

Exit Corporal.

STRANGER: Your talent for blackmail is remarkable.

MADAME: The place has a yellow barn. You had better wait some-where till evening, when the dogs are chained up.

STRANGER: I wish I had an aunt of your caliber.[15] All mine are au-thorities on crochet.

MADAME: I could wish you were my nephew. Good luck, and be careful. Perhaps one day, you will come back, and dine with me, and tell me the rest of the tale.

---

[15] *caliber:* here, value.

The sound of a running engine comes from outside.

STRANGER: Two years today, perhaps?

MADAME: One year today.

STRANGER [softly]: Who knows? [He lifts her hand to his lips.] Thank you, and *au revoir.* [16] [Turning at the door.] Being sped on my way by the enemy is a happiness I had not anticipated. I shall never be able to repay you for that. [He goes out.] [Off stage.] Ah, my coat—thank you, Simone.

Sound of car driving off. Madame pours out two glasses. As she finishes, Simone comes in, shutting the door correctly behind her and taking two paces into the room.

SIMONE: You wanted me, madame?

MADAME: You will drink a glass of wine with me, Simone.

SIMONE: With you, madame!

MADAME: You are a good daughter of France and a good servant to me. We shall drink a toast together.

SIMONE: Yes, madame.

MADAME [quietly]: To Freedom.

SIMONE [repeating]: To Freedom. May I add a bit of my own, madame?

MADAME: Certainly.

SIMONE [with immense satisfaction]: And a very bad end to that Corporal!

CURTAIN

[16] *au revoir* (ō rə-vwär′): until we meet again; good-bye.

DISCUSSION

1. Madame, Simone, and the Stranger are living in a dangerous situation requiring a great deal of courage. What different kinds of courage are shown by each?

2. Why does Madame feel fairly safe in asking the Corporal to give the Stranger a ride to St. Estèphe?

3. A "collaborator" is one who willingly works with one's enemies. Madame's real nephew, whom we do not meet, is evidently such a collaborator, explaining his actions as a belief in the "Brotherhood of Man" (pages 355 and 357). What kind of "brotherhood" does he believe in? What kind of belief in human beings does Madame have?

For further activities, see page 364.

VOCABULARY

The Driver and the Demon (page 341)

Here are five words that are used in the story to describe the engineer. With the help of your dictionary, check their meanings, and find five *antonyms*—words that have opposite meanings from the first words. Using these new words, write several sentences describing an imaginary person.

abhorrent   cynical   grotesque   mocking   squat

The Pen of My Aunt (page 348)

Use each of these words in a sentence. If you are unsure of their meanings, turn back to the pages indicated and check the footnotes, if they are defined. If some are not, try to determine their meanings from the way they are used.

anathema (p. 351)   hypothetical (p. 352)   absurd (p. 361)
caliber (p. 362)   consigned (p. 354)   conformity (p. 351)

COMPOSITION

Growing Up (page 340)

This poem is written from the son's point of view. Write a poem or a short account of the same experience told from the father's point of view.

The Driver and the Demon (page 341)

The author tells us how his faith in human beings is strengthened by his experience with the driver. We are not told what happens to the "demon" engineer who believes that "all men are by nature thieves and murderers" (page 342). Write another ending to this story from the point of view of the engineer. What does he think? What does he do? What are his feelings? What do you think happens to him? Start your ending as the author started his own on page 345: "I was alone, without food or water, in the middle of the huge steppe."

The Pen of My Aunt (see page 348)

If a play is to be successful, good characterization (see page 102) is important; the people in it should seem alive to the audience or reader. Do you have a clear picture of the characters in this play? Write a short paragraph describing one of them, according to the picture you have in your mind.

READING

Learn to Say Good-bye (page 324)

In literature as in life, what people say and do can affect others' lives in ways they never intended. The reader of a story, however, knowing more than the characters know, can pick up the clues that foreshadow events to come (see page 147). Here is a list of clues (1. through 4.) that lead you to certain conclusions (a. through d., below). On separate paper, write the number of each clue. After each number, write the letter that indicates the conclusions it foreshadows.

1. "I know for sure Curly's best."
2. The heat made Jo sleepy.
3. "Oh, Johnny's all right. He knows what the score is."
4. "The steers will be auctioned to the highest bidder."
    a. Dad had not prepared Johnny for Curly's fate.
    b. Jo missed most of the judging.
    c. Johnny knew Curly would win the blue ribbon.
    d. Curly would be sold for beefsteak.

The Driver and the Demon (page 348)

Indicating whether the statement was made by the driver, the demon, or the author, write a sentence explaining what each statement reveals about that person.

1. "Keep an eye on him, he's done time."
2. "He won't get lost. That kind always fall on their feet—unfortunately."
3. "I don't believe you! I don't believe you!"
4. "I'll take the money with me because you never know who might turn up."

The Perfect Shot

BILLIE JEAN KING with KIM CHAPIN

I expect to win every time I step on the tennis court and I'm truly surprised when I don't. That attitude, I'm pretty sure, goes all the way back. It was already there the day I made that (I suspect) less than marvelous catch as the hotshot ten-year-old shortstop on the Houghton Park girls' softball team. When the other kids congratulated me and patted me on the back, I just couldn't handle it. I turned red, I hung my head—the whole bit. I didn't think about it at all because I'd expected to make that kind of catch and double up that runner at third. Big deal.

I've been successful in tennis basically because of something I had nothing to do with—my talent. I was born with the physical and—to some degree—the mental ability to hit a tennis ball with accuracy and power, and that's all there is to it. Maybe I can be praised a little for using that talent, I believe, to its fullest, but not at all for having it in the first place. When everything is right on and I know I'm playing my absolute best tennis, I really don't believe there are very many players who can come close to me. Not Evert, Goolagong, Court, or anybody else. I'm sure they all feel the same way about themselves, too, and I'm sure that Laver and Gonzalez felt like that when they were at the absolute peak of their games. On my very best days I have this fantastic, utterly unself-conscious feeling of invincibility.

I still get that charge out of winning, and even from just hitting one great shot. If I didn't get that charge and suddenly found myself asking, "Is this really worth it?" that would probably be a good reason to stop playing. But that hasn't happened, not yet. Something inside keeps pushing me to go on. That restlessness, drive, motivation, or whatever you want to call it hasn't gone away yet. I'm not sure how to explain it; except I have a funny feeling it's probably the same thing that makes people go crazy too.

The more I play the more I'm amazed by this desire, that I and other top players apparently have, to succeed and accomplish something. Ken Rosewall has been around now for over twenty years. Laver's been a world-class player for fifteen, Court for thirteen. I've been playing internationally since 1961, and I don't know why I still want to be Number One. Maybe there's some basic insecurity beyond the simple fear of losing. All I know is that it's a part of me and I can't repress it. I can't say, "Okay, I'm not gonna go to work today." No way. I still love to play; every time I walk on the court I feel the need to prove myself all over again. Being Number One isn't everything to me, but for those few hours on the

court it's way ahead of whatever's in second place.

Sometimes I find it hard to motivate myself. I've got to have a goal. If I start to play and find myself asking, "What does this match really mean?" I know I'm in trouble. Long-range goals are the best. In those years when Wimbledon[1] was the most important thing in the world to me, just thinking about the place was enough to get me on the practice court months and months before the tournament.

I like to play on emotion, any emotion at all. The best days are those when I can feel the excitement of the crowd—it doesn't have to be a big crowd, either, although they're the best—and get a sense of the drama. There are times, however, when everything comes up just flat no matter how much I goad myself, and when that happens I have to force myself to just hang in the match until something—anything—happens to set off a spark and get me on the track.

But good tennis also requires a lot of self-discipline and sometimes the two things—emotion and discipline—get in the way of each other.

It's been said many times before that one of the real marks of a champion is not the ability to win when you're playing well, but the ability to pull out matches when you're playing badly. And raising your game that essential notch or two when your emotions are asking you "Why bother

with all this nonsense?" is a pretty difficult trick. Sometimes I'm successful at that, sometimes I'm not.

I guess I'm pretty disciplined, but it's not really my bag. I hate regimentation,[2] and training has always been difficult for me. I hate to lift weights even though I know it helps my legs. Jogging for the sake of jogging bores me to tears. I love to stay up late although I know I need my sleep. I go crazy around candy bars and ice cream even though my weight has always been borderline. I love to read and go to the movies, but I know that's bad for my eyes. I'd like to be able to just play competition tennis and not have to worry about any of the other stuff at all. If I hadn't been raised by parents with a pretty strong sense of discipline themselves, I would have been hopeless, absolutely hopeless.

I'm a music nut, and I sing to myself all the time on the court, especially if there's a song that relates to my immediate situation—whether I'm happy or sad, or winning or losing, or feeling good or feeling lousy. I'll go over the lyrics, or at least some fragments, or just let the tunes drift through my mind.

When I'm doing that—singing on the court—I know I'm playing good tennis. This isn't as crazy as it sounds. It means that I'm not thinking consciously about tennis and that as far as the plain mechanics of hitting the ball go, my mind is at a sort of zero

---

[1] *Wimbledon:* site of annual international tennis matches.

[2] *regimentation:* any enforced system ordering people's daily lives.

point. Neutral. Because instinct is everything, and that's exactly how I want it to be. If I'm thinking too much during a match, it's a dead giveaway that something isn't quite right with my game.

Instinct is what allows me to make the instantaneous connection between knowing what I ought to do on a certain shot and actually doing it. It's sort of a shorthand connection between the brain—the unconscious brain—and the body, because when I'm playing on instinct alone I have no idea what I'm doing physically on any of my shots. I really don't. I've been told, for example, that I hit my backhand, which I feel is one of my best shots, in a very strange way. I agree, but only because I've seen films of myself. At the time I'm actually hitting one, I have no idea what my body's doing. I know my backswing is normal and that my follow-through isn't too unusual, but somewhere in between I do this sort of odd thing with my wrist that allows me both to disguise the direction of the shot very nicely, and to be able to come over the ball or to slice it, or to hit it flat, whichever's right.

It's really amazing. I've asked a lot of the other players to analyze what exactly it is they do during a shot: "How do you hit your forehand?" And the better they are, the more likely they are to not know the answer.

Knowing that I'm playing totally by instinct gives me tremendous self-confidence. I'm sure, just positive, that since my instincts are basically

good, nothing can go wrong. What I do think about on those super days are things like my patterns—what shots I'm going to hit in a certain situation—my own movements, and how I'm playing generally. I don't worry about how I'm hitting the ball, and I hardly notice my opponent at all. It's like I'm out there by myself. I've talked with Laver and Rosewall about this, and even Court a little, and on their great days their attitude is exactly the same. I concentrate only on the ball in relationship to the face of my racket, which is a fulltime job anyway, since no two balls ever come over the net the same way. I appreciate what my opponent is doing, but in a very detached, abstract way, like an observer in the next room. I see her moving to her left or right, but it's almost as though there weren't any real opponent, as though I didn't know—and certainly didn't care—whom I was playing against.

When I'm in that kind of state (and sometimes even when I'm not), I feel that tennis is an art form that's capable of moving both the players and the audience—at least a knowledgeable audience—in emotional, almost sensual [3] ways. Tennis is a personal expression on my part, certainly the most complete and maybe the only way I can express myself. When I'm performing at my absolute best, I think that some of the euphoria [4] that I feel must be transmitted to the audience. That may be a pretty

[3] *sensual:* affecting the senses.
[4] *euphoria* (yōō-fôr'ē-ə): a feeling of great happiness.

feeble definition of art, but for me, the rhythms of tennis are very similar to the movements of a ballet, and the emotion that comes from a great match or even a single great shot is like the emotion you feel when you hear a moving piece of music.

There's a real conflict within me sometimes between what might be called the aesthetics[5] of tennis and the need to win. In certain situations I'm really tempted to try and hit a flashier, more fun shot than is smart. But I hate to lose so much that I involuntarily revert to the percentage shots and patterns that I know will work best. It kills me to admit it, but I'm a duller player because of my need to win.

I think I'll concentrate on winning, for a few more years, at least, but there is something to be said for the aesthetic approach to the game. If I didn't get a pure, abstract pleasure from just hitting that ball solidly, time after time, there's no way I'd continue playing. Who in her right mind would live out of a suitcase for thirteen years or more, check in and out of hotels and motels constantly, and go through all the other daily hassles, if in the very end, she just didn't like to play and to constantly test herself against the best players in the world? In this respect, it's impossible to satisfy me totally. I know I'm a perfectionist, that no matter how well I play I'll always feel I could have played a lot better. Other players have asked

me whether I was ever satisfied, whether I had just once walked off the court and been able to say that was the absolute best I could do.

And the answer has honestly been "No."

The perfect match would be one in which I won every point and did that by hitting every shot exactly how and where I wanted. The real challenge, the real fun, is to see how close I can come to that.

The perfect *shot* is another matter. They don't come along very often, but when they do, they're great. It gives me a marvelous feeling of almost perfect joy—especially if I can pull one off on the last shot of the match.

I can almost feel it coming. It usually happens on one of those days when everything is just right, when the crowd is large and enthusiastic and my concentration is so perfect it almost seems as though I'm able to transport myself beyond the turmoil on the court to some place of total peace and calm. I know where the ball is on every shot, and it always looks as big and as well-defined as a basketball. Just a huge thing that I couldn't miss if I wanted to. I've got perfect control of the match, my rhythm and movements are excellent, and everything's just in total balance. That's the setup.

The perfect shot. It's just an, "Aaaahhh"—all those years of preparation, the moments of losing and of mis-hitting the ball, all those nights as a kid when I stayed out when the sun was going down until I couldn't see

---

5 *aesthetics* (ĕs-thĕt´ĭks): human thinking concerning the meaning of beauty.

the ball anymore—that indescribable feeling of meeting the ball right in the old pocket just the way you planned it. . . . No, you didn't plan anything, not really. It just happened.

It can happen anytime, and it can really catch you by surprise. But most players have a favorite shot or two that gives them a bigger kick than the others. The one shot I love to make is when my opponent lobs over me and I run back and pass her with a backhand. I love it, especially when I get her wrong-footed. I can always see my opponent on that shot—not really see her but sense where she is, and I really hide my backhand well. Like, I'll fake it down the line and snap it crosscourt, or I'll wait just long enough for her to think I've got to go crosscourt and then I'll go *boom* with it down the line. I love to cut loose on that. It's such a free feeling, like that film thing they always do in slow motion, where the two young people are running toward each other, that feeling of putting everything together and of being in perfect harmony.

But it doesn't have to be that one favorite shot, or even a shot on a crucial point. I remember a drop shot I hit against Nancy Gunter in Indianapolis one year that really didn't mean a thing as far as our match was concerned, but it was one of *those* shots and I turned absolutely cold inside. I got chills and goose pimples and my heart was pounding—over one single drop shot.

That perfect moment happens in all sports. In basketball, it might be

that split-second hesitation just before a player gets off a jump shot that you know is gonna go swish. In baseball, players say they can't feel the ball on the bat at all when they've hit a home run, but they know, they just know.

Whenever I get to talking about drugs, I always say, "I get high just by hitting a backhand," and it's always worth a laugh. But it's true, absolutely true. And more and more club players, even, are telling me, "I know what you mean. I hit *one* shot out of a whole doubles match the other day, and it was the greatest feeling."

It is, it is. It's a perfect combination of a violent action taking place in an atmosphere of total tranquility. My heart pounds, my eyes get damp, and my ears feel like they're wiggling, but it's also just totally peaceful. And when it happens I want to stop the match and grab the microphone and shout, "*That's* what it's all about." Because it is. It's not the big prize I'm going to win at the end of the match or anything else. It's just having done something that's totally pure and having experienced the perfect emotion, and I'm always a little sad that I can't communicate that feeling right at the moment it's happening. I can only hope the people realize what's going on.

DISCUSSION

1. How do the author's feelings when playing tennis compare with those of champions in other fields?

2. "Long-range goals are the best." What does the author mean? Give an instance when short-range goals are important.

3. How does the author feel about discipline and training? What kind of training program does she carry out?

4. When the author is perfectly in touch with what she is doing, with total concentration but without mental strain, "the perfect shot" is possible. Give an instance in which you have experienced this in some activity.

For further activities, see page 392.

Say It with Flowers

TOSHIO MORI

He was a queer one to come to the ship and ask Mr. Sasaki[1] for
a job, but at the time I kept my mouth shut. There was something about this young man's appearance which I could not altogether harmonize with a job as a clerk in a flower shop. I was
a delivery boy for Mr. Sasaki then. I had seen clerks come and
go, and although they were of various sorts of temperaments
and conducts, all of them had the technique of waiting on the
customers or acquired one eventually. You could never tell
about a new one, however, and to be on the safe side I said
nothing and watched our boss readily take on this young man.
Anyhow we were glad to have an extra hand because the busy
season was coming around.

Mr. Sasaki undoubtedly remembered last year's rush when
Tommy, Mr. Sasaki and I had to do everything and had our
hands tied behind our backs from having so many things to do
at one time. He wanted to be ready this time. "Another clerk
and we'll be all set for any kind of business," he used to tell us.
When Teruo[2] came around looking for a job, he got it, and
Morning-Glory Flower Shop was all set for the year as far as
our boss was concerned.

When Teruo reported for work the following morning Mr.
Sasaki left him in Tommy's hands. Tommy had been our number one clerk for a long time.

"Tommy, teach him all you can," Mr. Sasaki said. "Teruo's
going to be with us from now on."

"Sure," Tommy said.

"Tommy's a good florist. You watch and listen to him," the
boss told the young man.

"All right, Mr. Sasaki," the young man said. He turned to
us and said, "My name is Teruo." We shook hands.

We got to know one another pretty well after that. He was
a quiet fellow with very little words for anybody, but his smile

---

Toshio Mori: pronounced tō-shē-ō mō-rē. Japanese words have no accented syllables.
[1] *Sasaki:* pronounced sä-sä-kī.
[2] *Teruo:* pronounced tə-rū-ō.

disarmed a person. We soon learned that he knew nothing about the florist business. He could identify a rose when he saw one, and gardenias and carnations too; but other flowers and materials were new to him.

"You fellows teach me something about this business and I'll be grateful. I want to start from the bottom," Teruo said.

Tommy and I nodded. We were pretty sure by then he was all right. Tommy eagerly went about showing Teruo the florist game. Every morning for several days Tommy repeated the prices of the flowers for him. He told Teruo what to do on telephone orders; how to keep the greens fresh; how to make bouquets, corsages, and sprays. "You need a little more time to learn how to make big funeral pieces," Tommy said. "That'll come later."

In a couple of weeks Teruo was just as good a clerk as we had had in a long time. He was curious almost to a fault, and was a glutton for work. It was about this time our boss decided to move ahead his yearly business trip to Seattle. Undoubtedly he was satisfied with Teruo, and he knew we could get along without him for a while. He went off and left Tommy in full charge.

During Mr. Sasaki's absence I was often in the shop helping Tommy and Teruo with the customers and the orders. One day Teruo learned that I once worked in the nursery and had experience in flower-growing.

"How do you tell when a flower is fresh or old?" he asked me. "I can't tell one from the other. All I do is follow your instructions and sell the ones you tell me to sell first, but I can't tell one from the other."

I laughed. "You don't need to know that, Teruo," I told him. "When the customers ask you whether the flowers are fresh, say yes firmly. 'Our flowers are always fresh, madam.'"

Teruo picked up a vase of carnations. "These flowers came in four or five days ago, didn't they?" he asked me.

"You're right. Five days ago," I said.

"How long will they keep if a customer bought them today?" Teruo asked.

"I guess in this weather they'll hold a day or two," I said.

"Then they're old," Teruo almost gasped. "Why, we have fresh ones that last a week or so in the shop."

"Sure, Teruo. And why should you worry about that?"

Tommy said. "You talk right to the customers and they'll believe you. 'Our flowers are always fresh? You bet they are! Just came in a little while ago from the market.' "

Teruo looked at us calmly. "That's a hard thing to say when you know it isn't true."

"You've got to get it over with sooner or later," I told him. "Everybody has to do it. You too, unless you want to lose your job."

"I don't think I can say it convincingly again," Teruo said. "I must've said yes forty times already when I didn't know any better. It'll be harder next time."

"You've said it forty times already so why can't you say yes forty million times more? What's the difference? Remember, Teruo, it's your business to live," Tommy said.

"I don't like it," Teruo said.

"Do we like it? Do you think we're any different from you?" Tommy asked Teruo. "You're just a green kid. You don't know any better so I don't get sore, but you got to play the game when you're in it. You understand, don't you?"

Teruo nodded. For a moment he stood and looked curiously at us for the first time, and then went away to water the potted plants.

In the ensuing weeks we watched Teruo develop into a slick salesclerk but for one thing. If a customer forgot to ask about the condition of the flowers Teruo did splendidly. But if someone should mention about the freshness of the flowers he wilted right in front of the customers. Sometimes he would splutter. He would stand gaping speechless on other occasions without a comeback. Sometimes, looking embarrassedly at us, he would take the customers to the fresh flowers in the rear and complete the sales.

"Don't do that any more, Teruo," Tommy warned him one afternoon after watching him repeatedly sell the fresh ones. "You know we got plenty of the old stuff in the front. We can't throw all that stuff away. First thing you know the boss'll start losing money and we'll all be thrown out."

"I wish I could sell like you," Teruo said. "Whenever they ask me, 'Is this fresh?' 'How long will it keep?' I lose all sense about selling the stuff, and begin to think of the difference between the fresh and the old stuff. Then the trouble begins."

"Remember, the boss has to run the shop so he can keep it going," Tommy told him. "When he returns next week you better not let him see you touch the fresh flowers in the rear."

On the day Mr. Sasaki came back to the shop we saw something unusual. For the first time I watched Teruo sell some old stuff to a customer. I heard the man plainly ask him if the flowers would keep good, and very clearly I heard Teruo reply, "Yes, sir. These flowers'll keep good." I looked at Tommy, and he winked back. When Teruo came back to make it into a bouquet he looked as if he had a snail in his mouth. Mr. Sasaki came back to the rear and watched him make the bouquet. When Teruo went up front to complete the sale Mr. Sasaki looked at Tommy and nodded approvingly.

When I went out to the truck to make my last delivery for the day Teruo followed me. "Gee, I feel rotten," he said to me. "Those flowers I sold to the people, they won't last longer than tomorrow. I feel lousy. I'm lousy. The people'll get to know my word pretty soon."

"Forget it," I said. "Quit worrying. What's the matter with you?"

"I'm lousy," he said, and went back to the store.

Then one early morning the inevitable happened. While Teruo was selling the fresh flowers in the back to a customer Mr. Sasaki came in quietly and watched the transaction. The boss didn't say anything at the time. All day Teruo looked sick. He didn't know whether to explain to the boss or shut up.

While Teruo was out to lunch Mr. Sasaki called us aside. "How long has this been going on?" he asked us. He was pretty sore.

"He's been doing it off and on. We told him to quit it," Tommy said. "He says he feels rotten selling old flowers."

"Old flowers!" snorted Mr. Sasaki. "I'll tell him plenty when he comes back. Old flowers! Maybe you can call them old at the wholesale market but they're not old in a flower shop."

"He feels guilty fooling the customers," Tommy explained.

The boss laughed impatiently. "That's no reason for a businessman."

When Teruo came back he knew what was up. He looked at us for a moment and then went about cleaning the stems of the old flowers.

"Teruo," Mr. Sasaki called.

Teruo approached us as if steeled for an attack.

"You've been selling fresh flowers and leaving the old ones go to waste. I can't afford that, Teruo," Mr. Sasaki said. "Why don't you do as you're told? We all sell the flowers in the front. I tell you they're not old in a flower shop. Why can't you sell them?"

"I don't like it, Mr. Sasaki," Teruo said. "When the people ask me if they're fresh I hate to answer. I feel rotten after selling the old ones."

"Look here, Teruo," Mr. Sasaki said. "I don't want to fire you. You're a good boy, and I know you need a job, but you've got to be a good clerk here or you're going out. Do you get me?"

"I get you," Teruo said.

In the morning we were all at the shop early. I had an eight o'clock delivery, and the others had to rush with a big funeral order. Teruo was there early. "Hello," he greeted us cheerfully as we came in. He was unusually highspirited, and I couldn't account for it. He was there before us and had already filled out the eight o'clock package for me. He was almost through with the funeral frame, padding it with wet moss and covering all over with brake fern, when Tommy came in. When Mr. Sasaki arrived, Teruo waved his hand and cheerfully went about gathering the flowers for the funeral piece. As he flitted here and there he seemed as if he had forgotten our presence, even the boss. He looked at each vase, sized up the flowers, and then cocked his head at the next one. He did this with great deliberation, as if he were the boss and the last word in the shop. That was all right, but when a customer soon came in, he swiftly attended him as if he owned all the flowers in the world. When the man asked Teruo if he was getting fresh flowers Teruo without batting an eye escorted the customer into the rear and eventually showed and sold the fresh ones. He did it with so much grace, dignity and swiftness that we stood around like his stooges. However, Mr. Sasaki went on with his work as if nothing had happened.

Along toward noon Teruo attended his second customer. He fairly ran to greet an old lady who wanted a cheap bouquet around fifty cents for a dinner table. This time he not only went back to the rear for the fresh ones but added three or four extras. To make it more irritating for the boss, who was watching every move, Teruo used an extra lot of maidenhair because the old lady was appreciative of his art of making bouquets. Tommy and I watched the boss fuming inside of his office.

When the old lady went out of the shop Mr. Sasaki came out furious. "You're a blockhead. You have no business sense.

What are you doing here?" he said to Teruo. "Are you crazy?"

Teruo looked cheerful. "I'm not crazy, Mr. Sasaki," he said. "And I'm not dumb. I just like to do it that way, that's all."

The boss turned to Tommy and me. "That boy's a sap," he said. "He's got no head."

Teruo laughed and walked off to the front with a broom. Mr. Sasaki shook his head. "What's the matter with him? I can't understand him," he said.

While the boss was out to lunch Teruo went on a mad spree. He waited on three customers at one time, ignoring our presence. It was amazing how he did it. He hurriedly took one customer's order and had him write a birthday greeting for it; jumped to the second customer's side and pursuaded her to buy Columbia roses because they were the freshest of the lot. She wanted them delivered so he jotted it down on the sales book, and leaped to the third customer.

"I want to buy that orchid in the window," she stated without deliberation.

"Do you have to have orchid, madam?" Teruo asked the lady.

"No," she said. "But I want something nice for tonight's ball, and I think the orchid will match my dress. Why do you ask?"

"If I were you I wouldn't buy that orchid," he told her. "It won't keep. I could sell it to you and make a profit but I don't want to do that and spoil your evening. Come to the back, madam, and I'll show you some of the nicest gardenias in the market today. We call them Belmont and they're fresh today."

He came to the rear with the lady. We watched him pick out three of the biggest gardenias and make them into a corsage. When the lady went out with her package a little boy about eleven years old came in and wanted a twenty-five-cent bouquet for his mother's birthday. Teruo waited on the boy. He was out in the front, and we saw him pick out a dozen of the two-dollar-a-dozen roses and give them to the kid.

Tommy nudged me. "If he was the boss he couldn't do those things," he said.

"In the first place," I said, "I don't think he could be a boss."

"What do you think?" Tommy said. "Is he crazy? Is he trying to get himself fired?"

"I don't know," I said.

When Mr. Sasaki returned, Teruo was waiting on another customer, a young lady.

"Did Teruo eat yet?" Mr. Sasaki asked Tommy.

"No, he won't go. He says he's not hungry today," Tommy said.

We watched Teruo talking to the young lady. The boss shook his head. Then it came. Teruo came back to the rear and picked out a dozen of the very fresh white roses and took them out to the lady.

"Aren't they lovely?" we heard her exclaim.

We watched him come back, take down a box, place several maidenhairs and asparagus, place the roses neatly inside, sprinkle a few drops, and then give it to her. We watched him thank her, and we noticed her smile and thanks. The girl walked out.

Mr. Sasaki ran excitedly to the front. "Teruo! She forgot to pay!"

Teruo stopped the boss on the way out. "Wait, Mr. Sasaki," he said. "I gave it to her."

"What!" the boss cried indignantly.

"She came in just to look around and see the flowers. She likes pretty roses. Don't you think she's wonderful?"

"What's the matter with you?" the boss said. "Are you crazy? What did she buy?"

"Nothing, I tell you," Teruo said. "I gave it to her because she admired it, and she's pretty enough to deserve beautiful things, and I liked her."

"You're fired! Get out!" Mr. Sasaki spluttered. "Don't come back to the store again."

"And I gave her fresh ones too," Teruo said.

Mr. Sasaki rolled out several bills from his pocketbook. "Here's your wages for this week. Now, get out," he said.

"I don't want it," Teruo said. "You keep it and buy some more flowers."

"Here, take it. Get out," Mr. Sasaki said.

Teruo took the bills and rang up the cash register. "All right, I'll go now. I feel fine. I'm happy. Thanks to you." He waved his hand to Mr. Sasaki. "No hard feelings."

On the way out Teruo remembered our presence. He looked back. "Good-bye. Good luck," he said cheerfully to Tommy and me.

He walked out of the shop with his shoulders straight, head high, and whistling. He did not come back to see us again.

DISCUSSION

1. How did Teruo feel about being fired? Why did he feel this way?

2. Teruo had a difficult choice to make. What did he have to decide, and exactly what did he do?

3. Mr. Sasaki called Teruo "a blockhead . . . a sap." Was Teruo stupid? Why did Mr. Sasaki feel that he was?

4. What kind of work do you think Teruo should look for? Under what conditions could he be a florist somewhere else?

5. What is the **theme** (see page 339) of this story?

For further activities, see page 392.

THE GIFT OF THE MAGI

O. HENRY

One dollar and eighty-seven cents. That was all. And sixty cents of it was in pennies. Pennies saved one and two at a time by bulldozing the grocer and the vegetable man and the butcher until one's cheeks burned with the silent imputation of parsimony[1] that such close dealing implied. Three times Della counted it. One dollar and eighty-seven cents. And the next day would be Christmas.

There was clearly nothing to do but flop down on the shabby little couch and howl. So Della did it. Which instigates[2] the moral reflection that life is made up of sobs, sniffles, and smiles, with sniffles predominating.

While the mistress of the home is gradually subsiding from the first stage to the second, take a look at the home. A furnished flat at eight dollars per week. It did not exactly beggar description,[3] but it certainly had that word on the lookout for the mendicancy squad.[4]

In the vestibule below was a letter box into which no letter would go, and an electric button from which no mortal finger could coax a ring. Also appertaining thereunto was a card bearing the name "Mr. James Dillingham Young."

The "Dillingham" had been flung to the breeze during a former period of prosperity when its possessor was being paid thirty dollars per week. Now, when the income was shrunk to twenty dollars, the letters of "Dillingham" looked blurred, as though they were thinking seriously of contracting to a modest and unassuming D. But whenever Mr. James Dillingham Young came home and reached his flat above, he was called "Jim" and greatly hugged by Mrs. James Dillingham Young, already introduced to you as Della. Which is all very good.

Della finished her cry and attended to her cheeks with the powder rag. She stood by the window and looked out dully at a

---

[1] *imputation of parsimony:* accusation of stinginess.
[2] *instigates:* stirs up.
[3] *beggar description:* exhaust the powers of description.
[4] *mendicancy squad:* police who arrested illegal beggars. A play on the word just used.

gray cat walking a gray fence in a gray back yard. Tomorrow would be Christmas Day, and she had only $1.87 with which to buy Jim a present. She had been saving every penny she could for months, with this result. Twenty dollars a week doesn't go far. Expenses had been greater than she had calculated. They always are. Only $1.87 to buy a present for Jim. Her Jim. Many a happy hour she had spent planning something nice for him. Something fine and rare and sterling—something just a little bit near to being worthy of the honor of being owned by Jim.

There was pier glass[5] between the windows of the room. Perhaps you have seen a pier glass in an eight-dollar flat. A very thin and very agile person may, by observing his reflection in a rapid sequence of longitudinal strips, obtain a fairly accurate conception of his looks. Della, being slender, had mastered the art.

Suddenly she whirled from the window and stood before the glass. Her eyes were shining brilliantly, but her face had lost its color within twenty seconds. Rapidly she pulled down her hair and let it fall to its full length.

Now, there were two possessions of the James Dillingham Youngs in which they both took a mighty pride. One was Jim's gold watch that had been his father's and his grandfather's. The other was Della's hair. Had the Queen of Sheba lived in the flat across the air shaft, Della would have let her hair hang out the window some day to dry just to depreciate Her Majesty's jewels and gifts. Had King Solomon been the janitor, with all his treasures piled up in the basement, Jim would have pulled out his watch every time he passed, just to see him pluck at his beard from envy.

So now Della's beautiful hair fell about her, rippling and shining like a cascade of brown waters. It reached below her knee and made itself almost a garment for her. And then she did it up again nervously and quickly. Once she faltered for a minute and stood still while a tear or two splashed on the worn red carpet.

On went her old brown jacket; on went her old brown hat. With a whirl of skirts and with the brilliant sparkle still in her eyes she fluttered out the door and down the stairs to the street.

Where she stopped, the sign read, "Mme. Sofronie. Hair Goods of All Kinds." One flight up Della ran and collected herself, panting. Madame, large, too white, chilly, hardly looked the "Sofronie."

---

[5] *pier glass:* a high, thin mirror.

"Will you buy my hair?" asked Della.

"I buy hair," said Madame. "Take yer hat off and let's have a sight at the looks of it."

Down rippled the brown cascade.

"Twenty dollars," said Madame, lifting the mass with a practiced hand.

"Give it to me quick," said Della.

Oh, and the next two hours tripped by on rosy wings. Forget the hashed metaphor.[6] She was ransacking the stores for Jim's present.

She found it at last. It surely had been made for Jim and no one else. There was no other like it in any of the stores, and she had turned all of them inside out. It was a platinum fob chain,[7] simple and chaste in design, properly proclaiming its value by substance alone and not by meretricious[8] ornamentation—as all good things should do. It was even worthy of The Watch. As soon as she saw it, she knew that it must be Jim's. It was like him. Quietness and value—the description applied to both. Twenty-one dollars they took from her for it, and she hurried home with the eighty-seven cents. With that chain on his watch Jim might be properly anxious about the time in any company. Grand as the watch was, he sometimes looked at it on the sly on account of the old leather strap that he used in place of a chain.

When Della reached home her intoxication gave way a little to prudence and reason. She got out her curling irons and lighted the gas and went to work repairing the ravages made by generosity added to love. Which is always a tremendous task, dear friends—a mammoth task.

Within forty minutes her head was covered with tiny, close-lying curls that made her look wonderfully like a truant schoolboy. She looked at her reflection in the mirror long, carefully, and critically.

"If Jim doesn't kill me," she said to herself, "before he takes a second look at me, he'll say I look like a Coney Island chorus girl. But what could I do—oh! what could I do with a dollar and eighty-seven cents?"

At seven o'clock the coffee was made and the frying pan was

---

[6] *hashed metaphor:* confused figure of speech; reference to the previous sentence: hours would trip on *feet*, not *wings*.

[7] *fob chain:* short chain attached to a pocket watch.

[8] *meretricious* (mĕr-ə-trĭsh'əs): cheap and gaudy.

on the back of the stove, hot and ready to cook the chops.

Jim was never late. Della doubled the fob chain in her hand and sat on the corner of the table near the door that he always entered. Then she heard his step on the stair away down on the first flight, and she turned white for just a moment. She had a habit of saying little silent prayers about the simplest everyday things, and now she whispered, "Please, God, make him think I am still pretty."

The door opened, and Jim stepped in and closed it. He looked thin and very serious. Poor fellow, he was only twenty-two—and to be burdened with a family! He needed a new overcoat, and he was without gloves.

Jim stopped inside the door, as immovable as a setter at the scent of quail. His eyes were fixed upon Della, and there was an expression in them that she could not read, and it terrified her. It was not anger, nor surprise, nor disapproval, nor horror, nor any of the sentiments that she had been prepared for. He simply stared at her fixedly with that peculiar expression on his face.

Della wriggled off the table and went for him.

"Jim, darling," she cried, "don't look at me that way. I had my hair cut off and sold it because I couldn't have lived through Christmas without giving you a present. It'll grow out again—you won't mind, will you? I just had to do it. My hair grows awfully fast. Say 'Merry Christmas!' Jim, and let's be happy. You don't know what a nice—what a beautiful, nice gift I've got for you."

"You've cut off your hair?" asked Jim, laboriously, as if he had not arrived at that patent fact yet even after the hardest mental labor.

"Cut it off and sold it," said Della. "Don't you like me just as well, anyhow? I'm me without my hair, ain't I?"

Jim looked about the room curiously.

"You say your hair is gone?" he said, with an air almost of idiocy.

"You needn't look for it," said Della. "It's sold, I tell you— sold and gone, too. It's Christmas Eve, boy. Be good to me, for it went for you. Maybe the hairs of my head were numbered," she went on with a sudden serious sweetness, "but nobody could ever count my love for you. Shall I put the chops on, Jim?"

Out of his trance Jim seemed quickly to wake. He enfolded his Della. For ten seconds let us regard with discreet scrutiny some inconsequential object in the other direction. Eight dollars a week or a million a year—what is the difference? A mathematician or a wit would give you the wrong answer. The Magi brought valuable gifts, but that was not among them. This dark assertion will be illuminated later on.

Jim drew a package from his overcoat pocket and threw it upon the table.

"Don't make any mistake, Dell," he said, "about me. I don't think there's anything in the way of a haircut or a shave or a shampoo that could make me like my girl any less. But if you'll unwrap that package, you may see why you had me going a while at first."

White fingers and nimble tore at the string and paper. And then an ecstatic scream of joy; and then, alas! a quick feminine change to hysterical tears and wails, necessitating the immediate employment of all the comforting powers of the lord of the flat.

For there lay The Combs—the set of combs, side and back, that Della had worshiped for long in a Broadway window. Beautiful combs, pure tortoise shell, with jeweled rims—just the shade to wear in the beautiful vanished hair. They were expensive combs, she knew, and her heart had simply craved and yearned over them without the least hope of possession. And now they were hers, but the tresses that should have adorned the coveted adornments were gone.

But she hugged them to her bosom, and at length she was able to look up with dim eyes and a smile and say, "My hair grows so fast, Jim!" And then Della leaped up like a little singed cat and cried, "Oh, oh!"

Jim had not yet seen his beautiful present. She held it out to him eagerly upon her open palm. The dull precious metal seemed to flash with a reflection of her bright and ardent spirit.

"Isn't it a dandy, Jim? I hunted all over town to find it. You'll have to look at the time a hundred times a day now. Give me your watch. I want to see how it looks on it."

Instead of obeying, Jim tumbled down on the couch and put his hands under the back of his head and smiled.

"Dell," said he, "let's put our Christmas presents away and keep 'em a while. They're too nice to use just at present. I sold the watch to get the money to buy your combs. And now suppose you put the chops on."

The Magi, as you know, were wise men—wonderfully wise men—who brought gifts to the Babe in the manger. They invented the art of giving Christmas presents. Being wise, their gifts were no doubt wise ones, possibly bearing the privilege of exchange in case of duplication. And here I have lamely related to you the uneventful chronicle of two foolish children in a flat who most unwisely sacrificed for each other the greatest treasures of their house. But in a last word to the wise of these days let it be said that of all who give gifts these two were the wisest. Of all who give and receive gifts, such as they are wisest. Everywhere they are wisest. They are the Magi.

DISCUSSION

1.   "Of all who give and receive gifts, such as they are wisest. . . . They are the Magi." Why does the author say this of Jim and Della, whose presents for each other are now useless?

2.   When Della and Jim each learned what the other had done, is it possible that they could have become angry with each other? How might the story have ended then?

3.   **Irony.**   Irony is a way of using words so that their intended meaning is opposite from the meaning usually expected. The author is being ironic when he describes Jim and Della as "two foolish children . . ." (last paragraph). What does he really mean?

Another way irony is used is in presenting events so that their outcome is opposite from that expected. However, when you are in a position to look back over all the events, you usually can see that the outcome is a reasonable one.

Explain how the author uses irony in presenting the events of this story.

For further activities, see page 392.

Stopping by Woods on a Snowy Evening

ROBERT FROST

Whose woods these are I think I know.
His house is in the village though;
He will not see me stopping here
To watch his woods fill up with snow.

My little horse must think it queer   5
To stop without a farmhouse near
Between the woods and frozen lake
The darkest evening of the year.

He gives his harness bells a shake
To ask if there is some mistake.   10
The only other sound's the sweep
Of easy wind and downy flake.

The woods are lovely, dark and deep,
But I have promises to keep,
And miles to go before I sleep,   15
And miles to go before I sleep.

DISCUSSION

1. Why does the speaker of this poem decide to leave this place he has been enjoying?

2. **Diction.** Diction is the particular choice of words an author makes to communicate a particular mood or feeling. In a poem with only a limited number of words, each word becomes even more important. In the last stanza, what three words describe the woods? What do these particular words tell us of the speaker's feelings?

3. What feeling are we left with as the speaker repeats line 15?

VOCABULARY

The Perfect Shot (page 366)

Listed below are eight words that the author uses in describing tennis and her feelings about playing. Write a short paragraph about any art, sport, or science in which you participate, or which interests you, using at least six of these eight words in your paragraph. Be sure you know what they mean!

invincibility	regimentation	insecurity	perfectionist
motivation	euphoria	discipline	emotion

The Gift of the Magi (page 382)

Synonyms are words which have the same meaning. On separate paper, list a synonym for each of the nine words from the story that are listed below. Choose the simplest word with the same meaning that you can think of. If you don't know the word, consult your dictionary, but first look back at the story for help.

imputation (p.382)	vestibule (p. 382)	discreet (p. 387)
parsimony (p. 382)	meretricious (p. 385)	intoxication (p. 385)
mendicancy (p. 382)	ecstatic (p. 388)	prudence (p. 385)

COMPOSITION

Say It with Flowers (page 373)

It takes character to stand alone and do what you think is right, especially when your friends or associates want you to do otherwise. Write several well-organized paragraphs describing a person you know, through fiction or real life, who has been able to do this. For help in organizing your thoughts, turn to page 320.

The Gift of the Magi (page 382)

Suppose that only Jim or only Della had sacrificed to buy the other's gift, while the other had given only a small present, and was therefore able to use the wonderful gift when it was given. How would each feel? Write such an ending for the story. How does the story change? Can you still use the same title?

READING

The Gift of the Magi (page 382)

Seven statements or circumstances from the story are given below. Below each is a choice of reasons. On separate paper, write the letter that indicates the correct cause of each statement or circumstance.

1. Della only had $1.87 left because:
   a. She spent too much at the grocery store.
   b. She didn't save all her extra money.
   c. She was poor, and that was all she could save.

2. Della was sad the day before Christmas because:
   a. Her husband wouldn't be home.
   b. She didn't have enough money to buy his present.
   c. She didn't pay the grocery bill.

3. After shopping, Della was happy because:
   a. She bought a chain for Jim's watch.
   b. She bought a new dress.
   c. She had a new haircut.

4. Della sold her only prized possession because:
   a. She was angry with Jim because they were poor.
   b. She loved Jim and wanted to give him a fine present.
   c. She knew Jim wanted her to sell it.

5. Jim was shocked when he saw Della because:
   a. She was wearing a wig.
   b. Her hair was short and curly.
   c. She was wearing ribbons in her hair.

6. Della said, ''My hair grows so fast, Jim,'' because:
   a. She didn't want him to be hurt because she couldn't use the combs now.
   b. He yelled at her for cutting her hair.
   c. She had had a permanent, and her hair looked frizzy.

7. Jim said, ''Let's put our Christmas presents away and keep 'em'' because:
   a. He was hungry and was tired of talking.
   b. The presents were too nice to use everyday.
   c. He had sold his watch to buy her a present.

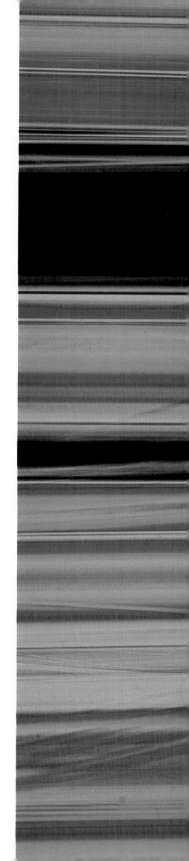

COMPOSITION

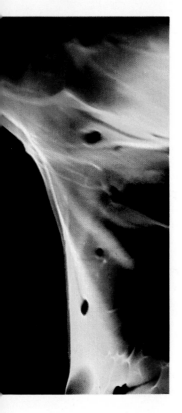

COHERENCE

When someone has received a bad shock—seen a crime or an accident—the person may become temporarily *incoherent*. Whatever he or she is trying to say relates to what has caused the shock, and so has unity. But the ideas come out jumbled.

In much the same way, some paragraphs that are unified (page 320) may lack *coherence*. *Cohere* means to "hold together." In a coherent paragraph, each sentence is closely related to the sentence that follows it.

The paragraph below has unity. Every sentence is about Billie Jean King's drive to win at tennis. But the order of sentences within the paragraph is incoherent, unintelligible:

Something inside keeps pushing me to go on. If I didn't get that charge and suddenly found myself asking, "Is this really worth it?" that would probably be a good reason to stop playing. I still get that charge out of winning, and even from just hitting one great shot. But that hasn't happened, not yet. I'm not sure how to explain it; except I have a funny feeling it's probably the same thing that makes people go crazy too. That restlessness, drive, motivation, or whatever you want to call it hasn't gone away yet.

Compare this version with the original one on page 366. The original opens with a statement that the author still likes to win. If she didn't, she tells us coherently, it would be time to quit tennis. But so far that hasn't happened. Something drives her on. Whatever it is, the feeling stays with her. She can't explain the restlessness, but maybe it's the same thing that drives some people crazy.

Her version is coherent. But why are some paragraphs *incoherent*? What happens is that our thoughts may outrace our pen. We write down thought A, and while we are writing, B passes though our mind and thought C enters it. Having finished writing A, we move directly to C, and maybe before we finish C, our mind has raced on past D to E, which we write next, sensing as we do so that something is missing—idea B back there—which we then add after E. The result, instead of A B C D E, is A C E B—confusion.

Make sure to keep your mind and pen together. Develop ideas clearly, step by step, according to some plan. That way your paragraphs will have unity *and* coherence.

ABOUT THE SELECTIONS

1.   Suppose that any one of the various choices made in these selections had been made the other way. For example, the driver in "The Driver and the Demon" might have chosen not to return, or Teruo might have chosen to become a high-powered salesman in "Say It with Flowers." In a page, describe what the consequences of such a choice would be. Try to imitate the writing of whichever selection you choose to develop, with only the outcome altered.

2.   Should John Thomas make a pet of Curly (page 324)? Should Madame in occupied France help the Stranger (p. 348)? Should Mr. Sasaki let Teruo go on working for him (p. 373)? Try to see both sides of such questions. Then, in a thoughtful letter, offer advice to any one of the several people in this unit faced with a decision to make. Be specific as to what the consequences of following your advice might be.

3.   Choose one of the following:

   a.   Describe in prose one of the people you have met in the poetry of this unit—the father in "Growing Up," for instance, or the person stopping by woods on a snowy evening (page 391).

   b.   Write a further reflection by archy the cockroach, in the manner of "The Lesson of the Moth" (page 346).

4.   There are four sentences in the paragraph on page 329 that begins "When Jo came downstairs, ten minutes later, . . ." In a paragraph of your own, explain why that paragraph is coherent.

ON YOUR OWN

1.   What is the most difficult choice you have ever had to make? In a page, describe the situation, indicate what your choices were, and justify why you chose as you did.

2.   Think about whom you would turn to for advice in a jam. Why would you turn to that person? In two or three paragraphs, explain the most important qualities that you would look for in an adviser or counselor.

3.   Suppose at some point in your past a choice had been made that suddenly altered your life. Your family, say, moved to another city. Or a person you barely knew willed you a million dollars. Put yourself in the place of that other "you," altered by circumstances. In a page, describe the feelings and attitudes of that different you.

4.   Rearrange the following sentences to make a coherent paragraph. When you finish, check your version with West's on page 337.

   The judge put out a hand intended for the boy's shoulder, but before it could settle there, Johnny was pressing his cheek against Curly's big, flat jowl. Jo was proud of the easy, happy way Johnny ran over to his side. This delighted the spectators, who laughed and cheered again. The steer seemed actually to lower his head for the caress and to move his cheek against Johnny's in loving recognition.

CHALLENGES

Through the Tunnel

DORIS LESSING

Going to the shore on the first morning of the vacation, the young English boy stopped at a turning of the path and looked down at a wild and rocky bay, and then over the crowded beach he knew so well from other years. His mother walked on in front of him, carrying a bright striped bag in one hand. Her other arm, swinging loose, was very white in the sun. The boy watched that white, naked arm, and turned his eyes, which had a frown behind them, toward the bay and back again to his mother. When she felt he was not with her, she swung around. "Oh, there you are, Jerry!" she said. She looked impatient, then smiled. "Why, darling, would you rather not come with me? Would you rather—" She frowned, conscientiously worrying over what amusements he might secretly be longing for, which she had been too busy or too careless to imagine. He was very familiar with that anxious, apologetic smile. Contrition[1] sent him running after her. And yet, as he ran, he looked back over his shoulder at the wild bay; and all morning, as he played on the safe beach, he was thinking of it.

Next morning, when it was time for the routine of swimming and sunbathing, his mother said, "Are you tired of the usual beach, Jerry? Would you like to go somewhere else?"

"Oh, no!" he said quickly, smiling at her out of that unfailing impulse of contrition—a sort of chivalry. Yet, walking down the path with her, he blurted out, "I'd like to go and have a look at those rocks down there."

She gave the idea her attention. It was a wild-looking place, and there was no one there; but she said, "Of course, Jerry. When you've had enough, come to the big beach. Or just go straight back to the villa, if you like." She walked away, that bare arm, now slightly reddened from yesterday's sun, swinging. And he almost ran after her again, feeling it unbearable that she should go by herself, but he did not.

She was thinking, Of course he's old enough to be safe without me. Have I been keeping him too close? He mustn't feel he ought to be with me. I must be careful.

He was an only child, eleven years old. She was a widow. She

---

[1] *contrition:* sincere regret for having hurt another.

was determined to be neither possessive nor lacking in devotion. She went worrying off to her beach.

As for Jerry, once he saw that his mother had gained her beach, he began the steep descent to the bay. From where he was, high up among red-brown rocks, it was a scoop of moving bluish green fringed with white. As he went lower, he saw that it spread among small promontories and inlets of rough, sharp rock, and the crisping, lapping surface showed stains of purple and darker blue. Finally, as he ran sliding and scraping down the last few yards, he saw an edge of white surf and the shallow, luminous movement of water over white sand, and, beyond that, a solid, heavy blue.

He ran straight into the water and began swimming. He was a good swimmer. He went out fast over the gleaming sand, over a middle region where rocks lay like discolored monsters under the surface, and then he was in the real sea—a warm sea where irregular cold currents from the deep water shocked his limbs.

When he was so far out that he could look back not only on the little bay but past the promontory that was between it and the big beach, he floated on the buoyant surface and looked for his mother. There she was, a speck of yellow under an umbrella that looked like a slice of orange peel. He swam back to shore, relieved at being sure she was there, but all at once very lonely.

On the edge of a small cape that marked the side of the bay away from the promontory was a loose scatter of rocks. Above them, some boys were stripping off their clothes. They came running, naked, down to the rocks. The English boy swam toward them, but kept his distance at a stone's throw. They were of that coast; all of them were burned smooth dark brown and speaking a language he did not understand. To be with them, of them, was a craving that filled his whole body. He swam a little closer; they turned and watched him with narrowed, alert dark eyes. Then one smiled and waved. It was enough. In a minute, he had swum in and was on the rocks beside them, smiling with a desperate, nervous supplication.[2] They shouted cheerful greetings at him; and then, as he preserved his nervous, uncomprehending smile, they understood that he was a foreigner strayed from his own beach, and they proceeded to forget him. But he was happy. He was with them.

They began diving again and again from a high point into a well of blue sea between rough, pointed rocks. After they had

---

[2] *supplication:* asking for earnestly and humbly, begging.

dived and come up, they swam around, hauled themselves up, and waited their turn to dive again. They were big boys—men, to Jerry. He dived, and they watched him; and when he swam around to take his place, they made way for him. He felt he was accepted and he dived again, carefully, proud of himself.

Soon the biggest of the boys poised himself, shot down into the water, and did not come up. The others stood about, watching. Jerry, after waiting for the sleek brown head to appear, let out a yell of warning; they looked at him idly and turned their eyes back toward the water. After a long time, the boy came up on the other side of a big dark rock, letting the air out of his lungs in a sputtering gasp and a shout of triumph. Immediately the rest of them dived in. One moment, the morning seemed full of chattering boys; the next, the air and the surface of the water were empty. But through the heavy blue, dark shapes could be seen moving and groping.

Jerry dived, shot past the school of underwater swimmers, saw a black wall of rock looming at him, touched it, and bobbed up at once to the surface, where the wall was a low barrier he could see across. There was no one visible; under him, in the water, the dim shapes of the swimmers had disappeared. Then one, and then another of the boys came up on the far side of the barrier of rock, and he understood that they had swum through some gap or hole in it. He plunged down again. He could see nothing through the stinging salt water but the blank rock. When he came up the boys were all on the diving rock, preparing to attempt the feat again. And now, in a panic of failure, he yelled up, in English, "Look at me! Look!" and he began splashing and kicking in the water like a foolish dog.

They looked down gravely, frowning. He knew the frown. At moments of failure, when he clowned to claim his mother's attention, it was with just this grave, embarrassed inspection that she rewarded him. Through his hot shame, feeling the pleading grin on his face like a scar that he could never remove, he looked up at the group of big brown boys on the rock and shouted, *"Bonjour! Merci! Au revoir! Monsieur, monsieur!"* [3] while he hooked his fingers round his ears and waggled them.

Water surged into his mouth; he choked, sank, came up. The rock, lately weighted with boys, seemed to rear up out of the water as their weight was removed. They were flying down past him, now, into the water; the air was full of falling bodies. Then the rock was empty in the hot sunlight. He counted one, two, three. . . .

At fifty, he was terrified. They must all be drowning beneath him, in the watery caves of the rock! At a hundred, he stared around him at the empty hillside, wondering if he should yell for help. He counted faster, faster, to hurry them up, to bring them to the surface quickly, to drown them quickly—anything rather than the terror of counting on and on into the blue emptiness of the morning. And then, at a hundred and sixty, the water beyond the rock was full of boys blowing like brown whales. They swam back to the shore without a look at him.

He climbed back to the diving rock and sat down, feeling the hot roughness of it under his thighs. The boys were gathering up their bits of clothing and running off along the shore to another promontory. They were leaving to get away from him. He cried openly, fists in his eyes. There was no one to see him, and he cried himself out.

It seemed to him that a long time had passed, and he swam

---

[3] *"Bonjour . . . monsieur"*: French for "Hello! Thank you! Good-bye! Sir, Sir!"

out to where he could see his mother. Yes, she was still there, a yellow spot under an orange umbrella. He swam back to the big rock, climbed up, and dived into the blue pool among the fanged and angry boulders. Down he went, until he touched the wall of rock again. But the salt was so painful in his eyes that he could not see.

He came to the surface, swam to shore and went back to the villa to wait for his mother. Soon she walked slowly up the path, swinging her striped bag, the flushed, naked arm dangling beside her. "I want some swimming goggles," he panted, defiant and beseeching.

She gave him a patient, inquisitive look as she said casually, "Well, of course, darling."

But now, now, now! He must have them this minute, and no other time. He nagged and pestered until she went with him to a shop. As soon as she had bought the goggles, he grabbed them from her hand as if she were going to claim them for herself, and was off, running down the steep path to the bay.

Jerry swam out to the big barrier rock, adjusted the goggles, and dived. The impact of the water broke the rubber-enclosed vacuum, and the goggles came loose. He understood that he must swim down to the base of the rock from the surface of the water. He fixed the goggles tight and firm, filled his lungs, and floated, face down, on the water. Now, he could see. It was as if he had eyes of a different kind—fish eyes that showed everything clear and delicate and wavering in the bright water.

Under him, six or seven feet down, was a floor of perfectly clean, shining white sand, rippled firm and hard by the tides. Two grayish shapes steered there, like long, rounded pieces of wood or slate. They were fish. He saw them nose toward each other, poise motionless, make a dart forward, swerve off, and come around again. It was like a water dance. A few inches above them the water sparkled as if sequins were dropping through it. Fish again—myriads of minute fish, the length of his fingernail, were drifting through the water, and in a moment he could feel the innumerable tiny touches of them against his limbs. It was like swimming in flaked silver. The great rock the big boys had swum through rose sheer out of the white sand—black, tufted lightly with greenish weed. He could see no gap in it. He swam down to its base.

Again and again he rose, took a big chestful of air, and went down. Again and again he groped over the surface of the rock, feeling it, almost hugging it in the desperate need to find the entrance. And then, once, while he was clinging to the black wall, his knees came up and he shot his feet out forward and they met no obstacle. He had found the hole.

He gained the surface, clambered about the stones that littered the barrier rock until he found a big one, and, with this in his arms, let himself down over the side of the rock. He dropped, with the weight, straight to the sandy floor. Clinging tight to the anchor of stone, he lay on his side and looked in under the dark shelf at the place where his feet had gone. He could see the hole. It was an irregular, dark gap; but he could not see deep into it. He let go of his anchor, clung with his hands to the edges of the hole, and tried to push himself in.

He got his head in, found his shoulders jammed, moved them in sidewise, and was inside as far as his waist. He could see nothing ahead. Something soft and clammy touched his mouth; he saw a dark frond moving against the grayish rock, and panic filled him. He thought of octopuses, of clinging weed. He pushed himself out backward and caught a glimpse, as he retreated, of a harmless tentacle of seaweed drifting in the mouth of the tunnel. But it was enough. He reached the sunlight, swam to shore, and lay on the diving rock. He looked down into the blue well of water. He knew he must find his way through that cave, or hole, or tunnel, and out the other side.

First, he thought, he must learn to control his breathing. He let himself down into the water with another big stone in his arms, so that he could lie effortlessly on the bottom of the sea. He counted. One, two, three. He counted steadily. He could hear the movement of blood in his chest. Fifty-one, fifty-two. . . . His chest was hurting. He let go of the rock and went up into the air. He saw that the sun was low. He rushed to the villa and found his mother at her supper. She said only "Did you enjoy yourself?" and he said "Yes."

All night the boy dreamed of the water-filled cave in the rock, and as soon as breakfast was over he went to the bay.

That night, his nose bled badly. For hours he had been underwater, learning to hold his breath, and now he felt weak and dizzy. His mother said, "I shouldn't overdo things, darling, if I were you."

That day and the next, Jerry exercised his lungs as if everything, the whole of his life, all that he would become, depended upon it. Again his nose bled at night, and his mother insisted on his coming with her the next day. It was a torment to him to waste a day of his careful self-training, but he stayed with her on that other beach, which now seemed a place for small children, a place where his mother might lie safe in the sun. It was not his beach.

He did not ask for permission, on the following day, to go to his beach. He went, before his mother could consider the complicated rights and wrongs of the matter. A day's rest, he discovered, had improved his count by ten. The big boys had made the passage while he counted a hundred and sixty. He had been counting fast, in his fright. Probably now, if he tried, he could get through the long tunnel, but he was not going to try yet. A curious, most unchildlike persistence, a controlled impatience, made him wait. In the meantime, he lay underwater on the white sand, littered now by stones he had brought down from the upper air, and studied the entrance to the tunnel. He knew every jut and corner of it, as far as it was possible to see. It was as if he already felt its sharpness about his shoulders.

He sat by the clock in the villa, when his mother was not near, and checked his time. He was incredulous and then proud to find he could hold his breath without strain for two minutes. The words "two minutes," authorized by the clock, brought close the adventure that was so necessary to him.

In another four days, his mother said casually one morning, they must go home. On the day before they left, he would do it. He would do it if it killed him, he said defiantly to himself. But two days before they were to leave—a day of triumph when he increased his count by fifteen—his nose bled so badly that he turned dizzy and had to lie limply over the big rock like a bit of seaweed, watching the thick red blood flow on to the rock and trickle slowly down to the sea. He was frightened. Supposing he turned dizzy in the tunnel? Supposing he died there, trapped? Supposing—his head went around, in the hot sun, and he almost gave up. He thought he would return to the house and lie down, and next summer, perhaps, when he had another year's growth in him—*then* he would go through the hole.

But even after he had made the decision, or thought he had, he found himself sitting up on the rock and looking down into the water; and he knew that now, this moment, when his nose had only just stopped bleeding, when his head was still sore and throbbing—this was the moment when he would try. If he did not do it now, he never would. He was trembling with fear that he would not go; and he was trembling with horror at that long, long tunnel under the rock, under the sea. Even in the open sunlight, the barrier rock seemed very wide and very heavy; tons of rock pressed down on where he would go. If he died there, he would lie until one day—perhaps not before next year—those big boys would swim into it and find it blocked.

He put on his goggles, fitted them tight, tested the vacuum. His hands were shaking. Then he chose the biggest stone he could carry and slipped over the edge of the rock until half of him was in the cool, enclosing water and half in the hot sun. He looked up once at the empty sky, filled his lungs once, twice, and then sank fast to the bottom with the stone. He let it go and began to count. He took the edges of the hole in his hands and drew himself into it, wriggling his shoulders in sidewise as he remembered he must, kicking himself along with his feet.

Soon he was clear inside. He was in a small rockbound hole filled with yellowish-gray water. The water was pushing him up against the roof. The roof was sharp and pained his back. He pulled himself along with his hands—fast, fast—and used his legs as levers. His head knocked against something; a sharp pain dizzied him. Fifty, fifty-one, fifty-two. . . . He was without light, and the water seemed to press upon him with the weight of rock. Seventy-one, seventy-two. . . . There was no strain on his lungs. He felt like an inflated balloon, his lungs were so light and easy, but his head was pulsing.

He was being continually pressed against the sharp roof, which felt slimy as well as sharp. Again he thought of octopuses, and wondered if the tunnel might be filled with weed that could tangle him. He gave himself a panicky, convulsive kick forward, ducked his head, and swam. His feet and hands moved freely, as if in open water. The hole must have widened out. He thought he must be swimming fast, and he was frightened of banging his head if the tunnel narrowed.

A hundred, a hundred and one. . . . The water paled. Victory filled him. His lungs were beginning to hurt. A few more strokes and he would be out. He was counting wildly; he said a hundred and fifteen, and then, a long time later, a hundred and fifteen again. The water was a clear jewel-green all around him. Then he saw, above his head, a crack running up through the rock. Sunlight was falling through it, showing the clean, dark rock of the tunnel, a single mussel shell, and darkness ahead.

He was at the end of what he could do. He looked up at the crack as if it were filled with air and not water, as if he could put his mouth to it to draw in air. A hundred and fifteen, he heard himself say inside his head—but he had said that long ago. He must go on into the blackness ahead, or he would drown. His head was swelling, his lungs cracking. A hundred and fifteen, a hundred and fifteen pounded though his head, and he feebly clutched at rocks in the dark, pulling himself forward, leaving the brief space of sunlit water behind. He felt he was dying. He was

no longer quite conscious. He struggled on in the darkness between lapses into unconsciousness. An immense, swelling pain
filled his head, and then the darkness cracked with an explosion of
green light. His hands, groping forward, met nothing; and his feet,
kicking back, propelled him out into the open sea.

He drifted to the surface, his face turned up to the air. He
was gasping like a fish. He felt he would sink now and drown; he
could not swim the few feet back to the rock. Then he was clutching it and pulling himself up on to it. He lay face down, gasping.
He could see nothing but a red-veined, clotted dark. His eyes must
have burst, he thought; they were full of blood. He tore off his
goggles and a gout of blood went into the sea. His nose was bleeding, and the blood had filled the goggles.

He scooped up handfuls of water from the cool, salty sea, to
splash on his face, and did not know whether it was blood or salt
water he tasted. After a time, his heart quieted, his eyes cleared,
and he sat up. He could see the local boys diving and playing half

a mile away. He did not want them. He wanted nothing but to get back home and lie down.

In a short while, Jerry swam to shore and climbed slowly up the path to the villa. He flung himself on his bed and slept, waking at the sound of feet on the path outside. His mother was coming back. He rushed to the bathroom, thinking she must not see his face with bloodstains, or tearstains, on it. He came out of the bathroom and met her as she walked into the villa, smiling, her eyes lighting up.

"Have a nice morning?" she asked, laying her hand on his warm brown shoulder a moment.

"Oh, yes, thank you," he said.

"You look a bit pale," And then, sharp and anxious, "How did you bang your head?"

"Oh, just banged it," he told her.

She looked at him closely. He was strained; his eyes were glazed-looking. She was worried. And then she said to herself, Oh, don't fuss! Nothing can happen. He can swim like a fish.

They sat down to lunch together.

"Mummy," he said, "I can stay under water for two minutes—three minutes, at least." It came bursting out of him.

"Can you, darling?" she said. "Well, I shouldn't overdo it. I don't think you ought to swim any more today."

She was ready for a battle of wills, but he gave in at once. It was no longer of the least importance to go to the bay.

DISCUSSION

1. Why does Jerry feel he has to go through the tunnel? At the end of the story, why does he feel that it is ''no longer of the least importance to go to the bay''?

2. After the native boys swim through the tunnel, their attitude toward Jerry appears changed. Describe and account for this change.

3. The **setting** (see page 57) of the story is an essential part of the **plot** (see page 31). What elements of the story help create the suspense of the story? What is the most frightening part of Jerry's experience? Why?

4. Describe, as precisely as you can, the changing relationship between Jerry and his mother, using details from the story to support your observations. How do the events in the story change this relationship?

For further activities, see page 430.

INVICTUS

WILLIAM ERNEST HENLEY

Out of the night that covers me,
Black as the Pit from pole to pole,
I thank whatever gods may be
For my unconquerable soul.

In the fell clutch of circumstance   5
I have not winced nor cried aloud.
Under the bludgeonings of chance
My head is bloody, but unbowed.

Beyond this place of wrath and tears
Looms but the horror of the shade,   10
And yet the menace of the years
Finds, and shall find me, unafraid.

It matters not how strait the gate,
How charged with punishments the scroll,
I am the master of my fate: 15
I am the captain of my soul.

Invictus: Latin for unconquerable.   5. *fell:* cruel.   10. *shade:*
world of the dead.   13. *strait:* narrow.

DISCUSSION

1. "Invictus" is an expression of courage and determination. What kinds of experiences are referred to in the second **stanza** (see page 10)? How is the thought advanced in the third stanza?

2. Henley is referring specifically to his illness of tuberculosis. Do you think "Invictus" is meaningful even if the reader knows nothing whatever of the poet's life? Explain.

3. **Denotation** and **Connotation.** Every word has a literal, dictionary meaning—denotation—and associated or suggested meanings—connotation. What are the suggested meanings of "pole," "winced," and "unbowed"? Would the poem be as effective if the poet had used different words? Explain.

The Four Directions

EMERSON BLACKHORSE MITCHELL

A century and eight more years,
   Since Kit Carson rode from four directions,
Deep into the heart of nomadic Navajos,
   Burning, ravishing the Land of Enchantment.

Prairie grasses are once more   5
   Growing as high as the horse's belly.
Cradles of wrapped babies in colors
   Of the rainbow again span the land.

I know my people will stand and rise again.
   Now it is time.   10
Pollen of yellow grain,
   Scatter in the four directions.

DISCUSSION

1.   This poem describes the effects of two different forces "from four directions" on "the Land of Enchantment." What are the two forces? How do they differ?

2.   How does the second stanza serve as a bridge for the ideas in the first and last stanzas?

One Sunday in December

DANIEL K. INOUYE with LAWRENCE ELLIOTT

The family was up by 6:30 that morning, as we usually were on
Sunday, to dress and have a leisurely breakfast before setting
out for 9 o'clock services at church. Of course anyone who has
some memory of that shattering day can tell you precisely what
he was doing at the moment when he suddenly realized that an
era was ending, that the long and comfortable days of peace
were gone, and that America and all her people had been
abruptly confronted with their most deadly challenge since the
founding of the Republic.

As soon as I finished brushing my teeth and pulled on my
trousers, I automatically clicked on the little radio that stood on
the shelf above my bed. I remember that I was buttoning my
shirt and looking out the window—it would be a magnificent
day; already the sun had burned off the morning haze and
glowed bright in a blue sky—when the hum of the warming set
gave way to a frenzied voice. "This is no test!" the voice cried
out. "Pearl Harbor[1] is being bombed by the Japanese! I repeat:
this is not a test or a maneuver! Japanese war planes are attack-
ing Oahu!"

"Papa!" I called, then froze into immobility, my fingers
clutching that button. I could feel blood hammering against my
temple, and behind it the unspoken protest, like a prayer—*It's
not true! It is a test, or a mistake! It can't be true!*—but somewhere in the core of my being I knew that all my world was
crumbling as I stood motionless in that little bedroom and listened to the disembodied voice of doom.

Now my father was standing in the doorway listening,
caught by that special horror instantly sensed by Americans of
Japanese descent as the nightmare began to unfold. There was a
kind of agony on his face and my brothers and sister, who had
pushed up behind him, stopped where they were and watched
him as the announcer shouted on:

". . . not a test. This is the real thing! Pearl Harbor has been
hit and now we have a report that Hickam Field and Schofield

Inouye: pronounced ē-nō′oo-ĕ.
[1] *Pearl Harbor:* site of U.S. Naval base on Oahu (ō-ä′hoo) Island, Hawaii.

Barracks have been bombed, too. We can see the Japanese planes . . ."

"Come outside!" my father said to me, and I plunged through the door after him. As my brothers John and Bob started out, too, he turned and told them: "Stay with your mother!"

We stood in the warm sunshine on the south side of the house and stared out toward Pearl Harbor. Black puffs of anti-aircraft smoke littered the pale sky, trailing away in a soft breeze, and we knew beyond any wild hope that this was no test, for practice rounds of anti-aircraft, which we had seen a hundred times, were fleecy white. And now the dirty gray smoke of a great fire billowed up over Pearl and obscured the mountains and the horizon, and if we listened attentively we could hear the soft *crrrump* of the bombs amid the hysterical chatter of the ack-ack.[2]

And then we saw the planes. They came zooming up out of that sea of gray smoke, flying north toward where we stood and climbing into the bluest part of the sky, and they came in twos and threes, in neat formations, and if it hadn't been for that red ball on their wings, the rising sun of the Japanese Empire, you could easily believe that they were Americans, flying over in precise military salute.

I fell back against the building as they droned near, but my father stood rigid in the center of the sidewalk, and stared up into that malignant sky, and out of the depths of his shock and torment came a tortured cry: "You fools!"

We went back into the house and the telephone was ringing. It was the secretary of the Red Cross aid station where I taught. "How soon can you be here, Dan?" he said tensely.

"I'm on my way," I told him. I felt a momentary surge of elation—he wanted me! I could do something!—and I grabbed a sweater and started for the door.

"Where are you going?" my mother cried. She was pointing vaguely out the window, toward the sky, and said, "They'll kill you."

"Let him go," my father said firmly. "He must go."

I went to embrace her. "He hasn't had breakfast," she whispered. "At least have some breakfast."

---

[2] *ack-ack:* anti-aircraft fire.

"I can't, Mama. I have to go." I took a couple of pieces of bread from the table and hugged her.

"When will you be back?" she said.

"Soon. As soon as I can."

But it would be five days, a lifetime, before I came back. The kid who set out on his bicycle for the aid station at Lunalilo School that morning of December 7 was lost forever in the debris of the war's first day, lost among the dead and the dying, and when I finally did come home I was a seventeen-year-old man.

The planes were gone as I pumped furiously toward the aid station, more than a mile away. The acrid smell of the smoke had drifted up from Pearl and people, wide-eyed with terror, fumbling for some explanation, something to do, had spilled into the streets. What would become of them, I agonized, these thousands, suddenly rendered so vulnerable and helpless by this monstrous betrayal at the hands of their ancestral land? In those first chaotic moments, I was absolutely incapable of understanding that I was one of them, that I, too, had been betrayed, and all of my family.

An old Japanese grabbed the handlebars of my bike as I tried to maneuver around a cluster of people in the street. "Who did it?" he yelled at me. "Was it the Germans? It must have been the Germans!"

I shook my head, unable to speak, and tore free of him. My eyes blurred with tears, tears of pity for that old man, because he could not accept the bitter truth, tears for all these frightened people in teeming, poverty-ridden McCully and Moiliili. They had worked so hard. They had wanted so desperately to be accepted, to be good Americans. And now, in a few cataclysmic minutes, it was all undone, for in the marrow of my bones I knew that there was only deep trouble ahead. And then, pedaling along, it came to me at last that I would face that trouble, too, for my eyes were shaped just like those of that poor old man in the street, and my people were only a generation removed from the land that had spawned those bombers, the land that sent them to rain destruction on America, death on Americans.

Why had they done it? Why couldn't they let us live in peace? My mind reeled with tormented, confused, unanswerable questions. Once, with the sharp pain of a fresh wound

being freshly plucked, it came to me that any one of the men in that armada of planes flaunting the rising sun could be my cousin, and to this day I do not know but what it might have been so, for I have never wanted to find out. I remembered my teacher in Japanese language school preaching, "When Japan calls, you must know that it is Japanese blood that flows in your veins." And in a spasm of fury I muttered, "Fool! Blind and bigoted fool, see what the likes of you have brought us!"

And so I rode on, filled with grief and shame and anger, not knowing how they would receive me at the aid station, uncertain even if they would let me stay in school. All my dreams seemed to be spiraling out of reach, like the great, greasy billows of smoke from the oil fires at Pearl Harbor, and by the time I reached my destination, I carried the full and bitter burden shared by every one of the 158,000 Japanese-Americans in Hawaii: not only had our country been wantonly attacked, but our loyalty was certain to be called into question, for it took no great effort of imagination to see the hatred of many Americans for the enemy turned on us, who looked so much like him. And no matter how hard we worked to defeat him, there would always be those who would look at us and think—and some would say it aloud—"Dirty Jap."

It was past 8:30—the war was little more than half an hour old—when I reported in at the aid station, two classrooms in the Lunalilo Elementary School. I had gained the first six years of my education in this building and before the day was out it would be half-destroyed by our own anti-aircraft shells which had failed to explode in the air. Even now confusion was in command, shouting people pushing by each other as they rushed for litters and medical supplies. Somewhere a radio voice droned on, now and then peaking with shrill excitement, and it was in one such outburst that I learned how the *Arizona* had exploded in the harbor. Many other vessels were severely hit.

And then, at 9 A.M., the Japanese came back. The second wave of bombers swooped around from the west and the anti-aircraft guns began thundering again. Mostly the planes hammered at military installations—Pearl, Hickam, Wheeler Field— and it was our own ack-ack that did the deadly damage in the civilian sectors. Shells, apparently fired without timed fuses, and finding no target in the sky, exploded on impact with the ground. Many came crashing into a three-by-five-block area of crowded McCully, the first only moments after the Japanese planes reappeared. It hit just three blocks from the aid station and the explosion rattled the windows. I grabbed a litter and rounded up a couple of fellows I knew.

"Where're we going?" one yelled at me.

"Where the trouble is! Follow me!"

In a small house on the corner of Hauoli and Algaroba Streets we found our first casualties. The shell had sliced through the house. It had blown the front out and the tokens of a lifetime—dishes, clothing, a child's bed—were strewn pathetically into the street.

I was propelled by sheerest instinct. Some small corner of my mind worried about how I'd react to what lay in that carnage—there would be no textbook cuts and bruises, and the blood would be real blood—and then I plunged in, stumbling over the debris, kicking up clouds of dust and calling, frantically calling, to anyone who might be alive in there. There was no answer. The survivors had already fled and the one who remained would never speak again. I found her half-buried in the rubble, one of America's first civilian dead of the Second World War. And all at once it was as though I had stepped out of my skin; I moved like an automaton, hardly conscious of what I was doing and totally oblivious of myself. I felt nothing. I did what I had been taught to do and it was only later, when those first awful hours had become part of our history, that I sickened and shuddered as the ghastly images of war flashed again and again in my mind's eye, as they do to this day.

By the time we had removed the dead to a temporary morgue set up in Lunalilo School, more shells had fallen. It was now, by one of those bitter ironies, that our aid station was hit by our own shells, and we lost precious minutes evacuating what was left of our supplies. Nearby, a building caught fire and as the survivors came stumbling out, we patched their wounds as best we could and commandeered whatever transportation that passed to get them to the hospital. For those still trapped inside there was nothing in the world anyone could do. The flames drove us back to the far side of the street, and by the time the firemen brought them under control, there was nothing left alive in that burned-out hulk. Then, carrying corrugated boxes, it became our melancholy duty to pick our way through the smouldering beams and hot ashes and collect the

charred, barely-recognizable remains of those who had perished.

There are moments I can never forget. An empty-eyed old
lady wandered screaming through the wreckage of a house on
King street. A boy of twelve or so, perhaps her grandson, tried
to lead her from danger, for she could scarcely keep her footing
in the ruins. But the old woman would not be budged. "Where
is my home?" she would cry out hysterically in Japanese, or
"Where are my things?"

I climbed up to where she tottered on a mountain of
wreckage and took hold of her shoulders. "Go with the boy," I
said to her.

But it was as though I wasn't there. She looked right
through me and wailed, "What have they done to my home?"
And without thinking about it, for if I had thought about it I
could never have done it, I slapped her twice across the face,
sharply. Later, I would be awed by my audacity—my whole life
had been a lesson in reverence for my elders—but at that instant I remembered only what I had been taught to do in cases
of uncontrollable hysteria. And it worked.

"Go with the boy," I said again, and the light of reason returned to her eyes, and she went.

We worked on into the night, and were working still when
the new day broke. There was so much to be done—broken
bodies to be mended, temporary shelter to be found for
bombed-out families, precautions against disease, food for the
hungry and comfort for the bereaved—that even our brief re-
spites for a sandwich or a cup of coffee were tinged with feelings of guilt. We worked on into the following night and
through the day after that, snatching some broken moments of
sleep wherever we happened to be when we could move no
further, and soon there was no dividing line between day and
night at all. Now and then my mother or father would appear
with a change of clothes, or some food, and they would look at
me, worried: "Are you all right? Will you come home soon?"

"Yes," I'd tell them. "I'm fine. I'll be home as soon as I
can."

I had been listed as a part-time volunteer. But right after
the bombing, the aid station was absorbed into the civil defense command and most of us were put on a full-time basis. I
was designated a medical aide, given the night shift, 6 P.M. to 6

A.M., so I could go to school in the daytime, and put on salary of $125 a month.

It was a wildly incongruous life. In the morning I was a senior at McKinley High, just as before, trying to be concerned with congruent triangles and passive verbs and the French Revolution. In the afternoon, I fell exhausted into my bed and slept like a dead man until 5:30, when my mother would shake me awake and, as I dashed for the door, hand me a sandwich to munch on while I bicycled to the aid station. And all through the night I tried to cope with the real problems of innocent people caught up in a tragedy of terrifying proportions. And always, day and night, I expected at any moment to hear the wailing air raid sirens signaling the return of those Japanese planes.

I was amazed at myself. Overnight I had been thrust into a position of leadership: in charge of a litter squad, training new volunteers at the aid station and directing the high school first aid program. Like everyone else in the military or civil defense command, I wore a steel helmet, carried a gas mask and a special identity card that permitted me on the streets after curfew. Me, Dan Inouye! Only a few weeks before, my biggest worries had been marks and dates and whether I'd get that neat saxophone riff in "Little Brown Jug" just right. And now I was earning $125 a month, more money than I'd ever seen in my life. It meant less than nothing to me. All I could really focus on was that I was at war.

DISCUSSION

1. "Let him go. . . . He must go." Explain why Dan's father says this.

2. Why did Daniel feel that his loyalty to the U.S. was certain to be called into question? How would you explain his saying that he is filled with "grief and shame and anger?"

3. How is Daniel challenged to grow up overnight? Does he meet this challenge? Explain.

4. Daniel Inouye went on to become a U.S. senator. If you are interested in reading more about his life, look in your library for the book *Journey to Washington* by Daniel K. Inouye.

For further activities, see page 430.

STAKEOUT

CHET HUNTLEY

In my third year of high school I worked in the Whitehall State Bank after classes and on Saturdays. My responsibilities were somewhat varied, ranging from the pedestrian tasks of sweeping out, dusting, filling inkwells and stoking the furnace, to posting the statements, sometimes posting the ledger as well, numbering checks and seeing to it that the outgoing mail got to the post office.

Mr. Roberts, the bank manager, graciously consented to my playing football that autumn and that necessitated a slight alteration of my schedule. I practiced with the team after classes, ate a hurried dinner at home and then went to the bank to discharge my responsibilities. Why Mr. Roberts put up with it, I was never certain, unless he felt it was his patriotic contribution to the excellence of the football team. If so, I hasten to add that Mr. Roberts's gift to the team was modest. My absence at right tackle would have left no gaping hole in the line.

One Thursday evening as I unlocked the front door of the bank and stepped inside, I was certain I heard a movement of some sort. I switched on the lights, looked into the toilet, the backrooms, and searched the basement. It was nothing. I finished my work and went home.

On Friday evening as I was posting the statements, I heard a slight scuffling and scraping which seemed to come from the ceiling. I concluded that something had evidently fallen onto the roof and was flapping about in the wind. I would go up there the following morning.

A slight skiff of snow fell that night and began to melt the next morning as the sun came up. However, as I opened the bank door, prepared to get the furnace going and to set up the establishment for a busy Saturday, I saw that water was trickling from the ceiling and forming a pool in the middle of the floor. I mopped up the puddle of water and then dragged a long ladder out of the basement, leaned it against the back of the building and climbed to the roof.

Near the skylight lay an old blanket. I picked it up and uncovered a yawning hole in the roof! Peering down into the dark attic, I saw the top of the vault, from which a generous number of the bricks had been removed and stacked to one side. As my eyes adjusted to the darkness I detected a tin can hanging from the electric wiring. Dropping through the opening in the roof, I found that the tin can contained a light bulb, which I turned in its socket. In the light there at my feet was the whole story!

Drills, hammers, chisels, and tools of all description were laid out neatly on top of the vault. Where the bricks had been removed, the workman was down to the steel lining, and an acetylene torch had cut a gash of about eight inches.

I think my first bewildered reaction was one of utter disbelief mixed with a recollection of a sign which was hung prominently in the window of the bank: $4,000 REWARD FOR THE APPREHENSION OF ANYONE ATTEMPTING TO ROB THIS BANK. It also occurred to me that the project might be weeks old and that the bandit might have given up or had been frightened off and that the whole thing would end in just a tedious cleanup job.

I unscrewed the bulb, hoisted myself up through the hole in the roof, made certain that I left the blanket as I had found it, and returned to the bank.

But I had a genuine problem. Should I keep this electrifying information to myself, or did I have a solemn duty to report it to my employers?

The teller and assistant manager was a little gnome of a man, Mr. Hardin; but he was kind and gentle, almost repulsively neat and efficient, timid and grossly underpaid. Mr. Hardin had never been casual in his life; saying "Good morning" was a project to be well thought out and tidied up afterward.

Furiously, I debated with myself and realized that the longer I delayed the more I was inviting censure. Finally, I decided to take Mr. Hardin into my confidence.

Mr. Roberts was out of town that day, leaving Mr. Hardin in complete charge. When I told him what I had found on the roof, he began to flutter. To my disgust and consternation he went to the telephone to relay the information to the bank president, Mr. McKay, a white-haired and tight-fisted old Scotsman who had a rather substantial stake in virtually every enterprise in town. I could see that the whole adventure was about to be taken out of my hands and that I was going to be reduced to a most obscure role. Over the telephone, Mr. McKay said that he would summon the sheriff in Boulder, the county seat, and that we employees in the bank were to continue with our work as though nothing were amiss.

At noon, I slipped out and called my classmate and friend Bob Manlove, whose father was the town butcher. Bob agreed with me that he and I could play no important part in this impending drama, but he did propose that he would sneak his older brother's National Guard .45 pistol out of the house and he would come "armed" and join me after work.

Late that afternoon the sheriff and a deputy arrived from Boulder, and I was assigned to take them up to the roof of the bank building for an inspection. The two law-enforcement officers casually looked down through the hole in the roof and then began to discuss their strategy. They agreed that the chances of the bandit returning to his work that night—a Saturday night, when most of the stores were open to accommodate the ranchers—were very slight. No cautious robber, they reasoned, would venture to complete a job like this one on a Saturday night, but that he might undertake it the following night, on Sunday. Perhaps the project was an abortive one—abandoned for weeks. However, they did agree that a lookout should be posted, and that was my opportunity. I suggested that my friend Bob and I would hide behind the skylight and if the bandit appeared we could summon the sheriff and his deputy. The deputy wanted to know how I proposed getting off the roof of the building without alerting the robber. I had had the foresight to prepare for that. Bob and I could actually be on the roof of the adjoining building and yet be hidden behind the skylight. By walking across the roof of the adjoining building toward the alley, we could reach a telephone pole at the rear, climb down the convenient steel rungs and run to the hotel for the sheriff.

The two officers, candidly acknowledging no taste whatsoever for a cold night on a Whitehall rooftop, quickly agreed. Bob and I could hide behind the skylight. They airily told Mr. Hardin of the plans and retired to the hotel. Mr. Hardin went home, and the town settled down to a normal Saturday evening.

Bob and I choked down some food at my house. His brother's .45 was safely in a dresser drawer in my room. Mother inquired why we seemed to be in such a hurry, and we said we wanted to be sure to be on time for the movie that night. Safely out of the house with the .45 and a flashlight, Bob and I walked down to Main Street. We loitered for a while in front of the movie house and offered thin excuses to our friends why we were not quite ready to buy our tickets and go inside. Finally, we reasoned that we might as well see the movie because the robber, if he should appear that night, would probably arrive rather late and certainly we could hear him at work if we should arrive on the roof after he did. We went inside and enjoyed the picture—convinced, I believe, that the sheriff was quite correct: the bank robber, if he were to return at all, would certainly choose not to work on a Saturday night.

The movie came to an end, and Bob and I sauntered around the block, and approached the alley. On the corner, just inside the alley, Bob inserted a clip of ammunition in the .45, which had been bulging inside his shirt front all evening, pulled on the loading device, and a bullet slid noisily into the chamber. Cautiously we made our way down the dark alley to the telephone pole which was set where the bank and movie house joined. On up the alley were the drab backsides of J. C. Penney's, the grocery store and the drugstore on the corner. The far end of the alley was faintly lit by the small electric sign which hung over the side entrance of the hotel.

I recall having one spasm of misgiving as I gripped the cold steel rungs on the telephone pole and crept up toward the roof. Although I was protected by a heavy shirt and a warm jacket, it was going to be cold up there behind the skylight. I wished we had brought a blanket, but how would we have stolen it out of our homes without some serious questions?

As I raised my head above the level of the roof I paused to listen for a moment. No sound came from the bank building. In the dim light reflected from Main Street, I could see that the blanket over the hole in the roof was in place. Silently I lifted myself up, Bob behind me, and we edged to our post behind the skylight and crouched down.

Our vigil was brief. We had been in position no more than two or three minutes when I felt Bob's elbow in my side. On a telephone pole in back of the drugstore, at the far end of the

alley, silhouetted against the light from the hotel sign, a figure loomed up. I could see the bill on his cap, a high collar turned up on a long heavy overcoat reaching well below the knees. Crouching, he made his way along the rear edges of the building, kicked the blanket away from the hole, stood and looked about for a long moment. Not more than twelve feet away, we lay terrorized behind the skylight. I could see him through the glass . . . ten feet tall . . . and mean! What had I got myself into?

It seemed like hours before the figure somehow decided not to look behind the skylight, dropped down and disappeared through the hole. He took a long time adjusting both the blanket and his overcoat over the aperture he had cut in the roof. Presently, he went to work. The noise he made was unbelievable. He was a confident workman, assuming that anyone hearing his hammering and scraping would conclude it was coming from the garage or perhaps the railroad station across Main Street.

Bob nodded to me, and I edged toward the point of exit . . . the telephone pole. Once the roof creaked under my knee, and it sounded like an avalanche, but the noise of illicit industry from the cranny of the bank went on without interruption. As I crept down the pole my hands shook on the steel spikes. Safely on the ground, I sprinted up the alley, burst through the lobby of the hotel and shouted to the sleepy old clerk that I had to get to the sheriff. What was his room number? Infuriatingly, old Tom wanted to know what all the excitement was about and I had to placate him with a promise I would let him know right away, if he would only tell me where the sheriff was.

I raced down the upstairs hall and banged on the door. A sleepy voice from inside mumbled a response.

"He's there," I shouted. "He's in the bank!"

The weary, indifferent voice said, "Okay, okay. We'll be along." There followed the sounds of body getting slowly and deliberately out of bed and fumbling about for a light switch.

I waited for a long moment and realized that the sheriff was going to take his time. He would probably then awaken the deputy and wait for him to get dressed. Bob, meanwhile, was alone on the roof.

I ran back down the stairs and past old Tom, who was peering out of the front door. As I sped down the alley and approached the bank building I realized that the pounding and scraping had ceased. Had he discovered something? What had happened to Bob? I dared not call out. I knew I had to climb back up that pole!

I peered over the top of the building. Bob was still there, the .45 clutched in his hand and aimed over the top of the skylight in the direction of the hole. But the silence was overwhelming. Not a sound came from the hole in the roof. Inch by inch I made my way to Bob.

"He's found out something," he whispered.

We lay there for a long time. I can recall how my pulse was banging in my ears.

Then the strain was somehow relieved by the obvious fact that something was going to happen . . . and quickly, as the overcoat and blanket over the hole began to move and then disappeared down into the chamber of horrors. Presently the bill on the cap and the high collar arose out of the opening, and then the shoulders of the man. Could we let him get away? Would he come looking for us?

Bob made the decision. The .45 vomited a tongue of flame and shook the town. No artillery piece ever made that much noise.

Like a gopher the bandit ducked down in the hole, and the tragicomedy was galvanized.

Bob leaped from behind the skylight, shouting, "Come out of there! Put your hands up! Come out!"

Silence. Not a sound came out of the black cavern at our feet. I switched on the flashlight and beamed it into the hole and caught a glimpse of heavy boots and trouser legs.

"Come out of there!" we shouted.

Nothing happened.

Bob thrust the .45 into the hole, and again it roared and echoed over the sleepy little town.

A voice came out of the blackness—a defiant, angry voice. "I'm coming, just stop that shootin!"

In the beam of the flashlight a stooped figure appeared beneath us, then straightened up until his head protruded out of the opening.

"Put your hands up," I yelled.

My flashlight was all over the place, on the bandit, in Bob's face, and on myself. Bob was waving the .45 about.

"Get your hands out of there," I demanded.

But he was fumbling about and no hands appeared.

In an outburst of hopeless desperation I shouted, "Get your hands up or I'll kick you right in the face!"

In the beam of the flashlight a strong rugged countenance looked up, and the bank robber replied with nerve-racking calm, "You kick me in the face, kid, and it'll be the last guy you kick in the face!"

He put his hands up through the hole!

Now what? We had brought nothing with which to tie up a prisoner. There was a momentary delay in further orders to our captive, and he waited patiently. But I had it! Furiously, I tore at my belt, unbuckled it and whipped it out of the trouser loops. Another moment of uncertainty developed. What to do with the flashlight while I tied his hands, and my trousers began to slide down over my hips. Bob was jumping about, still brandishing the enormous .45 and trying to prevent me from getting between him and the bandit.

At last rescue came! There were shouts, and the sheriff, the deputy, old Tom and a half dozen others came running across the rooftops. I was still holding the flashlight and belt in one hand and my trousers in the other. Quickly, the sheriff took charge. Bob was relieved of his .45, and the flashlight was snatched out of my hands. The robber was lifted out of the pit, and the entire entourage descended the telephone pole one by one. We marched up the alley, around the block, down Main Street, and burst into the pool hall.

The robber was in handcuffs by this time, and he sat quietly and confidently in a chair by one of the card tables. In response to the sheriff's questions, he said his name was Chester Casey, that his home was in Butte. Asked how long he had been working on the bank job, he said it had taken him longer than he had judged and that it sure was not worth it. He volunteered the information that shortly after starting his "work" that night, he had detected that it had been discovered. He did not say how.

About that moment, Dad walked into the pool hall and saw me standing near the handcuffed prisoner. He demanded to know "what the devil" was going on, what was I doing there, and what was this all about? Graciously, the sheriff said I had captured a bank robber

Dad had heard the cannonading of the .45 and was convinced that a gunfight had broken out in the pool hall.

Finally, someone thought to search the prisoner. A .38 was removed from the top of his boot.

Dad's shift at the depot had ended and we walked home. Both Bob and I were given rather stern lectures that night concerning the important distinction between heroism and plain foolishness. Dad vowed he was going to let the sheriff know what he thought about permitting two kids to maintain a lookout for a bank bandit. The whole affair was singularly lacking in heroics. The placid little farm and railroad town paid scant attention. I think we were denigrated by the somewhat universal conviction of the community that Casey the bankrobber was a bumbling idiot or he had simply spared a couple of brash kids.

Several weeks later, Bob and I were summoned out of class by an emissary from Mr. McKay. In a most generous manner we were told that since we were minors, Mr. McKay, in order to insure the payment of the $4,000 reward money, would make the application in his name, and would we therefore sign the document which had been prepared? I believe the same paper, containing a most sketchy description of the capture, was submitted to our parents. In any event, a courteous note arrived ultimately from Mr. McKay and to it was attached a check for $50!

DISCUSSION

1. What did the authorities discover on the thief, Chester Casey, when they searched him? Were you surprised by the discovery? Explain.

2. What does the boys' going to the movie just before they went up on the roof tell you about the way they felt about the situation?

3. What was the reaction of Chet's father to the news that his son had captured a bandit? Was his father's reaction justified?

4. If you are interested in finding out more about Chet Huntley's experiences, look for the book *The Generous Years* in your library.

For further activities, see page 430.

VOCABULARY

One Sunday in December (page 412)

On separate paper, match the words in the left column with the sentences in the right column that best reflect their meaning.

1. automaton   a. I remembered what I had been taught to do when people were uncontrollable.

2. audacity   b. We had removed the dead to a temporary place.

3. hysteria   c. I was hardly conscious of what I was doing and totally oblivious of myself.

4. respite   d. I slapped her twice across the face. I was awed by my action.

5. morgue   e. Our brief time for a sandwich was tinged with feelings of guilt.

Stakeout (page 421)

On a separate piece of paper, write the word from the list below that completes the following sentences.

1. Mr. Hardin was a little——of a man.
2. To my disgust and——, Mr. Hardin called the bank president.
3. He looked through the——he had cut in the roof.
4. The noise of the——industry went on without interruption.
5. The bandit ducked down in the hole, and the tragicomedy was——.
6. His head——out of the opening.
7. Bob was jumping about, still——the enormous .45.
8. The——little farm and railroad town paid scant attention.

brandishing   protruded
galvanized   gnome
placid   consternation
aperture   illicit

COMPOSITION

Through the Tunnel (page 398)

The title of this story does not really suggest that the story will be about a trial under water. It could be about any number of subjects. Using this title write several descriptive and imaginative paragraphs about an incident that is completely unrelated to swimming or water.

Stakeout (page 421)

1. Write an account of the incident as it might appear in a small-town weekly newspaper. Then write the same story as it might appear in a large daily paper.

2. Write your version of Mr. McKay's "polite note" to the boys.

READING

Through the Tunnel (page 398)

Below are five sentences that contain similes (see page 110). On separate paper write down each simile and then rewrite each sentence inserting your simile. Be as imaginative as you can.

1. A few inches above them the water sparkled as if sequins were dropping through it.
2. And then, at a hundred and sixty, the water beyond the rock was full of boys blowing like brown whales.
3. He felt like an inflated balloon, his lungs were so light and easy, but his head was pulsing.
4. There she was, a speck of yellow under an umbrella that looked like a slice of orange peel.
5. Through his hot shame, feeling the pleading grin on his face like a scar that he could never remove. . . .

One Sunday in December (page 412)

Indicate on separate paper which of the following statements are true and which are false. Correct the false statements.

1. Dan did not believe the reality of the war at first.
2. After the bombing began, Dan was afraid to go to the Red Cross station.
3. Dan showed strength and maturity.
4. Because she was mean to him, Dan slapped the old woman.
5. Dan was put into a position of leadership because he was strong.
6. Money became more important than deeds for Dan.
7. Being Japanese was not easy for Dan during the war.

400-Meter Freestyle   MAXINE KUMIN

```
THE GUN full swing the swimmer catapults and cracks
                                                   s
                                                     i
                                                       x
feet  away  onto  that  perfect  glass  he  catches  at
a
  n
    d
throws behind him scoop after scoop cunningly moving
                                                    t
                                                      h
                                                        e
water back to move him forward. Thrift is his wonderful
s
  e
    c
ret;  he  has  schooled  out  all  extravagance.  No muscle
                                                        r
                                                          i
                                                            p
ples without compensation wrist cock to heel snap to
                                                    h
  i
    s
mobile  mouth  that  siphons  in  the  air  that  nurtures
                                                        h
                                                          i
                                                            m
at  half  an  inch  above  sea  level  so  to  speak.
```

T
h
e
astonishing whites of the soles of his feet rise
                                                  a
                                                   n
                                                    d
salute us on the turns. He flips, converts, and is gone
a
l
l
in one. We watch him for signs. His arms are steady at
                                                      t
                                                       h
                                                        e
catch, his cadent feet tick in the stretch, they know
t
h
e
lesson well. Lungs know, too; he does not list for
                                                        a
                                                         i
                                                          r
he drives along on little sips carefully expended
b
u
t
that plum red heart pumps hard cries hurt how soon
                                                        i
                                                         t
                                                          s
near one more and makes its final surge   TIME: 4:25:9

DISCUSSION

1. How is the printed form of this poem related to the subject matter? Why do you think the first two words and the last word are capitalized?

2. What does the line "he has schooled out all extravagance" mean?

For further activities, see page 480.

Black Water and Bright Air

CONSTANCE CARRIER

Skaters upon thin ice,
how weightlessly they leap,
like figures seen in sleep;
how rhythmic, how precise
the pattern of their skates   5
upon the frozen floor—
the shell that separates
black water and bright air,
the shell beneath which waits,
dreadful and disavowed,   10
an element forsworn.
Oh, but the skaters know
the sullen depths below;
they test what can be borne;
their bodies, like their breath,   15
floating on winter air,
lightly they skim and soar
from shore to barren shore,
lightness their one device,
their article of faith.   20

O summer, come once more!
Season of innocence,
under the summer cloud,
join air and water, let
the severed elements,   25
with no more parting, fuse;
set the bound water loose,
let those who feared its threat
dare to plunge downward, straight
through waters warm and bright   30
into that cold unknown,
deeper and deeper down,
terrified, into black,
until they touch the stone,
touch the bleak stone at last;   35
then, only then, turn back,
turn toward the sky, released,
borne upward toward the sun
through layers of lessening weight,
back into summer light,   40
back into lucid air.

DISCUSSION   1.   How are the skaters in stanza 1 and the divers in stanza 2 alike?

2.   **Metaphor.**   An implied comparison between two dissimilar objects is called a metaphor. Everyday speech is full of metaphors: starry-eyed, rosy-cheeked, sunny disposition, evening of life. In each case the intended meaning is not the literal one. A starry-eyed person does not literally have stars in his or her eyes, but the brightness of the eyes is like the brightness of stars.

In line 6, Carrier uses the metaphor "the frozen floor." What is being compared to what in that metaphor? See if you can find other metaphors in the poem.

Marian Anderson is an American singer who has won acclaim in all parts of the world. Conductor Arturo Toscanini said, "A voice like hers comes once in a century." However, her musical career was made more difficult because of racial prejudice.

SHOCK

MARIAN ANDERSON

If I had it all to do over again, I would wish to study at least in part at an established school of music for the extra benefits beyond individual vocal training. A pianist, a violinist, any sort of instrumentalist must follow a prescribed course of standard studies if he is to belong. A singer starts by having his instrument as a gift of God. Nowadays most singers attend conservatories, and it is well that they do. Some do not and manage to have careers, though they must scramble and learn musicianship the hard way.

I sensed the need for a formal musical education when I was in my teens and was beginning to make my first modest tours. I decided, in fact, to see if I could not go to a music school. I did not know whether we could afford it, but I thought that I ought to find out. Mother encouraged me, and so did other friends, but I had no idea where to turn until a person who had shown some interest in my problem suggested a school.

That music school no longer exists in Philadelphia, and its name does not matter. I went there one day at a time when enrollments were beginning, and I took my place in line. There was a young girl behind a cage who answered questions and gave out application blanks to be filled out. When my turn came she looked past me and called on the person standing behind me. This went on until there was no one else in line. Then she spoke to me, and her voice was not friendly. "What do *you* want?"

I tried to ignore her manner and replied that I had come to make inquiries regarding an application for entry to the school.

She looked at me coldly and said, "We don't take colored."

I don't think I said a word. I just looked at this girl and was shocked that such words could come from one so young. If she had been old and sour-faced I might not have been startled. I cannot say why her youth shocked me as much as her words. On second thought, I could not conceive of a person surrounded as she was with the joy that is music without having some sense of its beauty and understanding rub off on her. I did not argue with her or ask to see her superior. It was as if a cold, horrifying hand had been laid on me. I turned and walked out.

It was my first contact with the blunt, brutal words, and this school of music was the last place I expected to hear them. True enough, my skin was different, but not my feelings.

It must be remembered that we grew up in a mixed neighborhood. White and Negro lived side by side and shared joys and sorrows. At school and on the street we encountered all kinds of children. Did we live in a poor neighborhood? "Poor" is relative. Some people owned their homes in that street and considered themselves well off. We had enough to eat and we dressed decently. We were not so poor that we had nothing, and our neighbors were in the same situation.

There were times when we heard our relatives and friends talking, and we knew we might come in contact with this, that, or the other thing. In some stores we might have to stand around longer than other people until we were waited on. There were times when we stood on a street corner, waiting for a trolley car, and the motorman would pass us by. There were places in town where all people could go, and there were others where some of us could not go. There were girls we played with and others we didn't. There were parties we went to, and some we didn't. We were interested in neither the places nor the people who did not want us.

I tried to put the thought of a music school out of my mind, for I could not help thinking of other music schools and wondering whether this would be their attitude too. I would not risk rejection again, and for some years the idea was not mentioned.

Of course I came to Mother with the story of what had happened. Mother was reassuring: there would be another way to get what I wanted and needed. I don't want to give the impression that she was placid and passive, however. It is true that she was not as aggressive as my aunt was, and I did not tell my aunt about the incident. If I had, she would have gone straight to that music school, I am sure, and demanded to see someone higher up and to be told why and wherefore. Mother had her own opinions of the rights and wrongs of things, but she believed profoundly that somehow someone would be raised up who would be understanding, and that another way would be found to accomplish what might have been accomplished at the conservatory.

There were other shocks to come. Though I was prepared for them, so I thought, the contact with reality never ceased to have its disturbing impact. Mother had grown up in Virginia, and we had friends who had come from farther south, so I had heard about Jim Crow, but meeting it bit deeply into the soul.

I was still in high school when I took my first long trip to participate in a gala concert. Mother went with me. At Washington we changed trains, and this time our bags were taken to the first coach—the Jim Crow car!

The windows were badly in need of washing; inside and outside the car was not clean, and the ventilation and lighting were poor. When the air became much too stuffy and windows were raised it just might happen that you would get, along with your fresh air, smoke and soot from the train's engine. At mealtime containers of all shapes and sizes were brought down from the racks, and the train vendor had a sizable supply of soft drinks, fruit, and packaged cookies.

The night seemed interminably long as we sat through it. On arrival in Savannah we were given a warm welcome by a small group of school officials, and later at the home of the president we became acquainted first-hand with genuine Southern hospitality. Our bedroom was quite large, with a fireplace and an adjoining bath. In the morning a girl came in and lit the fire so that the room was most comfortable when we arose.

Throughout our stay in Savannah my thoughts went often to that first coach. We returned to Washington under the same conditions, a bit wiser but sadder and so ashamed. I had looked closely at my people in that train. Some seemed to be embarrassed to the core. Others appeared to accept the situation as if it were beyond repair. Of course some fitted neither of these classes. Habit, I thought, can be good if it has an elevated aim; it can be devastating if it means taking bad things for granted; and I wondered how long it would take people on both sides to see a change. I have lived long enough to see some progress and to realize something of the great work being done by so many people, sincere in their efforts, to bring about better understanding.

It was shortly after that first long trip that I had my second experience. This time I traveled with Billy King, a young man who was my accompanist. Billy spoke to a porter who happened to be passing through our car, and inquired about the chances of getting some hot food in the dining car. The porter was kind enough to go to the dining room to makes inquiries for us, and he returned with the message that if we appeared at a given time we would be served.

At the fixed time Billy King and I started from our coach to the dining car. We passed through a coach occupied by white people, and we noticed immediately that the accommodations, though not first class, were much better than in our car. The dining car was empty when we reached it. Nevertheless we were seated at one end of it, where curtains could be drawn. Our seats were those occupied by the waiters when they ate, and the curtains no doubt were there to be drawn if a waiter should happen to be finishing his meal when the guests began to arrive.

We had fine hot meals, and the service was excellent. The chef and the waiters, it seemed to me, put themselves out to make us comfortable; there were extra things at our table, and even extra-large portions. This was their way of saying that they were glad we had had the courage to come back and be served.

I had more opportunity to observe other things on this trip. I knew about the separate waiting rooms, but no matter how much you are prepared and steeled for them they have their effect on you. I noticed that facilities in the Negro waiting rooms were indifferent. Some might have places where you could purchase a magazine or newspaper; some might not. Probably the Negro trade in some stations was meager, for those who could afford other modes of travel used them to avoid the humiliation. But there are plenty of persons who must make journeys and have no other resort than train travel. I suppose it was naive of me to think then, as I think now—and it has been said by many people in more eloquent ways—that if one only searched one's heart one would know that none of us is responsible for the complexion of his skin, and that we could not change it if we wished to, and many of us don't wish to, and that this fact of nature offers no clue to the character or quality of the person underneath.

In the next few years I had occasion to do much more traveling. My tours were modest, but the concerts were increasing in number, and many of these engagements were in the south. Billy King still traveled with me, and we were giving full programs. I did not have the attention that a big managerial office can provide for a performer, and it was important to have travel conditions as convenient and comfortable as possible. I tried to make my own travel arrangements, but I found that often if I presented myself at a railroad ticket window, sometimes even in Philadelphia, there would be no reservations available.

After a while we learned that it was wisest not to arrange for our own transportation. We began to rely on a man in Philadelphia to make as many advance arrangements as possible. He looked after the entire itinerary, and if he foresaw that some leg of a journey would not be comfortable for one reason or another, he warned us in advance, and we tried to make this part of the trip by auto. This we could afford to do only on short runs.

Many years later I happened to be on my way to appear in Hampton, Virginia. There had been a storm and the roadbed below Washington had been partly washed out. All trains were delayed, and we sat around in the Washington station through the entire night, waiting for a train to be made up and sent out. In the morning a train was finally ready, and people filled every space in every car. This was an emergency situation, and no effort was made to enforce the usual Jim Crow rules. I saw a white woman take a Negro child and hold it on her lap to give the mother a few minutes of rest. I saw other expressions of brotherhood. Negroes and whites talked to one another; they shared their newspapers and even their food. The world did not crumble.

Things are changing in our country, and I am hopeful. But I cannot suppress a private regret. I still wish that I could have gone to a music school.

DISCUSSION

1. Why is Marian Anderson shocked by the attitude of the young girl taking applications at the music school?

2. What are the differences between the responses to racism by Marian's mother and her aunt? Which response do you share? Why?

3. **Biography** and **Autobiography.** A book or a piece of writing that one person writes about another is called biography. But what a person writes about herself or himself is called autobiography. People can have many different reasons for writing autobiography. What is one reason Marian Anderson might have had for writing her autobiography?

If you would like to read the book this excerpt is taken from, look in your library for *My Lord, What a Morning* by Marian Anderson.

For further activities, see page 480.

O Black and Unknown Bards

JAMES WELDON JOHNSON

O black and unknown bards of long ago,
How came your lips to touch the sacred fire?
How, in your darkness, did you come to know
The power and beauty of the minstrel's lyre?
Who first from midst his bonds lifted his eyes?   5
Who first from out the still watch, lone and long,
Feeling the ancient faith of prophets rise
Within his dark-kept soul, burst into song?

Heart of what slave poured out such melody
As "Steal away to Jesus"? On its strains   10
His spirit must have nightly floated free,
Though still about his hands he felt his chains.
Who heard great "Jordan roll"? Whose starward eye
Saw chariot "swing low"? And who was he
That breathed that comforting, melodic sigh,   15
"Nobody knows de trouble I see"?

What merely living clod, what captive thing,
Could up toward God through all its darkness grope,

Bards: poets.

And find within its deadened heart to sing
These songs of sorrow, love and faith, and hope?   20
How did it catch that subtle undertone,
That note in music heard not with the ears?
How sound the elusive reed so seldom blown,
Which stirs the soul or melts the heart to tears.

Not that great German master in his dream   25
Of harmonies that thundered amongst the stars
At the creation, ever heard a theme
Nobler than "Go down, Moses." Mark its bars
How like a mighty trumpet-call they stir
The blood. Such are the notes that men have sung   30
Going to valorous deeds; such tones there were
That helped make history when Time was young.

There is a wide, wide wonder in it all,
That from degraded rest and servile toil
The fiery spirit of the seer should call   35
These simple children of the sun and soil.
O black slave singers, gone, forgot, unfamed,
You—you alone, of all the long, long line
Of those who've sung untaught, unknown, unnamed,
Have stretched out upward, seeking the divine.   40

You sang not deeds of heroes or of kings;
No chant of bloody war, no exulting paean
Of arms-won triumphs; but your humble strings
You touched in chord with music empyrean.
You sang far better than you knew; the songs   45
That for your listeners' hungry hearts sufficed
Still live,—but more than this to you belongs:
You sang a race from wood and stone to Christ.

42. *paean* (pē'ən): song of joy or praise.   44. *empyrean* (ĕm-pī-rē'ən): highest reaches
of heaven.

DISCUSSION   Why does Johnson praise the unknown black slave
singers of Negro spirituals? How does he do so? Include specific words and lines in your answer.

For further activities, see page 480.

Twelve Angry Men

REGINALD ROSE

CAST

FOREMAN
JURORS (Two—Twelve)

JUDGE
GUARD

DESCRIPTIONS OF
JURORS

FOREMAN: A small, petty man who is impressed with the authority he has and handles himself quite formally. Not overly bright, but dogged.

JUROR NUMBER TWO: A meek, hesitant man who finds it difficult to maintain any opinions of his own. Easily swayed and usually adopts the opinion of the last person to whom he has spoken.

JUROR NUMBER THREE: A very strong, very forceful, extremely opinionated man within whom can be detected a streak of sadism. A humorless man who is intolerant of opinions other than his own and accustomed to forcing his wishes and views upon others.

JUROR NUMBER FOUR: Seems to be a man of wealth and position. A practiced speaker who presents himself well at all times. Seems to feel a little bit above the rest of the jurors. His only concern is with the facts in this case, and he is appalled at the behavior of the others.

JUROR NUMBER FIVE: A naive, very frightened young man who takes his obligations in this case very seriously, but who finds it difficult to speak up when his elders have the floor.

JUROR NUMBER SIX: An honest but dull-witted man who comes upon his decisions slowly and carefully. A man who finds it difficult to create positive opinions, but who must listen to and digest and accept those opinions offered by others which appeal to him most.

JUROR NUMBER SEVEN: A loud, flashy, glad-handed salesman type who has more important things to do than to sit on a jury. He is quick to show temper, quick to form opinions on things about which he knows nothing. Is a bully and, of course, a coward.

JUROR NUMBER EIGHT: A quiet, thoughtful, gentle man. A man who sees all sides of every question and constantly seeks the truth. A man of strength tempered with compassion. Above all, a man who wants justice to be done and will fight to see that it is.

JUROR NUMBER NINE: A mild, gentle old man, long since defeated by life and now merely waiting to die. A man who recognizes himself for what he is and mourns the days when it would have been possible to be courageous without shielding himself behind his many years.

JUROR NUMBER TEN: An angry, bitter man. A man who antagonizes almost at sight. A bigot who places no values on any human life save his own. A man who has been nowhere and is going nowhere and knows it deep within him.

JUROR NUMBER ELEVEN: A refugee from Europe who had come to this country in 1941. A man who speaks with an accent and who is ashamed, humble, almost subservient to the people around him, but who will honestly seek justice because he has suffered through so much injustice.

JUROR NUMBER TWELVE: A slick, bright advertising man who thinks of human beings in terms of percentages, graphs, and polls and has no real understanding of people. A superficial snob, but trying to be a good fellow.

Act One

Fade in on a jury box. Twelve men are seated in it, listening intently to the voice of the judge as he charges[1] them. We do not see the judge. He speaks in slow, measured tones, and his voice is grave. The camera drifts over the faces of the jurymen as the judge speaks, and we see that most of their heads are turned to camera's left. Seven looks down at his hands. Three looks off in another direction, the direction in which the defendant would be sitting. Ten keeps moving his head back and forth nervously. The judge drones on.

JUDGE: Murder in the first degree—premeditated homicide—is the most serious charge tried in our criminal courts. You've heard a long and complex case, gentlemen, and it is now your duty to sit down to try and separate the facts from the fancy. One man is dead. The life of another is at stake. If there is a reasonable doubt in your minds as to the guilt of the accused . . . then you must declare him not guilty. If, however, there is no reasonable doubt, then he must be found guilty. Whichever way you decide, the verdict must be unanimous. I urge you to deliberate honestly and thoughtfully. You are faced with a grave responsibility. Thank you, gentlemen.

There is a long pause.

CLERK [droning]: The jury will retire.

And now, slowly, almost hesitantly, the members of the jury begin to rise. Awkwardly, they file out of the jury box and off camera to the left. Camera holds on jury box, then fades out.

Fade in on a large, bare, unpleasant-looking room. This is the jury room in the county criminal court of a large Eastern city. It is about 4:00 P.M. The room is furnished with a long conference table and a dozen chairs. The walls are bare, drab, and badly in need of a fresh coat of paint. Along one wall is a row of windows which look out on the skyline of the city's financial district. High on another wall is an electric clock. A washroom opens off the jury room. In one corner of the room is a water fountain. On the table are pads, pencils, ashtrays. One of the windows is open. Papers blow across the table and onto the floor as the door opens. Lettered on the outside of the door are the words "Jury Room." A uniformed guard holds the door open. Slowly, almost self-consciously, the twelve jurors file in. The guard counts them as they enter the door, his lips moving, but no sound coming forth. Four or five of the jurors light cigarettes as they enter the room. Juror Five lights his pipe, which he smokes constantly throughout the

---

[1] *he charges them:* he tells them what their duties are as jurors.

play. Jurors Two and Twelve go to the water fountain. Nine goes into the washroom, the door of which is lettered "Men." Several of the jurors take seats at the table. Others stand awkwardly around the room. Several look out the windows. These are men who are ill at ease, who do not really know each other to talk to, and who wish they were anywhere but here. Seven, standing at window, takes out a pack of gum, takes a piece, and offers it around. There are no takers. He mops his brow.

SEVEN [to Six]: Y'know something? It's hot. [Six nods.] You'd think they'd at least air-condition the place. I almost dropped dead in court.

Seven opens the window a bit wider. The guard looks them over and checks his count. Then, satisfied, he makes ready to leave.

GUARD: Okay, gentlemen. Everybody's here. If there's anything you want, I'm right outside. Just knock.

He exits, closing the door. Silently they all look at the door. We hear the lock clicking.

FIVE: I never knew they locked the door.
TEN [blowing nose]: Sure, they lock the door. What did you think?
FIVE: I don't know. It just never occurred to me.

Some of the jurors are taking off their jackets. Others are sitting down at the table. They still are reluctant to talk to each other. Foreman is at head of table, tearing slips of paper for ballots. Now we get a close shot of Eight. He looks out the window. We hear Three talking to Two.

THREE: Six days. They should have finished it in two. Talk, talk, talk. Did you ever hear so much talk about nothing?
TWO [nervously laughing]: Well . . . I guess . . . they're entitled.
THREE: Everybody gets a fair trial. [He shakes his head.] That's the system. Well, I suppose you can't say anything against it.

Two looks at him nervously, nods, and goes over to water cooler. Cut to shot of Eight staring out window. Cut to table. Seven stands at the table, putting out a cigarette.

SEVEN [to Ten]: How did you like that business about the knife? Did you ever hear a phonier story?
TEN [wisely]: Well, look, you've gotta expect that. You know what you're dealing with.
SEVEN: Yeah, I suppose. What's the matter, you got a cold?
TEN [blowing]: A lulu. These hot-weather colds can kill you.

Seven nods sympathetically.

FOREMAN [briskly]: All right, gentlemen. Let's take seats.

SEVEN: Right. This better be fast. I've got tickets to *The Seven Year Itch* tonight. I must be the only guy in the whole world who hasn't seen it yet. [He laughs and sits down.] Okay, your honor, start the show.

They all begin to sit down. The foreman is seated at the head of the table. Eight continues to look out the window.

FOREMAN [to Eight]: How about sitting down? [Eight doesn't hear him.] The gentleman at the window.

Eight turns, startled.

FOREMAN: How about sitting down?

EIGHT: Oh. I'm sorry.

He heads for a seat.

TEN [to Six]: It's tough to figure, isn't it? A kid kills his father. Bing! Just like that. Well, it's the element. They let the kids run wild. Maybe it serves 'em right.

FOREMAN: Is everybody here?

TWELVE: The old man's inside.

The foreman turns to the washroom just as the door opens. Nine comes out, embarrassed.

FOREMAN: We'd like to get started.

NINE: Forgive me, gentlemen. I didn't mean to keep you waiting.

FOREMAN: It's all right. Find a seat.

Nine heads for a seat and sits down. They look at the foreman expectantly.

FOREMAN: All right. Now, you gentlemen can handle this any way you want to. I mean, I'm not going to make any rules. If we want to discuss it first and then vote, that's one way. Or we can vote right now to see how we stand.

SEVEN: Let's vote now. Who knows, maybe we can all go home.

TEN: Yeah. Let's see who's where.

THREE: Right. Let's vote now.

FOREMAN: Anybody doesn't want to vote? [He looks around the table. There is no answer.] Okay, all those voting guilty raise your hands.

Seven or eight hands go up immediately. Several others go up more slowly. Everyone looks around the table. There are two hands not raised, Nine's and Eight's. Nine's hand goes up slowly now as the foreman counts.

FOREMAN: . . . Nine . . . ten . . . eleven . . . That's eleven for guilty. Okay. Not guilty? [Eight's hand is raised.] One. Right. Okay. Eleven to one, guilty. Now we know where we are.

THREE: Somebody's in left field. [To Eight] You think he's not guilty?

EIGHT [quietly]: I don't know.

THREE: I never saw a guiltier man in my life. You sat right in court and heard the same thing I did. The man's a dangerous killer. You could see it.

EIGHT: He's nineteen years old.

THREE: That's old enough. He knifed his own father. Four inches into the chest. An innocent little nineteen-year-old kid. They proved it a dozen different ways. Do you want me to list them?

EIGHT: No.

TEN [to Eight]: Well, do you believe his story?

EIGHT: I don't know whether I believe it or not. Maybe I don't.

SEVEN: So what'd you vote not guilty for?

EIGHT: There were eleven votes for guilty. It's not so easy for me to raise my hand and send a boy off to die without talking about it first.

SEVEN: Who says it's easy for me?

EIGHT: No one.

SEVEN: What, just because I voted fast? I think the guy's guilty. You couldn't change my mind if you talked for a hundred years.

EIGHT: I don't want to change your mind. I just want to talk for a while. Look, this boy's been kicked around all his life. You know, living in a slum, his mother dead since he was nine. That's not a very good head start. He's a tough, angry kid. You know why slum kids get that way? Because we knock 'em on the head once a day, every day. I think maybe we owe him a few words. That's all.

He looks around the table. Some of them look back coldly. Some cannot look at him. Only Nine nods slowly. Twelve doodles steadily. Four begins to comb his hair.

TEN: I don't mind telling you this, mister. We don't owe him a thing. He got a fair trial, didn't he? You know what that trial cost? He's lucky he got it. Look, we're all grownups here. You're not going to tell us that we're supposed to believe him, knowing what he is. I've lived among 'em all my life. You can't believe a word they say. You know that.

NINE [to Ten very slowly]: I don't know that. What a terrible thing for a man to believe! Since when is dishonesty a group characteristic? You have no monopoly on the truth——

THREE [interrupting]: All right. It's not Sunday. We don't need a sermon.

NINE: What this man says is very dangerous. . . .

Eight puts his hand on Nine's arm and stops him. Somehow his touch and his gentle expression calm the old man. He draws a deep breath and relaxes.

FOUR: I don't see any need for arguing like this. I think we ought to be able to behave like gentlemen.

SEVEN: Right!

FOUR: If we're going to discuss this case, let's discuss the facts.

FOREMAN: I think that's a good point. We have a job to do. Let's do it.

ELEVEN [with accent]: If you gentlemen don't mind, I'm going to close the window. [He gets up and does so.] [Apologetically] It was blowing on my neck.

Ten blows his nose fiercely.

TWELVE: I may have an idea here. I'm just thinking out loud now, but it seems to me that it's up to us to convince this gentleman [indicating Eight] that we're right and he's wrong. Maybe if we each took a minute or two, you know, if we sort of try it on for size. . . .

FOREMAN: That sounds fair enough. Supposing we go once around the table.

SEVEN: Okay, let's start it off.

FOREMAN: Right. [To Two] I guess you're first.

TWO [timidly]: Oh. Well . . . [long pause] I just think he's guilty. I thought it was obvious. I mean nobody proved otherwise.

EIGHT [quietly]: Nobody has to prove otherwise. The burden of proof is on the prosecution. The defendant doesn't have to open his mouth. That's in the Constitution. The Fifth Amendment. You've heard of it.

TWO [flustered]: Well, sure, I've heard of it. I know what it is. I . . . what I meant . . . well, anyway, I think he was guilty.

THREE: Okay, let's get to the facts. Number one, let's take the old man who lived on the second floor right underneath the room where the murder took place. At ten minutes after twelve on the night of the killing he heard loud noises in the upstairs apartment. He said it sounded like a fight. Then he heard the kid say to his father, "I'm gonna kill you." A second later he heard a body falling, and he ran to the door of his apartment, looked out, and saw the kid running down the stairs and out of the house. Then he called the police. They found the father with a knife in his chest.

FOREMAN: And the coroner fixed the time of death at around midnight.

THREE: Right. Now what else do you want?

FOUR: The boy's entire story is flimsy. He claimed he was at the movies. That's a little ridiculous, isn't it? He couldn't even remember what pictures he saw.

THREE: That's right. Did you hear that? [To Four] You're absolutely right.

TEN: Look, what about the woman across the street? If her testimony don't prove it, then nothing does.

TWELVE: That's right. She saw the killing, didn't she?

FOREMAN: Let's go in order.

TEN [loud]: Just a minute. Here's a woman who's lying in bed and can't sleep. It's hot, you know. [He gets up and begins to walk around, blowing his nose and talking.] Anyway, she looks out the window, and right across the street she sees the kid stick the knife into his father. She's known the kid all his life. His window is right opposite hers, across the el tracks, and she swore she saw him do it.

EIGHT: Through the windows of a passing elevated train.

TEN: Okay. And they proved in court that you can look through the windows of a passing el train at night and see what's happening on the other side. They proved it.

EIGHT: I'd like to ask you something. How come you believed her? She's one of "them" too, isn't she?

Ten walks over to Eight.

TEN: You're a pretty smart fellow, aren't you?

FOREMAN [rising]: Now take it easy.

Three gets up and goes to Ten.

THREE: Come on. Sit down. [He leads Ten back to his seat.] What're you letting him get you all upset for? Relax.

Ten and Three sit down.

FOREMAN: Let's calm down now. [To Five] It's your turn.

FIVE: I'll pass it.

FOREMAN: That's your privilege. [To Six] How about you?

SIX [slowly]: I don't know. I started to be convinced, you know, with the testimony from those people across the hall. Didn't they say something about an argument between the father and the boy around seven o'clock that night? I mean, I can be wrong.

ELEVEN: I think it was eight o'clock. Not seven.

EIGHT: That's right. Eight o'clock. They heard the father hit the boy twice and then saw the boy walk angrily out of the house. What does that prove?

SIX: Well, it doesn't exactly prove anything. It's just part of the picture. I didn't say it proved anything.

FOREMAN: Anything else?

SIX: No.

Six goes to the water fountain.

FOREMAN [to Seven]: All right. How about you?

SEVEN: I don't know, most of it's been said already. We can talk all day about this thing, but I think we're wasting our time. Look at the kid's record. At fifteen he was in reform school. He stole a car. He's been arrested for mugging. He was picked up for knife-fighting. I think they said he stabbed somebody in the arm. This is a very fine boy.

EIGHT: Ever since he was five years old his father beat him up regularly. He used his fists.

SEVEN: So would I! A kid like that.

THREE: You're right. It's the kids. The way they are—you know? They don't listen. [Bitter] I've got a kid. When he was eight years old, he ran away from a fight. I saw him. I was so ashamed, I told him right out, "I'm gonna make a man out of you or I'm gonna bust you up into little pieces trying." When he was fifteen he hit me in the face. He's big, you know. I haven't seen him in three years. Rotten kid! You work your heart out. . . . [Pause] All right. Let's get on with it.

Looks away embarrassed.

FOUR: We're missing the point here. This boy—let's say he's a product of a filthy neighborhood and a broken home. We can't help that. We're not here to go into the reasons why slums are breeding grounds for criminals. They are. I know it. So do you. The children who come out of slum backgrounds are potential menaces to society.

TEN: You said it there. I don't want any part of them, believe me.

There is a dead silence for a moment, and then Five speaks haltingly.

FIVE: I've lived in a slum all my life——

TEN: Oh, now wait a second!

FIVE: I used to play in a back yard that was filled with garbage. Maybe it still smells on me.

FOREMAN: Now let's be reasonable. There's nothing personal——

Five stands up.

FIVE: There is something personal!

Then he catches himself and seeing everyone looking at him, sits down, fists clenched.

THREE [persuasively]: Come on, now. He didn't mean you, feller. Let's not be so sensitive. . . .

There is a long pause.

ELEVEN: I can understand this sensitivity.

FOREMAN: Now let's stop the bickering. We're wasting time. [To Eight] It's your turn.

EIGHT: All right. I had a peculiar feeling about this trial. Somehow I felt that the defense counsel never really conducted a thorough cross-examination. I mean, he was appointed by the court to defend the boy. He hardly seemed interested. Too many questions were left unasked.

THREE [annoyed]: What about the ones that were asked? For instance, let's talk about that cute little switch-knife. You know, the one that fine, upright kid admitted buying.

EIGHT: All right. Let's talk about it. Let's get it in here and look at it. I'd like to see it again, Mr. Foreman.

The foreman looks at him questioningly and then gets up and goes to the door. During the following dialogue the foreman knocks, the guard comes in, the foreman whispers to him, the guard nods and leaves, locking the door.

THREE: We all know what it looks like. I don't see why we have to look at it again. [To Four] What do you think?

FOUR: The gentleman has a right to see exhibits in evidence.

THREE [shrugging]: Okay with me.

FOUR [to Eight]: This knife is a pretty strong piece of evidence, don't you agree?

EIGHT: I do.

FOUR: The boy admits going out of his house at eight o'clock after being slapped by his father.

EIGHT: Or punched.

FOUR: Or punched. He went to a neighborhood store and bought a switch-knife. The storekeeper was arrested the following day when he admitted selling it to the boy. It's a very unusual knife. The storekeeper identified it and said it was the only one of its kind he had in stock. Why did the boy get it? [Sarcastically] As a present for a friend of his, he says. Am I right so far?

EIGHT: Right.

THREE: You bet he's right. [To all] Now listen to this man. He knows what he's talking about.

FOUR: Next, the boy claims that on the way home the knife must have fallen through a hole in his coat pocket, that he never saw it again. Now there's a story, gentlemen. You know what actually happened. The boy took the knife home and a few hours later stabbed his father with it and even remembered to wipe off the fingerprints.

The door opens, and the guard walks in with an oddly designed knife with a tag on it. Four gets up and takes it from him. The guard exits.

FOUR: Everyone connected with the case identified this knife. Now are you trying to tell me that someone picked it up off the street and went up to the boy's house and stabbed his father with it just to be amusing?

EIGHT: No, I'm saying that it's possible that the boy lost the knife and that someone else stabbed his father with a similar knife. It's possible.

Four flips open the knife and jams it into the table.

FOUR: Take a look at that knife. It's a very strange knife. I've never seen one like it before in my life. Neither had the storekeeper who sold it to him.

Eight reaches casually into his pocket and withdraws an object. No one notices this. He stands up quietly.

FOUR: Aren't you trying to make us accept a pretty incredible co-incidence?

EIGHT: I'm not trying to make anyone accept it. I'm just saying it's possible.

THREE [shouting]: And I'm saying it's not possible.

Eight swiftly flicks open the blade of a switch-knife and jams it into the table next to the first one. They are exactly alike. There are several gasps and everyone stares at the knife. There is a long silence.

THREE [slowly amazed]: What are you trying to do?

TEN [loud]: Yeah, what is this? Who do you think you are?

FIVE: Look at it! It's the same knife!

FOREMAN: Quiet! Let's be quiet.

They quiet down.

FOUR: Where did you get it?

EIGHT: I got it last night in a little junk shop around the corner from the boy's house. It cost two dollars.

THREE: Now listen to me! You pulled a real smart trick here, but you proved absolutely zero. Maybe there are ten knives like that, so what?

EIGHT: Maybe there are.

THREE: The boy lied and you know it.

EIGHT: He may have lied. [To Ten] Do you think he lied?

TEN [violently]: Now that's a stupid question. Sure he lied!

EIGHT [to Four]: Do you?

FOUR: You don't have to ask me that. You know my answer. He lied.

EIGHT [to Five]: Do you think he lied?

Five can't answer immediately. He looks around nervously.

FIVE: I . . . I don't know.

SEVEN: Now wait a second. What are you, the guy's lawyer? Listen, there are still eleven of us who think he's guilty. You're alone. What do you think you're gonna accomplish? If you want to be stubborn and hang this jury, he'll be tried again and found guilty, sure as he's born.

EIGHT: You're probably right.

SEVEN: So what are you gonna do about it? We can be here all
    night.

NINE: It's only one night. A man may die.

Seven glares at Nine for a long while, but has no answer. Eight looks closely at
Nine, and we can begin to sense a rapport between them. There is a long silence. Then suddenly everyone begins to talk at once.

THREE: Well, whose fault is that?

SIX: Do you think maybe if we went over it again? What I mean
    is. . . .

TEN: Did anyone force him to kill his father? [To Three] How do you
    like him? Like someone forced him!

ELEVEN: Perhaps this is not the point.

FIVE: No one forced anyone. But listen. . . .

TWELVE: Look, gentlemen, we can spitball all night here.

TWO: Well, I was going to say——

SEVEN: Just a minute. Some of us've got better things to do than sit
    around a jury room.

FOUR: I can't understand a word in here. Why do we all have to
    talk at once?

FOREMAN: He's right. I think we ought to get on with it.

Eight has been listening to this exchange closely.

THREE [to Eight]: Well, what do you say? You're the one holding up
    the show.

EIGHT [standing]: I've got a proposition to make.

We catch a close shot of Five looking steadily at him as he talks. Five, seemingly
puzzled, listens closely.

EIGHT: I want to call for a vote. I want eleven men to vote by secret
    ballot. I'll abstain. If there are still eleven votes for guilty, I
    won't stand alone. We'll take in a guilty verdict right now.

SEVEN: Okay. Let's do it.

FOREMAN: That sounds fair. Is everyone agreed?

They all nod their heads. Eight walks over to the window, looks out for a moment
and then faces them.

FOREMAN: Pass these along.

The foreman passes ballot slips to all of them, and now Eight watches them
tensely as they begin to write. Fade out.

Act Two

Fade in on same scene, no time lapse. Eight stands tensely watching as the jurors write on their ballots. He stays perfectly still as one by one they fold the ballots and pass them along to the foreman. The foreman takes them, riffles through the folded ballots, counts eleven, and now begins to open them. He reads each one out loud and lays it aside. They watch him quietly, and all we hear is his voice and the sound of Two sucking on a cough drop.

FOREMAN: Guilty. Guilty. Guilty. Guilty. Guilty. Guilty. Guilty. Guilty. Guilty. [He pauses at the tenth ballot and then reads it.] Not Guilty. [Three slams down hard on the table. The foreman opens the last ballot.] Guilty.

TEN [angry]: How do you like that!

SEVEN: Who was it? I think we have a right to know.

ELEVEN: Excuse me. This was a secret ballot. We agreed on this point, no? If the gentleman wants it to remain secret——

THREE [standing up angrily]: What do you mean? There are no secrets in here! I know who it was. [He turns to Five.] What's the matter with you? You come in here and you vote guilty and then this slick preacher starts to tear your heart out with stories about a poor little kid who just couldn't help becoming a murderer. So you change your vote. If that isn't the most sickening——

Five stares at Three, frightened at this outburst.

FOREMAN: Now hold it.

THREE: Hold it? We're trying to put a guilty man into the chair where he belongs—and all of a sudden we're paying attention to fairy tales.

FIVE: Now just a minute. . . .

ELEVEN: Please. I would like to say something here. I have always thought that a man was entitled to have unpopular opinions in this country. This is the reason I came here. I wanted to have the right to disagree. In my own country, I am ashamed to say——

TEN: What do we have to listen to now—the whole history of your country?

SEVEN: Yeah, let's stick to the subject. [To Five] I want to ask you what made you change your vote.

There is a long pause as Seven and Five eye each other angrily.

NINE [quietly]: There's nothing for him to tell you. He didn't change

his vote. I did. [There is a pause.] Maybe you'd like to know
why.

THREE: No, we wouldn't like to know why.

FOREMAN: The man wants to talk.

NINE: Thank you. [Pointing at Eight] This gentleman chose to stand
alone against us. That's his right. It takes a great deal of courage to stand alone even if you believe in something very
strongly. He left the verdict up to us. He gambled for support,
and I gave it to him. I want to hear more. The vote is ten to
two.

TEN: That's fine. If the speech is over, let's go on.

Foreman gets up, goes to door. Knocks, hands guard the tagged switch-knife
and sits down again.

THREE [to Five]: Look, buddy, I was a little excited. Well, you know
how it is. I . . . I didn't mean to get nasty. Nothing personal.

Five looks at him.

SEVEN [to Eight]: Look, supposing you answer me this. If the kid
didn't kill him, who did?

EIGHT: As far as I know, we're supposed to decide whether or not
the boy on trial is guilty. We're not concerned with anyone
else's motives here.

NINE: Guilty beyond a reasonable doubt. This is an important thing
to remember.

THREE [to Ten]: Everyone's a lawyer. [To Nine] Supposing you explain
what your reasonable doubts are.

NINE: This is not easy. So far, it's only a feeling I have. A feeling.
Perhaps you don't understand.

TEN: A feeling! What are we gonna do, spend the night talking
about your feelings? What about the facts?

THREE: You said a mouthful. [To Nine] Look, the old man heard the
kid yell, "I'm gonna kill you." A second later he heard the
father's body falling, and he saw the boy running out of the
house fifteen seconds after that.

TWELVE: That's right. And let's not forget the woman across the
street. She looked into the open window and saw the boy stab
his father. She saw it. Now if that's not enough for you. . . .

EIGHT: It's not enough for me.

SEVEN: How do you like him? It's like talking into a dead phone.

FOUR: The woman saw the killing through the windows of a moving elevated train. The train had five cars, and she saw it

through the windows of the last two. She remembers the most insignificant details.

Cut to close shot of Twelve who doodles a picture of an el train on a scrap of paper.

THREE: Well, what have you got to say about that?

EIGHT: I don't know. It doesn't sound right to me.

THREE: Well, supposing you think about it. [To Twelve] Lend me your pencil.

Twelve gives it to him. He draws a tic-tac-toe square on the same sheet of paper on which Twelve has drawn the train. He fills in an X, hands the pencil to Twelve.

THREE: Your turn. We might as well pass the time.

Twelve takes the pencil. Eight stands up and snatches the paper away. Three leaps up.

THREE: Wait a minute!

EIGHT [hard]: This isn't a game.

THREE [angry]: Who do you think you are?

SEVEN [rising]: All right, let's take it easy.

THREE: I've got a good mind to walk around this table and belt him one!

FOREMAN: Now, please. I don't want any fights in here.

THREE: Did ya see him? The nerve! The absolute nerve!

TEN: All right. Forget it. It don't mean anything.

SIX: How about sitting down?

THREE: This isn't a game. Who does he think he is?

He lets them sit him down. Eight remains standing, holding the scrap of paper. He looks at it closely now and seems to be suddenly interested in it. Then he throws it back toward Three. It lands in center of table. Three is angered again at this, but Four puts his hand on his arm. Eight speaks now and his voice is more intense.

EIGHT [to Four]: Take a look at that sketch. How long does it take an elevated train going at top speed to pass a given point?

FOUR: What has that got to do with anything?

EIGHT: How long? Guess.

FOUR: I wouldn't have the slightest idea.

EIGHT [to Five]: What do you think?

FIVE: About ten or twelve seconds, maybe.

EIGHT: I'd say that was a fair guess. Anyone else?

ELEVEN: I would think about ten seconds, perhaps.

TWO: About ten seconds.

FOUR: All right. Say ten seconds. What are you getting at?

EIGHT: This. An el train passes a given point in ten seconds. That given point is the window of the room in which the killing took place. You can almost reach out of the window of that room and touch the el. Right? [Several of them nod.] All right. Now let me ask you this. Did anyone here ever live right next to the el tracks? I have. When your window is open and the train goes by, the noise is almost unbearable. You can't hear yourself think.

TEN: Okay. You can't hear yourself think. Will you get to the point?

EIGHT: The old man heard the boy say, "I'm going to kill you," and one second later he heard a body fall. One second. That's the testimony, right?

TWO: Right.

EIGHT: The woman across the street looked through the windows of the last two cars of the el and saw the body fall. Right? The *last two* cars.

TEN: What are you giving us here?

EIGHT: An el takes ten seconds to pass a given point or two seconds per car. That el had been going by the old man's window for at least six seconds, and maybe more, *before the body fell,* according to the woman. The old man would have had to hear the boy say, "I'm going to kill you," while the front of the el was roaring past his nose. It's not possible that he could have heard it.

THREE: What d'ya mean! Sure he could have heard it.

EIGHT: Could he?

THREE: He said the boy yelled it out. That's enough for me.

NINE: I don't think he could have heard it.

TWO: Maybe he didn't hear it. I mean with the el noise. . . .

THREE: What are you people talking about? Are you calling the old man a liar?

FIVE: Well, it stands to reason.

THREE: You're crazy. Why would he lie? What's he got to gain?

NINE: Attention, maybe.

THREE: You keep coming up with these bright sayings. Why don't you send one in to a newspaper? They pay two dollars.

Eight looks hard at Three and then turns to Nine.

EIGHT [softly]: Why might the old man have lied? You have a right to be heard.

NINE: It's just that I looked at him for a very long time. The seam of his jacket was split under the arm. Did you notice that? He was a very old man with a torn jacket, and he carried two canes. I think I know him better than anyone here. This is a quiet, frightened, insignificant man who has been nothing all his life, who has never had recognition—his name in the newspapers. Nobody knows him after seventy-five years. That's a very sad thing. A man like this needs to be recognized. To be questioned, and listened to, and quoted just once. This is very important.

TWELVE: And you're trying to tell us he lied about a thing like this just so that he could be important?

NINE: No. He wouldn't really lie. But perhaps he'd make himself believe that he heard those words and recognized the boy's face.

THREE [loud]: Well, that's the most fantastic story I've ever heard. How can you make up a thing like that? What do you know about it?

NINE [low]: I speak from experience.

There is a long pause. Then the foreman clears his throat.

FOREMAN [to Eight]: All right. Is there anything else?

Eight is looking at Nine. Two offers the foreman a box of cough drops. The foreman pushes it away.

TWO [hesitantly]: Anybody . . . want a cough . . . drop?
FOREMAN [sharply]: Come on. Let's get on with it.
EIGHT: I'll take one. [Two almost gratefully slides him one along the table.] Thanks.

Two nods, and Eight puts the cough drop into his mouth.

EIGHT: Now. There's something else I'd like to point out here. I think we proved that the old man couldn't have heard the boy say, "I'm going to kill you," but supposing he really did hear it? This phrase: how many times has each of you used it? Probably hundreds. "If you do that once more, Junior, I'm going to murder you." "Come on, Rocky, kill him!" We say it every day. This doesn't mean that we're going to kill someone.
THREE: Wait a minute. The phrase was "I'm going to kill you," and the kid screamed it out at the top of his lungs. Don't try and tell me he didn't mean it. Anybody says a thing like that the way he said it—they mean it.
TEN: And how they mean it!
EIGHT: Well, let me ask you this. Do you really think the boy would shout out a thing like that so the whole neighborhood would hear it? I don't think so. He's much too bright for that.
TEN [exploding]: Bright! He's a common, ignorant slob. He don't even speak good English!
ELEVEN [slowly]: He *doesn't* even speak good English.

Ten stares angrily at Eleven, and there is silence for a moment. Then Five looks around the table nervously.

FIVE: I'd like to change my vote to not guilty.

Three gets up and walks to the window, furious, but trying to control himself.

FOREMAN: Are you sure?
FIVE: Yes. I'm sure.
FOREMAN: The vote is nine to three in favor of guilty.
SEVEN: Well, if that isn't the end. [To Five] What are you basing it on? Stories this guy [indicating Eight] made up! He oughta write

for *Amazing Detective Monthly*. He'd make a fortune. Listen, the kid had a lawyer, didn't he? Why didn't his lawyer bring up all these points?

FIVE: Lawyers can't think of everything.

SEVEN: Oh, brother! [To Eight] You sit in here and pull stories out of thin air. Now we're supposed to believe that the old man didn't get up out of bed, run to the door, and see the kid beat it downstairs fifteen seconds after the killing. He's only saying he did to be important.

FIVE: Did the old man say he *ran* to the door?

SEVEN: Ran. Walked. What's the difference? He got there.

FIVE: I don't remember what he said. But I don't see how he could run.

FOUR: He said he *went* from his bedroom to the front door. That's enough, isn't it?

EIGHT: Where was his bedroom again?

TEN: Down the hall somewhere. I thought you remembered everything. Don't you remember that?

EIGHT: No. Mr. Foreman, I'd like to take a look at the diagram of the apartment.

SEVEN: Why don't we have them run the trial over just so you can get everything straight?

EIGHT: Mr. Foreman. . . .

FOREMAN [rising]: I heard you.

The foreman gets up, goes to door during following dialogue. He knocks on door, guard opens it, he whispers to guard, guard nods and closes door.

THREE [to Eight]: All right. What's this for? How come you're the only one in the room who wants to see exhibits all the time?

FIVE: I want to see this one, too.

THREE: And I want to stop wasting time.

FOUR: If we're going to start wading through all that nonsense about where the body was found. . . .

EIGHT: We're not. We're going to find out how a man who's had two strokes in the past three years, and who walks with a pair of canes, could get to his front door in fifteen seconds.

THREE: He said twenty seconds.

TWO: He said fifteen.

THREE: How does he know how long fifteen seconds is? You can't judge that kind of a thing.

NINE: He said fifteen. He was very positive about it.

THREE [angry]: He's an old man. You saw him. Half the time he was confused. How could he be positive about . . . anything?

Three looks around sheepishly, unable to cover up his blunder. The door opens and the guard walks in, carrying a large pen-and-ink diagram of the apartment. It is a railroad flat. A bedroom faces the el tracks. Behind it is a series of rooms off a long hall. In the front bedroom is a diagram of the spot where the body was found. At the back of the apartment we see the entrance into the apartment hall from the building hall. We can see a flight of stairs in the building hall. The diagram is clearly labeled, and included in the information on it are the dimensions of the various rooms. The guard gives the diagram to the foreman.

GUARD: This what you wanted?
FOREMAN: That's right. Thank you.

The guard nods and exits. Eight goes to Foreman and reaches for it.

EIGHT: May I?

The foreman nods. Eight takes the diagram and sets it up on a chair so that all can see it. Eight looks it over. Several of the jurors get up to see it better. Three, Ten, and Seven, however, barely bother to look at it.

SEVEN [to Ten]: Do me a favor. Wake me up when this is over.
EIGHT [ignoring him]: All right. This is the apartment in which the killing took place. The old man's apartment is directly beneath it and exactly the same. [Pointing] Here are the el tracks. The bedroom. Another bedroom. Living room. Bathroom. Kitchen. And this is the hall. Here's the front door to the apartment. And here are the steps. [Pointing to front bedroom and then front door] Now, the old man was in bed in this room. He says he got up, went out into the hall, down the hall to the front door, opened it, and looked out just in time to see the boy racing down the stairs. Am I right?
THREE: That's the story.
EIGHT: Fifteen seconds after he heard the body fall.
ELEVEN: Correct.
EIGHT: His bed was at the window. It's [looking closer] twelve feet from his bed to the bedroom door. The length of the hall is forty-three feet, six inches. He had to get up out of bed, get his canes, walk twelve feet, open the bedroom door, walk forty-three feet, and open the front door—all in fifteen seconds. Do you think this possible?
TEN: You know it's possible.

ELEVEN: He can only walk very slowly. They had to help him into the witness chair.

THREE: You make it sound like a long walk. It's not.

Eight gets up, goes to the end of the room, and takes two chairs. He puts them together to indicate a bed.

NINE: For an old man who uses canes, it's a long walk.

THREE [to Eight]: What are you doing?

EIGHT: I want to try this thing. Let's see how long it took him. I'm going to pace off twelve feet—the length of the bedroom.

He begins to do so.

THREE: You're crazy. You can't recreate a thing like that.

ELEVEN: Perhaps if we could see it . . . this is an important point.

THREE [mad]: It's a ridiculous waste of time.

SIX: Let him do it.

EIGHT: Hand me a chair. [Someone pushes a chair to him.] All right. This is the bedroom door. Now how far would you say it is from here to the door of this room?

SIX: I'd say it was twenty feet.

TWO: Just about.

EIGHT: Twenty feet is close enough. All right, from here to the door and back is about forty feet. It's shorter than the length of the hall, wouldn't you say that?

NINE: A few feet, maybe.

TEN: Look, this is absolutely insane. What makes you think you can——

EIGHT: Do you mind if I try it? According to you, it'll only take fifteen seconds. We can spare that. [He walks over to the two chairs now and lies down on them.] Who's got a watch with a second hand?

TWO: I have.

EIGHT: When you want me to start, stamp your foot. That'll be the body falling. Time me from there. [He lies down on the chair.] Let's say he keeps his canes right at his bedside. Right?

TWO: Right!

EIGHT: Okay. I'm ready.

They all watch carefully. Two stares at his watch, waiting for the second hand to reach 60. Then, as it does, he stamps his foot loudly. Eight begins to get up. Slowly he swings his legs over the edges of the chairs, reaches for imaginary canes, and struggles to his feet. Two stares at the watch. Eight walks as a crippled old man would walk, toward the chair which is serving as the bedroom door. He gets to it and pretends to open it.

TEN [shouting]: Speed it up. He walked twice as fast as that.

Eight, not having stopped for this outburst, begins to walk the simulated forty-foot hallway.

ELEVEN: This is, I think, even more quickly than the old man walked in the courtroom.

EIGHT: If you think I should go faster, I will.

He speeds up his pace slightly. He reaches the door and turns now, heading back, hobbling as an old man would hobble, bent over his imaginary canes. They watch him tensely. He hobbles back to the chair, which also serves as the front door. He stops there and pretends to unlock the door. Then he pretends to push it open.

EIGHT [loud]: Stop.

TWO: Right.

EIGHT: What's the time?

TWO: Fifteen . . . twenty . . . thirty . . . thirty-one seconds exactly.

ELEVEN: Thirty-one seconds.

Some of the jurors ad-lib their surprise to each other.

EIGHT: It's my guess that the old man was trying to get to the door, heard someone racing down the stairs, and *assumed* that it was the boy.

SIX: I think that's possible.

THREE [infuriated]: Assumed? Now, listen to me, you people. I've seen all kinds of dishonesty in my day . . . but this little display takes the cake. [To Four] Tell him, will you?

Four sits silently. Three looks at him, and then he strides over to Eight.

THREE: You come in here with your heart bleeding all over the floor about slum kids and injustice and you make up these wild stories, and you've got some softhearted old ladies listening to you. Well, I'm not. I'm getting real sick of it. [To all] What's the matter with you people? This kid is guilty! He's got to burn! We're letting him slip through our fingers here.

EIGHT [calmly]: Our fingers. Are you his executioner?

THREE [raging]: I'm one of 'em.

EIGHT: Perhaps you'd like to pull the switch.

THREE [shouting]: For this kid? You bet I'd like to pull the switch!

EIGHT: I'm sorry for you.

THREE [shouting]: Don't start with me.

EIGHT: What it must feel like to want to pull the switch!

THREE: Shut up!

EIGHT: You're a sadist.

THREE [louder]: Shut up!

EIGHT [strong]: You want to see this boy die because you personally want it—not because of the facts.

THREE [shouting]: Shut up!

He lunges at Eight, but is caught by two of the jurors and held. He struggles as Eight watches calmly.

THREE [screaming]: Let me go! I'll kill him. I'll kill him!

EIGHT [softly]: You don't really mean you'll kill me, do you?

Three stops struggling now and stares at Eight. All the jurors watch in silence as we fade out.

Act Three

> Fade in on same scene. No time lapse. Three glares angrily at Eight. He is still held by two jurors. After a long pause, he shakes himself loose and turns away. He walks to the windows. The other jurors stand around the room now, shocked by this display of anger. There is silence. Then the door opens and the guard enters. He looks around the room.

GUARD: Is there anything wrong, gentlemen? I heard some noise.

FOREMAN: No. There's nothing wrong. [He points to the large diagram of the apartment.] You can take that back. We're finished with it.

> The guard nods and takes the diagram. He looks curiously at some of the jurors and exits. The jurors still are silent. Some of them slowly begin to sit down. Three still stands at the window. He turns around now. The jurors look at him.

THREE [loud]: Well, what are you looking at?

> They turn away. He goes back to his seat now. Silently the rest of the jurors take their seats. Twelve begins to doodle. Ten blows his nose, but no one speaks. Then, finally——

FOUR: I don't see why we have to behave like children here.

ELEVEN: Nor do I. We have a responsibility. This is a remarkable thing about democracy. That we are . . . what is the word? . . . Ah, notified! That we are notified by mail to come down to this place and decide on the guilt or innocence of a man we have not known before. We have nothing to gain or lose by our verdict. This is one of the reasons why we are strong. We should not make it a personal thing.

> There is a long, awkward pause.

TWELVE: Well—we're still nowhere. Who's got an idea?

SIX: I think maybe we should try another vote. Mr. Foreman?

FOREMAN: It's all right with me. Anybody doesn't want to vote?

> He looks around the table.

SEVEN: All right, let's do it.

THREE: I want an open ballot. Let's call out our votes. I want to know who stands where.

FOREMAN: That sounds fair. Anyone object? [No one does.] All right. I'll call off your jury numbers.

> He takes a pencil and paper and makes marks now in one of two columns after each vote.

FOREMAN: I vote guilty. Two?

TWO: Not guilty.

FOREMAN: Three?

THREE: Guilty.

FOREMAN: Four?

FOUR: Guilty.

FOREMAN: Five?

FIVE: Not guilty.

FOREMAN: Six?

SIX: Not guilty.

FOREMAN: Seven?

SEVEN: Guilty.

FOREMAN: Eight?

EIGHT: Not guilty.

FOREMAN: Nine?

NINE: Not guilty.

FOREMAN: Ten?

TEN: Guilty.

FOREMAN: Eleven?

ELEVEN: Not guilty.

FOREMAN: Twelve?

TWELVE: Guilty.

FOUR: Six to six.

TEN [mad]: I'll tell you something. The crime is being committed right in this room.

FOREMAN: The vote is six to six.

THREE: I'm ready to walk into court right now and declare a hung jury. There's no point in this going on any more.

SEVEN: I go for that, too. Let's take it in to the judge and let the kid take his chances with twelve other guys.

FIVE [to Seven]: You mean you still don't think there's room for reasonable doubt?

SEVEN: No, I don't.

ELEVEN: I beg your pardon. Maybe you don't understand the term "reasonable doubt."

SEVEN [angry]: What do you mean I don't understand it? Who do you think you are to talk to me like that? [To all] How do you like this guy? He comes over here running for his life, and before he can even take a big breath he's telling us how to run the show. The arrogance of him!

FIVE [to Seven]: Wait a second. Nobody around here's asking where you came from.

SEVEN: I was born right here.

FIVE: Or where your father came from. . . . [He looks at Seven, who doesn't answer but looks away.] Maybe it wouldn't hurt us to take a few tips from people who come running here! Maybe they learned something we don't know. We're not so perfect!

ELEVEN: Please—I am used to this. It's all right. Thank you.

FIVE: It's not all right!

SEVEN: Okay, okay, I apologize. Is that what you want?

FIVE: That's what I want.

FOREMAN: All right. Let's stop the arguing. Who's got something constructive to say?

TWO [hesitantly]: Well, something's been bothering me a little . . . this whole business about the stab wound and how it was made, the downward angle of it, you know?

THREE: Don't tell me we're gonna start that. They went over it and over it in court.

TWO: I know they did—but I don't go along with it. The boy is five feet eight inches tall. His father was six two. That's a difference of six inches. It's a very awkward thing to stab *down* into the chest of someone who's half a foot taller than you are.

Three jumps up, holding the knife.

THREE: Look, you're not going to be satisfied till you see it again. I'm going to give you a demonstration. Somebody get up.

He looks around the table. Eight stands up and walks toward him. Three closes the knife and puts it in his pocket. They stand face to face and look at each other for a moment.

THREE: Okay. [To Two] Now watch this. I don't want to have to do it again. [He crouches down now until he is quite a bit shorter than Eight.] Is that six inches?

TWELVE: That's more than six inches.

THREE: Okay, let it be more.

He reaches into his pocket and takes out the knife. He flicks it open, changes its position in his hand, and holds the knife aloft, ready to stab. He and Eight look steadily into each other's eyes. Then he stabs downward, hard.

TWO [shouting]: Look out!

He stops short just as the blade reaches Eight's chest. Three laughs.

SIX: That's not funny.

FIVE: What's the matter with you?

THREE: Now just calm down. Nobody's hurt, are they?

EIGHT [low]: No. Nobody's hurt.

THREE: All right. There's your angle. Take a look at it. Down and in. That's how I'd stab a taller man in the chest, and that's how it was done. Take a look at it and tell me I'm wrong.

Two doesn't answer. Three looks at him for a moment, then jams the knife into the table and sits down. They all look at the knife.

SIX: Down and in. I guess there's no argument.

Eight picks the knife out of the table and closes it. He flicks it open, and changing its position in his hand, stabs downward with it.

EIGHT [to Six]: Did you ever stab a man?

SIX: Of course not.

EIGHT [to Three]: Did you?

THREE: All right, let's not be silly.

EIGHT: Did you?

THREE [loud]: No, I didn't!

EIGHT: Where do you get all your information about how it's done?

THREE: What do you mean? It's just common sense.

EIGHT: Have you ever seen a man stabbed?

THREE [pauses and looks around the room nervously]: No.

EIGHT: All right. I want to ask you something. The boy was an experienced knife fighter. He was even sent to reform school for knifing someone, isn't that so?

TWELVE: That's right.

EIGHT: Look at this. [Eight closes the knife, flicks it open, and changes the position of the knife so that he can stab overhanded.] Doesn't it seem like an awkward way to handle a knife?

THREE: What are you asking me for?

Eight closes the blade and flicks it open, holds it ready to slash underhanded.

FIVE: Wait a minute! What's the matter with me? Give me that.

He reaches out for the knife.

EIGHT: Have you ever seen a knife fight?

FIVE: Yes, I have.

EIGHT: In the movies?

FIVE: In my back yard. On my stoop. In the vacant lot across the street. Too many of them. Switch-knives came with the neighborhood where I lived. Funny I didn't think of it before. I guess you try to forget those things. [Flicking the knife open]

Anyone who's ever used a switch-knife would never have stabbed downward. You don't handle a switch-knife that way. You use it underhanded.

EIGHT: Then he couldn't have made the kind of wound which killed his father.

FIVE: No. He couldn't have. Not if he'd ever had any experience with switch-knives.

THREE: I don't believe it.

TEN: Neither do I. You're giving us a lot of mumbo jumbo.

EIGHT [to Twelve]: What do you think?

TWELVE [hesitantly]: Well . . . I don't know.

EIGHT [to Seven]: What about you?

SEVEN: Listen, I'll tell you something. I'm a little sick of this whole thing already. We're getting nowhere fast. Let's break it up and go home. I'm changing my vote to not guilty.

THREE: You're what?

SEVEN: You heard me. I've had enough.

THREE: What do you mean, you've had enough? That's no answer.

ELEVEN [angry]: I think perhaps you're right. This is not an answer. [To Seven] What kind of a man are you? You have sat here and voted guilty with everyone else because there are some theater tickets burning a hole in your pocket. Now you have changed your vote for the same reason. I do not think you have the right to play like this with a man's life. This is an ugly and terrible thing to do.

SEVEN: Now wait a minute . . . you can't talk like that to me.

ELEVEN [strong]: I can talk like that to you! If you want to vote not guilty, then do it because you are convinced the man is not guilty. If you believe he is guilty, then vote that way. Or don't you have the . . . the . . . guts—the guts to do what you think is right?

SEVEN: Now listen. . . .

ELEVEN: Is it guilty or not guilty?

SEVEN [hesitantly]: I told you. Not . . . guilty.

ELEVEN [hard]: Why?

SEVEN: I don't have to ——

ELEVEN: You have to! Say it! Why?

They stare at each other for a long while.

SEVEN [low]: I . . . don't think . . . he's guilty.

EIGHT [fast]: I want another vote.

FOREMAN: Okay, there's another vote called for. I guess the quickest way is a show of hands. Anybody object? [No one does] All right. All those voting not guilty, raise your hands.

Two, Five, Six, Seven, Eight, Nine, and Eleven raise their hands immediately. Then, slowly, Twelve raises his hand. The foreman looks around the table carefully, and then he too raises his hand. He looks around the table, counting silently.

FOREMAN: Nine. [The hands go down.] All those voting guilty.

Three, Four, and Ten raise their hands.

FOREMAN: Three. [They lower their hands.] The vote is nine to three in favor of acquittal.

TEN: I don't understand you people. How can you believe this kid is innocent? Look, you know how those people lie. I don't have

to tell you. They don't know what the truth is. And lemme tell you, they—[Five gets up from table, turns his back to it, and goes to window.]—don't need any real big reason to kill someone either. You know, they get drunk, and *bang*, someone's lying in the gutter. Nobody's blaming them. That's how they are. You know what I mean? Violent!

Nine get up and does the same. He is followed by Eleven.

TEN: Human life don't mean as much to them as it does to us. Hey, where are you going? Look, these people are drinking and fighting all the time, and if somebody gets killed, so somebody gets killed. They don't care. Oh, sure there are some good things about them, too. Look, I'm the first to say that.

Eight gets up, and then Two and Six follow him to the window.

TEN: I've known a few who were pretty decent, but that's the exception. Most of them, it's like they have no feelings. They can do anything. What's going on here?

The foreman gets up and goes to the windows, followed by Seven and Twelve.

TEN: I'm speaking my piece, and you—Listen to me! They're no good. There's not a one of 'em who's any good. We better watch out. Take it from me. This kid on trial. . . .

Three sits at table toying with the knife, and Four gets up and starts for the window. All have their backs to Ten.

TEN: Well, don't you know about them? Listen to me! What are you doing? I'm trying to tell you something. . . .

Four stands over him as he trails off. There is a dead silence. Then Four speaks softly.

FOUR: I've had enough. If you open your mouth again, I'm going to split your skull.

Four stands there and looks at him. No one moves or speaks. Ten looks at him, then looks down at the table.

TEN [softly]: I'm only trying to tell you. . . .

There is a long pause as Four stares down at Ten.

FOUR [to all]: All right. Sit down everybody.

They all move back to their seats. When they are all seated, Four then sits down.

FOUR [quietly]: I still believe the boy is guilty of murder. I'll tell you why. To me, the most damning evidence was given by the woman across the street who claimed she actually saw the murder committed.
THREE: That's right. As far as I'm concerned, that's the most important testimony.
EIGHT: All right. Let's go over her testimony. What exactly did she say?
FOUR: I believe I can recount it accurately. She said that she went to bed at about eleven o'clock that night. Her bed was next to the open window, and she could look out of the window while lying down and see directly into the window across the street. She tossed and turned for over an hour, unable to fall asleep. Finally she turned toward the window at about twelve-ten and as she looked out, she saw the boy stab his father. As far as I can see, this is unshakable testimony.
THREE: That's what I mean. That's the whole case.

Four takes off his eyeglasses and begins to polish them, as they all sit silently watching him.

FOUR [to the jury]: Frankly, I don't see how you can vote for acquittal. [To Twelve] What do you think about it?

TWELVE: Well . . . maybe . . . there's so much evidence to sift.

THREE: What do you mean, maybe? He's absolutely right. You can throw out all the other evidence.

FOUR: That was my feeling.

Two, polishing his glasses, squints at clock, can't see it. Six watches him closely.

TWO: What time is it?

ELEVEN: Ten minutes of six.

TWO: It's late. You don't suppose they'd let us go home and finish it in the morning. I've got a kid with mumps.

FIVE: Not a chance.

SIX [to Two]: Pardon me. Can't you see the clock without your glasses?

TWO: Not clearly. Why?

SIX: Oh, I don't know. Look, this may be a dumb thought, but what do you do when you wake up at night and want to know what time it is?

TWO: What do you mean? I put on my glasses and look at the clock.

SIX: You don't wear them to bed.

TWO: Of course not. No one wears eyeglasses to bed.

TWELVE: What's all this for?

SIX: Well, I was thinking. You know the woman who testified that she saw the killing wears glasses.

THREE: So does my grandmother. So what?

EIGHT: Your grandmother isn't a murder witness.

SIX: Look, stop me if I'm wrong. This woman wouldn't wear her eyeglasses to bed, would she?

FOREMAN: Wait a minute! Did she wear glasses at all?

ELEVEN [excited]: Of course she did! The woman wore bifocals. I remember this very clearly. They looked quite strong.

NINE: That's right. Bifocals. She never took them off.

FOUR: She did wear glasses. Funny. I never thought of it.

EIGHT: Listen, she wasn't wearing them in bed. That's for sure. She testified that in the midst of her tossing and turning she rolled over and looked casually out the window. The murder was taking place as she looked out, and the lights went out a split second later. She couldn't have had time to put on her glasses. Now maybe she honestly thought she saw the boy kill his father. I say that she saw only a blur.

THREE: How do you know what she saw? Maybe she's far-sighted.

He looks around. No one answers.

THREE [loud]: How does he know all these things?

There is silence.

EIGHT: Does anyone think there still is not a reasonable doubt?

He looks around the room, then squarely at Ten. Ten looks down and shakes his head no.

THREE [loud]: I think he's guilty!
EIGHT [calmly]: Does anyone else?
FOUR [quietly]: No. I'm convinced.
EIGHT [to Three]: You're alone.
THREE: I don't care whether I'm alone or not! I have a right.
EIGHT: You have a right.

There is a pause. They all look at Three.

THREE: Well, I told you I think the kid's guilty. What else do you
    want?
EIGHT: Your arguments.

They all look at Three.

THREE: I gave you my arguments.
EIGHT: We're not convinced. We're waiting to hear them again. We
    have time.

Three runs to Four and grabs his arm.

THREE [pleading]: Listen. What's the matter with you? You're the guy.
    You made all the arguments. You can't turn now. A guilty
    man's gonna be walking the streets. A murderer. He's got to
    die! Stay with me.
FOUR: I'm sorry. There's a reasonable doubt in my mind.
EIGHT: We're waiting.

Three turns violently on him.

THREE [shouting]: Well, you're not going to intimidate me! [They all
    look at Three.] I'm entitled to my opinion! [No one answers him.]
    It's gonna be a hung jury! That's it!
EIGHT: There's nothing we can do about that, except hope that some
    night, maybe in a few months, you'll get some sleep.
FIVE: You're all alone.
NINE: It takes a great deal of courage to stand alone.

Three looks around at all of them for a long time. They sit silently, waiting for him to speak, and all of them despise him for his stubbornness. Then, suddenly, his face contorts as if he is about to cry, and he slams his fist down on the table.

THREE [thundering]: All right!

Three turns his back on them. There is silence for a moment and then the foreman goes to the door and knocks on it. It opens. The guard looks in and sees them all standing. The guard holds the door for them as they begin slowly to file out. Eight waits at the door as the others file past him. Finally he and Three are the only ones left. Three turns around and sees that they are alone. Slowly he moves toward the door. Then he stops at the table. He pulls the switch-knife out of the table and walks over to Eight with it. He holds it in the approved knife-fighter fashion and looks long and hard at Eight, pointing the knife at his belly. Eight stares back. Then Three turns the knife around. Eight takes it by the handle. Three exits. Eight closes the knife, puts it away and taking a last look around the room, exits, closing the door. The camera moves in close on the littered table in the empty room, and we clearly see a slip of crumpled paper on which are scribbled the words ''Not guilty.''

FADE OUT

DISCUSSION   1.   At the very beginning of the play, before the first vote is taken, what is Eight doing? How is what he is doing important to the play?

2.   Major characters in a play can be divided into *protagonists*—persons with whom the audience sympathizes—and *antagonists*—the hero's opponents. Who are the protagonists and the antagonists in this play? Explain.

3.   How do the opinions of the protagonists and antagonists differ on the following: (a) innocent until proven guilty; (b) past behavior indicates present behavior; and (c) justice is a slow and deliberate process? Which opinions do you share? Why?

4.   **Types.**   The characters you have just met in *Twelve Angry Men* are types. They are not shown as full, complete people. Basically, we see only one side of them. One trait is highlighted. Using types makes a character easy to remember, especially when there are time limitations as there are in a television play. So Rose deliberately portrayed these characters as types—a bigot (Ten), a just man (Eight), a humble immigrant (Eleven). What types do Three and Seven represent? How is the device heightened by the characters being numbered rather than named?

For further activities, see page 480.

VOCABULARY

400-Meter Freestyle (page 432)

There are several metaphors (see page 435) in the poem. On a separate piece of paper rewrite the three metaphors listed below in your own words. Then find two other metaphors in the poem and rewrite those.

1. His cadent feet tick in the stretch.
2. He has schooled out all extravagance.
3. The swimmer catapults and cracks six feet away.

O Black and Unknown Bards (page 442)

On a separate piece of paper, match the numbers in the left column with the letters in the right column.

1. lyre   a. evasive
2. minstrel   b. song of praise or joy
3. elusive   c. harplike instrument
4. valorous   d. highest reaches of heaven
5. paean   e. musician
6. empyrean   f. being brave

Shock (page 436)

There are many slang words or expressions that are used as accepted English. One example is the expression "Jim Crow" which you encountered in this selection. Below are other slang words that are used often. On a separate piece of paper write the definition of each expression and use it appropriately in a sentence. Try to find out how some of these expressions came into use.

1. long green   8. gyp joint
2. hotshot   9. kickback
3. Mickey Finn   10. hot seat
4. speakeasy   11. kick up a storm
5. kick the bucket   12. Bronx cheer
6. tin lizzie   13. cop out
7. old man   14. hot rod

COMPOSITION

Shock (page 436)

1. Imagine that you are interviewing Marian Anderson after she was refused admission to the music school. Write your interview as you think it would appear in a one-page magazine article.

2. Imagine that you are a news reporter for either television, radio, or newspaper. Write your coverage of Marian Anderson singing on the steps of the Lincoln Memorial to thousands of people in 1939. Do some research in the library so that you have as many facts regarding the occurrence as you think necessary to make it vivid.

Twelve Angry Men (page 444)

Jurors Three and Twelve are quite different in their appearances, attitudes, and beliefs. Write a character analysis in which you compare these two men.

READING

Twelve Angry Men (page 444)

Rose makes use of irony (see page 389) quite often throughout the play. On a separate piece of paper explain the irony of the following statements.

1. Ten: Human life don't mean as much to them as it does to us (page 475).
2. Three: He's an old man. You saw him. Half the time he was confused. How could he be positive about . . . anything (p. 465)?
3. Eleven: We have nothing to gain or lose by our verdict. This is one of the reasons why we are strong (p. 469).
4. Ten: Bright! He's a common, ignorant slob. He don't even speak good English (p. 463).
5. Three: Everybody gets a fair trial. . . . That's the system (p. 447).

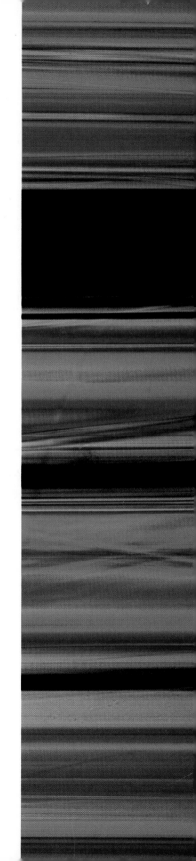

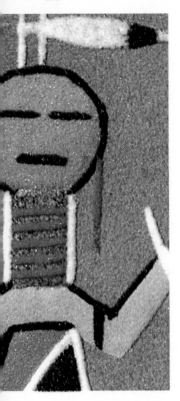

COMPOSITION

To be coherent, the second sentence of a paragraph should grow out of something that was written in the first, the third out of something written in the second, and so on.

A famous singer writes the following sentence:

I sensed the need for a formal musical education when I was in my teens and was beginning to make my first modest tours.

Having expressed that idea, she might then move in any one of several directions. For example, why did she sense the need at that time? Or, what does she mean by a "formal musical education"? Or, what kind of education had she had before then? Or, what details might be recalled about those first modest tours? But the direction the writer chooses is different from any of those. However, it is still coherent. She explains what she did about the need.

I decided, in fact, to see if I could not go to a music school.

The phrase "in fact" makes the *transition,* carries the reader forward from the need sensed in the first sentence to the decision in the second to do something about it. Now, having chosen to move in that direction, the writer must continue along that path to the end of the paragraph—must not, for instance, write now (in *this* paragraph) about why she sensed the need, or about the education received earlier. She must follow through on what she has begun to develop.

She senses a need, and decides to go to music school.

I did not know whether we could afford it, but I thought that I ought to find out.

What does "it" in that sentence refer to? To the music school in the preceding sentence of the paragraph. Thus, the transition to the third sentence is made by the pronoun "it."

Mother encouraged me, and so did other friends, but I had no idea where to turn until. . . .

That final sentence of the paragraph on page 437 grows out of the preceding idea, "I ought to find out." But, the paragraph concludes, I didn't know where to turn—how to find out—until someone mentioned a specific music school.

Thus, each sentence in Marian Anderson's paragraph leads into the next, as your sentences should. And all her transitions are clear—as yours, too, should be.

**MAKING
TRANSITIONS**

ABOUT THE SELECTIONS

1. What was the most challenging single moment you encountered in this section? Was it with eleven-year-old Jerry in the depths of the tunnel (page 398)? Was it one of the fateful moments at Pearl Harbor in 1941 that Daniel Inouye describes? Was it at some point during the deliberations in *Twelve Angry Men?* Decide which moment in your opinion required the most courage to live through, then write two or three unified and coherent paragraphs giving specific reasons for your choice.

2. *Twelve Angry Men* unfolds its story in the form of a play. Choose some other appropriate selection in the section and relate a portion of it as a play, entirely through stage directions and dialogue. Marian Anderson applying to music school (page 436) would be one of several possibilities.

3. Choose one of the following:

   a. Write a brief poem with a shape that imitates what it is describing, as the lines of ''400-Meter Freestyle'' imitate the back-and-forth path of a swimmer in a race.

   b. Write a poem of two stanzas that contrasts the same spot in two different seasons of the year. The idea is suggested by ''Black Water and Bright Air,'' but yours may be much simpler than that poem. Make your contrasting scenes vivid, though.

4. Consider the paragraph in ''Through the Tunnel'' beginning, ''As for Jerry, once he saw that his mother had gained her beach . . .'' (page 399). Specifically, what words carry the thought forward from sentence to sentence, to the end of the paragraph? In a paragraph of your own, identify and explain the transitional words or expressions that give coherence to the paragraph in the story.

ON YOUR OWN

1. Think of some challenge you have undertaken—and either overcome or failed to surmount. Write about it accurately and coherently. Be specific about what the challenge was, what was at stake and why it mattered, and how you succeeded or why you failed in meeting it.

2. Imagine yourself faced with some challenge—walking on the moon, winning a medal in the Olympics, auditioning for a play. Write an account of what happens and how you feel about it. Include details to make the experience seem real. What do you hear, see, think, feel? A little research at the library will help you make your account sound authentic.

3. Here are four transitional expressions—*however, consequently, for example, moreover.* Place them appropriately in the following paragraph.

   Grace hates doing most household chores. _____, she hates cleaning windows, washing clothes, scrubbing woodwork, polishing silver. _____, she earns enough money at her job to hire a cleaning service to come in once a week. _____, she does feel that some part of life should be spent doing what you don't necessarily enjoy, just for the discipline of it. _____, she does most of the housework herself.

THE FLOW

OF TIME

From ECCLESIASTES

To every thing there is a season,
And a time to every purpose under the heaven:
A time to be born, and a time to die;
A time to plant, and a time to pluck up that which is planted;
A time to kill, and a time to heal;
A time to break down, and a time to build up;
A time to weep, and a time to laugh;
A time to mourn, and a time to dance;
A time to cast away stones, and a time to gather stones together;
A time to embrace, and a time to refrain from embracing;
A time to get, and a time to lose;
A time to keep, and a time to cast away;
A time to rend, and a time to sew;
A time to keep silence, and a time to speak;
A time to love, and a time to hate;
A time of war, and a time of peace.

THE KING JAMES BIBLE

Something Bright

ZENNA HENDERSON

Do you remember the Depression? That black shadow across time? That hurting place in the consciousness of the world? Maybe not. Maybe it's like asking do you remember the Dark Ages. Except what would I know about the price of eggs in the Dark Ages? I knew plenty about prices in the Depression.

If you had a quarter—*first find your quarter*—and five hungry kids, you could supper them on two cans of soup and a loaf of day-old bread, or two quarts of milk and a loaf of day-old bread. It was filling and—in an after-thoughty kind of way—nourishing. But if you were one of the hungry five, you eventually began to feel erosion set in, and your teeth ached for substance.

But to go back to eggs. Those were a precious commodity. You savored them slowly or gulped them eagerly—unmistakably as eggs—boiled or fried. That's one reason why I remember Mrs. Klevity. She had eggs for *breakfast!* And *every day!* That's *one* reason why I remember Mrs. Klevity.

I didn't know about the eggs the time she came over to see Mom, who had just got home from a twelve-hour day, cleaning up after other people at thirty cents an hour. Mrs. Klevity lived in the same court as we did. Courtesy called it a court because we were all dependent on the same shower house and two toilets that occupied the shack square in the middle of the court.

All of us except the Big House, of course. It had a bathroom of its own and even a radio blaring "Nobody's Business" and "Should I Reveal" and had ceiling lights that didn't dangle nakedly at the end of a cord. But then it really wasn't a part of the court. Only its back door shared our area, and even that was different. It had *two* back doors in the same frame—a screen one and a wooden one!

Our own two-room place had a distinction, too. It had an upstairs. One room the size of our two. The Man Upstairs lived up there. He was mostly only the sound of footsteps overhead and an occasional cookie for Danna.

Anyway, Mrs. Klevity came over before Mom had time to put her shopping bag of work clothes down or even to unpleat the folds of fatigue that dragged her face down ten years or more of time to come. I didn't much like Mrs. Klevity. She made me uncomfortable. She was so solid and slow-moving and so nearly blind that she peered frighteningly wherever she went. She stood in the doorway as though she had been stacked there

like bricks and a dress drawn hastily
down over the stack and a face
sketched on beneath a fuzz of hair.
Us kids all gathered around to watch,
except Danna who snuffled wearily
into my neck. Day nursery or not, it
was a long, hard day for a four-year-
old.

"I wondered if one of your girls
could sleep at my house this week."
Her voice was as slow as her steps.

"At your house?" Mom massaged
her hand where the shopping-bag
handles had crisscrossed it. "Come in.
Sit down." We had two chairs and a
bench and two apple boxes. The
boxes scratched bare legs, but surely
they couldn't scratch a stack of
bricks.

"No, thanks." Maybe she
couldn't bend! "My husband will be

away several days and I don't like to be in the house alone at night."

"Of course," said Mom. "You must feel awfully alone."

The only aloneness *she* knew, what with five kids and two rooms, was the taut secretness of her inward thoughts as she mopped and swept and ironed in other houses. "Sure, one of the girls would be glad to keep you company." There was a darting squirm and LaNell was safely hidden behind the swaying of our clothes in the diagonally curtained corner of the Other room, and Kathy knelt swiftly just beyond the dresser, out of sight.

"Anna is eleven." I had no place to hide, burdened as I was with Danna. "She's old enough. What time do you want her to come over?"

"Oh, bedtime will do." Mrs. Klevity peered out the door at the darkening sky. "Nine o'clock. Only it gets dark before then——" Bricks can look anxious, I guess.

"As soon as she has supper, she can come," said Mom, handling my hours as though they had no value to me. "Of course she has to go to school tomorrow."

"Only when it's dark," said Mrs. Klevity. "Day is all right. How much should I pay you?"

"Pay?" Mom gestured with one hand. "She has to sleep anyway. It doesn't matter to her where, once she's asleep. A favor for a friend."

I wanted to cry out: whose favor for what friend? We hardly passed the time of day with Mrs. Klevity. I couldn't even remember Mr. Klevity except that he was straight and old and wrinkled. Uproot me and make me lie in a strange house, a strange dark, listening to a strange breathing, feeling a strange warmth making itself part of me for all night long, seeping into me. . . .

"Mom——" I said.

"I'll give her breakfast," said Mrs. Klevity. "And lunch money for each night she comes."

I resigned myself without a struggle. Lunch money each day—a whole dime! Mom couldn't afford to pass up such a blessing, such a gift from God, who unerringly could be trusted to ease the pinch just before it became intolerable.

"Thank you, God," I whispered as I went to get the can opener to open supper. For a night or two I could stand it.

I felt all naked and unprotected as I stood in my flimsy crinkle cotton pajamas, one bare foot atop the other, waiting for Mrs. Klevity to turn the bed down.

"We have to check the house first," she said thickly. "We can't go to bed until we check the house."

"Check the house?" I forgot my starchy stiff shyness enough to question. "What for?"

Mrs. Klevity peered at me in the dim light of the bedroom. They had *three* rooms for only the two of them! Even if there was no door to shut between the bedroom and the kitchen.

"I couldn't sleep," she said, "unless I looked first. I have to."

So we looked. Behind the closet curtain, under the table—Mrs. Klevity even looked in the portable oven that sat near the two-burner stove in the kitchen.

When we came to the bed, I was moved to words again. "But we've been in here with the doors locked ever since I got here. What could possibly——"

"A prowler?" said Mrs. Klevity nervously, after a brief pause for thought. "A criminal?"

Mrs. Klevity pointed her face at me. I doubt if she could see me from that distance. "Doors make no difference," she said. "It might be when you least expect, so you have to expect all the time."

"I'll look," I said humbly. She was older than Mom. She was nearly blind. She was one of God's *Also Unto Me's.*

"No," she said. "I have to. I couldn't be sure, else."

So I waited until she grunted and groaned to her knees, then bent stiffly to lift the limp spread. Her fingers hesitated briefly, then flicked the spread up. Her breath came out flat and finished. Almost disappointed, it seemed to me.

She turned the bed down and I crept across the gray, wrinkled sheets and, turning my back to the room, I huddled one ear on the flat tobacco-smelling pillow and lay tense and uncomfortable in the dark, as her weight shaped and reshaped the bed around me. There was a brief silence before I heard the soundless breathy shape of her words, "How long, O God, how long?"

I wondered through my auto-

matic *Bless Papa and Mama*—and the automatic back-up because Papa had abdicated from my specific prayers—*bless Mama and my brother and sisters*—what it was that Mrs. Klevity was finding too long to bear.

After a restless waking, dozing sort of night that strange sleeping places held for me, I awoke to a thin, chilly morning and the sound of Mrs. Klevity moving around. She had set the table for breakfast, a formality we never had time for at home. I scrambled out of bed and into my clothes with only my skinny, gooseflesh back between Mrs. Klevity and me for modesty. I felt uncomfortable and unfinished because I hadn't brought our comb over with me.

I would have preferred to run home to our usual breakfast of canned milk and shredded wheat, but instead I watched, fascinated, as Mrs. Klevity struggled with lighting the kerosene stove. She bent so close, peering at the burners with the match flaring in her hand that I was sure the frowzy brush of her hair would catch fire, but finally the burner caught instead and she turned her face toward me.

"One egg or two?" she asked.

"Eggs! Two!" Surprise wrung the exclamation from me. Her hand hesitated over the crumpled brown bag on the table. "No, no!" I corrected her thought hastily. "One. One is plenty." And sat on the edge of a chair watching as she broke an egg into the sizzling frying pan.

"Hard or soft?" she asked.

"Hard," I said casually, feeling

very woman-of-the-worldish, dining
out—well, practically—and for breakfast, too! I watched Mrs. Klevity
spoon the fat over the egg, her hair
swinging stiffly forward when she
peered. Once it even dabbled briefly
in the fat, but she didn't notice and,
as it swung back, it made a little
shiny curve on her cheek.

"Aren't you afraid of the fire?" I
asked as she turned away from the
stove with the frying pan. "What if
you caught on fire?"

"I did once." She slid the egg out
onto my plate. "See?" She brushed
her hair back on the left side and I
could see the mottled pucker of a

large old scar. "It was before I got
used to Here," she said, making Here
more than the house, it seemed to
me.

"That's awful," I said, hesitating
with my fork.

"Go ahead and eat," she said.
"Your egg will get cold." She turned
back to the stove and I hesitated a
minute more. Meals at a table you
were supposed to ask a blessing, but
. . . I ducked my head quickly and
had a mouthful of egg before my
soundless amen was finished.

After breakfast I hurried back to
our house, my lunch-money dime
clutched securely, my stomach not
quite sure it liked fried eggs so early

in the morning. Mom was ready to leave, her shopping bag in one hand, Danna swinging from the other, singing one of her baby songs. She *liked* the day nursery.

"I won't be back until late tonight," Mom said. "There's a quarter in the corner of the dresser drawer. You get supper for the kids and try to clean up this messy place. We don't have to be pigs just because we live in a place like this."

"Okay, Mom," I struggled with a snarl in my hair, the pulling making my eyes water. "Where you working today?" I spoke over the clatter in the other room where the kids were getting ready for school.

She sighed, weary before the day began. "I have three places today, but the last is Mrs. Paddington." Her face lightened. Mrs. Paddington sometimes paid a little extra or gave Mom discarded clothes or leftover food she didn't want. She was nice.

"You get along all right with Mrs. Klevity?" asked Mom as she checked her shopping bag for her work shoes.

"Yeah," I said. "But she's funny. She looks under the bed before she goes to bed."

Mom smiled. "I've heard of people like that, but it's usually old maids they're talking about."

"But, Mom, nothing coulda got in. She locked the door after I got there."

"People who look under beds don't always think straight," she said. "Besides, maybe she'd *like* to find something under there."

"But she's *got* a husband," I cried after her as she herded Danna across the court.

"There are other things to look for beside husbands," she called back.

"Anna wants a husband! Anna wants a husband!" Deet and LaNell were dancing around me, teasing me singsong. Kathy smiled slowly behind them.

"Shut up," I said. "You don't even know what you're talking about. Go on to school."

"It's too early," said Deet, digging his bare toes in the dust of the front yard. "Teacher says we get there too early."

"Then stay here and start cleaning house," I said.

They left in a hurry. After they were gone, Deet's feet reminded me I'd better wash my own feet before I went to school. So I got a washpan of water from the tap in the middle of the court and, sitting on the side of the bed, I eased my feet into the icy water. I scrubbed with the hard, gray, abrasive soap we used and wiped quickly on the tattered towel. I threw the water out the door and watched it run like dust-covered snakes across the hard-packed front yard.

I went back to put my shoes on and get my sweater. I looked at the bed. I got down on my stomach and peered under. *Other things to look for.* There was the familiar huddle of cardboard cartons we kept things in and the familiar dust fluffs and one green sock LaNell had lost last week, but nothing else.

I dusted my front off. I tied my

lunch-money dime in the corner of a handkerchief and, putting my sweater on, left for school.

I peered out into the windy wet semi-twilight. "Do I have to?"

"You said you would," said Mom. "Keep your promises. You should have gone before this. She's probably been waiting for you."

"I wanted to see what you brought from Mrs. Paddington's." La-Nell and Kathy were playing in the corner with a lavender hug-me-tight and a hat with green grapes on it. Deet was rolling an orange on the floor, softening it preliminary to poking a hole in it to suck the juice out.

"She cleaned a trunk out today," said Mom, "Mostly old things that belonged to her mother, but these two coats are nice and heavy. They'll be good covers tonight. It's going to be cold. Someday when I get time, I'll cut them up and make quilts." She sighed. Time was what she never had enough of. "Better take a newspaper to hold over your head."

"Oh, Mom!" I huddled into my sweater. "It isn't raining now. I'd feel silly!"

"Well, then, scoot!" she said, her hand pressing my shoulder warmly, briefly.

I scooted, skimming quickly the flood of light from our doorway, and splishing though the shallow run-off stream that swept across the court. There was a sudden wild swirl of wind and a vindictive splatter of heavy, cold raindrops that swept me, exhilarated, the rest of the way to Mrs. Klevity's house and under the shallow little roof that was just big enough to cover the back step. I knocked quickly, brushing my disordered hair back from my eyes. The door swung open and I was in the shadowy, warm kitchen, almost in Mrs. Klevity's arms.

"Oh!" I backed up, laughing breathlessly. "The wind blew——"

"I was afraid you weren't coming." She turned away to the stove. "I fixed some hot cocoa."

I sat cuddling the warm cup in my hands, savoring the chocolate sip by sip. She had made it with milk instead of water, and it tasted rich and wonderful. But Mrs. Klevity was sharing my thoughts with the cocoa. In that brief moment when I had been so close to her, I had looked deep into her dim eyes and was feeling a vast astonishment. The dimness was only on top. Underneath—underneath——

I took another sip of cocoa. Her eyes—almost I could have walked into them, it seemed like. Slip past the gray film, run down the shiny bright corridor, into the live young sparkle at the far end.

I looked deep into my cup of cocoa. Were all grownups like that? If you could get behind their eyes, were they different, too? Behind Mom's eyes, was there a corridor leading back to youth and sparkle?

I finished the cocoa drowsily. It was still early, but the rain was drumming on the roof and it was the kind of night you curl up to if you're warm and fed. Sometimes you feel thin and cold on such nights, but I was feeling curl-uppy. So I groped under the bed for the paper bag that had my jammas in it. I couldn't find it.

"I swept today," said Mrs. Klevity, coming back from some far country of her thoughts. "I musta pushed it farther under the bed."

I got down on my hands and knees and peered under the bed. "Ooo!" I said. "What's shiny?"

Something snatched me away from the bed and flung me to one side. By the time I had gathered myself up off the floor and was rubbing a banged elbow, Mrs. Klevity's bulk was pressed against the bed, her head under it.

"Hey!" I cried indignantly, and then remembered I wasn't at home. I heard an odd whimpering sob and then Mrs. Klevity backed slowly away, still kneeling on the floor.

"Only the lock on the suitcase," she said. "Here's your jammas." She handed me the bag and ponderously pulled herself upright again.

We went silently to bed after she had limped around and checked the house, even under the bed again. I heard that odd breathy whisper of a prayer and lay awake, trying to add up something shiny and the odd eyes and the whispering sob. Finally I shrugged in the dark and wondered what I'd pick for funny when I grew up. All grownups had some kind of funny.

The next night Mrs. Klevity couldn't get down on her knees to look under the bed. She'd hurt herself when she

plumped down on the floor after yanking me away from the bed.

"You'll have to look for me tonight," she said slowly, nursing her knees. "Look good. Oh, Anna, look good!"

I looked as good as I could, not knowing what I was looking for.

"It should be under the bed," she said, her palms tight on her knees as she rocked back and forth. "But you can't be sure. It might miss completely."

"What might?" I asked, hunkering down by the bed.

She turned her face blindly toward me. "The way out," she said. "The way back again——"

"Back again?" I pressed my cheek to the floor again. "Well, I don't see anything. Only dark and suitcases."

"Nothing bright? Nothing? Nothing——" She tried to lay her face on her knees, but she was too unbendy to manage it, so she put her hands over her face instead. Grownups aren't suppose to cry. She didn't quite, but her hands looked wet when she reached for the clock to wind it.

I lay in the dark, one strand of her hair tickling my hand where it lay on the pillow. Maybe she was crazy. I felt a thrill of terror fan out on my spine. I carefully moved my hand from under the lock of hair. How can you find a way *out* under a *bed?* I'd be glad when Mr. Klevity got home, eggs or no eggs, dime or no dime.

Somewhere in the darkness of the night, I was suddenly swimming to wakefulness, not knowing what was waking me but feeling that Mrs. Klevity was awake too.

"Anna." Her voice was small and light and silver. "Anna——"

"Hummm?" I murmured, my voice still drowsy.

"Anna, have you ever been away from home?" I turned toward her, trying in the dark to make sure it was Mrs. Klevity. She sounded so different.

"Yes," I said. "Once I visited Aunt Katie at Rocky Butte for a week."

"Anna." I don't know whether she was even hearing my answers; her voice was almost a chant. "Anna, have you ever been in prison?"

"No! Of course not!" I recoiled indignantly. "You have to be awfully bad to be in prison."

"Oh, no. Oh, no!" she sighed. "Not jail, Anna. Prison, prison. The weight of the flesh—bound about——"

"Oh," I said, smoothing my hands across my eyes. She was talking to a something deep in me that never got talked to, that hardly even had words. "Like when the wind blows the clouds across the moon and the grass whispers along the road and all the trees pull like balloons at their trunks and one star comes out and

says 'Come' and the ground says 'Stay' and part of you tries to go and it hurts——" I could feel the slender roundness of my ribs under my pressing hands. "And it hurts——"

"Oh, Anna, Anna!" The soft, light voice broke. "You feel that way and you *belong* Here. You won't ever——"

The voice stopped and Mrs. Klevity rolled over. Her next words came thickly, as though a gray film were over them as over her eyes. "Are you awake, Anna? Go to sleep, child. Morning isn't yet."

I heard the heavy sigh of her breathing as she slept. And finally I slept too, trying to visualize what Mrs. Klevity would look like if she looked like the silvery voice-in-the-dark.

I sat savoring my egg the next morning, letting thoughts slip in and out of my mind to the rhythm of my jaws. What a funny dream to have, to talk with a silver-voiced someone. To talk about the way blowing clouds and windy moonlight felt. But it wasn't a dream! I paused with my fork raised. At least not my dream. But how can you tell? If you're part of someone else's dream, can it still be real for you?

"Is something wrong with the egg?" Mrs. Klevity peered at me.

"No—no——" I said, hastily snatching the bite on my fork. "Mrs. Klevity——"

"Yes." Her voice was thick and heavy-footed.

"Why did you ask me about being in prison?"

"Prison?" Mrs. Klevity blinked blindly. "Did I ask you about prison?"

"Someone did—I thought——" I faltered, shyness shutting down on me again.

"Dreams." Mrs. Klevity stacked her knife on her plate. "Dreams."

I wasn't quite sure I was to be at Mrs. Klevity's the next evening. Mr. Klevity was supposed to get back sometime during the evening. But Mrs. Klevity welcomed me.

"Don't know when he'll get home," she said. "Maybe not until morning. If he comes early, you can go home to sleep and I'll give you your dime anyway."

"Oh, no," I said, Mom's teaching solidly behind me. "I couldn't take it if I didn't stay."

"A gift," said Mrs. Klevity.

We sat opposite one another until the silence stretched too thin for me to bear.

"In olden times," I said, snatching at the magic that drew stories from Mom, "when you were a little girl——"

"When I was a girl——" Mrs. Klevity rubbed her knees with reflective hands. "The other Where. The other When."

"In olden times," I persisted, "things were different then."

"Yes." I settled down comfortably, recognizing the reminiscent tone of voice. "You do crazy things when you are young." Mrs. Klevity leaned heavily on the table. "Things you have no business doing. You volunteer when you're young." I jerked as she lunged across the table and grabbed both my arms. "But I *am* young! Three years isn't an eternity. I *am* young!"

I twisted one arm free and pried at her steely fingers that clamped my other one.

"Oh." She let go. "I'm sorry. I didn't mean to hurt you."

She pushed back the tousled brush of her hair.

"Look," she said, her voice was almost silver again. "Under all this— this grossness, I'm still me. I thought I could adjust to anything, but I had no idea that they'd put me in such——" She tugged at her sagging dress. "Not the clothes!" she cried. "Clothes you can take off. But this——" Her fingers dug into her heavy shoulder and I could see the bulge of flesh between them.

"If I knew *anything* about the setup maybe I could locate it. Maybe I could call. Maybe——"

Her shoulders sagged and her eyelids dropped down over her dull eyes.

"It doesn't make any sense to you," she said, her voice heavy and thick again. "To you I'd be old even There. At the time it seemed like a perfect way to have an odd holiday and help out with research, too. But we got caught."

She began to count her fingers mumbling to herself. "Three years There,

but Here that's—eight threes are——" She traced on the table with a blunt forefinger, her eyes close to the old, wornout cloth.

"Mrs. Klevity." My voice scared me in the silence, but I was feeling the same sort of upsurge that catches you sometimes when you're playing-like and it gets so real. "Mrs. Klevity, if you've lost something, maybe I could look for it for you."

"You didn't find it last night," she said.

"Find what?"

She lumbered to her feet. "Let's look again. Everywhere. They'd surely be able to locate the house."

"What are we looking for?" I asked, searching the portable oven.

"You'll know it when we see it," she said.

And we searched the whole house. Oh, such nice things! Blankets, not tattered and worn, and even an extra one they didn't need. And towels with wash rags that matched—and weren't rags. And uncracked dishes that matched! And glasses that weren't jars. And books. And money. Crisp new-looking bills in the little box in the bottom drawer— pushed back under some *extra* pillow cases. And clothes—lots and lots of clothes. All too big for any of us, of course, but my practiced eye had already visualized this, that, and the other cut down to dress us all like rich people.

I sighed as we sat wearily looking at one another. Imagine having so much and still looking for something else! It was bedtime and all we had for our pains were dirty hands and tired backs.

I scooted out to the bath house before I undressed. I gingerly washed the dirt off my hands under the cold of the shower and shook them dry on the way back to the house. Well, we had moved everything in the place, but nothing was what Mrs. Klevity looked for.

Back in the bedroom, I groped under the bed for my jammas and again had to lie flat and burrow under the bed for the tattered bag. Our moving around had wedged it back between two cardboard cartons. I squirmed under farther and tried to ease it out after shoving the two cartons a little farther apart. The bag tore, spilling out my jammas, so I grasped them in the bend of my elbow and started to back out.

Then the whole world seemed to explode into brightness that pulsated and dazzled, that splashed brilliance into my astonished eyes until I winced them shut to rest their seeing and saw the dark inversions of the radiance behind my eyelids.

I forced my eyes open again and looked sideways so the edge of my seeing was all I used until I got more accustomed to the glory.

Between the two cartons was an opening like a window would be, but little, little, into a wonderland of things I could never tell. Colors that had no names. Feelings that made windy moonlight a puddle of dust. I felt tears burn out of my eyes and

start down my cheeks, whether from brightness or wonder, I don't know. I blinked them away and looked again.

Someone was in the brightness, several someones. They were leaning out of the squareness, beckoning and calling—silver signals and silver sounds.

"Mrs. Klevity," I thought. "Something bright."

I took another good look at the shining people and the tree things that were like music bordering a road, and grass that was the song my evening grass hummed in the wind—a last, last look, and began to back out.

I scrambled to my feet, clutching my jammas. "Mrs. Klevity." She was still sitting at the table, as solid as a pile of bricks, the sketched face under the wild hair a sad, sad one.

"Yes, child." She hardly heard herself.

"Something bright . . ." I said.

Her heavy head lifted slowly, her blind face turned to me. "What, child?"

I felt my fingers bite into my jammas and the cords in my neck getting tight and my stomach clenching itself. "Something bright!" I thought I screamed. She didn't move. I grabbed her arm and dragged her off-balance in her chair. "Something bright!"

"Anna." She righted herself on the chair. "Don't be mean."

I grabbed the bedspread and yanked it up. The light sprayed out like a sprinkler on a lawn.

Then *she* screamed. She put both hands up to her heavy face and screamed, "Leolienn! It's here! Hurry, hurry!"

"Mr. Klevity isn't here," I said. "He hasn't got back."

"I can't go without him! Leolienn!"

"Leave a note!" I cried. "If you're there, you can make them come back again and I can show him the right place!" The upsurge had passed make-believe and everything was realer than real.

Then, quicker than I ever thought she could move, she got paper and a pencil. She was scribbling away at the table as I stood there holding the spread. So I dropped to my knees and then to my stomach and crawled under the bed again. I filled my eyes with the brightness and beauty and saw, beyond it, serenity and orderliness and—and uncluttered cleanness. The miniature landscape was like a stage setting for a fairy tale—so small, so small—so lovely.

And then Mrs. Klevity tugged at my ankle and I slid out, reluctantly stretching my sight of the bright square until the falling of the spread broke it. Mrs. Klevity worked her way under the bed, her breath coming pantingly, her big, ungainly body inching along awkwardly.

She crawled and crawled and crawled until she should have come up short against the wall, and I knew she must be funneling down into the brightness, her face, head, and shoulders, so small, so lovely, like her silvery voice. But the rest of her, still

gross and ugly, like a butterfly trying to skin out of its cocoon.

Finally only her feet were sticking out from under the bed and they thrashed and waved and didn't go anywhere, so I got down on the floor and put my feet against hers and braced myself against the dresser and pushed. And pushed and pushed. Suddenly there was a going, a finishing, and my feet dropped to the floor.

There, almost under the bed, lay Mrs. Klevity's shabby old-lady black shoes, toes pointing away from each other. I picked them up in my hands, wanting, somehow, to cry. Her saggy lisle stockings were still in the shoes.

Slowly I pulled all of the clothes of Mrs. Klevity out from under the bed. They were held together by a thin skin, a sloughed-off leftover of Mrs. Klevity that only showed, gray and lifeless, where her bare hands and face would have been, and her dull gray filmed eyes.

I let it crumple to the floor and sat there, holding one of her old shoes in my hand.

The door rattled and it was gray, old, wrinkled Mr. Klevity.

"Hello, child," he said. "Where's my wife?"

"She's gone," I said, not looking at him. "She left you a note there on the table."

"Gone——?" He left the word stranded in mid-air as he read Mrs. Klevity's note.

The paper fluttered down. He yanked a dresser drawer open and snatched out spool-looking things, both hands full. Then he practically dived under the bed, his elbows thudding on the floor, to hurt hard. And there was only a wiggle or two and *his* shoes slumped away from each other.

I pulled his cast-aside from under the bed and crawled under it myself. I saw the tiny picture frame—bright, bright, but so small.

I crept close to it, knowing I couldn't go in. I saw the tiny perfection of the road, the landscape, the people—the laughing people who crowded around the two new rejoicing figures—the two silvery, lovely young creatures who cried out in tiny voices as they danced. The girl-one threw a kiss outward before they all turned away and ran up the winding white road together.

The frame began to shrink, faster, faster, until it squeezed to a single bright bead and then blinked out.

All at once the house was empty and cold. The upsurge was gone. Nothing was real any more. All at once the faint ghost of the smell of eggs was frightening. All at once I whimpered, "My lunch money!"

I scrambled to my feet, tumbling Mrs. Klevity's clothes into a disconnected pile. I gathered up my jammas and leaned across the table to get my sweater. I saw my name on a piece of paper. I picked it up and read it.

Everything that is ours in this house now belongs to Anna-across-the-court, the little girl that's been staying with me at night.

Ahvlaree Klevity

I looked from the paper across the room. All for me? All for us? All this richness and wonder of good things? All this and the box in the bottom drawer, too? And a paper that said so, so that nobody could take them away from us.

A fluttering wonder filled my chest and I walked stiffly around the three rooms, visualizing everything without opening a drawer or door. I stood by the stove and looked at the frying pan hanging above it. I opened the cupboard door. The paper bag of eggs was on the shelf. I reached for it, looking back over my shoulder almost guiltily.

The wonder drained out of me with a gulp. I ran back over to the bed and yanked up the spread. I knelt and hammered on the edge of the bed with my clenched fists. Then I leaned my forehead on my tight hands and felt my knuckles bruise me. My hands went limply to my lap, my head drooping.

I got up slowly and took the paper from the table, bundled my jammas under my arm and got the eggs from the cupboard. I turned the lights out and left.

I felt tears wash down from my eyes as I stumbled across the familiar yard in the dark. I don't know why I was crying—unless it was because I was homesick for something bright that I knew I would never have, and because I knew I could never tell Mom what really happened.

Then the pale trail of light from our door caught me and I swept in on an astonished Mom, calling softly, because of the sleeping kids, "Mom! Mom! Guess what!"

Yes, I remember Mrs. Klevity because she had eggs for *breakfast! Every day!* That's *one* of the reasons I remember her.

DISCUSSION

1. What does Mrs. Klevity mean by "prison" when she asks, "Anna, have you ever been in prison?" Once Anna understands that Mrs. Klevity does not mean a literal jail, how does she react? Does she feel that she is in "prison" in any way? Explain.

2. Anna remembers Mrs. Klevity because she had eggs for breakfast. "That's *one* of the reasons," Anna says. Another is of course Mrs. Klevity's unusual exit. Why else might Anna remember Mrs. Klevity? What do you think Anna learned from the experience?

For further activities, see page 532.

Metropolitan Nightmare

STEPHEN VINCENT BENÉT

It rained quite a lot that spring. You woke in the morning
And saw the sky still clouded, the streets still wet,
But nobody noticed so much, except the taxis
And the people who parade. You don't, in a city.
The parks got very green. All the trees were green   5
Far into July and August, heavy with leaf,
Heavy with leaf and the long roots boring and spreading,
But nobody noticed that but the city gardeners
And they don't talk.
                         Oh, on Sundays, perhaps you'd notice: 10
Walking through certain blocks, by the shut, proud houses
With the windows boarded, the people gone away,

You'd suddenly see the queerest small shoots of green
Poking through cracks and crevices in the stone
And a bird-sown flower, red on a balcony,   15
But then you made jokes about grass growing in the streets
And politics and grass-roots—and there were songs
And gags and a musical show called "Hot and Wet."
It all made a good box for the papers. When the flamingo
Flew into a meeting of the Board of Estimate,   20
The new mayor acted at once and called the photographers.
When the first green creeper crawled upon Brooklyn Bridge,
They thought it was ornamental. They let it stay.

That was the year the termites came to New York
And they don't do well in cold climates—but listen, Joe,   25
They're only ants, and ants are nothing but insects.

It was funny and yet rather wistful, in a way
(As Heywood Broun pointed out in the *World-Telegram*)
To think of them looking for wood in a steel city.
It made you feel about life. It was too divine.   30
There were funny pictures by all the smart, funny artists
And Macy's ran a terribly clever ad:
"The Widow's Termite" or something.
                                          There was no
Disturbance. Even the Communists didn't protest   35
And say they were Morgan hirelings. It was too hot,
Too hot to protest, too hot to get excited,
An even African heat, lush, fertile and steamy,
That soaked into bone and mind and never once broke.
The warm rain fell in fierce showers and ceased and fell.   40
Pretty soon you got used to its always being that way.

You got used to the changed rhythm, the altered beat,
To people walking slower, to the whole bright
Fierce pulse of the city slowing, to men in shorts,
To the new sun-helmets from Best's and the cops' white uniforms,   45
And the long noon-rest in the offices, everywhere.
It wasn't a plan or anything. It just happened.
The fingers tapped slower, the office-boys
Dozed on their benches, the bookkeeper yawned at his desk.
The A.T.&T. was the first to change the shifts   50
And establish an official siesta-room;
But they were always efficient. Mostly it just
Happened like sleep itself, like a tropic sleep,
Till even the Thirties were deserted at noon
Except for a few tourists and one damp cop.   55
They ran boats to see the big lilies on the North River
But it was only the tourists who really noticed
The flocks of rose-and-green parrots and parakeets
Nesting in the stone crannies of the Cathedral.
The rest of us had forgotten when they first came.   60
There wasn't any real change, it was just a heat spell,
A rain spell, a funny summer, a weather-man's joke,
In spite of the geraniums three feet high
In the tin-can gardens of Hester and Desbrosses.

36. *Morgan hirelings:* people hired by J.P. Morgan, an extremely rich and powerful man.

New York was New York. It couldn't turn inside out.   65
When they got the news from Woods Hole about the Gulf Stream,
The *Times* ran an adequate story.
But nobody reads those stories but science-cranks.

Until, one day, a somnolent city-editor
Gave a new cub the termite yarn to break his teeth on.   70
The cub was just down from Vermont, so he took his time.
He was serious about it. He went around.
He read all about termites in the Public Library
And it made him sore when they fired him.
                        So, one evening,   75
Talking with an old watchman, beside the first
Raw girders of the new Planetopolis Building
(Ten thousand brine-cooled offices, each with shower)
He saw a dark line creeping across the rubble
And turned a flashlight on it.   80
                  "Say, buddy," he said,
"You better look out for those ants. They eat wood, you know,
They'll have your shack down in no time."
                      The watchman spat.
"Oh, they've quit eating wood," he said, in a casual voice,   85
"I thought everybody knew that."
                —And, reaching down
He pried from the insect jaws the bright crumb of steel.

70. *cub:* nickname for a beginning newspaper reporter.

DISCUSSION

1. Is this poem about the beginning or the end of the "nightmare"? Explain.

2. What lines tell you how the people reacted to what was happening?

3. **Understatement.** Understatement is the opposite of exaggeration. Understatement can be very effective, because the difference between *what* is being said and the low-toned *way* it is said can create surprise or shock in the listener. Find the understatement near the end of the poem. Then put it into different words. Is your version more or less effective than the writer's? Explain.

For further activities, see page 532.

POMPEII

ROBERT SILVERBERG

Not very far from Naples a strange city sleeps under the hot Italian sun. It is the city of Pompeii, and there is no other city quite like it in all the world. No one lives in Pompeii but crickets and beetles and lizards, yet every year thousands of people travel from distant countries to visit it.

Pompeii is a dead city. No one has lived there for nearly 2,000 years—not since the summer of the year A.D. 79, to be exact.

Until that year Pompeii was a prosperous city of 25,000 people. Nearby was the Bay of Naples, an arm of the blue Mediterranean. Rich men came down from wealthy Rome, 125 miles to the north, to build luxurious seaside villas. Fertile farmlands occupied the fields surrounding Pompeii. Rising sharply behind the city was the 4,000-foot bulk of Mount Vesuvius, a grass-covered slope where the shepherds of Pompeii took their goats to graze. Pompeii was a busy city and a happy one.

It died suddenly, in a terrible rain of fire and ashes.

The tragedy struck on the 24th of August, A.D. 79. Mount Vesuvius, which had slumbered quietly for centuries, exploded with savage violence. Death struck on a hot summer afternoon. Tons of hot ashes fell on Pompeii, smothering it, hiding it from sight. For three days the sun did not break through the cloud of volcanic ash that filled the sky. And when the eruption ended, Pompeii was buried deep. A thriving city had perished in a single day.

Centuries passed . . . Pompeii was forgotten. Then, 1,500 years later, it was discovered again. Beneath the protecting shroud of ashes, the city lay intact. Everything was as it had been the day Vesuvius erupted. There were still loaves of bread in the ovens of the bakeries. In the wine shops, the wine jars were in place, and on one counter could be seen a stain where a customer had thrown down his glass and fled.

Modern archaeology began with the discovery of buried Pompeii. Before then, the digging of treasures from the ground had been a haphazard and unscholarly affair. But the excavation of Pompeii was done in a systematic, scientific manner, and so the science of serious archaeology can be said to have begun there. Since the year 1748, generations of skilled Italian workmen have been carefully removing the ashes that buried Pompeii, until today almost four-fifths of the city has been uncovered.

Other Roman cities died more slowly. Wind and rain and fire wore them away. Later peoples tore down the ancient monuments, using the stone to build houses and churches. Over the centuries, the cities of the Caesars vanished, and all that is left of them today are scattered fragments.

Not so with Pompeii. It was engulfed in an instant, and its people's tragedy was our great gain. The buildings of Pompeii still stand as they stood 2,000 years ago, and within the houses we can still see the pots and pans, the household tools, the hammers and nails. On the walls of the buildings are election slogans and the scrawlings of unruly boys. Pompeii is like a photograph in three dimensions. It shows us exactly what a city of the Roman Empire was like, down to the smallest detail of everyday life.

To go to Pompeii today is to take a trip backward in a time machine. The old city comes to vivid life all around you. You can almost hear the clatter of horses' hoofs on the narrow streets, the cries of children, the loud hearty laughter of the shopkeepers. You can almost smell meat sizzling over a charcoal fire. The sky is cloudlessly blue, with the summer sun almost directly overhead. The grassy slopes of great Vesuvius pierce the heavens behind the city, and sunlight shimmers on the water of the bay a thousand yards from the city walls. Ships from every nation are in port, and the babble of strange languages can be heard in the streets.

Such was Pompeii on its last day. And so it is today, now that the volcanic ash has been cleared away. A good imagination is all you need to restore it to bustling vitality.

As its last day of life dawned, in A.D. 79, Pompeii found itself in the midst of a long, sleepy Mediterranean summer. It was a city several hundred years old. Its founders were an Italian people

called the Oscans, who had built the city long before Rome had carved out its worldwide empire. Greeks from Naples had settled in Pompeii, too, and the walls that surrounded the city were built in the Greek style.

For more than 150 years, Pompeii had been part of the Roman Empire. The Roman dictator Sulla had besieged and captured the town in 89 B.C., giving it to his soldiers and making it a Roman colony. By A.D. 79, it had become a fashionable seaside resort, an Atlantic City or a Miami Beach of its day. Important Romans had settled there. The great orator Cicero had been very proud of his summer home in Pompeii. It was a city of merchants and bankers, too.

Pompeii had not had unbroken peace. Twenty years earlier, in the year 59, a contest of gladiators had been held in the big outdoor stadium of Pompeii. A team of gladiators from the neighboring town of Nocera had come to fight against Pompeii's best gladiators. Tempers grew hot as local favorites were pitted against each other in combat to the death. Men from Pompeii began to hurl insults at Nocerans. Words led to blows. Then daggers flashed. A terrible massacre resulted, in which dozens of Nocerans perished and only a few escaped.

Nocera appealed to Rome, and the Roman Senate issued a stern decree: the amphitheater of Pompeii would be closed for ten years. No more gladiatorial games! It was like having our Congress declare that neither the Yankees nor the Dodgers could play baseball for a decade.

The ruling was considered a great tragedy in sports-loving Pompeii. But an even greater one was in store four years later, in A.D. 63, for an earthquake rocked the town. Nearly every building in Pompeii toppled. Hundreds of people died.

One who survived the earthquake of 63 was the banker, Caecilius Jucundus. He was a plump, well-fed man with a harsh smile and beady eyes and a big wart on his left cheek. At the moment the earth shook, Caecilius was in the Forum, the main square of Pompeii. Much business was transacted in the Forum, which was lined with imposing stone columns arranged in a double row, one above the other.

As statues of the gods and slabs of marble tumbled to the ground, fat Caecilius sank to his knees in terror. "If my life is spared," he cried to the heavens, "I'll sacrifice a bull to the gods!"

We know that Caecilius escaped—and that he kept his vow. For when he rebuilt his house after the earthquake, he added a little strip of marble above his family's altar, and on it was a scene showing the earthquake and depicting the bull he had sacrificed. Next to the altar the fat moneylender kept his treasure chest, crammed full with gold coins—and, facing it, a portrait of himself, wart and all.

Sixteen years passed after the dreadful earthquake of 63. Sixteen years later, signs of the catastrophe could still be seen everywhere, for the Pompeiians were slow to rebuild. The private homes were back in order, of course, but the big public places still showed the effects of the quake. The columns of the Forum remained fallen. The Basilica, or law court, still looked devastated. The Temple of Apollo was not yet restored to its former glory. Such repairs took time and cost a great deal of money. The Pompeiians were in no hurry. Time passes slowly along the Mediterranean coast. The columns could be rebuilt next year, or the year after next, or the year after that. In time, everything would be attended to. Commerce and daily life were more important.

But time was running short.

At dawn, on the 24th of August, in the year 79, Pompeii's 25,000 people awakened to another hot day in that hot summer. There was going to be a performance in the arena that night, and the whole town was looking forward to the bloody contests of the gladiators, for the Senate's ban had long since ended. The rumble of heavy wooden wheels was heard as carts loaded with grain entered the city from the farms outside the walls. Over the centuries the steady stream of carts had worn ruts deep into the pavement of Pompeii's narrow streets.

Wooden shutters were drawn back noisily. The grocers and sellers of fruit opened their shops, displaying their wares on trays set out on the sidewalk. In the wine shops, the girls who sold wine to the thirsty sailors got ready for another busy day.

Outside, children headed toward school, carrying slates and followed by their dogs. Nearly everyone in Pompeii had a dog, and barking could be heard everywhere as the Pompeiian pets greeted one another. A small boy who had just learned the Greek alphabet stopped in front of a blank wall and took a piece of charcoal from his tunic. Hastily he scribbled the Greek letters: *alpha, beta, gamma. . . .*

In the Forum, the town's important men had gathered after breakfast to read the political signs that were posted during the night. Elsewhere in the Forum, the wool merchants talked business and the men who owned the vineyards were smiling to each other about the high quality of this year's wine, which would fetch a good price in other countries.

The quiet morning moved slowly along. There was nothing very unusual about Pompeii. Hundreds of other towns just like it dotted the rolling plains of Italy.

But tragedy was on its way. Beneath Vesuvius' vinecovered slopes, a mighty force was about to break loose.

No one in Pompeii knew the dangerous power imprisoned in Vesuvius. For 1,500 years the mountain had slept quietly; but far beneath the crest a boiling fury of molten lava had gradually been gathering strength. The solid rock of Vesuvius held the hidden forces in check. The earthquake 16 years before had been the first sign that the trapped fury beneath the mountain was struggling to break free. Pressure was building up. In the city at the base of the mountain, life went on in complete ignorance of the looming catastrophe.

At 1 o'clock in the afternoon on the 24th of August, 79, the critical point was reached. The walls of rock could hold no longer.

The mountain exploded, raining death on thousands.

Like many tragedies, this one was misunderstood at first. Down in Pompeii, four miles from Vesuvius, a tremendous explosion was heard, echoing ringingly off the mountains on the far side of the city.

"What was that?" people cried from one end of town to another. They stared at each other, puzzled, troubled. Were the gods fighting in heaven? Is that what the loud explosion was?

"Look!" somebody shouted. "Look at Vesuvius!"

Thousands of eyes swiveled upward. Thousands of arms pointed. A black cloud was rising from the shattered crest of the mountain. Higher and higher it rose. An eyewitness, the Roman philosopher Pliny, described the cloud as he saw it from Misenum, 22 miles from Pompeii on the opposite side of the Bay:

"Better than any other tree, the pine can give an idea of the shape and appearance of this cloud," Pliny wrote in his notebook later that day. "In fact it was projected into the air like an enormous trunk and then spread into many branches, now white, now black, now spotted, according to whether earth or ashes were thrown up."

Minutes passed. The sound of the great explosion died away, but it still tingled in everyone's ears. The cloud over Vesuvius still rose, black as night, higher and higher.

"The cloud is blotting out the sun!" someone cried in terror.

Still no one in Pompeii had perished. The fragments of rock thrown up when the mountain exploded all fell back on the volcano's slopes. Within the crater, sizzling masses of molten rock were rushing upward, and upwelling gas drove small blobs of liquefied stone thousands of feet into the air. They cooled, high above the gaping mouth of the volcano, and plummeted earthward.

A strange rain began to fall on Pompeii—a rain of stone.

The stones were light. They were pumice stones, consisting mostly of air bubbles. They poured down as though there had been a sudden cloudburst. The pumice stones, or lapilli, did little damage. They clattered against the wooden roofs of the Pompeiian houses. They fell by the hundreds in the streets. The people who had rushed out of houses and shops and thermopolia to see what had caused the explosion now scrambled to take cover as the weird rain of lapilli continued.

"What is happening?" Pompeiians asked one another. They rushed to the temples—the Temple of Jupiter, the Temple of Apollo, the Temple of Isis. Bewildered priests tried to calm bewildered citizens. Darkness had come at midday, and a rain of small stones fell from the sky, and who could explain it?

Some did not wait for explanation. In a tavern near the edge of the city, half a dozen gladiators who were scheduled to compete in that night's games decided to flee quickly. They had trumpets with them that were used to sound a fanfare at the amphitheater. But they tossed the trumpets aside, leaving them to be found centuries later. Covering their heads with tiles and pieces of wood, the gladiators rushed out into the hail of lapilli and sprinted toward the open country beyond the walls, where they hoped they would be safe.

Vesuvius was rumbling ominously, now. The sky was dark. Lapilli continued to pour down, until the streets began to clog with them.

"The eruption will be over soon!" a hopeful voice exclaimed.

But it did not end. An hour went by and darkness still shrouded everything, and still the lapilli fell. All was confusion now. Children struggled home from school, panicky in the midday darkness.

The people of Pompeii knew that doom was at hand, now. Their fears were doubled when an enormous rain of hot ashes began to fall on them, along with more lapilli. Pelted with stones, half smothered by the ashes, the Pompeiians cried out to the gods for mercy. The wooden roofs of some of the houses began to catch fire as the heat of the ashes reached them. Other buildings were collapsing under the weight of the pumice stones that had fallen on them.

In those first few hours, only the quickwitted managed to escape. Vesonius Primus, the wealthy wool merchant, called his family together and piled jewelry and money into a sack. Lighting a torch, Vesonius led his little band out into the nightmare of the streets. Overlooked in the confusion was Vesonius' black watchdog, chained in the courtyard. The terrified dog barked wildly as lapilli struck and drifting white ash settled around him.

The animal struggled with his chain, battling fiercely to get free, but the chain held, and no one heard the dog's cries. The humans were too busy saving themselves.

Many hundreds of Pompeiians fled in those first few dark hours. Stumbling in the darkness, they made their way to the city gates, then out, down to the harbor. They boarded boats and got away, living to tell the tale of their city's destruction. Others preferred to remain within the city, huddling inside the temples, or in the public baths, or in the cellars of their homes. They still hoped that the nightmare would end— that the tranquillity of a few hours ago would return.

It was evening, now. And new woe was in store for Pompeii. The earth trembled and quaked! Roofs that had somehow withstood the rain of lapilli went crashing in ruin, burying hundreds who had hoped to survive the eruption. In the Forum, tall columns toppled as they had in 63. Those who remembered that great earthquake screamed in new terror as the entire city seemed to shake in the grip of a giant fist.

Three feet of lapilli now covered the ground. Ash floated in the air. Gusts of poisonous gas came drifting from the belching crater, though people could still breathe. Roofs were collapsing everywhere. The cries of the dead and dying filled the air. Rushing throngs, blinded by the darkness and the smoke, hurtled madly up one street and down the next, trampling the fallen in a crazy, fruitless dash toward

safety. Dozens of people plunged into dead-end streets and found themselves trapped by crashing buildings. They waited there, too frightened to run farther, expecting the end.

The rich man Diomedes was another of those who decided not to flee at the first sign of alarm. Rather than risk being crushed by the screaming mobs, Diomedes calmly led the members of his household into the solidly built basement of his villa. Sixteen people altogether, as well as his daughter's dog and her beloved little goat. They took enough food and water to last for several days.

But for all his shrewdness and foresight, Diomedes was undone anyway. Poison gas was creeping slowly into the underground shelter! He watched his daughter begin to cough and struggle for breath. Vesuvius was giving off vast quantities of deadly carbon monoxide, that was now settling like a blanket over the dying city.

The poison gas thickened as the terrible night continued. It was possible to hide from the lapilli, but not from the gas, and Pompeiians died by the hundreds. Carbon monoxide gas keeps the body from absorbing oxygen. Victims of carbon monoxide poisoning get sleepier and sleepier, until they lose consciousness, never to regain it. All over Pompeii, people lay down in the beds of lapilli, overwhelmed by the gas, and death came quietly to them.

Two prisoners, left behind in the jail when their keepers fled, pounded on the sturdy wooden doors. "Let us out!" they called. But no one heard, and the gas entered. They died, not knowing that the jailers outside were dying as well.

In a lane near the Forum, a hundred people were trapped by a blind-alley wall. Others hid in the stoutly built public bathhouses, protected against collapsing roofs but not against the deadly gas. Near the house of Diomedes, a beggar and his little goat sought shelter. The man fell dead a few feet from Diomedes' door; the faithful goat remained by his side, its silver bell tinkling, until its turn came.

All through the endless night, Pompeiians wandered about the streets or crouched in their ruined homes or clustered in the temples to pray. By morning, few remained alive. Not once had Vesuvius stopped hurling lapilli and ash into the air, and the streets of Pompeii were filling quickly. At midday on August 25th, exactly twenty-four hours after the beginning of the holocaust, a second eruption racked the volcano. A second cloud of ashes rose above Vesuvius' summit. The wind blew ash as far as Rome and Egypt. But most of the new ashes descended on Pompeii.

The deadly shower of stone and ashes went unslackening into its second day. But it no longer mattered to Pompeii whether the eruption continued another day or another year. For by midday on August 25th, Pompeii was a city of the dead.

Arriving at Pompeii today, you leave your car outside and enter through an age-old gate. Just within the entrance is a museum that has been built in recent years to house many of the smaller antiquities found in the ruins. Here are statuettes and toys, saucepans and loaves of bread. The account books of the banker Caecilius Jucundus are there, noting all the money he had lent at steep interest rates. Glass cups, coins, charred beans and peas and turnips, baskets of grapes and plums and figs, a box of chestnuts—the little things of Pompeii have all been miraculously preserved for your startled eyes.

Then you enter the city proper. The streets are narrow and deeply rutted with the tracks of chariot wheels. Only special narrow Pompeiian chariots could travel inside the town. Travelers from outside were obliged to change vehicles when they reached the walls of the city. This provided a profitable monopoly for the Pompeiian equivalent of cab drivers, twenty centuries ago!

At each intersection, blocks of stone several feet high are mounted in the roadway, so designed that chariot wheels could pass on either side of them.

"Those are steppingstones for the people of Pompeii," your guide tells you. "Pompeii had no sewers, and during heavy rainfalls the streets were flooded with many inches of water. The Pompeiians could keep their feet dry by walking on those stones."

The houses and shops are of stone. The upper stories, which were wooden, were burned away in the holocaust or simply crumbled with the centuries. The biggest of the shops are along the Street of Abundance, which must have been the Fifth Avenue of its day. Silversmiths, shoemakers, manufacturers of cloth—all had their shops here. And every few doors, there is another thermopolium, or wine shop. In many of these, the big jars of wine are still intact, standing in holes in marble counters just the way bins of ice cream are stored in a soda fountain today.

The center of the city's life was the Forum, a large square which you enter not far from the main gate of the city. Before the earthquake of 63, Pompeii's Forum must have been a truly imposing place, enclosed on three sides by a series of porticoes supported by huge columns. At the north end, on the fourth side, stood the temple of Jupiter, Juno, and Minerva, raised on a podium ten feet high. But the earthquake toppled the temple and most of the columns, and not much rebuilding had been done at the time of the eruption. Pompeii's slowness to rebuild was our eternal loss, for little remains of the Forum except the stumps of massive columns.

Other public buildings were also on the main square: the headquarters of the wool industry, and several other temples, including one dedicated to Vespasian (father of Titus), a Roman emperor who was worshiped as a deity. Near the Forum was a macellum, or market, where food-stuffs were sold and where beggars wandered.

Pompeii had many beggars. One of them was found in April, 1957, at the gate of the road leading to the town of Nocera. A cast taken of him shows him to have been less than five feet tall, and deformed by the bone disease known as rickets. On the last day of Pompeii's life, this beggar had gone about asking for alms, and some generous citizen had given him a bone with a piece of meat still adhering to it. When the eruption came, the beggar tried to flee, jealously guarding his precious sack containing the cutlet—and he was found with it, 2,000 years later.

Pompeii was a city of many fine temples, both around the Forum and in the outlying streets. One of the most interesting is one dating from the sixth century B.C., the oldest building in the city. Only the foundation and a few fragmented columns remain, but this temple was evidently regarded with great reverence, since it was located in the center of a fairly large triangular space adjoining the main theater. Nearby is the Temple of Isis, which was rebuilt after the earthquake and so is in fairly good preservation. Isis, an Egyptian goddess, was one of the many foreign gods and goddesses who had come to be worshiped in the Roman Empire by the time of the destruction of Pompeii. Her gaudily decorated temple at Pompeii is the only European temple of Isis that has come down to us from the ancient world.

But many temples, bathhouses, amphitheaters, and government buildings have survived in other places. What makes Pompeii uniquely significant is the wealth of knowledge it gives us about the *private* lives of its people. Nowhere else do we have such complete information about the homes of the ancients, about their customs and

living habits, about their humble pots and pans.

The houses in Pompeii show the evolution of styles over a period of several centuries. Many of the houses are built to the same simple plan: a central court, known as the atrium, around which a living room, bedrooms, and a garden are arrayed. This was the classic Roman style of home. Some of the later and more impressive houses show the influence of Greek styles, with paintings and mosaic decorations as well as baths, reception rooms, huge gardens, and sometimes a second atrium.

The houses of Pompeii are known by name, and a good deal is known of their occupants. One of the most famous is the House of the Vetti Brothers, which is lavishly decorated with paintings, mosaics, and sculptures. The inscriptions on these houses are often amusing today. One businessman had written on the walls of his villa, WELCOME PROFITS! Another greeted his visitors with the inscribed words, PROFITS MEAN JOY!

At the so-called House of the Tragic Poet, a mosaic shows a barking dog, with the inscription *cave canem*— "Beware of the dog." On the building known as the House of the Lovers, which received its name because the newly married Claudius Elogus lived there, someone had written a line of verse dedicated to the newlyweds on the porch: *Amantes, ut apes, vitam mellitem exigunt.* ("Lovers, like bees, desire a life full of honey.")

One interesting house uncovered since World War II is the Villa of Giulia Felix ("Happy Julia") which was of exceptional size. Apparently Giulia found the expense of this elegant house too much for her budget, because she had opened her baths to the public and advertised the fact with a sign on the gate. For a fee, Pompeiians who scorned the crowds at the public baths could bathe at Giulia's in privacy and comfort. Even this income does not seem to have been enough, for another sign uncovered in 1953 announced that the magnificent villa was for rent.

One of the truly fascinating aspects of Pompeii is the multitude of scribbled street signs. Notices were painted directly on the stone, and have come down to us. At the big amphitheater, an inscription tells us, "The troupe of gladiators owned by Suettius Centus will give a performance at Pompeii on May 31st. There will be an animal show. The awnings will be used." And at the theater where plays were given, a message to a popular actor reads, "Actius, beloved of the people, come back soon; fare thee well!"

There are inscriptions at the taverns, too. "Romula loves Staphyclus" is on one wall. Elsewhere there is a poem that sounds like one of today's hit tunes: "Anyone could as well stop the winds blowing, / And the waters from flowing, / As stop lovers from loving."

DISCUSSION

1. What finally killed the people of Pompeii?

2. Suppose that a complete catastrophe, like an earthquake or an atomic accident, happened to a city you live in or near. And suppose that you were reading an article written 2,000 years later about the people you knew about and the event that wiped them out. Would you like to see all this described in the way this writer describes Pompeii? Does the writer make you feel that the Pompeiians were real people? Back up your answer with examples of where he succeeded or failed.

For further activities, see page 532.

THE HAMMERS

RALPH HODGSON

Noise of hammers once I heard
Many hammers, busy hammers,
Beating, shaping night and day,
Shaping, beating dust and clay
To a palace; saw it reared;   5
Saw the hammers laid away.

And I listened, and I heard
Hammers beating, night and day,
In the palace newly reared,
Beating it to dust and clay: 10
Other hammers, muffled hammers,
Silent hammers of decay.

DISCUSSION

1.   What is the difference between the hammers in stanza one and the hammers in stanza two?

2.   Both the rhythm and the rhyme of this poem are very regular, like the steady beat of hammers. But the rhythm is also like the regular tick-tock of a clock. How might the rhythm of a ticking clock be related to the meaning of this poem?

WHERE ARE THE CHILDREN?

COLETTE

The house was large, topped by a lofty garret. The steep gradient of the street compelled the coachhouses, stables, and poultry-house, the laundry and the dairy, to huddle on a lower level all round a closed courtyard.

By leaning over the garden wall, I could scratch with my finger the poultry-house roof. The Upper Garden overlooked the Lower Garden—a warm, confined enclosure reserved for the cultivation of aubergines and pimentos—where the smell of tomato leaves mingled in July with that of the apricots ripening on the walls. In the Upper Garden were two twin firs, a walnut tree whose intolerant shade killed any flowers beneath it, some rose-bushes, a neglected lawn and a dilapidated arbor. At the bottom, along the Rue des Vignes, a boundary wall reinforced with a strong iron railing ought to have ensured the privacy of the two gardens, but I never knew those railings other than twisted and torn from their cement foundations, and grappling in mid-air with the invincible arms of a hundred-year-old wisteria.

In the Rue de l'Hospice, a two-way flight of steps led up to the front door in the gloomy façade with its large bare windows. It was the typical burgher's house in an old village, but its dignity was upset a little by the steep gradient of the street, the stone steps being lopsided, ten on one side and six on the other.

A large solemn house, rather forbidding, with its shrill bell and its carriage-entrance with a huge bolt like an ancient dungeon, a house that smiled only on its garden side. The back, invisible to passers-by, was a sun trap, swathed in a mantle of wisteria and bignonia too heavy for the trellis of worn ironwork, which sagged in the middle like a hammock and provided shade for the little flagged terrace and the threshold of the sitting room.

Is it worthwhile, I wonder, seeking for adequate words to

describe the rest? I shall never be able to conjure up the splendor that adorns, in my memory, the ruddy festoons of an autumn vine borne down by its own weight and clinging despairingly to some branch of the fir trees. And the massive lilacs, whose compact flowers—blue in the shade and purple in the sunshine—withered so soon, stifled by their own exuberance. The lilacs long since dead will not be revived at my bidding, any more than the terrifying moonlight—silver, quicksilver, leaden gray, with facets of dazzling amethyst or scintillating points of sapphire—all depending on a certain pane in the blue glass window of the summerhouse at the bottom of the garden.

Both house and garden are living still, I know; but what of that, if the magic has deserted them? If the secret is lost that opened to me a whole world—light, scents, birds and trees in perfect harmony, the murmur of human voices now silent for ever—a world of which I have ceased to be worthy?

It would happen sometimes long ago, when this house and garden harbored a family, that a book lying open on the flagstones of the terrace or on the grass, a skipping-rope twisted like a snake across the path, or perhaps a miniature garden, pebble-edged and planted with decapitated flowers, revealed both the presence of children and their varying ages. But such evidence was hardly ever accompanied by childish shouts or laughter, and my home, though warm and full, bore an odd resemblance to those houses which, once the holidays have come to an end, are suddenly emptied of joy. The silence, the muted breeze of the enclosed garden, the pages of the book stirred only by invisible fingers, all seemed to be asking, "Where are the children?"

It was then, from beneath the ancient iron trellis sagging to the left under the wisteria, that my mother would make her appearance, small and plump in those days when age had not yet wasted her. She would scan the thick green clumps and raising her head, fling her call into the air: "Children! Where are the children?"

Where indeed? Nowhere. My mother's cry would ring through the garden, striking the great wall of the barn and returning to her as a faint exhausted echo. "Where . . . ? Children . . . ?"

Nowhere. My mother would throw back her head and gaze heavenwards, as though waiting for a flock of winged children to

alight from the skies. After a moment she would repeat her call; then, grown tired of questioning the heavens, she would crack a dry poppy-head with her finger-nail, rub the greenfly from a rose shoot, fill her pockets with unripe walnuts, and return to the house shaking her head over the vanished children.

And all the while, from among the leaves of the walnut tree

above her, gleamed the pale, pointed face of a child who lay
stretched like a tomcat along a big branch, and never uttered a
word. A less short-sighted mother might well have suspected
that the spasmodic salutations exchanged by the twin tops of
the two firs were due to some influence other than that of the

sudden October squalls! And in the square dormer, above the pulley for hauling up fodder, would she not have perceived, if she had screwed up her eyes, two pale patches among the hay —the face of a young boy and the pages of his book?

But she had given up looking for us, had despaired of trying to reach us. Our uncanny turbulence was never accompanied by any sound. I do not believe there can ever have been children so active and so mute. Looking back at what we were, I am amazed. No one had imposed upon us either our cheerful silence or our limited sociability. My nineteen-year-old brother, engrossed in constructing some hydrotherapeutic apparatus out of linen bladders, strands of wire and glass tubes, never prevented the younger, aged fourteen, from disembowelling a watch or from transposing on the piano, with never a false note, a melody or an air from a symphony heard at a concert in the county town. He did not even interfere with his junior's incomprehensible passion for decorating the garden with little tombstones cut out of cardboard, and each inscribed, beneath the sign of the cross, with the names, epitaph, and genealogy[1] of the imaginary person deceased.

My sister with the too long hair might read forever with never a pause; the two boys would brush past her as though they did not see the young girl sitting abstracted and entranced, and never bother her. When I was small, I was at liberty to keep up as best I could with my long-legged brothers as they ranged the woods in pursuit of swallow tails, White Admirals, Purple Emperors, or hunted for grass snakes, or gathered armfuls of the tall July foxgloves which grew in the clearings already aglow with patches of purple heather. But I followed them in silence, picking blackberries, bird-cherries, a chance wild flower, or roving the hedgerows and waterlogged meadows like an independent dog out hunting on its own.

"Where are the children?" She would suddenly appear like an oversolicitous mother dog breathlessly pursuing her constant quest, head lifted and scenting the breeze. Sometimes her white linen sleeves bore witness that she had come from kneading dough for cakes or making the pudding that had a velvety hot sauce of rum and jam. If she had been washing the Havanese

---

[1] *epitaph . . . genealogy:* a statement about the dead person and a list of her or his ancestors.

dog, she would be enveloped in a long blue apron, and some-times she would be waving a banner of rustling yellow paper, the paper used round the butcher's meat, which meant that she hoped to reassemble, at the same time as her elusive children, her carnivorous family of vagabond cats.

To her traditional cry she would add, in the same anxious and appealing key, a reminder of the time of day. "Four o'clock, and they haven't come in to tea! Where are the children? . . ." "Half-past six! Will they come home to dinner? Where are the children? . . ." That lovely voice; how I should weep for joy if I could hear it now! Our only sin, our single misdeed, was silence, and a kind of miraculous vanishing. For perfectly innocent rea-sons, for the sake of a liberty that no one denied us, we clam-bered over the railing, leaving behind our shoes, and returned by way of an unnecessary ladder or a neighbor's low wall.

Our anxious mother's keen sense of smell would discover on us traces of wild garlic from a distant ravine or of marsh mint from a treacherous bog. The dripping pocket of one of the boys would disgorge the bathing slip worn in malarial ponds, and the "little one," cut about the knees and skinned at the elbows, would be bleeding complacently under plasters of cobweb and wild pepper bound on with rushes.

"Tomorrow I shall keep you locked up! All of you, do you hear, every single one of you!"

Tomorrow! Next day the eldest, slipping on the slated roof where he was fitting a tank, broke his collarbone and remained at the foot of the wall waiting, politely silent and half uncon-scious, until someone came to pick him up. Next day an eigh-teen-rung ladder crashed plumb on the forehead of the younger son, who never uttered a cry, but brought home with becoming modesty a lump like a purple egg between his eyes.

"Where are the children?"

Two are at rest. The others grow older day by day. If there be a place of waiting after this life, then surely she who so often waited for us has not ceased to tremble for those two who are yet alive.

For the eldest of us all, at any rate, she has done with look-ing at the dark window pane every evening and saying, "I feel that child is not happy. I feel she is suffering." And for the elder of the boys she no longer listens, breathlessly, to the wheels of a doctor's trap[2] coming over the snow at night, or to the hoof beats of the gray mare.

But I know that for the two who remain she seeks and wanders still, invisible, tormented by her inability to watch over them enough.

"Where, oh where are the children? . . ."

[2] *trap:* a light, two-wheeled carriage.

DISCUSSION

1. "Looking back at what we were, I am amazed," the writer says. How would you describe these children? Why didn't they answer their mother's call?

2. At first the writer describes the house and the garden that she grew up in, but then she says, "Is it worthwhile, I wonder, seeking for adequate words to describe the rest?" What is troubling her? (Rereading paragraphs five and six should help you answer.)

3. **Tone.** Sometimes it is hard to tell how a writer feels about what he or she is writing about. Sometimes the opposite is true—you can tell that someone is writing mainly out of feeling. Usually, however, you can have some idea of the writer's attitude, and this attitude is called the tone of the story or poem. What is this writer's tone—what feeling does she have about her subject? In what ways does the mother's call, "Where are the children?" reflect the tone of the story?

For further activities, see page 532.

UPHILL

CHRISTINA ROSSETTI

Does the road wind uphill all the way?
   Yes, to the very end.
Will the day's journey take the whole long day?
   From morn to night, my friend.

But is there for the night a resting place?   5
   A roof for when the slow dark hours begin.
May not the darkness hide it from my face?
   You cannot miss that inn.

Shall I meet other wayfarers at night?
   Those who have gone before.   10
Then must I knock, or call when just in sight?
   They will not keep you standing at that door.

Shall I find comfort, travel sore and weak?
   Of labor you shall find the sum.
Will there be beds for me and all who seek?   15
   Yea, beds for all who come.

DISCUSSION

1. How would you describe the two speakers?

2. **Symbol.** An object that stands for something else, usually something more abstract, is called a symbol. A flag, for example, can be thought of as a symbol for a country. In this poem the road is a symbol for life. What is night a symbol for?

3. What is the meaning of the line, "You cannot miss that inn"?

LAMENT

EDNA ST. VINCENT MILLAY

Listen, children:
Your father is dead.
From his old coats
I'll make you little jackets;
I'll make you little trousers   5
From his old pants.
There'll be in his pockets
Things he used to put there,
Keys and pennies
Covered with tobacco;   10
Dan shall have the pennies
To save in his bank;
Anne shall have the keys
To make a pretty noise with.
Life must go on,   15
And the dead be forgotten;
Life must go on,
Though good men die;
Anne, eat your breakfast;
Dan, take your medicine;   20
Life must go on;
I forget just why.

DISCUSSION   1. Who is the speaker in this poem?

2. A lament is an expression of sorrow. Where in the poem does the speaker express the greatest sorrow?

VOCABULARY

Something Bright (page 488)

There are many millions of possible word combinations. This means that a writer—or you—can put words together in completely new ways to make fresh, vivid images, or to get the reader's attention. Look at these unusual word combinations from "Something Bright."

"the folds of fatigue that dragged her face down"
"She stood in the doorway as though she had been stacked there like bricks."
"a face sketched on beneath a fuzz of hair"
"I forgot my starchy shy stiffness."

Make up some interesting ways to describe the following things, or make up four or five of your own.

1. feeling very hungry
2. an interesting, attractive face
3. the face of someone who is feeling seasick
4. unexpectedly seeing someone you love
5. somebody walking very slowly

Metropolitan Nightmare (page 504)

Imagine a *different* change in climate—the city drying up and turning into desert, or slowly freezing. Go back over the poem and substitute words that would describe a different climate change.

COMPOSITION

Something Bright (page 488)

At some time or another, everyone is wrong about a first impression. Write a few paragraphs about someone you changed your mind about. Describe the person as vividly as you can as you first saw her or him; then tell how and why your impression changed.

Where Are the Children? (page 522)

Is there anything that you miss that you had when you were a child—a place, a pet, a feeling about things? Write about this thing that you used to have in a way that shows how you feel about it.

READING

Metropolitan Nightmare (page 504)

According to the poem, many unusual events or happenings went almost unnoticed. On separate paper, match the number of the events with the letter of the people that did notice them. Or, if no one in particular did, use the letter *i*.

1. There was a lot of rain.
2. The trees were very green and heavy leafed.
3. The tree roots were spreading.
4. Grass grew in the streets.
5. A flamingo flew into the mayor's office.
6. Termites invaded New York.
7. There were parrots and parakeets in the city.
8. There was a change in the Gulf Stream.
9. The termites ate steel.

a. the mayor
b. "science-cranks"
c. people walking
d. taxi drivers and paraders
e. a reporter
f. city gardeners
g. watchman and cub reporter
h. the tourists
i. no one in particular

Pompeii (page 508)

Read the details below. On separate paper write an *F* (false) after the number of the incorrect items. Renumber the remaining details in the order in which they occurred.

1. Until A.D. 79, Pompeii was a poor city of 25,000.
2. The tragedy began with an explosion.
3. The fateful day dawned cool and cloudy.
4. A few days before the volcano, an earthquake destroyed much of the town.
5. There was a rain of stone.
6. It was blazing bright at midday.
7. Hot ashes rained down.
8. The earth trembled and quaked.
9. The houses caught fire or collapsed from the weight of the stones and ashes.
10. Poisonous gas blanketed the city.

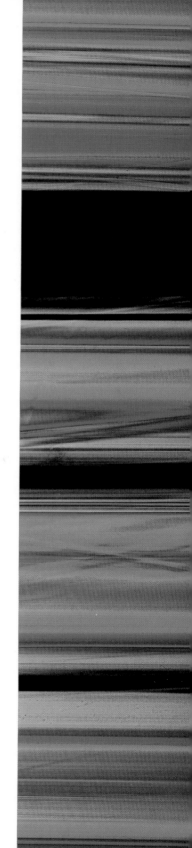

FROM # High, Wide and Lonesome

HAL BORLAND

It was late April before Spring really came. It came first as a
greenness in the hollows beside the shallow ponds of snowmelt,
but soon it began to spread like a faint green mist on all the
hillsides and across the flats. After that the chilly days and the
raw nights didn't seem quite so raw or chilly.

Timbered country has Spring subtleties:[1] rising sap and
first buds, florets on trees and bushes, half-hidden flowers
among the rocks and leaf mold. But the plains are a vast simplicity at any season, their moods and changes swift, evident,
and decisive. On that boundless open grassland neither Spring
nor any other season can hide or creep up slowly. Spring comes
in a vast green wave rolling northward, a wave as evident as
were the buffalo millions that once swept northward with new
grass, as evident as the Winter-hungry Indians that once swept
northward with the buffalo. Spring on the plains has little more
subtlety than a thunder storm.

Winter ends, March drags its cold, muddy feet but finally
passes, and there is Spring, a rebirth that assaults all your
senses. The surge of life at the grass roots penetrates your soles,
creeps up through your bones, your marrow, and right into your
heart. You see it, you feel it, you smell it, you taste it in every
breath you breathe. You partake of Spring. You are a part of it,
even as you were a part of Winter. Spring is all around you and
in you, primal, simple as the plains themselves. Spring is, and
you know it.

I rode over to the Bromleys to return *David Copperfield*
and get *A Tale of Two Cities.* . . . On the way home I saw a
badger cleaning out his den. He was down in the hole kicking
dirt out with his hind feet almost as fast as a man could toss it
out with a shovel. Then I saw a flock of meadowlarks. Most of
them were busy looking for beetles, but two of them were so full
of song they just strutted around whistling at each other. And
when I got to the head of our draw I saw the first of the lark
buntings, which we called prairie bobolinks. Half a dozen of
them flew up, singing on the wing, and I knew that before long

---

[1] *subtleties* (sŭt′əl-tēz): aspects so delicate or slight as to escape notice.

I would be finding their nests in the grass, and light blue eggs in the nests.

A few days later I rode over to the big prairie dog town. Even there, where the prairie dogs had eaten the soil bare last Summer, the grass was beginning to come back. The prairie dogs were out by the hundred, chipper and noisy as though they hadn't an enemy in the world. Over at the far side of the town an old badger was waddling along, watching me over one shoulder. The dogs over there were all out of sight, but a hundred yards from the badger other prairie dogs paid him no attention.

Two little owls were bobbing and screaming at each other; they saw me and forgot their own quarrel and screamed at me, but the minute I was past they began hopping at each other again.

Most of the old mother prairie dogs were fat with pup. The pups would be born in another week or two, but would stay in the dens for a month. The thin old males were feeding greedily on the grass, truculent and quarrelsome among themselves.

I dismounted to watch an ant hill, and I saw two tumble-bugs pushing each other around in the grass. They butted and rolled and nipped and got to their feet and butted each other again, until one of them drove the other off. The victor pursued a little way, then came back and began rolling the ball of dung over which they probably had been fighting. They were strange creatures with the mark of antiquity on them, though I didn't know then that they were close cousins of the ancient Egyptian scarabs. All I knew was that these big, dark, timeless-looking beetles fashioned balls of cow manure three quarters of an inch. in diameter and rolled them from place to place, walking backward and rolling the balls with their hind legs. They laid eggs in the balls and the eggs hatched into grubs which ate their way out and eventually turned into beetles which laid their own eggs in other dung balls. It seemed to me that the way the birds did it, laying eggs in nests, eggs with shells on them and food inside, was much simpler.

I watched the tumblebug maneuver his ball to the edge of the bare space around the ant hill, and I watched the ants gather to repel the invader, who paid almost no attention to them. The tumblebug rolled his ball across the little clearing and into the grass beyond, the ants rubbed feelers in a conference as though telling each other that they had driven off a major threat to the colony, and everybody went back to work.

The sun was warm. Even the ground was beginning to lose its March chill. I lay there thinking about the beetles and the ants and the prairie dogs and the badgers and the owls and the meadowlarks. They had been here a long time, all of them. They were here when the buffalo first came, and that was so long ago that the Indians couldn't remember that far back. Time was a strange thing. It was days and nights and months and years, and then it stretched out into something else. Into grass, maybe, or into clouds. Or into the earth itself. You lay watching a cloud overhead, and you closed your eyes and pretty soon the cloud moved over the sun. You felt the coolness and the darkness of the shadow. You lay and waited for the brightness and the sun's warmth again. You could count, slowly, and that was time. You counted slowly, and the cloud passed the sun. The shadow was gone.

Time was strange. A prairie dog pup was born in May, and by Fall it was practically grown up. A meadowlark laid an egg in a nest in May and before frost in the Fall the baby bird hatched from that egg was as big as its mother and it flew south with the other birds. But it took years for a boy to grow up.

We had been out there two years. When we first came I was so short I had to stand on a manger or a cut-bank to get on a horse. Now I could mount Mack from the ground, just put my hands on his withers and jump and throw my leg over his back.

I wondered how many ants had grown old and died while I was growing up enough to get on a horse from the ground. A year must be a long time to an ant. Or a beetle. Or a prairie dog. Even a day must be a long time. Maybe time was like distance. If an ant got twenty feet away from the ant hill, he was a long way from home, much farther than I was right now from the house. And it probably would take a tumblebug all day to roll that ball of dung fifty feet, especially with all the obstacles it had to get over or around.

Some day, I told myself, I would find a tumblebug early in the morning and watch him all day and see just how far he did go. I would catch him and tie a thread around him, or mark him some way, so I could be sure to know which one he was if he had a fight with another beetle.

But not today. I caught Mack and whistled to Fritz, who

was still trying to catch a prairie dog, and I rode west, to circle back toward our place.

I rode only a little way when a kit fox jumped not fifty yards ahead of me. He had been catching ground squirrels until I startled him. A kit fox was like a small coyote with a very bushy tail. He was really a fox, but not much bigger than a good-sized cat. There weren't many of them around, and most of them were here on these South Flats. This one jumped and ran like a streak, its bushy tail floating behind, graceful as a bird. It ran maybe twenty yards; then, without slackening pace, it veered and ran off at an angle another twenty-five yards or so, then changed directions again. That's the way a kit fox always ran, zigzag. Dogs would seldom run kit foxes, and anyone who ever watched one knew why. It made you dizzy just watching that zigzagging. I yelled, and the kit veered again. One more turn and it vanished in a little hollow.

I rode over to the hollow, but I couldn't find the kit fox. It must have darted down the little wash and out onto the flats again where I wasn't watching. But as I rode down the hollow I came to a fresh cut-bank that had washed out in the Spring melt. The grass had caved away, leaving a bank of fresh gravelly soil. Such a place was always worth searching for arrowheads. I got off and began poking through the gravel.

It was different from the gravel on our land, coarser and full of lumps of sandstone. The sandstone was grayish yellow. There was a thin ledge of it reaching back under the grass. I sifted a few handfuls through my fingers and stood up, about to leave. Then I scuffed at it with my toe and a smooth, rounded flat piece caught my eye. It wasn't a pebble. It was almost the size of a silver dollar, but smooth and rounded.

Even as I picked it up, I sensed that here was something out of time so remote that my mind could not quite grasp the distance. It was a fossil clam, and the place I found it was fifteen hundred miles from the nearest ocean.

There it was, a clam turned to stone, a petrified clam with fluting around the edges of the twin shells, with bits of sandstone still clinging to it. Different from the fresh-water clams of the Missouri River, but still a shellfish, something from an ocean that once had been where I stood. And somehow, standing in the warm Spring sunlight on the high plains, I comprehended the matter of eons and ages. Without knowing geology,

I sensed geologic time. I touched the beat of the big rhythm, the coming and going of oceans and the rise and fall of mountains. And, for a little while, I was one not only with the Indians who had been there before me, but with those who were there before the Indians; not only with the grass which had greened with a thousand Springs, but with that which was there before the grass.

There had been ranchmen before we came, and Indians before the ranchmen, and buffalo before the Indians. And long before the buffalo there had been an ocean, and clams. Back, back—how far back? And how far ahead? Time was indeed a strange thing. The time of the ant, the time of the tumblebug, the time of the prairie dog, the time of a boy. The time of a fossil clam.

I got on my horse and rode slowly home in the late afternoon of that Spring day, with a strange, hard, smooth fragment of time in my pocket.

Mother said, "You've just got time to get the chores done before supper."

DISCUSSION

1.   "Time [is] strange," Hal thinks, because living things experience it differently. How does he see that time is different for a prairie dog pup, a meadowlark, and a boy?

2.   Hal finds a fossil clam and comprehends the "matter of eons and ages." What kind of time is he then in touch with? What kind of time did these suggest to Hal: the tumblebug, the ants, his mother?

3.   Spring, in this author's description of its coming, "assaults all your senses." What does he mean? What does he see and hear and smell?

For further activities, see page 572.

Buffalo Dusk

CARL SANDBURG

The buffaloes are gone
And those who saw the buffaloes are gone.
Those who saw the buffaloes by thousands and how they
     pawed the prairie sod into dust with their hoofs, their
     great heads down pawing on in a great pageant of dusk,
Those who saw the buffaloes are gone.
And the buffaloes are gone.

The Eagle's Song

TRADITIONAL INDIAN SONG

Translated by Mary Austin

Said the Eagle:

I was astonished
When I heard that there was death.

My home, alas,
Must I leave it!   5
All beholding summits,
Shall I see thee no more!

North I went,
Leaning on the wind;
Through the forest resounded   10
The cry of the hunted doe.

East I went,
Through the hot dawning;
There was the smell of death in my nostrils.

South I went, seeking   15
The place where there is no death.
Weeping I heard
The voice of women
Wailing for their children.

West I went,   20
On the world encompassing water;
Death's trail was before me.

People, O people,
Needs be that we must die!

Therefore let us make   25
Songs together.
With a twine of songs to bind us
To the middle Heaven,
The white way of souls.

There we shall be at rest,   30
With our songs
We shall roam no more!

DISCUSSION

1. As the Eagle searches in all directions, it meets death in different forms. What different forms of death does it confront?

2. What answer does the Eagle offer to people, who "needs must die"?

Buffalo Grass

ALICE MARRIOTT

For Leah the south porch of the big house was the best part of home. Here you could sit and watch sunrise or sunset; watch the shapes of the earth change and move as the sun moved. Then you knew, when you sat out there, that the earth was alive itself.

Spear Woman sat beside her granddaughter and thought that the earth had gone dead. Lights played and moved, and cloud shadows came and went, but the earth itself had somehow died. It was all one color now; not like the old days when its shades really changed and flickered like flames under the wind. She stirred and sighed and spoke.

"When the buffalo moved across it, there were other colors and other lights."

The thought was near enough Leah's own to startle her. "There are lots of colors there now."

Her father spoke behind them. "Not like there used to be. In the days that even I remember, there was one color when the wind was from the north and another when it was from the south, one from the east and another from the west. Now the grass is all one color on every side, and it doesn't change with the wind."

"Sometimes the colors change. Down near Lawton there is a prairie where the grass takes different colors."

"In Buffalo Park. The government made it to be like the old days."

"Is it, Father?"

"Pretty much. Grandmother would know better than I do. The buffalo were gone already when I was a young man."

"Is it, Grandmother? Is that buffalo park like the old days?"

Spear Woman shook her head. "How do I know? I have never seen it. A buffalo park—Are there buffalo there?"

Leah's father nodded. "Lots of buffalo. They were there last autumn when I went with the army officers, looking for old battlefields. We saw the buffalo. They came close."

Spear Woman was sitting straight up now, like a young

woman. "Lots of buffalo and they came close. I wish I could see them. I want to see them."

Leah stared. Grandmother often said "I wish," but never "I want."

"Do you really want to see them, Grandmother?"

"I need to see them. I am an old woman, and soon it will be too late. I want to see the buffalo."

Father nodded. "I guess you better. Daughter, can you take your grandmother?"

Leah spoke English. "Casings are pretty bad, and it will take just about all our gasoline."

"You make it. Just one-day trip. Leave here early in the morning, be back that night. You don't got to hurry."

Leah thought. "All right. I never saw a whole lot of buffalo myself. Just two one time, in a circus." She changed into Kiowa. "When do you want to go, Grandmother?"

Spear Woman thought. "You can't hurry with these things.

Buffalo don't hurry. Got to plan buffalo hunt ahead. I guess we go four sleeps from now."

"All right." Her son rose slowly. "I fix the car. Leah will make a lunch. Then you can go."

It didn't sound like much to do, just to fix the car and a lunch, but Spear Woman kept them at it for the whole four days. Everything had to be just right. "You owe respect to buffalo. They kept us alive," she said when Leah protested that the upholstery didn't need scrubbing. Even her son went so far as to suggest tying a rawhide saddle on the hood, so that she could ride the car like a horse. "In the old days, you wouldn't make fun of the buffalo, wouldn't make fun of your mother. You'd know you needed them both."

But by the next morning she had got over her hurt feelings. Even after the four days of getting ready, she still had things to see to at the last minute. She brought her best Pendleton blanket from the trunk and spread it over the seat. She put on her very best clothes and painted her face. Leah, already thinking of fifty miles of dust each way, of the crowds of white people that hung around government parks, of all the things that could happen to a car with two women in it, wished that the paint had been left off. But Grandmother would have to show respect for the buffalo.

The sun was low in the morning, and the shadows of the little hills were on the grass, changing its color in Leah's eyes. Grandmother looked at it and said, "All brown," and got into the car. She arranged her dress carefully and set her moccasins firm on the floor of the car, as if they were in stirrups. Then she said, "All ready," and Leah let out the clutch, and they started.

She took the back road, down through Cutthroat Gap and around Saddle Mountain. It was longer than the highway, but it was pretty. Grandmother showed her places as they went along.

"That big bend there, by the river, Buffalo River. That's where they held the Sun Dance the year I was born. That little butte over there. That's where the three boys froze to death, the time they ran away from the first government school. See where that hole is, where the ground kind of dips down? That's where the old trading post stood."

On and on. Every little dip, every bend and curve—the spring where they stopped to drink and water the radiator, even the beds of water cress below it—had their histories and their names. It was all alive, this country; people walked across it that Leah could not see, but Spear Woman could. She did not call their names, for they were dead, but she told to whom they were related, and how that made them kin to her and to Leah. Some places were happy; there had been Sun Dances and ceremonies. Other places were unhappy; people had died there, and been mourned. Leah could feel the mourning, even now. On, with the sun rising higher and the shadows drawing up under the objects that cast them. On and on.

Two lines of high, tight fence spread across the prairie from a gate, and Spear Woman sat stiff, suddenly. "What is that? That is grass like the old days. Real grass. All different colors."

It was, too. It was like changeable silk, the kind the Delawares used to trim their blankets. Yellow as the wind struck it; rose-color as it died away; then a sort of in-between color, with patterns that moved like the patterns in silk when you folded it.

"That's the buffalo park. Buffalo ought to be here. I don't see them."

Spear Woman looked quickly overhead. "Not now. Nearly noon. Sun's too high. Now's the time when the buffalo lie down by the creeks and rest. They're wise. They don't run about in the sun as we do."

Leah nodded. "I guess you're right. We'll go find some shade, too. Lie down ourselves."

All these past four days she had been in a hurry. Her plans had been pushing her. It had been the most important thing in the world to get her here quickly, to find the buffalo and look at them, and to be gone. That the buffalo might not be there to be seen had not come into her thoughts. Now the hurry had rushed itself away; she was no more pushed for time than her grandmother or the buffalo themselves. She could find shade and lie down and sleep. It would take until late at night to get home. That was all right. They could sleep again when they were there.

Shade was not even in sight, and when they had driven through the gates, with the lines of fence on either hand, it was still not easy to find. Spear Woman didn't care. She sat and watched the grass turn over in the sun, flickering and bending and straightening like little campfire flames, and was happy. It was the old kind of grass, the old, rippling, running prairies, even if there were fences. She was glad her eyes were dim, because she didn't always see the fences, and could forget about them. It was all peaceful and alive again.

There was a creek, with a pebble bank, shelving down to clear, shallow water. Spear Woman took her Pendleton blanket from the seat of the car and spread it on the ground for them to lie on. Leah brought the lunch from the car, to find that her grandmother had gathered up little sticks and twigs and boughs, and built a fire. "Long ago I camped here. I had forgotten. Your grandfather and I were hunting for some horses that had run off. We stopped and ate here, and built a little clear fire like this."

They did not really need the fire, for coffee would stay warm a long time in the thermos jug, but it was nice to heat it in tin cups. They let the coffee get stone cold to cool the handles, and sipped it, and slipped into sleep as if eating and drinking and sleeping and being were all one thing.

Shadows were running away from the things that cast them, and there was blue light in the wonderful rose color of the prairie when Leah waked. Spear Woman was sitting still beside her, just watching the wind walk across the grass. Leah stretched, and her grandmother nodded at her. "You had a sleep. That's good. Now we will go and see the buffalo."

It had taken a long time to put things in the car this morning, but it seemed to take only a minute now. Their fire was out, everything packed away, and the blanket spread on the car seat almost without their moving. They started back along the fence.

There was a little draw ahead of them, across the blueing prairie, and there was something dark moving along it. Spear Woman saw it before Leah did. "There they are. You'd better stop. I'll call them this way."

She stood up in the car and lifted her voice out of her throat, not loud, but clear and high and true. It ran across the grass to stop the herd and turn them, and Leah understood why women always went on the hunts in the old days. It was to draw with their voices the herds to them. No man had a voice that could do that.

The buffalo had changed their course, and were moving jerkily along and up the draw. They were coming nearer, and Spear Woman called to them again. They actually began to hurry then.

Spear Woman stood in the car beside her granddaughter. Tears ran down her face, and her mouth tasted salt, but she was singing; she who had never made a song before, found words in her heart and sang them aloud.

Once we were all free on the prairies together.
Blue and rose and yellow prairies like this one.
We ran and chased and hunted.
You were good to us.
You gave us food and clothes and houses.
Now we are all old.
We are tied.
But our minds are not tied.
We can remember the old days.
We can say to each other,
Those times were good.

Something had happened to the buffalo. They were near to the fence, now, but they had stopped. The clear, high call they had obeyed; the song puzzled them. The herd broke apart, shuffling and snorting against the wire, and Spear Woman, dropped from her song, stared at them.

Then she saw. They were yearlings, little more than calves. And she had been singing to them about the old days. The tears were still on her cheeks, but she began to laugh. She laughed and laughed, and Leah stared at her, in wonder and fright.

"Of course you don't understand my singing," Spear Woman said. "Of course you don't know what it's about when I sing about the old days. You're just calves. You don't remember. You were born inside the fence, like my own grandchildren."

Then she sat down in the car and waited to be driven home.

DISCUSSION

1. "Of course you don't understand my singing," Spear Woman says to the buffalo. Why did she sing? Why does she laugh when they fail to understand her song?

2. Why is it important to Spear Woman to see the buffalo? "You owe respect to buffalo. They kept us alive." What does she mean?

3. Leah also learns something from the trip to see the buffalo. What does she learn? How does her attitude change? Why?

For further activities, see page 572.

OREGON TRAIL

LOREN EISELEY

It is spring somewhere beyond
        Chimney Rock
        on the old
        Oregon trail now.
I remember the time   5
        when the ruts of the wagons
          could still be seen across
               a half mile
      of unbroken short-grass prairie
as though   10
      in that high air
      they had just passed,
the rolling Conestoga wagons
      heavy-freighted
        for the Sierras,   15
        as though time was
only yesterday,
      as though, if one hurried,
a fast horse
      with good wind   20
      would bring you
        to the buckskinned outriders
        and the lined brown women
        with sunbonnets,
the grandmothers,   25
        the fathers,
        children who became
        the forest cutters,
        wheat raisers,
            gold seekers,   30
          sharpshooters,
        range killers,
         users of
         the first Colts in
         the cattle wars   35
         or at the gamblers' tables—

a time a fast horse
> might still catch up with
almost anything.

I whirl my animal 40
three times about
and bend over the tracks
trampling uncertainly.
> It is time to go home.
But the other time is there 45
> tempting
> just beyond the horizon.
I back off reluctantly
> and out of some shamed courtesy
> slip my spectacles 50
> into my pocket
> and raise my hand
> saying a wordless
> > goodbye.

DISCUSSION   1.   What does the speaker feel about the Oregon Trail? Explain your answer.

2.   At about what time in our nation's history was there such a trail? What details in the poem tell you?

For further activities, see page 572.

The Marginal World

RACHEL CARSON

The edge of the sea is a strange and beautiful place. All through
the long history of Earth it has been an area of unrest where
waves have broken heavily against the land, where the tides have
pressed forward over the continents, receded, and then returned.
For no two successive days is the shore line precisely the same.
Not only do the tides advance and retreat in their eternal rhythms,
but the level of the sea itself is never at rest. It rises or falls as the
glaciers melt or grow, as the floor of the deep ocean basins shifts
under its increasing load of sediments, or as the earth's crust along
the continental margins warps up or down in adjustment to strain
and tension. Today a little more land may belong to the sea, tomorrow a little less. Always the edge of the sea remains an elusive
and indefinable boundary.

The shore has a dual nature, changing with the swing of the
tides, belonging now to the land, now to the sea. On the ebb tide
it knows the harsh extremes of the land world, being exposed to
heat and cold, to wind, to rain and drying sun. On the flood tide it
is a water world, returning briefly to the relative stability of the
open sea.

Only the most hardy and adaptable can survive in a region so
mutable, yet the area between the tide lines is crowded with plants
and animals. In this difficult world of the shore, life displays its
enormous toughness and vitality by occupying almost every con-
ceivable niche. Visibly, it carpets the intertidal rocks; or half hidden, it descends into fissures and crevices, or hides under boulders,
or lurks in the wet gloom of sea caves. Invisibly, where the casual
observer would say there is no life, it lies deep in the sand, in burrows and tubes and passageways. It tunnels into solid rock and
bores into peat and clay. It encrusts weeds or drifting spars or the
hard, chitinous shell of a lobster. It exists minutely, as the film of
bacteria that spreads over a rock surface or a wharf piling; as
spheres of protozoa, small as pinpricks, sparkling at the surface of
the sea; and as Lilliputian beings swimming through dark pools
that lie between the grains of sand.

The shore is an ancient world, for as long as there has been
an earth and sea there has been this place of the meeting of land

and water. Yet it is a world that keeps alive the sense of continuing creation and of the relentless drive of life. Each time that I enter it, I gain some new awareness of its beauty and its deeper meanings, sensing that intricate fabric of life by which one creature is linked with another, and each with its surroundings.

The sense of creation comes with memories of a southern coast, where the sea and the mangroves, working together, are building a wilderness of thousands of small islands off the southwestern coast of Florida, separated from each other by a tortuous pattern of bays, lagoons, and narrow waterways. I remember a winter day when the sky was blue and drenched with sunlight; though there was no wind one was conscious of flowing air like cold clear crystal. I had landed on the surf-washed tip of one of those islands, and then worked my way around to the sheltered bay side. There I found the tide far out, exposing the broad mud flat of a cove bordered by the mangroves with their twisted branches, their glossy leaves, and their long prop roots reaching down, grasping and holding the mud, building the land out a little more, then again a little more.

The mud flats were strewn with the shells of that small, exquisitely colored mollusk, the rose tellin, looking like scattered petals of pink roses. There must have been a colony nearby, living buried just under the surface of the mud. At first the only creature visible was a small heron in gray and rusty plumage—a reddish egret that waded across the flat with the stealthy, hesitant movements of its kind. But other land creatures had been there, for a line of fresh tracks wound in and out among the mangrove roots, marking the path of a raccoon feeding on the oysters that gripped the supporting roots with projections from their shells. Soon I found the tracks of a shore bird, probably a sanderling, and followed them a little; then they turned toward the water and were lost, for the tide had erased them and made them as though they had never been.

Looking out over the cove I felt a strong sense of the interchangeability of land and sea in this marginal world of the shore, and of the links between the life of the two. There was also an awareness of the past and of the continuing flow of time, obliterating much that had gone before, as the sea had that morning washed away the tracks of the bird.

The sequence and meaning of the drift of time were quietly summarized in the existence of hundreds of small snails—the mangrove periwinkles—browsing on the branches and roots of the trees. Once their ancestors had been sea dwellers, bound to the salt waters by every tie of their life processes. Little by little over the thousands and millions of years the ties had been broken, the snails had adjusted themselves to life out of water, and now today they were living many feet above the tide to which they only occasionally returned. And perhaps, who could say how many ages hence, there would be in their descendants not even this gesture of remembrance for the sea.

The spiral shells of other snails—these quite minute—left winding tracks on the mud as they moved about in search of food. They were horn shells, and when I saw them I had a nostalgic moment when I wished I might see what Audubon[1] saw, a century and more ago. For such little horn shells were the food of the flamingo, once so numerous on this coast, and when I half closed my eyes I could almost imagine a flock of these magnificent flame birds feeding in that cove, filling it with their color. It was a mere yesterday in the life of the earth that they were there; in nature, time and space are relative matters, perhaps most truly perceived subjectively in occasional flashes of insight, sparked by such a magical hour and place.

[1] *Audubon:* John James Audubon, American naturalist and artist best known for his paintings of birds.

DISCUSSION   1.   The shore, the meeting place of land and water, is to Rachel Carson a "strange and beautiful place." What does she reveal of it that is strange? What does she find beautiful?

2.   The tracks a shore bird left in the sand give the author a sense of the flow of time. How did the bird tracks link the land and sea, the marginal world, to the author's experience of life?

For further activities, see page 572.

THE NEGRO SPEAKS OF RIVERS

To W.E.B. DuBois

LANGSTON HUGHES

I've known rivers:
I've known rivers ancient as the world and older than
 the flow of human blood in human veins.

My soul has grown deep like the rivers.

I bathed in the Euphrates when dawns were young. 5
I built my hut near the Congo and it lulled me to sleep.
I looked upon the Nile and raised the pyramids above it.
I heard the singing of the Mississippi when Abe Lincoln
 went down to New Orleans, and I've seen its
 muddy bosom turn all golden in the sunset. 10
I've known rivers:
Ancient, dusky rivers.

My soul has grown deep like the rivers.

DISCUSSION 1. What words suggest ancient times? What words
suggest a broad geographic range?

2. How might the flow of rivers and the flow of time
be similar?

By the Waters of Babylon

STEPHEN VINCENT BENÉT

The north and the west and the south are good hunting ground, but it is forbidden to go east. It is forbidden to go to any of the Dead Places except to search for metal and then he who touches the metal must be a priest or the son of a priest. Afterward, both the man and the metal must be purified. These are the rules and the laws; they are well made. It is forbidden to cross the great river and look upon the place that was the Place of the Gods—this is most strictly forbidden. We do not even say its name though we know its name. It is there that spirits live, and demons—it is there that there are the ashes of the Great Burning. These things are forbidden—they have been forbidden since the beginning of time.

My father is a priest; I am the son of a priest. I have been in the Dead Places near us, with my father—at first, I was afraid. When my father went into the house to search for the metal, I stood by the door and my heart felt small and weak. It was a dead man's house, a spirit house. It did not have the smell of man, though there were old bones in a corner. But it is not fitting that a priest's son should show fear. I looked at the bones in the shadow and kept my voice still.

Then my father came out with the metal—a good, strong piece. He looked at me with both eyes but I had not run away. He gave me the metal to hold—I took it and did not die. So he knew that I was truly his son and would be a priest in my time. That was when I was very young—nevertheless, my brothers would not have done it, though they are good hunters. After that, they gave me the good piece of meat and the warm corner by the fire. My father watched over me—he was glad that I should be a priest. But when I boasted or wept without a reason, he punished me more strictly than my brothers. That was right.

After a time, I myself was allowed to go into the dead houses and search for metal. So I learned the ways of those houses—and if I saw bones, I was no longer afraid. The bones are light and old—sometimes they will fall into dust if you touch them. But that is a great sin.

I was taught the chants and the spells—I was taught how to stop the running of blood from a wound and many secrets. A priest must know many secrets—that was what my father said. If the hunters think we do all things by chants and spells, they may believe so—it does not hurt them. I was taught how to read in the old books and how to make the old writings—that was hard and took a long time. My knowledge made me happy—it was like a fire in my heart. Most of all, I liked to hear of the Old Days and the stories of the gods. I asked myself many questions that I could not answer, but it was good to ask them. At night, I would lie awake and listen to the wind—it seemed to me that it was

the voice of the gods as they flew through the air.

We are not ignorant like the Forest People—our women spin wool on the wheel, our priests wear a white robe. We do not eat grubs from the tree, we have not forgotten the old writings, although they are hard to understand. Nevertheless, my knowledge and my lack of knowledge burned in me—I wished to know more. When I was a man at last, I came to my father and said, "It is time for me to go on my journey. Give me your leave."

He looked at me for a long time, stroking his beard, then he said at last, "Yes. It is time." That night, in the house of the priesthood, I asked for and received purification. My body hurt but my spirit was a cool stone. It was my father himself who questioned me about my dreams.

He bade me look into the smoke of the fire and see—I saw and told what I saw. It was what I have always seen—a river, and, beyond it, a great Dead Place and in it the gods walking. I have always thought about that. His eyes were stern when I told him—he was no longer my father but a priest. He said, "This is a strong dream."

"It is mine," I said, while the smoke waved and my head felt light. They were singing the Star song in the outer chamber and it was like the buzzing of bees in my head.

He asked me how the gods were dressed and I told him how they were dressed. We know how they were dressed from the book, but I saw them as if they were before me. When I had finished, he threw the sticks three

times and studied them as they fell.

"This is a very strong dream," he said. "It may eat you up."

"I am not afraid," I said and looked at him with both eyes. My voice sounded thin in my ears but that was because of the smoke.

He touched me on the breast and the forehead. He gave me the bow and the three arrows.

"Take them," he said. "It is forbidden to travel east. It is forbidden to cross the river. It is forbidden to go to the Place of the Gods. All these things are forbidden."

"All these things are forbidden," I said but it was my voice that spoke and not my spirit. He looked at me again.

"My son," he said. "Once I had young dreams. If your dreams do not eat you up, you may be a great priest. If they eat you, you are still my son. Now go on your journey."

I went fasting, as is the law. My body hurt but not my heart. When the dawn came, I was out of sight of the village. I prayed and purified myself, waiting for a sign. The sign was an eagle. It flew east.

Sometimes signs are sent by bad spirits. I waited again on the flat rock, fasting, taking no food. I was very still—I could feel the sky above me and the earth beneath. I waited till the sun was beginning to sink. Then three deer passed in the valley going east—they did not mind me or see me. There was a white fawn with them—a very great sign.

I followed them, at a distance, waiting for what would happen. My heart was troubled about going east, yet I knew that I must go. My head hummed with my fasting—I did not even see the panther spring upon the white fawn. But, before I knew it, the bow was in my hand. I shouted and the panther lifted his head from the fawn. It is not easy to kill a panther with one arrow but the arrow went through his eye and into his brain. He died as he tried to spring—he rolled over, tearing at the ground. Then I knew I was meant to go east—I knew that was my journey. When the night came, I made my fire and roasted meat.

It is eight suns journey to the east and a man passes by many Dead Places. The Forest People are afraid of them but I am not. Once I made my fire on the edge of a Dead Place at night and, next morning, in the dead house, I found a good knife, little rusted. That was small to what came afterward but it made my heart feel big. Always when I looked for game, it was in front of my arrow, and twice I passed hunting parties of the Forest People without their knowing. So I knew my magic was strong and my journey clean, in spite of the law.

Toward the setting of the eighth sun, I came to the banks of the great river. It was half-a-day's journey after I had left the god-road—we do not use the god-roads now for they are falling apart into great blocks of stone, and the forest is safer going. A long way off, I had seen the water through trees but the trees were thick. At last, I came out upon an open place at the top of a cliff. There was the great river below, like a giant in the sun. It is very long, very wide. It could eat all the streams we know and still be thirsty. Its name is Ou-dis-sun, the Sacred, the Long. No man of my tribe had seen it, not even my father, the priest. It was magic and I prayed.

Then I raised my eyes and looked south. It was there, the Place of the Gods.

How can I tell what it was like— you do not know. It was there, in the red light, and they were too big to be houses. It was there with the red light upon it, mighty and ruined. I knew that in another moment the gods would see me. I covered my eyes with my hands and crept back into the forest.

Surely, that was enough to do, and live. Surely it was enough to spend the night upon the cliff. The Forest People themselves do not come near. Yet, all through the night, I knew that I should have to cross the river and walk in the places of the gods, although the gods ate me up. My magic did not help me at all and yet there was a fire in my bowels, a fire in my mind. When the sun rose, I thought, "My journey has been clean. Now I will go home from my journey." But, even as I thought so, I knew I could not. If I went to the Place of the Gods, I would surely die; if I did not go, I could never be at peace with my spirit again. It is better to lose one's life than one's spirit, if one is a priest and the son of a priest.

Neverthelesss, as I made the raft, the tears ran out of my eyes. The Forest People could have killed me without a fight, if they had come upon me

then, but they did not come. When the raft was made, I said the sayings for the dead and painted myself for death. My heart was cold as a frog and my knees like water, but the burning in my mind would not let me have peace. As I pushed the raft from the shore, I began my death song—I had the right. It was a fine song.

> "I am John, son of John," I sang. "My people are the Hill People. They are the men.
> I go into the Dead Places but I am not slain.
> I take the metal from the Dead Places but I am not blasted.
> I travel upon the god-roads and am not afraid. E-yah! I have killed the panther, I have killed the fawn!
> E-yah! I have come to the great river. No man has come there before.
> It is forbidden to go east, but I have gone, forbidden to go on the great river, but I am there.
> Open your hearts, you spirits, and hear my song.
> Now I go to the place of the gods, I shall not return.
> My body is painted for death and my limbs weak, but my heart is big as I go to the Place of the Gods!"

All the same, when I came to the Place of the Gods, I was afraid, afraid. The current of the great river is very strong—it gripped my raft with its hands. That was magic, for the river itself is wide and calm. I could feel evil spirits about me, in the bright morning; I could feel their breath on my neck as

I was swept down the stream. Never have I been so much alone—I tried to think of my knowledge, but it was a squirrel's heap of winter nuts. There was no strength in my knowledge any more and I felt small and naked as a new-hatched bird—alone upon the great river, the servant of the gods.

Yet, after a while, my eyes were opened and I saw. I saw both banks of the river—I saw that once there had been god-roads across it, though now they were broken and fallen like broken vines. Very great they were, and wonderful and broken—broken in the time of the Great Burning when the fire fell out of the sky. And always the current took me nearer to the Place of the Gods, and the huge ruins rose before my eyes.

I do not know the customs of rivers—we are the People of the Hills. I tried to guide my raft with the pole but it spun around. I thought the river meant to take me past the Place of the Gods and out into the Bitter Water of the legends. I grew angry then—my heart felt strong. I said aloud, "I am a priest and the son of a priest!" The gods heard me—they showed me how to paddle with the pole on one side of the raft. The current changed itself—I drew near to the Place of the Gods.

When I was very near, my raft struck and turned over. I can swim in our lakes—I swam to the shore. There was a great spike of rusted metal sticking out into the river—I hauled myself up upon it and sat there, panting. I had saved my bow and two arrows and the knife I found in the Dead Place but that was all. My raft went whirling downstream toward the Bitter Water. I looked after it, and thought if it had trod me under, at least I would be safely dead. Nevertheless, when I had dried my bowstring and re-strung it, I walked forward to the Place of the Gods.

It felt like ground underfoot; it did not burn me. It is not true what some of the tales say, that the ground there burns forever, for I have been there. Here and there were the marks and stains of the Great Burning, on the ruins, that is true. But they were old marks and old stains. It is not true either, what some of our priests say, that it is an island covered with fogs and enchantments. It is not. It is a great Dead Place—greater than any Dead Place we know. Everywhere in it there are god-roads, though most are cracked and broken. Everywhere there are the ruins of the high towers of the gods.

How shall I tell what I saw? I went carefully, my strung bow in my hand, my skin ready for danger. There should have been the wailings of spirits and the shrieks of demons, but there were not. It was very silent and sunny where I had landed—the wind and the rain and the birds that drop seeds had done their work—the grass grew in the cracks of the broken stone. It is a fair island—no wonder the gods built there. If I had come there, a god, I also would have built.

How shall I tell what I saw? The towers are not all broken—here and there one still stands, like a great tree in a forest, and the birds nest high. But the towers themselves look blind, for the gods are gone. I saw a fish hawk, catching fish in the river. I saw a little dance of white butterflies over a great heap of broken stones and columns. I went there and looked about me— there was a carved stone with cut-letters, broken in half. I can read letters but I could not understand these. They said UBTREAS. There was also the shattered image of a man or a god. It had been made of white stone and he wore his hair tied like a woman's. His name was ASHING, as I read on the cracked half of a stone. I thought it wise to pray to ASHING, though I do not know that god.

How shall I tell what I saw? There was no smell of man left, on stone or metal. Nor were there many trees in that wilderness of stone. There are many pigeons, nesting and dropping in the towers—the gods must have loved them, or, perhaps, they used them for sacrifices. There are wild cats that roam the god-roads, green-eyed, unafraid of man. At night they wail like demons but they are not demons. The wild dogs are more dangerous, for they hunt in a pack, but them I did not meet un-til later. Everywhere there are the carved stones, carved with magical numbers or words.

I went north—I did not try to hide myself. When a god or a demon saw me, then I would die, but meanwhile I was no longer afraid. My hunger for knowledge burned in me—there was so much that I could not understand. Af-ter a while, I knew that my belly was hungry. I could have hunted for my meat, but I did not hunt. It is known that the gods did not hunt as we do— they got their food from enchanted boxes and jars. Sometimes these are still found in the Dead Places—once, when I was a child and foolish, I opened such a jar and tasted it and found the food sweet. But my father found out and punished me for it strictly, for, often, that food is death. Now, though, I had long gone past what was forbidden, and I entered the likeliest towers, looking for the food of the gods.

I found it at last in the ruins of a great temple in the mid-city. A mighty temple it must have been, for the roof was painted like the sky at night with its stars—that much I could see, though the colors were faint and dim. It went down into great caves and tunnels— perhaps they kept their slaves there. But when I started to climb down, I heard the squeaking of rats, so I did not go—rats are unclean, and there must have been many tribes of them, from the squeaking. But near there, I found food, in the heart of a ruin, be-hind a door that still opened. I ate only the fruits from the jars—they had a very sweet taste. There was drink, too, in bottles of glass—the drink of the gods was strong and made my head swim. After I had eaten and drunk, I slept on the top of a stone, my bow at my side.

When I woke, the sun was low. Looking down from where I lay, I saw a dog sitting on his haunches. His tongue was hanging out of his mouth; he looked as if he were laughing. He was a big dog, with a gray-brown coat, as big as a wolf. I sprang up and shouted at him but he did not move—he just sat there as if he were laughing. I did not like that. When I reached for a stone to throw, he moved swiftly out of the way of the stone. He was not afraid of me; he looked at me as if I were meat. No doubt I could have killed him with an arrow, but I did not know if there were others. Moreover, night was falling.

I looked about me—not far away there was a great, broken god-road, leading north. The towers were high enough, but not so high, and while many of the dead-houses were wrecked, there were some that stood. I went toward this god-road, keeping to the heights of the ruins, while the dog followed. When I had reached the god-road, I saw that there were others behind him. If I had slept later, they would have come upon me asleep and torn out my throat. As it was, they were sure enough of me; they did not hurry. When I went into the dead-house, they kept watch at the entrance—doubtless they thought they would have a fine hunt. But a dog cannot open a door and I knew, from the books, that the gods did not like to live on the ground but on high.

I had just found a door I could open when the dogs decided to rush. Ha! They were surprised when I shut the door in their faces—it was a good door, of strong metal. I could hear their foolish baying beyond it but I did not stop to answer them. I was in darkness—I found stairs and climbed. There were many stairs, turning around till my head was dizzy. At the top was another door—I found the knob and opened it. I was in a long small chamber—on one side of it was a bronze door that could not be opened, for it had no handle. Perhaps there was a magic word to open it but I did not have the word. I turned to the door in the opposite side of the wall. The lock of it was broken and I opened it and went in.

Within, there was a place of great riches. The god who lived there must have been a powerful god. The first room was a small anteroom—I waited there for some time, telling the spirits of the place that I came in peace and not as a robber. When it seemed to me that they had had time to hear me, I went on. Ah, what riches! Few, even, of the windows had been broken—it was all as it had been. The great windows that looked over the city had not been broken at all though they were dusty and streaked with many years. There were coverings on the floors, the colors not greatly faded, and the chairs were soft and deep. There were pictures upon the walls, very strange, very wonderful—I remember one of a bunch of flowers in a jar—if you came close to it, you could see nothing but bits of color, but if you stood away from it, the flowers might have been picked yesterday. It made my heart feel strange to look at this picture—and to look at the figure of a bird, in some hard clay, on a table and see it so like our birds. Everywhere there were books and writings, many in tongues that I could not read. The god who lived there must have been a wise god and full of knowledge. I felt I had a right there, as I sought knowledge also.

Nevertheless, it was strange. There was a washing-place but not water—perhaps the gods washed in air. There was a cooking-place but no wood, and though there was a machine to cook food, there was no place to put fire in it. Nor were there candles or lamps—there were things that looked like lamps but they had neither oil nor wick. All these things were magic, but I touched them and lived—the magic had gone out of them. Let me tell one thing to show. In the washing-place, a thing said "Hot" but it was not hot to the touch—another thing said "Cold" but it was not cold. This must have been a strong magic but the magic was gone. I do not understand—they had ways—I wish that I knew.

It was close and dry and dusty in their house of the gods. I have said that the magic was gone but that is not true—it had gone from the magic things but it had not gone from the place. I felt the spirits about me, weighing upon me. Nor had I ever slept in a Dead Place before—and yet, tonight, I must sleep there. When I thought of it, my tongue felt dry in my throat, in spite of my wish for knowledge. Almost I would have gone down again and faced the dogs, but I did not.

I had not gone through all the rooms when the darkness fell. When it fell, I went back to the big room looking over the city and made fire. There was a place to make fire and a box with wood in it, though I do not think they cooked there. I wrapped myself in a floor-covering and slept in front of the fire—I was very tired.

Now I tell what is very strong magic. I woke in the midst of the night. When I woke, the fire had gone out and I was cold. It seemed to me that all around me there were whisperings and voices. I closed my eyes to shut them out. Some will say that I slept again, but I do not think that I slept. I could feel the spirits drawing my spirit out of my body as a fish is drawn on a line.

Why should I lie about it? I am a priest and the son of a priest. If there are spirits, as they say, in the small Dead Places near us, what spirits must there not be in that great Place of the Gods? And would not they wish to speak? After such long years? I know that I felt myself drawn as a fish is drawn on a line. I had stepped out of my body—I could see my body asleep in front of the cold fire, but it was not I. I was drawn to look out upon the city of the gods.

It should have been dark, for it was night, but it was not dark. Everywhere there were lights—lines of light—circles and blurs of light—ten thousand torches could not have been the same. The sky itself was alight—you could barely see the stars for the glow in the sky. I thought to myself "This is strong magic" and trembled. There was a roaring in my ears like the rushing of rivers. Then my eyes grew used to the light and my ears to the

sound. I knew that I was seeing the city as it had been when the gods were alive.

That was a sight indeed—yes, that was a sight: I could not have seen it in the body—my body would have died. Everywhere went the gods, on foot and in chariots—there were gods beyond number and counting and their chariots blocked the streets. They had turned night to day for their pleasure—they did not sleep with the sun. The noise of their coming and going was the noise of many waters. It was magic what they could do—it was magic what they did.

I looked out of another window—the great vines of their bridges were mended and the god-roads went east and west. Restless, restless, were the gods and always in motion! They burrowed tunnels under rivers—they flew in the air. With unbelievable tools they did giant works—no part of the earth was safe from them, for, if they wished for a thing, they summoned it from the other side of the world. And always, as they labored and rested, as they feasted and made love, there was a drum in their ears—the pulse of the giant city, beating and beating like a man's heart.

Were they happy? What is happiness to the gods? They were great, they were mighty, they were wonderful and terrible. As I looked upon them and their magic, I felt like a child—but a little more, it seemed to me, and they would pull down the moon from the sky. I saw them with wisdom beyond wisdom and knowledge beyond knowledge. And yet not all they did was well done—even I could see that—and yet their wisdom could not but grow until all was peace.

Then I saw their fate come upon them and that was terrible past speech. It came upon them as they walked the streets of their city. I have been in the fights with the Forest People—I have seen men die. But this was not like that. When gods war with gods, they use weapons we do not know. It was fire falling out of the sky and a mist that poisoned. It was the time of the Great Burning and the Destruction. They ran about like ants in the streets of their city—poor gods, poor gods! Then the towers began to fall. A few escaped—yes, a few. The legends tell it. But, even after the city had become a Dead Place, for many years the poison was still in the ground. I saw it happen, I saw the last of them die. It was darkness over the broken city and I wept.

All this, I saw. I saw it as I have told it, though not in the body. When I woke in the morning, I was hungry, but I did not think first of my hunger for my heart was perplexed and confused. I knew the reason for the Dead Places but I did not see why it had happened. It seemed to me it should not have happened, with all the magic they had. I went through the house looking for an answer. There was so much in the house I could not understand—and yet I am a priest and the son of a priest. It was like being on one side of the great river, at night, with no light to show the way.

Then I saw the dead god. He was sitting in his chair, by the window, in a room I had not entered before and, for the first moment, I thought that he was alive. Then I saw the skin on the back of his hand—it was like dry leather. The room was shut, hot and dry—no doubt that had kept him as he was. At first I was afraid to approach him— then the fear left me. He was sitting looking out over the city—he was dressed in the clothes of the gods. His age was neither young nor old—I could not tell his age. But there was wisdom in his face and great sadness. You could see that he would have not run away. He had sat at his window, watching his city die—then he himself had died. But it is better to lose one's life than one's spirit—and you could see from the face that his spirit had not been lost. I knew that, if I touched him, he would fall into dust—and yet, there was something unconquered in the face.

That is all of my story, for then I knew he was a man—I knew then that they had been men, neither gods nor demons. It is great knowledge, hard to tell and believe. They were men—they went a dark road, but they were men. I had no fear after that—I had no fear going home, though twice I fought off the dogs and once I was hunted for two days by the Forest People. When I saw my father again, I prayed and was purified. He touched my lips and my breast, he said, "You went away a boy. You come back a man and a priest." I said, "Father, they were men! I have been in the Place of the Gods and seen it! Now slay me, if it is the law—but still I know they were men."

He looked at me out of both eyes. He said, "The law is not always the same shape—you have done what you have done. I could not have done it in my time, but you come after me. Tell!"

I told and he listened. After that, I wished to tell all the people but he showed me otherwise. He said, "Truth is a hard deer to hunt. If you eat too much truth at once, you may die of the truth. It was not idly that our fathers forbade the Dead Places." He was right—it is better the truth should come little by little. I have learned that, being a priest. Perhaps, in the old days, they ate knowledge too fast.

Nevertheless, we make a beginning. It is not for the metal alone we go to the Dead Places now—there are the books and the writings. They are hard to learn. And the magic tools are broken—but we can look at them and wonder. At least, we make a beginning. And, when I am chief priest we shall go beyond the great river. We shall go to the Place of the Gods—the place newyork—not one man but a company. We shall look for the images of the gods and find the god ASHING and the others—the gods Lincoln and Biltmore and Moses. But they were men who built the city, not gods or demons. They were men. I remember the dead man's face. They were men who were here before us. We must build again.

DISCUSSION

1. Where is the Place of the Gods? How do you know? What has happened before this story begins?

2. This John, son of John, is a leader. Because of his action, his people will probably advance. What personal characteristics does he possess that make his journey possible?

3. How is the young priest's civilization different from the one he learns about in the Place of the Gods?

4. Why does the father urge the young priest to delay telling all? What is the significance of the son's thought, "Perhaps, in the old days, they ate knowledge too fast"? This story was written before the Atomic Age, but it still has a special significance today. Why?

For further activities, see page 572.

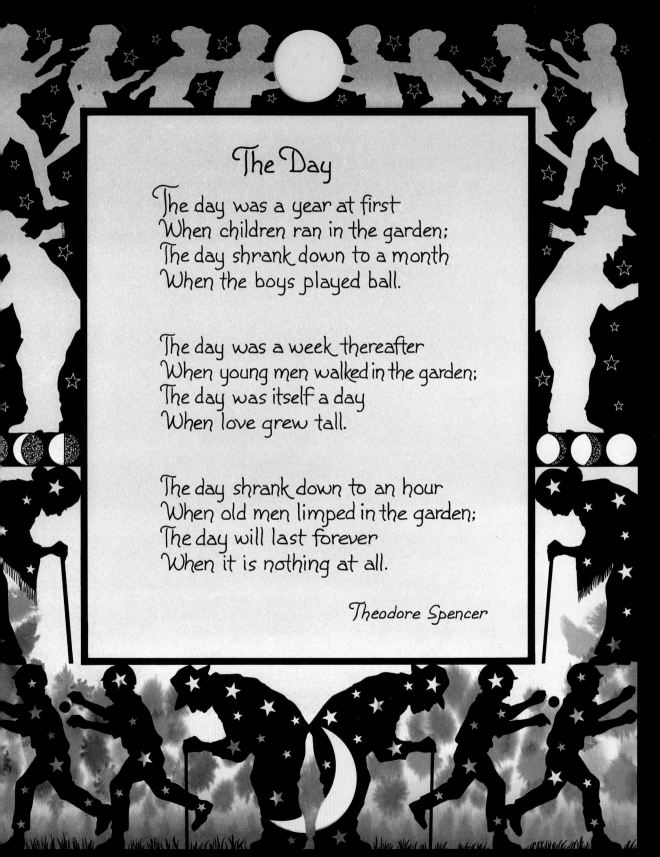

The Day

The day was a year at first
When children ran in the garden;
The day shrank down to a month
When the boys played ball.

The day was a week thereafter
When young men walked in the garden;
The day was itself a day
When love grew tall.

The day shrank down to an hour
When old men limped in the garden;
The day will last forever
When it is nothing at all.

Theodore Spencer

VOCABULARY

Buffalo Grass (page 542)

During the days of buffalo hunts, people found it often very difficult to kill these animals because of the buffalo's great speed and strength. Today, our language contains the word *buffaloed,* a feeling of frustration, bewilderment, and hopelessness. What do these "animal" words mean?

outfoxed	elephantine	catty	pigheaded	lionize
dogged	owlish	mousy	mulish	harebrained

Oregon Trail (page 549)

In line 34, the word *Colts* refers to a type of gun, not to its inventor, Samuel Colt. In our language we have many words that are the result of something that a particular person did. Look up these words to find out what they mean and where they came from.

boycott	sandwich	chauvinism	pasteurize
mesmerize	macadamize	sideburns	gardenia

COMPOSITION

High, Wide and Lonesome (page 534)

Hal Borland used many metaphors in describing the seasons. For example, he wrote "March drags its cold, muddy feet. . . ." Choose a season that you especially like or dislike. Describe it briefly and use metaphors to help convey your feelings.

Buffalo Grass (page 542)

1. Going to see the buffalo was a meaningful experience for Leah. Write a letter as she might write it to a friend in which she explains how she felt before the trip and how she felt afterward.

2. Interview an older person to find out what that person's life was like when he or she was the age you are now. Think of questions you want to ask and phrase them tactfully, in ways that will help the person you are interviewing remember what it was like being your age. Use the notes you take to write about another person's life at a moment in the past that corresponds to your life at this time.

READING

The Marginal World (page 552)

On separate paper, write the number of each sentence that is true.

1. The level of the sea is never constant, just as the shoreline is never the same on two successive days.
2. Shoreline life survives by occupying every available nook and cranny.
3. The author compares the dual nature of the marginal sea and its linking of life between land and water with man's awareness of the past and the constant, continuing flow of time into the future.
4. Carson compares the edge of the sea with time; both are elusive and have indefinable boundaries.
6. She compares the sequence and flow of time with the existence of mangrove periwinkles, which were once land dwellers that have now become adjusted to life in the water.

By the Waters of Babylon (page 558)

Rewrite the following sentences so that in each group of three, the sentences are in the order in which they occur in the story.

1. I was afraid.
   I ate a good piece of roasted meat.
   I held the metal and knew I would be a priest in time.

2. The sticks were thrown three times and their arrangement signified a very strong dream that could destroy me.
   The sign of the eagle suggested that I go east.
   I left without eating my food.

3. I swam ashore to the Dead Place.
   I made my raft, painted myself, and sang my death song.
   I looked for the food of the gods.

4. I saw the dead god in his chair.
   I slept in the dusty and close and dry house of the gods.
   I saw coverings that were not faded, pictures on the walls, flowers, but I understood that the magic had gone out of the machines.

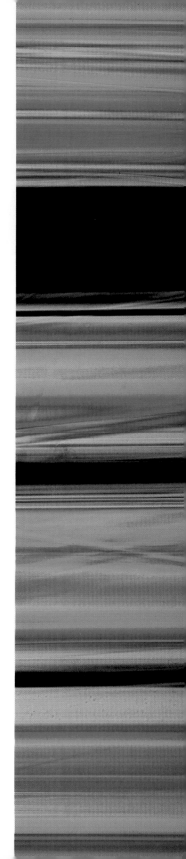

COMPOSITION

Having written a first draft, what do you check as you read it over? Spelling, of course, and punctuation. Take a good look at agreements: is a plural subject being used with a singular verb, or vice versa? ("Every one of the tenth-graders have a cold." One *have*?) And check for any of the kinds of mistakes that past experience has taught you to be on the lookout for in your own writing: dangling modifiers ("Waving good-bye, the plane took off"), pronouns without clear antecedents ("This was hard to put up with." *What* was?), and the like.

But those are obvious matters to watch for. Your revision should go farther. Check *word choice*. Can a single, specific word replace a less precise phrase? Can one exact noun ("meadowlark") serve the same purpose as a vague adjective-and-noun combination ("yellow bird"), or one clear verb ("March *drags* along") serve for a verb and adverb ("March *moves slowly* along")? Have you repeated yourself, using two words that mean the same thing? Get rid of one of them. And get rid of redundancies ("She shouted *loudly*." How else *could* she shout?).

Next, check your paragraphs for *unity*. Does each paragraph develop a central idea, and does *every* sentence in the paragraph relate to that idea? Remove any sentences that are irrelevant.

Check for *coherence*. Has your mind outraced your pen, so that some vital idea in your head never got down on the page? Insert the idea where it ought to appear. Does each sentence lead into the one that follows it? Are transitions from sentence to sentence clear?

Check for *emphasis*. Have you used a variety of sentence patterns and types, in ways that subordinate less important ideas? A single short sentence ("Time was strange") among longer sentences is emphatic. So is a question ("And how far does time stretch ahead?") among a series of statements. Use such devices to stress what should stand out.

The final step—and time should be allowed for this, too—is transcribing the results of your revision to make a fair copy, free of mistakes and blemishes. When you have proofread that version and corrected any last slips of the pen, only then is your composition finished.

REVISING

ABOUT THE SELECTIONS

1.   Which selection in this unit most effectively awakened for you a sense of time passing? In a paragraph discuss the way in which the awareness of time was expressed. What images or details helped make you conscious of how the past is yesterday's present, how the present is tomorrow's past?

2.   Try your hand at writing an advertisement to lure people to one of the places described in these selections. New York City, the prairies, Pompeii, seaside pools, and the Oregon Trail are among the possibilities. Look at some travel advertisements in magazines and newspapers. Then, by choosing appropriate details, and by using language that is urgent and persuasive, let your reader know of the wonders that await the traveler who goes to the destination you are promoting.

3.   Which of the several poems in this section impressed you most? Write two or three paragraphs accounting for your preference. Quote specific words and phrases from the poem to support your general statements. Be sure your paragraphs are both unified and coherent, and leave time for revising, recopying, and proofreading what you have written.

4.   Reporters send cablegrams over great distances to report news fast. But such messages are charged by the word: the longer the message, the more expensive it is. Using language efficiently and economically, write a cablegram to communicate the essential facts of either the Pompeii disaster or the disaster befalling New York in "Metropolitan Nightmare." Revise your first draft to remove unnecessary words. Hold your final account to fifty words or fewer.

ON YOUR OWN

1.   For the dentist absorbed in working, time may be speeding by. For the patient being worked on in the chair, it may be dragging and dragging. Describe a scene in which two people are experiencing the same space of time differently. You might arrange your description in two paragraphs, using the transitional expression *meanwhile.*

2.   Find out everything you can about the day you were born. Ask your parents or relatives to share with you any details they can recollect of that day. If possible, read at the library a newspaper for the day, or check out the appropriate newsmagazine. Take notes. Then assemble the facts you have gathered in some logical order to bring the day back into the present. Revise the paragraphs you have written.

3.   "By the Waters of Babylon" describes such objects as faucets and elevators from the point of view of someone who does not understand their function. Describe an object with which you are familiar (a typewriter or refrigerator, for instance) as an English-speaking visitor from another planet might perceive it. The visitor would see what the object did, but would not understand why, or for what purpose.

ABOUT THE authors

Leonard Adamé (born 1947) Born in the San Joaquin Valley in California, Leonard Adamé spent his early years in his father's restaurant where he "grew to hate dishes." He worked a few summers on his uncle's farm, disliked high school although he managed to finish, and toured the U.S. with a rock group. Now married, he has three daughters.

Marian Anderson (born 1908) A contralto who once drew a crowd of 75,000 to hear her sing at the Lincoln Memorial, Marian Anderson was born to a poor family in South Philadelphia. At the age of six she joined the junior choir of the Union Baptist Church and later helped support her family by singing with other choirs. Her talent was recognized early and she studied under the best vocal teachers, winning a contest which allowed her to sing with the New York Philharmonic at Lewishon Stadium. Disappointed with a lack of concert bookings at home, Anderson traveled to Europe where she sang before the Swedish and Danish kings and for the Finnish composer Sibelius. Upon her triumphant return she was entertained by President Franklin Roosevelt and gave her now famous concert at the Lincoln Memorial.

W. H. Auden (1907–1973) The most influential English-born poet of the twentieth century, W. H. Auden became an American citizen during his maturity. His work defies categorization. He has written plays, librettos, ballads, lyrics, and narratives. With *The Age of Anxiety* (1947), he not only won a Pulitzer Prize but bestowed a descriptive name on a decade and a generation. The imagery in Auden's poetry, drawn from such unlikely sources as science and slang, makes it fresh, challenging, and representative of the concerns and many of the attitudes of our times. A year or so before his death, he returned to England to teach at Oxford University.

Jacqueline Auriol (born 1917) On May 12, 1951, Jacqueline Auriol became "the fastest woman in the world," setting the international women's speed record in a Havilland Vampire jet fighter plane. She grew up as Jacqueline Douet, the daughter of a wealthy ship builder in Challans, France, and shocked her parents by marrying Paul Auriol, the son of the leader of the Socialist Party. Later she met a flyer who introduced her to airplanes. Learning to fly quickly, she performed in air shows and worked as a test pilot. When she first soloed in the new jet in which she was to try for the world's record, she said, "That day I experienced a sense of completeness . . . a sense of being in complete possession of myself."

Maralyn Bailey (born 1941) Born in Nottingham, England, Maralyn Bailey received her education in Derby and later worked as a government tax clerk. She has received numerous awards for outstanding seamanship and is currently working on a book about her voyage to Patagonia.

Maurice Bailey (born 1932) Born and educated in Derby, England, Maurice Bailey worked for a time as a printer's clerk and was later managing director of Maulyn Ltd. of Jersey. He is a contributor to *Sail* and *Yachting Monthly* and with his wife Maralyn is currently working on a book about their voyage to Patagonia.

Stephen Vincent Benét (1898–1943) Only in his mid-forties at the time of his death, Stephen Vincent Benét had already made his mark on modern American literature. Always fascinated by America's unique heritage, Benét in many of his stories and poems recreated that heritage and the people who shaped it. Two of his long poems, *Western Star* and *John Brown's Body,* were awarded Pulitzer Prizes.

William Rose Benét (1886–1950) Christopher Morley once wrote of his friend William Rose Benét, "Old Bill Benét, Old Bill Benét / Born in a Fort on Groundhog Day." Benét was indeed born at Fort Hamilton, New York, where his father was stationed. Both William and his younger brother Stephen graduated from Yale University and pursued literary careers. William regarded himself primarily as a poet, but he also wrote a novel, essays, and short stories. He edited several anthologies, including the *Oxford Anthology of American Literature,* and enjoyed making eccentric drawings of fantastic animals.

Philip Booth (born 1925) Booth considers himself a New Hampshireman not only by birth but "by instinct." His boyhood ambition was to become a member of the Dartmouth College ski team, an ambition he later made a reality. He earned a master's degree at Columbia University and served with the Air Force during World War II. A teacher by profession, he has taught at Bowdoin College, Dartmouth, and Wellesley College, remaining as much as possible in his native New England and continuing to write poetry.

Hal Borland (1900–1978) "I grew up on the American frontier," wrote Hal Borland. "I was born . . . ninety-six years to the day after Lewis and Clark left St. Louis on their expedition." In terms of historical progress, he continues, "I have lived close to 150 years, simply because I grew up . . . during the tag end of the big cattle-ranch and sod-house days." Completing high school in three years, he earned his way through the University of Colorado by working as a newspaper correspondent and ever since graduation has combined newspaper work with the writing of books. Borland is known for his nature writing in particular. On his hundred-acre farm he has written the "outdoor" editorials that have been appearing in Sunday editions of *The New York Times* for more than twenty years.

High, Wide and Lonesome derives its name from the author's description of the country he knew as a boy. His latest book is *A Place to Begin: The New England Experience.*

Gwendolyn Brooks (born 1917) Awarded the Pulitzer Prize in 1950 for *Annie Allen,* her second book of poetry, Gwendolyn Brooks is also a fine novelist. Both her fiction and her poetry are characterized by a directness and restraint that make all the more moving the seemingly uneventful lives she explores. Although her own life has been comfortable, she writes frequently and sympathetically of the poor, doomed to squalor while dreaming of something better. Her verse, as one critic has noted, draws on the world she understands but records insights about that world in such a way that they become "not merely personal or racial but universal in their implications." She is a member of The National Institute of Arts and Letters and edits a magazine, *The Black Position.*

Heywood Broun (1888–1939) Heywood Broun lived an active life. Primarily he was a journalist—and a courageous and controversial one. After college at Harvard, he became a sports writer for a New York newspaper. Later he earned a reputation as a drama critic. In the 1930s Broun crowned a long interest in politics by running for Congress—and being defeated. Then he became a good painter; on several occasions his paintings were exhibited in museums. In his spare time he wrote novels, biographies, and short stories.

Constance Carrier (born 1908) Known both as a poet and as a translator of Latin poetry, Constance Carrier taught Latin in high schools in New Britain, and Hartford, Connecticut for thirty-eight years. Her book of poems *The Middle Voice* won the Lamont Poetry Prize and she has been awarded several fellowships at the MacDowell Colony in New Hampshire.

Rachel Carson (1907–1964) Rachel Carson's book *Silent Spring,* published in 1962, aroused such public interest in the potential dangers of pesticides that it is credited with helping the eventual passage of laws limiting their use. Carson had long been known as a popular writer of marine life, and her book *The Sea Around Us* was a best seller. Born in Springdale, Pennsylvania, Carson enrolled in Pennsylvania College for Women intending to become a writer. But a course in biology aroused her interest and she became a science major. After graduate work at Johns Hopkins University, she taught zoology there and later at the University of Maryland, and for sixteen years she worked as aquatic biologist for the U.S. Bureau of Fisheries in Washington.

Robert P. Tristram Coffin (1892–1955) "I am a New Englander by birth, by bringing up, by spirit," Coffin once wrote. He was raised on a Maine coastal farm: "I began being a poet there among lighthouses and barns and boats, tides and fogs and apples and hired men." After graduating from Bowdoin College, he attended Oxford University as a Rhodes Scholar. For many years he taught English while writing poetry, novels, essays, and biographies. Among the most popular of his books of poetry are *Ballads of Square-Toed Americans* and *Maine Ballads*. His prose works include *Lost Paradise,* his autobiography.

Colette (1873–1954) A prolific career as a writer of novels and short stories spanned over fifty years of Sidone-Gabrielle Colette's life. She grew up in Burgundy, France, and her first novels, centered around a character called Claudine, draw upon her early experiences. Later she concentrated on journalism and novels, becoming a prominent figure in Paris society and an author with an important literary reputation. Probably the Colette novel best known to Americans is *Gigi,* which was made into a popular movie.

John Collier (born 1901) English author John Collier began his literary career by writing poetry. But he later switched to novels. Perhaps his most interesting novel is *Full Circle,* a story about England in 1955 after it has been destroyed by war. John Collier has served as poetry editor for a leading British magazine.

Richard Connell (1893–1949) Summing up his career this way, Richard Connell once said, "My first writing was done for the daily newspaper my father edited in Poughkeepsie, New York. I covered baseball games. I was ten years old and got ten cents a game. I have been a professional writer ever since." At Harvard University in Massachusetts, Connell was editor of two student publications, and during World War I he edited his army camp's weekly newspaper. After the war he devoted all his time to writing fiction, concentrating for the most part on short stories. About 300 of his stories were published in various English and American magazines.

Roald Dahl (born 1916) Born of Norwegian parents in Wales, Dahl is one of the contemporary short story masters of the English language. His wildly improbable plots, unique characters, and acid humor have gained him international acclaim. His collections, *Kiss Kiss* and *Someone Like You,* consist of bizarre stories a reader is not likely ever to forget.

Borden Deal (born 1922) A writer of novels as well as short stories, Borden Deal has also fought forest fires, worked for a circus, and been a government skip tracer (tracer of people who fail to pay bills). Born and raised in Mississippi, he served in the navy during World War II and now lives in Florida. Mr. Deal began his writing career when he won first prize in a short-story contest while a student at the University of Alabama.

Walter de la Mare (1873–1956) The British author Walter de la Mare began his writing career at sixteen with the founding of a school magazine. The magazine was short-lived, but the career was not. Before de la Mare was widely known, he supported himself with a job as a bookkeeper in a large oil company—routine work that he left as soon as he could. As growing popularity brought greater financial security, he was able to move his family to the country, where he devoted himself entirely to his books.

Emily Dickinson (1830–1886) Except for a few brief trips to nearby cities, Emily Dickinson spent her life in the New England village of Amherst, Massachusetts. She lived much to herself, and when asked who her companions were, she would reply, "Hills, sir, and the sundown, and a dog as large as myself." Her thoughts, too, were her companions. "How do most people live without any thoughts?" she once asked a friend. Emily Dickinson wrote hundreds of poems, often jotting them down on any available piece of paper: a brown paper bag, a used envelope, the back of a recipe. All of them she saved in little packets tied with ribbon, tucked away in boxes and drawers. The poems were discovered and published shortly after her death, but forty years went by before their excellence was recognized.

Annie Dillard (born 1945) The author of *Pilgrim at Tinker Creek,* Annie Dillard, was born in Pittsburgh, Pennsylvania, and educated at Hollins College. Later she married a poet and novelist, Richard Dillard. Since 1973 she has been a contributing editor for *Harper's Magazine* and has published poems and articles in other magazines, including the *Atlantic Monthly* and *Sports Illustrated.* She also writes a regular column for *Living Wilderness.* In 1974 she published a book of poems, *Tickets for a Prayer Wheel.*

Sir Arthur Conan Doyle (1859–1930) Sherlock Holmes came into being while a struggling young doctor waited vainly for patients. Scottish-born Sir Arthur Conan Doyle amused himself during those long hours by writing stories about a "scientific" detective who solved cases by his amazing powers of deduction. The physician modeled Holmes on a real person, a tall, wiry surgeon who had the reputation of being able to tell a person's occupation just by looking at him. Later, growing tired of writing Holmes stories, Sir Arthur Conan Doyle wrote a story in which the detective was killed by a Professor Moriarty. But Holmes was so popular that public demand forced the author to bring him back to life.

Loren Eiseley (1907–1977) Contributing verse and prose to literary anthologies and magazines, and articles to scientific and anthropological journals, Loren Eiseley has managed to synthesize his interests in the humanities and science. After earning his Ph.D. from the University of Pennsylvania, he went on to teach anthropology at Oberlin College and the University of Pennsylvania and to act as head of the latter university's department of history and philosophy of science. His academic honors have been numerous and he received awards for his books *Darwin's Century* and *The Firmament of Time.*

T. S. Eliot (1888–1965) Although he became a British subject in 1927, Eliot was born in the Midwest of an established New England family. Born and raised in St. Louis, Eliot entered Harvard in 1906, returning to the region of his ancestors. After continuing his studies in Europe, he finally settled in England, where he was first a schoolteacher, then a banker, and finally a member of the English publishing firm of Faber & Faber. Meanwhile, he had written a number of controversial poems expressing his pessimistic view of modern life. His verse is not "pretty"; for a poet, he insisted, should "be able to see beneath both beauty and ugliness—to see the boredom, and the horror, and the glory." At forty he became an "Anglo-Catholic in religion" and almost all of his later poetry dealt with religious themes.

Mari Evans A native of Toledo, Ohio, Mari Evans was a John Hay Whitney Fellow, 1965–66, and a Consultant for the National Endowment of the Arts. Her poetry has been used extensively in textbooks and anthologies. Formerly producer/director of a weekly half-hour television series "The Black Experience," she is Writer-in-Residence and assistant professor in Black Literature at Indiana University, Bloomington, Indiana. She is the author of several juvenile books and her poems have been collected in two volumes, *Where is All the Music* and *I Am A Black Woman.*

Robert Francis (born 1901) On the edge of town in Amherst, Massachusetts, Robert Francis lives in a white house that he calls Fort Juniper. Although he has taught high school English and the violin, he is primarily a poet. Robert P. Tristram Coffin once commented that Robert Francis uses "the simplest kind of words . . . but the poem is there."

Robert Frost (1874–1963) The only American poet to be awarded the Pulitzer Prize four times, Robert Frost charmed and challenged readers for half a century. His poems, often set against a rural New England landscape, are notable for their conversational style and realistic portraits. Beneath their seeming simplicity, however, lies an irony and subtlety which exemplify Frost's belief that poetry is a question of "saying one thing and meaning another."

Susan Glaspell (1882–1948) Love of the theater led Susan Glaspell to become an amateur actress, a dramatist, and one of the founders of the Provincetown Players—a group that began producing plays in 1915 on a fishing wharf in Provincetown, Massachusetts. Here many aspiring American playwrights, including Eugene

O'Neill, had their first successful efforts performed.

Born in Davenport, Iowa, Susan Glaspell earned a degree at Drake College before starting work as a reporter and free-lance writer. In 1931, she was awarded a Pulitzer Prize for her play *Alison's House,* based on the life of Emily Dickinson. In addition to plays, she wrote several short stories, novels, and biographies. *Trifles,* which she adapted from her own short story "A Jury of Her Peers," was suggested by a true incident which Glaspell encountered as a news reporter.

Arthur Gordon (born 1912) Born in Georgia, Arthur Gordon graduated from Yale University in New Haven, Connecticut, and studied later at Oxford University in England. After three years in the air force overseas, he returned to this country and worked for a while as an editor. When he writes, his working hours are comfortable: "I try to work about three hours a day, roughly from nine till noon. Then I put on such a show of exhaustion that I convince everybody—including myself."

Lady Gregory (1852–1932) Born in Ireland, Lady Gregory lived a quiet life on her family's estate in Galway until her marriage at twenty-eight. Introduced by her husband to the literary world, she took up writing to support herself after his death. Ireland at that time was in the midst of a literary revival, and Lady Gregory's translations of Irish sagas from Gaelic to English soon made her a principal figure in it. For the rest of her life she wrote plays, raised funds, encouraged new playwrights, and fed hungry actors—acting as godmother of the Abbey Theater, which she helped to establish.

Thomas Hardy (1840–1928) Born in a thatched-roof cottage in a tiny English town, Thomas Hardy received all his formal schooling between the ages of eight and sixteen. Then he was apprenticed to a draftsman, despite the fact that he wanted to be a writer. Although poetry was his first love, he soon found that publishers were not interested in the poems he wrote; accordingly he began to write novels and eventually achieved wide recognition. After more than twenty years as a successful novelist he once again turned to poetry and spent his remaining thirty years writing more than a thousand lyrics and a long epic-drama called *The Dynasts.*

Roy Helton (born 1886) As a young man Roy Helton, a graduate of the University of Pennsylvania, tried several occupations. After color blindness thwarted an artistic career, Helton became a radio commentator and then a teacher. An interest in primitive folk poetry led him to travel among the hill people of South Carolina and Kentucky, searching for folk material at its source. Three volumes of poems, particularly *Lonesome Water,* reflect this interest. In addition Helton has written two novels and held several state offices.

Zenna Henderson (born 1917) Having taught in schools throughout Arizona, for the U.S. Air Force in France, and at a tuberculosis sanitorium for children, Zenna Henderson has now settled down to teach in Eloy, Arizona, her home state. Her stories, mostly science fiction, have been included in many anthologies of this genre and have been collected in her own volumes *The Anything Box,* and *The People: No Different Flesh.* A member of the Science Fiction Writers of America, she won second prize in the Ellery Queen Contest of 1954.

William Ernest Henley (1849–1903) Early in his life William Ernest Henley was stricken with tuberculosis of the bone and had to have one foot amputated. Later the same disease infected the other foot, but Henley refused to submit to a second operation. Lying in a hospital bed for nearly two years, he battled the disease and

won, his courage and determination prevailing in spite of his poor health. One of his close friends was Robert Louis Stevenson, who used him as a model for the pirate Long John Silver in *Treasure Island.*

O. Henry (1862–1910) William Sydney Porter, better known by his pen name O. Henry, grew up in North Carolina. As a young man in Ohio he served a three-year prison term for embezzlement, although his innocence was later established beyond a reasonable doubt. He spent the last part of his life in New York, writing prolifically. *Cabbages and Kings* and *The Four Million* are two of his most popular collections of stories.

Ralph Hodgson (1871–1962) This English poet was a recluse who believed that his private life was not the public's concern. He was a quiet man, fond of dogs and billiards. It is known, however, that he was an editor of *Fry's Magazine* in London and that he lived in the United States during two periods of his life, once in youth and once in old age. He wrote several books of poetry before 1917, and then published nothing more until 1941. He was the winner of several poetry awards and in 1954 received the Queen's Medal for Poetry.

Langston Hughes (1902–1967) Born in Joplin, Missouri, Langston Hughes traveled so widely that he titled his autobiography *I Wonder As I Wander.* After high school Hughes lived for a year in Mexico and then went to New York City to attend college. A year later he was on the move again, this time as a sailor. On one transatlantic voyage he ceremoniously broke free from his past ideas; he stood on the deck of the ship and, one by one, threw his books into the ocean. Back in America in 1926 Hughes published his first book of poems. That work won both wide acclaim and a college scholarship for him. Once he finished college, he began to write seriously for a living. A versatile as well as a talented writer, he published poems, short stories, novels, plays, movie scripts, songs, and several nonfiction studies of the American Negro.

Chet Huntley (1911–1974) During his thirty-one-year career as a broadcast journalist, Huntley worked first as a radio newscaster and correspondent and later in the same capacity on television. *The Huntley-Brinkley Report,* an NBC nightly news program in which he appeared for fourteen years, won numerous awards, and Huntley himself won two Peabody awards. He stated that he hoped it would be said of him that "he had a great respect, almost an awe, of the medium in which he worked. He regarded it as a privilege, not a license."

Daniel K. Inouye (born 1924) From his beginning as the oldest son of a Japanese laborer in the Hawaiian canefields, Daniel Inouye rose to the office of U.S. Senator—discovering as he says "that there is no limit to the aspirations of an American boy." During World War II Inouye repeatedly demonstrated his loyalty to the U.S. by volunteering for military service; he was finally accepted by the 442nd Regiment and fought with them in Europe, losing an arm in battle. In 1962 he was the first Japanese-American to be elected to the U.S. Senate. His book *Journey to Washington* recounts his experiences overcoming racial prejudice.

Dorothy M. Johnson (born 1905) After a fifteen-year career as a magazine editor in New York, Dorothy Johnson moved to Montana and began to write the western novels for adults and young people which have won her renown. Among these are *Lawmen of the Old West, Some Went West,* and *A Biography of Sitting Bull.* The motion pictures *The Hanging Tree, The Man Who Shot Liberty Valence,* and *A Man Called Horse* were based on her stories, and several television plays have been adapted from her writings. She is an honorary member of the

Blackfeet tribe in Montana and has won the Spur Award from the Western Writers of America.

James Weldon Johnson (1871–1938) Johnson had a remarkably varied career. While studying for his law degree he became a high school teacher and principal. At thirty he went to New York to become a successful writer of popular songs; later he was appointed U.S. Consul to Venezuela and Nicaragua. But above all Johnson was a writer. *God's Trombones* is probably his best-known book, in addition to the anthologies of American Negro poetry and spirituals that he edited. Here as elsewhere a feeling of responsibility to the Negro American is the keynote of his work. Late in life Johnson returned to teaching at Fisk University and New York University.

Billy Jean King (born 1943) Six-time winner of England's Wimbledon Women's Tennis Championship, Billie Jean King grew up in Long Beach, California, in a sports-loving family. At first she concentrated on softball, but realizing the limited opportunities for women in this sport, she switched to tennis. From her first tournament at age eleven, Billie Jean has devoted her life to tennis. Winning her first title in 1958, she went on to become the number one ranked woman player in the U.S. and to win the South African Championship, the U.S. Indoor Tennis Championship, and the Eastern Grass Courts Championship.

Galway Kinnell (born 1927) A career as poet and university professor has taken Galway Kinnell to many places around the world. After earning his B.A. from Princeton University and M.A. from the University of Rochester, Kinnell began a teaching career which included two years at the University of Grenoble, France, a year at the University of Iran as Fulbright Professor, and periods at the University of Chicago and Colorado State College. In 1963 he acted as field worker for CORE. His poetry has won him numerous prizes as well as a Guggenheim fellowship and a Rockefeller Foundation grant. His other work includes translations of books and poems from the French and a novel, *Black Light.*

Maxine Kumin (born 1925) Although she has written a novel and several books for children, Maxine Kumin is best known and most highly regarded as a poet. Born in Philadelphia, she received her B.A. and M.A. from Radcliffe College and was a scholar of the Radcliffe Institute for Independent Study. She also taught English for three years at Tufts University. Her books of poems include *Halfway, The Beach Before Breakfast,* and *The Privilege.*

Doris Lessing (born 1919) Born of British parents in Iran, Doris Lessing grew up in Southern Rhodesia and never even visited England until 1949. Her writings express her concern with two major issues: the conflict between the races in Africa and the problems of an intelligent woman seeking to maintain her identity in a man's world. Her *African Stories,* according to one reviewer, are beautifully wrought "by a sensitive and thoughtful but fiercely honest writer. . . ." Playwright, poet, journalist, writer of fiction, Doris Lessing has been called by the *London Times* "one of the most serious, intelligent, and honest writers of the whole post-war generation."

Henry Wadsworth Longfellow (1807–1882) The best-loved poet of his time, Longfellow saw beauty in everything from a ruined castle on the Rhine to a blacksmith shop in Cambridge. In such familiar things as the old clock on the stairs, the bridge from Cambridge to Boston, or a fire of driftwood, he found unexpected meanings. He created poetry out of everyday experiences. But Longfellow also loved the romantic memories of America's past which he recaptured and immortalized in poems such as "The Courtship of Miles Standish," *Evangeline,* and *Hiawatha.* He remains the most quoted of American poets. He wrote on profound as well as simple themes; he embraced both American and European subjects; and he used with melodious skill a wide variety of poetic forms.

Phyllis McGinley (1905–1978) "The vanishing West had not quite vanished," recalled Phyllis McGinley about her childhood on a Colorado ranch. She and her brother rode ponies three miles to school at which they were sometimes the only students. Later McGinley spent a year in Utah as a teacher. Her selected poems, *Times Three,* won the Pulitzer Prize. Other collections include *A Pocketful of Wry, A Short Walk from the Station,* and *The Love Letters of Phyllis McGinley.* She has described her writing as "outwardly amusing, but inwardly serious."

Don Marquis (1878–1937) Don Marquis began his journalism career in earnest when he joined the editorial staff of the *Atlanta Constitution.* But he is best known for "archy" (a cockroach) and "mehitabel" (a cat). Through these characters Marquis told satiric stories of life in America.

Alice Marriott (born 1910) Alice Marriott's strong interest in Indians developed when she was a librarian for a period after graduating from Oklahoma City University. She decided to study Indian culture at the University of Oklahoma and was the first woman to receive a degree in anthropology from that institution. Since then she has done field work with the Modoc, Kiowa, Cheyenne, Arapaho and Cherokee tribes and has worked with Indians in forty-six states in her capacity as field representative for the Indian Arts and Crafts Board of the Department of the Interior. She has helped arrange displays of Indian art at the San Francisco World's Fair, the Museum of Modern Art in New York, and many other museums and has published fifteen books as well as articles in *The New Yorker* and *Southwest Review.*

Guy de Maupassant (1850–1893) Guy de Maupassant was born in France, the son of a Paris stockbroker. His parents' separation when he was eleven left the young boy to grow up in the care of his mother, through whom he met the literary circle that was later to have a great influence on his writing career. Maupassant's education was interrupted by army service during the Franco-Prussian War. After the war he began to take an interest in writing, soon finding that his talent lay in the short story. Before illness cut short his career, Maupassant's many books had earned him a place among the world's best short-story writers.

Edna St. Vincent Millay (1892–1950) By the time she was twenty, Edna St. Vincent Millay had achieved fame with "Renascence." The poem marked the beginning of a career that was to see her become probably the most popular poet in America between the two World Wars. Her poems expressed the disillusionment of the postwar generation and struck a tone that appealed to public tastes. Although usually working within traditional stanza forms, she often expressed a romantic protest against traditions and conventions. Her early concern with her own identity—her relationship to others and to the universe—gradually shifted to a concern with broader social issues.

Emerson Blackhorse Mitchell (born 1945) A Navajo Indian, Emerson Blackhorse Mitchell was born near Shiprock, New Mexico, where he was brought up by his grandparents, speaking only the Navajo language until he was six. He attended public schools and then went on to the Institute of American Indian Arts in Santa Fe. There, his creative writing teacher, Mrs. Terry Allen, encouraged him to write about his childhood. From these efforts emerged the book *Miracle Hill: The Story of a Navajo Boy*.

Toshio Mori (born 1910) Toshio Mori writes about first-generation Japanese immigrants who refused to be crushed by disillusionment and about second-generation Japanese-Americans, some of whom faced a terrible crisis of loyalty brought on by World War II. His heroes all come from San Leandro, California, where Mori was born and where he augmented his public school education with self-education in libraries and secondhand book stores. He was relocated for three years during the war and returned to San Leandro to find his mother dead and his brother injured in combat. His stories have been published in many magazines, and one was selected for the *Best American Short Stories* for 1943.

Pauli Murray (born 1910) Combining a career in law with writing poetry, Pauli Murray has distinguished herself in both fields. She graduated from Hunter College in New York, received her law degree from Howard University, and her LL.M. from the California School of Jurisprudence. Practicing law in California and New York, she has worked for civil rights and women's rights, becoming a "freedom rider" in the 1940s to protest segregated buses and bringing suits against universities for refusing to admit women to their graduate schools. She has also taught law at Ghana School of Law and at Brandeis University. Her poetry has appeared in magazines and been collected in the volume *Dark Testament. Proud Shoes,* a chronicle of her family history, was published in 1956.

Liam O'Flaherty (born 1896) The Irish author Liam O'Flaherty was born in the Aran Islands, tiny windswept points of land off the west coast, where fishermen and farmers struggle against the violence of nature and still speak the ancient language of their ancestors. His first language was Gaelic (Irish), not English. Leaving college to enlist in the British army during World War I, O'Flaherty was seriously injured in action. After his discharge he knocked about the world, working for a while in the United States as a Western Union messenger, factory hand, and fisherman. O'Flaherty was in Ireland during part of the political upheaval of the early 1920s. *The Informer,* his best-known novel, is set in Dublin during the same period as "The Sniper."

Elder Olson (born 1909) Born in Chicago and educated there, Olson became a professor of English at the University of Chicago in 1953. *Things of Sorrow,* an early collection of poetry, received the Friends of Literature award in 1935. In addition, Olson has written a prize-winning study, *The Poetry of Dylan Thomas.* His *Collected Poems* appeared in 1963.

Américo Paredes (born 1915) A descendant of the settlers who colonized the Rio Grande area, Américo Paredes was born in Brownsville, Texas. After graduating from the University of Texas, he returned to earn his M.A. and Ph.D. in English and Spanish and is now professor of English and anthropology at the same university. Dr. Paredes is a contributing editor for the Chicano journal *Aztlán* and writes short stories and poems. Two of his books are *With His Pistol in His Hand* and *Folktales of Mexico.*

Patricia Parker Publishing her poems in such magazines as *Loveletter* and *Black Dialogue,* Patricia Parker has also given readings of her work throughout the San Francisco Bay area. She was born in Texas and now lives in Berkeley, California. One of her poems was included in *Dices or Black Bones,* an anthology of black poetry of the 1970s.

Marge Piercy (born 1936) *Breaking Camp,* Marge Piercy's first book of poems won for her a University of Michigan award for poetry and drew admiration from critics who saw her poems as a courageous rejecting of easy cynicism and modish cool to "believe again in language as thought and feeling and in metaphor as possibility." Piercy was born in Detroit, graduated from the University of Michigan, and earned her

M.A. from Northwestern University. In 1973 she published the novel *Small Changes* and a book of poems, *To Be of Use.*

Edgar Allan Poe (1809–1849) In his short life, Poe achieved fame, but his story is tragic, full of frustration and sadness, poverty and loneliness. He lost both of his parents before he was three, one by death and the other by desertion. Foster parents brought him up, but as he grew older there were many quarrels at home. After a short stay at the University of Virginia he began a career as a soldier, then as a writer and editor. While Poe was writing his tales of the supernatural and suspense, his young wife was hopelessly ill. In 1847 she—like his mother—died of tuberculosis. Two years later Poe was found unconscious on a Baltimore street and was taken to the charity hospital where he died. "The saddest and strangest figure in American literary history," one biographer has said of Poe.

Leroy Quintana Born and raised in New Mexico, Leroy Quintana fought in the Vietnam War and attended the University of New Mexico, the University of Denver, and New Mexico State University. He has taught at New Mexico State University and currently is an instructor at El Paso Community College. His book of poems is titled *Hijo del Pueblo.*

Santha Rama Rau (born 1923) A background part eastern, part western prepared Santha Rama Rau to write sensitive and perceptive travel books interpreting the Orient to Western readers. She was born in Madras, India, educated at St. Paul's Girls' School in London and Wellesley College, and now lives in Bombay, India. Some of her titles are *Home to India, My Russian Journey,* and *Gifts of Passage.*

Reginald Rose (born 1921) Before he won fame as a television playwright, Reginald Rose worked for an advertising firm in his native New

York City. At the same time he was writing plays nights and weekends. He has been most successful with his hour-long dramas. While serving on a New York jury, he conceived the idea of a play that would take place entirely within a jury room. The result was the award-winning *Twelve Angry Men.*

Christina Rossetti (1830–1894) The daughter of an Italian political refugee, Christina Rossetti lived nearly all of her life in London. Educated at home, she was fluent in Italian and English and began to write in both languages while still a girl. She also helped her mother teach and run a school, and from time to time sat as a model for her brother, Dante Gabriel Rossetti, who was an artist as well as a writer. Her verse is varied, ranging from children's rhymes to love poems.

Norman H. Russell (born 1921) Norman H. Russell says of his Cherokee ancestry "that part of me which is Indian dominates that part of me which is European. It gives me a pride and a pleasure and especially a wisdom I could not find in cities, books, and universities. . . ." He was trained as an ecologist and now teaches biology at Central State College, Edmund, Oklahoma. His poems have been published in *Southwest Review* and *The South Dakota Review,* and his first book of poems, *At the Zoo,* was published in 1969.

Saki (1870–1916) Saki is the pen name of an Englishman named H. H. Munro. Born in Burma, Munro was sent to England as a child and grew up there. He traveled widely during his youth before starting a career as news writer and foreign correspondent. In time he began writing novels and the famous Saki short stories which contain a unique blend of horror and humor that has made them favorites with readers since they first appeared in print. When World War I began, Munro—at forty-four—enlisted as

a private. Refusing the chance to be an officer, he went to France as a corporal, and met his death in action.

Carl Sandburg (1878–1967) Milkman, dishwasher, harvest hand, sign painter, brickmaker, and barbershop porter—all these jobs Carl Sandburg had tried before enrolling in Lombard College not far from his Illinois home. With the publication of "Chicago" in 1914, Sandburg at last found the role for which he had unconsciously been preparing all his life. In many books which followed, Sandburg demonstrated his remarkable command of American speech, rhythms, and colloquial idiom, as well as an uncanny ability to convey what it feels like to live in a modern industrial civilization.

William Saroyan (born 1908) Born in California of Armenian parents, William Saroyan early displayed a spirit of independence. Before he went to work to help his mother support the family, he earned himself a reputation for playing hookey from school. But books appealed to him, even if school did not, and his wide reading encouraged him to write his own stories. Saroyan has tried almost every kind of writing: stories, plays, novels. It is the writing itself, not the various forms, that interests him: "What difference does it make what you call it, just so it breathes?" he once asked.

Helen Sekaquaptewa (born 1898) A Hopi Indian born at Old Oraibi, Arizona, Helen Sekaquaptewa was named Dowawisnima, which means "a trail marked by sand." After a childhood spent absorbing the legends and culture of her people, she attended Keams Canyon boarding school and Phoenix Indian School, becoming acquainted with Anglo culture. In 1919 she married Emory Sekaquaptewa who later became a tribal judge. Their eight children and two foster sons have all graduated from high school and four went on to college. Baptised into the Mormon church in 1953, Helen Seka-quaptewa has been active in the women's organization of the church.

Robert Silverberg Dividing his writing career between science fiction and nonfiction, Robert Silverberg has published over forty books. His nonfiction books include works on such subjects as underwater archeology, scientific biography, space exploration, and military and ancient history; while his science fiction books have titles like *To Worlds Beyond, Lost Race of Mars,* and *The Plot Against Earth.* Silverberg was born in New York and graduated from Columbia University.

Theodore Spencer (1902–1949) The American poet and scholar Theodore Spencer grew up in Haverford, Pennsylvania. After his graduation from college he studied at Cambridge University in England. In 1939 he was invited to return to Cambridge as a professor, but the outbreak of World War II prevented his leaving. Accepting a post at Harvard University in Massachusetts instead, Spencer taught there until his death of a heart attack.

Wallace Stegner (born 1909) Born in Iowa, Wallace Stegner grew up traveling all over the West. Until he was in high school, the longest time he had lived in one place was a five-year stay in a Canadian prairie town. These five years Stegner calls the most important of his life; during them he learned firsthand what rough pioneer living was like. Stegner became a teacher after college and graduate school, and today is a professor of English at Stanford University, in California. His work has won several awards, including three O. Henry prizes for the best American short story of the year.

May Swenson (born 1919) Although Swenson lives now in New York, she was born in Logan, Utah, and has served as Poet in Residence at Purdue University in the Midwest. During a distinguished career she has been honored by many awards and grants, including both Guggenheim and Ford Fellowships. Her first collection of verse appeared in 1954, *Another Animal;* since then she has published several other volumes, including *A Cage of Spines* and *Half Sun Half Sleep.*

Josephine Tey (1897–1952) Elizabeth Mackintosh, the Scottish novelist and playwright, wrote her mystery novels under the pen name Josephine Tey, her great-great-grandmother's name, and her historical plays under the name of Gordon Daviot. She was born and educated in Inverness, Scotland, and refusing to enroll in a university, took a course in physical culture instead. She trained for three years at the Anstey Physical Training College in Birmingham and went on to teach physical education all over England. Gradually however, she turned to writing, publishing *The Man in the Queue* in 1929 which introduced Inspector Grant, the central character in her later mysteries. Inspector Grant's last case is recorded in *The Singing Sands,* published after the author's death.

Piri Thomas (born 1928) Piri Thomas grew up in the streets of Harlem's Puerto Rican barrio, the oldest of seven children. He served a four-year prison term, during which time he became interested in serious reading and started to write. After his release he worked in a drug rehabilitation center and later went to Puerto Rico to organize a similar center. There he attended the University of Puerto Rico. Thomas wrote the narration for the film *Petey and Johnny* about Spanish Harlem, and later an autobiographical novel, *Down These Mean Streets.*

David Wagoner (born 1926) Having earned his B.A. from Pennsylvania State University and his M.A. from Indiana University, David Wagoner embarked on a career as college teacher. He has taught at De Pauw University and Pennsylvania State University; currently he is a professor at the University of Washington. He was born in Massillon, Ohio, and served in the navy for two years during World War II. His writings, including *The Man in the Middle, Rock, The Escape Artist,* and *Staying Alive,* have won him both Guggenheim and Ford fellowships, and he has acted as editor of *Poetry Northwest.*

Jessamyn West (born 1907) "From the age of twelve," writes Jessamyn West, "I kept notebooks filled with story ideas." But for a long time she was too busy to write. In high school she edited the school paper, was a member of the debating team, and held two student-body offices at once—although the school constitution had to be amended to allow her to do so. After graduating from Whittier College, she took an advanced degree from the University of California. When illness forced her into leisure, she finally began writing stories. Her first book was warmly praised, and she has been writing ever since.

Keith Wilson (born 1927) Keith Wilson is a widely published modern poet who is best known for his powerful war poetry and poems of his native Southwest. A graduate of the U.S. Naval Academy, Wilson turned to poetry after the Korean War. He received a Master's degree in English from the University of New Mexico, and is now a resident poet and associate professor of English at New Mexico State University. He has published many volumes of poetry and has given readings of his work throughout the West.

Chiang Yee (1903–1977) Son of the painter Chiang Ho-an, Chiang Yee was born in Kiukiang, China. In 1935 he became a lecturer in Chinese at London University. It was at that time that he also gained recognition as an artist of some renown. Some years later Chiang Yee came to the United States. He is the author of many novels, children's books, and poems. Perhaps his most well-known book is *The Silent Traveller,* which contains poems, paintings, and comments on the author's travels.

Yevgeny Yevtushenko (born 1933) After the death of Stalin in 1953, the Soviet Union for a time underwent a period of liberalization in the arts known as "the Thaw." One of the youngest and most vigorous of the new Soviet poets was Yevtushenko, who, before he was thirty, was internationally known as the voice of the post-Stalin generation in Russia. "Let us be extremely outspoken," he proclaimed. In a famous poem, "Babi Yar," named after a place where the Nazis killed thousands of Jews during World War II, he condemns by implication anti-Semitism in Soviet Russia. In recent years Yevtushenko's voice has been heard less often, but his vigorous and lyrical poetry and his *Precocious Autobiography* continue to circulate widely in his own country and in the West.

Al Young (born 1939) For seven years Al Young was a free-lance musician playing guitar and flute and singing across the U. S., and for a time he was a disk jockey in Alameda, California. Then, winning a fellowship for creative writing, he concentrated on writing the poems which were later published in his book *Dancing.* At the same time he taught creative writing for the Berkeley Neighborhood Youth Corps and for Stanford University. *Snakes,* his first novel, he calls "a prose-movie centered in the emerging consciousness of a black teenager out of the urban Midwest." Young says of his writing, "I write out of spiritual need. I consider it a religious experience," and lists his interests as contemporary mythology, pop culture and mysticism.

AUTHORS AND TITLES

Titles of selections are in italics. Biographical information for the authors can be found in *About the Authors,* beginning on page 576.

LITERARY SKILLS

The page number given indicates where the term is first introduced and defined.

ART CREDITS

ILLUSTRATIONS

pp. 12, 17, 20, 26, 30 Ken Longtemps

pp. 37, 40 Kyuzo Tsugami

pp. 48, 53, 56, Les Morrill

pp. 62, 65, 68, 72 George Ulrich

p. 75 Bob Dacey

pp. 87, 90 Marc Brown

pp. 95, 98 Ann Toulmin-Rothe

pp. 114, 117 George Ulrich

p. 123 sculptures by Carol Anthony

pp. 124, 129 Robert Byrd

p. 133 calligraphy by Candy Kaihlanin

pp. 136, 141, 142–3 Richard Loehle

p. 150 Ann Grifalconi

pp. 155, 158, 162, 164 John Whalley

pp. 177, 180–1, 185 Floyd Sowell

p. 188 Laszlo Gal

pp. 190–1 sculpture "Reginald" by Walter Einsel

pp. 194, 197, 200 Bill Oakes

p. 203 calligraphy by Candy Kaihlanin

pp. 208, 212, 214 Gordon Laite

p. 217 woodcut by David Frampton

p. 218 Harvey Kidder

pp. 221, 226 David Calver

pp. 228, 233, 236 James Watling

pp. 245, 249, 252 John Wallner

p. 257 David Garland

pp. 259, 262 Joseph Smith

p. 268 Robert Andrew Parker

pp. 271, 272–3 Molly Bang

pp. 280, 284, 289, 292, 296 Tom Hamilton

p. 302 Ken Maryanski

pp. 305, 310 Errol Le Cain

p. 314 Ron Carreiro

pp. 342, 344 Bill Carroll

pp. 350, 356, 359 Bill Greer

pp. 375, 380 Patricia Bargielski

pp. 383, 386 Jeannette Kehl

pp. 400, 402, 407 Arvis Stewart

pp. 413, 416 Hal Frenck

pp. 421, 425 Bruce MacDonald

p. 442 woodcut by David Frampton

pp. 444, 450, 456, 461, 466, 474–5 Randall McKissick

p. 486 calligraphy by Edward A. Karr

pp. 489, 492, 501 John Whalley

pp. 504, 506 Robert Lo Grippo

pp. 524–5 Charles Waller

p. 530 collage sculpture by Jill Weber

p. 540 William Jacob Hays, *Herd of Buffalo,* oil, courtesy of Denver Art Museum, Denver.

pp. 543, 547 Dorothea Sierra

p. 571 Sue Thompson

PHOTOGRAPHS

Cover: Van Bucher, Photo Researchers, Inc.

pp. i (44, 80, 120, 168, 206, 238, 274, 318, 364, 392, 430, 480, 532, 572) Terry Walker

pp. ii–iii Rebuffat, Photo Researchers Inc.

pp. iv (45, 81, 121, 169, 207, 239, 275, 319, 364, 393, 431, 481, 533, 573) Manfred P. Kage, Peter Arnold

pp. xiv–1 Outward Bound, Inc.

p. 5 Aviaplans, Paris

p. 9 Charles Bonna, Black Star

p. 33 Sarah Benham

p. 58 George Sheng

pp. 84–5 George Holton, Photo Researchers, Inc.

p. 93 Ken Hyman

p. 103 Harvard College Observatory

p. 105 George Sheng

p. 109 George Sheng

p. 110 Cary Wolinsky, Stock/ Boston

p. 148 Grant Heilman

pp. 172–3 Pamela Perry, Stock/ Boston

p. 174 Starr Ockenga

p. 204 John Running

p. 242–3 Terry Walker

p. 255 Peter Southwick, Stock/ Boston

p. 277 Bill Sumner

pp. 322–3 Susan McCartney, Photo Researchers, Inc.

p. 325 James R. Smith

p. 330, 335 Paul Fortin

p. 340 Olen S. Hanson, Photo Researchers, Inc.

pp. 346–7 George Sheng

pp. 367, 371 Bruce Curtis, Peter Arnold

p. 390 Angelo Lomeo, Photo Researchers, Inc.

p. 396–7 Frank Siteman, Stock/ Boston

p. 410 Michal Heron

p. 434 William Finch, Stock/Boston

p. 436 Nemo Warr, Hurok Concerts, Inc.

pp. 484–5 David Muench

p. 487 David Muench

p. 509 John Ross, Photo Researchers, Inc.

p. 514 Fritz Henle, Photo Researchers, Inc.

p. 518 Werner Forman Archive

p. 521 Joe Weiler, Stock/Boston

p. 535 David Muench

p. 550 David Hiser

p. 553 Dan McCoy, Rainbow

p. 556 Grant Heilman

p. 560 Bill Sumner

p. 563 John Hay, Stock/Boston

p. 568 Ellis Herwig, Stock/Boston

GLOSSARY

Many unfamiliar words in this text have been footnoted. Other words that may be unfamiliar to you are defined in this glossary. If you look for a word and find it not listed in the glossary, reread the sentence or paragraph in which the word appeared. The word may not have been included here because the context gives clues to its meaning.

Guide words at the top of each page will help you locate the word you want. Use the pronunciation key found at the bottom of each page to learn how to pronounce a word correctly.

The pronunciations and definitions in this glossary are from *The American Heritage Dictionary of the English Language* and are used with permission.

A

a·ban·don (ə-băn′dən) *tr.v.* **-doned, -doning, -dons.** To yield (oneself) completely, as to emotion. —*n.* A complete surrender of inhibitions.

a·bash (ə-băsh′) *tr.v.* **abashed, abashing, abashes.** To make ashamed or uneasy; disconcert.

ab·di·cate (ăb′dĭ-kāt′) *v.* **-cated, -cating, -cates.** —*tr.* To relinquish (power or responsibility) formally.

ab·hor·rent (ăb-hôr′ənt, -hŏr′ənt) *adj.* Disgusting; loathsome; repellent.

ab·ject (ăb′jĕkt′, ăb-jĕkt′) *adj.* Of the most miserable kind; wretched.

a·brade (ə-brād′) *tr.v.* **abraded, abrading, abrades.** To rub off or wear away by friction; erode.

ab·ra·sive (ə-brā′sĭv, -zĭv) *adj.* Causing abrasion; harsh; rough.

ab·stain (ăb-stān′) *intr.v.* **-stained, -staining, -stains.** To refrain from something by one's own choice.

ab·stract (ăb-străkt′, ăb′ străkt′) *adj.* **1.** Theoretical; not applied or practical. **2.** Not easily understood; abstruse.

ab·stract·ed (ăb-străk′tĭd) *adj.* Lost or deep in thought; preoccupied; meditative.

ab·surd (ăb-sûrd′, -zûrd′) *adj.* Ridiculously incongruous or unreasonable.

ac·cli·mate (ə-klī′mĭt, ăk′lə-māt′) *v.* **-mated, -mating, -mates.** —*tr.* To accustom (something or someone) to a new environment or situation; adapt; acclimatize.

ac·cli·ma·tize (ə-klī′mə-tīz′) *v.* **-tized, -tizing, -tizes.** —*tr.* To acclimate (someone or something).

ac·cost (ə-kôst′, ə-kŏst′) *tr.v.* **-costed, -costing, -costs.** To approach and speak to first.

ac·rid (ăk′rĭd) *adj.* **1.** Harsh to the taste or smell. **2.** Caustic in language or tone.

a·cute (ə-kyōot′) *adj.* **1.** Of great importance or consequence; crucial. **2.** Extremely severe or sharp; intense: *acute pain.*

a·dapt (ə-dăpt′) *v.* **adapted, adapting, adapts.** —*tr.* To adjust to a specified use or situation.

a·dapt·a·ble (ə-dăp′tə-bəl) *adj.* Capable of adapting or of being adapted.

ad·here (ăd-hîr′) *intr.v.* **-hered, -hering, -heres.** To stick fast or together by or as if by grasping, suction, or being glued.

ad·mi·ral·ty (ăd′mər-əl-tē) *n. Capital* **A.** The department of the British government (Board of Admiralty) having control over naval affairs.

aer·o·bat·ics (âr′ō-băt′ĭks) *n.* Plural in form, used with a singular or plural verb. The performance of stunts, such as rolls and loops, with an airplane or glider.

af·fa·ble (ăf′ə-bəl) *adj.* **1.** Easy to speak to; approachable; amiable. **2.** Mild; gentle; benign.

af·flu·ent (ăf′lōo-ənt) *adj.* Rich; opulent.

ag·ile (ăj′əl, ăj′ īl) *adj.* Able to move in a quick and easy fashion; active.

a·gil·i·ty (ə-jĭl′ə-tē) *n.* The state or quality of being agile; nimbleness; briskness.

al·i·bi (ăl′ə-bī′) *n., pl.* **-bis. 1.** *Law.* A form of defense whereby a defendant attempts to prove that he was elsewhere when the crime in question was committed. **2.** *Informal.* An excuse.

ă pat/ā pay/âr care/ä father/b bib/ch church/d deed/ĕ pet/ē be/f fife/g gag/h hat/hw which/ĭ pit/ī pie/îr pier/j judge/k kick/l lid, needle/m mum/n no, sudden/ng thing/ŏ pot/ō toe/ô paw, for/oi noise/ou out/ŏŏ took/ōō boot/p pop/r roar/s sauce/sh ship, dish/ t tight/th thin, path/*th* this, bathe/ŭ cut/ûr urge/v valve/w with/y yes/z zebra, size/zh vision/ə about, item, edible, gallop, circus/ à *Fr.* ami/œ *Fr.* feu, *Ger.* schön/ü *Fr.* tu, *Ger.* über/KH *Ger.* ich, *Scot.* loch/N *Fr.* bon.

alms (ämz) *pl.n.* Money or goods given to the poor in charity.

a·mend (ə-měnd′) *v.* **amended, amending, amends.** —*tr.* **1.** To improve; better. **2.** To remove the faults or errors of; correct; rectify. **3.** To alter (a legislative measure, for example) formally by adding, deleting, or rephrasing.

a·men·i·ty (ə-měn′ə-tē, ə-mē′nə-) *n., pl.* **-ties.** *Plural.* Social courtesies; pleasantries; civilities.

an·a·lyt·ic (ăn′ə-lĭt′ĭk) *adj.* Also **an·a·lyt·i·cal** (-ĭ-kəl). **1.** Of or pertaining to analysis. **2.** Dividing into elemental parts or basic principles. **3.** Reasoning from a perception of the parts and interrelations of a subject; using analysis.

an·es·thet·ic (ăn′ĭs-thĕt′ĭk) Also **an·aes·thet·ic.** *n.* Any agent that causes unconsciousness or insensitivity to pain.

an·i·mate (ăn′ə-māt′) *tr.v.* **-mated, -mating, -mates.** **1.** To give life to; fill with life. **2.** To impart interest or zest to; enliven.

an·te·room (ăn′tĭ-rōōm′, -rŏŏm′) *n.* A waiting room.

an·tiq·ui·ty (ăn-tĭk′wə-tē) *n., pl.* **-ties.** *Usually plural.* Something belonging to or dating from a time long past.

ap·er·ture (ăp′ər-chŏŏr′, -chər) *n.* A hole, gap, slit, or other opening; an orifice.

ap·pall (ə-pôl′) *tr.v.* **-palled, -palling, -palls.** To fill with consternation or dismay.

ap·pall·ing (ə-pô′lĭng) *adj.* Causing dismay; frightful; horrifying.

ap·pa·ra·tus (ăp′ə-rā′təs, -răt′əs) *n.* **a.** A machine. **b.** A group of machines used together or in succession to accomplish a task.

ap·point·ment (ə-point′mənt) *n.* *Usually plural.* Fittings or equipment.

ap·praise (ə-prāz′) *tr.v.* **-praised, -praising, -praises.** **1.** To evaluate, especially in an official capacity. **2.** To estimate the quality, amount, size, and other features of; to judge.

ap·pre·hen·sion (ăp′rĭ-hĕn′shən) *n.* A fearful or uneasy anticipation of the future; dread.

ap·pre·hen·sive (ăp′rĭ-hĕn′sĭv) *adj.* Anxious or fearful about the future; uneasy.

apt (ăpt) *adj.* Exactly suitable; appropriate.

ar·bor (är′bər) *n.* A shady garden shelter or bower, often made of rustic work or latticework on which vines, roses, or the like are grown.

arc (ärk) *n.* Anything shaped like a bow, curve, or arch.

ar·dent (är′dənt) *adj.* Displaying or characterized by strong enthusiasm or devotion; fervent; zealous.

ar·son (är′sən) *n.* The crime of maliciously burning the building or property of another, or of burning one's own for some improper purpose, as to collect insurance.

ar·tic·u·late (är-tĭk′yə-lāt′) *v.* **articulated, -lating, -lates.** —*tr.* **1.** To utter (a speech sound or sounds) by moving the necessary organs of speech. **2.** To pronounce distinctly and carefully; enunciate.

as·cet·ic (ə-sĕt′ĭk) *n.* A person who renounces the comforts of society and leads a life of austere self-discipline, especially as an act of religious devotion. —*adj.* Pertaining to or characteristic of an ascetic; self-denying; austere.

as·sail (ə-sāl′) *tr.v.* **-sailed, -sailing, -sails.** **1.** To attack with or as if with violent blows; assault. **2.** To attack verbally, as with ridicule or censure.

as·ser·tion (ə-sûr′shən) *n.* **1.** The act of asserting or declaring. **2.** A declaration stated positively but with no support or attempt at proof.

a·stray (ə-strā′) *adv.* Away from the correct path or direction.

at·trib·ute (ăt′rə-byōōt′) *n.* A quality or characteristic belonging to a person or thing; a distinctive feature.

au·dac·i·ty (ô-dăs′ə-tē) *n., pl.* **-ties.** **1.** Boldness; daring; intrepidity. **2.** Unrestrained impudence; insolence; presumption. **3.** An instance of boldness or presumption.

aug·ment (ôg-mĕnt′) *v.* **-mented, -menting, -ments.** —*tr.* To make greater, as in size, extent, or quantity; enlarge; increase.

au·tom·a·ton (ô-tŏm′ə-tən, -tŏn′) *n., pl.* **-tons** or **-ta** (-tə). **1.** A robot. **2.** One that behaves in an automatic or mechanical fashion.

a·venge (ə-vĕnj′) *v.* **avenged, avenging, avenges.** —*tr.* **1.** To take revenge or exact satisfaction for (a wrong, injury, or the like). **2.** To take vengeance on behalf of.

a·verse (ə-vûrs′) *adj.* Opposed; reluctant.

awn·ing (ô′nĭng) *n.* A rooflike structure, as of canvas, stretched over a frame as a shelter from weather.

ax·is (ăk′sĭs) *n., pl.* **axes** (ăk′sēz′). A center line to which parts of a structure or body may be referred.

B

bade. A past tense of **bid.**

baf·fle (băf′əl) *tr.v.* **-fled, -fling, -fles.** **1.** To foil; thwart; frustrate. **2.** To check (someone) in his efforts at solution by confusing; perplex to the point of helplessness; stymie. —**baf′fle·ment** *n.*

ban·ish (băn′ĭsh) *tr.v.* **-ished, -ishing, -ishes.** **1.** To force to leave a country or place by official decree; exile. **2.** To drive away; expel.

bar·ba·rous (bär′bər-əs) *adj.* **1.** Primitive in culture and customs; uncivilized. **2.** Characterized by savagery; cruel; brutal. **3.** Lacking refinement or culture; coarse; boorish.

bar·on (băr′ən) *n.* A lord or nobleman; peer.

ba·ro·ni·al (bə-rō′nē-əl) *adj.* **1.** Of or pertaining to a baron or barony. **2.** Suited for or befitting a baron; stately; grand.

bar·ri·er (băr′ē-ər) *n.* **1.** A fence, wall, or other structure built to bar passage. **2.** Anything, material or immaterial, that acts to obstruct or prevent passage.

bay (bā) *n.* **1.** A deep, prolonged barking, espe-

ă pat/ā pay/âr care/ä father/b **bib**/ch **church**/d **deed**/ĕ pet/ē be/f **fife**/g **gag**/h hat/hw **which**/ĭ pit/ī pie/îr pier/j **judge**/k **kick**/l lid, needle/m **mum**/n no, sudden/ng **thing**/ŏ pot/ō toe/ô paw, for/oi noise/ou out/ŏŏ took/ōō boot/p **pop**/r roar/s sauce/sh **ship, dish**/

cially of hounds closing in on prey. **2.** The position of one cornered by pursuers and forced to turn and fight at close quarters. —*v.* **bayed, baying, bays.** —*intr.* To utter a deep, prolonged bark or howl.

be·guile (bĭ-gīl') *tr.v.* **-guiled, -guiling, -guiles.** To deceive by guile; delude.

be·lat·ed (bĭ-lā'tĭd) *adj.* Tardy; too late.

be·lea·guer (bĭ-lē'gər) *tr.v.* **-guered, -guering, -guers.** To besiege by surrounding with troops.

ben·e·fac·tor (bĕn'ə-făk'tər) *n.* One who gives financial or other aid.

be·seech (bĭ-sēch') *tr.v.* **-sought** (-sôt') or **-seeched, -seeching, -seeches. 1.** To address an earnest or urgent request to; implore. **2.** To request earnestly; beg for.

be·siege (bĭ-sēj') *tr.v.* **-sieged, -sieging, -sieges.** To surround with aggressive intent; lay siege to.

bid (bĭd) *v.* For transitive sense: **bade** (băd, bād) or *archaic* **bad** (băd), **bidden** (bĭd'ən) or **bid, bidding, bids.** —*tr.* To direct; command; enjoin.

bi·zarre (bĭ-zär') *adj.* Strikingly unconventional and far-fetched in style or appearance; odd; grotesque.

bluff (blŭf) *n.* A steep headland, promontory, river bank, or cliff.

blun·der (blŭn'dər) *n.* A stupid and grave mistake; a clumsy, foolish act or remark.

bog (bôg, bŏg) *n.* Soft, waterlogged ground; a marsh; swamp.

bond (bŏnd) *n.* Anything that binds, ties, or fastens together: **a.** *Usually plural.* A shackle; a fetter. **b.** A cord, rope, or band.

bout (bout) *n.* A period of time spent in a particular way.

bran·dish (brăn'dĭsh) *tr.v.* **-dished, -dishing, -dishes. 1.** To wave or flourish menacingly, as a weapon. **2.** To display ostentatiously.

bra·va·do (brə-vä'dō) *n., pl.* **-does** or **-dos. 1.** Defiant or swaggering show of courage; false bravery. **2.** An instance of such behavior.

bris·tle (brĭs'əl) *v.* **bristled, -tling, -tles.** —*intr.* To react with agitation to anger, excitement, or fear. Often used with *up: He bristled up in anger.*

bul·lock (bŏŏl'ək) *n.* **1.** A castrated bull; a steer. **2.** A young bull.

bul·wark (bŏŏl'wərk, bŭl'-, -wôrk') *n. Usually plural.* The part of a ship's side that is above the upper deck.

buoy·an·cy (boi'ən-sē, bōō'yən-) *n.* The upward force of a fluid upon a floating or immersed object.

buoy·ant (boi'ənt, bōō'yənt) *adj.* Having buoyancy.

bur·ro (bûr'ō, bŏŏr'ō) *n., pl.* **-ros.** A small donkey, especially one used as a pack animal.

bur·row (bûr'ō) *n.* **1.** A hole or tunnel dug in the ground by a small animal, such as a rabbit or a mole, for habitation or refuge. **2.** Any similar narrow or snug place. —*v.* **burrowed, -rowing, -rows.** —*intr.* **1.** To dig a burrow. **2.** To live or hide in a burrow.

butte (byōōt) *n.* A hill rising abruptly above the surrounding area and having sloping sides and a flat top.

C

ca·dence (kād'əns) *n., pl.* **-cies.** The measure or beat of movement, as in dancing or marching.

ca·dent (kād'ənt) *adj.* Having cadence or rhythm.

cal·cu·late (kăl'kyə-lāt') *v.* **-lated, -lating, -lates.** —*tr.* To make an estimate of; evaluate.

cal·i·ber (kăl'ə-bər) *n.* The diameter of the bore of a gun.

can·did (kăn'dĭd) *adj.* Without pretense or reserve; straightforward; open.

can·is·ter (kăn'ĭs-tər) *n.* A container, usually of thin metal, for holding dry foods.

can·o·py (kăn'ə-pē) *n., pl.* **-pies.** A cloth covering fastened or held horizontally above a person or an object for protection or ornamentation.

cas·cade (kăs-kād') *n.* A waterfall or a series of small waterfalls over steep rocks. —*intr.v.* **cascaded, -cading, -cades.** To fall from one level to another in a continuous series.

cas·se·role (kăs'ə-rōl') *n.* **1.** A dish, usually of earthenware, glass, or cast iron, in which food is both baked and served. **2.** Food prepared and served in such a dish.

cast (kăst, käst) *v.* **cast, casting, casts.** —*intr.* To throw; especially, to throw out a lure or bait at the end of a fishing line.

caste (kăst, käst) *n.* Any social class separated from others by distinctions of hereditary rank, profession, or the like.

cat·a·clysm (kăt'ə-klĭz'əm) *n.* **1.** A violent and sudden change in the earth's crust. **2.** Any violent upheaval. **3.** A devastating flood. —**cat'a·clys'mic** (-klĭz'mĭk),

cat·a·pult (kăt'ə-pŭlt') *n.* A mechanism for launching aircraft without a runway, as from the deck of a ship.

cause·way (kôz'wā') *n.* **1.** A raised roadway, as across water or marshland. **2.** A paved highway.

cen·sure (sĕn'shər) *n.* An expression of blame or disapproval.

cen·trif·u·gal (sĕn-trĭf'yə-gəl, -trĭf'ə-gəl) *adj.* Moving or directed away from a center or axis.

chafe (chāf) *v.* **chafed, chafing, chafes.** —*tr.* To wear away or irritate by rubbing.

cha·os (kā'ŏs) *n.* Any condition or place of total disorder or confusion. —**cha·ot'ic** (kā-ŏt'ĭk) *adj.*

chaste (chāst) *adj.* **chaster, chastest.** Pure or simple in literary or artistic style; not ornate or extreme.

cha·teau (shă-tō') *n., pl.* **chateaux** (shă-tōz'; *French* shà-tō'). Also *French* **châ·teau** (shà-tō'). **1.** A French castle or manor house. **2.** A country house, especially one resembling a French castle.

chi·tin (kī'tĭn) *n.* A semitransparent horny substance, primarily a mucopolysaccharide, forming the principal component of crustacean shells, insect exoskeletons, and the cell walls of certain fungi. —**chi'tin·ous** adj.

chiv·al·ry (shĭv'əl-rē) n., pl. **-ries. 1. a.** The medieval institution of knighthood. **b.** The principles and customs of this institution. **2.** The qualities idealized by knighthood, such as bravery, courtesy, and honesty.

chron·i·cle (krŏn'ĭ-kəl) n. A chronological record of historical events.

chron·o·log·i·cal (krŏn'ə-lŏj'ĭ-kəl, krō'nə-) adj. Arranged in order of time of occurence.

cir·cum·fer·ence (sər-kŭm'fər-əns) n. **1.** The boundary line of a circle. **2.** The boundary line of any closed curvilinear figure; perimeter. **3.** The length of such a boundary.

cir·cum·scribe (sûr'kəm-skrīb') tr.v. **-scribed, -scribing, -scribes. 1.** To draw a line around; encircle. **2.** To confine within bounds; to limit; restrict.

civ·il (sĭv'əl) **1.** Of or in accordance with organized society and government; civilized. **2.** Observing or befitting accepted social usages; proper; polite.

col·league (kŏl'ēg') n. A fellow member of a profession, staff, or academic faculty; associate.

co·los·sal (kə-lŏs'əl) adj. Enormous in size, extent, or degree; gigantic; tremendous.

com·man·deer (kŏm'ən-dîr') tr.v. **-deered, -deering, -deers. 1.** To seize (property) for public use; confiscate. **2.** Informal. To take arbitrarily or by force.

com·mend (kə-měnd') tr.v. **-mended, -mending, -mends.** To represent as worthy, qualified, or desirable; recommend.

com·mune (kə-myōōn') intr.v. **-muned, -muning, -munes.** To converse intimately; exchange thoughts and feelings.

com·pas·sion (kəm-pǎsh'ən) n. The deep feeling of sharing the suffering of another in the inclination to give aid or support, or to show mercy.

com·ply (kəm-plī') intr.v. **-plied, -plying, -plies.** To act in accordance with a command, request, rule, wish, or the like.

com·pro·mise (kŏm'prə-mīz') n. A settlement of differences in which each side makes concessions.

com·pul·sion (kəm-pŭl'shən) n. **1.** The act of compelling or forcing; coercion; constraint. **2.** The state of being compelled.

con·done (kən-dōn') tr.v. **-doned, -doning, -dones.** To forgive, overlook, or disregard (an offense) without protest or censure.

con·fed·er·ate (kən-fěd'ər-ĭt) n. A member of a confederacy; an ally.

con·fla·gra·tion (kŏn'flə-grā'shən) n. A large and destructive fire.

con·form (kən-fôrm') v. **-formed, -forming, -forms.** —intr. **1.** To come to have the same form or character. **2.** To act or be in accord or agreement; comply. Used with to. **3.** To act in accordance with current customs or modes.

con·form·i·ty (kən-fôr'mə-tē) n., pl. **-ties.** Action or behavior in correspondence with current customs, rules, or styles.

con·gen·ial (kən-jēn'yəl) adj. Suited to one's needs; agreeable.

con·ic (kŏn'ĭk) adj. Also **con·i·cal** (-ĭ-kəl) Shaped like a cone.

con·jure (kŏn'jər, kən-jōōr') v. **-jured, -juring, -jures.** —tr. To cause or effect by or as by magic.

con·nois·seur (kŏn'ə-sûr') n. A person with informed and astute discrimination, especially concerning the arts or matters of taste. —**con'nois·seur'ship'** n.

con·sci·en·tious (kŏn'shē-ěn'shəs) adj. **1.** Governed by or accomplished according to conscience; scrupulous. **2.** Thorough and painstaking; careful. —**con'sci·en'tious·ly** adv.

con·ser·va·to·ry (kən-sûr'və-tôr'ē, -tōr'ē) n., pl. **-ries.** A school of music or dramatic art.

con·sign (kən-sīn') v. **-signed, -signing, -signs.** —tr. To set apart, as for a special use or purpose; assign.

con·spir·a·cy (kən-spîr'ə-sē) n., pl. **-cies.** An agreement to perform together an illegal, treacherous, or evil act.

con·ster·na·tion (kŏn'stər-nā'shən) n. Sudden confusion, amazement, or frustration.

con·tort (kən-tôrt') v. **-torted, -torting, -torts.** —tr. To twist, wrench, or bend severely out of shape. —intr. To become twisted into a strained shape or expression.

con·tri·tion (kən-trĭsh'ən) n. Sincere remorse for wrongdoing.

con·ven·tion (kən-věn'shən) n. General agreement on or acceptance of certain practices or attitudes.

con·ven·tion·al (kən-věn'shən-əl) adj. **1.** Developed, established, or approved by general usage; customary. **2.** Conforming to established practice or accepted standards.

con·verge (kən-vûrj') v. **-verged, -verging, -verges.** —intr. **1.** To approach the same point from different directions; tend toward a meeting or intersection. **2.** To tend or move toward union or toward a common conclusion or result.

con·vic·tion (kən-vĭk'shən) n. A fixed or strong belief.

con·vul·sion (kən-vŭl'shən) n. An intense paroxysmal involuntary muscular contraction.

con·vul·sive (kən-vŭl'sĭv) adj. Marked by or of the nature of convulsions.

cord·age (kôr'dĭj) n. The ropes in the rigging of a ship.

cor·rob·o·rate (kə-rŏb'ə-rāt') tr.v. **-rated, -rating, -rates.** To strengthen or support (other evidence); attest the truth or accuracy of.

cor·sage (kôr-säzh') n. A small bouquet of flowers worn by a woman at the shoulder, waist, or on the wrist.

coun·te·nance (koun'tə-nəns) n. Aspect; appearance; especially, the expression of the face.

cove (kōv) n. A small, sheltered bay in the shoreline of a sea, river, or lake.

cov·ert (kŭv'ərt, kō'vərt) adj. Concealed; hidden; secret.

cov·et (kŭv'ĭt) tr.v. **-eted, -eting, -ets. 1.** To desire

ă pat/ā pay/âr care/ä father/b bib/ch church/d deed/ě pet/ē be/f fife/g gag/h hat/hw which/ĭ pit/ī pie/îr pier/j judge/k kick/l lid, needle/m mum/n no, sudden/ng thing/ŏ pot/ō toe/ô paw, for/oi noise/ou out/ōō took/ōō boot/p pop/r roar/s sauce/sh ship, dish/

(that which is another's). **2.** To wish for excessively and culpably; crave.

cow·er (kou'ər) *intr.v.* **-ered, -ering, -ers.** To cringe or shrink away from cold or in fear.

craft·y (krăf'tē, kräf'-) *adj.* **-ier, -iest.** Skilled in underhandedness and deception; shrewd; cunning.

cra·ven (krā'vən) *adj.* Characterized by abject fear; cowardly. —*n.* A coward.

cre·den·tial (krĭ-děn'shəl) *n.* **1.** That which entitles one to confidence, credit, or authority. **2.** *Usually plural.* **a.** A letter attesting one's right to credit, confidence, or authority. **b.** Written evidence of qualifications.

crest (krĕst) *n.* **a.** The top of something, as a mountain or wave; peak; summit. **b.** A ridge.

crev·ice (krĕv'ĭs) *n.* A narrow crack or opening; fissure; cleft.

cro·chet (krō-shā') *v.* **-cheted** (-shād'), **-cheting** (-shā'ĭng), **-chets** (-shāz'). —*intr.* To make a piece of needlework by looping thread with a hooked needle.

cue (kyōō) *n.* *Theater.* A word or bit of stage business signaling the beginning of another action or speech.

cun·ning (kŭn'ĭng) *adj.* Shrewd; crafty; artful. —**cun'ning·ly** *adv.*

cu·rate (kyŏŏr'ĭt) *n.* **1.** A clergyman who has charge of a parish. **2.** A clergyman who assists a rector or vicar.

cu·ri·o (kyŏŏr'ē-ō') *n., pl.* **-os.** A curious or unusual object of art or bric-a-brac.

cus·to·dy (kŭs'tə-dē) *n., pl.* **-dies.** **1.** The act or right of guarding, especially such a right granted by a court to a guardian of a minor. **2.** The state of being kept or guarded.

cyn·i·cal (sĭn'ĭ-kəl) *adj.* Scornful of the motives or virtue of others; bitterly mocking; sneering.

D

dachs·hund (däks'hŏŏnt', däks'hŏŏnd') *n.* A small dog of a breed developed in Germany for hunting badgers, having a long body with a usually short-haired brown or black and brown coat, drooping ears, and very short legs.

dank (dăngk) *adj.* **danker, dankest.** Uncomfortably damp; chilly and wet.

de·ba·cle (dĭ-bä'kəl, -băk'əl) *n.* A sudden, disastrous overthrow or collapse; rout; ruin.

de·bris (də-brē', dā'brē') *n.* The scattered remains of something broken or destroyed; ruins; rubble; fragments.

de·ceive (dĭ-sēv') *v.* **-ceived, -ceiving, -ceives.** —*tr.* To delude; mislead.

de·cep·tive (dĭ-sĕp'tĭv) *adj.* Intended or tending to deceive; disingenuous.

de·ci·sive (dĭ-sī'sĭv) *adj.* **1.** Having the power to settle a dispute or doubt; conclusive. **2.** Characterized by decision and firmness; resolute; determined. **3.** Beyond doubt; unmistakable; unquestionable.

de·co·rum (dĭ-kôr'əm, kĭ-kō'əm) *n.* Conformity to social conventions; propriety.

de·duce (dĭ-dōōs', -dyōōs') *tr.v.* **-duced, -ducing, -duces.** To reach (a conclusion) by reasoning.

de·fer (dĭ-fûr') *v.* **-ferred, -ferring, -fers.** —*tr.* To put off until a future time; postpone.

de·fi·ance (dĭ-fī'əns) *n.* **1.** The disposition to defy or resist an opposing force or authority; resolute resistance. **2.** Intentionally provocative behavior or attitude; a challenge.

de·fi·ant (dĭ-fī'ənt) *adj.* Marked by defiance.

de·grade (dĭ-grād') *tr.v.* **-graded, -grading, -grades. 1.** To lower in moral or intellectual character; debase; corrupt. **2.** To expose to contempt, dishonor, or disgrace.

de·mur (dĭ-mûr') *intr.v.* **-murred, -murring, -murs.** To take exception; raise objections; object. —*n.* **1.** An objection. **2.** A delay.

den·i·grate (děn'ĭ-grāt') *tr.v.* **-grated, -grating, -grates.** To belittle or calumniate the character or reputation of; defame.

de·plete (dĭ-plēt') *tr.v.* **-pleted, -pleting, -pletes.** To use up or exhaust.

de·plor·a·ble (dĭ-plôr'ə-bəl, dĭ-plōr'ə-) *adj.* **1.** Worthy of severe reproach. **2.** Lamentable; grievous. **3.** Wretched; bad.

dep·re·cate (dĕp'rĭ-kāt') *tr.v.* **-cated, -cating, -cates. 1.** To express disapproval of; protest or plead against. **2.** To depreciate; belittle.

de·pre·ci·ate (dĭ-prē'shē-āt') *v.* **-ated, -ating, -ates.** —*tr.* To lessen the price or value of.

de·ri·sion (dĭ-rĭzh'ən) *n.* **1. a.** Scoffing; ridicule. **b.** A state of being derided. **2.** An object of ridicule; laughingstock.

des·e·crate (dĕs'ə-krāt') *tr.v.* **-crated, -crating, -crates.** To abuse the sacredness of; subject to sacrilege; profane.

des·ig·nate (dĕz'ĭg-nāt') *tr.v.* **-nated, -nating, -nates. 1.** To give a name or title to; characterize. **2.** To select for a particular duty, office, or purpose; appoint.

de·tach·ment (dĭ-tăch'mənt) *n.* **1.** The act or process of disconnecting or detaching; separation. **2.** The state or condition of being separate or apart. **3.** Dissociation from surroundings, the concerns of others, or wordly affairs; aloofness.

dev·as·tate (dĕv'ə-stāt') *tr.v.* **-tated, -tating, -tates.** To lay waste.

de·vour (dĭ-vour') *tr.v.* **-voured, -vouring, -vours. 1.** To swallow or eat up greedily. **2.** To destroy, consume, or waste.

dex·ter·i·ty (dĕk-stĕr'ə-tē) *n.* Skill in the use of the hands or body; adroitness.

di·ag·o·nal (dī-ăg'ə-nəl) *adj.* **1.** Having a slanted or oblique direction. **2.** Having oblique lines or markings. —**di·ag'o·nal·ly** *adv.*

dif·fuse (dĭ-fyōōs') *adj.* Characterized by profusion or excess of words; verbose; long-winded.

di·lap·i·dat·ed (dĭ-lăp'ə-dā'tĭd) *adj.* Fallen into a state of disrepair; broken-down.

di·late (dī-lāt', dī'lāt', dī-lāt') *v.* **-lated, -lating, -lates.** —*intr.* To become wider or larger; expand.

ă tight/th thin, path/*th* this, bathe/ŭ cut/ûr urge/v valve/w with/y yes/z zebra, size/zh vision/ə about, item, edible, gallop, circus/ à *Fr.* ami/œ *Fr.* feu, *Ger.* schön/ü *Fr.* tu, *Ger.* über/кн *Ger.* ich, *Scot.* loch/N *Fr.* bon.

di·lem·ma (dĭ-lĕm'ə) *n.* A situation that requires one to choose between two equally balanced alternatives.

dirge (dûrj) *n.* A funeral hymn or lament.

dis·arm (dĭs-ärm') *v.* **-armed, -arming, -arms.** —*tr.* To overcome or allay the suspicion, hostility, or antagonism of; win the confidence of.

dis·a·vow (dĭs'ə-vou') *tr.v.* **-vowed, -vowing, -vows.** To disclaim knowledge of, responsibility for, or association with; disown.

dis·cern (dĭ-sûrn', -zûrn') *v.* **-cerned, -cerning, -cerns.** —*tr.* **1.** To perceive (something obscure or concealed); detect. **2.** To perceive the distinctions of; to discriminate.

dis·course (dĭs'kôrs', -kōrs') *n.* **1.** Verbal expression in speech or writing. **2.** Verbal exchange; conversation. **3.** A formal and lengthy discussion of a subject, either written or spoken.

dis·creet (dĭs-krēt') *adj.* **1.** Having or showing a judicious reserve in one's speech or behavior; respectful of propriety. **2.** Lacking ostentation or pretension; unobtrusive; modest.

dis·em·bod·y (dĭs'ĭm-bŏd'ē) *tr.v.* **-ied, -ying, -ies.** To free (the soul or spirit) from the body.

di·shev·eled (dĭ-shĕv'əld) *adj.* **1.** Hanging in loose disarray; unkempt, as hair. **2.** Disarranged; untidy.

dis·sen·tient (dĭ-sĕn'shənt) *adj.* Dissenting, especially from the sentiment or policies of a majority.

dis·tract·ed (dĭs-trăk'tĭd) *adj.* Having the attention diverted.

di·ver·sion (dĭ-vûr'zhən, -shən, dī-) *n.* In military strategy, a maneuver that draws the attention of the enemy away from the planned point of attack.

di·vine (dĭ-vīn') *v.* **-vined, -vining, -vines.** —*tr.* **a.** To know by inspiration, intuition, or reflection. **b.** To guess.

doc·ile (dŏs'əl) *adj.* **1.** Capable of being taught; ready and willing to receive training; teachable. **2.** Submissive to training or management; tractable.

dog·ged (dô'gĭd, dŏg' ĭd) *adj.* Not yielding readily; willful; stubborn.

dol·drums (dōl'drəmz, dôl'-, dŏl'-) *n.* Ocean regions near the equator, characterized by calms or light winds.

do·main (dō-mān') *n.* A territory or range of rule or control; realm.

dor·mer (dôr'mər) *n.* **1.** A window set vertically in a small gable projecting from a sloping roof. Also called "dormer window." **2.** The gable holding such a window.

dow·ry (dour'ē) *n., pl.* **-ries.** Money or property brought by a bride to her husband at marriage.

draft (drăft, dräft) *n.* Also *chiefly British* **draught** (drăft). The amount taken in by a single act of drinking or inhaling.

draught. *Chiefly British.* Variant of **draft.**

draw (drô) *v.* **drew** (drōo), **drawn, drawing, draws.** —*tr.* A natural drainage basin; gully.

drawn (drôn). Past participle of **draw.** —*adj.* Haggard, as from fatigue or ill health.

droll (drōl) *adj.* Amusingly odd; whimsically comical.

drought (drout) *n.* **1.** A long period with no rain, especially during a planting season. **2.** A dearth of anything; scarcity.

du·al (dōo'əl, dyōo'-) *adj.* **1.** Composed of two parts; double; twofold. **2.** Pertaining or relating to two.

dum·found (dŭm'found') *tr.v.* **-founded, -founding, -founds.** To strike dumb with astonishment or amazement; stun; nonplus.

E

ear·nest (ûr'nĭst) *adj.* Showing deep sincerity or feeling; serious.

ebb (ĕb) *n.* A period of fading away, declining, or diminishing.

ec·cen·tric (ĕk-sĕn'trĭk, ĭk-) *adj.* **a.** Departing or deviating from the conventional or established norm, model, or rule. **b.** Departing from a direct or charted course; erratic; irregular.

ec·stat·ic (ĕk-stăt' ĭk) *adj.* **1.** Of, relating to, induced by, or inducing ecstasy. **2.** In a state of ecstasy; enraptured.

e·la·tion (ĭ-lā'shən) *n.* An exalted feeling arising typically from a sense of triumph, power, or relief.

el·e·ment (ĕl'ə-mənt) *n.* An environment naturally occupied, preferred, or regarded as being preferred by an individual.

e·lude (ĭ-lōod') *tr.v.* **eluded, eluding, eludes.** **1.** To avoid or escape from, as by cunning, daring, or artifice; evade. **2.** To escape understanding or detection by; baffle.

e·ma·ci·ate (ĭ-mā'shē-āt') *tr.v.* **-ated, -ating, -ates.** To make thin, as by starvation or illness.

em·a·nate (ĕm'ə-nāt') *v.* **-nated, -nating, -nates.** —*intr.* To come forth or proceed, as from a source or origin; issue; originate.

em·is·sar·y (ĕm'ə-sĕr'ē) *n., pl.* **-ies.** A messenger or agent sent to represent or advance the interests of another.

en·gross (ĕn-grōs', ĭn-) *tr.v.* **-grossed, -grossing, -grosses.** To occupy the complete attentions of; absorb wholly.

en·hance (ĕn-hăns', -häns', ĭn-) *tr.v.* **-hanced, -hancing, -hances.** To increase or make greater, as in value, cost, beauty, or reputation; augment.

en·ig·mat·ic (ĕn'ĭg-măt' ĭk) *adj.* Also **en·ig·mat·i·cal** (-ĭ-kəl). Of or resembling an enigma; puzzling.

en·nui (än'wē') *n.* Listlessness and dissatisfaction resulting from lack of interest; boredom.

en·ter·prise (ĕn'tər-prīz') *n.* An undertaking, especially one of some scope, complication, and risk.

en·ti·tle (ĕn-tīt'l, ĭn-) *tr.v.* **-tled, -tling, -tles. a.** To give (one) a right to do or have something; allow; qualify. **b.** To give (one) a legal right or claim to something.

ă pat/ā pay/âr care/ä father/b bib/ch church/d deed/ĕ pet/ē be/f fife/g gag/h hat/hw which/ĭ pit/ī pie/îr pier/j judge/k kick/l lid, needle/m mum/n no, sudden/ng thing/ŏ pot/ō toe/ô paw, for/oi noise/ou out/ŏŏ took/ōō boot/p pop/r roar/s sauce/sh ship, dish/

en·tou·rage (än′tŏŏ-räzh′; *French* äN-tŏŏ-räzh′) *n.* A train of attendants, followers, or associates.

en·trance (ĕn-trăns′, -träns′, ĭn-) *tr.v.* **-tranced, -trancing, -trances.** To fill with great pleasure, wonder, or enchantment; fascinate.

en·treat (ĕn-trēt′, ĭn-) *v.* **-treated, -treating, -treats.** —*tr.* **1.** To ask (someone) earnestly; beseech; implore; beg. **2.** To ask for (something) earnestly; petition for.

en·treat·y (ĕn-trē′tē, ĭn-) *n., pl.* **-ies.** An earnest request or petition; plea.

e·on (ē′ŏn′, ē′ən) *n.* An indefinitely long period of time; an age; eternity.

e·qua·nim·i·ty (ē′kwə-nĭm′ə-tē, ĕk′wə-) *n.* The quality or characteristic of being calm and eventempered; composure.

e·qui·lib·ri·um (ē′kwə-lĭb′rē-əm) *n.* Any condition in which all acting influences are cancelled by others resulting in a stable, balanced, or unchanging system.

e·ra (îr′ə, ĕr′ə) *n.* A period of time that utilizes a specific point in history as the basis of its chronology.

e·rode (ĭ-rōd′) *v.* **eroded, eroding, erodes.** —*tr.* **1.** To wear away by or as if by abrasion, dissolution, and transportation. **2.** To make or form by wearing away.

e·ro·sion (ĭ-rō′zhən) *n.* The state of being eroded or the process of eroding.

eth·ics (ĕth′ĭks) *pl.n.* **1.** The study of the general nature of morals and of the specific moral choices to be made by the individual in his relationship with others; the philosophy of morals. **2.** Any set of moral principles or values.

e·voke (ĭ-vōk′) *tr.v.* **evoked, evoking, evokes.** To summon or call forth (memories, for example); reawaken; inspire.

ex·hil·a·rate (ĕg-zĭl′ə-rāt′, ĭg-) *tr.v.* **-rated, -rating, -rates.** **1.** To make cheerful; elate. **2.** To invigorate; stimulate.

ex·ot·ic (ĕg-zŏt′ĭk, ĭg-) *adj.* From another part of the world; not indigenous; foreign.

ex·pan·sive (ĕk-spăn′sĭv, ĭk-) *adj.* **1.** Wide; sweeping; comprehensive. **2.** Disposed to be open and generous; outgoing.

ex·plic·it (ĕk-splĭs′ĭt, ĭk-) *adj.* **1.** Expressed with precision; clearly defined; specific. **2.** Forthright in expression; unreserved; outspoken.

ex·u·ber·ant (ĕg-zŏŏ′bər-ənt, ĭg-) *adj.* Full of unrestrained high spirits; abandonedly joyous.

ex·ult (ĕg-zŭlt′, ĭg-) *intr.v.* **-ulted, -ulting, -ults.** To rejoice greatly; be jubilant or triumphant.

F

fa·çade (fə-säd′) *n.* Also **fa·cade.** The face or front part of anything; especially, an artificial or false front.

fac·et (făs′ĭt) *n.* An aspect; phase.

fa·ce·tious (fə-sē′shəs) *adj.* Playfully jocular; humorous and flippant.

fac·ul·ty (făk′əl-tē) *n., pl.* **-ties.** **1.** An inherent power or ability. **2.** Any of the powers or capacities possessed by the human mind.

fal·ter (fôl′tər) *intr.v.* **-tered, -tering, -ters.** **1.** To waver in confidence; hesitate. **2.** To speak hesitatingly; stammer. **3.** To move ineptly or haltingly; stumble.

fa·nat·ic (fə-năt′ĭk) *n.* A person possessed by an excessive and irrational zeal, especially for a religious or political cause.

fan·fare (făn′fâr′) *n.* **1.** A loud flourish of trumpets. **2.** *Informal.* A clamorous or spectacular public display, ceremony, or reaction; a stir.

fan·ta·sy (făn′tə-sē, -zē) *n., pl.* **-sies.** The realm of vivid imagination, reverie, depiction, illusion, and the like; the natural conjurings of mental invention and association; the visionary world; make-believe.

fast (făst, fäst) *intr.v.* **fasted, fasting, fasts.** To abstain from eating all or certain foods, especially as a religious observance or as a means of protest.

fat·u·ous (făch′ŏŏ-əs) *adj.* **1.** Complacently or unconsciously stupid; asinine; inane. **2.** Delusive; self-deceiving.

fe·line (fē′līn) *adj.* Resembling or suggestive of a cat, as in suppleness, slyness, or stealthiness.

fe·ro·cious (fə-rō′shəs) *adj.* Extremely savage; fierce.

fe·roc·i·ty (fə-rŏs′ə-tē) *n., pl.* **-ties.** The condition or quality of being ferocious.

fes·toon (fĕs-tŏŏn′) *n.* A string or garland of leaves, flowers, ribbon, or the like, suspended in a loop or curve between two points.

fet·ter (fĕt′ər) *n.* **1.** A chain or shackle attached to the ankles to restrain movement. **2.** *Usually plural.* Anything that serves to restrict; restraint. —*tr.v.* **fettered, -tering, -ters.** To put fetters on; to shackle.

fi·as·co (fē-ăs′kō) *n., pl.* **-coes** or **-cos.** A complete failure.

fierce (fîrs) *adj.* **fiercer, fiercest.** Intense or ardent; extreme: *fierce loyalty.*

fis·sure (fĭsh′ər) *n.* A narrow crack or cleft, as in a rock face.

fit·ful (fĭt′fəl) *adj.* Occurring in or characterized by fits; intermittent; spasmodic; irregular. —**fit′ful·ly** *adv.*

flaunt (flônt) *v.* **flaunted, flaunting, flaunts.** —*tr.* To exhibit ostentatiously; show off.

flax·en (flăk′sən) *adj.* Having the color of flax fiber; pale-yellow.

flot·sam (flŏt′səm) *n.* **1.** Any wreckage or cargo that remains afloat after a ship has sunk. **2.** Unemployed and vagrant people; drifters.

floun·der (floun′dər) *intr.v.* **-dered, -dering, -ders.** **1.** To move clumsily, as to regain balance. **2.** To proceed clumsily and in confusion.

flout (flout) *v.* **flouted, flouting, flouts.** —*tr.* To show contempt for; scoff at; scorn. —*intr.* To be scornful; jeer.

fluc·tu·a·tion (flŭk′chŏŏ-ā′shən) *n.* Irregular variation.

t tight/th thin, path/*th* this, bathe/ŭ cut/ûr urge/v valve/w with/y yes/z zebra, size/zh vision/ə about, item, edible, gallop, circus/ à *Fr.* ami/œ *Fr.* feu, *Ger.* schön/ü *Fr.* tu, *Ger.* über/KH *Ger.* ich, *Scot.* loch/N *Fr.* bon.

flut·ing (floo'tĭng) *n.* A decorative motif consisting of a series of long, rounded, parallel grooves, such as those incised in the surface of a column.

fod·der (fŏd'ər) *n.* Feed for livestock, often consisting of coarsely chopped stalks and leaves of corn mixed with hay, straw, and other plants.

fray (frā) *v.* **frayed, fraying, frays.** —*tr.* To unravel, wear away, or tatter (the edges of fabric, for example) by rubbing.

fren·zied (frĕn'zēd) *adj.* Affected with or filled with frenzy; frantic.

fren·zy (frĕn'zē) *n., pl.* **-zies.** a seizure of violent agitation or wild excitement, often accompanied by manic activity.

fru·gal (froo'gəl) *adj.* Costing little; inexpensive.

fur·row (fûr'ō) *n.* A long, narrow, shallow trench made in the ground by a plow or other implement.

fuse (fyooz) *v.* **fused, fusing, fuses.** —*intr.* To become mixed or united by or as if by melting together.

fu·tile (fyoot'l, fyoo'tīl') *adj.* Having no useful result; ineffectual; useless; vain.

G

gaff (găf) *n.* An iron hook attached to a pole and used to land and maneuver large fish. —*tr.v.* **gaffed, gaffing, gaffs.** To hook or land (a fish) using a gaff.

gait (gāt) *n.* A way of moving on foot; a particular fashion of walking, running, or the like.

gal·lant·ry (găl'ən-trē) *n., pl.* **-ries. 1.** Nobility of spirit or action; courage. **2.** Chivalrous attention toward women; courtliness; courteousness.

gal·va·nize (găl'və-nīz') *tr.v.* **-nized, -nizing, -nizes.** To arouse to awareness or action; to spur; startle.

gape (gāp, găp) *intr.v.* **gaped, gaping, gapes.** To become widely open or separated.

gar·goyle (gär'goil') *n.* **1.** A roof spout carved to represent a grotesque human or animal figure, and projected from a gutter to carry rainwater clear of the wall. **2.** Any grotesque ornamental figure or projection.

gar·ret (găr'ĭt) *n.* A room on the top floor of a house, typically immediately under a pitched roof; an attic; a loft.

gaud·y (gô'dē) *adj.* **-ier, -iest.** Characterized by tasteless or showy colors; garish.

gaunt (gônt) *adj.* **gaunter, gauntest.** Bleak and desolate; barren. —**gaunt'ly** *adv.*

ges·tic·u·late (jĕ-stĭk'yə-lāt') *v.* **-lated, -lating, -lates.** —*intr.* To make deliberate and vigorous motions or gestures, especially as an expression complementing or substituting for speech.

ghast·ly (găst'lē, gäst'-) *adj.* **-lier, -liest. 1.** Terrifying; dreadful. **2.** Extremely unpleasant or bad.

gib·ber (jĭb'ər, gĭb'-) *intr.v.* **-bered, -bering, -bers.** To prattle and chatter unintelligibly.

gird·er (gûr'dər) *n.* A horizontal beam, as of steel

or wood, used as a main support for a vertical load.

glut·ton (glŭt'n) *n.* One that has inordinate capacity to receive or withstand something.

gnarled (närld) *adj.* Having gnarls; knotty or misshapen: *gnarled branches.*

gnome (nōm) *n.* **1.** One of a fabled race of dwarflike creatures who live underground and guard treasure hoards. **2.** A shriveled old man.

goad (gōd) *tr.v.* **goaded, goading, goads.** To prod with or as if with a goad; give impetus to; incite.

gra·di·ent (grā'dē-ənt) *n.* **1.** A rate of inclination; slope. **2.** An ascending or descending part; an incline.

gris·ly (grĭz'lē) *adj.* **-lier, -liest.** Horrifying; repugnant; gruesome.

gro·tesque (grō-tĕsk') *adj.* **1.** Characterized by ludicrous or incongruous distortion. **2.** Extravagant; outlandish; bizarre.

gun·wale (gŭn'əl) *n.* The upper edge of a ship's side.

H

hag·gard (hăg'ərd) *adj.* Appearing worn and exhausted from or as if from suffering or deprivation; emaciated; gaunt.

har·bor (här'bər) *tr.v.* **harbored, -boring, -bors.** To entertain or nourish (a specified thought or feeling).

har·mo·nize (här'mə-nīz') *v.* **-nized, -nizing, -nizes.** —*intr.* To be in agreement; be harmonious.

heark·en (här'kən) *v.* **-ened, -ening, -ens.** Also **hark·en.** —*intr.* To listen attentively; give heed.

her·ald (hĕr'əld) *tr.v.* **heralded, -alding, -alds.** To proclaim; announce; usher in.

her·i·tage (hĕr'ĭ-tĭj) *n.* **1.** Property that is or can be inherited; inheritance. **2.** Something other than property passed down from preceding generations; legacy; tradition.

hid·e·ous (hĭd'ē-əs) *adj.* **1.** Physically repulsive; revolting; ugly. **2.** Repugnant to the moral sense; despicable; odious.

hi·lar·i·ous (hĭ-lâr'ē-əs, hī-) *adj.* Boisterously funny, gay, or merry.

hogs·head (hôgz'hĕd', hŏgz'-) *n.* **1.** Any of various units of volume or capacity ranging from 62.5 to 140 gallons; especially, a unit of capacity used in liquid measure in the United States, equal to 63 gallons. **2.** A large barrel or cask with such capacity.

hu·mil·i·ate (hyoo-mĭl'ē-āt') *tr.v.* **-ated, -ating, -ates.** To lower the pride, dignity, or status of; to humble or disgrace; degrade.

hu·mil·i·a·tion (hyoo-mĭl'ē-ā'shən) *n.* **1.** The act of humiliating; degradation. **2.** The state or condition of being humiliated; disgrace; shame.

hy·poth·e·sis (hī-pŏth'ə-sĭs) *n., pl.* **-ses** (-sēz') **1.** A premise from which a conclusion is drawn. **2.** An assumption used as the basis for action.

ă pat/ā pay/âr care/ä father/b bib/ch church/d deed/ĕ pet/ē be/f fife/g gag/h hat/hw which/ĭ pit/ī pie/îr pier/j judge/k kick/l lid,
needle/m mum/n no, sudden/ng thing/ŏ pot/ō toe/ô paw, for/oi noise/ou out/oo took/oo boot/p pop/r roar/s sauce/sh ship, dish/

I

il·lic·it (ĭ-lĭs′ĭt) *adj.* Not sanctioned by custom or law; illegal; unlawful.

im·mense (ĭ-mĕns′) *adj.* **1.** Extremely large; huge. **2.** Boundless.

im·mi·nent (ĭm′ə-nənt) *adj.* About to occur; impending.

im·pair (ĭm-pâr′) *tr.v.* **-paired, -pairing, -pairs.** To diminish in strength, value, quantity, or quality. —**im·pair′ment** *n.*

im·pen·e·tra·ble (ĭm-pĕn′ə-trə-bəl) *adj.* Incomprehensible; inscrutable; unfathomable.

im·per·a·tive (ĭm-pĕr′ə-tĭv) *adj.* Obligatory; mandatory.

im·pet·u·ous (ĭm-pĕch′ŏŏ-əs) *adj.* Characterized by sudden energy, emotion, or the like; impulsive; brash. —**im·pet′u·ous·ly** *adv.*

im·plore (ĭm-plôr′, -plōr′) *v.* **-plored, -ploring, -plores.** —*tr.* To appeal to in supplication; entreat; beseech.

im·pose (ĭm-pōz′) *v.* **-posed, -posing, -poses.** —*tr.* To obtrude or force (oneself, for example) upon another or others. —*intr.* To take unfair advantage of something or someone.

im·pos·ing (ĭm-pō′zĭng) *adj.* Impressive or awesome.

im·pos·ture (ĭm-pŏs′chər) *n.* Deception or fraud; especially, assumption of a false identity.

im·pound (ĭm-pound′) *tr.v.* **-pounded, -pounding, -pounds.** To seize and retain in legal custody.

im·promp·tu (ĭm-prŏmp′tōō, -tyōō) *adj.* Not rehearsed; extempore. —*adv.* Without rehearsal or preparation; spontaneously.

im·pru·dent (ĭm-prōō′dənt) *adj.* Not prudent; unwise or injudicious; rash.

im·pu·ni·ty (ĭm-pyōō′nə-tē) *n., pl.* **-ties. 1.** Exemption from punishment or penalty. **2.** Immunity or preservation from recrimination, regret, or the like; escape from what is probable, certain, or just.

in·a·ni·tion (ĭn′ə-nĭsh′ən) *n.* Exhaustion, as from lack of nourishment.

in·au·di·ble (ĭn-ô′də-bəl) *adj.* Incapable of being heard; not audible. —**in·au′di·bly** *adv.*

in·con·gru·ous (ĭn-kŏng′grōō-əs) *adj.* **1.** Made up of disparate, inconsistent, or discordant parts or qualities. **2.** Not consistent with what is correct, proper, or logical; unsuitable; inappropriate.

in·cred·u·lous (ĭn-krĕj′ə-ləs) *adj.* **1.** Disbelieving; skeptical. **2.** Expressing disbelief: *an incredulous stare.* —**in·cred′u·lous·ly** *adv.*

in·dig·nant (ĭn-dĭg′nənt) *adj.* Characterized by or filled with indignation. —**in·dig′nant·ly** *adv.*

in·dig·na·tion (ĭn′dĭg-nā′shən) *n.* Anger aroused by something unjust, mean, or unworthy.

in·dis·crim·i·nate (ĭn′dĭs-krĭm′ə-nĭt) *adj.* **1.** Random; haphazard. **2.** Confused; motley. —**in′dis·crim′i·nate·ly** *adv.*

in·do·lent (ĭn′də-lənt) *adj.* Disinclined to work; habitually lazy.

in·dul·gent (ĭn-dŭl′jənt) *adj.* Showing, character-

ized by, or given to indulgence; lenient. —**in·dul′gent·ly** *adv.*

in·ert (ĭn-ûrt′) *adj.* **1.** Unable to move or act. **2.** Resisting motion or action.

in·ev·i·ta·ble (ĭn-ĕv′ə-tə-bəl) *adj.* Incapable of being avoided or prevented.

in·ex·o·ra·ble (ĭn-ĕk′sər-ə-bəl) *adj.* Not capable of being persuaded by entreaty; unyielding.

in·fal·li·ble (ĭn-făl′ə-bəl) *adj.* **1.** Incapable of erring; dependable: *an infallible source of information.* **2.** Incapable of failing: *an infallible antidote.* —**in·fal′li·bly** *adv.*

in·fi·nite (ĭn′fə-nĭt) *adj.* Having no boundaries or limits. —**in′fi·nite·ly** *adv.*

in·quis·i·tive (ĭn-kwĭz′ə-tĭv) *adj.* Unduly curious and inquiring; prying.

in·sight (ĭn′sīt′) *n.* **1.** The capacity to discern the true nature of a situation; penetration. **2.** An elucidating glimpse.

in·so·lence (ĭn′sə-ləns) *n.* **1.** The quality of being insolent. **2.** An instance of insolent behavior.

in·so·lent (ĭn′sə-lənt) *adj.* Audaciously impudent; impertinent.

in·suf·fer·a·ble (ĭn-sŭf′ər-ə-bəl) *adj.* Not endurable; intolerable. —**in·suf′fer·a·bly** *adv.*

in·su·lar (ĭn′sə-lər, ĭn′syə-) *adj.* Circumscribed and detached in outlook and experience.

in·te·gral (ĭn′tə-grəl) *adj.* Essential for completion; necessary to the whole; constituent.

in·ter·mi·na·ble (ĭn-tûr′mə-nə-bəl) *adj.* Tiresomely protracted; endless. —**in·ter′mi·na·bly** *adv.*

in·ter·pret·er (ĭn-tûr′prə-tər) *n.* One who translates orally from one language into another.

in·tim·i·date (ĭn-tĭm′ə-dāt′) *tr.v.* **-dated, -dating, -dates. 1.** To make timid; frighten. **2.** To discourage or inhibit by or as if by threats.

in·tone (ĭn-tōn′) *v.* **-toned, -toning, -tones.** —*tr.* **1.** To recite in a singing voice. **2.** To utter in a monotone.

in·tri·cate (ĭn′trĭ-kĭt) *adj.* **1.** Having many complexly arranged elements. **2.** Soluble or comprehensible only with painstaking effort.

in·vin·ci·ble (ĭn-vĭn′sə-bəl) *adj.* Unconquerable.

i·so·late (ī′sə-lāt′, ĭs′ə-) *tr.v.* **-lated, -lating, -lates.** To separate from a group or whole and set apart.

J

jade (jād) *n.* Either of two distinct minerals, nephrite and jadeite, that are generally pale green or white and are used mainly as gemstones or in carving.

ju·di·cial (jōō-dĭsh′əl) *adj.* Relative to, characterized by, or expressing judgment.

K

kink (kĭngk) *n.* A tight curl, as in a hair, or a sharp twist in a line or wire, typically caused by the tensing of a looped section.

---

t tight/th thin, path/*th* this, bathe/ŭ cut/ûr urge/v valve/w with/y yes/z zebra, size/zh vision/ə about, item, edible, gallop, circus/ à *Fr.* ami/œ *Fr.* feu, *Ger.* schön/ü *Fr.* tu, *Ger.* über/KH *Ger.* ich, *Scot.* loch/N *Fr.* bon.

kip·per (kĭp′ər) *n.* A herring that has been split, salted, and smoked.

knead (nēd) *tr.v.* **kneaded, kneading, kneads. 1.** To mix and work (a substance) into a uniform mass, especially to fold, press, and stretch dough with the hands. **2.** To make (bread) by kneading.

L

lac·er·ate (lăs′ə-rāt′) *tr.v.* **-ated, -ating, -ates.** To tear. *—adj.* **1.** Torn; mangled. **2.** Having jagged, deeply cut edges.

lag (lăg) *v.* **lagged, lagging, lags.** *—intr.* To fail to keep up a pace; fall behind; straggle; loiter.

la·goon (lə-gōōn′) *n.* A body of brackish water, especially one separated from the sea by sandbars or coral reefs.

la·ment·ed (lə-mĕn′tĭd) *adj.* Mourned for.

lan·guid (lăng′gwĭd) *adj.* **1.** Lacking energy or vitality; faint; weak. **2.** Unwilling to stir or exert oneself.

lan·guor (lăng′gər) *n.* Languidness; lassitude; sluggishness.

lar·der (lär′dər) *n.* A room, cupboard, or the like where meat and other foods are kept.

la·va (lä′və, lăv′ə) *n.* **1.** Molten rock that issues from a volcano or a fissure in the earth's surface. **2.** The rock formed by the cooling and solidifying of this substance.

le·git·i·mate (lə-jĭt′ə-mĭt) *adj.* **1.** In accordance with traditional or established patterns and standards. **2.** Based on logical reasoning; reasonable.

le·ver·age (lĕv′ər-ĭj, lē′vər-) *n.* Positional advantage; power to act effectively.

lev·i·tate (lĕv′ə-tāt′) *v.* **-tated, -tating, -tates.** *—intr.* To rise into the air and float, in apparent defiance of gravity. *—tr.* To cause to rise into the air and float. *—lev′i·ta′tion n.*

lev·y (lĕv′ē) *v.* **-ied, -ying, -ies.** *—tr.* To impose or collect (a tax, for example).

Lil·li·pu·tian (lĭl′ə-pyōō′shən) *n.* **1.** One of the tiny inhabitants of an island in Jonathan Swift's *Gulliver's Travels.* **2.** *Often small* **l.** A very small person or being.

list·less (lĭst′lĭs) *adj.* Marked by a lack of energy or enthusiasm; disinclined toward any effort; indifferent; languid. *—list′less·ly adv.*

lit·er·al (lĭt′ər-əl) *adj.* **1.** Concerned chiefly with facts; prosaic. **2.** Avoiding exaggeration, metaphor, or embellishment; plain.

lit·ter (lĭt′ər) *n.* A stretcher for the sick or wounded. *—v.* **littered, -tering, -ters.** *—tr.* To make untidy by discarding rubbish carelessly.

loft·y (lôf′tē, lŏf′-) *adj.* **-ier, -iest.** Of imposing height; towering.

lore (lôr, lōr) *n.* Accumulated fact, tradition, or belief about a particular subject.

lu·cid (lōō′sĭd) *adj.* Easily understood; clear.

lu·mi·nous (lōō′mə-nəs) *adj.* **1.** Emitting light; especially, emitting self-generated light. **2.** Full of light; illuminated.

M

mal·ice (măl′ĭs) *n.* The desire to harm others, or to see others suffer; ill will; spite.

ma·lig·nant (mə-lĭg′nənt) *adj.* Showing great malevolence; actively evil in nature.

ma·neu·ver (mə-nōō′vər, -nyōō′-) *n.* A calculated and skillful movement, act, or stratagem.

man·ger (mān′jər) *n.* A trough or open box in which feed for horses or cattle is placed.

man·grove (măn′grōv′, măng′grōv′) *n.* Any of various tropical evergreen trees or shrubs of the genus *Rhizophora*, having stiltlike roots and stems, and forming dense thickets along tidal shores.

mar (mär) *tr.v.* **marred, marring, mars. 1.** To damage or deface. **2.** To spoil the quality of.

mar·row (măr′ō) *n.* The soft material that fills bone cavities, consisting, in varying proportions, of fat cells and maturing blood cells, together with supporting connective tissue and numerous blood vessels.

mar·tyr (mär′tər) *n.* **1.** One who chooses to suffer death rather than renounce religious principles. **2.** One who sacrifices something very important to him in order to further a belief, cause, or principle. **3.** A person who endures great suffering.

mas·sa·cre (măs′ə-kər) *n.* Savage and indiscriminate killing.

ma·tron (mā′trən) *n.* A woman who supervises a public institution, such as a school, hospital, or prison.

mea·ger (mē′gər) *adj.* Conspicuously deficient in quantity, fullness, or extent; scanty.

men·ace (mĕn′ĭs) *n.* **1.** A threat. **2.** A troublesome or annoying person.

mer·it (mĕr′ĭt) *n.* Value, excellence, or superior quality. *—v.* **merited, -iting, -its.** *—tr.* To earn; deserve; warrant.

mi·nute (mī-nōōt′, -nyōōt′, mĭ-) *adj.* Characterized by careful scrutiny and close examination.

mi·rage (mĭ-räzh′) *n.* **1.** An optical phenomenon that creates the illusion of water, often with inverted reflections of distant objects. It results from distortion of light by alternate layers of hot and cool air. Also called "fata morgana." **2.** Something that is illusory or insubstantial like a mirage.

mis·cre·ant (mĭs′krē-ənt) *n.* An evildoer or villain.

mock (mŏk) *v.* **mocked, mocking, mocks.** *—tr.* To treat with scorn or contempt; deride; ridicule.

mol·ten (mōlt′n) *adj.* Made liquid by heat; melted.

mon·i·tor (mŏn′ə-tər) *n.* Any device used to record or control a process.

mo·rale (mə-răl′) *n.* The state of the spirits of an individual or group, as shown in willingness to perform assigned tasks, confidence, cheerfulness, and discipline.

mor·sel (môr′səl) *n.* A small piece or bite of food.

mo·sa·ic (mō-zā′ĭk) *n.* **1.** A picture or decorative design made by setting small colored pieces, such as tile, in mortar. **2.** Anything that resembles a piece of mosaic work.

ă pat/ā pay/âr care/ä father/b bib/ch church/d deed/ĕ pet/ē be/f fife/g gag/h hat/hw which/ĭ pit/ī pie/îr pier/j judge/k kick/l lid, needle/m mum/n no, sudden/ng thing/ŏ pot/ō toe/ô paw, for/oi noise/ou out/ōō took/ōō boot/p pop/r roar/s sauce/sh ship, dish/

mot·ley (mŏt′lē) *adj.* Exhibiting or having many colors; multicolored.

mot·tle (mŏt′l) *n.* A spot of color or shading contrasting with the rest of the surface on which it is found.

muf·fle (mŭf′əl) *tr.v.* **-fled, -fling, -fles.** To wrap or pad in order to deaden a sound.

mu·ta·ble (myōō′tə-bəl) *adj.* **1.** Subject to change or alteration. **2.** Prone to frequent change; inconstant; fickle.

N

na·ive, na·ïve (nä-ēv′) *adj.* **a.** Lacking worldliness and sophistication; artless; unaffected. **b.** Simple and credulous as a child; ingenuous.

nape (nāp) *n.* The back of the neck.

ne·go·ti·ate (nĭ-gō′shē-āt′) *v.* **-ated, -ating, -ates.** —*tr.* To succeed in passing over, accomplishing, or coping with.

niche (nĭch) *n.* **1.** A recess in a wall for holding a statue or other ornament. **2.** Any steep, shallow recess or concavity, as in a rock or hill.

no·mad·ic (nō-măd′ĭk) *adj.* Leading the life of a nomad; wandering; roving.

non·cha·lance (nŏn′shə-läns′) *n.* Debonair lack of concern.

nos·tal·gi·a (nō-stăl′jə, nə-) *n.* A longing for things, persons, or situations that are not present. —**nos·tal′gic** *adj.*

nov·el·ty (nŏv′əl-tē) *n., pl.* **-ties.** Something that is novel; a new or unusual thing; an innovation.

nur·ture (nûr′chər) *n.* Anything that nourishes; sustenance; food. —*tr.v.* **nurtured, -turing, -tures.** To nourish.

O

o·bei·sance (ō-bā′səns, ō-bē′-) *n.* A gesture or movement of the body expressing reverence or respect, such as a bow or curtsy.

o·blit·er·ate (ə-blĭt′ə-rāt′) *tr.v.* **-ated, -ating, -ates.** To do away with completely; destroy so as to leave no trace.

o·bliv·i·ous (ə-blĭv′ē-əs) *adj.* Unaware or unmindful.

ob·sti·nate (ŏb′stə-nĭt) *adj.* Stubbornly adhering to an attitude, opinion, or course of action; resistant to argument or entreaty; inflexible; obdurate.

o·di·ous (ō′dē-əs) *adj.* Exciting hatred or repugnance; abhorrent; offensive.

om·i·nous (ŏm′ə-nəs) *adj.* **1.** Being or pertaining to an evil omen; portentous; foreboding. **2.** Menacing; threatening.

o·paque (ō-pāk′) *adj.* Impenetrable by light; neither transparent nor translucent. —**o·paque′ness** *n.*

o·pi·ate (ō′pē-ĭt, -āt′) *n.* Anything that relaxes or that induces sleep or torpor.

or·gan·ic (ôr-găn′ĭk) *adj.* Of, pertaining to, or affecting an organ of the body.

or·na·ment (ôr′nə-mənt) *n.* **1.** Anything that decorates or adorns; an embellishment. **2.** Decorations or adornments collectively.

P

pag·eant (păj′ənt) *n.* **1.** A spectacular procession or celebration. **2.** Colorful display; pageantry.

pain·ter (pān′tər) *n. Nautical.* A rope attached to the bow of a boat, used for tying up.

pal·ate (păl′ĭt) *n.* The sense of taste.

pa·la·tial (pə-lā′shəl) *adj.* **1.** Of or suitable for a palace. **2.** Of the nature of a palace; spacious and ornate.

pal·lid (păl′ĭd) *adj.* Lacking intensity of hue or luminousness.

par·al·lel (păr′ə-lĕl′) *adj.* Being an equal distance apart at every point.

par·a·pet (păr′ə-pĭt, -pĕt′) *n.* A low, protective wall or railing along the edge of a roof, balcony, or similar structure.

par·ox·ysm (păr′ək-sĭz′əm) *n.* A spasm or fit; convulsion.

pat·ent (pāt′ənt) *adj.* Obvious; plain.

paunch (pônch, pänch) *n.* The belly; especially, a potbelly.

pa·vil·ion (pə-vĭl′yən) *n.* A temporary, ornamental, and often open structure, used at parks or fairs for amusement or shelter.

peak·ed (pē′kĭd) *adj.* Having a sickly, pale, or emaciated appearance; drawn.

peat (pēt) *n.* Partially carbonized vegetable matter, usually mosses, found in bogs, and used as fertilizer and fuel.

pe·des·tri·an (pə-dĕs′trē-ən) *n.* Commonplace; undistinguished; ordinary.

pen·sive (pĕn′sĭv) *adj.* **1.** Engaged in deep thoughtfulness. **2.** Suggesting or expressing deep, often melancholy thoughtfulness.

per·emp·to·ry (pə-rĕmp′tə-rē) *adj.* **1.** Having the nature of or expressing a command; urgent. **2.** Offensively self-assured; dictatorial; imperious. —**per·emp′to·ri·ly** *adv.*

pe·rim·e·ter (pə-rĭm′ə-tər) *n.* **a.** *Mathematics.* A closed curve bounding a plane area. **b.** The length of such a boundary.

per·pe·trate (pûr′pə-trāt′) *tr.v.* **-trated, -trating, -trates.** **1.** To be guilty of; commit: *perpetrate a crime.* **2.** To carry out; perform: *perpetrate a practical joke.* —**per′pe·tra′tor** (-trā′tər) *n.*

per·sist (pər-sĭst′, -zĭst′) *intr.v.* **-sisted, -sisting, -sists.** To hold firmly and steadfastly to some purpose, state, or undertaking, despite obstacles, warnings, or setbacks.

per·sist·ence (pər-sĭs′təns, -zĭs′təns) *n.* **1.** The act of persisting. **2.** The quality of being persistent; perseverance; tenacity.

per·sist·ent (pər-sĭs′tənt, -zĭs′tənt) *adj.* Refusing to give up or let go; persevering obstinately.

---

t tight/th thin, path/*th* this, bathe/ŭ cut/ûr urge/v valve/w with/y yes/z zebra, size/zh vision/ə about, item, edible, gallop, circus/ à *Fr.* ami/œ *Fr.* feu, *Ger.* schön/ü *Fr.* tu, *Ger.* über/KH *Ger.* ich, *Scot.* loch/N *Fr.* bon.

per·verse (pər-vûrs′) *adj.* Obstinately persisting in an error or fault; wrongly self-willed or stubborn.

pet·tish (pĕt′ ĭsh) *adj.* Ill-tempered; peevish; petulant. —**pet′tish·ly** *adv.*

pet·u·lant (pĕch′ŏŏ-lənt) *adj.* Unreasonably irritable or ill-tempered; peevish.

phos·pho·res·cence (fŏs′fə-rĕs′əns) *n.* Persistent emission of light following exposure to and removal of incident radiation.

pike (pīk) *n.* A long spear formerly used by infantry.

pil·fer (pĭl′fər) *v.* **-fered, -fering, -fers.** —*tr.* To steal (a small amount or item); filch. —*intr.* To steal or filch.

pin·ion (pĭn′yən) *tr.v.* **pinioned, -ioning, -ions.** To restrain or immobilize (a person) by binding the arms.

pit·tance (pĭt′əns) *n.* **1.** A meager allowance of money. **2.** A very small salary or remuneration. **3.** A small amount or portion of anything.

pla·cate (plā′kāt′, plăk′āt′) *tr.v.* **-cated, -cating, -cates.** To allay the anger of, especially by yielding concessions; appease.

plac·id (plăs′ĭd) *adj.* Having an undisturbed surface or aspect; outwardly calm or composed.

plain·tive (plān′tĭv) *adj.* Expressing sorrow; mournful; melancholy.

pli·ant (plī′ənt) *adj.* **1.** Easily bent or flexed; supple; limber. **2.** Easily altered or modified to fit conditions; adaptable. **3.** Yielding readily to influence or domination; docile; compliant.

plum·met (plŭm′ĭt) *intr.v.* **plummeted, -meting, -mets.** To drop straight down; plunge.

po·di·um (pō′dē-əm) *n., pl.* **-dia** (-dē-ə) or **-ums.** An elevated platform for an orchestra conductor, lecturer, or the like; dais.

pom·pous (pŏm′pəs) *adj.* **1.** Characterized by an exaggerated show of dignity or self-importance; pretentious. **2.** Bombastic or self-important in speech or manner.

pon·der (pŏn′dər) *v.* **-dered, -dering, -ders.** —*tr.* To weigh mentally; consider carefully. —*intr.* To meditate; deliberate; reflect.

pon·der·ous (pŏn′dər-əs) *adj.* Graceless or unwieldy from weight. —**pon′der·ous·ly** *adv.*

por·ti·co (pôr′tĭ-kō′, pōr′-) *n., pl.* **-coes or -cos.** A porch or walkway with a roof supported by columns, often leading to the entrance of a building.

po·tent (pōt′nt) *adj.* **1.** Possessing inner or physical strength; powerful. **2.** Capable of commanding attention; able to convince: *potent arguments.* **3.** Having great control or authority.

po·ten·tial (pə-tĕn′shəl) *adj.* Possible but not yet realized; capable of being but not yet in existence; latent.

pre·clude (prĭ-klŏŏd′) *tr.v.* **-cluded, -cluding, -cludes.** To make impossible or impracticable by previous action; prevent.

preen (prēn) *v.* **preened, preening, preens.** —*tr.* To smooth or clean (feathers) with the beak or bill. Used of a bird.

pre·lim·i·nar·y (prĭ-lĭm′ə-nĕr′ē) *adj.* Prior to or preparing for the main matter, action, or business; introductory; prefatory.

pre·ma·ture (prē′mə-chŏŏr′, -tŏŏr′, -tyŏŏr′) *adj.* Occurring, growing, or existing prior to the customary, correct, or assigned time; uncommonly or unexpectedly early.

pre·med·i·tate (prē-mĕd′ə-tāt′) *v.* **-tated, -tating, -tates.** —*tr.* To plan, arrange, or plot (a deed or events) in advance.

pre·pos·ter·ous (prĭ-pŏs′tər-əs) *adj.* Contrary to nature, reason, or common sense; absurd.

pre·scribe (prĭ-skrīb′) *v.* **-scribed, -scribing, -scribes.** —*tr.* To set down as a rule or guide; ordain; enjoin.

pre·text (prē′tĕkst′) *n.* An ostensible or professed purpose; pretense; excuse.

pri·va·tion (prī-vā′shən) *n.* An act, condition, or result of deprivation or loss.

pro·ce·dure (prə-sē′jər) *n.* **1.** A manner of proceeding; way of performing or effecting something. **2.** An act composed of steps; course of action. **3.** A set of established forms or methods for conducting the affairs of a business, legislative body, or court of law.

pro·found (prə-found′, prō-) *adj.* Unqualified; absolute; complete. —**pro·found′ly** *adv.*

prom·on·to·ry (prŏm′ən-tôr′ē, -tōr′ē) *n., pl.* **-ries.** A high ridge of land or rock jutting out into a sea or other expanse of water.

pro·tract (prō-trăkt′) *tr.v.* **-tracted, -tracting, -tracts.** To draw out or lengthen in time; prolong.

prov·i·den·tial (prŏv′ə-dĕn′shəl) *adj.* **1.** Of or resulting from divine providence. **2.** Happening as if through divine intervention; fortunate; opportune.

pro·vin·cial (prə-vĭn′shəl) *adj.* **1.** Of or pertaining to a province. **2.** Of or characteristic of people from the provinces; not fashionable or sophisticated.

pru·dence (prŏŏd′əns) *n.* **1.** The state, quality, or fact of being prudent; discretion. **2.** Careful management; economy.

pry (prī) *tr.v.* **pried, prying, pries. 1.** To raise, move, or force open with a lever. **2.** To obtain with effort or difficulty.

pul·sate (pŭl′sāt′) *intr.v.* **-sated, -sating, -sates. 1.** To expand and contract rhythmically; throb. **2.** To quiver.

pu·ri·fi·ca·tion (pyŏŏr′ə-fĭ-kā′shən) *n.* The act or process of cleansing or purifying.

pu·ri·fy (pyŏŏr′ə-fī′) *v.* **-fied, -fying, -fies.** —*tr.* To free from sin, guilt, or other defilement.

Q

quack (kwăk) *n.* **1.** An untrained person who pretends to have medical knowledge. **2.** A charlatan; mountebank.

quaff (kwŏf, kwăf, kwôf) *v.* **quaffed, quaffing, quaffs.** —*tr.* To drink heartily. —*intr.* To drink something heartily.

ă pat/ā pay/âr care/ä father/b **bib**/ch **church**/d **deed**/ĕ pet/ē be/f **fife**/g **gag**/h **hat**/hw **which**/ĭ pit/ī pie/îr pier/j **judge**/k **kick**/l **lid**,
needle/m **mum**/n no, sudden/ng thing/ŏ pot/ō toe/ô paw, for/oi noise/ou out/ŏŏ took/ōō boot/p **pop**/r roar/s sauce/sh ship, dish/

quar·ry (kwôr′ē, kwŏr′ē) *n., pl.* **-ries. 1.** A bird or animal hunted; prey; game. **2.** Any object of pursuit.

quay (kē) *n.* A wharf or reinforced bank where ships are loaded or unloaded.

quest (kwĕst) *n.* The act or instance of seeking or pursuing something; a search.

R

ra·di·al (rā′dē-əl) *adj.* **a.** Of, pertaining to, or arranged like rays or radii. **b.** Radiating from or converging to a common center.

ra·di·us (rā′dē-əs) *n., pl.* **-dii** (-dē-ī′) or **-uses. a.** A line segment that joins the center of a circle with any point on its circumference. **b.** A line segment that joins the center of a sphere with any point on its surface.

rank (răngk) *adj.* **ranker, rankest.** Growing profusely or with excessive vigor: *rank weeds.*

ran·kle (răng′kəl) *v.* **-kled, -kling, -kles.** *—intr.* To cause persistent irritation or resentment.

ran·sack (răn′săk′) *tr.v.* **-sacked, -sacking, -sacks. 1.** To search or examine thoroughly. **2.** To search carefully for plunder; to pillage.

ra·pa·cious (rə-pā′shəs) *adj.* Greedy; avaricious.

rap·port (ră-pôr′, -pōr′) *n.* Relationship; especially, one of mutual trust or emotional affinity.

ra·vine (rə-vēn′) *n.* A deep, narrow cleft or gorge in the earth's surface, especially one worn by the flow of water.

re·cede (rĭ-sēd′) *intr.v.* **-ceded, -ceding, -cedes.** To become or seem to become more distant.

re·cess (rē′sĕs′, rĭ-sĕs′) *n.* **a.** An indentation or small hollow. **b.** An alcove.

re·coil (rĭ-koil′) *intr.v.* **-coiled, -coiling, -coils.** To shrink back in fear or repugnance.

re·fec·to·ry (rĭ-fĕk′tə-rē) *n., pl.* **-ries.** A room where meals are served.

re·fute (rĭ-fyoōt′) *tr.v.* **-futed, -futing, -futes. 1.** To prove (a statement or argument) to be false or erroneous; disprove. **2.** To prove (a person) to be wrong.

rel·a·tive (rĕl′ə-tĭv) *adj.* Considered in comparison to or relationship with something else.

re·lent·less (rĭ-lĕnt′lĭs) *adj.* **1.** Unyielding; pitiless. **2.** Steady and persistent; unremitting.

rel·e·vant (rĕl′ə-vənt) *adj.* Related to the matter at hand; to the point; pertinent. **rel′e·van·cy** *n.*

rem·i·nis·cent (rĕm′ə-nĭs′ənt) *adj.* **1.** Having the quality of or containing reminiscence. **2.** Tending to recall or talk of the past.

re·mon·strance (rĭ-mŏn′strəns) *n.* **1.** The act of remonstrating. **2.** A speech or gesture of protest, opposition, or reproof.

re·morse (rĭ-môrs′) *n.* Moral anguish arising from repentance for past misdeeds; bitter regret.

rend (rĕnd) *v.* **rent** (rĕnt) or **rended, rending, rends.** *—tr.* To tear apart or into pieces violently; to split.

rent (rĕnt). Past tense and past participle of **rend.** *—n.* An opening made by rending; a rip or gap.

re·past (rĭ-păst′, -päst′) *n.* A meal, or the food eaten or provided at a meal.

re·signed (rĭ-zīnd′) *adj.* Feeling or marked by resignation; acquiescent. **—re·sign′ed·ly** (rĭ-zī′nĭd-lē) *adv.*

res·pite (rĕs′pĭt) *n.* A temporary cessation or postponement, usually of something disagreeable; an interval of rest or relief.

res·tive (rĕs′tĭv) *adj.* Impatient or nervous under restriction, delay, or pressure; uneasy; restless.

re·tain (rĭ-tān′) *tr.v.* **-tained, -taining, -tains.** To keep or hold in one's possession.

re·ten·tion (rĭ-tĕn′shən) *n.* **1.** The act of retaining. **2.** The condition of being retained.

re·tort (rĭ-tôrt′) *v.* **-torted, -torting, -torts.** *—tr.* **1.** To return in kind; pay back. **2.** To reply; especially, to answer in a quick, direct manner.

re·treat (rĭ-trēt′) *n.* A quiet, private, or secure place; a refuge.

ret·ri·bu·tion (rĕt′rə-byoō′shən) *n.* Something given or demanded in repayment; especially, punishment.

rev·er·ence (rĕv′ər-əns) *n.* A feeling of profound awe and respect and often of love; veneration.

rev·er·ent (rĕv′ər-ənt) *adj.* Feeling or showing reverence. **—rev′er·ent·ly** *adv.*

re·vert (rĭ-vûrt′) *intr.v.* **-verted, -verting, -verts.** To return to a former condition, practice, subject, or belief.

riff (rĭf) *n. Music.* A short rhythmic phrase repeated constantly.

rit·u·al (rĭch′oō-əl) *adj.* **1.** Of or characterized by a rite or rites. **2.** Practiced as a rite.

row·el (rou′əl) *n.* A sharp-toothed wheel inserted into the end of the shank of a spur.

rue·ful (roō′fəl) *adj.* Causing, feeling, or expressing sorrow or regret.

ru·in·ous (roō′ĭ-nəs) *adj.* Causing or apt to cause ruin; destructive.

rum·mage (rŭm′ĭj) *v.* **-maged, -maging, -mages.** *—tr.* To search thoroughly by handling, turning over, or disarranging the contents of.

ruse (roōz) *n.* An action or device meant to confuse or mislead.

S

saf·fron (săf′rən) *n.* Moderate or strong orange-yellow to moderate orange.

sa·gac·i·ty (sə-găs′ə-tē) *n.* Keen intelligence; shrewdness.

sal·low (săl′ō) *adj.* **-lower, -lowest.** Of a sickly yellowish hue or complexion.

sal·vage (săl′vĭj) *tr.v.* **-vaged, -vaging, -vages.** To save (a ship or its cargo, for example) from loss or destruction. *—n.* The act of saving any imperiled property from loss.

sap (săp) *v.* **sapped, sapping, saps.** *—tr.* To deplete or weaken gradually; devitalize.

---

t tight/th thin, path/*th* this, bathe/ŭ cut/ûr urge/v valve/w with/y yes/z zebra, size/zh vision/ə about, item, edible, gallop, circus/ â *Fr.* ami/œ *Fr.* feu, *Ger.* schön/ü *Fr.* tu, *Ger.* über/KH *Ger.* ich, *Scot.* loch/N *Fr.* bon.

saun·ter (sôn'tər) *intr.v.* **-tered, -tering, -ters.** To walk at a leisurely pace; to stroll.

scal·lop (skŏl'əp, skăl'-) *n.* Any of a series of variously curved projections forming an ornamental border, as on fabrics or lace.

scep·ter (sĕp'tər) *n.* A staff held by a sovereign on ceremonial occasions as an emblem of authority.

scin·til·late (sĭn'tə-lāt') *v.* **-lated, -lating, -lates.** —*intr.* **1.** To throw off sparks; flash. **2.** To sparkle or shine. **3.** To be animated and brilliant.

scour (skour) *v.* **scoured, scouring, scours.** —*tr.* **1.** To range over (an area) quickly and energetically. **2.** To search through or over thoroughly.

scru·ple (skrōō'pəl) *n.* Ethical objection to certain actions; principle; dictate of conscience.

scud (skŭd) *intr.v.* **scudded, scudding, scuds.** To run or skim along swiftly and easily.

se·cu·ri·ty (sĭ-kyŏŏr'ə-tē) *n., pl.* **-ties.** *Plural.* Written evidence of ownership or creditorship; especially, a stock certificate.

se·date (sĭ-dāt') *adj.* Serenely deliberate in character or manner; composed; collected. —**se·date'ly** *adv.*

sed·a·tive (sĕd'ə-tĭv) *adj.* Having a soothing, calming, or tranquilizing effect. —*n.* A sedative agent or drug.

sed·i·ment (sĕd'ə-mənt) *n.* Material that settles to the bottom of a liquid; dregs; lees.

sen·ti·nel (sĕnt'n-əl) *n.* One that keeps guard; a sentry. —*tr.v.* **sentineled, -neling, -nels.** To watch over as a sentinel.

ser·vile (sûr'vəl, -vīl') *adj.* Slavish in character or attitude; obsequious; submissive.

sex·tant (sĕks'tənt) *n.* A navigational instrument used for measuring the altitudes of celestial bodies.

sham·rock (shăm'rŏk') *n.* Any of several plants, such as a clover or wood sorrel, having compound leaves with three small leaflets, considered the national emblem of Ireland.

shrewd (shrōōd) *adj.* **shrewder, shrewdest. 1.** Having keen insight; discerning; astute. **2.** Artful; cunning; tricky. **3.** Sharp; penetrating.

si·dle (sīd'l) *intr.v.* **-dled, -dling, -dles.** To move sideways; edge along furtively or indirectly.

sil·hou·ette (sĭl'ōō-ĕt') *n.* A representation of the outline of something, usually filled in with black or another solid color. —*tr.v.* **silhouetted, -etting, -ettes.** To cause to be seen as a silhouette; to outline.

sim·u·late (sĭm'yə-lāt') *tr.v.* **-lated, -lating, -lates.** To have or take on the appearance, form, or sound of; imitate.

sin·ew (sĭn'yōō) *n.* **1.** A tendon. **2.** Vigorous strength; muscular power.

sin·ew·y (sĭn'yōō-ē) *adj.* Like or consisting of sinew.

singe (sĭnj) *tr.v.* **singed, singeing, singes.** To burn superficially; scorch.

sin·gu·lar (sĭng'gyə-lər) *adj.* **a.** Being only one; separate; individual. **b.** Deviating strongly from a norm; rare; extraordinary.

sin·is·ter (sĭn'ĭ-stər) *adj.* **1.** Suggesting an evil force or motive: *a sinister smile.* **2.** Presaging trouble; ominous.

si·phon (sī'fən) *v.* **siphoned, -phoning, -phons.** Also **sy·phon.** —*tr.* To draw off or convey through or as if through a siphon.

skiff (skĭf) *n. Nautical.* A flat-bottomed open boat of shallow draft, having a pointed bow and a square stern and propelled by oars, sail, or motor.

sloop (slōōp) *n. Nautical.* A single-masted, fore-and-aft-rigged sailing boat with a short standing bowsprit or none at all and a single headsail set from the forestay.

slug·gish (slŭg'ĭsh) *adj.* Slow to perform or respond to stimulation.

sluice (slōōs) *v.* **sluiced, sluicing, sluices.** —*tr.* To wash with a sudden flow of water.

smug (smŭg) *adj.* **smugger, smuggest.** Complacent or self-righteous.

sod (sŏd) *n.* **1.** A section of grass-covered surface soil held together by matted roots; turf. **2.** The ground, especially when covered with grass.

so·lic·i·tous (sə-lĭs'ə-təs) *adj.* Anxious and concerned; attentive.

so·lic·i·tude (sə-lĭs'ə-tōōd', -tyōōd') *n.* The state of being solicitous; care; concern.

som·no·lent (sŏm'nə-lənt) *adj.* **1.** Drowsy; sleepy. **2.** Inducing or tending to induce sleep; soporific.

son·ic (sŏn'ĭk) *adj.* **1.** Of or relating to audible sound: *a sonic wave.* **2.** Having a speed approaching or being that of sound in air, approximately 738 miles per hour at sea level.

span (spăn) *tr.v.* **spanned, spanning, spans.** To reach or extend over or from one side to the other of.

spas·mod·ic (spăz-mŏd'ĭk) *adj.* Happening intermittently; fitful: *spasmodic rifle fire.* —**spas·mod'i·cal·ly** *adv.*

spec·u·la·tion (spĕk'yə-lā'shən) *n.* Engagement in risky business transactions on the chance of quick or considerable profit.

squall·y (skwôl'ē) *adj.* **-ier, -iest.** Characterized by squalls; stormy; gusty.

stac·ca·to (stə-kä'tō) *adj.* Composed of abrupt, distinct, emphatic parts or sounds. —*n., pl.* **staccatos** or **-ti** (-tĭ). An abrupt, emphatic manner or sound.

stalk (stôk) *v.* **stalked, stalking, stalks.** —*intr.* To track game. —*tr.* To pursue by tracking.

star·board (stär'bərd) *n.* The right-hand side of a ship or aircraft as one faces forward.

state·ly (stāt'lē) *adj.* **-lier, -liest. 1.** Dignified; formal. **2.** Majestic; lofty.

stealth·y (stĕl'thē) *adj.* **-ier, -iest.** Characterized by clandestine or secret movement; avoiding notice.

steel (stēl) *tr.v.* **steeled, steeling, steels.** To make hard, strong, or obdurate; strengthen.

sti·fle (stī'fəl) *v.* **-fled, -fling, -fles.** —*tr.* To keep or hold back; suppress; repress.

stir·rup (stûr'əp, stĭr'-) *n.* A flat-based loop or ring

ă pat/ā pay/âr care/ä father/b **bib**/ch **church**/d **deed**/ĕ pet/ē be/f **fife**/g **gag**/h **hat**/hw **which**/ĭ pit/ī pie/îr pier/j **judge**/k **kick**/l lid,
needle/m **mum**/n no, sudden/ng **thing**/ŏ pot/ō toe/ô paw, for/oi noise/ou out/ŏŏ took/ōō boot/p **pop**/r roar/s sauce/sh **ship, dish**/

hung from either side of a horse's saddle to support the rider's foot in mounting and riding.

stol·id (stŏl'ĭd) *adj.* Having or showing little emotion; impassive.

stow·age (stō'ĭj) *n.* The act, manner, or process of stowing.

stren·u·ous (strĕn'yōō-əs) *adj.* Requiring or characterized by great effort, energy, or exertion: *a strenuous task.*

strew (strōō) *tr.v.* **strewn** (strōōn) or **strewed, strewing, strews. 1.** To spread here and there; scatter; sprinkle. **2.** To cover (a surface) with things scattered or sprinkled.

strin·gent (strĭn'jənt) *adj.* Imposing rigorous standards of performance; severe.

suave (swäv, swāv) *adj.* Smoothly gracious in social manner; urbane. —**suav'i·ty** *n.*

sub·jec·tive (səb-jĕk'tĭv) *adj.* **a.** Proceeding from or taking place within an individual's mind such as to be unaffected by the external world. **b.** Particular to a given individual; personal.

sub·ser·vi·ent (səb-sûr'vē-ənt) *adj.* **1.** Useful as a means or instrument; serving to promote some end. **2.** Subordinate in capacity or function. **3.** Obsequious; servile.

sub·tle (sŭt'l) *adj.* **-tler, -tlest. a.** So slight as to be difficult to detect or analyze; elusive. **b.** Not immediately obvious; abstruse.

sub·tle·ty (sŭt'l-tē) *n., pl.* **-ties.** The quality or state of being subtle.

suf·fice (sə-fīs') *v.* **-ficed, -ficing, -fices.** —*intr.* To meet present needs or requirements; be sufficient or adequate.

sul·len (sŭl'ən) *adj.* **1.** Showing a brooding ill humor or resentment; morose; sulky. **2.** Gloomy or somber in tone, color, or portent.

sul·try (sŭl'trē) *adj.* **-trier, -triest.** Very hot and humid.

su·per·fi·cial (sōō'pər-fĭsh'əl) *adj.* Concerned with or comprehending only what is apparent or obvious; shallow.

sup·press (sə-prĕs') *tr.v.* **-pressed, -pressing, -presses.** To hold back (an impulse, for example); to check.

sur·cease (sûr'sēs', sər-sēs') *v.* **-ceased, -ceasing, -ceases.** *Archaic.* —*intr.* To cease; stop. —*n. Archaic.* Cessation; end.

sur·mount (sər-mount') *tr.v.* **-mounted, -mounting, -mounts.** To overcome (an obstacle, for example); conquer.

swerve (swûrv) *v.* **swerved, swerving, swerves.** —*intr.* To turn aside from a straight course; veer. —*tr.* To cause to veer; deflect; turn aside.

T

tac·i·turn (tăs'ə-tərn) *adj.* Habitually untalkative; laconic; uncommunicative.

taint (tānt) *v.* **tainted, tainting, taints.** —*tr.* **1.** To stain the honor of someone or something. **2.** To infect with or as with a disease.

tan·gi·ble (tăn'jə-bəl) *adj.* Discernible by the touch; capable of being touched; palpable.

tap·es·try (tăp'ĭ-strē) *n., pl.* **-tries.** A heavy textile fabric having a varicolored design woven across the warp, used for wall hangings, furniture coverings, and the like.

teem (tēm) *v.* **teemed, teeming, teems.** —*intr.* To be full and, usually, in motion; abound or swarm.

tem·per (tĕm'pər) *v.* **-pered, -pering, -pers.** —*tr.* To modify by the addition of some moderating agent or quality; moderate.

te·na·cious (tə-nā'shəs) *adj.* **1.** Holding or tending to hold firmly; persistent; stubborn. **2.** Holding together firmly; cohesive. —**te·na'cious·ly** *adv.*

ten·don (tĕn'dən) *n.* A band of tough, inelastic fibrous tissue that connects a muscle with its bony attachment; a sinew.

ten·ta·cle (tĕn'tə-kəl) *n.* **1.** *Botany.* One of the hairs on the leaves of insectivorous plants, such as the sundew. **2.** Something resembling a tentacle, especially in ability to grasp or hold.

ter·mi·na·tion (tûr'mə-nā'shən) *n.* A result or outcome of something.

tes·ty (tĕs'tē) *adj.* **-tier, -tiest.** Irritable; touchy; peevish. —**tes'ti·ly** *adv.*

tier (tîr) *n.* One of a series of rows placed one above another.

tim·or·ous (tĭm'ər-əs) *adj.* Full of apprehensiveness; timid.

tor·rent (tôr'ənt, tŏr'-) *n.* A raging flood; deluge.

tor·ren·tial (tô-rĕn'shəl, tə-) *adj.* **1.** Of or pertaining to a torrent. **2.** Resembling a torrent; turbulent; wild.

tor·tu·ous (tôr'chōō-əs) *adj.* **1.** Having or marked by repeated turns or bends; winding; twisting. **2.** Not straightforward; deceitful; devious.

tou·sle (tou'zəl) *tr.v.* **-sled, -sling, -sles.** To disarrange or rumple; dishevel. —*n.* A disheveled mass, as of hair.

tran·quil (trăn'kwəl) *adj.* **-quiler** or **-quiller, -quilest** or **-quillest.** Free from agitation or other disturbance; calm; unruffled; serene.

tran·quil·li·ty, tran·quil·i·ty (trăn-kwĭl'ə-tē) *n.* The state or quality of being tranquil; serenity.

trea·cle (trē'kəl) *n.* **a.** *British.* Molasses. **b.** A kind of syrup.

trel·lis (trĕl'ĭs) *n.* **1.** A frame supporting open latticework, used for training vines and other creeping plants. **2.** An arbor or arch made with this structure.

trem·u·lous (trĕm'yə-ləs) *adj.* Vibrating or quivering; trembling.

truc·u·lent (trŭk'yə-lənt) *adj.* **1.** Savage and cruel; fierce. **2.** Vitriolic; scathing. **3.** Disposed to fight; pugnacious; defiant.

tu·mul·tu·ous (tə-mŭl'chōō-əs) *adj.* Noisy and disorderly; riotous.

tur·bu·lence (tûr'byə-ləns) *n.* The state or quality of being agitated, violently disturbed, or in commotion.

twine (twīn) *v.* **twined, twining, twines.** —*tr.* To twist together; intertwine, as threads. —*n.* **1.** A

---

t tight/th thin, path/*th* this, bathe/ŭ cut/ûr urge/v valve/w with/y yes/z zebra, size/zh vision/ə about, item, edible, gallop, circus/ à *Fr.* ami/œ *Fr.* feu, *Ger.* schön/ü *Fr.* tu, *Ger.* über/KH *Ger.* ich, *Scot.* loch/N *Fr.* bon.

strong string or cord formed of two or more threads twisted together. **2.** Any thing or part formed by twining.

U

ul·cer (ŭl'sər) *n.* An inflammatory, often suppurating lesion on the skin or an internal mucous surface of the body, resulting in necrosis of the tissue.

ul·cer·ate (ŭl'sə-rāt') *v.* **-ated, -ating, -ates.** —*intr.* To become affected with or as if with an ulcer.

un·can·ny (ŭn'kăn'ē) *adj.* **-nier, -niest.** So keen and perceptive as to seem preternatural: *uncanny insight.*

un·daunt·ed (ŭn'dôn'tĭd, -dän'tĭd) *adj.* Not discouraged or disheartened; resolute; fearless.

un·der·mine (ŭn'dər-mīn') *tr.v.* **-mined, -mining, -mines.** To weaken, injure, or impair, often by degrees or imperceptibly; to sap.

un·err·ing (ŭn'ûr'ĭng, -ĕr'ĭng) *adj.* Committing no mistakes; consistently accurate; errorless. —**un'err'ing·ly** *adv.*

un·gain·ly (ŭn'gān'lē) *adj.* **-lier, -liest. 1.** Without grace or ease of movement; clumsy. **2.** Difficult to move or use; unwieldy.

u·ni·ver·sal (yōo'nə-vûr'səl) *adj.* Of, pertaining to, extending to, or affecting the entire world or all within the world; worldwide.

un·ru·ly (ŭn'rōo'lē) *adj.* **-lier, -liest.** Difficult or impossible to govern; not amenable to discipline.

up·surge (ŭp'sûrj') *n.* A rapid upward swell or rise.

us·age (yōo'sĭj, -zĭj) *n.* Customary practice; habitual use.

ut·ter·ance (ŭt'ər-əns) *n.* **1.** The act of uttering or expressing vocally. **2.** Something that is uttered or expressed.

V

vain (vān) *adj.* **vainer, vainest.** —**in vain.** Without effect or avail; to no use or purpose: *Our labor was in vain.*

val·iant (văl'yənt) *adj.* Possessing or acting with valor; brave; courageous; stouthearted.

val·id (văl'ĭd) *adj.* Well-grounded; sound; supportable.

val·or·ous (văl'ər-əs) *adj.* Possessing or marked by personal bravery; valiant.

ven·er·a·ble (vĕn'ər-ə-bəl) *adj.* Worthy of reverence or respect by virtue of dignity, character, position, or age.

ve·ran·dah, ve·ran·da (və-răn'də) *n.* A porch or balcony, usually roofed and often partly enclosed, extending along the outside of a building; piazza; gallery.

ver·sa·tile (vûr'sə-təl) *adj.* Having varied uses or serving many functions.

vig·il (vĭj'əl) *n.* A watch kept during normal sleeping hours.

vin·dic·tive (vĭn-dĭk'tĭv) *adj.* **1.** Disposed to seek revenge; revengeful. **2.** Unforgiving; bitter; spiteful.

vir·tu·al·ly (vûr'chōo-ə-lē) *adv.* In fact or to all purposes; essentially; practically.

vir·tu·o·so (vûr'chōo-ō'sō) *n.* One with masterly skill or technique in any field, especially in the arts.

vi·tal·i·ty (vī-tăl'ə-tē) *n.* Vigor; energy; exuberance.

vol·u·ble (vŏl'yə-bəl) *adj.* Characterized by a ready flow of words in speaking; garrulous; fluent; loquacious.

vul·ner·a·ble (vŭl'nər-ə-bəl) *adj.* Susceptible to injury; unprotected from danger. —**vul'ner·a·bil'i·ty** *n.*

W

wa·ger (wā'jər) *n.* An agreement under which each bettor pledges a certain amount to the other depending upon the outcome of an unsettled matter.

wan (wŏn) *adj.* **wanner, wannest.** Unnaturally pale, as from physical or emotional distress.

wan·ton (wŏn'tən) *adj.* Maliciously cruel; merciless.

war·rant (wôr'ənt, wŏr'-) *n. Law.* A judicial writ authorizing an officer to make a search, seizure, or arrest or to execute a judgment.

wash (wŏsh, wôsh) *n. Western U.S.* The dry bed of a stream.

wax (wăks) *intr.v.* **waxed, waxing, waxes.** To grow or become as specified: *the seas wax calm.*

wel·ter (wĕl'tər) *intr.v.* **-tered, -tering, -ters.** To writhe, roll, or wallow. —*n.* Turbulence; tossing.

whim·si·cal (hwĭm'zĭ-kəl) *adj.* Capricious; playful; arbitrary.

wist·ful (wĭst'fəl) *adj.* Full of a melancholy yearning; longing pensively; wishful.

with·ers (wĭth'ərz) *pl.n.* The high point of the back of a horse, or of a similar or related animal, located at the base of the neck and between the shoulder blades.

wiz·en (wĭz'ən) *v.* **-ened, -ening, -ens.** —*intr.* To wither or sear; dry up; shrivel. —*adj.* Shriveled or dried up; withered.

wont (wônt, wōnt, wŭnt) *n.* Usage or custom.

work (wûrk) *v.* **worked** or *archaic* **wrought** (rôt), **working, works.** —*tr.* **1.** To cause or effect; bring about. **2.** To form or shape; mold.

wrath (răth, räth) *n.* Violent, resentful anger; rage; fury.

wrought (rôt). *Archaic.* Past tense and past participle of **work.**

ă pat/ā pay/âr care/ä father/b bib/ch church/d deed/ĕ pet/ē be/f fife/g gag/h hat/hw which/ĭ pit/ī pie/îr pier/j judge/k kick/l lid/ needle/m mum/n no, sudden/ng thing/ŏ pot/ō toe/ô paw, for/oi noise/ou out/ōo took/ōō boot/p pop/r roar/s sauce/sh ship, dish/ t tight/th thin, path/*th* this, bathe/ŭ cut/ûr urge/v valve/w with/y yes/z zebra, size/zh vision/ə about, item, edible, gallop, circus/ à *Fr.* ami/œ *Fr.* feu, *Ger.* schön/ü *Fr.* tu, *Ger.* über/KH *Ger.* ich, *Scot.* loch/N *Fr.* bon.